Todd,

The best lesson in this book is ...

If you have integrity, nothing else matters; and

If you *don't* have integrity, nothing else matters!

Dm Timmins

P9-EJU-373

Proof 30301

More Praise for
Conspiracy of Fools

"Quite simply the best business book I've ever read . . . One hell of a great read." —*Edmonton Journal*

"One of the best nonfiction investigative books I've read in years, with more plot twists than a John le Carré novel." —*Providence Journal*

"Better than most of the courtroom thrillers in bookstores, with an added bonus: It's a real-life drama." —*Pittsburgh Tribune-Review*

"A page-turner. . . . As with another business book, *Barbarians at the Gate*, this one succeeds not only in telling the story of a company in crisis, but in portraying the spirit of an era. In this case, the story of Enron's rise and fall captures the frothy, do-anything-to-win values that thrived during the dot-com bubble." —*USA Today*

"A prodigious feat of reporting. Eichenwald seems to have uncovered every surviving memo (despite the orgy of document shredding and deleting of e-mail messages that went on at both Arthur Andersen and Enron in the final days). He has also elicited candid revelations from many of the front-line executives, lawyers, accountants and investigators, and doggedly followed the money trail down all its byways, an achievement that in itself commands admiration. Moreover, his writing is reader-friendly. He manages to convey a sense of the dizzying confusion and nerve-racking tension that infused the company years before it fell. The narrative is broken up into short, cinematic takes, each a study in corporate stress, humiliation, envy and macho preening." —*New York Times Book Review*

"**Leaves the reader's heart racing** . . . You know what the terrible ending will be, but each time you must put the book down, you can't wait to get back to it to see what the next installment will bring." —*Washington Post*

"**A scene-by-scene cinematic thriller** . . . a riveting slice of business journalism that bursts with chaos, adrenaline and despair." —*Salon*

"A comprehensive, compellingly written narrative that employs novelistic techniques while never straying from the facts . . . A good mix of accounting shenanigans, prosecutorial decisions, sexual innuendo, marriages in trouble, marriages that survived and—above all—greed, greed and more greed." —*Houston Chronicle*

"**A rip-roaring account** . . . Kurt Eichenwald has ploughed through a mountain of suspect, complicated wheeling and dealing to provide a clear-eyed account of one of the great man-made disasters on Wall Street." —*The Tennessean*

"**An irresistible read** . . . **Riveting** . . . will no doubt one day make a highly entertaining film . . . Mr. Eichenwald appears to have talked to everyone more extensively and scoured the documents more exhaustively than anyone else. The book is organized chronologically in a sequence of short but powerfully vivid scenes, complete with dramatic dialogue and detailed descriptions." —*New York Observer*

"**A gripping account** . . . Reads like a good airport novel." —*The Economist*

"**A riveting page-turner** . . . *Conspiracy of Fools* should be required reading in every business school in America." —*Providence Journal*

"**I couldn't put it down** . . . It's pretty hard to read Kurt Eichenwald's history of the economic disaster known as 'Enron' without feeling one's jaw drop." —*Wisconsin State Journal*

"**Unfolds like a suspense novel** . . . **A really good read** . . . Eichenwald's meticulously researched volume will captivate readers . . . His book is chilling exploration of how far down the road to destruction any venture can travel when a collection of supremely self-assured but wrongheaded minds are given enough power." —*Washington Monthly*

"**Engrossing** . . . an excellent, entertaining tale. Mr. Eichenwald writes the book in a chain of ear-to-the-keyhole anecdotes of Enron meetings and conversations that show readers how the scandal unfolded." —*Dallas Morning News*

"**Grade: A+** . . . **One of the best nonfiction books of the year** . . . **Must reading** . . . so well crafted that events leap off of the written page much like in a Grisham thriller. This is one of the most outstanding books ever written about corporate depravity and is almost certain to be nominated for a Pulitzer Prize . . . *Conspiracy of Fools* is nothing less than a stunning achievement. Kurt Eichenwald again proves he is one of the nation's most influential financial reporters and is a seasoned journalist at the top of his game." —*Tucson Citizen*

"Not only does [Eichenwald] make the book read like a John Grisham thriller, it provides a fascinating insight into some of the sheer ineptitude that led to the company's collapse." —*Daily Telegraph* (London)

"**A can't-put-it-down tale** of how arrogance, greed and competitive drive ran amok in the meteoric rise and cataclysmic implosion of Enron . . . *Conspiracy of Fools* will likely stand as the last word on turn-of-the-century corporate chaos."
—*Newsweek*

"**This is a book you will *want* to read.** One big reason is that Eichenwald has given his material the structure and drive of a good suspense novel."
—*Rocky Mountain News*

"**Relentless** . . . Eichenwald tells the story like a thriller, vividly re-creating scene after scene."
—*Baltimore Sun*

"**I could not stop reading it. It's really gripping** . . . *Conspiracy of Fools* has more in common with *The Bonfire of the Vanities* or a John le Carré novel than with other books about business."
—NPR, *All Things Considered*

"**A page-turning financial thriller** . . . This book compares with *Liar's Poker* and *Barbarians at the Gate* in its breadth and depth of coverage of esoteric corporate culture and financial practices, recognizing the compelling human drama beneath the scandal."
—*Booklist*

"**Puts the reader in the center of the action** . . . Even if you've read innumerable accounts of the Enron scandal, you'll find the meltdown depicted in Kurt Eichenwald's *Conspiracy of Fools* to be an eye-opener. His you-are-there narrative and fastidious attention to detail bring this Byzantine saga to life as never before."
—*Business Week*

"Only this white-collar-crime reporter for the *New York Times* could turn the Enron scandal into a book that reads like a Joel Schumacher script (starring Gene Hackman as glad-handing Ken Lay?) . . . Eichenwald's style, which worked so well in *The Informant*, carries the day."   —*Details*

"This enormous, intimate blow-by-blow of Enron's implosion gets as close to what actually happened, in terms of people making (bad) decisions in real time, as anyone who wasn't there with a concealed video-phone possibly could . . . [P]resented in a rat-a-tat style thick with corporate anxiety, keeping pages turning . . . As an unadorned attempt to get into the heads of some major manipulators, this book can hardly be bettered."
                                                        —*Publishers Weekly*

"If it's an inside look at corporate malfeasance you're after, look no further than *Conspiracy of Fools*."   —*New York Post*

"Meticulous and impressive."   —*Orlando Sentinel*

"Will rightly be judged as the definitive book to date."
                                                        —*Library Journal*

"A thriller disguised as a nonfiction account of a financial implosion that affected the federal government, Wall Street and millions of investors."
                                                        —MSNBC

"There is much to love in this account . . . *Conspiracy of Fools* may be the most comprehensive [book about Enron], with a sophisticated grasp of the big picture tempered by considerable human drama."
                                                        —*Fort Worth Star-Telegram*

"Eichenwald's narrative approach makes it easier to understand how Enron's esoteric business deals and accounting chicanery came about. The mounting layers of bogus transactions, incompetence, venality and a contempt for business basics created inexorable pressures that carried the company to its demise."
—*San Diego Union-Tribune*

"The most comprehensive—and the most readable—of the dozen [books] that have come out since Enron collapsed."
—*Portland Oregonian*

"Eichenwald dissects [the story] with the swift strokes of a Robert Ludlum page-turner . . . exhaustively researched . . . Other reporters pried the lid off Enron, but Eichenwald spills out the contents. What tumbles into view is all the corruption you might expect, some boneheaded incompetence, and a surprising degree of honor."
—*Buffalo News*

"**A first-rate ripper** . . . the author is as sure-footed as a trapeze artist when he describes the crazed internal dynamics of Enron's dysfunctional corporate culture, and the toxic criminal schemes that led to its inevitable implosion."
—*Edmonton Journal*

"**It's very, very good.** I started reading it on a Tuesday, thinking it would take about two weeks to wade through all 675 pages. Instead, I was finished in four days."
—*National Post*

"Author Kurt Eichenwald reconstructs the story of the fall of energy giant Enron with a zestful knack for storytelling and reporting . . . Eichenwald's narrative is an engaging and engrossing look at corporate malfeasance and ineptitude."
—*Pittsburgh Tribune-Review*

"I've been up well past midnight this week reading Kurt Eichenwald's riveting account of the destruction of Enron . . . well written and exhaustively researched."
—*Kansas City Star*

"**Massive and gripping** . . . Very much like a mystery, with tension building throughout."
—*San Antonio Express-News*

"Greed. Arrogance. Lavish evening gowns. Kurt Eichenwald's new book on the rise and fall of Enron has all the trappings of a season of 'Dynasty' . . . Eichenwald chops the bogus deals and accounting distortions into bite-size scenes and adds cliffhangers on every page. You know how this story ends, but you can't stop reading."
—*The News & Observer* (Raleigh, N.C.)

CONSPIRACY OF FOOLS

ALSO BY KURT EICHENWALD

THE INFORMANT

SERPENT ON THE ROCK

CONSPIRACY OF FOOLS

A TRUE STORY

KURT EICHENWALD

BROADWAY BOOKS
NEW YORK

BROADWAY

A hardcover edition of this book was published in 2005 by Broadway Books.

CONSPIRACY OF FOOLS. Copyright © 2005 by Kurt Eichenwald. All rights reserved.
No part of this book may be reproduced or transmitted in any form or by any means,
electronic or mechanical, including photocopying, recording, or by any information
storage and retrieval system, without written permission from the publisher. For
information, address Broadway Books, a division of Random House, Inc.

PRINTED IN THE UNITED STATES OF AMERICA

BROADWAY BOOKS and its logo, a letter B bisected on the diagonal, are trademarks
of Random House, Inc.

Visit our website at www.broadwaybooks.com

First trade paperback edition published 2005.

Book design by Lovedog Studio

The Library of Congress has cataloged the hardcover edition as:
Eichenwald, Kurt, 1961–
    Conspiracy of fools : a true story / Kurt Eichenwald.— 1st ed.
       p. cm.
    1. Enron Corp.—Corrupt practices. 2. Energy industries—Corrupt practices—United States.
3. Lay, Kenneth L. 4. Business failures—United States. I. Title.
    HD9502.U54E5736 2005
    333.79'0973—dc22   2004058216

ISBN 0-7679-1179-2

20 19 18 17 16 15 14

To my parents,

Elva Eichenwald and Heinz Eichenwald,

Who encouraged me to fight my windmills

And cheered me when I won.

Reason dreams of an empire of knowledge, a mansion of the mind. Yet sometimes we end up living in a hovel by its side.

—Heinz R. Pagels, *The Dreams of Reason*

If I remember, I predicted fence integrity would fail.

—The character of Ian Malcolm,
in Michael Crichton's *Jurassic Park*

AUTHOR'S NOTE

This narrative account is based on more than a thousand hours of interviews with over a hundred participants in these events as well as a review of tens of thousands of confidential corporate and government documents. Those include FBI notes of interviews and testimony before federal grand juries, the SEC, and other federal bodies. The dialogue comes from those documents and contemporaneous records—including personal diaries—or from the best recollections of participants. This, then, is the full story of America's biggest corporate scandal, one that, in the end, involved events that even now may seem difficult to believe. But they're all real.

THE CAST OF CHARACTERS
and Their Primary Roles

WITH THE ENRON CORPORATION, HOUSTON, TEXAS

The Top Officers

Kenneth Lay, chairman and CEO

Jeffrey Skilling, president (1997–2001), CEO (2001)

Rich Kinder, president (1989–1996)

Greg Whalley, president (2001)

In the Finance Division

Andrew Fastow, chief financial officer (1998–2001)

Michael Kopper, head of special projects

Jeffrey McMahon, treasurer (1999–2000), CFO (2001–2002)

Ben Glisan Jr., treasurer (2000–2001)

Raymond Bowen Jr., treasurer (2001–2002)

Jordan Mintz, general counsel

Lea Fastow, assistant treasurer

Michael Jakubik, vice president

Jim Timmins, director, private equity

Tim Despain, vice president

Bill Brown, vice president

The Internal Accountants

Richard Causey, chief accounting officer

David Woytek, vice president, corporate auditing

Rodney Faldyn, vice president, transaction accounting group

Ryan Siurek, member, transaction accounting group

In Risk Assessment

Richard Buy, chief risk officer

Vince Kaminski, vice president of research

Stinson Gibner, analyst

Vasant Shanbhogue, analyst

Rakesh Bharati, analyst

Kevin Kindall, analyst

In Corporate Development

J. Clifford Baxter, executive vice
president

Mark Muller, senior vice president
Sherron Watkins, vice president (2001)

The Corporate Staff

Rebecca Carter, investor relations
representative, corporate secretary
Mark Palmer, head of corporate
communications
Stephen Kean, head of government affairs
(1998), chief of staff (1999–2001)

Mark Koenig, head of investor relations
Cindy Olson, head of community
relations

In the Legal Department

James Derrick, general counsel
Rob Walls, deputy general counsel

Rex Rogers, associate general counsel

In Wholesale Energy

Kenneth Rice, chief executive
Kevin Hannon, president
Greg Whalley, president (2000)
Amanda Martin, managing director,
asset management
Mark Haedicke, general counsel
Kristina Mordaunt, co-head of finance
legal cluster (1997–1999)

Timothy Belden, managing director,
west power trading division
John Forney, manager, west power real
time trading desk
Stuart Zisman, senior counsel
Mark Frevert, president, London
(1998), unit chairman (2000–2001)

In Retail Energy

Andrew Fastow, managing director (1996)
Lou Pai, chief executive (1996–2001)

David Delainey, chief executive (2001)
Raymond Bowen Jr., vice president

In the International Division

Rebecca Mark, chief executive

Joseph Sutton, deputy

In the Broadband Division

Kenneth Rice, co-chief executive (1999),
chief commercial officer (2000)
Joseph Hirko, co-chief executive
Kevin Hannon, chief operating
officer

Rex Shelby, senior vice president
Kristina Mordaunt, general counsel
(1999–2001)

At Portland General, an Electric Utility

Kenneth Harrison, chairman

Joseph Hirko, chief financial officer
(1991–1996)

At Azurix, a Water Company

Rebecca Mark, chief executive

Amanda Martin, executive director

Colin Skellett, executive director

On the Board of Directors

John Duncan

Herbert "Pug" Winokur Jr.

Norman Blake

Charles "Mickey" LeMaistre

Robert Jaedicke

Robert Belfer

Wendy Gramm

William Powers

WITH ARTHUR ANDERSEN & CO.

Joseph Berardino, managing partner
(2001–2002)

Andrew Pincus, general counsel

John Riley, practice director

Rich Corgel, practice director

In the Houston Office

David Duncan, partner

Stephen Goddard, partner

Thomas Bauer, partner

Carl Bass, partner

Debra Cash, partner

Patricia Grutzmacher, partner

Gary Goolsby, global managing partner

James Hecker, partner

In the Professional Standards Group, Chicago, Illinois

John Stewart, partner

Ben Neuhausen, partner

In the Litigation Group, Chicago, Illinois

Nancy Temple, lawyer

WITH DYNEGY CORPORATION, HOUSTON, TEXAS

Chuck Watson, chairman and chief
executive

Stephen Bergstrom, president

Keith Fullenweider, deputy general
counsel

Rob Doty, chief financial officer

WITH MERRILL LYNCH & COMPANY

Daniel Bayly, head of global investment banking

James Brown, head of strategic asset lease and finance

Schuyler Tilney, relationship banker, Houston office

Robert Furst, relationship banker, Dallas office

John Olson, securities analyst

WITH GREENWICH NATWEST, GREENWICH, CONNECTICUT, AND LONDON, ENGLAND

Gary Mulgrew, managing director

Giles Darby, managing director

David Bermingham, banker

WITH J. P. MORGAN CHASE

James (Jimmy) Lee, vice chairman

Rick Walker, relationship banker

WITH KYNIKOS ASSOCIATES

James Chanos, president

THE OTHER CHIEF EXECUTIVES

Dennis Kozlowski, Tyco International

Rupert Murdoch, News Corporation

Sumner Redstone, Viacom

WITH THE LAW FIRMS

At Vinson & Elkins, Houston, Texas

Joseph Dilg, managing partner

Ronald Astin, partner

Max Hendrick III, partner

At Wilmer, Cutler & Pickering, Washington, D.C.

William McLucas, partner

Charles Davidow, partner

Joseph Brenner, partner

William Joor, partner

Reed Brodsky, counsel

At Weil, Gotshal & Manges, New York City

Thomas Roberts, partner

Mary Korby, partner

THE PRESIDENTS

George H. W. Bush (1988–1992)   George W. Bush (2001–2004)
Bill Clinton (1992–2001)

AT THE WHITE HOUSE OF GEORGE W. BUSH, WASHINGTON, D.C.

Dick Cheney, Vice President   Andrew Card, Chief of Staff

AT THE UNITED STATES DEPARTMENT OF JUSTICE, WASHINGTON, D.C.

John Ashcroft, Attorney General   Michael Chertoff, head of the criminal
Larry Thompson, Deputy Attorney   division
General

On the Enron Task Force

Leslie Caldwell, director   Andrew Weissmann, deputy director

With the Federal Bureau of Investigation

Robert Mueller, director   Joseph Ford, special agent

AT THE SECURITIES AND EXCHANGE COMMISSION, WASHINGTON, D.C.

Arthur Levitt, chairman (1993–2001)   Stephen Cutler, director of
Harvey Pitt, chairman (2001–2002)   enforcement (2001–2004)
Richard Walker, director of   Linda Chatman Thomsen, deputy
enforcement (1998–2001)   director of enforcement

In the Fort Worth Regional Office

Spencer Barasch, associate district   Robert Hannan, lawyer
administrator

AT THE UNITED STATES DEPARTMENT OF THE TREASURY, WASHINGTON, D.C.

Lawrence Summers, Secretary   Paul O'Neill, Secretary (2001–2002)
(1999–2001)

AT THE UNITED STATES DEPARTMENT OF COMMERCE, WASHINGTON, D.C.

Donald Evans, Secretary

AT THE UNITED STATES DEPARTMENT OF STATE, WASHINGTON, D.C.

Colin Powell, Secretary

IN CALIFORNIA STATE GOVERNMENT, SACRAMENTO, CALIFORNIA

Gray Davis, Governor

IN THE UNITED STATES CONGRESS

In the Senate

Trent Lott, Majority Leader, Republican of Mississippi

Phil Gramm, Republican of Texas

In the House of Representatives

W. J. (Billy) Tauzin, Republican of Louisiana

James Greenwood, Republican of Pennsylvania

Staff, House Energy and Commerce Committee's Subcommittee on Oversight and Investigations

Mark Paoletta
David Cavicke

Ken Johnson

AT *THE WALL STREET JOURNAL*

Jonathan Weil, reporter
John Emshwiller, reporter

Rebecca Smith, reporter

AT *FORTUNE* MAGAZINE

Bethany McLean, reporter

OTHERS

Bal Thackeray, leader, Shiv Sena, Mumbai, India

Arnold Schwarzenegger, actor, Los Angeles, California

THE PRIMARY DEALS

JEDI

Joint Energy Development Investments. A fund—jointly owned by Enron and the California Public Employees Retirement System, or Calpers—to invest in oil and gas properties.

JEDI II

Also formed between Enron and Calpers, for investments in a wider range of assets.

CHEWCO

An off-books partnership controlled by an Enron executive. Used to purchase Calpers's interest in JEDI to allow for the retirement system to invest in JEDI II.

LJM CAYMAN

Also known as LJM1. An investment fund managed by Enron's chief financial officer. Used mainly to provide Enron with a protection against a decline in the price of its investment in a technology company, Rhythms NetConnections.

LJM2

A far larger investment fund, also managed by Enron's CFO. Used primarily to purchase investments and assets that Enron wanted to sell, and to provide cash to off-books entities that were also doing deals with the company.

THE RAPTORS

A quartet of off-books entities which were, at one point, partly owned by LJM2. They were created for the purpose of providing Enron with a protection against losses from certain investments in other companies and assets.

BRAVEHEART

The code name for a deal involving the sale by Enron of a portion of its video-on-demand business, formed in a joint venture with Blockbuster. Again, the sale was to an off-books entity created by the company.

CONSPIRACY OF FOOLS

PROLOGUE

Ken Lay settled into his black Mercedes 600 SL, easing out of his reserved parking space at the Huntingdon condominiums. From the lot's entrance, he turned right onto Kirby Drive, the tree-lined road that served as a main thoroughfare through River Oaks, Houston's wealthiest and most prestigious neighborhood.

The eight-year-old convertible cruised past the mansions bordering the street, homes that testified to the financial success of the city's oilmen and corporate barons. Many estates peeked out from behind manicured shrubs and wrought-iron gates, or were far from the road on a ridge sloping down to the Buffalo Bayou. But Lay made no effort to peer beyond those veils of privacy. As Houston's most influential businessman, he had already been welcomed in most every River Oaks mansion that might interest him.

The neighborhood's elegance melted into Allen Parkway, a winding stretch of road that offered the most direct route downtown. Ahead, the morning sun was a blazing orange ball, rising behind a glittering glass-and-aluminum tower that defined the architectural rhythm of Houston's skyline. It was the headquarters of Enron—*his* Enron—the once-obscure pipeline company that in a matter of years had been transformed into a politically connected energy colossus. Enron was now at the epicenter of Houston's life, a ubiquitous player in everything from the city's politics to its sports teams. But for locals, the sprawling giant would probably just always be known as Ken Lay's company.

Lay lowered his car visor and glanced at the dashboard clock. Shortly before seven, early for his commute. But already he knew this would not be a normal day. His company was under attack; Lay was sure of it. Stock traders who had bet that Enron's share price would fall were whispering rumors— no, *lies*—about his company. *The Wall Street Journal* was publishing a drumbeat of articles suggesting Enron had played games with its finances. It infuriated him.

They just don't understand.

By all rights, Lay shouldn't even have been stuck with the mess. He had stepped down as chief executive the prior February, handing the reins to his handpicked successor, Jeffrey Skilling, the brains behind Enron's spectacular growth. With market power came world influence, and—as Skilling's profit machine rumbled along—Lay had emerged as a confidant of presidents, a media celebrity, and, at least in Houston, a household name. When Lay bowed out, he was celebrated as a man of vision who got things done. By year's end, he was supposed to be ensconced in a new job at Kohlberg Kravis Roberts & Company, the buyout firm, basking in the glory of the empire he had left behind.

Then, with almost no warning, Skilling had up and resigned. Just like that, only months after winning the job. Lay had suspected for weeks that something was wrong with his successor; he had even quietly told a few Enron directors that Skilling seemed emotionally overwhelmed by his new responsibilities. Still, he had never imagined the man would just *leave*. The bombshell had left Lay with little choice. He contacted KKR's principals, passing up their offer, and headed back to his old post.

But nothing was the same. Inside Enron, Skilling's departure unleashed a torrent of anger and demands for change; outside, it fanned suspicions that there were some terrible secrets harbored within the company.

Rapidly, the press had lit into the company's chief financial officer, Andrew Fastow, criticizing him for holding a second job as manager of investment funds that did deals with Enron. The allegations of a conflict of interest angered Lay; he had listened to Fastow reluctantly take on the additional responsibilities, just to benefit the company. And it had. The Fastow funds provided partners that knew Enron's business, that could transact deals quickly. As far as Lay was concerned, Fastow had gone the extra mile for Enron and now was getting tarred for his loyalty.

We had every protection in place. We disclosed it all. They just don't understand.

Lay turned in to the Allen Center Garage, parking one space from the walkway to the Enron building. He hurried to the company's sleek metallic lobby, approaching a security checkpoint installed after the September 11 attacks. Holding up a magnetic card, he hesitated until the green light flashed, and then pushed past to the elevator.

The huge, mahogany-paneled reception area on the fiftieth floor was quiet and empty. Lay strode through, past a multicolored statue of an elephant colleagues had acquired on one of their many trips to India. Using a card key, he released an electronic lock and pushed open the heavy wooden door to the executive offices. He saw Rosalee Fleming, his assistant, busy at her desk.

"Morning, Rosie," Lay said.

"Good morning, Ken. Andy Fastow called a few minutes ago. He said that he needs to meet with you urgently."

"All right. Let him know I'm here."

Lay slipped off his suit jacket as he walked into his office. He pressed a panel in the wall, popping open a hidden closet, where he hung the jacket. Lay pulled out his chair, but before he could sit, Fastow appeared in the doorway.

"Good morning, Andy," Lay said.

Fastow nodded. "We need to talk, Ken."

"Well, come in. Sit down."

Fastow shuffled toward a circular conference table bolted to the office floor. Lay reached inside his desk drawer and touched a button, sending a radio signal across the room to a release in the door. It shut automatically.

As Lay took his seat, he glanced across the table. Fastow looked awful, showing the strains of the last few days. Usually, he was neatly coiffed, everything about him fresh and tailored. But today his face sagged, his brow furrowed. He looked as if he hadn't slept most of the night.

"I've got some information I need to share with you," Fastow said. "Last night Ben Glisan met with some of the bankers, and they told him that they couldn't proceed with a loan to us so long as I was chief financial officer."

That was grim news. Glisan, Enron's young treasurer, was a devotee of Fastow. If he couldn't persuade the bankers to do business with the man, no one could.

It was a difficult moment. Lay had been fighting for days to keep Fastow in his job, fending off efforts by the company's new president, Greg Whalley, to oust him. Lay respected Fastow, and the board almost revered him; he couldn't just fire his CFO because of a few nasty newspaper articles. But this was different. If bankers wouldn't do business with him, Enron itself was in peril.

"You know, Andy, we talked about this possibility," Lay said. "Certainly the board and I have been very supportive of you, both publicly and privately. But we've also said that if you ever lost the confidence of the financial community, we would have to rethink the whole thing."

Fastow nodded, his eyes downcast.

"So I need to call a board meeting and see what they think we ought to do," Lay said. "I'll do that as soon as I can, because, obviously, we've got a lot going on."

Fastow was silent. "Well," he said finally, standing as he spoke, "thank you for meeting with me, Ken."

It pained Lay to watch Fastow trudge out of the room, back to a desk they both knew he would soon be vacating. Lay was certain that in no time, the squall about Enron would pass, but by then, it would be too late to save the career of this talented young executive. Fastow would be a victim. It just wasn't right.

Lay had no idea that Fastow had failed to tell him the most devastating news of all—news he wouldn't learn for years to come.

At almost that very moment across town, Ray Bowen was standing naked in his upstairs bathroom, checking the shower temperature with his hand. As he lifted his foot to step inside, the telephone rang. In the bedroom, his wife answered the line and put the call on hold.

"Hey, Ray!" she called. "It's Jeff!"

This couldn't be good, not at this hour. His boss, Jeff McMahon, head of Enron's paper-market business, would only call this early with a problem. And Bowen knew Enron's recent chaos had created plenty of those. Wrapping a towel around his waist, he stepped into a toilet room where he had installed a Panasonic phone system.

"Hey, Jeff. What's up?"

"It's bad, man," McMahon said. "The shit really hit the fan last night."

Bowen listened in disbelief as McMahon told the ugly story. Enron had reached the precipice of collapse. The markets for the billions of dollars in day-to-day credit that large companies need—to pay salaries, to meet obligations to vendors, to keep *the lights* on—had shut out Enron. The institutions that ponied up the cash in short-term loans known as commercial paper no longer believed the company was worth the risk. The marketplace—that living, breathing entity whose judgment its executives hailed as infallible—was passing its harsh, unemotional verdict: Enron could not be trusted to survive the week.

"How . . . how can that be?" Bowen stuttered.

"Don't know, but that's what I'm hearing."

McMahon paused. "I think that's it," he said. "I think they're going to fire Andy today."

No kidding. Fastow had so mismanaged the books that nobody trusted Enron with an overnight loan? Of course he was gone. And if Lay let sentimentality get in the way of that obvious decision, then Whalley would pull the trigger.

"So what's the plan?" Bowen asked.

"I need your help. Whalley wants you and me to come in and help him figure it out. Can you be there by eight?"

Fifty-five minutes later, McMahon was in the offices of his division on the fourth floor of Enron's new building when he saw Bowen hurrying toward him.

"What do you think?" McMahon called out.

"We've gotta draw down the revolvers right away," Bowen replied brusquely.

The revolvers. The billions of dollars in standing lines of credit that Enron had available from its major banks. That was disaster money, the financial equivalent of a nuclear fallout shelter. And Enron needed it now.

The two men hustled to the fiftieth floor of the main Enron building. They headed to Skilling's old office, where Whalley had recently set up shop. A few others were already gathered there. Whalley's door was closed, and his secretary told the men they needed to wait.

"Greg's meeting with Andy Fastow," she said.

Minutes passed. Finally the doorknob clicked and Fastow emerged, flashing a nervous smile. Whalley pushed past and took command.

"Okay," he said. "We're meeting upstairs. Go on up, and I'll be there in a few minutes."

The men rode a small internal elevator to the mezzanine level and made their way to a tiny conference room, crowding around an oblong table. Fastow and McMahon—who had long treated each other with an antipathy bordering on contempt—drifted to the seats farthest away from each other. Fifteen minutes later, Whalley blew into the room.

"Okay, let's get going," he said as he took his seat. "Let's start with the organization first."

Whalley shot a look at Fastow, pointing at him.

"Andy," he said rapidly, "as we discussed, you're no longer CFO, effective right now."

Fastow's face fell. "Wait . . ."

Ignoring Fastow, Whalley swept his arm across the table, pointing at McMahon.

"Jeff, you're now CFO of this company."

What was that? McMahon wasn't sure he heard Whalley correctly. He was chief financial officer? Just like that?

"Excuse me?" McMahon said. "I'm CFO?"

"Yes, you're CFO."

McMahon glanced across the table. Fastow was shaking his head, looking shocked. The moment was surreal.

Are other companies like this? You get promoted and the guy you replace gets fired, all in front of everybody?

"Wait a minute!" Fastow sputtered, anger in his voice. "That was not my understanding of the deal!"

Whalley held up a hand. "Andy, I don't have time for this. I don't know your arrangement; I don't know the legal stuff. You get with Ken and work it out. But you're not CFO. That decision's made."

That was it. Whalley turned away from Fastow.

"Okay, Jeff, commercial paper. What should we do?"

"Well," McMahon said, "I need to assemble a team to figure out where we are. But I think there's a good chance we'll need to draw down the revolvers."

Bowen jumped in. "People, from my experience, if a company has a cash crisis, it either draws its revolvers immediately or gets ready for the banks to come in and find lots of reasons to delay sending the cash."

The group tossed around the idea. Fastow shook his head, leaning forward in his chair. "Wait a minute, Ray," he said, looking at Bowen. "I really disagree with you. I think drawing down the revolvers will send a terrible message to the market."

Fastow pressed a forefinger against the table.

"You do this," he said forcefully, "and people are going to think there's really something *wrong* at Enron."

Three hours later, Fastow sat in a rich leather chair at the credenza behind his desk, typing an e-mail to his wife, Lea. They had planned to have lunch together that day, but now that was impossible. Too much needed to be done; he had to get some things settled. He finished typing his apologies to Lea and hit the "send" button.

Fastow pushed back from the credenza and stood. Ken Lay appeared in his office doorway, his face stern.

"I need to talk to you, Andy," Lay said.

"Okay, Ken. Come on in."

Fastow touched the button on his remote, closing his office door, while Lay sat at the conference table. As Fastow joined him, Lay eyed the man he had trusted for so long. In the hours since their first meeting that day, he had learned new information, disturbing details that had made Lay question his steadfast confidence in Fastow. But no matter. The problem was out of Lay's hands now.

"Andy, I just left a meeting of the board. And based on the information you provided this morning, the board decided that we can't continue with you as CFO. We've decided to put you on a leave of absence and make Jeff McMahon the new chief financial officer."

Fastow didn't flinch. Lay was surprised; no one had bothered to tell him that Whalley had already delivered the news with far less formality.

"I understand," he said.

Before Lay could speak again, Fastow plowed ahead.

"We need to work out a severance agreement," he said.

Lay shook his head. "We're not ready for that, Andy."

"It won't take long. I won't be unrealistic. I know I'm entitled to nine or ten million dollars. But I think for three or four million, we can all agree that I'm leaving and I'm not going to be a problem."

What? Was this some kind of threat?

"Andy, we're not doing it that way," Lay said. "First of all, there's a lot I need to do other than negotiate your severance. But I also need the board involved."

Fastow leaned in, his voice above a whisper. "Well, let's just have a handshake on something now, you and me, just so it's done."

Lay almost recoiled in disgust.

"No, Andy. We'll talk about it in a few days, but right now we're not going to do anything."

Lay didn't wait for a response. He rose to let Fastow know that the meeting had ended.

"Andy, I think the sooner you exit the building, the better," he said. "I'm sorry about what's happened, but it's necessary. Obviously, I wish you and Lea the best."

Lay strode out of the room, confident he had done the right thing. With Fastow going, he felt a tinge of hope that Enron would soon right itself. Still, the news he had learned at that day's board meeting, coupled with Fastow's sordid scheming for a secret severance, left him shaken.

Had his chief financial officer, a man he had trusted implicitly, really been a snake all along?

OCTOBER 27, 2001—MIAMI BEACH, FLORIDA

The jazz guitarist shuffled toward the front of the small stage at the Jazid club, easing into a sensual blues solo. The bar was woody and intimate, illuminated by long-stemmed candles resting on a handful of marble-topped tables. On this night the place was packed, the crowd swaying to the rhythm of each soulf riff.

On one side of the room Jeff Skilling sat at a crow glass of white wine. None of the revelers spoke to hi ognize him as someone who, weeks before, had b America's top companies. And none realized that on th riorating, a man approaching a nervous breakdown.

There's no way out of this.

Skilling ran it through his mind. Enron, his company—for years, his life—was imploding. Other traders were refusing to do business with it. Capital was evaporating. Confidence was shattered. Regardless of Lay's happy talk about its prospects, Skilling knew his baby was dying.

Oh, fuck! There's got to be something. Got to be. Outside equity, find investors. How? No time. Talk to the banks. Look 'em in the eye, tell them you'll pay them back. Shit! It's too late. Should have had the planes headed to New York last week. Fuck! Why aren't they doing anything?

He breathed deeply. Again and again, he walked through Enron's maze of financial problems in his mind, hoping to find some means of escape he had overlooked. But the answer was always the same. Enron was gone. It couldn't be saved.

Skilling wiped a hand up his cheek, smearing a tear. Fatigue shadowed his red-rimmed eyes. He picked up his glass, then glanced at a passing waitress.

"One more," he told her. "Pinot Grigio."

Rebecca Carter, Skilling's longtime girlfriend and recent fiancée, sat next to him with a growing sense of alarm. The two had met at Enron, and had both left the company in August. For weeks, things had been wonderful; Skilling had spent time with his kids, did some traveling. Just the day before, the couple had come to Florida to visit a friend. But with Enron's sudden troubles on his mind, Jeff was coming apart. Carter had never seen him drink this much. *What was it now? Eight glasses? Ten?* She reached out and touched his shoulder.

"Jeff, can we please just leave?"

"No." He didn't even look at her.

"Jeff . . ."

"No."

"Jeff, you need to stop drinking."

"*No.*" Skilling was stone-faced, unflinching.

The wine kept coming, as many as fifteen glasses. Skilling sat stock-still, tranquilizing his frayed emotions, growing angry. He was thinking of the ones he blamed for the troubles. *It was the international division,* he thought. *They* were the ones who wasted billions on lousy projects. *They* were the ones who tied up Enron's capital. Skilling tossed them out when Enron stock was soaring; the longtime international chief, Rebecca Mark, had made tens of millions of dollars selling her shares.

I kicked them out and saved them, he thought bitterly. *They destroyed Enron's ~~wealth~~, and I made them rich.*

Hours passed as Skilling veered between despondency and fury. Finally he'd had enough.

"Let's get out of here," he said suddenly, grabbing Carter's hand.

Skilling stumbled out to the street, and Carter wrapped an arm around him, struggling to hold him up in the crisp October evening. The couple brushed past crowds as they staggered down Washington Street toward their hotel. With each tormented step, Skilling fell deeper into incoherence.

"It's going down," he mumbled rapidly, his voice hollow and detached. "It's going down."

Carter tugged at his arm to keep him moving, astonished. "Jeff, come on. You're talking about Enron."

"It's all going down . . ." The words trailed off.

For ten minutes they lurched along, until the elegant Delano Hotel loomed ahead, its gleaming white facade serving as a beacon. Carter maneuvered her fiancé up the terrazzo steps and into the hotel's high-ceilinged lobby.

"Come on," she said. "Let's just go to bed."

Skilling jerked away from her.

"No fucking way," he growled.

He stumbled across the lobby, collapsing on a sofa. Catching sight of the bar in the back, he motioned for a waitress to bring him a drink. Carter sat next to him, closing her eyes as he downed another glass of wine. Finally, she gave in to her fury and frustration.

"Damn it, Jeff!" she said, standing up. "This is stopping right now! You're not going to kill yourself tonight. We are going upstairs and we're going to bed."

Chastened, Skilling placed his wineglass on a table, following Carter meekly to the elevators. But his mind was churning. He had no control anymore. He was giving up.

Carter dragged him into their room, and Skilling fell onto the bed. Lying sideways, he sobbed uncontrollably. He tried to speak, but his words came out as gibberish; he pulled his knees into a fetal position. Carter brought her hands to her head. *What the hell is going on?*

"Jeff, what's happening? You're scaring me."

She sat beside him, stroking his back, murmuring reassurances that Skilling didn't want to hear. Minutes ticked by, until finally he crushed the pillow.

"It's not going to be okay!" he shouted. "It's all going down!"

He sat up, pushing Carter back as he moved.

"Everything I worked for my whole life is gone, just destroyed! Everything is gone!"

Skilling shook his head, tears streaming down his face. The enormity of it all suddenly crashed down on him.

"You don't understand what's going to happen!" he cried in a raspy voice. "Everyone's going to get hit by this! I'll never be able to show my face in Houston again! I mean, just the impact on all the people. Everything I've worked for is cratering!"

Reaching out to him, Carter muttered some soothing words. Skilling breathed deeply and tried to think. *It's too late*. His world was gone, he would be a pariah. Everyone close to him would be caught in the wreckage. *Rebecca*. He couldn't marry her. He couldn't.

Skilling pulled away, a look of terror in his face. He was wide-awake now, wild-eyed and breathing rapidly.

"Rebecca, you need to go," he said.

"Jeff . . . ," Carter said, reaching for him again.

Skilling recoiled. "Get the fuck away from me!"

Carter stood, astonished. "What?"

"Get the fuck out of here! Get away from me!"

"Jeff . . ."

"Leave me alone! I don't want to see you!"

Carter stared at her fiancé, her eyes welling up. Nothing, not a sound or movement, interrupted the moment.

Grimacing, Skilling stood and flailed his arms. "Get the fuck out! Go back to Houston! I don't want you here!"

Hesitation. Carter shuddered, then silently turned to leave. The door clicked closed behind her. Skilling stayed motionless for a moment, then crumpled into the bed. He pulled his knees to his chest again, his body shaking.

"Oh, God!" he wailed, crushing a pillow to his face.

———

It was the scandal that seemed to come out of nowhere, the scandal that changed everything. In the fall of 2001, the Enron Corporation—a politically powerful company whose business was only vaguely understood even by its own competitors—imploded, falling so far from its pedestal that its once-respected name transformed in a matter of weeks into shorthand for corporate wrongdoing.

The implications of the Enron debacle were so vast that even years in hindsight, they are still coming into view. It set off what became a cascading collapse in public confidence, sealing the final days of an era of giddy markets and seemingly painless, riskless wealth. Soon Enron appeared to be just the first symptom of a disease that had somehow swept undetected through corporate America, felling giants in its wake from WorldCom to Tyco, from Adelphia to Global Crossing. What emerged was a scandal of scandals, all seemingly interlinked in some mindless spree of corporate greed.

As investors fled the marketplace, terrified of where the next eruption might emerge, trillions of dollars in stock values vanished, translating into untold numbers of second jobs, postponed retirements, lost homes, suspended educations, and shattered dreams.

But nothing was quite what it appeared. The Enron scandal did not burst out, fully grown, from the corporate landscape in a matter of days. Across corporate America, widespread corner cutting, steadily falling standards, and compromised financial discipline had been festering for close to a decade. Warnings about funny numbers, about unrealistic expectations, about the coming pain of economic reality, went unheeded as investors celebrated corporations pursuing reckless or incomprehensible business strategies that helped their stock prices defy the laws of gravity.

It was in that environment, and only that environment, that the Enron debacle could emerge. It was not simply the outgrowth of rampant lawbreaking. The true story was more complex, and certainly more disturbing. For crime at Enron—and, no doubt, there was crime—was just one ingredient in the toxic stew that poisoned the company. Shocking incompetence, unjustified arrogance, compromised ethics, and an utter contempt for the market's judgment all played decisive roles. Ultimately, it was Enron's tragedy to be filled with people smart enough to know how to maneuver around the rules, but not wise enough to understand why the rules had been written in the first place.

No single person bore responsibility for the debacle; no single person possibly could. Instead, the shortcomings of a handful of executives—along with a community of bankers, lawyers, and accountants eager to win the company's fees; a government willing to abide absurdly lax rules; and an investor class more interested in quick wealth than long-term rewards—merged to create an enterprise destined to fail. But in the end, for all the mind-numbing accounting ploys and financial maneuvers that came to light in Enron's wake, the underlying cause of the collapse was fairly simple: the company spent much of its money on lousy businesses. And the market exacted its revenge.

The repercussions were ugly. Arthur Andersen, the once-revered accounting firm, evaporated overnight as its role in the debacle led to a subsidiary scandal of its own. A President and members of his Administration, already struggling with a new threat to national security, found themselves on the defensive because of their close association with Enron. The new chairman of the Securities and Exchange Commission saw his dream job slip through his fingers amid the recriminations. And members of Congress, reacting to their constituents' fear and anger, pushed through what proved to be the most dramatic revision since the Great Depression in the laws protecting investors.

This, then, is more than the tale of one company's fall from grace. It is, at its base, the story of a wrenching period of economic and political tumult as revealed through a single corporate scandal. It is a portrait of an America in upheaval at the turn of the twenty-first century, a country torn between its worship of fast money and its zeal for truth, between greed and high-mindedness, between Wall Street and Main Street. Ultimately, it is the story of the untold damage wreaked by a nation's folly—a folly that, in time, we are all but certain to see again.

BOOK ONE

THE WINE OF ASPIRATION

CHAPTER 1

THE TWO MEN PUSHED through the glass-and-chrome doors of the Enron building and hurried down the polished granite steps outside. Across the street, a white fountain resembling a mammoth three-tiered wedding cake bubbled in the brilliant winter morning. The sounds of splashing receded as the men crossed Smith Street, a main artery for downtown Houston. Rounding a corner, the older man, David Woytek, glanced at his watch. *Fifteen minutes to go.* Fifteen minutes, he felt sure, till all hell broke loose.

Without a word, he picked up the pace, followed in step by John Beard, a colleague from Enron's internal-audit department. On that morning, February 2, 1987, the two were eager to meet with Ken Lay, to finally prove that two of his underlings had cheated his company. Beard carried the damning evidence—bank records showing millions of dollars siphoned from Enron into personal accounts, transactions so suspicious that the bank itself raised a red flag to Woytek. But, most delicious of all, the executives under investigation—Louis Borget and Thomas Mastroeni, two top officers in Enron's oil-trading unit in Valhalla, New York—would be at the meeting, defending themselves with what Woytek and Beard were certain would be a tangle of lies.

The proof was strong, but the auditors knew it would need to be. Borget was Enron's earnings Svengali, a man whose business reliably brought in tens of millions of dollars in badly needed annual profits. He and Mastroeni, his top finance executive, were rumored to consort with the rulers of Saudi Arabia and Kuwait, contacts everyone believed gave them strong knowledge about the inner workings of OPEC, the Arab petroleum cartel. Taking them down would mean losing their connections and dismantling their profit machine at a time when Enron was struggling.

But Woytek and Beard believed Lay would have no choice; their case was ironclad. Mastroeni had opened an Enron corporate account at Eastern Savings Bank, listing himself and Borget as the signers. But neither had bothered to tell Enron about the account, and it was not recorded in the company's books. Millions in corporate cash had been wired there, about half of which ended up in Mastroeni's personal accounts. The dealings had all the earmarks of some multimillion-dollar scam, with Enron as the mark.

Woytek and Beard turned onto Dallas Street, two blocks from their destination, Enron's other offices at the Houston Natural Gas building. The streets of downtown seemed almost abandoned that morning, with only a smattering of cars around, a reminder that the years-long oil bust was still wreaking its havoc on Houston.

The two auditors walked into the lobby, taking the elevator to the sixteenth floor. There, a receptionist directed them to the office of Mick Seidl, Enron's president. Lay had borrowed the office for the morning meeting while Seidl was on the road.

They arrived in the doorway of the large, wood-paneled office. Borget and Mastroeni were already inside, deep in discussion with John Harding and Steve Sulentic, the home office's nominal supervisors of the oil unit. When the auditors walked in, the conversation stopped.

"Hey," Harding said. "Good to see you."

There were handshakes all around. Borget picked up a thick stack of documents and slid them across the table.

"This is a memo with everything you need to know about these transactions," he said. "All the relevant banking records and other material are attached."

"Thanks," Woytek replied. "We'll look through it."

Beard picked up the documents and left Seidl's office, following Woytek to an unoccupied secretary's desk. He set the documents down, leaning over as he read them. "CONFIDENTIAL," the first page blared. "Memo for the File."

Step by step, the memo described how the transactions came about. In one paragraph it mentioned some attached bank statements. Beard thumbed through the pages and found the records. He studied them for an instant.

Wait a minute.

He scanned the records again, fearful he had made some mistake. No, there was no doubt. He glanced over at Woytek.

"Dave, come here," he said. "Take a look at these."

Woytek strolled over and skimmed through the statements. They were from Eastern Savings Bank, in the name of the oil-trading division. Nothing seemed surprising; the discovery of that account had set off the investigation. With an almost imperceptible shrug, Woytek looked at Beard, waiting to hear what he was missing.

"These are the same statements we already have from the bank," Beard said. "But this copy has been altered."

"You've gotta be kidding me. Show me our copy."

Beard fished through his briefcase, pulling out an almost-identical set of the statements. Woytek laid the pages side by side with the records from Borget.

Unbelievable. The statements were from the same account on the same date, but the numbers were different. The original records showed hundreds of thousands of dollars sloshing in and out. In this new copy, those transactions had simply disappeared. Woytek held Borget's records up to the light. No lines. No shadows. No telltale signs anywhere of an alteration. Somebody had put a lot of effort into this.

Woytek chuckled. These traders were planning to defend themselves to Lay—*using dummied-up records?* This meeting was going to be even more interesting than he had thought.

"Well," he said, looking up, "that settles it. Those two are gonna be fired *today.*"

As the two auditors spoke, they saw Lay and Rich Kinder, Enron's general counsel, walking toward Seidl's office. Woytek and Beard gathered up their papers and stood to greet them. Everyone immediately followed Lay into the office and took a seat around the conference table.

After some chitchat, Lay opened things up. "Well, we know why we're here. So, Lou, why don't you go ahead?"

Borget handed out copies of the memo with the attached bank records. "As everyone's aware," he began, "questions have been raised about some of the trading operation's financial transactions. We want to go through them so that you know why these were done. I think everyone will be very satisfied with what they hear."

Borget and Mastroeni took turns laying out the story. Because of their huge profits in 1986, they explained, company managers had asked them to find a way to shift income into 1987, the current year; that way, Enron would have a jump on hitting its profit projections.

"Now, we were told to get that done using whatever legitimate business practice we could," Borget said, moving his hands as he spoke. "So we set up a system that's used by lots of other trading companies."

The idea was to conduct twinned trades that canceled each other out, known as a "book-out" or a "net-out." So, Mastroeni explained, they tracked down three trading companies—Isla Petroleum, Southwest Oil & Commodities, and Petropol Energy—that wanted to boost their 1986 earnings. Then, that December, Mastroeni and Borget entered into trades that gave profits to the competitors and losses to Enron. The plan was to reverse the trades in 1987, with Enron gaining the profits and the three others getting the losses. All the parties would walk away even and with exactly the results they wanted. The Eastern Savings account had been opened as a precaution, Mastroeni explained, to hold the money until the trades were completed. But since it was in the company's name, Mastroeni said, he had transferred the money to personal accounts, ready to be returned to Enron once the 1987 trades were conducted.

"How many other transactions have you guys done off the books?" Woytek asked.

"This is it," Mastroeni replied.

As the traders' words tumbled out, Woytek breathed deeply. *This is the stupidest thing I've ever heard.*

Sulentic broke in, looking Lay in the eye. "This was all just a misunderstanding, Ken. Lou and Tom really believed they were acting in Enron's interest. I say we accept that mistakes were made, do what needs to be done to correct them, and move on to a profitable 1987."

Lay nodded grimly, seeming lost in thought. "This is obviously not the type of thing we want to have happen," he said finally. "I understand what you were trying to do, but this is not the way to accomplish that."

Everything would be undone, Lay ordered. The transactions must be reversed and the off-books bank account shut down. And there would be other consequences. New controls, new oversight. This would not happen again.

Lay sat back. "Does anybody else have anything?"

"Well," Woytek said, "I have a couple of problems."

There was a short discussion about taxes and when the income would be reported. Heads nodded all around; they agreed Enron would report all of its 1986 profits in that year and pay the taxes. Woytek glanced at the traders. By raising such a tangential issue first, he seemed to have lowered their guard. They looked relaxed, confident.

Time to move in for the kill.

He held up the banking records from the memo. "But the real problem I have is that these bank statements you guys brought here today have been altered."

Woytek pulled out the second set of statements, describing the discrepancies. All the while, he stared at the traders, looking in their eyes for a flicker of shame or embarrassment. *None.* Just pure, controlled fury.

"Now, wait a minute!" Borget snapped.

"I can explain that," Mastroeni interrupted.

There was this trader, Mastroeni said, who had been fired at the end of 1985. After Enron paid out its bonuses for the year, the trader had hired a lawyer, threatening to sue the company if he didn't receive a bonus.

"There was so much going on at Enron at the time we didn't want to start a new political problem internally," Mastroeni said. "So we set up a closeout transaction for him and paid him a $250,000 bonus. But that was it."

"So why alter the records?" Woytek asked.

Borget scowled. "We just didn't want to cloud up this meeting with this stuff about bonuses. It has nothing to do with what we're talking about. So we just took it out."

The back-and-forth continued for several minutes. Lay just watched, expressionless as he listened. Woytek wrapped up his interrogation and sat back, ready for the hammer to drop.

Lay clasped his hands on the table. "Well," he said finally. "Okay."

Oh, shit, Woytek thought. These guys had just presented forged documents, and they're going to get away with it?

"I just don't want this to happen again," Lay continued. "If something like this comes up again, call us. We can handle this bonus situation. But these profits have got to be reported properly."

The meeting ended, and the traders, somehow, had survived. Everyone began filing out.

"Dave, John, stay behind a minute."

The two auditors looked back at Lay, who was signaling for them to return to the conference table. They took their seats; Lay stayed silent until the office door closed.

"Okay," Lay said. "Go to Valhalla and look through their records. If I find out Borget is trading on inside information, on tips he's getting from somebody in OPEC, I'll make sure he never works in the industry again."

Woytek and Beard nodded, taking notes.

"So, John," Lay continued, "you go ahead and get that going, and Dave and I will run through some details."

Beard gathered his papers and strode out of the room. Lay leaned in, his eyes boring in on Woytek.

"I want you to go up there and take your top people," Lay said. "Make sure every penny of this money is returned to the company, even this bonus Borget was talking about. I want all of it back. And I want you to go today, now."

"All right," Woytek replied. "We're on it."

Both men stood, and Lay escorted Woytek to the door. He felt confident that his message had been heard. He wasn't going to stand by and be played for a fool. Besides, the trading unit had always struck him as a little wild and woolly; maybe this was the chance to get the place under some more watchful eyes. Lay liked that idea; he liked to see the possibilities, the upside. As anyone who knew Enron would say, Lay and his company had long ago learned that every challenge could be transformed into opportunity.

The dilapidated black truck rumbled over the rural Missouri road, veering ever closer to the edge. In the flatbed, dozens of crated-up chickens squawked, scratched, and clucked as the truck headed out of a speck of a town called Raymondville. It was 1948, and Ken Lay's father, Omer, was struggling for the second time to keep a general store afloat. Omer had taken to purchasing chickens from local farmers, selling them at a profit in nearby cities, and on this day he had gambled everything on a single shipment. But his driver had knocked back a few drinks and now was weaving all over the road. The weight of the truck shifted, until it flipped over in a terrible crunch of metal and wood. The driver survived, but most of the chickens were killed—right along with Omer's business.

The accident was a turning point for the struggling, deeply religious Lay family. With two daughters and Kenny, their six-year-old middle child, Omer and his wife, Ruth, had hoped the store might allow them to settle down, maybe own their own place. Now those dreams were gone.

Omer took a job in Mississippi selling stoves door-to-door, bouncing his family around the state but never seeing enough success to make ends meet. The family hit bottom one Thanksgiving when Ruth—the spark plug of the household who delighted in nothing more than whipping up family feasts— could only afford to serve luncheon meat. Admitting defeat, the Lays moved to a Missouri farm with some of Ruth's family until Omer could get back on his feet. Soon he found work in sales and a spot preaching at a church.

Around that time, young Kenny—he was usually "Kenny" as a child, never "Ken" and rarely "Kenneth"—scouted up some jobs for before and after school so that he could help the family. He delivered newspapers, mowed grass, baled hay, anything he could find. Between Omer and Kenny, money was coming in, and the Lays were able to settle in a home just off a dirt road cutting through Rush Hill.

Within a few years the financial troubles returned. Lay's older sister, Bonnie, headed to college, and the cost was far more than the family had anticipated. The only way the family could scrape together the money for college, they decided, was for the kids to live at home. So the Lays moved again, this time some fifty miles southwest to Columbia, the college town for the University of Missouri.

Lay's big moment in college came in his sophomore year, when he signed up for introductory economics, taught by a popular professor, Pinkney Walker. Lay found himself mesmerized by Walker's lectures laying out free-market theories; *this*, he decided, was what he wanted to study. Walker was impressed with the smart young man and became a mentor for young Lay.

With Walker's encouragement, Lay stayed on at school after his senior year to obtain his master's degree. But that was enough for Lay; he was eager to get out and start earning some money.

He took a job with Houston-based Humble Oil & Refining, later part of Exxon, helping set up the company's corporate-development department for what seemed a princely salary of thirteen thousand dollars a year. With his career blooming, Lay felt ready to settle down, and in June 1966 he married his college sweetheart, Judith Ayers.

Lay took to the job, enthralled as he debated topics like the future growth rate of the American economy. But soon a new opportunity emerged. His company's chief executive was looking for a speechwriter, and Lay got the assignment, winning the chance for a close-up view of life at the top of the corporate world. He liked what he saw.

For many young American men, the late 1960s were a time for putting plans on hold. The Vietnam War was escalating, deferments were running out, and the draft loomed. Lay did his best to avoid the military, keeping the job that gave him a deferment and studying nights for his doctorate. Still, he found the arrangement distasteful and wound up attending the Navy's officer candidate school in Rhode Island starting in January 1968. From there, it was on to the Pentagon, where he was hired to apply his economics knowledge. Lay soon found himself assembling econometric models and later analyzed the economic effects of military spending for his doctoral thesis.

When his time in the military was up, Lay was eager to return to the corporate world. But then Pinkney Walker, his old economics professor, was named to the Federal Power Commission, and he persuaded his star student to join him as his technical assistant. After eighteen months, Lay was asked to serve as deputy undersecretary of energy for the Department of the Interior; he accepted and was named to the post in October 1972 at the age of thirty. In a little more than a year, he was ready to move on.

He latched on to a senior-level position at Florida Gas, a sleepy pipeline company in Winter Park, thanks to an old acquaintance, W. J. "Jack" Bowen, its chief executive. Lay found the smaller company suited him. But the following year his pal Bowen left for Transco Energy, a pipeline giant in Houston, turning the top job over to Selby Sullivan, his second in command. Over the next seven years, Lay moved up the corporate ladder until he was president.

Still, at times he chafed under Sullivan, whose management style he found unnervingly erratic. One night Lay received a phone call at home from Sullivan, asking him to handle an early-morning meeting in Orlando. Lay agreed, and the next morning attended the meeting. But when he called in to the office, a panicked assistant told him Sullivan was pacing the halls, screaming, "Where's Lay?"

Sullivan's frequent explosions were always followed by long apologies, a habit Lay began to exploit. When important decisions needed to be made, Lay would anger his boss on purpose, then wait for the inevitable mea culpa. Only then would he present the issue that needed a decision, making clear how he wanted things to go. More often than not, the contrite Sullivan agreed, not knowing he had been manipulated by his young president.

In Washington, D.C., the group of energy-industry executives milled about the hallway of the Capitol Hill office building, grabbing refreshments between meetings of the American Gas Association. Ken Lay scooped up a couple of hors d'oeuvres and noticed his old pal Jack Bowen. They chatted a few minutes, with Bowen asking about life in Florida. It was the spring of 1981, and Lay intimated he didn't plan to hang around Winter Park much longer. While he didn't mention it, Lay was tiring of Sullivan's antics and was eager to run his own show. He also had personal issues; his marriage was troubled and was on the verge of falling apart. Bowen walked away convinced he might be able to steal his former colleague for Transco.

Two weeks later, Bowen called, asking Lay to join Transco as his number two and heir apparent. Lay agreed and, days before his departure, filed for divorce.

It seemed a glorious time to live in Houston. The oil shocks of the 1970s had pushed energy prices through the roof, levitating the town in a bubble of economic growth. Throughout the industry it became a matter of faith that oil prices, which had already tripled, would do it again, surpassing one hundred dollars a barrel. But just after the thirty-nine-year-old Lay arrived, the good times stopped rolling. Oil prices cracked, and soon crashed.

Pipeline companies like Transco suddenly found themselves in a bind. Under old regulations, they were required to have adequate supplies to fill their pipelines before expanding their markets or capacity. To accomplish that, they entered into "take or pay" contracts with producers, committing to buy a set percentage of a well's production over years—whether customers needed it or not. And they agreed to pay ever increasing rates. After all, if energy companies could sell oil at a hundred a barrel, they sure wouldn't spend time looking for gas selling at thirty.

Reality wasn't quite that simple. When oil prices fell, the contracts kept gas at high prices, meaning that while producers might want to drill it, customers didn't want to use the more expensive fuel. Pipeline companies were left with contracts worth billions for gas that nobody wanted.

The problem hit Transco hard. Shortly after Lay joined, he found that the company, which had assured him it had no take-or-pay exposure, had failed to properly account for its contracts. If oil prices kept falling, he figured, his new employer would go bust. So Lay corralled a group of Transco analysts and urged them to play around with a new idea: setting up a spot market for gas. That would jettison the old system in which producers sold gas to pipeline operators, who sold it to distributors, who sold it to the final customers. Instead, in a spot market, producers—or at least the ones who released Transco from its contracts—would sell directly to customers; Transco would then be paid to move the gas through its pipeline.

It seemed like a great idea. Lay worked for months obtaining the necessary regulatory approvals, and then sat back to watch it succeed. Problem was, no one was interested. On the first day of trading, Lay was on vacation in Florida with his new wife, the former Linda Phillips Herrold, his onetime secretary at Florida Gas. After some time puttering around the hotel, he called in to hear how things had gone. Not a single trade had taken place. Same on the second day. And the third. No one was willing to be the first producer to break ranks and utilize the new system.

By the fifth day of failure, Lay headed back to Houston. He and his team worked the phones, persuading a few independent producers to try the new market. From there, Lay reached out to other contacts; the breakthrough came when Shell Oil announced it would use the spot market. Within eighteen months, the spot market had pretty much taken over all new contracts, and Lay emerged as an industry legend, a man who had transformed certain disaster into a new business. Plenty of other companies took notice.

On a Thursday afternoon in May 1984, Lay was in the Woodlands, a part of suburban Houston, playing tennis with a Transco banker, when he heard he had a call. He ambled off the court and picked up the phone. On the line was John Duncan, chairman of the executive committee of Transco's smaller rival Houston Natural Gas, or HNG. Duncan said that the HNG board was eager to meet with Lay for breakfast that Saturday; Lay thought the suggestion sounded suspiciously like the opening gambit in an effort to persuade Transco to purchase HNG.

That Saturday, Lay drove over to Duncan's home near the Houston Country Club for breakfast. Over eggs and toast, Duncan lobbed in a surprise: the HNG board wasn't interested in Transco; they were interested in Lay. They wanted to bring him in as chairman and chief executive. Lay was flattered but dubious. Over the weekend, though, Duncan and other HNG directors kept up the pressure, throwing all kinds of incentives into the mix.

By Sunday, Lay agreed to come aboard, so long as Bowen, who was counting on him to take over Transco, gave his blessing.

The next morning, Monday, Lay arranged to have a private lunch with Bowen and spent the entire meal spelling out the details of the HNG approach. Bowen seemed a little disappointed HNG hadn't asked *him*. On the other hand, he wasn't about to block the move.

"I'm not going to stand in your way," Bowen said. "So you go ahead, become a CEO right now."

The decision was made. Ken Lay, the kid from rural Missouri, became chairman and chief executive of a major corporation in June 1984, at the age of forty-two.

It could be argued that the creation of Enron was set in motion on April 21, 1985, when a thirteen-year-old Texas boy decided to phone Zurich.

Earlier that day, the teenager, Beau Herrold, had taken a message for his stepfather from Sam Segnar, chief executive of InterNorth, an Omaha energy company. Beau told the caller that his stepfather, Ken Lay, was traveling with his mother, Linda. As instructed, he refused to say where Lay was or how to reach him. Still, Beau chewed over the call; it somehow seemed urgent enough that he decided to let his stepfather know about it right away. He checked his parents' itinerary and saw that they would be arriving at the Dolder Grand Hotel in Zurich. Beau called and left a message for Lay with the front desk.

That evening at eleven, the Lays arrived at the hotel from the latest meeting with European investors. At the front desk, Lay picked up Beau's message and, after checking in, called the boy. Lay knew Segnar's name, and certainly knew his company, InterNorth, a rival, but he had no idea why the man was calling. Taking a seat at a small desk in the one-bedroom suite, he dialed Segnar at home. As the phone rang, Lay glanced out the window, admiring the lights of Zurich twinkling under a cloud-filled sky. Segnar answered, and the two men spent a moment exchanging pleasantries. Then Segnar sprang the question.

"Ken," Segnar said, "would you have any interest in putting our two companies together?"

The idea struck Lay out of the blue. He barely knew what to say. "Well, Sam," Lay finally replied, "truthfully, I've never really thought about it before."

There were plenty of reasons to do it, Segnar said. Both companies were pursuing a strategy based on the idea that fully deregulated markets were coming in the gas industry. Both understood that the biggest pipeline systems would be the winners. Both had been snapping up smaller pipelines and were often competing bidders. Fighting over scraps made no sense when they both could achieve their shared goal through a single merger—with each other.

Segnar had plenty of other justifications for pushing the deal, but many of those went unmentioned. Irwin Jacobs, the feared corporate raider, was loading up on InterNorth stock. If Segnar didn't take control of his own destiny, Jacobs might do it for him. A major acquisition, like HNG, would load the company up with debt and make it far less attractive as a candidate for a hostile takeover.

Intrigued, Lay asked some questions and said he would get his best people working on the idea. For the next few days, he traveled through Europe with almost no sleep. During the day he met investors; all night he held strategy sessions by phone with his team. HNG wanted seventy dollars a share, InterNorth haggled for sixty-five. Segnar caved on everything, including a commitment that Lay could take over in a matter of years. The seventy-dollars-a-share deal was announced on May 2, just eleven days after the phone call to Zurich.

There was little time for celebration. Lay had acquired new problems, as he discovered at a September reception in Houston. He hosted the get-together for the InterNorth crowd, giving them a chance to meet the city's big oilmen. But instead, the directors trooped off to another room to verbally beat up Sam Segnar. They had grown angry about the HNG deal, which they thought had put the company too deeply in debt. Worse, they had heard rumors that Lay and Segnar had secretly agreed to move the headquarters from Omaha to Houston. Segnar denied there was any such deal, but the directors wanted to hear it from Lay—that night.

As the last of the guests filed out of the reception, Lay headed over to meet the angry directors. He was not in a mood to play nice; a lot of effort had gone into organizing the reception, and the directors had basically insulted everyone in Houston's energy industry. But before he could speak, the directors started in, making it clear that there was more at stake than some bruised feelings; apparently, the directors distrusted Segnar, their own CEO.

Lay assured them that no secret deal existed, yet at the same time pushed the idea of moving the headquarters to Houston. The directors decided to hire a consultant to analyze the option. They turned to John Sawhill—a former Nixon Administration official now with McKinsey & Company, the management consulting firm—who had done work for InterNorth in the past.

It was a decision that would bring to the company the man who ultimately redefined its future.

————

"What, are you kidding me? No way."

Jeff Skilling almost laughed. His boss, John Sawhill, had just phoned to tell him about the HNG/InterNorth headquarters study. Skilling, at thirty-one already a rising star in McKinsey's Houston office, was incredulous.

"Jeff, it's an important assignment," Sawhill said. "It's something the company really wants."

Skilling could only shake his head. He knew about the battles at HNG/InterNorth in the Houston-versus-Omaha debate. Whatever the answer, somebody at the company would be furious—and almost certainly blame the consultants.

"How do you win this one, John? How do you decide this? I want nothing to do with it."

Sawhill implored his underling to reconsider, but Skilling was adamant. Finally, the two agreed to turn the job over to McKinsey's Washington office, effectively shielding Houston from the company's inevitable wrath.

For most young businessmen, such a refusal of a client request might seem risky. But not for Skilling; he was already viewed as a McKinsey wunderkind—brash and arrogant, but with the intellectual firepower to justify his lofty self-image. Born in Pittsburgh in 1953, he was the second of four children, the son of a valve salesman. The family eventually settled in Aurora, Illinois, where Skilling's father worked with a company called Henry Pratt.

Aurora was a typical Midwestern town, with wide-open plains and endless enthusiasm for the high-school sports teams. But Skilling, who arrived at the age of twelve, didn't go in much for sports—or many other school activities. He was a shy, awkward kid, horribly intimidated by girls and largely bored by his teachers.

Home life wasn't much better. His father, Thomas, was happy-go-lucky, but he wasn't around much; his mother, Betty, was a chronic complainer who seemed to blame her husband for a life that didn't work out the way she hoped. Even positive events in Jeff's life—a stellar report card, an aced test—fueled her pessimism. "You think things are going well now," she often said. "Just wait. Things'll fall apart. Sooner or later, they'll get you."

Skilling ached for something to enthrall him and finally found his answer in the working world. His older brother Tom fancied himself an expert on weather patterns, and as a teenager found a spot doing the weather on WLXT-TV, a struggling local television station. The place was nothing much to look at; its crumbling offices had previously been a Moose Lodge. Tom persuaded the managers to hire his younger brother to fix it up. Jeff showed up every day—painting walls, scrubbing floors, doing odd jobs—but would often steal away during his break time, asking the technicians about the broadcast equipment.

His big chance came when he was about thirteen. The station was hosting an event to celebrate its early success, and a number of local politicians were on hand. When one part of the broadcast didn't come off properly, the station's anxious general manager screamed at the young man running the control booth, who quit on the spot.

The evening looked doomed. Then the chief electrician came up with a suggestion: since Jeff Skilling had learned to work the equipment, why not let him try his hand? Within minutes the teenager was running the broadcast, and he was so successful he kept the job. Skilling was thrilled; here he was, a kid dropped at the station in his mom's car, bossing around grown-ups. He found that he loved being in charge, dictating how the work should be accomplished.

The television station went bankrupt just before Skilling left for Southern Methodist University in Dallas, where he had been granted a full scholarship. While there, Skilling had his first real exposure to the vagaries of the business world—and showed his own disposition toward gambling in the markets. He had invested his savings in the company that employed his dad, and watched with delight as the price climbed year after year. It seemed like a painless way to wealth; Skilling even borrowed against the stock to buy his first car. But the early 1970s ushered in a bear market, the price collapsed, and Skilling was broke. He was forced to get a bank loan just to purchase new tires for his car.

But his investment failure only spurred him to deepen his knowledge of business by studying esoteric investments, like options and warrants. Ultimately, he dreamed up a theory of how to turn commodities like gold into securities like stock and wrote a school paper about the idea. Exhilarated by the intellectual challenge, Skilling abandoned his plans to become an engineer and instead focused on preparing for a career in business.

Skilling skipped his college graduation, instead driving up to Chicago to marry his girlfriend, Susan Long, whom he met at SMU. From there, he found his first full-time job at First City National Bank in Houston, where he figured out a way to identify sophisticated crooks who were defrauding the bank with bad checks; he was bursting with pride when an equation he devised helped catch a couple of bad guys.

Despite his success, he decided that the place that could help him really shine was Harvard Business School. He applied and was notified that a dean from the school would be in Houston for another event and would interview him. Freshly scrubbed and in a suit, Skilling headed for the meeting at the downtown Hyatt Hotel, but things got awkward quickly. The dean drilled Skilling with questions for about forty-five minutes; Skilling gave prepared, formulaic answers and sensed things were going badly.

"Skilling," the dean finally said. "Are you smart?"

Skilling smiled. *I've probably blown this anyway. What the hell?* "I'm fucking smart," he shot back.

"That's what I would guess. So why are you giving me all these bullshit answers?"

"I thought that was what you were supposed to do."

"Okay, so drop that. Tell me what you really think. Why do you want to go to Harvard?"

Skilling breathed in deeply. "I want to be a businessman," he said. "I really want it bad."

The conversation began anew, continuing for another hour, and this time Skilling sensed everything was clicking. And he was right; before the day was out, he learned that he had been admitted.

Harvard transformed him. At first intimidated by his classmates, he soon found he outscored most of them on classroom tests. His conceit began to show, alienating some potential friends. But his professors considered Skilling brilliant, and in 1979 he graduated as a Baker Scholar, a designation bestowed on the top five percent of the class.

He was offered a position at McKinsey & Company, the consulting firm with a reputation for arrogance that matched his own, and leaped at it. After wheedling his way back to Texas—first in McKinsey's Dallas office, then in Houston—he focused on energy, an industry whose approach to business struck him as hopelessly outdated and, more important, just plain screwy. He attacked its problems with a vehemence that won him the reputation of a brilliant but self-important strategist.

By 1985, Skilling had been working with John Sawhill on InterNorth for more than three years, long enough to understand the company's internal politics and steer clear of the headquarters debate. After fobbing the assignment off on Washington, Skilling thought little about it again until a draft copy landed on his desk. He picked it up and flipped through the pages.

What the hell?

He couldn't believe what he was reading. The thing was *junk*—more like a travelogue than a real report. *Which city had more professional sports teams? Which had more nonstop flights?* What businessman would relocate his business solely on the basis of such trivia?

Skilling snapped up a pen and started writing. He wasn't about to turn over such a shoddy piece of work to a client—suicide mission or not. If the Washington office couldn't handle the assignment, then he'd do it himself.

Skilling and Sawhill walked past the front desk at the Omaha Marriott on their way to the first-floor meeting rooms. On this day, November 12, 1985, a film crew—in town to make a movie about Boys Town—had taken over, lending the usually businesslike place an air of frivolity. Still, Skilling and Sawhill barely noticed. Not this morning, on the day of their formal report to the HNG/InterNorth board.

The two men arrived at ten o'clock at the door of the Columbus Room, where the board was meeting. An aide told them to wait. They wandered over to chairs outside the door and sat. Minutes passed, followed by hours.

Then, fireworks. Directors started yelling at one another. Skilling and Sawhill glanced at each other. Neither could quite make out the words. Finally, sometime after one o'clock, the door opened. Sam Segnar emerged, his eyes red-rimmed. Sawhill and Skilling stood.

"Listen," Segnar said, "I just want you to know I've been replaced as the chief executive of the company."

Sawhill and Skilling were too stunned to speak.

"It's been nice knowing you," Segnar said. He headed down the hallway, tears in his eyes. The two consultants just stood there; all this over *the headquarters*? This assignment might be more lethal than even Skilling had thought.

The door opened again; the board was ready for them. Most of the directors were looking sheepish. On one side, Ken Lay, a man Skilling had met in passing only a few weeks before, was wide-eyed and a little pale.

Sawhill and Skilling found their seats, and the situation was laid out for them. Segnar was gone; Ken Lay was now president and chief executive. Bill Strauss, InterNorth's sixty-three-year-old former chairman, had returned to his old job and would be running the meeting.

"All right," Strauss said. "Now we want to hear your advice on the corporate headquarters location."

Sawhill stood, straightening his coat. "Thank you," he said. He spoke for a few minutes, then gestured toward his colleague. "Let me introduce Jeff Skilling, who's handling this presentation."

Oh, thanks, John. Skilling launched into the report. The conclusions were simple: HNG/InterNorth's business was in Houston. Its key pipeline there had numerous problems, and its contracts required renegotiation; management needed to be there to oversee the work.

"Now," Skilling said, "the worst possible outcome would be to maintain dual headquarters. So you need to decide, Houston or Omaha, and we would recommend Houston."

A pause. Charles Harper, the chairman and chief executive of ConAgra, an Omaha-based food company, gestured that he wished to speak. Strauss recognized him.

"This," Harper said, fury in his voice, "is the biggest pile of bullshit I have ever heard in my life!"

For several minutes Harper and other directors raged. The company was a major Omaha employer; it couldn't just pick up and leave. Harper turned red as he stormed, and Skilling feared the man was building up to a heart attack.

"Okay," Skilling said, holding up his hands. "Listen, I'm just a consultant. I'm just giving my advice."

One director moved that the company maintain dual headquarters. Another seconded the motion.

"Fine," said Strauss, the chairman. "All in favor?"

A chorus of ayes filled the room.

"Opposed?" Silence.

Jesus Christ, Skilling thought.

"The ayes have it," Strauss said.

Defeated, Skilling and Sawhill made their way out of the room as the directors called a break. Lay hustled to the hallway to find the consultants.

"Jeff! John!" he called.

The two consultants waited as Lay hurried up to them.

"I want to apologize for what happened here," he said. "The work you did was very good, we appreciate the thought that went into it. I think you're probably right, but we just can't do it now."

Skilling nodded, mumbling his thanks. For all the trouble the board had given him, he thought, at least this fellow Lay was a class act.

HNG/InterNorth descended into chaos. The ousting of Segnar was supposed to calm the waters at the company; instead, it set in motion an endless drama of backstabbing and one-upmanship as longtime InterNorth employees prepared for a final battle with the interlopers from HNG. Many viewed Lay as one misstep away from Segnar's fate.

Topping it off, the newly merged company was still struggling through the basics, including the selection of its independent accounting firm. HNG had long relied on Deloitte Haskins & Sells; Lay and his top management were recommending that firm. But InterNorth had used the prestigious Arthur

Andersen & Company, and the directors were frightened that changing firms would leave Andersen no choice but to shut down its Omaha office.

The issues came to a head in late January 1986 at a series of directors' meetings in the sixteenth-floor boardroom of the Omaha headquarters. Lay easily won the battles with subordinates; the directors accepted his appeal to terminate two longtime InterNorth executives he believed were sowing discontent. But the selection of auditors proved to be far stickier. The audit committee—which would make the final recommendation of accountants to the full board—listened in silence as Keith Kern, the chief financial officer, presented management's recommendation of Deloitte as auditors and Andersen as consultants.

When Kern was finished, Lay spoke up. "Now, the management committee is not unanimous here," he said. "But I personally agree with the recommendation."

The first shot from the directors was a surprise: it was aimed at Andersen. James Renier, who worked at Honeywell, said he was worried about that firm. He knew Andersen had been clobbered in recent years by malpractice lawsuits; it had paid about $140 million in such cases over five years, seven times more than any other firm.

That would not be an issue, Kern replied. "They've discussed those cases with us in detail. The amount of money is large, but, really, the number of cases is relatively small. We don't think it's a concern."

The signal of support for Andersen was all the other directors needed. Of course the lawsuits weren't a problem, several said. In fact, one suggested, why take the auditing away from Andersen? With all the difficulties that HNG/InterNorth was facing, why go to the trouble of a switch? Why not rely on Andersen for everything?

Georgiana Sheldon, formerly head of the Federal Energy Regulatory Commission, felt uncomfortable with the suggestion. "Wait," she said. "I don't like the idea of giving all the work to Arthur Andersen. I'd be concerned about a possible conflict of interest if the same firm performed both the consulting and the auditing."

The directors understood. Auditors might need to examine the outcomes of consultants' strategies. Who would want an adviser grading its own papers?

"I agree," said Robert Jaedicke, the Stanford Business School dean who served as the committee chair. "I'd be concerned if Andersen was appointed auditor and a transition wasn't made quickly to another consultant."

The bantering left Lay uneasy. Once again the board members seemed to be undercutting their managers in favor of their own parochial interests. "I need to point something out," he said. "Our CFO made this recommendation to me, and I agreed with it. So it's the recommendation of the CFO and the CEO that this proposal, as outlined, be accepted."

The room went silent. Finally, someone took the bait. "I'm concerned about the message we'd send if this committee doesn't support management," Renier said.

The dynamic of the discussion was shifting. But Jaedicke asked for a forty-eight-hour recess. Lay walked out frustrated. It was a stupid squabble, one that, if he lost, would once again undercut his authority.

Some battles are just not worth fighting.

The only way to win, Lay decided, was to adopt the board's position as his own. He would be victorious in defeat. Two days later, Lay went back to the boardroom to speak with the directors by conference call.

"It is very important at this stage in the company's history to have unanimity from this committee," Lay said. "In view of the fact of the virtual equality of the two firms, management has revised its recommendation."

He paused for a moment. "We are now recommending that Arthur Andersen be retained as our independent auditor."

The directors unanimously agreed. Arthur Andersen was retained as auditor and consultant; Deloitte was abandoned. No one raised the concerns again about the possible problems of Andersen serving in two conflicting roles.

Lay's defeat on the accounting issue set Bill Strauss to thinking. His reappointment as chairman was supposed to help the company come together. Instead, it was pulling itself apart. Already he thought Lay was spending too much time on internal politics; the man had been given the CEO title but received little of the respect that the job deserved. Something needed to be done, Strauss decided. Everything was put in motion in early February 1986, when Strauss ambled down to Lay's office.

"Look, Ken, I know these are tough times, and they're probably not going to get any easier," Strauss said.

"That's probably an understatement," Lay said, chuckling.

"Well, we need to resolve a few things. I need to know your hands are tied to the steering wheel, that you're here for good."

One problem, Strauss said, was that Lay's contract from HNG allowed him to pull the rip cord on a golden parachute up to a year after the company merged. So there was still plenty of time left for Lay to walk away from his job with about three years' worth of salary and bonus.

"If everybody is going to get behind you, Ken, we need to know there's no escape hatch," Strauss said. "I'd like you to give up your golden parachute, and I'd like to be able to tell the board at the next meeting that you did."

Lay asked for the weekend to think about it, and talked it over with his wife, Linda. On Monday he returned with the verdict: Strauss could let the directors know he was giving up the pay package.

The board met on February 11, 1986, at an office building in Orlando, Florida. The directors gathered around the table, and Strauss started things off. Lay figured he would open with the announcement about the pay package.

"I have something to tell you," Strauss began. "I'm going to tell you something that only my wife and I know."

What? Strauss's wife sure wasn't the only one to know about Lay's decision. What was going on?

"In the last few weeks I've met with each of you individually. I've talked to you about what ought to happen at this company. I've asked you about the management team, and the problems and all of that."

Strauss looked over at Lay. "I've reached the conclusion that I should step down as chairman and Ken should become chairman."

No one spoke; no one moved.

"This company needs one leader and one leader only," Strauss continued. "There has to be no doubt about that. So, effective right now, I resign as chairman, I resign from the board, and I am going back to Omaha."

Strauss walked out—no good-byes, no handshakes. In that moment Lay understood Strauss's request from the week before; he had tied Lay's hands to the steering wheel before jumping out of the car. It was the ultimate rebuke to the board; the company had only one driver now, and the board could either support him or crash.

The directors sat in silence, until finally one of them spoke up. "I nominate Ken Lay as chairman."

The vote was immediate and unanimous. Lay assumed total control. Before the year was out, his own supporters had a majority on the board—enough to succeed in moving the headquarters to Houston. But the tumult that surrounded the creation of his company was far from over.

"Enteron." The decision seemed final. HNG/InterNorth would abandon its awkward name and be rechristened "Enteron." It would be the strongest signal of the company's emergence into the new Lay era. On February 19, 1986, eight days into Lay's chairmanship, the company announced that the new name would be put to a shareholder vote in April.

The name had been proposed by Lippincott & Margulies, a pricey New

York consulting firm that had spent three months and millions of dollars on the project. It derived from an analysis of the company's business—"En" for "energy," "ter" for "international" and "InterNorth," and "on" because it sounded cool. After thinking it up, the consultants had checked around the world to be sure no other company was using the name and that it did not have some vulgar meaning in another language.

Problem was, no one bothered to check *Webster's*. "Enteron" is also a word for the digestive tube running from the mouth to the anus—particularly unfortunate, given that Lay's company produced natural gas. Within days of the announcement, the soon-to-be Enteron was a laughingstock.

It all came to a head one Saturday as Lay and his two top advisers—Mick Seidl, his president, and Rich Kinder, his general counsel—jogged three miles in Houston's Memorial Park, debating what to do. Seidl and Kinder believed that the issue would blow over in little time; Lay was equally adamant that the new name had to go.

Two days later, Lay contacted the naming consultants, informing them that either they needed to figure out a new name quickly or it would stay HNG/InterNorth. Somehow, the work that took three months for the first name was repeated in little more than a week. Lay liked the new suggestion immediately; the shareholders overwhelmingly approved it.

HNG/InterNorth would from then on be known as Enron, a name that in its first days was already on its way to being bound up in scandal.

———

The limousine eased along the sidewalk outside the New York airport, stopping where David Woytek and two other auditors were waiting. It was days after the big showdown in Houston over the secret bank accounts, and Woytek and his colleagues—including John Beard and Carolyn Kee, an Arthur Andersen partner—had come to New York to conduct the inspection of the trading unit that Lay ordered. They loaded their luggage and climbed in the limo—provided by Borget, the unit's head—which took them to the offices at the Mount Pleasant Corporate Center. But they were forbidden to enter without being announced, and once they were inside, Borget ordered them not to speak to his traders.

"I don't want you stirring them up and making me lose people," Borget told them.

For three days, the auditors played cat and mouse, with Borget and Mastroeni providing the bare minimum of the records they requested. Finally, on the third day, Woytek had had enough. He flagged down Borget.

"What's the matter?" Borget asked.

"We want to see the backup for these trades," Woytek replied, holding up some trading records.

"What do you mean?"

"The telexes, the wire transfers. All of these trades had to create a paper trail. We want to see it."

Borget tightened. "Okay, we'll get it for you."

The records never arrived. Instead, Borget phoned Houston to complain about the auditors' disruptions. A few hours later, Mick Seidl, Enron's president, called Woytek.

"You guys need to pack up and come home," Seidl said.

"What? Why?"

"Borget is getting upset, the traders are getting upset. You need to pull out. We're going to turn this over to Arthur Andersen instead."

Woytek couldn't believe it. *Borget's got them hoodwinked again.* But he knew there was no fighting a direct order. "Fine," he said. "We'll come back."

The investigation in Valhalla was turned over to Carolyn Kee, who summoned a number of young Andersen auditors to help her dig through the paperwork. Still, Woytek and his team had rifled through enough records to know things in oil trading were bad. For one thing, Borget had sold a company car for seventy-eight hundred dollars and stolen the proceeds, depositing them in the Eastern Savings account.

And then there was M. Yass, a broker from another firm identified as part of the profit shifting. About $106,000 from the bank account had been converted into cash and supposedly paid to Yass, a man described by Borget as a Lebanese national working with Southwest Oil & Commodities. But the auditors were convinced that Yass was a ghost, a creation of the traders' imagination, invented for the purpose of shifting money around. Even his name—Woytek figured it stood for "My Ass"—suggested that the traders were thumbing their noses at Houston.

The team had tried to track down Yass and Southwest Oil. Beard hired a private investigations firm called Intertect to check the backgrounds of Borget and Mastroeni, and to locate Yass, Southwest Oil, and the other companies that supposedly helped in the profit-shifting scheme.

The report arrived at Enron in the second week of February. Southwest Oil, Isla Petroleum, and Petropol Energy did not exist. The telex numbers for them provided by Borget and Mastroeni were bogus. Worst of all, the report said, Mastroeni, the unit's top finance executive, had been personally sued by banks for using fraudulent documents to obtain loans.

Woytek took the devastating report up the line, hurrying over to the office of Keith Kern, Enron's chief financial officer. He gave Kern a copy, laying out everything the private investigators had uncovered.

"Why did we hire these people?" Kern asked, "We don't need to be doing this. Arthur Andersen is up there; they're looking into everything."

Kern tossed the report on his desk. "I want you guys to drop it."

At four o'clock on the afternoon of April 29, Enron's audit committee gathered in the boardroom of the new Houston headquarters. For an hour the directors heard about the company's internal-audit work for 1986. They could not have been more pleased; after months of tumult, it sounded as if Enron's controls were finally falling into place.

"I think you would agree that this is a remarkable turnaround in a very short period of time," Robert Jaedicke, the committee chairman, said during a presentation from accountants with Arthur Andersen.

"Absolutely, yes," replied Jack Tompkins, an Andersen partner. "I would agree with that."

Once all the happy talk was out of the way, the directors turned to the matter of Enron Oil. Andersen had submitted its final report a week earlier, loading it with caveats about their inability to determine whether crimes had been committed. The report was breathtaking in what it failed to reveal—nothing about Mastroeni's past problems with fraud, or the nonexistent trading partners, or the forged documents. It *did* caution that the potential losses in the oil-trading business seemed far larger than the directors believed, but that point went by with little comment.

Instead, Mick Seidl held up the report as evidence that the swirl of suspicions about the goings-on in oil trading could be dispelled. "While there appear to have been some errors in judgment, there are no indications that anything was done for personal gain," he said.

The directors asked questions signaling deep discomfort with Mastroeni. Lay listened, disturbed by the direction of the discussion. Before the meeting, Borget had called him personally, pleading to save Mastroeni's job. The unit wouldn't work without him, Borget had said, and Lay took the warnings seriously. It was clear to him that he needed to make a decisive move to avert an action by the directors. He began to speak.

"I hear your concerns, and I understand them. But I've made the decision. I've got to put my CEO hat on and do what is in the best interest of Enron. We cannot afford to be disrupting our trading operations unnecessarily. It is too important to our financial performance."

Lay's tone was resolute. "I've decided we're not firing anyone. But we will make changes. We will keep Tom Mastroeni on the payroll, but he will be relieved of his financial responsibilities. We're going to name a new chief financial officer for the unit and move that person up there to take control. And all of the banking and financial activities will report through Houston from now on. That's my decision."

Ron Roskens, one of the directors, was the first to respond. "Well, I have to tell you, this bothers me."

Other directors agreed, but Lay held firm. None of the directors seemed willing to start up the sort of battle that had infected Enron in the years before. So, with their reservations clear, the committee voted to back Lay.

After so many months of controversy, the oil-trading-unit scandal appeared all but over.

Lay stretched out his legs as he sat in a soft, upholstered seat on an Enron corporate jet. It was the afternoon of October 9, 1987. He and a few colleagues were somewhere over the Atlantic, flying back from meetings with European investors. Lay was feeling a little sleepy when he noticed one of the pilots coming his way.

"Mr. Lay?" the pilot said. "We just got a message from Mr. Seidl. He's getting on a plane, and he's going to meet you in Gander."

Lay nodded. "Okay, thanks."

This wasn't good. Lay and the others were already on their way to Houston. What could be so urgent that his president would fly to meet him at a refueling stop in Newfoundland?

More than an hour later, the plane landed at the Gander International Airport. Lay and the other executives traveling with him—Forrest Hoglund from the oil and gas group and Kern, who had recently been named chief financial officer of that division—huddled in a corner of the terminal, waiting for Seidl. His plane arrived in less than an hour, and Seidl hustled off, finding his colleagues at a small table. He grabbed a chair and sat down with them.

"I was just up in New York with Lou Borget," Seidl said. He had gone there for a social lunch at the Pierre Hotel, hoping to repair the relations strained by the investigations months before. But over the meal Borget had dropped a bombshell. His group's bets on the direction of oil prices had been going badly. The group had been trading on expectations that prices would fall, but then they rose. When Borget doubled his bet, hoping to make up the loss, they rose again. To hide the problem, Seidl said, Valhalla kept two sets of books, never revealing their position to Houston.

"Now the trading desk has got some very, very large exposed positions that we didn't know about," Seidl said.

"How much are we talking about?" Lay asked.

Seidl took a breath. "Hundreds of millions, maybe more than a billion if the market goes the wrong way."

Lay was speechless. *A billion dollars in potential trading losses?* With Enron still struggling under all the debt it had assumed in the merger, this could bring the company down. Immediately, the pilots were told that Lay's flight plans were changing; he was heading to Valhalla.

Before getting on the plane, he contacted Mike Muckleroy, an experienced Enron oil trader in Houston who for months had been warning—just as the Andersen report had cautioned might be the case—that Borget had to be busting through his trading limits. But Lay hadn't listened, chalking Muckleroy's complaints up to jealousy. Now he needed Muckleroy to help save the company by cleaning up Borget's mess.

By Saturday morning, Lay had arrived in Valhalla and summoned Borget to a nearby hotel conference room. Borget sauntered in, all smooth and self-confident.

"Okay, Ken," he said. "I know we've got a problem here, but it's manageable, and we're going to solve it."

"How did the problem happen, Lou?"

"Ken, I just saw it as a great opportunity for the company, a real chance to hit a super home run. I figured everybody in Houston would be nervous about it, but I didn't think we could afford to pass up the opportunity."

Borget pressed his charm offensive, but this time Lay wasn't buying. Instead, he pumped Borget for information to help Enron minimize the disaster. Finally, when he figured he had heard everything Borget had to offer, Lay lowered the boom.

"Lou, you know you violated a lot of company policies in all of this," he said. "And you've really exposed us to possibly horrendous downsides here."

"Well, again, Ken, I'm very confident we can work all of this out without any harm to the company."

Lay ignored him. "Lou, I have no choice but to terminate you."

Borget sat back, speechless. "*What?*" he sputtered. "You can't work your way out of this problem without me!"

"Yeah, Lou, we can."

Borget pushed him to change his mind, but Lay was unbending. Finally Lay's message sank in. Borget stood and made his way to the door, then stopped and turned.

"Well, if you decide you need my help, I'll be at home. You can call me."

With that, Borget strode away, leaving Enron forever.

———

The second scandal in the oil-trading division transformed Enron, destroying old internal alliances and reshaping the corporate leadership structure.

For three weeks, Mike Muckleroy led a group of traders in gradually shrinking the size of Enron's oil-market position. They were in constant fear that competitors would realize the gravity of Enron's situation and bid up the price of oil; after all, the company had to pay pretty much any price to save itself. But they pulled it off. By late October, Enron's after-tax losses had shrunk to a manageable eighty-five million dollars.

In the months that followed, the Valhalla unit was shut down. Within a few years, Borget and Mastroeni were charged with fraud and tax crimes; Borget was also charged with aiding Enron in filing false income-tax returns through the profit shifting. Both men pleaded guilty; Borget was sentenced to a year in prison, and Mastroeni received a suspended sentence and probation.

Lay and Seidl knew someone had to pay the price for the debacle, and it certainly was not going to be Lay. While Seidl continued at Enron for a couple of years, his responsibilities gravitated to Rich Kinder, now working as chief of staff, sort of a roving Mr. Fixit. While Seidl was viewed internally as indecisive, Kinder was a barn-burning man of action who inspired fear in Enron's executive ranks—just the sort of manager the company needed.

Lay acknowledged soon after the announcement of the trading losses that Enron would have to change its ways. In late October 1987, he called an all-employee meeting in Houston. He held himself up as a victim of Borget and Mastroeni, as someone who had no reason to suspect the problems in Valhalla. But, he said, he walked away from the scandal having learned an important lesson.

"We became involved in a business with risks that we did not appreciate well enough," Lay told the assembled crowd. "And I promise you, we will never again risk Enron's credibility in business ventures without first making sure we thoroughly understand the risks."

It was a commitment he would fail to keep.

CHAPTER 2

THE ELEVATOR DOORS OPENED, and Jeff Skilling stepped into the broad hallway on the forty-ninth floor of the Enron building. He walked past a few inexpensive, nondescript paintings and turned left toward a solid-oak door. Fishing out his wallet, he rubbed it against a sensor in the wall and waited for the magnetic card inside to be read. The electronic lock clicked almost instantly.

Behind the door was a drab corridor with row upon row of empty offices and cubicles—space Enron had paid for but had little hope of filling anytime soon. Striding down the stark hallway, Skilling did not cut an impressive figure. At thirty-five, he was of medium height with a receding hairline and a few unnecessary pounds, the image of just another anonymous consultant working in the dreary surroundings of another besieged American corporation.

It was December 1988. For weeks Skilling and his team from McKinsey had been working here, struggling with Enron's growing and maddeningly complex challenges. Deregulation had upended the game board for gas pipelines, but Enron had yet to devise a strategy to flourish in the new world. McKinsey was supposed to fix that, but after weeks of work Skilling's team was no closer to an answer.

Skilling reached a large, open area lined with empty offices. His was the first on the right; a large conference table filled the room, piled high with stacks of paper—reports, memos, and other remnants of dozens of rejected strategies. He sat, reaching for a pad of quadrille paper. Something was tugging at the back of his mind—an idea, a thought, something Skilling had ruminated about for years. Maybe if he wrote it down, it would become clearer.

Pulling a pen out of his shirt pocket, Skilling sketched an axis, then drew a declining curve. He divided the curve into sections—at five years, ten years, twenty. He tore off the sheet and scribbled calculations on the next page. After about thirty minutes, he set down his pen and studied what he had written.

This is fucking brilliant.

Could it be this simple? Here, on a couple of pages, was the answer to

Enron's problems—hell, to the *industry's* problems. Over the years, Skilling had often been electrified by his own ideas, but this one, *this* one was a gold mine. It was so elegant. It had to work.

Tearing the second sheet off the pad, Skilling scrambled out of the office in search of Rich Kinder, who was just moving up to the job of Enron's vice chairman. As a consultant, Skilling couldn't just take an idea and run with it; somebody at Enron needed to give the green light. He figured Kinder not only would understand his brainstorm but would have the guts to get it done.

On the other side of the building, Skilling rode a small executive elevator to fifty, then walked past the boardroom into Kinder's office.

"Rich . . ."

"Jeff. What's up?"

Skilling laid his quadrille paper on a small conference table. "Look at this."

Kinder strode over to the table and skimmed the page. A bunch of numbers. He shrugged. So?

"Let's say we go out and buy gas reserves," Skilling said. "Give me a number, Rich. How much is it going to cost to buy gas reserves?"

"I don't know, one dollar per mcf."

A dollar for every thousand cubic feet of gas. Just as Skilling had figured. "Okay," Skilling said. "So if we bought reserves at a dollar, we could take them and carve them up, send them to different term markets."

Kinder didn't know where this was going.

"Different contract terms," Skilling continued. "Twenty years, ten years, five years, it doesn't matter. And then we lock in their price with the contract."

Skilling scribbled his graph again. Kinder recognized it as a standard gas-production curve. Gas wells are a lot like a shaken-up bottle of soda; when they are first tapped, built-up pressure pushes out fuel, but over time that force—and the volume of gas coming out—drop. That was reflected in the curve Skilling sketched, showing declining production over many years. But, he said, if Enron owned reserves with a production curve of two decades, it could calculate a fixed price for gas sales over periods of years. The longer the term of the contract—the further out on the production curve—the more expensive the price. The market movement for gas prices wouldn't matter, since Enron would already have locked in its costs at one dollar.

Kinder understood the implications immediately. With deregulation, the old world of fixed gas rates was gone, and prices were now dictated by the open market—meaning a cold snap, a shortage, anything could drive them up rapidly. Suddenly industrial customers couldn't anticipate fuel costs, pipelines couldn't be sure they could guarantee delivery on a long-term contract, and producers were only as good as their last well. The uncertainty was already driving industry toward dirtier fuels—coal, oil—with more reliable pricing. This Skilling idea might change all that. Enron could transform cleaner natural gas into a dependable choice, buying it at fixed, rock-bottom prices, selling it for more, and pocketing the difference.

It would be like a bank, Skilling said, but instead of taking in and sending out money, Enron would traffic in gas. Producers would be depositors, gas customers would be borrowers, and Enron would be rich. To attract the business, he said, Enron would need a marketing division, but from there everything should come together.

"Rich," Skilling said. "What if I told you that I can construct a twenty-year contract, right now, at $2.20."

Kinder stood back. "You're fucking kidding me."

"No, I'm not fucking kidding you."

It was one of those rare eureka moments. Industrial customers were having enough trouble obtaining twenty-year contracts, and finding one at less than four dollars per thousand cubic feet was thought to be impossible. A guaranteed fixed price from Enron of just over two dollars would bring every customer to the company's doorstep.

"If that's true," Kinder said, "then we will own the power-generation market in North America."

Skilling beamed. "Yep," he said, nodding.

Word of some gangbuster new McKinsey idea crackled through Enron, and soon everyone wanted to hear the details. Within days, a group of about twenty Enron executives gathered in conference room 49C1 for their own briefing from Skilling. Most were ready to give up much of their afternoon; typically, McKinsey reports ran on for as long as a hundred pages and took hours to review.

Once everyone was seated, Skilling stepped forward and placed a single transparency on an overhead projector. It was a more professional version of his original scribbles.

"The concept is pretty simple," Skilling began, launching into his analysis. After about twenty minutes, he stepped away from the projector.

The room was silent.

"That's it?" Kinder asked. He had been expecting a beefed-up presentation this time.

"Yeah, that's it."

Kinder nodded. "Okay, let's go around and see what everybody thinks."

To one side, Jim Rogers Jr., head of the interstate pipeline operation, waved a hand. Kinder nodded his way.

"Yeah," Rogers said. "I've got to say, that's the dumbest idea I've ever heard in my life."

Skilling's face fell.

"Who's going to do this?" Rogers continued. "Why is somebody going to sell at those prices? Why will customers come to us? That's not our business."

Rogers's scorn unleashed a torrent of doubts and criticism from other executives in the room. Skilling had failed to take a proper account of the take-or-pay contracts, they said; worse, it forced Enron to be responsible for maintaining a market for gas, making its pipelines almost beside the point. It just wouldn't work.

The meeting ended, and Skilling, downcast, followed Kinder to the elevator for the fiftieth floor. Kinder pulled out an unlit cigar, chewing it as the doors opened. He pushed the button for fifty.

"Rich, I'm sorry," Skilling said. "I thought it was a great idea, but I guess it came up short."

Kinder pulled the cigar out of his mouth. "As soon as I heard Rogers say it was the dumbest idea he's ever heard, I knew it's exactly what we need to do."

The elevator doors opened, and Kinder walked out into the hallway, again clenching the cigar in his teeth.

"Put a team on this," he growled. "Make it happen."

The Gas Bank was an instant success—and failure.

After months of pulling together the logistics, Enron set up its new gas-marketing division. Kinder and Skilling flew around the country, delivering sales pitches to big industrial customers. Many were wowed by the idea; obtaining a predictable price for a clean-burning fuel was a factory owner's dream, even at above the current market. In less than two weeks Kinder and Skilling lined up multiyear contracts for more than a billion dollars of gas.

Then, problems. Despite the demand, gas producers weren't eager to offer a supply. Gas was selling at low levels, and drillers had always survived on faith that prices would rise in the future. Why lock in low prices today, they argued, for gas being used tomorrow? But Enron executives didn't want to abandon the customers they had rounded up, so they temporarily tossed some of the Gas Bank's founding principles. Instead of locking up gas at a fixed cost, Enron purchased fuel on the open market—a gamble, since a price rise could force large losses. Enron won that initial roll of the dice; prices held steady.

The hot concept needed tinkering, and Skilling plunged into the task. A breakthrough came during a meeting with Kaiser Aluminum and Chemical Corporation. Kaiser wanted a five-year fixed-price gas contract for a Louisiana aluminum plant, but Enron had no gas in the state. The fuel,

Skilling said, would have to come from Texas, adding thirty cents to the price. Kaiser nixed the idea as too expensive. Then, as everyone was leaving, Skilling had a thought. Why did Enron even need to deliver gas?

"Wait a minute," he said. "Sit down."

Skilling asked the Kaiser executives some questions. They could already obtain gas in Louisiana, right? Yes, by purchasing it off of a Texaco pipeline.

"So let's do this," Skilling said. Kaiser would buy from Texaco. But Enron would guarantee that Kaiser would never pay more than $2.50 for every thousand cubic feet. If prices climbed, Enron would deliver gas to Kaiser in Texas at $2.50, which Kaiser could then sell at the higher price. If prices fell below $2.50, Kaiser would pay Enron the difference. Rather than agreeing to actually deliver fuel, Skilling was proposing that Enron be paid for assuming the price risk. Kaiser jumped at the proposal.

Over time, Skilling and his team were even able to solve their gas-supply problems. The recalcitrant wildcatters perked up when Enron came to the table with something they needed: loans. After years of turmoil in the energy markets, banks had tightened the purse strings on exploration and drilling. So, with Skilling's urging, Enron offered the financing that the banks withheld in exchange for access to fixed-price gas. Yet another new division, Enron Finance Corporation, was set up to provide the credit.

By late 1989, the Gas Bank was carrying matched orders on its books between five customers and five suppliers. Now Skilling was ready to add the final tweak that would send his idea into the stratosphere. What Enron had created was, in truth, nothing more than a predictable future flow of cash, not much different from a mortgage or a bond. And for more than a decade, Wall Street had been pooling such cash flows together and trading them. Why, Skilling asked, couldn't the cash flows from the Gas Bank be traded, too?

Almost imperceptibly, Skilling's innovations were transforming Enron into a radically different beast. This company of pipelines and rigs, populated by rugged leathernecks with dirty fingernails, was grabbing on to intangible concepts of risk, attracting buttoned-down investment bankers with manicures. The changes were transforming the very nature of Enron, but few people inside or outside the company recognized it.

Late that year, Skilling figured his work was done and headed back to his office at McKinsey. Enron, he thought, was on the precipice of greatness. Then the Gas Bank began falling apart. Except with Kinder, the idea still generated little enthusiasm among Enron's top ranks; it just seemed too foreign. Skilling watched with dismay as his program languished from indifference. Repeatedly, he visited Kinder, by then company president, and pounded his desk, saying Enron was squandering its one great opportunity.

"You guys have got to get going on this," Skilling raged. "Somebody else is going to figure this out, and right now you've got a huge head start."

Kinder agreed, but also understood that Skilling was the only one with a personal stake in seeing the Gas Bank succeed. So in December 1989, he approached Skilling with a proposal: join Enron. Skilling dismissed the offer out of hand. The previous summer he had been elected a McKinsey director; he was on the track for great wealth. It seemed ridiculous now to take a flier on Enron.

But as the months wore on, Kinder—and then Lay—came to believe that the great idea was destined to fail without Skilling. Finally, in early 1990, Lay ran out of patience. He headed to Kinder's office and announced that Skilling had to be persuaded to take charge of the effort.

The timing was perfect. By then, Skilling had glimpsed his future at McKinsey and didn't like the view. He had recently joined the partner election committee and had grown frustrated with the meetings. Nothing ever changed; nothing was ever resolved. At one meeting, Skilling listened in dismay as the head of the German office mouthed the same arguments he had made months before.

Skilling scowled and crossed his arms. *Ten years from now, I'm going to be sitting in this same room, listening to these same guys saying exactly the same things.*

Despite the money he was making, despite the respect he commanded, Skilling was bored. He wanted a new challenge, a new vista, something to make his future more than just a repetition of his past.

At the peak of Skilling's dissatisfaction, in April 1990, Kinder called. This time Skilling jumped at the chance. *This* was his challenge. He would be at the forefront of redefining American energy markets—maybe the international energy markets. That night he discussed the idea with his wife, Susan. With their third child on the way, he feared she would resist, but she said she would support whichever path he chose. The pay would be less—something Skilling glossed over—but Kinder had suggested Enron might give him a piece of the business. If his project worked, Skilling could become very rich; if not, joining Enron could turn out to be professional suicide.

On June 11, 1990, his wife went into labor, and he drove her to St. Luke's Episcopal Hospital. After six hours his second son still had not arrived, and Skilling wandered into the hallway. He tracked down a pay phone and called Kinder. He was ready to finalize everything, Skilling said, and the two men haggled through the last details of the contract. Skilling would be chairman and chief executive of the division Enron Finance. His annual salary would be $275,000—a huge pay cut—but he would be granted his ownership stake in the division.

"Okay," Skilling said. "That's it. We're done."

The call ended, and Enron's newest hire returned to his wife's side.

Exactly one month later, on July 11, a line of black limousines eased out of the wooded campus of Rice University near downtown Houston. The cars moved northeast, passing tens of thousands of people on Main Street who were cheering, waving placards, and releasing hundreds of yellow balloons. It was one big celebration of Houston and of its special visitors, the leaders of the industrialized nations, there for the World Economic Summit.

In one limo, President George H. W. Bush watched through the passenger window. It was a glorious moment, a reward for the gamble he had taken pushing his adopted hometown as a summit site. At the time, Houston had still been struggling with the image of a weakened giant, knocked on its knees by the oil crash. It had failed in its bid for the national political conventions, large parts of the city were dirty, and its people were demoralized. But this week Houston sparkled. It had even parlayed a heat wave to its advantage with a new slogan for the summit: "Houston's Hot."

Bush could only smile. For months, planning had been at the brink of disaster. So in January, with seven months to go, Bush had phoned his friend Ken Lay and asked him to take charge, joining another Houston businessman, George Strake, as summit co-chair. But Bush had made it clear that the success or failure of the event rested with Lay.

In turning to Lay, Bush was reaching out to a man who had slowly become a friend over many years. Lay had been a Florida supporter during Bush's first presidential run in 1980, but had really become part of the inner circle through his ties with other Bush associates. He had been longtime friends with Robert Mosbacher, a Texas oilman who was now Secretary of Commerce. Lay also had a close relationship with Jim Baker, the Houston lawyer who served as Bush's most trusted adviser. Lay solidified his connections to Bush in 1988, when he hosted one of Bush's first big fund-raisers for his successful presidential bid.

After Bush assumed the presidency, Lay had cultivated his relationship, often sending letters of support and playing roles large and small in the Administration. With the friendship blossoming, no one on the White House staff was surprised when Bush chastised them for failing to deliver a letter from Lay directly to the Oval Office. Lay was welcomed as a guest in the White House family quarters, where he had met with Bush, urging him to locate his presidential library in Houston; when Bush leaned toward another choice, Lay had traveled to the Dallas office of the President's oldest son, George W., to lobby the family. Young George had greeted Lay warmly but cautioned that the decision would be made by his parents. Still, President Bush appreciated his friend's effort and told him so during personal visits.

By the time of the summit, Bush had come to consider Lay a go-getter who could take charge of the big event. With little more than the force of will, Lay and his team had recruited some fifty-two hundred volunteers to clean up Houston, removing three million pounds of trash. Buildings were painted, flowers and trees planted, logos designed, traffic patterns altered. Now, with the meetings wrapping up, there was *this*—this seemingly impromptu celebration of the city and the summit. Bush could not have been prouder.

The procession of limousines pulled up to the George R. Brown Convention Center on the other side of town. One at a time, the world's leaders emerged from their cars—Bush, Margaret Thatcher from England, Helmut Kohl from Germany, François Mitterrand from France, and on and on. Inside, the dignitaries congratulated Bush on what they had just witnessed. That warm outpouring on Houston's streets, Bush was told, had been nothing short of miraculous.

Later that afternoon, the world leaders traveled to the "Thank You Houston Celebration," held on the campus of the University of Houston. Thousands of people gathered in front of a sprawling stage that held bleachers for VIPs. Plenty of entertainers were on hand, including the singers Randy Travis and Marilyn McCoo and the actress Jaclyn Smith. But the stars of the evening were Bush and his powerful guests. Just after seven, the crowd broke into sustained applause as the procession of cars carrying the dignitaries pulled behind the stage.

A Secret Service agent popped open a limousine door, and George and Barbara Bush emerged, the President in a brown suit with a maroon tie, the First Lady in a dark blue dress with her trademark pearls. Ahead, they saw a large tent where everyone scheduled to be onstage—whether performing or watching from the bleachers—was supposed to gather. Waiting inside the doorway beside his wife, Linda, was Ken Lay, wearing a seersucker jacket with a red tie.

Bush beamed; this was his first chance that day to speak with Lay. The two men shook hands eagerly.

"Mr. President," Lay said.

"Ken, I'm overwhelmed," Bush said. "Our guests were incredibly impressed and were really left with a positive image of Houston. I can't tell you how thankful I am."

"Thank you, Mr. President," Lay replied. "Everyone in the city worked very hard to make this happen."

Barbara Bush approached Lay and spoke softly in his ear. "Ken, I really appreciate you taking all this on. You really bailed George out."

The Lays escorted the Bushes around, introducing them to volunteers. Bush took a moment to speak with George Strake, Lay's co-chair, and Fred Malek, the summit director. Finally, an aide announced it was time to head out on the stage. Everyone had been assigned a place on the bleachers, the aide announced, and they needed to line up in the order they would be seated. The aide approached Lay.

"Mr. Lay," the aide said, "you're between the President and the First Lady."

Lay was astonished; the President's gesture could not have been more generous. He walked to his spot behind Bush and struck up a conversation as they waited.

"Did you see anything we missed or should have done differently?" Lay asked.

Bush smiled. "No, Ken. We keep looking for glitches, and we haven't found any."

With the line formed, everyone strode onto the stage. The crowd burst into renewed applause. At 7:13, as the cheers continued, Bush stepped up to a podium. Lay remained in his seat next to Barbara on the bleachers.

"Listen, Barbara and I really want to come over and say 'thank you' to all of you," Bush said. "To Ken Lay and George Strake and Fred Malek and so many others. I am so very, very grateful—and so is Bar."

It had been three historic days, Bush said, for Houston and the world. And it had all happened because of the town's hard work. "So, in short, you've shown the world what Houston hospitality is all about," he continued. "And you made this Houstonian very, very proud of his hometown tonight. Thank you all very, very much."

Cheers again, louder than before—for Bush, for the summit, for Houston. It was as if the town were basking in the respect that had been so elusive for a decade. Bush headed back to the bleachers, shaking Lay's hand again.

"Just wonderful, Ken," Bush said. "Just wonderful."

It was a day that, years later, would be remembered as a turning point. The day Houston emerged from its years of desperation. The day a deep appreciation for Lay spread through the city. And the day the world realized that Enron and its chairman had acquired some very influential allies.

A little more than two weeks later, on August 1, Jeff Skilling started his new job at Enron—and hit the place like a hurricane. He arrived with fixed ideas on organizing and running his business, but a lot of those plans ran headlong into the company's calcifying bureaucracy.

Out went the rows of offices on the edges of endless corridors. Instead, Skilling pushed to build a central work area modeled on a trading room. Any surviving offices would have glass walls so that everything in the division would be visible to everyone. The ideas appalled the people in charge of Enron's office standards—the Building Nazis, Skilling took to calling them—but he got his way.

Same with the changes in personnel management. Enron employed a system where every job description was assigned a certain number of points, which could be used to "purchase" an office with a bigger window or a better chair. Not in Skilling's group. There would be no job descriptions; he didn't want anyone locked in to some predetermined list of duties.

With every step and every idea, Skilling won legions of enemies among Enron's administrators. He reduced the company's dozens of titles to just four in his division—associate, manager, director, and vice president. Seniority-based compensation was chucked out, too; instead, pay would be based solely on annual performance.

Skilling thought he was on his way to building a perfect meritocracy, where smart, gifted—and richly compensated—people would be pitted against one another in an endless battle for dominance, creating a free flow of ideas that could push the business past its competitors.

As his dream office space was being constructed on the thirty-ninth floor, Skilling started scouring around for talent. Gene Humphrey, Skilling's first hire, was brought in from Citibank to head the effort providing financing to gas developers; Lou Pai, a former SEC economist, jumped from Enron's marketing organization. George Posey, from the corporate division, was assigned to handle accounting and finance. Within a month, Skilling had filled almost every important position—except one.

The last piece Skilling needed on his game board was an expert in a form of finance known as securitization. In such deals an institution pools similar loans, and then sells interests in them to outside investors. That gives the institution new money, which can then be used to make new loans. Better still, loans sold in a securitization can be removed from the company's balance sheet, since the risk of ownership has been shifted to the outside investors. With his plans to push loans into the gas market, Skilling knew a securitization expert could give his fledgling business access to an almost endless supply of capital.

The only question was, could he find somebody creative enough for the job?

The telephone rang in the Chicago office of Andrew Fastow, a young senior director with Continental Bank, on a morning in early October. On the line was Jonathan Crystal, a corporate recruiter from the Houston office of Spencer Stuart, one of the world's largest executive search firms.

"There's an opportunity available that I think you will find very interesting," Crystal said.

Spencer Stuart had been hired by Skilling to track down his securitization expert, and Fastow, a twenty-eight-year-old banker, seemed to fit the bill. In the last few years, Fastow had specialized in such financings, working on some high-profile, complex deals. The second son of a buyer for drugstores and a homemaker, Fastow had grown up in New Providence, New Jersey. His family was comfortable, though hardly wealthy. But Fastow, who graduated summa cum laude in 1984 from Tufts University, soon came to be more familiar with the world of the well-heeled. He married his college sweetheart, Lea—an heiress to the Weingarten fortune, earned with grocery stores—and set off for Chicago to launch his business career. While working, he earned his MBA at the Kellogg School and eventually found his niche at Continental Bank.

Andy worked hard, but his personal style could be grating, even pompous. He was the type to take a stand in quicksand, making demands with shouts and temper tantrums, at times costing him more in reputation than he gained in deal points. Even a simple cab ride had once transformed into a fracas, with a hotheaded driver ultimately punching Fastow in the face in a dispute over seventy cents.

Still, the Fastows were restless. For months they had considered moving to Houston if the right jobs came along, but the idea seemed like a long shot. New York and Chicago were the hot spots for securitization; Houston wasn't even on the industry's map. But with this call from Crystal, suddenly it seemed like that might be changing.

Fastow listened as Crystal gave the rundown on the position. Enron needed someone who knew about securitization to join their new finance business; it sounded, Crystal said, like a great fit.

For a moment Fastow said nothing.

"Who," he finally asked, "is Enron?"

On the morning of October 3, a Wednesday, Lou Rieger, head of Spencer Stuart's Houston office, called Skilling. "We've found a good candidate," Rieger said. "There's a guy who wants to move to Houston. He's been working at Continental Bank in Chicago."

"You're kidding me. He wants to move to Houston?" Skilling asked. "Send over his résumé. Let me look at it."

Minutes later, at 9:36, the fax machine near Skilling's office hummed to life, and three pages of paper scrolled into a tray. His assistant, Sherri Reinartz, brought it in. Skilling flipped through the pages, reading quickly.

"Andrew S. Fastow."

Education. "Kellogg, Tufts."

Experience. "Continental Bank . . . Sold first security backed solely by senior LBO debt . . . named 1989 'Deal of the Year' . . . directly responsible for pre-tax profit contribution of $12.8 million . . . structured and arranged leveraged buyouts . . . proficient in Chinese . . ."

"Holy shit," Skilling said. *The perfect guy.*

He picked up the phone and dialed Rieger's office.

"Lou, hey, home run," Skilling said. "This guy is dead-on what we're looking for."

Fastow traveled to Houston later that month to visit a company that still made no sense to him. His world was one of esoteric deals, derivatives, wealthy bankers with business degrees. But from what he could tell, Enron worked in *pipelines*—expensive, dirty pipelines. It sounded like nothing more than a big step down.

Fastow arrived at the building early that morning and rode up to the thirty-ninth floor, where he asked for Skilling. A receptionist placed a call, and a minute later an energetic man in his late thirties—a little nerdy-looking, with steely eyes—came bounding toward him.

"Andy? Jeff Skilling."

"Good to meet you," Fastow replied, shaking hands.

Skilling smiled as he glanced around the room. "Well, welcome to Enron. Follow me, we'll go talk."

Fastow trailed Skilling to a bullpen that housed most of the department's professionals and support staff. The place bristled with energy, the staccato rhythms of computer keyboards punctuating a low hum of activity. Fastow had expected the place to be sleepy and dull. But here, no one dawdled or wandered about. There was work to be done, and Team Skilling seemed thrilled by the challenge.

The two men walked into Skilling's glass-encased office and took seats at the table. Fastow didn't smile and was a little standoffish; he still didn't understand what role he could play in this corporation.

"So," Fastow said, an edge of condescension in his voice, "what are you guys doing here?"

Skilling launched into his now-familiar speech about the irrationality of the natural-gas business and how his team was building a marketplace balanced between buyers and sellers. It was all about gathering risks and spreading them around, so that no one player got stuck if the music stopped. That's where securitization came in; the division couldn't be constrained by Enron's capital or its balance sheet. New investors meant new money, new money meant more business, and more business was sure to mean more profit.

As Skilling spoke, Fastow's eyes lit up. This wasn't some company trying to hire a showcase executive it couldn't use; for someone with his background, Enron's new venture was right on the center of the fairway.

"Wait a minute," Fastow interrupted. "Why is this going on at a pipeline company? What you're talking about is finance and almost banking activities."

"Having the pipelines gives us a jump, a place to start, and a knowledge of the business we can use."

Made sense. Still, Fastow had trouble accepting that a corporation in such an old-line industry could harbor cutting-edge visions. Maybe this was all some fad.

"Is this company really going to stand behind this?" he asked. "Are they really committed?"

"Talk to Kinder," Skilling replied. "He gets it. He knows this is the future, and he's committed to it."

Fastow sat back. This was all coming too fast, and this guy Skilling seemed to be at the center of it all. Fastow had already heard that Skilling abandoned a lucrative career at McKinsey to take on this new business. That stumped him more than anything.

"You walked away from McKinsey?"

"I did," Skilling replied.

Fastow didn't know how else to put it. "Why?"

Skilling smiled and turned up his hands. "Hey," he said, "how often do you get a chance to change the world?"

The interview clinched it. The conversation transformed into a free-flowing exchange of ideas as Fastow brainstormed about how Enron could utilize securitizations. In about an hour, Fastow pushed the thinking further than anyone in the building had ever dreamed. Skilling was enthralled.

Afterward, Skilling telephoned Lou Rieger, telling him that Enron was very interested. Not long after, Fastow called the Spencer Stuart Houston office, too, equally enthusiastic. But there was a problem. If they were going to move, his wife also needed a job in Houston. Rieger phoned Skilling, telling him about the roadblock.

"Fine. Send me her résumé," Skilling said. "I'll see if we can find something for her here."

The résumé arrived that same day by fax. Skilling read it through quickly; her background seemed perfect for Enron's treasury department. In no time, both Fastows were offered jobs at Enron, with Andy's paying a salary of seventy-five thousand dollars, a signing bonus of twenty thousand, and a guaranteed bonus for the following year of at least twenty-five thousand.

On December 3, 1990, Andy Fastow returned to Enron as a newly minted employee, one who would play a far greater role in its history than anyone could have possibly imagined.

The slime ball zipped across the room, splatting against a window before slowly oozing down the glass. Fastow grabbed another one of the green globs, going into a slow windup.

"Heads up!" he yelled, heaving the ball past his colleagues in the bullpen.

Skilling and his team kept talking, ignoring the mess from another typical late-night session at Enron Finance. No longer was Fastow the zipped-up banker he had been at his job interview; instead, he had emerged as a prankster, adept at lending the frequent after-hours discussions the feel of a college bull session. The bottom left-hand drawer of his desk had become known as the toy store; Skilling's children always made a beeline there whenever they visited. Throughout the day—and into the night—the place descended into toy chaos; footballs flew, slime balls splatted, and Nerf-gun wars raged.

The mischievousness was all part of the division's character, one that quickly made the thirty-ninth floor a central attraction for other employees. The executives there often spoke with messianic fervor about the new order they hoped to create: they were going to take power away from the monopolies, finance the dying gas industry, create markets that had never existed before.

The early years were a time of discovery, and Skilling's division evolved into an idea factory. One of the earliest changes was a reorganization. The separation of Enron Finance, which worked with producers, from Enron Gas Marketing, which arranged long-term contracts, was simply illogical; both were different ends of the same business. So in January 1991, the two were melded into Enron Gas Services, with Skilling its top executive.

The business also evolved. Buying reserves outright made no sense; in order to get the gas it needed, Enron was paying for intangible things it didn't want, like drilling opportunities and exploratory potential. But writing a contract to purchase the gas would limit securitization efforts; most producers were in lousy financial shape, and investors wouldn't be eager to buy interests in contracts struck with businesses on the brink of bankruptcy.

The remedy was found in century-old laws, which created something called a production payment. In essence, the production payment was nothing more than the gas that a company could pump out of the ground; if a wildcatter sold production payments to Enron, then the company owned the fuel. It didn't matter if the wildcatter went bankrupt, as several did; Enron's ownership of the gas production would survive any challenge from the producer's creditors.

With a solid asset available, Fastow went into action. The first securitization idea, named Cactus, was hatched in 1991, utilizing an accounting device called a special-purpose entity—the critical piece of such financings. Essentially, Enron could legally use special-purpose entities to transfer risks and debt off its books by selling interests in them to independent investors. The vehicle was like a sponge that soaked up the acquired gas before Enron tore it into bits for sale to investors.

But the rules governing what constituted an off-books special-purpose entity—and what instead would just be another part of the company itself—were detailed.

So in 1991, Fastow and his team met with lawyers from the Houston firm of Vinson & Elkins and accountants from Arthur Andersen. The rules, recited by a young Andersen accountant named Rick Causey, were fairly simple. First, loan sales to the special-purpose entity had to be real, with ownership transferring to outside investors. Enron couldn't agree to compensate investors for losses; doing so meant the company retained the risk of ownership, and the loans would have to stay on its books. Plus, Enron could not control the entity; strategic decisions had to be made by third parties. The independent investors also had to invest at least three percent of the entity's capital.

Eventually the accountants and lawyers left the room, and Fastow broke into laughter. The three percent rule struck him as hilarious.

"Who comes up with these ridiculous rules?" he laughed. "This is such bullshit! Your gardener could hold the three percent! I could get my brother to do it!"

Fastow set to putting Cactus together. With it, Enron pooled loan commitments to gas producers in exchange for a deal on their production payments, placed them in the Cactus special-purpose entity, and sold stakes to heavy-hitting institutional investors. Cactus investors would then resell the gas back to Enron, which in turn would use it to meet its obligations under the long-term supply contracts with customers. It was the Gas Bank in its final form; outsiders provided cash, producers received financing, customers obtained gas at a reliable price—all with Enron in the middle, profiting handsomely.

Or so it seemed. But a problem emerged. The accounting for the two sides of the transaction—buying production payments and selling fixed-price contracts—followed different rules. Enron could be forced to report a loss simply because it couldn't count the two parts of the deal in the same way. Skilling thought the result absurd: how could things of the same value be worth different amounts?

The issue came to a head at a meeting between Skilling's team, the accountants from Arthur Andersen, advisers from Bankers Trust, and lawyers from Vinson & Elkins. Steve Goddard, an Andersen partner, brought along a number of other accountants, including a young graduate from Texas A&M named David Duncan, who was working on the Cactus deals.

Skilling took the floor. He wanted his group's accounting to shift from the old oil-and-gas rules to mark-to-market, a method commonly used by trading houses. It allowed a company to record the value of a transaction at the beginning; any changes over time—caused by anything from flawed assumptions to variations in market value—would be recorded as a profit or a loss. If a brokerage owned a stock that went up in price, it reported a profit—even if it didn't sell the stock. If the value went down, it reported a loss. That was the beauty of mark-to-market, Skilling said. It reflected market reality.

"Wait," Goddard said. "But this is an oil-and-gas transaction. You need to use oil-and-gas accounting."

Around and around they went. The auditors with Andersen's energy group were far more familiar with old-line oil-and-gas accounting; this new stuff was hard to get their heads around. Everyone became frustrated.

"You guys are just stupid," Lou Pai finally railed in exasperation. "You're fucking stupid!"

Skilling pushed Goddard to check with Andersen's top accounting experts in Chicago; after that, he flew there to see them and to present his arguments in person. A few weeks later, Goddard dropped by Skilling's office.

"Well, I talked to Chicago," he said. "They agree mark-to-market is the appropriate treatment."

Skilling clapped his hands. "Great!"

"Well, I still don't feel up to speed on this. But they like it, and they think it's the right way to go."

"Okay," Skilling said.

Goddard hesitated. "But they don't think we can do this unilaterally."

"What do you mean?"

"We've got to go to the SEC with this," Goddard said. "This is a change in accounting methodology, so we've got to convince the SEC to approve it."

Skilling flopped back in his chair. *The SEC.* The Securities and Exchange Commission. *All we have to do is convince the government to reverse course.*

Skilling was silent for a moment, then sat up.

"Okay," he said. "Let's go convince the SEC."

"This is the stupidest accounting I've ever heard of. It's just crazy."

As he spoke, David Woytek stared across a conference table at Jack

Tompkins, Enron's chief financial officer. It was June 1991, and Woytek, the accountant who investigated the Valhalla oil-trading scandal, was attending a monthly meeting of Enron's top financial executives. Now chief financial officer of Enron's liquid-fuels division, Woytek had just heard George Posey, Skilling's finance chief, explain the new accounting his team was pushing.

"Mark-to-market makes much more sense for what we're doing," Posey replied.

"Mark-to-market is all fine and good, but that's not what you're describing," Woytek shot back.

"We're describing mark-to-market."

"No, you're not. You're saying you want to recognize revenues from twenty-year contracts in the first year. I don't know what that is, but *that's* not mark-to-market."

Posey held up a hand. "We're talking mark-to-market," he said. "It's the accounting the investment banks use."

That wasn't the same thing, Woytek argued. Those institutions were valuing their portfolios based on current, actively traded markets. If they owned stock in Exxon and Exxon's share price rose two dollars, then the value of their investment went up. There was logic to it; the market was independently assessing the value. If an investment bank needed cash, the stock could be sold at the price recorded on its books. But *this* was different, he said. They were making estimates about the total revenues a contract would produce, and then reporting the whole thing right away. There was no independent judgment involved. It wasn't mark-to-market; it was mark-to-guess.

"How can you book twenty years of revenue in the first year?" Woytek asked. "That goes against everything I was ever taught in accounting. You never recognize revenue in advance, only when title passes from one owner to the next. And title doesn't pass on this until you deliver the gas, over the next twenty years."

There were other problems, Woytek said. The strange accounting idea would make the profits from Skilling's division unpredictable from one year to the next. If it sold fifty contracts in the first year—requiring gas deliveries over, say, five years—and recognized all future revenues up front, the next year it would start out at zero, with no revenues. In fact, it would start out at less than zero, since it would have already presumably done business with its stable of customers. So the second year, it would have to sell as many contracts as in the first year—and then more—just to beat its first year's earnings. Year after year, it would be the same thing, forever. An investment bank using mark-to-market just needed market prices to rise to grow profits; but Skilling's group was almost guaranteed to someday hit a wall.

Worse, the reported earnings would be huge, but the cash wouldn't finish trickling in for years. Earnings without cash are anathema to investors; how would the company explain it?

"We've always sold long-term contracts, and we always took into earnings the amount of gas we delivered each month," Woytek said. "Why should this be different?"

Posey didn't back down. Woytek, he said, was looking at this from the old oil-and-gas method, which was affected by fluctuating energy prices. But Gas Services was matching its purchases and sales, and then marking to market the entire position. It made sense, Posey argued.

Woytek smiled. There were other reasons to use this accounting idea that nobody was mentioning. He had already heard that as part of his compensation, Skilling received an ownership stake in his division. When the division's earnings went up, the value of that stake would, too. If that division started booking twenty years of contracts in a single year, its earnings would go through the roof.

And then—even if those profits came from fancy accounting—Jeff Skilling would be one very rich man.

The following month, on July 26, Jack Tompkins was sitting at his desk when a call came in from the SEC. It was Jack Albert from the agency's office of the chief accoutant, calling about the Skilling accounting proposal. Tompkins asked Albert to hold for a moment and patched in Posey from Skilling's group.

"I've kept very close contact with this, but George has been the one carrying the ball," Tompkins explained.

Albert acknowledged Posey, and then started. "The bottom line is that we don't believe you can make a case with the preferability to change at this time," he said. "I know this is not the best news to give you."

The Enron executives spoke simultaneously for a second. What was the issue?

"The reasons vary," Albert replied. "But at the present time we think accounting for oil and gas is locked into this historical cost model."

Posey was almost speechless. Because Enron had an oil-and-gas business, it should use oil-and-gas accounting—*even for its finance division*? "Let me just maybe understand your point a little better," he said. "This doesn't include our oil-and-gas exploration company."

"I understand that."

"Okay," Posey continued. So one division's accounting should be dictated by another division's business?

"This is a dramatic change for anyone in the oil-and-gas business," Albert responded. "I don't think you really have anyone analogous to Enron Gas Services out there."

Tompkins jumped in, trying to play conciliator. "We certainly don't want to be argumentative," he said. "The more information we can get why and what we can do sometime down in the future as far as—"

Albert interrupted. "I think you've made an excellent point right there with 'sometime down in the future.' We think it is premature at this time."

The call ended, and Posey rushed to Skilling's office. He found him at his desk, engrossed in work.

"The SEC turned us down," Posey announced.

Skilling sank in his chair. "*What?* That's stupid."

Furious, Skilling threw questions at Posey and learned the details of the call with the SEC. He phoned Tompkins, warning that he was coming up. Minutes later, in Tompkins's office, Skilling could barely contain himself.

"What the hell happened?"

Tompkins shrugged. "They turned us down."

"Did you give them the reasons that was the wrong thing to do?" Skilling barked. "Did you talk to them?"

"About how this compares with other companies, and I explained that other companies use it."

"Did you explain why this is important?"

"I think our application was very clear about that."

Skilling fumed in silence, then turned on his heel and stormed out. Back in his office, he called Steve Goddard from Andersen.

"Is this normal?" Skilling asked. "Mark-to-market makes all the sense in the world. Why wouldn't they just automatically do this?"

"Well," Goddard replied, "they are very conservative, and this is a big change."

"It's *not* a big change," Skilling shot back. Lots of investment banks used the accounting, he said. It was ridiculous that competing companies would be forced to treat the same deals differently. The whole thing had been mishandled, Skilling said. Andersen needed to fix it.

"We can't just send a letter and say, 'Oh, we want to switch to mark-to-market,' " Skilling said. "We need a full-blown presentation about why it's the right thing."

Goddard agreed to call the SEC and set up a meeting. Skilling said he would make the presentation himself, but asked Andersen to be there ready to answer any questions on the technical accounting issues. Goddard said he would give the job to Rick Causey.

It was the assignment that set Causey on the path to becoming a power in his own right at Enron.

On September 17, 1991, SEC staffers gathered in a conference room at the agency's Washington headquarters. Already the place was packed, with people standing along the walls or sitting on the carpet, eager to hear the presentation from Enron and Andersen. After all, it wasn't every day a big company lobbied to fundamentally change the way it reported revenues and profits. This was as close to a financial wonk's version of Woodstock as there could be.

With the place filled, Skilling and his team were escorted into the room. Goddard walked to the front of the assembled group, gave a few greetings, and introduced Skilling, who strode to an overhead projector.

"Thank you, Steve," he said. "As Steve suggested, our business is changing radically. What has traditionally been a very fixed structure is now turning into a traded commodity. And with that, the accounting has to change."

Skilling placed a series of transparencies on the projector, describing the history of his unit and the growth of the natural gas trading market. But it was the eighteenth transparency that captivated the room. It showed two gas portfolios—one with matched purchases and sales handled the way Enron did business, and another with a long-term supply contract satisfied by buying fuel in the open market. At first, since short-term prices were lower than long-term prices, such a deal might look good. But of course, Skilling said, the approach was reckless, since the company taking the position could be forced to sell gas at a loss if prices climbed. It was the kind of shortsighted strategy—lending long-term and buying short-term—that blew up the savings-and-loan industry, he said.

A new transparency appeared, showing how the two portfolios would be reported under the traditional, accrual accounting and the mark-to-market approach. With mark-to-market, the matched portfolio was worth the current value of all the cash it would generate over its life; the mismatched, dangerous portfolio was worth less. But with accrual accounting, the matched portfolio showed a loss while the dangerous portfolio showed big profits. Worse, traditional accounting provided benefits to companies that sold winning positions while holding on to losers.

Skilling glanced at the assembled faces. "Accrual accounting lets you pretty much create the outcome you want, by keeping the bad stuff and selling the good," he said. "Mark-to-market doesn't let you do this."

An SEC staffer sitting in front of Skilling stopped taking notes. He was from the financial-institutions group, and Skilling's words had sounded a familiar chord.

"That's gains trading," the staffer said. "That's what our banks do all the time."

"Of course they do," Skilling said. "Under accrual accounting, it's a no-brainer. It's a simple, easy way to report profits, but they don't reflect reality."

"Wait a minute," the staffer continued. "Let me get this right. You're *asking* to go to mark-to-market?"

"Yeah, we're asking to go to mark-to-market."

A pause. "Why?"

"Because," Skilling said, "we think it's a more accurate reflection of what is going on in the business."

The staffer shook his head. "We've been trying to get the banks to go to mark-to-market accounting for years."

"Well . . . ," Skilling began.

"I think this makes all the sense in the world," the staffer interrupted, gathering his notes as he stood. "Sorry, I've gotta go."

Skilling smiled as the staffer headed out of the room.

"Well," he said, "I think *he* gets it."

The SEC ruminated over the idea for months, calling Enron periodically for more material—copies of Skilling's presentation, information about other market participants. More meetings were held in Washington to review details.

Finally, on January 30, 1992, a call came to Skilling from Jack Tompkins. "Jeff, I just got a letter from the SEC, and they've agreed with our accounting change."

"Really?"

"Yeah, they put some conditions in place, but they signed off on the idea."

Skilling hurried upstairs to see the two-page letter. Posey was already there and handed Skilling a copy. Reading it, Skilling broke into a smile.

"Thank God," he said. "There's some logic in the world after all."

After a round of congratulations, Skilling and Posey headed to their offices, now on the thirty-third floor. Skilling walked into the bullpen and called for everyone's attention.

"We got mark-to-market!" he crowed.

The announcement elicited a burst of congratulatory chatter from the Enron executives. At last, their business was ready to take off. "Folks," Posey announced, "I'm going out and getting us all some beer to celebrate."

Still, there were loose ends. In its letter the SEC said it would allow Enron to use mark-to-market accounting beginning in January 1992. Days later, Tompkins wrote back, informing the SEC that Enron would be applying the new accounting treatment for 1991, although he said that the effect on earnings would not be material.

As far as the executives at Enron were concerned, they had no choice. They needed the profits they would gain from collapsing the estimated lifetime revenues of their gas contracts into a single year. Without them, under traditional accounting the company could miss the earnings targets Wall Street was projecting for the year just ended.

Accounting techniques—approved by the nation's top securities regulator—now allowed Enron to report fast-growing profits. But the related cash would not finish flowing in for years. With high earnings and low cash, about the worst thing Enron could do at that moment was start throwing money into another risky business.

Rebecca Mark pushed open the door to a conference room for a group of dignitaries from India. The delegation, led by the country's Power Secretary, Srinivas Rajgopal, had been in America almost a week and had flown to Houston on this day in May 1992 specifically to meet with her. The thirty-seven-year-old onetime Missouri farm girl had made a name for herself helping Enron build power plants in several countries—just what the Indian delegation wanted.

The meeting this day came at a time of transition for both India and Mark. After decades of shunning foreign investment, the Indian government had begun aggressively seeking overseas capital; in particular, it needed power plants to overcome chronic energy shortfalls that often paralyzed the country's factories.

Enron had almost no track record in the developing world, but Mark wanted to change that. An attractive woman with a wave of blond hair that illuminated her face, Mark had just lost an internal political battle. Despite her work on a number of plant projects—including one constructed in Massachusetts while she attended Harvard Business School and a hugely successful plant in Teesside, England—she had drawn the short straw when the company split its power business into three units. The lucrative deals in Europe and the United States were divvied up to others. Mark and her team handled what was left—the riskier developing world. India was right in her bailiwick.

The Indian delegation took their seats and quickly got to the point. Rajgopal said that Enron had come to his attention because of its plant in Teesside. India needed such a project, he said. Mark listened, with reservations. She knew India mostly relied on high-polluting, coal-fired power plants, a business she wanted nothing to do with.

"I must tell you," she said, "we don't do coal, we do gas. We have some ethical issues about coal."

"We understand that," Rajgopal said. "That is why we're here. We want you to bring gas into India."

Ludicrous. India had no reserves, no infrastructure of a gas industry. Gas would have to be imported, but that seemed unlikely, she told her guests. A pipeline through Pakistan was too risky, and the only other alternative—shipped liquid natural gas, or LNG—was pricey. Plus, the investments required—gas field drilling, liquefaction technology, ports—meant that to justify the costs, an LNG plant would have to be huge, at least two thousand megawatts.

"The size would drive up the cost of electricity," Mark said. "In my view, you can't afford LNG."

Rajgopal shook his head. "We think we can."

Mark still was dubious. The cost of electricity would be almost double that from a coal plant, she said. How could India possibly handle that?

"We're very power short," Rajgopal responded. "Our industries need power. We want to look at LNG."

The government was willing to make whatever commitments were necessary to ensure such a project worked, Rajgopal said. Mark sat back in her chair. These were determined people. Could this be the break her team needed?

It was almost a magical moment. After losing the internal battles, her group might well be stumbling into the lead role on one of the world's biggest projects. It would cost billions. And it would shower cash on Mark and her team. Enron effectively paid the power-plant developers a percentage of their deals, based on estimates of the money they would bring in. The larger the project, the more electricity it produced, and—consequently—the bigger the bonuses, often running into millions. Enron would invest the cash, and the international team would get rich.

"Okay," Mark said. "We'll take a look at it."

With that, the fuse was lit. Enron would soon be pursuing wildly contradictory strategies. One brought in huge earnings but little cash, and depended on Enron's credit rating to survive. The other would devour cash while producing next to no earnings for years, potentially putting the credit rating at risk.

Enron was on a collision course with itself.

CHAPTER 3

ROWS OF LUXURY CARS lined Wroxton Road near Andy Fastow's house in the upscale neighborhood of Southampton Place. It was a weekend evening in December 1992, the night of the Fastows' holiday party for Enron's executives and bankers. Already the crowded street was forcing latecomers to park more than a block away; the crisp evening air whipped by as they scurried back, past historic bungalows and Victorian-style lampposts that battled feebly against the darkness. From the Fastows' front walk, new arrivals could see a huge crowd through the shutters on the Georgian home's first-floor windows.

Just inside, Lea Fastow stood near a staircase in the entry hallway, playing hostess to perfection. She greeted new arrivals personally, dispensing warm smiles and cheerful words. Framed artwork and delicate knickknacks lent the house a sumptuous air of class. Many of the guests complimented Lea on her decorating skills, already the stuff of legend around the office. Andy wandered from room to room, chatting up the revelers.

The mood was relaxed and celebratory, capping a fantastically successful year. Gas Services had taken off; following the accounting change, the division had blown through its projected numbers, the bottom line rising in an unswerving, near-vertical climb. After years of stumbling from one embarrassment to the next, Enron now inspired awe and fear in competitors, thanks largely to the cocksure, bubbly young people packed shoulder to shoulder at Fastow's house. That evening everyone felt successful, smart, and richer than they had ever dreamed.

One late arrival, Amanda Martin, headed up the Fastows' front walk, watching the festivities with a sense of wonder. A lawyer by training, Martin, thirty-six, was blond and attractive, but it was her smarts that wowed Enron executives. Although her job was to clear away legal land mines in Enron's deals, she never hesitated to challenge transactions she thought wrongheaded; her pointed questions, raised in her lilting Afrikaner accent, could deflate the most arrogant of deal makers.

Martin found Enron a delight. Skilling and his vision for the industry captivated her. The staid old pipeline company was, in Skilling's group, more like a Wall Street deal factory, attracting young, smart people on the make. Martin and the rest became Skilling's youthful acolytes, eager to shatter the constraints of the old world.

From the start, Martin formed a close bond with Andy Fastow and relished his seeming lack of pretension. He would schmooze with colleagues into the wee hours. And on weekends, when Martin sometimes brought her young son to work, Fastow thought nothing of getting down on the floor to horse around with the boy. True, Fastow had a dark side—yelling when things didn't go his way, shoving a banker in the heat of negotiations—but Martin viewed those outbursts as standard fare in a high-pressure profession.

But if Fastow the sour deal maker put Martin off, Andy the bubbly games player was always a delight. Just the other day, Fastow's wicked sense of humor had taken one of Enron's outside lawyers down a peg. All week, the lawyer had been bragging about the deal he had struck on a Jaguar. The jabbering only stopped when the lawyer was told that he had a call from the police. The lawyer had purchased a stolen car, the caller informed him, faxing over the evidence to prove it. Only then did everyone listening to the escapade collapse in laughter; the lawyer had been taken in by one of Fastow's elaborate practical jokes.

Tonight, Martin was confident that Fastow the fun loving would be waiting inside. As she rang the front bell, a truck pulled up and a delivery man climbed out, carrying a large object to the Fastows' entryway. Lea opened the door, greeting Martin as the delivery man arrived. He set down a giant, hideous bust of Elvis Presley.

"Mrs. Fastow?" he said. "We're delivering that bust you ordered."

"I'm sorry?" Lea said, looking mortified. "That's not mine. We never ordered it."

"No," the delivery man said. "It's for you. It's all paid up. Where do you want it?"

Lea glanced around at her guests as her husband walked over to see what was going on. Martin had already figured it out: the Jaguar lawyer was getting his revenge, right in the middle of Fastow's holiday party. She shook with laughter. God, she loved working for this place.

The tall, patrician man walked casually through the lobby of the Enron building toward the elevators. He was dressed in a finely tailored, top-of-the-line suit and a muted tie. It was the kind of look that seemed calculated to attract notice, but the man paid no attention to the stares set off by his arrival. As someone with one of the world's most recognizable faces, James

Baker III, the former Secretary of State in the Bush Administration, was pretty much used to them, particularly in his hometown of Houston. After being ushered through security, Baker headed to the fiftieth floor, where a beaming Ken Lay waited, eager to hear the thoughts of Enron's newest consultant.

"Jim, thanks for coming to see us today," Lay said, pumping Baker's hand.

"Well, Ken, it's an honor."

It was early 1993, not long after Bill Clinton's inauguration as President. While Lay had been disappointed by Bush's defeat, he also viewed it as an opportunity to attract top-flight talent to Enron. Baker—and Lay's old friend Robert Mosbacher, the former Commerce Secretary—were offered consulting contracts to lend their international expertise to Enron's overseas power projects.

The deals were signed on February 22, 1993, and Baker and Mosbacher soon began examining company projects. One caught Baker's attention: the Indian power plant that Rebecca Mark had contracted to build. Constructing the plant in Dabhol, about a hundred miles south of Bombay on the rocky coast of the Arabian Sea, struck Baker as tricky business. Enron had made efforts to protect its interests, winning agreements from the Maharashtra State Electricity Board to purchase virtually all of the plant's power, securing guarantees from the state and national governments, bringing in contractors involved in the construction as part owners. But Baker saw dangers that appeared to have escaped Enron's attention.

He dashed off a one-and-a-half-page memo, raising red flags. Enron, he cautioned, seemed to be assuming that the politicians negotiating the deal would be around to enforce it; the company was betting on a single horse, without forging alliances with other political factions. Worse, the company had failed to give locals a sense of ownership in the plant, say, by bringing in an Indian company as a corporate partner. It would be a serious error, he warned, to underestimate the potency of Indian nationalism and its potential to harm the deal.

Baker sent the memo to Enron's officers, who promptly filed it away and largely forgot about it.

The hunt had lasted almost three years. But now, having found Enron, Christopher Bower was ready to bring down the big game.

Bower, founder of the Pacific Corporate Group in La Jolla, California, held one of the country's most intriguing jobs—helping Calpers, the giant retirement system for government employees in California, invest more than two billion dollars in private deals. With that kind of money jangling in his pocket, Bower was welcome in most any corporate or Wall Street office and had heard hundreds of investment ideas. But time and again, he and his team of eleven professionals found the proposals unexciting.

Then, paydirt. Bower came to Houston, meeting with Fastow and his finance executives, and pushed a simple idea. Enron wanted to finance gas producers through off-books entities but needed outside money to meet the accounting rules. The Cactus deals had been fine but required Enron to wander around, tin cup in hand, scaring up investors. Calpers was ready to fill the gap. It could provide cash custom-fit for Enron's needs, up to half of a $500 million fund. Enron, already cash starved, could use its own stock to finance the other half.

"This is an approach that would give you guys a real leg up on your competitors," Bower said.

"It's great," Fastow replied. "It's exactly the kind of deal Enron wants to do."

Months of work ensued. Then, on May 17, 1993, Skilling, Fastow, and Amanda Martin appeared in the glass-and-mahogany corporate boardroom before the executive committee of Enron's directors. John Duncan called the meeting to order and asked Lay to open things up.

"We have several items," Lay said. "But the primary purpose of our meeting is to consider a joint venture with Calpers that Andy and his team have been working on."

The broad outlines of the deal were left for Kinder to describe. It all sounded too good to be true. What, one of the directors asked, were the potential profits?

Fastow studied a sheaf of papers. "We've done a detailed analysis of the estimated impact this would have on our financial reporting for the next few years."

He laid out the numbers and the directors' eyes lit up. The potential was huge. With little additional debate, the directors unanimously approved the concept. The joint venture was named JEDI—ostensibly for Joint Energy Development Investments, but in truth as a tip of the hat to Fastow's affection for *Star Wars*.

The project would soon be well known within Enron. It would take almost a decade for it to become infamous.

Just blocks from Enron's headquarters, on the twenty-third floor of Two Shell Plaza, Toni Mack was going through her mail. A reporter at *Forbes*, Mack had written for years about the travails of the energy industry, early on spotting Lay's efforts to solve the take-or-pay problems. Long ago she had decided

Enron was about the only company putting together a crackerjack strategy for deregulation, and always made sure to keep an eye on its business.

Sitting at her steel-case desk, Mack picked up a long envelope stamped with a logo she recognized. *Enron.* Probably the company's annual report to shareholders for the prior year, 1992. She tore open the envelope and pulled out the document. A splash of colors danced across the cover in an illustration depicting Enron's impact on the world.

Mack grabbed a highlighter and began reading. On page fifty she saw a summary of Enron's accounting policies. The usual boilerplate, until she reached the seventh entry: *Enron accounts for its price-risk management activities under the mark-to-market method of accounting.*

"Huh?" Mack said aloud.

In the next two paragraphs Enron spelled out its methods for counting profits in Skilling's division. Mack's highlighter marked almost every word.

What the heck does that mean?

Mack hit the phones, calling sources in the industry. But the more questions she asked, the more puzzled she became. While the accounting was mark-to-market, it wasn't being handled the old-fashioned way, with trading prices dictating values; instead, Enron was using its own projections to fold anticipated income from decades-long contracts into the current year. It struck her as horribly aggressive. What if the other party to the contract went bankrupt? What if energy taxes changed? If, oh, natural gas was outlawed? This newfangled accounting seemed highly risky, and Mack thought investors needed to know about it.

Mack's article appeared in the May 24, 1993, issue of *Forbes.* While acknowledging Enron's business successes, the piece focused on its accounting risk—the potential for unexpected events to erode previously reported profits. She pointed out that with profits of each contract reported the first year, Enron needed to sign up increasing numbers of contracts each year to keep growing.

Mack believed she had untangled the threads of a complicated corporate tale. But Wall Street analysts—many at firms already lapping up banking fees from Enron—issued reports saying mark-to-market made no difference. None confronted the substance of Mack's analysis.

Days later, Mack received a hand-delivered letter from Ken Lay. How could Mack criticize mark-to-market, he asked, when the SEC and Arthur Andersen had approved the approach? Mack wrote back, appealing to Lay's sense of history. The take-or-pay debacle proved the industry's shortcomings in making long-term assumptions; imagine, she wrote, how bad that episode would have been if gas companies had been forced to reverse previously reported profits.

But Lay—and Skilling—were unmoved. The risks *Forbes* was warning about were imaginary, they told colleagues. Mack, they insisted, just didn't get it.

Could Enron use mark-to-market accounting in a business that, at this point, had no real market?

That was the question bedeviling executives in Skilling's group. By mid-1993, Enron had a division running that seemed to fit no place: clean fuels, which manufactured methanol and MTBE, a gasoline additive. Skilling thought the business made no sense and put Enron in danger of losing big money. But maybe, he thought, if he could re-create Enron's approach to the gas business in clean fuels, there were dollars to be made.

To get the ball rolling, Skilling tapped Ken Rice, a top-notch marketer in his division. Skilling knew Rice's zest for salesmanship and figured he was just what the business needed—an executive who produced results.

Skilling summoned Rice to his office. The young executive walked in and flopped down on a chair. Tall and fit with a cap of brown hair, he wore his usual outfit—jeans, a faded shirt, and boots. Skilling bluntly broke the news that he wanted Rice to take over clean fuels.

"You're kidding, right?" Rice said. "I don't know anything about this business."

It didn't matter, Skilling said. The division was a disaster, but it had a couple of valuable contracts. "If we can create a market and renegotiate those contracts," he said, "maybe we can get mark-to-market earnings on them."

At that point the fuels group was making profits the old-fashioned way: it made stuff and sold it at a profit. The plants were connected by pipeline to the factories that used the fuels—hardly an arrangement, Rice thought, conducive to creating a market. But if Enron could switch the accounting, big profits from the contracts could be booked right away.

Rice took a few days to think about it, then accepted Skilling's request. By his first day on the new job, he had devised his strategy. He would build a market for the fuels. Then, once the traders had some traction, he would consult Andersen and propose switching to mark-to-market accounting. It seemed logical, similar to the path set by the original foray into gas trading.

Within days Rice figured he had it backward, at least as far as his bosses were concerned. Rick Causey, Skilling's top accounting guru, assigned a controller to Rice, and she arrived with marching orders. The controller brought copies of the unit's big contracts into Rice's office and laid them out on his desk.

"Let's talk about how we can make these mark-to-market," she said.

Rice didn't get it. How could plants servicing two customers through direct pipelines be a market? The controller assured him it could be handled.

Just shift the corporate entity that signed the contracts and persuade customers to agree to allow the fuels to come from any source. True, it was an artifice—why would Enron get MTBE anyplace other than the plant connected directly to the customer? But with the changes, the controller said, Enron could argue it had established a rudimentary marketplace.

"But we'll still have only two big contracts," Rice said. "How many will we need to be considered a market?"

The controller shrugged. "All we need to show is two or three independent deals. Causey says that will be enough to get Arthur Andersen's approval."

That's all? A little renegotiating, and suddenly Enron had hundreds of millions in new profits—on the same deals? Still, Rice figured the accountants knew what they were doing. "All right," he said. "Let's get on it."

Storm clouds and tendrils of mist drifted across the summit of Arrowhead Mountain in Edwards, Colorado, tempering the summer heat. On the golf course below, Ken Lay was climbing into a cart, ready to ride out to the driving range. It was early on August 14, 1993, and Lay had just arrived at the Country Club of the Rockies following a ten-minute flight from his Aspen vacation home on one of Enron's Hawker jets. He was eager to get in a few practice swings; after all, it wasn't every day he teed off in front of the White House press corps alongside the President.

Weeks before, Lay had received a call from the White House inviting him to join President Clinton in a game. Lay figured Clinton was inviting an assortment of business executives, maybe to spend the time seeking support on some economic issue. But days ago, his assistant had checked for final details and learned that only three people were joining Clinton. Lay would be the sole businessman. The others were Lay's friend Gerald Ford, the former President, and Jack Nicklaus, the pro golfer. For someone like Lay, a sometime golfer, the lineup was unnerving.

As Lay's small white cart approached the driving range, he saw Ford hitting a few warm-up balls. The cart circled to a stop and Lay hopped out. The former President set the head of his club on the ground and smiled.

"Jerry, nice to see you," Lay said. "Looks like we're going to have an interesting foursome today."

"That's an understatement," Ford replied with a smile. "Thanks for agreeing to play, Ken."

After a few minutes of conversation, the two men hit some practice balls. Another cart came around, carrying Nicklaus, and everyone exchanged greetings.

The first sign of Clinton's arrival was the sudden emergence of reporters. He showed up on a cart driven by the course's golf pro and spoke a few kind words to Ford before turning to Lay and clasping his hand.

"Ken, I'm delighted you could join us," Clinton said.

"Well," Lay said, glancing around at the famous men, "it certainly looks like it's going to be interesting."

They climbed into two carts and rode out to the first tee, Clinton and Nicklaus in the lead, Ford and Lay following. The four men teed up, but only two balls made it on the fairway—one from Nicklaus and one from Lay. The presidents' had both veered off: the Democratic President's ball to the left, the Republican's to the right.

After nine holes riding with Ford, Clinton invited Lay to accompany him in his cart. The two men spent time discussing their lives, their thoughts, and their games as the press corps snapped photos.

The game ended hours later, and all the players went on their way. Any thoughts that the defeat of President Bush would significantly blunt Enron's influence at the White House had evaporated with the first swing of a club.

Skilling threw his arms up in disgust.

"Why wouldn't they do this?" he shouted. "It makes all the sense in the world!"

Two of Skilling's lieutenants had just delivered the bad news: the electric utilities had no desire to hitch themselves to his latest idea. Since 1994, Skilling had been trying to build on Enron's success in gas by expanding into electricity. It was an audacious, if logical, move. While the folks at Enron could spout chapter and verse about gas, they didn't know much about electricity trading. But that business dwarfed the gas industry, with transactions totaling close to $100 billion a year. Baby steps toward deregulation were forcing utilities to open their transmission lines to anyone, and Skilling wanted Enron to jump in with both feet.

He tossed the trading business to Lou Pai; the first transactions began in June. He pulled Rice back from clean fuels and put him in charge of negotiating long-term power contracts with the utilities.

Then it struck him—*the Idea*. Enron should form a consortium with, say, half a dozen electric utilities. Skilling hated owning assets, so the utilities would be responsible for building and operating the power plants. Enron would stick with what it did best—marketing and trading the power that the plants produced. It seemed breathtaking in its simplicity and moneymaking promise.

Skilling summoned Cliff Baxter, an investment banker who had joined

Enron years before. The two had become close friends, despite Baxter's penchant for challenging Skilling's views, a cocksureness that few others in the building dared display. This time was no different.

"Jeff," he scoffed on hearing the idea, "you're out of your fucking mind."

A deal involving at least seven parties? Laughable. It was hard enough to get *two* to agree on anything. Skilling's vision might be shrewd, but it could never be implemented.

Undaunted, Skilling assigned Baxter and Rice to get out on the road and pitch the idea to utilities. They did—and came back empty-handed, just as Baxter had predicted. The utilities' response had been blunt: they could handle their own business, thank you very much. They didn't need some upstart coming in to tell them how things should be done.

Baxter and Rice reported the reaction to Skilling and tried hard not to roll their eyes as he railed about the stupidity of utilities executives.

For years to come, Rice and Baxter would joke about Skilling's brainstorm. Funny or not, it revealed to them something essential about Skilling's character: he might not always be right, but he was never in doubt.

The battle lines had been drawn.

The pitched competition between Jeff Skilling and Rebecca Mark was rapidly becoming almost mythic inside Enron. He thought her international projects were mismanaged and undermined the company; she thought his trading business nothing more than air and bluster.

None of the sniping was a secret; the two would fight each other face-to-face. But increasingly Mark was hearing criticism around the company that her projects were lousy, that her team never sweated the details, that they were all rushing to close the next deal simply to cash in on a big payday.

On some levels, Mark thought there was room for criticism; the setup was all wrong. Her team was charged solely with developing the projects, never operating them. If they were operators, too, her team could learn firsthand about what was needed on the front end for the deals to work. They would be less tied financially to just developing the next project. The pace of new projects would slow down, but Enron would improve operations.

After one deal closed, Mark went up to see Kinder. "Rich, I'm always hearing everybody bitching that we don't have enough of a long-term interest in these projects," she said. "Give us control of the operations. Then we'll have a long-term interest."

But that wasn't what Kinder wanted. "You can't possibly be developing at the rate you're developing and run day-to-day operations as well," he said.

That was it. Developers would be paid to develop. Nothing else.

Following a short introduction, Fastow walked to the front of the Enron conference room. Around the room was a collection of Enron's best and brightest—analysts who tore apart the company in search of excessive risks.

It was their job to play doomsayer, to run the numbers through complex mathematical models that showed the effect different events could have. Recently, one analyst had completed a report proving the obvious: because of the amount of profits from trading—which in turn relied on the willing-ness of others to strike multimillion-dollar transactions on the promise of payment—Enron was uniquely dependent on its credit rating, meaning a downgrade could set off a death spiral. Far-fetched, sure, but dreaming up that kind of scenario was why the analysts were paid.

Today, the analysts had gathered for one of their informal meetings with executives from other parts of the building, to get a better understanding about their businesses. This time Fastow was the featured speaker.

For twenty minutes, Fastow described his division's deals. He showed charts spelling out the cash flow from them—oftentimes going from zero in the early years to fat sums in the later ones. Eventually he asked for questions.

"Yes," one analyst began. "How do you manage your interest-rate expo-sure?"

Fastow shrugged. "I don't have any."

The room went uncomfortably silent. *Fastow was wrong.* Enron booked fu-ture cash flows based on their present value—basically, the net result of a multiyear investment expressed in current dollars. Interest rates were critical to that calculation. And apparently, Fastow didn't grasp that.

The questions wound down, and Fastow departed. One of the analysts, Jeff Kinneman, broke into a smile. "That guy has already lost the company a few million dollars," Kinneman said. "And he doesn't even know it."

The analysts cracked up.

"Ken, you're not going to believe this!"

Amanda Martin stormed into Ken Rice's twenty-ninth-floor office, keep-ing a tight rein on her fury. It was the fall of 1994, a time when suspicions were spreading inside Enron about deep, fundamental problems with some of the power projects. Few seemed to be producing their projected profits, and Kinder had shuffled responsibility for the North American plants to Rice's electricity business, with Martin assigned to clean them up.

What she found appalled her. Plants had been built on a foundation of poor business judgments—overestimating demand, ignoring technical problems. Even the plant in Milford, Massachusetts—the centerpiece of Rebecca Mark's legend, the one built during her time at Harvard Business School—had been a debacle, constructed with assumptions of a growth in demand that never materialized.

With so many disasters, Martin began to question Enron's compensation system for the plant developers. They received their bonuses when someone—a bank, a government—agreed to finance the projects, leaving them with no stake in their ultimate success. Could it be, Martin wondered, that developers put together deals that could be financed rather than projects that could work?

Now, on this day, Martin thought she had found the unsettling answer. Minutes before, she had been reviewing records from the plant in Richmond, Virginia, and stumbled across a consultant's report. After reading it, she bolted from her desk, heading straight for Rice's office.

As soon as Martin walked in, grim-faced, Rice leaned back in his chair and plopped his feet on the desk.

"What's up, Mandy?"

"Ken, these people are outrageous," she said. "I want to show you something on Richmond."

"Okay," Rice sighed. "What did they do now?"

Martin slid the consultant's report across Rice's desk. "Look," she said, pointing at the page. "They *knew* this wasn't going to work. They knew it and did it anyway!"

Rice skimmed through the document. Richmond, he knew, had been an embarrassment. The plant had been designed to provide extra electricity to the local utility, Virginia Power, whenever demand dictated. But the contract required the juice to flow in less time than it took for the plant to start running. As a result, the plant repeatedly violated its contract, costing buckets of money. Everyone wondered how such an obvious problem had been missed.

Now here, in black and white, was the answer: it hadn't. A consultant had warned Enron that the contract requirements and technical constraints of the plant were not in sync. But nobody on the development team sent up a warning flare; instead, they hunkered down, got their bonuses, and left Enron stuck with the mess.

"You've got to be kidding me," Rice said.

Martin laughed. The developer on the deal got a six-figure bonus for this, she exclaimed, and now was working on the big international deals.

A bulb went off in Rice's head. *Skilling would love to have something like this in his battle with Rebecca.*

He stood up. "Come on. Let's go talk to Jeff."

Skilling looked up from his desk when they arrived.

"We want to show you something we found in the Richmond documents," Rice said.

Again Martin turned to the relevant page and showed it to Skilling. He took a moment reading through it.

"This is unbelievable," Skilling said softly.

"The thing in Milford was sloppy," Rice said. "But this one to me is just blatant fraud."

Skilling nodded, hiding his thoughts.

"But, Jeff, there's a bigger problem," Rice continued.

"What's that?"

"These people can't put together little plants in North America without messing it up," Rice said. "Now they're running around the world with a billion dollars to spend on big projects."

Rice paused. "You gotta ask, how bad are those deals gonna be?"

By 1994, complaints about the dysfunctional arrangement in the international division's development business had grown too heated to ignore. Those projects were eating up cash and having a significant impact on Enron's balance sheet. The company's ability to grow and protect its trading operation was being threatened by its overseas excursions. And capping it all, the exorbitant bonuses Enron paid the developers were enraging people throughout the building. Lay was dead set on expanding Enron's presence around the globe, but Kinder wanted to bring the monster under control.

By that time, Amanda Martin had made progress on the domestic plants; maybe she should clean up the international ones, too. Kinder summoned her to his office.

"I don't know what the hell international is doing," he said. "That whole organization needs to be reeled in."

"What do you see as the main problem?" Martin asked.

"We don't know what we've got!" Kinder growled. "We pay millions in bonuses based on projections, and then end up with pieces of shit that don't look like what we started with. I don't know what Rebecca's thinking."

The company, Kinder decided, had to fix the overseas projects and shove them as far away from Enron as possible. Martin, he said, would head up a new division called Joint Venture Management, which would take control of some of the foreign projects. The second step was more complicated: Enron would transfer the plants to a new division, which would be spun off as a separate public company called Enron Global Power and Pipelines, or EPP.

Enron would still own just over half of the publicly traded shares but be able to treat sales to EPP as revenue.

Martin agreed to take on the job and organized meetings with the development teams. Downcast glances and uncomfortable silences punctuated every session as executives launched into cathartic confessions about their projects. Martin was horrified by what she heard.

China was a disaster in the making. Guatemala was an absurdity, with financial shenanigans that had all the appearances of illegal bribes to foreign officials—payments that, unknown to Martin, Enron was deducting from its taxes. Each story seemed worse than the last.

But it was the project in the Dominican Republic that left Martin's mouth agape. The plant was on a barge, near a hillside of local slums that produced streams of garbage. The currents drove trash straight to the plant, right into the intake valve where water flowed in to keep the plant running. Rubbish of every sort—boxes, food, tricycles, animal carcasses—was repeatedly sucked in with the water, wrapping around the equipment. Jury-rigged flaps were installed over the intake valves, but to no avail. So now Enron employed local villagers to float on boats near the plant, using long wooden poles to push the trash away from the water intake. Without them there, the multimillion-dollar power plant couldn't stay operational.

Not that it was making money anyway; the Dominicans weren't paying their bills. The plant's fuel contract had been negotiated with Enron itself, at a hugely profitable rate for the company. But high fuel costs drove up the electricity prices to the point where the Dominicans refused to open their wallets for the power. And somehow, no one at Enron thought to write provisions into the contract to ensure payment, such as a standard term requiring the Dominicans to post a letter of credit.

"All right," Martin said. "Anything else?"

Well, one of the executives replied, there was this hotel near the Dominican plant, called the Bayside Inn. The plant had been built without anyone checking the prevailing winds—a problem, since its smokestacks belched out tons of soot. The wind carried the pollutants up a hill, where they showered down on the Bayside Inn and its guests. The hotel grounds were filthy, the rooms were filthy, even the food from its restaurant was covered with soot. The Bayside Inn promptly shut down and sued Enron for $200 million.

Martin rubbed her eyes. "Let me see if I understand this," she said. "The place shut down because our soot was landing in their food, *and now they're suing us for the value of the entire flipping hotel?*"

A sea of heads around the table nodded.

The slender, dark-haired man stepped onto Enron's twenty-ninth floor, ready for his first day of work. Everything about him was pressed and neat, his clothes an ensemble of elegance that belied his love of quirky discount stores. Michael Kopper was eager to make a good impression. This was his moment, his chance to strike it big, working at Enron alongside Andy Fastow and Rick Causey.

Kopper had been hired almost by happenstance. Enron had been on the prowl for new executives and had found Kathy Lynn, a senior banker at Toronto Dominion. When Enron offered her a job, Lynn suggested bringing along Kopper, one of the brightest lights on Dominion's structure-finance staff. Fastow himself handled the recruiting.

Kopper bristled with credentials; he was a twenty-nine-year-old graduate of the London School of Economics with a laser focus for negotiating deals. He was smart and cosmopolitan; he'd lived in London and New York and was well traveled.

At Enron his creativity shone through quickly. He proved adept at structured deals, and his star soon rose in the division. In negotiations he was sometimes a little too eager to play bad cop. Causey at times worried that Kopper didn't know when to leave something on the table, to ensure that the deal got done.

But in his personal life Kopper was something of an enigma. He never forgot his roots in Long Island, or the times he had struggled to bring in cash. In his younger days he waited tables, and now often regaled colleagues over business meals with critiques of the restaurant staff's performance. But in his early days at Enron, Kopper seemed surprisingly taciturn, almost withdrawn.

Whispers about Kopper started before his third month. Could it be, colleagues asked, that he was gay? By then, some of his colleagues had already learned that he was, but said nothing. Others were curious but didn't really care one way or the other. At that point, Kopper was not in a long-term relationship and was far from eager to discuss his sexuality with his new colleagues. "Discretion," he often told friends, "is the better part of valor."

But over time, Kopper loosened up, allowing his personality to shine through; soon he had forged a close friendship with Andy and Lea Fastow. The anomalous relationship between boss and employee flourished, with Michael becoming Andy's second voice, speaking for him when he wasn't around. They worked deals together, dined together, and—when Kopper finally found a long-term relationship with William Dodson, a finance executive with Continental Airlines—double-dated.

The depth of their friendship was always something of a mystery, so years later their former colleagues could only guess when asked the obvious question: Was it Fastow who eventually corrupted Kopper? Or the other way around?

Thousands of Hindus packed an outdoor victory rally in Bombay, cheering and waving saffron-colored flags at a group of men on a makeshift stage. A small, owlish man with flowing white robes lifted his arms, sending the crowd into a frenzy. He was Bal Thackeray, a former cartoonist who now led Shiv Sena, one of India's extremist nationalist groups. At first glance, no one would think Thackeray the type to inspire the masses. But on this day, March 14, 1995, he had led a coalition of Hindu nationalists to electoral victory in the state of Maharashtra, where Enron had begun constructing its giant power project.

Though Thackeray held no elected office, he was recognized as the man who would dictate the decisions of those who did; he would rule, Thackeray promised, by remote control. He spoke openly of his admiration for Hitler and spewed words of hate that whipped up the passions of a violent mob. Now his followers had secured power through appeals to nationalism and attacks on the ruling party's deals with foreign corporations, particularly Enron.

Enron had handed the Indian people plenty of reason for opposition. The World Bank had refused to finance the project, calling it ill conceived—too big, too expensive, and economically irrational. To fight back, Enron had launched a public-relations campaign, boasting of spending twenty million dollars to educate local officials about the project. While no one had evidence of impropriety, on the streets of India "educate" became a synonym for "bribe." Then, weeks before the election, bulldozers had roared to life in Dabhol, flattening space for the plant. Locals were enraged, and the rhetoric of Thackeray and his followers grew more inflamed. If elected, the nationalists promised, they would push Enron and its plant into the Arabian Sea.

Now, thanks in large part to Enron's blunders, the dangers highlighted by James Baker years before had materialized. Here was Thackeray, newly infused with power, standing before the cheering masses, promising to deliver on the commitments of the nationalist campaign.

"We will pick and choose the foreign investors we want," Thackeray proclaimed. "Why do we need foreigners when we have so many resourceful Indian industrialists?"

The crowd exploded in cheers.

"We will first review Enron's power plant in Dabhol," Thackeray said. "We must make sure this project only serves to benefit our people."

Enron's big international project was on the chopping block. And no one at the company had seen it coming.

Skilling dragged himself out of bed, feeling lousy. It had been another night of restlessness, of wandering the house, jotting down ideas, knowing his life was falling apart. He felt awful. He was fat. Something had to give.

It was the spring of 1995, and Skilling was a man adrift. It wasn't the office; that was going great. His gambit to push Enron into the wholesale-electricity business was already a roaring success. Skilling and Enron had become the champions of electricity deregulation, arguing that the calcified industry was ready to be shattered by competition. The whole effort was thrilling.

No, Skilling's problems were personal. He and Susan had grown apart; the three children were the only thing they had in common anymore. Jeff was jamming more meetings into each day, traveling too much, spending time with clients in far-flung cities. Susan was a dedicated supermom, rushing from one packed schedule to the next. Their time together was spent competing over whose day had been more nerve-racking. The tenderness they had both once felt was gone. They were always angry and just plain tired.

A choice had to be made. Skilling had walked away from a job before, leaving McKinsey. Maybe he should again—at least partway. He laid out a plan to Sue: he would work at Enron part-time. She seemed gratified by the proposal. After days of mulling it over, Skilling headed to Kinder's office. Everything about his demeanor spelled trouble.

"Okay, Jeff," Kinder said, "what's the problem?"

"Look, Rich," Skilling said, "my family matters to me and it's falling apart. The company is doing great, and I'm not needed as much around anymore."

"What are you talking about, Jeff?"

"I want to go part-time."

Kinder sank back, as though he'd taken a sock in the gut. For a moment there was only silence. Then Kinder rested his arms on the desk.

"You are out of your fucking mind."

"I may be," Skilling said. "But I have to do this."

"You're head of your division!" Kinder sputtered. "Why would anyone walk away from that? You don't do that!"

"Well," Skilling said, "yeah, you do, Rich."

Unable to change Skilling's mind, Kinder caved. He rewrote Skilling's contract, allowing him to work two weeks on, two weeks off, starting October. Ron Burns was assigned the other half of the job. Burns wasn't the strategist Skilling was, but his management skills were sharper, with a delicate touch that left employees feeling respected rather than belittled.

Once all the pieces were in place, though, Skilling was besieged with second thoughts. Two weeks on, two weeks off—and then what? What were they going to do with the time? Go sailing? Homeschool the kids? He had no idea.

Skilling's distress reached a boiling point that summer during a Nantucket vacation. He and his wife were lying in bed; Sue was reading, Jeff was going crazy. Months had passed, and he still didn't know how he was going to spend all the free time. He didn't like giving up power; he had to figure out what he was getting from all this.

"Listen, Sue," he said, "we've got to talk about how we're going to work this out. What are we going to do? I'm giving up my company, and I don't know what I'm giving it up for. What am I moving over to?"

Sue closed her book and set it on the nightstand. She switched off the light before rolling over on her side.

"You figure it out," she muttered.

Darkness surrounded Skilling. He lay on his back, eyes wide, as he stared at a ceiling he could no longer see.

Oh, shit! What have I done?

The Enron corporate jet banked over the Gulf of Mexico, winging its way to Buenos Aires. Inside, James Alexander ignored the roar of the engines as he readied himself for what was sure to be a battle.

Months before, Alexander had been brought in as chief financial officer of Enron Global Power and Pipelines, the now-public company formed to purchase international assets from Enron. At first Alexander had been excited about the opportunity. But his exuberance quickly faded, replaced by a cold dread.

The international project development business, despite all its public accolades, was a disaster. Developers, he thought, were setting project values at absurdly high levels, just to increase their bonuses under Enron's bizarre compensation system. Worse, they used improper accounting, refusing to immediately book the costs associated with bids on projects that they lost; instead, they created a rolling, growing long-term expense item known internally as "the snowball."

Topping it all, Enron seemed to have no idea that EPP was obligated to act on behalf of its public shareholders. Too many people at Enron viewed EPP as the company's back pocket—a place to stuff junk, at ridiculous prices. Pressure was already being exerted for EPP to pay an off-the-charts price for a project in the Dominican Republic—one that had already destroyed a hotel, for heaven's sake.

Now, as he rode in the corporate jet alongside Rich Kinder, Alexander decided to raise some of his concerns.

"Rich," he said, "from the point of view of EPP—"

Kinder slammed down an open hand. "Me! My! That's the problem with this company! Everybody's saying, 'Me! My!' "

The tongue-lashing lasted another hour, with the flight ending before Alexander could speak his mind. All right then, he would go to Ken Lay instead and expose all of the abuses he had witnessed.

Alexander arrived in Lay's office on a sunny May afternoon. He spoke carefully, laying out his concerns in slightly more than ten minutes. The pressure to overpay for projects. The perverse compensation system. The snowball.

Lay nodded seriously. "Well, gee, Jim, I guess I'm going to have to call Rich about this," he said.

Within minutes, Alexander found himself ushered out the door. He never heard anything back. Lay, he feared, had been lulled by the overly rosy assurances from underlings, who themselves had embraced fundamental fallacies as truth.

Not only was nothing fixed, the problems worsened. Weeks later, Alexander was informed that Enron had decided to enter a cost-sharing arrangement with EPP, resulting in the elimination of certain staff members.

Alexander's finance team and his accountants—the ones who might be willing to battle on behalf of EPP's public shareholders—from now on worked for Enron, the company on the other side of the bargaining table.

In late July 1995, the elite of German society jammed the stately Max Joseph Platz in Munich, buzzing about the production opening that evening at the Bavarian State Opera House. A swirl of tuxedos and formal gowns painted the plaza, lit up amid the popping flashbulbs of photographers gathered near the performance center's pillared entryway.

A black Mercedes pulled in, joining a line of luxurious automobiles dispatching passengers. A regal-looking man with chiseled features stepped out, crossing over to open the car door for a lovely young woman. Some in the crowd recognized the man as Herbert Henzler, chairman of McKinsey & Company's German office, who had recently married the woman accompanying him. The couple strolled up the sweeping stone steps of the opera house, turning to wave amid a torrent of flashes.

A few feet away, a pale, overweight man hobbling on crutches watched the moment and seethed. It was Skilling, who had broken his leg just before leaving Houston and had refused to postpone his business meetings to give his doctors time to put on a cast. He knew Henzler from McKinsey and for a moment saw the life he had abandoned. Henzler was in the bright lights, with a pretty young wife and the world at his feet. Skilling shook his head.

That's the picture of bliss. That's success. And here I am, with a broken leg and everything falling apart.

Skilling tottered his way back to his nearby hotel. There, a message was waiting from Ron Burns, the man taking over half his work. He headed to his room and dialed Enron.

"Hey, Ron. It's Jeff. I got your message."

"Jeff, thanks for calling. Listen, I have something I have to tell you."

"Yeah?"

"I'm leaving the company. I'm taking a job as president of Union Pacific."

"Really?"

"I hope this doesn't leave you in the lurch, but I really think this is the right thing for me."

Skilling felt a wave of anger. His shoulders tensed, his first clenched. For a moment he sat absolutely still.

"Okay," he finally said. "Thanks for calling."

Then he hung up.

Over the weeks that followed, Skilling stopped functioning. He was unable to make decisions, uncertain of what he should be doing. His depression was as dark and overpowering as ever. He was weeks from starting his part-time schedule, but now no one was there to pick up the slack. Worse, he still had no idea what he was going to do at home. There had been no planning, no organizing, nothing. Finally, by late August, he found a new resolve; he couldn't be depressed the rest of his life. Before Labor Day, Skilling appeared in Kinder's office.

"Hey, Rich," Skilling said from the doorway. "Deal's off. I'm back full-time. Forget everything I said."

Kinder broke into a wide smile. "Great."

Somebody. Skilling needed somebody to shepherd his newest idea into a fully functioning business, one sure to bring Enron big profits. Somebody. But who?

The idea had kind of leaped off the page. Ken Rice was building a wholesale-electricity business dealing with utilities and was going great guns. But Enron was virtually ignoring the retail market. With deregulation spreading—cutting direct ties between utilities and the users of power—every customer could soon be up for grabs.

Enron already had a foothold in the business, thanks to Cliff Baxter. Years back, Baxter had engineered the purchase of an Ohio power company called Access Energy for corporate pocket change. But what caught Skilling's attention was Access Energy's direct-energy sales business to industrial customers; he had long ago assigned the Ohio executives the task of using that base to build a broader retail effort. But they had failed to deliver, and Skilling was tired of waiting. Enron needed to start this in Houston, he decided, under someone who wouldn't take any nonsense from Ohio.

Skilling turned in his chair, his hand on his chin, as he considered possible candidates. A thought came to him.

What about Andy Fastow?

Fastow had done a hell of a job in finance, getting Cactus going, pulling together JEDI. And Fastow made no secret that he considered himself underpaid; he griped about the huge paychecks going to those money losers in international development, when here he was, bringing real profits into Enron and not getting enough reward for it. The path to the big money was on the commercial side, and Fastow wanted to be there. He had appealed to Skilling repeatedly for his chance. Maybe this was the solution for everybody.

Skilling made an appointment with Fastow. On the designated day they met in Skilling's office.

"Andy," Skilling said, "we're getting ready to launch a significant effort in retail. It's an important business for us, one that I think really holds promise for us."

He smiled. "And I'd like you to head it up. Would you do that for me?"

Fastow's face lit up. "Yeah, Jeff," he enthused. "Gee, thanks for showing the confidence in me."

Skilling nodded. "Okay, well, here's what I need from you. We need a business strategy for this. Who are our customers? What's our approach? I want you to think it through and line it all up."

Fastow said he would take on the job quickly. Some things in finance needed to be wrapped up. But by December he'd be ready to go. That strategy would be on Skilling's desk early in the New Year, he promised.

A throng of beggar children swarmed a chauffeur-driven sedan, tapping on the car's windows as it inched forward in midday traffic. Hardened to the emotional battering that accompanied travel in India, Ken Lay and Rebecca Mark did their best to avoid reacting to the drumbeat of pleas. Slowly negotiating the sedan forward, the driver pulled away, leaving the children to flock to the next car.

Through the sedan's passenger windows, overpowering, contradictory images came into view. Animals wandering the streets. A vibrant city skyline.

Impoverished merchants hauling pushcarts. Here and there, games of street cricket. Every vivid sight, every blaring sound engendered a disquieting sense of a city bordering on chaos.

In recent weeks even the city's name had become part of the disarray. The nationalists who won office the previous February had ordered the colonial "Bombay" to be abandoned in favor of "Mumbai," in honor of the area's original Koli inhabitants. Even so, by this time, November 1, 1995, all but a handful of road signs still read "Bombay"; few outside the government uttered the new name in anything but the most formal conversations.

For Mark and Lay, the uncertainty about the name of India's largest financial center captured their own predicament. Would decisions of this new government stick?

After taking office, the nationalists had wasted little time in scrapping the Dabhol project. Enron was now on the hook for more than $116 million in loans—not including the tens of millions already spent—for a project that by all rights seemed dead.

As their car approached suburban Bandra, Lay and Mark felt hopeful Dabhol could get back on track. Mark had relentlessly pursued an effort to revive the project. She had spent weeks visiting dignitaries, practically begging for support, building to this day, this trip. She had secured an audience with Bal Thackeray, the extremist who controlled the nationalists. Lay and Mark could only hope that after today's meeting, the demagogue would smile on them and salvage their struggling investment.

The sedan turned onto the final stretch of road leading to Matoshri, Thackeray's suburban home. Outside, a phalanx of guards stood watch, protecting against potential reprisals against the Shiv Sena leader for the violence inflicted on Muslims by his followers.

"All right, Ken," Mark said, wrapping up her briefing. "Just remember, everything today is scripted. There shouldn't be any surprises."

"Fine," Lay replied.

The sedan pulled to a stop. Mark picked up a small bag containing an original Walt Disney animation; she knew Thackeray still had a love for his original career as a cartoonist. A gift of the animation, along with flowers she brought, would start things off on just the right tone.

Mark stepped out of the car first. She wore a formal *salwar kameez*—a traditional long dress with pants underneath—sandals, and no makeup. Lay followed, dressed in a formal business suit. A young woman answered the door. Once inside, Lay and Mark removed their shoes in a symbolic gesture of respect, and the young woman escorted them into a modest living room.

Minutes later, Thackeray appeared, wearing his trademark dark-rimmed glasses. Mark and Lay stood.

"Mr. Thackeray," Mark said, "good to see you again."

Thackeray nodded. "Yes, hello."

Mark motioned toward Lay. "I'd like to introduce you to Ken Lay, the chairman of Enron. We're here to visit you today and hear your views about the Dabhol project."

Mark presented her gifts to Thackeray's apparent delight. Afterward, he invited everyone to sit. An assistant wandered into the room, dispensing cups of tea.

Mark almost held her breath. Lay was old-school, with a gregarious personal style that often led him to engage in animated banter. But deference was critical today. She had told Lay during the car ride that he needed to stay quiet. This would be Thackeray's show. Thackeray sipped his tea, placing the cup on a small table beside his chair.

"Your company made mistakes," he finally said. "You have come in telling us what to do, rushing through without respect. You have demanded terms in your favor and not in the favor of this country."

Lay and Mark listened, saying nothing.

"We are not against Enron. We are against the Dabhol project in the form passed by the previous government. But the last few weeks you have come far. You have made clear your desire to work with us, to more fully take our interests into account. That is an important step."

Thackeray looked Lay in the eyes. "We have to do something to improve the electricity situation in our country. I know this."

For several minutes, Thackeray questioned how long it would take to get the power-plant deal back together. Then, glancing at a nearby table, he nodded toward a white-framed photograph of an older Indian woman.

"That is my wife, Meena," Thackeray said. "I am in mourning for her. She died in September."

"I'm so sorry," Lay said softly.

Thackeray nodded, then continued. "We were at our home outside of Bombay, in the evening, and she had a heart attack. The doctor had given her medicine, but the power was out. We looked for the medicine, but it was too dark. We could not find it."

Lay expressed condolences again, understanding the message. Thackeray had learned from personal experience the human toll of his country's electricity shortage.

The conversation continued for more than an hour, at which point Thackeray led the executives to the front of his house. Outside, reporters had gathered; the fate of the plant was big news in Maharashtra, and everyone knew this meeting was key. At the doorway, Thackeray turned to Lay.

"What would you like us to say?" Thackeray asked. "How can I be helpful getting this project going again?"

Lay glanced at Mark, suppressing a smile. Those words sealed it; they had again transformed setback into victory. Now—in part because of the death of an elderly woman whose name was unknown to almost everyone at Enron—the project that had seemed doomed was back in business.

November 22 dawned clear and cool in Washington, D.C., the rising sun bathing the city's landmarks in a golden glow. Inside the White House, Bill Clinton scanned a lengthy article in *The New York Times*. The previous day, it reported, the state of Maharashtra had reached a tentative pact allowing Enron to proceed with its Dabhol power project. Clinton thought the situation might call for additional attention from his Administration.

He picked up a pen, scribbling the letters "FYI" across the article. He then forwarded it to his chief of staff, Thomas "Mack" McLarty III, who once ran an Arkansas energy company. McLarty jumped on the assignment, contacting Lay to find out if the Administration could help. The government's international apparatus was put into play, with Frank Wisner, the Ambassador to India, visiting government officials to stress the White House's interest in seeing Enron treated fairly.

Final negotiations between Mark and Maharashtra had been intense, dispensing with the cautious structure of the first agreement. The original deal called for construction in two stages, with the first generating just 695 megawatts of power through the burning of fuel oil. India then had the option to commission the second phase—involving construction of the far more expensive liquefied-natural-gas facilities, which would generate an additional 1,300 megawatts.

Despite the project's troubles, Enron decided to double its bet on India. The plant size was increased, from 2,015 megawatts to 2,184 megawatts, even while Enron agreed to cut $300 million from its original $2.8 billion budget. And no longer was the expensive, complex second phase simply an option. Instead, Enron committed to building it no matter what.

Back in Houston, the revived deal was seen by the Enron board as a grand slam. The increased risk was barely considered; India was still sure to be a big winner. After all, the international division's projections said so.

The executives from international development trickled into a conference room on the mezzanine above the fiftieth floor. They rarely spent much time in Enron's headquarters, instead passing their days in the division's offices across the street in Allen Center. But on this day, guests from corporate wanted to attend their staff meeting, so they elected to gather in the executive offices.

Everyone found a place, with Rebecca Mark on the far side of the room, ready to hash through recent and projected performance data in what was known as the QBR, or quarterly business review. Nearby, two executives from investor relations—Mark Koenig and Rebecca Carter—sat quietly, eager to hear the latest numbers.

For Koenig and Carter, being in the room was something of a coup. The international development group had always jealously guarded its information; sure, developers *agreed* to turn over details of their projects, but they rarely followed through. Koenig and Carter had complained to Kinder about the secretiveness but didn't expect much help; Kinder had trouble getting the numbers himself.

There was a touch of buoyancy in the room as the last of the executives found their seats. "All right," Mark announced. "Let's get started."

The division was doing wonderfully, she told the assembled executives. Koenig and Carter took notes as Mark rattled off the financial details.

For several minutes, Mark gave a rundown on how returns had been calculated on a particular project. Koenig and Carter sat quietly, trying hard to disguise their growing horror. Carter shot a glance at Koenig, distress in her eyes. Koenig tapped her under the table, warning her to keep quiet. He understood.

The rates of return were wrong.

Oftentimes, Enron received management fees and other payments for operating power plants—an additional source of revenue, separate from the cash generated by selling electricity. But Mark was treating the fees as if they were a return of a portion of Enron's initial investment. Under such a calculation, the more the fees, the lower the capital investment, and in turn the higher the returns. It was a method wide of the mark, resulting in artificially large rates of return.

Carter glanced around the room. No one was objecting.

Oh, God, Rebecca, no! Carter thought. *Somebody's got to tell her she's wrong.*

About an hour later, the meeting wound down. Koenig and Carter gathered their things and hustled out the door.

"My God," Carter said. "Mark, did she really . . ."

"Yes. Yes."

Koenig pushed the button for the elevator.

"But you can't say anything, Rebecca," Koenig said.

"Mark . . ."

"Rebecca, we'll never be allowed back in their staff meetings again. You can't say anything."

Carter shook her head. "Well," she said, "we better not let her talk to investors with this kind of crap."

Christmas season, 1995. Time for the Fastows' annual party and a stream of other Enron celebrations. But this season things felt far different from years before.

The thrill, the sense of mission, had faded. No longer did the place seem fun-loving; the workday was a hazy, frenetic rush. Too many executives were tired and bitter. The department had gone through yet another one of its seemingly endless series of reorganizations, this time renamed Enron Capital & Trade. Skilling had suffered his near-breakdown over the summer. Fastow's playfulness had given way to the honing of his sharp edges. The team mentality had died amid a torrent of backstabbing as executives competed for a higher rung on the corporate ladder. Somehow, the matchup had shifted from *Enron versus the world* to just *Enron versus Enron*.

At a little past seven on the night of his division's big party, Skilling puffed on a cigarette in his living room, waiting for Susan. Since abandoning his plans to work part-time, he had lost weight on a starvation diet and taken up chain-smoking. He felt better about himself, but life at home had deteriorated even more. He and Susan were barely speaking, at best going through motions of civility. Skilling wasn't even spending time with his kids. Instead, he dedicated almost every available moment to work.

He poured himself a glass of wine and lit another cigarette. It was time to go, but Susan still hadn't come out of the bedroom. Thirty minutes passed. Forty-five. An hour. Skilling, by then on his third glass of wine, stewed in anger. Susan had never hidden her dislike of these holiday parties, but this year Skilling had taken on that problem weeks before. His people were important to him, he had told her; she was going to go to the party and be nice. Now, he felt sure, Sue was obtaining her silent revenge.

Finally, past 8:15, Sue walked into the living room.

"I can't do anything with my hair," she announced.

Skilling ground out his cigarette.

"Okay, fine," he said. "I'm not going."

"Oh yes you are."

"No," he said, standing. "I'm going out drinking."

Skilling headed to his car, and Susan followed. In silence, he drove over to Westheimer Road, near Loop 610, and pulled into a shopping center. He maneuvered toward Grotto, an Italian restaurant, and parked.

"I'm going in," he said.

"I'm staying here."

Skilling shrugged. "Fine."

He climbed out and stalked inside the restaurant, heading straight for the bar. After a number of drinks he returned to the car, where Sue still waited.

"Okay," he said. "Now I'm going someplace else."

The scene from the Grotto repeated itself, with Skilling drinking as his wife waited in the parking lot. When he lumbered back, he was fairly drunk, and Sue was angry.

"We have to go to the Christmas party," she said.

"No, I'm not going to let you go there and cause problems. I'm not going to let you screw that up."

"You have to go to the party."

Skilling gripped the steering wheel, rage and alcohol overtaking him. He closed his eyes for a second. Then he stared through the windshield, resolved.

"Sue, I've had it. I've just had it."

He took a breath.

"I want a divorce."

CHAPTER 4

THE WHITE MAZDA NAVAJO turned onto an inclined driveway off Westheimer Road, heading toward the purple-and-white stucco facade of Armando's Mexican restaurant. A valet watched the vehicle slow to a stop before hustling over to the driver-side door. Andy Fastow popped his seat belt and stepped out, handing over the keys as Lea emerged from the passenger side. He escorted her to the restaurant's wooden door and swept inside.

Minutes later, Ken Rice—with his wife, Teresa—pulled his red Porsche off Westheimer into Armando's, hitting the sloping driveway with a thud; he winced as metal scraped asphalt. Leaving the car with the valet, the Rices strolled inside. Andy Fastow waved from the bar.

It was January 1996, the first time the Fastows and the Rices had gone out together socially. Despite years of working in the same building, Rice and Fastow had only crossed paths a few times, and neither had come away with kind thoughts. Fastow considered Rice overindulged and overpaid, while Rice called Fastow an ambitious prick behind his back, a man who only invested time with colleagues if he thought they could help his career. But days before, Fastow had stunned Rice—and aroused his suspicions—by phoning with an invitation to dinner.

The couples met in the bar; all four were dressed chic-casual, with plenty of sweaters and knit shirts. The men shook hands. Rice introduced Teresa, then greeted Lea; the two already knew each other from the office.

"Listen," Fastow said. "They've got our table ready. You want to go over there?"

The couples left the bar and found the hostess. On either side, diners crowded tables in two small annexes—one painted blue, the other red. The hostess ignored the side rooms, leading the couples through a dimly lit central area with a decor faintly reminiscent of a French château. Their table was alongside a wall; the wives sat on one side together, the husbands on the other.

As the couples chatted, a waiter appeared. "Would you care for a libation?" he asked.

It was the classic Armando's pretension, but that, after all, was part of its appeal. There were orders for margaritas all around, and soon the table was loaded with drinks, baked chips, chicken enchiladas, and seafood.

As they ate, the couples chatted about children. Lea had recently given birth to her first child and spilled out questions to Teresa, a pediatrician. Ken bragged about his three kids' accomplishments, while Andy talked about his new son, Jeffrey—a name that had already led to jokes inside Enron about Fastow using his baby to kiss up to Skilling.

The conversation turned to the office. Fastow had just started running the retail-electricity unit; Rice figured that Fastow had set up the dinner to pick his brain about the wholesale-electricity business he ran.

"Hey," Rice said, "how are things in retail?"

Fastow broke into a smile. "Oh, just great. Really great. We're really going out, taking on some big stuff."

Rice sipped his margarita.

"We've got some really important challenges," Fastow continued. "We're trying to redefine how people buy electricity. We want to come up with ways to provide services that look nontraditional, that really open people's eyes with how we differentiate our product."

Rice nodded, saying nothing. A bunch of marketing buzzwords. Not a good sign.

"That's what we've got to do," Fastow went on. "We've got to come out with new and creative things."

"Okay," Rice said. "That sounds good."

"Like take M&M's."

M&M's? The candy?

Fastow's words tumbled out excitedly. "M&M's is now putting blue M&M's in the bags, and they're making a big deal out of blue just so they can sell more M&M's."

Rice vaguely knew what Fastow was talking about. Mars, the maker of M&M's, had just introduced a new color for the candy and had launched a big advertising blitz announcing its arrival. That was fine for a candy promotion, but what the hell did that have to do with selling electricity? Was Enron going to create new colors for it?

"Okay," Rice said. "I think that's a creative marketing strategy for M&M's, but what does it mean? What's the analogy for electricity?"

"I think we can come up with some products that really attract people's attention like that."

Rice nodded, trying to hide his dismay. Fastow might be good at finance, but he sure didn't understand commodities; there, price was everything. Rice decided to offer a little electricity primer before Fastow embarrassed himself in front of Skilling with all this talk of blue M&M's.

"Well," Rice said slowly. "Okay. But I think the real key for the electricity consumer is that they're interested in price and they're interested in convenience."

Fastow stared at Rice blankly.

"But consumers don't know what their comparative costs are," Rice continued. "Price signals aren't in their hands. If you figure out a way to let consumers understand their costs, they could make intelligent decisions, and then you could compete on price."

Silence. Fastow blinked. "We've got other creative ideas, too," he began, launching into a description of another marketing gimmick. Apparently, he hadn't listened to a word Rice had said.

Rice rocked back in his chair. *Okay, I get it.* Fastow liked Fastow's ideas and didn't care for what anyone else had to say. If this was how Fastow was going to run things, Rice figured, retail was probably doomed.

Some time later, Fastow paid the bill, and the two couples headed back to the valet. The Rices' car came around first; Armando's valets tended to favor expensive vehicles, so the Porsche had been sure to arrive before the Fastows' boxy, two-door SUV. The Rices thanked their hosts and piled into the car.

Teresa waited until they pulled away before saying anything. She had noticed Fastow jabbering at Ken a lot and not listening to his responses. It struck her as odd.

"What was that all about?" she asked.

Rice held the steering wheel.

"I have no idea," he said.

On the east side of downtown Portland stands the World Trade Center, a trio of buildings overlooking a promenade that opens to the Willamette River. A symphony of glass and concrete, the towers are the corporate epicenter for Portland General Electric, a utility that served Oregon and was pushing for the deregulation of electricity.

On the morning of January 17, 1996, a cab carrying Cliff Baxter and Ken Rice pulled alongside the brick sidewalk in front of the trade center. The two hustled out of the car and headed for a covered walkway. Brilliant stretches of deep blue peeked past a lattice of glass and aluminum overhead as they walked through a wave of pedestrian traffic. Baxter and Rice arrived at Tower One and boarded an elevator for the top floor.

This, they knew, was an important day for Enron's electricity business. Once Skilling gave up his idea for a massive energy consortium, Baxter began seeking a more reasonable alternative, an alliance with a single utility. If Enron was going to be a player, the thought went, it needed such a relationship in the West, where the industry was being shaped by the expectation of deregulation in the giant California market.

The hunt for a partner had been frustrating; too many utility executives seemed more interested in their golf games than in their corporate strategies. A bunch of nine-to-fivers wouldn't fit the Enron mold. What they needed was a company pushing for change, on the leading edge. Portland General seemed perfect, if only its chairman and chief executive, Ken Harrison, could be persuaded to deal.

The elevator stopped, and the Enron officials strode into Portland General's executive offices, a place that dripped with a woody and conservative style common to utilities. Rice approached the receptionist.

"Hi. Ken Rice and Cliff Baxter to see Mr. Harrison."

Fifteen minutes later, they were summoned into a conference room just off the lobby. Harrison was waiting at the large table, his back to an enormous picture window. Alongside him sat Joe Hirko, the company's chief financial officer. Baxter and Rice said their hellos and found their seats.

Rice took it from there, reminding everyone of the meeting more than a year earlier when they had discussed Skilling's now-abandoned idea for an electricity consortium. The utility executives nodded and smiled; the silliness of that proposal didn't need to be mentioned.

"We still believe there's a lot we could do together," Baxter said. "We're interested in talking about a formal strategic relationship with Portland General."

Rice set his arms on the table. "We've looked at your position in the market and what you guys are doing, and we think that we can bring in capabilities that complement what you're doing, and vice versa."

The Enron executives pressed hard. Deregulation was a force that couldn't be stopped, they said. Companies that prepared would flourish. Those that didn't would flounder. Harrison and Hirko listened attentively, nodding.

"We agree with you on the direction of the market," Harrison said. "We're already trading electricity; we know that area pretty well. But I think there are some things we should be doing together."

He smiled. "So let's talk some more," he said.

The strategy session in Fastow's retail group dragged on for hours.

Weeks into his new job, Fastow had yet to devise a business plan for Skilling. His ideas were vague, flighty, unmoored to the practical details of the real world. On this day in early 1996, he and his top team thrashed through various proposals, scribbling notes on a whiteboard, trying hard to cobble together *something*.

Fastow glanced through the room's glass wall and saw Vince Kaminski walking by. Kaminski was Enron's resident genius, a top risk analyst who had worked on Wall Street before coming to Houston. Now the Polish-born Kaminski was the man Enron most relied on to protect the company from unseen perils. When Enron held investments that could lose worth, it was Kaminski and his team of financial rocket scientists who concocted complex hedges, devices that—in the perfect world—went up in value as the price of the original investment declined. His advice, Fastow felt sure, would be an important part of any retail strategy.

"Hey," Fastow said, pointing to the hallway. "Get Vince in here."

Somebody pulled in Kaminski. He was soft-spoken yet excitable, a man who quickly assessed colleagues' brainpower—and Fastow had never made it high on his list of high-voltage intellects. Long ago, when Fastow had incorrectly boasted that his business was unaffected by interest rates, Kaminski had concluded the man was a lightweight.

Fastow stretched his legs under the table. "Vince, we're putting together the strategy for retail," he said, inadvertently punctuating every *s* sound with a slight whistle. "I wanted to see if we could get your input."

"Of course," Kaminski said. "What have you planned?"

The whole idea was based on the inevitability of electricity deregulation, Fastow said. "When that happens, electricity prices are sure to drop."

Kaminski nodded solemnly, already recognizing the flaw in Fastow's thinking. Electricity prices would go down under deregulation *in theory*. What if oil and gas prices spike upward? What if the deregulation is done badly? What if there's a nuclear meltdown, sounding the death knell for that part of the industry overnight, creating power shortages?

"Yes?" Kaminski said. Arguing was pointless.

"So, we offer consumers long-term contracts, below current rates. Then deregulation happens, prices drop, and our contract price will be above the market price. We'll make profits on the spread."

Kaminski folded his arms. Fastow hadn't disappointed; the idea was ridiculous. Basically, Enron would make a massive bet on the timing of deregulation, with losses piling up until new rules came about. Then—if prices dropped—Enron would charge *above market* rates? What about customers who went bankrupt? Was Enron going to sue everyone who switched providers? And once Enron spent a few years ripping off its retail customers, how would the company renew its contracts or attract new business?

Before Kaminski could respond, a Fastow deputy spoke.

"There is one problem with the idea," the executive said. "We're guaranteeing ourselves some pretty big losses in the first few years."

"That's right," Fastow nodded.

He glanced at Kaminski. "Vince, can you come up with a hedge that would offset losses in the initial years?"

Kaminski smiled to himself. *How could a man like this be in charge of a business?* A hedge could only offset declines in an asset's value, not operating losses from a failing business. The only hedge for a money-losing business was a moneymaking business—and one of those certainly wasn't going to be coming out of this meeting.

"If I could come up with such a hedge," Kaminski said patiently, "I would say forget about having customers. We can all just make money by hedging."

The cell phone on Ken Rice's belt rang as he walked through downtown Houston. He snapped it off its holder and pushed the answer button.

"I just got a call from Oejay Irkohay," a voice said, sounding conspiratorial.

Rice laughed. It was Cliff Baxter, with news on the Portland General talks. In a faint stab at security, Baxter had taken to speaking in pig latin whenever discussing the negotiations over a cell phone.

Oejay Irkohay. Joe Hirko, Portland General's CFO.

"Okay, Iffclay Axterbay," Rice responded. "What did Oejay have to say?"

The talks had not progressed much in the weeks after the first meeting in Portland. What started as a discussion about vague cooperation had turned into a proposal for a formal joint venture. But that idea was floundering; there were too many technical problems, too many opportunities for each side to rip the other off. Writing an agreement that surmounted the mutual wariness seemed impossible.

Hirko wanted to get together again, Baxter explained, and make another stab at a deal. Rice agreed, and the negotiation teams scheduled a new meeting at a hotel in Laguna Niguel, California.

Once everyone arrived, the talks went round without resolution. After several hours of effort Hirko called for a break and left the room.

Baxter rubbed his face in frustration. "This is never going to work."

"I know," Rice replied.

A pause. "The only thing that'll work is a full-out merger," Baxter said.

Rice nodded. "Let's go ask Hirko what he thinks."

Baxter and Rice walked out of the conference room and found Hirko in the hallway.

"Look, Joe, I don't think we're going to get there on a joint venture," Baxter said. "What about a merger?"

Hirko breathed in deep. "If anything is going to work," he said, "it's going to be a merger."

Sherron Smith flipped through the pages of an investment presentation, her face tightening in disgust.

A former accountant, Smith had worked at Enron since October 1993, when she was hired to manage JEDI, Enron's joint venture with Calpers. At first she had enjoyed Enron and her boss, Andy Fastow, who struck her as energetic and dynamic, with occasional touches of thoughtfulness. But over time, Fastow's shortcomings as a manager had alienated her. That year he had even failed to show up at the semiannual Performance Review Committee meeting, where managers pushed to get bonuses and promotions for their staff. As a result, Smith had come away with a disappointing fourteen-thousand-dollar bonus and a simmering anger toward Fastow. She had even considered quitting.

Then, salvation. Fastow moved to retail. Rick Causey, Skilling's favorite accountant, took over, and her world brightened. Causey was a friendly, doughy man who had already promised to get raises for Smith and her colleagues. The change rekindled her good feelings for Enron.

Her job, put simply, was to act as JEDI's gatekeeper. Executives around Enron were always looking for JEDI to invest in their deals. But too many proposals were fanciful—badly thought out, badly structured, or just plain bad.

When deal makers made a sloppy presentation to Smith, she savaged them. She delighted in shocking people with uncomfortable truths—about anything at all, including herself. The knock on Smith was that she tried too hard to be one of the boys—so long as the boys were truck drivers and longshoremen. Her foul mouth at meetings was legendary, and this day, no one expected things to be any different.

Smith closed up the presentation, staring hard across the table at the executives who brought it to her.

"What the fuck is this?" she snorted. "This thing looks like a circle jerk to me."

Smirks all around. Sherron was just being Sherron.

"Sherron, I know you've got strong opinions, but there's a lot of value—," one of the executives began.

"Oh, come on," Smith interrupted. "Let's not sit around blowing each other, okay?"

On one side of the table, a couple of Smith's colleagues, Shirley Hudler and Bill Brown, listened to the exchange and winced. They respected Smith but thought her salty approach to business discussions damaged her.

Oh, God, Sherron, Hudler thought. *Shut up.*

The deal team pushed hard for Smith to change her mind. Smith countered with responses about the problems with the transaction; her arguments were strong. The case for doing the deal crumpled.

Smith quashed another proposal—but, as always, at a price. Her colleagues whispered that her coarse language was undermining her credibility, that her penchant for one-upmanship was giving her the reputation as someone who wouldn't listen. If she didn't stop, if she didn't learn how to play nice in a corporate setting, if she didn't learn to be more of a team player, they had no doubt that Sherron Smith's future at Enron would be bleak.

None of her colleagues could have imagined that Smith would be one of Enron's few executives to emerge from the company in high stead, known worldwide under her then-married name as Sherron Watkins, the Enron whistle-blower.

Lea Fastow's voice almost purred over the phone line. "So, Ray," she said, "I hear you're looking for a job."

Over at Citibank's office in Houston, Ray Bowen cradled the phone to his ear and smiled. "Oh, really," he replied. "Is that what you heard?"

It was amazing how fast word traveled. Bowen, a hulking man whose size belied a soft-spoken, almost unflappable demeanor, had been considering a career change for only a short while. After almost a dozen years in banking, Bowen had won respect both from bosses and from clients, like Enron. But he had grown tired of Friday-afternoon phone calls about some other corporation going through some other crisis. He wanted control of his life, control of his weekends, time with his family. That meant chucking the banker's life and finding work on the corporate side. He had already put out a few feelers when the call came from Lea, Enron's assistant treasurer.

"I never thought you'd leave Citibank," Lea said.

"I'm on a plateau. I'm bored."

"Well, don't go anywhere without talking to us."

Interesting. "Have anything in mind?" Bowen asked.

"There are some good opportunities here. You know, Andy's off doing this new group."

Lea spelled out the details. Retail, a new Enron venture. Revolutionary stuff. Shattering old concepts.

"Okay," Bowen said. "If he's interested, I'll talk."

The interviewing started almost right away, and Bowen liked what he heard. The retail group struck him as dynamic, cutting-edge. Fastow might be a problem; he seemed to surround himself with yes-men, and Bowen tended to speak his mind. But the possibilities at Enron seemed too good to pass up. Bowen's pay and title wouldn't compare with Citibank, but the chances for advancement made up for the sacrifice. He decided to take the risk.

Bowen arrived for his first day in late February 1996. The retail offices were nothing much to look at, just desks in different quadrants of a large room. When Bowen walked in, Fastow was at a desk on the northwest side.

"Hey, Ray!" he called out. "How you doing?"

Bowen greeted his new boss and made his way to a desk across the room. Over the next few minutes Fastow's secretary, Bridget Maronge, provided him with a collection of electronic gadgetry—a cell phone, a pager, a laptop. Bowen was surprised. At Citi, he had purchased his own personal technology; here, it was provided before anyone asked if it was needed. Wasn't anybody watching expenses?

"Umm . . . I already have a cell phone," Bowen said softly.

"Well, we already bought it," Maronge replied. "You might as well take it."

Bowen sat at his desk for a few hours, fiddling with his computer and not quite sure what he was supposed to be doing. Around noon, Fastow approached.

"Hey, Ray, you want to go out to lunch?"

"Sure," Bowen said, standing. "I'd love to."

Bowen gathered his things and followed his new boss. Partway across the room, Fastow turned to him.

"I wanted to get together, Ray, because I wanted to tell you what's been going on," Fastow said. "We're not quite as far along as I may have led you to believe."

Somehow, Bowen had suspected he wasn't getting the full story from Fastow. But now it was too late to do anything about it; he had already cut his ties to Citi.

"This is really just a start-up, Ray," Fastow continued. "And we haven't figured it all out yet. But we gotta get there fast."

What did *that* mean? For the next few days, Bowen tried to find out, interviewing colleagues and examining records. The answer was disquieting. There was no cohesive strategy; people were off talking to ad agencies about marketing, running around scouting up deals, all without bothering to figure out what the division was trying to achieve.

Word got around the office about Bowen's questioning. Before the week was out, Gustav Beerel, a young Harvard MBA working in the division, dropped by Bowen's desk.

"I've been doing some analysis about our business," Beerel said. "I wanted to see what you think."

Beerel laid out a sheet of paper crammed with numbers. "Okay," he said. "Let's just walk through this. I think you'll see the problem pretty quickly."

The numbers were ballpark, but they told a damning story: The average retail customer paid about sixty dollars a month for electricity, with two-thirds of that covering fixed costs—expenses that couldn't change. That left one-third, or twenty dollars, related to the purchase of fuel or electricity, plus whatever profit there was. Even assuming Enron could buy the commodities for ten percent less than competitors, those savings didn't translate into much—just two dollars of average savings per month.

"Would you take the chance of switching to some unknown electricity provider for two dollars a month?" Beerel asked. "That's the issue we're facing."

Bowen stared at the data, reality hitting him hard.

"The numbers don't work," he said softly.

Fastow appeared pasty-faced and anxious as he signaled for his troops to gather round. In recent days, his nervous tics had grown more pronounced: his speech was laced with a rising number of whistles, he pulled more often at his collar while craning his neck, his eyes widened with panic. Time was running out, and he needed his staff's help.

As everyone straggled over, Fastow sat on a desk, trying awkwardly to project a casual look. "I've got a meeting coming up with Skilling," he said. "And we've got to knock his socks off. We've got to come up with a great story for what we're doing in our business plan."

The executives squirmed. There was no business plan.

"When do we have to get this done?" one asked.

Fastow flashed a smile. "Next week."

The staff members glanced around at one another.

The group went into action. Fastow and about a half-dozen members of his senior team took over an interior conference room on the twenty-fifth floor. Ideas were scribbled on a whiteboard, market studies assembled, research plans sketched out. Amid the feverish preparations, the conference table filled with reams of paper as everyone struggled to convey a message that no one quite understood.

Nowhere in the report being assembled did anyone suggest that the division's mission might be flawed. Bowen took Fastow aside and mentioned Beerel's dire findings. Maybe, he suggested, they should be in the report.

Fastow shook his head. "Gustav is full of shit," he said. "Don't believe everything you hear from him."

Discussion over. Bowen stepped back to the table, convinced Fastow simply didn't want to face—or didn't think Skilling wanted to hear—retail's real challenge.

The final report measured less than an inch thick. Half an hour before his meeting, Fastow was in his recently completed office, hefting the document in his hand. It felt insubstantial. He was terrified; Skilling was expecting a lot from this presentation, and Fastow couldn't shake his fear that he was missing the target. He closed the report and walked into the main room. All eyes were on him.

"Okay," he called out. "I'm off to see Skilling."

"Good luck, Andy," someone shouted back.

With copies of his report in hand, Fastow walked down to the elevators. Inside, he pushed the button for twenty-seven, where he had to change elevator banks to reach the thirty-third floor. There, he approached Skilling's modest-sized, glass-encased office and leaned in the open doorway.

"Jeff?"

"Hey, Andy. Come on in."

Fastow stepped inside, heading to a small conference table. Skilling came around from his desk and joined him.

"Okay," Skilling said. "What you got?"

Without a word, Fastow slid a copy of his report across the table. Skilling leafed through it. Words with boxes around them. "Sales and Marketing." "Profit Projections." Numbers floating all over with no explanation where they came from. *Page after page of gobbledygook.*

"Okay," Fastow began. "Well, we've taken a look at the business opportunities for our division and have assembled some profit projections—"

"Andy, this is junk," Skilling interrupted. "You can't build a business off something this general."

"Well, I think this is the concept of our strategy."

Skilling tossed the pages onto the table. "Andy, there's no plan here! How many people do you need to hire? What office space are you going to get? Which customers are you going to call on? I mean, how exactly do you make the profits in the profit projections?"

"This is how we calculated it . . ."

"Andy, come on! That's just stupid. There's a lot of stuff you don't know when you start a business. You may not know the outputs, but you sure can know the inputs."

Fastow swallowed, his face flushed.

"You have to understand how many telephones you need," Skilling continued, an edge still in his voice. "You have to know which customers you're gonna call. How frequently are you gonna call on them? And for God's sake, what's the pitch? What's the business proposition? You can't have a retail business if you don't know what you're selling. You've got to give me the plan."

"It's here," Fastow protested, holding up the report.

"No, it's not, Andy! I need details. I need to understand how you're going to go about this. You can't just put a few numbers and boxes on a piece of paper and tell me that you're done. You're not an idiot, Andy!"

A pause. "Look, Andy," Skilling said, "I can tell you're frustrated . . ."

"Well, I'm not sure what you want."

Oh, man, Skilling thought. This was bad. Fastow seemed to have a mental block. How could a guy put together complex financing deals but not understand basic business?

"Okay, Andy," he said. "You need to figure out specifically what it is you're going to do. You've got to make a compelling case to me that you have all the pieces in place and that we should fund this."

"Okay."

"So sit down with your people again and get them to articulate what they're going to do. Then come back next week and we'll talk about it again."

There was a moment of silence. Fastow couldn't shake the feeling that his career had just imploded.

"All right," Fastow said, standing. "I'll take another run at it."

Fastow plodded out the door. Skilling could tell the meeting had devastated him, but there was no sugarcoating the situation. Enron had built plenty of businesses, and the plans for them usually followed the same basic outline. But not Fastow's. The guy didn't know where he was going. *Maybe this little trip to the woodshed will help him straighten out,* Skilling thought.

Out in the hallway, the elevator arrived, and Fastow climbed on. He wasn't ready to head back to the office yet. He needed to clear his head, maybe walk around.

What am I going to do?

About an hour later, the elevator doors opened on twenty-five, and Fastow wandered out, heading back to his office. In the center of retail, he saw the crowds of employees gathered, waiting for the results. They studied his face for any suggestion of what had happened. *Nothing.* His expression, his demeanor, everything was just neutral.

Fastow surveyed the room, then made his way to his office. Inside, he tossed the report on his desk and flopped into his chair. He sat silently, unmoving, staring at the walls. There was a knock at the door.

"Yeah?" Fastow said.

Bowen peeked inside. "What happened?"

"It was okay."

Oh, sure. "Come on, Andy. You can't just ignore everybody out there and not tell them what happened."

Fastow closed his eyes.

"It didn't go well, Ray," he said. "I've never talked to Skilling like that before. He was pissed."

"What's he pissed about?"

"I don't think he's happy with our progress."

The brush-off from on high irked Bowen. "Well, this is a start-up," he said. "We're just figuring it out."

"That's what I thought," Fastow said. "But he asked questions I couldn't answer, and I didn't handle it well."

Pulling at his collar, Fastow stretched his neck. "It was awful, Ray. Skilling hated it. He basically told me I was an idiot, that I didn't understand the business."

Bowen searched Fastow's face for clues of his plans for the next step, and found none. The man seemed vacant.

"Okay," Bowen said. "So what are you going to do?"

Fastow shrugged. "He wants to meet with me again next week and go over this stuff."

"Okay," Bowen said. "So what do you want me to tell the rest of the staff?"

There was a very long silence. "I don't know," Fastow finally said. "What do you want to tell them?"

This guy is just not with it. "Well, I think you've gotta be honest and tell them that we've got work to do."

Fastow glanced out the window. "Yeah. Sure. Okay."

Again silence. Fastow seemed to have had the stuffing knocked out of him. He rubbed his fingertips across his eyes. "I'm a failure, I guess. Maybe I should have just stayed in finance. Maybe . . ." His words trailed off.

He looked away from the window, into Bowen's eyes.

"I don't know what I'm going to do," Fastow said. "I'm going to lose my job. My meeting with him next week might be my last meeting at Enron."

He fidgeted nervously. "Ray, I'm really sorry for bringing you here," he said. "I know you've got every reason to hate me. But please don't be pissed. You're a smart guy, you'll do fine. But I'm not sure if I'm going to be here anymore if this doesn't go well next week."

Bowen stared down at his boss. Until that moment, he would never have thought that he could pity Andy Fastow.

The days inched toward the deadline. The retail team worked through the week, but there was no repeat of the last feverish rush. They had done their best the week before. There were no miracles, no secret strategies hidden in desk drawers. There was, instead, a silent sense of futility, a recognition that, somehow, changes were coming.

The appointed day arrived, but the mood in the retail division was very different this time. There was no anticipation, no excitement. Few even noticed when Fastow slipped away, heading upstairs for what he was convinced would be his professional execution.

"Hey, Andy, how's it going?" Skilling said gently when Fastow arrived. "So what have you got for me?"

No rancor, no anger. Skilling's tone was softer than last time. Again Fastow handed him his report and sat at the conference table. Skilling thumbed through it for about ten seconds. Again boxes and numbers. The information he needed just wasn't in there. He closed it up.

"All right, Jeff," Fastow began. "I think—"

"Andy," Skilling interrupted. "I just don't think this is working."

Fastow stiffened, bracing for the blow. "Okay."

"You're just not giving me what I need to know to make the decision to commit the capital and people to this business," Skilling continued. "I'm just not comfortable with this being the game plan for a whole new business."

"Jeff, it's not like I haven't tried. I've tried. I just don't know what it is that you want."

Skilling could see Fastow was on edge. The message had been delivered. Maybe it was time to smooth things over.

"Andy, I don't know if it's what you're doing or if it's what I'm asking for. But this isn't what I need."

"Yeah, I can tell it's not clicking for you."

"Well," Skilling said, "I just don't think this is going to work out."

Fastow nodded, his shoulders sagging.

"We don't need to decide anything right now," Skilling continued. "Let's get together tomorrow and talk about it some more."

The two men set a time, and Fastow left the room.

When Fastow arrived the next day, Skilling was engaged in an animated phone conversation. He saw Fastow outside the door and raised his index finger. Fastow stayed almost motionless in the hallway, occasionally glancing down at his feet, until Skilling hung up and waved him in.

"Hey, man, how's it going?" Skilling said, standing.

Fastow shrugged. "Well, obviously, not too good," he said, dropping into one of the conference table chairs.

For a moment Skilling studied his young colleague. Shoulders slumped, hangdog face. Like a kid who had failed a school test and was now going to talk to Dad about it.

Skilling spread open his hands. "Hey, Andy, everything is fine. I love you. I have no problems here. This obviously just isn't the right thing. Hey, maybe it's me. Maybe we just weren't on the same wavelength."

No reaction. "Look, man," Skilling continued, "I'd really like you to go back and do what you were doing before in the finance group, 'cause you're great at it."

It was as if a weight was lifted from Fastow's shoulders.

"You mean I can have my old job back?" he asked.

"Yeah, if you want it, sure. I mean, you're the best in the world at what you do."

A wisp of a smile creased Fastow's face. "Okay, yeah," he said eagerly. "I would like my old job back."

"Fine," Skilling replied. "Done."

All that was left to do, Skilling said, was for Fastow to write up a memo, explaining that he had decided to go back to finance. Somebody else would be needed to run retail, Skilling said, probably Lou Pai from over at gas trading.

The meeting ended, and Fastow stammered out his thanks as he left the room. Skilling felt pretty good. Gave the guy a chance, didn't work, pulled him out. No harm, no foul.

Fastow arrived back at retail a few minutes later and walked over to Bowen's desk.

"I'm out of here," he announced. "Back to finance."

Stunned, Bowen sat in his chair. "And what do I do?"

"I think they'll want you to stay and hold this place together. Lou Pai's coming down and taking over."

For a moment, Fastow eyed Bowen. Then he turned away.

"See you later," he said.

News of Fastow's failure shot through the Enron building in a matter of hours. His enemies relished the moment, delighted to know that they had something to hold over his head for months—maybe years—to come. But a small band of sympathizers worried that his public humiliation would drive him from the company.

Shortly after his meeting with Skilling, one of his friends, Amanda Martin, bumped into Fastow in a hallway. She could see he was hurting. She touched his shoulder.

"Andy, are you all right?"

"Yeah, I'm fine."

"What are you going to do?"

"I'm in the process of figuring that out."

His initial relief had given way to the knowledge that he had just suffered a spectacular public failure.

"What does Jeff say?" Martin asked.

"He said I should go back to finance, because that's where I was good." Fastow shrugged. "He says he's going to be supportive and that he doesn't want me to leave."

"Okay. Well, that's good."

"But I don't know. He just fired my ass out of retail. So I'm considering my options, maybe other opportunities."

Martin could hear the anger in his barely veiled threat to bolt Enron. "I hope it doesn't come to that, Andy," she said. "I hope you stay."

Fastow said nothing. He continued on his way.

In reality, Fastow had narrowed his options considerably, and leaving Enron wasn't one of them. Quitting was defeat. It would only add to the disgrace. He knew there was something better.

Fastow had reached a resolve; he would claw his way back to the top. He wasn't going to let one fumble stop him from driving to the goal line—fulfilling his ambition for the wealth and influence commercial executives commanded. His path was clear. If he couldn't go to the commercial side, the commercial side would come to him.

Finance had always been considered a support function, raising the capital that fed commercial businesses. But then the commercial guys pulled in the profits and the glory—benefits that would never have happened without the behind-the-scenes work of the finance group.

But Skilling was always pushing everyone, even the support functions, to think creatively. Why should finance be merely "a cost of doing business"? Sure, capital had costs attached, but saving on such expenses meant profits. And what about Fastow's deals, like Cactus and JEDI? Those had translated into earnings, attributed to the commercial division. Why couldn't that be assigned to finance? Why couldn't finance be a *profit* center? And wouldn't that give Fastow everything he had wanted from retail?

With Skilling's backing, all Fastow needed was information about deals going on at Enron where finance could play a role, where finance could make a profit. Then he could be back on top.

The plan was simple. Execution was the hard part.

The same week he left retail, Fastow began scouting out Enron's managing directors. Office after office, the message was the same: he was there to help—with deals, with meeting their budgeted profits. They just had to let him know what they were doing; he'd take it from there.

But deal makers by their very nature are a cautious bunch. Bragging rights for transactions were hoarded at Enron because they translated into bonuses. If Fastow wanted to help, that could only mean that he was trying to snag credit. Everyone listened to the pitch politely—and then ignored him. Fastow needed to try another tack.

Later that week he was roaming the hallway in the finance division. He noticed Shirley Hudler, a young executive who helped with JEDI, sitting alone in Sherron Smith's office. Fastow knew Hudler as the sort who charmed people easily, a down-home Texas type. She was tight with some executives in the North American units. She was close with his buddy Michael Kopper. She might be perfect to help out. Fastow stuck his head in the door.

"Hey," he said cheerfully. "How's it going?"

Hudler looked up from her work. "Hey, Andy. Pretty well, how about you?"

He stepped into the room. For a minute he tossed out a few questions about her work. "So," he asked, "are you busy?"

"Yeah, but I could be busier," she replied, regretting the words as soon as they came out of her mouth.

"Well," Fastow replied, "we'll see if we can do something about that."

Fastow moved on. Not long after, he telephoned Hudler and asked her to come to his office. She hurried down.

"You know," he said from behind his desk, "now that I'm back, I'm thinking about getting somebody to work for me, sort of as a chief of staff."

Hudler listened. This didn't sound good.

"Somebody to run down deals for me," he continued. "Meet with people, figure out their transactions, and come back to communicate the structures to me."

It sounded worse. *Boy, this is going to be a dead end. Where does somebody go after a job like that?*

"And I don't just mean in this department," Fastow said. "Wherever there are deals going on, I'd want somebody to run down the information."

He leaned on his elbows. "What do you think?"

Hudler forced a smile. "Sounds interesting, Andy. I think I see what you want. And I think I'd be good at it."

For a few minutes she asked questions, doing her best impression of someone who was interested; she was too far down on the department totem pole to brush him off. Finally she stood, murmured a few cheery words about the opportunity, and left. Fastow promised to get back to her.

Hudler headed back down the hallway. *I'm not doing that job*, she thought. She tracked down her boss, Sherron Smith, and told her about Fastow's proposal.

Smith's reply was direct. "Wow, that sucks."

"Sherron, you've got to get me out of this. I can't tell Andy no. I'm doomed if I do that."

Smith told Hudler she would take care of it. Fastow had made the offer because he thought she was short of things to do. Well, then, Smith said, she'd load Hudler up with assignments and tell Fastow she couldn't afford to lose her. That would solve everything.

Fastow never got his secret office spy. In the end, it didn't matter. He got what he wanted another way.

Shafts of sunlight filtered through the windows in Ken Rice's office, illuminating the pennant behind his head from the University of Nebraska, his alma mater. Rice was leaning back in his chair, his feet propped up on the desk as he squeezed a blue stress ball. On one side of the room, Amanda Martin sat in a chair with her back to a glass wall while Cliff Baxter paced the floor in agitation.

They were known as the Three Musketeers, friends who gossiped endlessly about office goings-on. Their friendship seemed solid, but strains were developing. Rice and Martin had recently begun a romantic affair, keeping Baxter in the dark about it. The deception had injected tension into their dealings, requiring some playacting among three colleagues who supposedly told one another everything.

But today anger had displaced unease. A meeting of Enron's top managers was coming up and, as usual, word had been purposely leaked out about the agenda to make sure any vehement objections could be aired ahead of time, behind closed doors. Rumor had it that Fastow had persuaded Skilling to designate finance as a profit center and that the announcement would come at the next meeting.

The three friends found the concept ludicrous. Finance was a support function, not a business.

"This is just bullshit," Rice said, tossing the stress ball, and then catching it. "It makes no sense."

Baxter, his suit jacket unbuttoned, waved his hands in the air. "This is so fucking out of control!"

"Why is Skilling doing it?" Rice asked.

Baxter turned on his heel, pacing toward the back wall. "Fastow is such a little shit," he growled.

"He's just trying to make up for blowing it in retail," Rice said.

Baxter snapped around. Fastow's original elevation had long been a sore point with him. "Retail! Retail! What the fuck was that? What the fuck was Skilling thinking? You can't just take a guy out of finance and have him run a business! He's a goddamn banker! He doesn't know shit about running a business! What the fuck was he doing there?"

Martin jumped in. "Already half of my day is spent fighting with our traders over prices they want us to pay for commodities. They're gaming the system, they're jacking up the prices, but I have to use them."

She shook her head. "So now I've got to contend with finance charging us extra on our interest rates so that they can make some more profit?" she said. "All so we can charge each other for doing Enron business! Rather than meeting with customers or structuring deals, I'm just going to be fighting all the time."

Something had to be done, the three agreed. Someone had to tell Skilling that this idea was foolish. Baxter, the most mercurial of the bunch, would approach first, pounding him with his outrage. Rice would handle the follow-up, calmly reinforcing Baxter's objections.

They gave it their best shot, but the final proposal was different only in the details. Finance would still be a profit center, but its earnings would be reallocated to the various commercial divisions for the purpose of calculating bonuses. If finance actually brought earnings to the table—as opposed to just jacking up prices to the commercial division—the results could net out to everyone's benefit.

The day for the management committee meeting rolled around, and the top executives from Enron Capital & Trade assembled in a thirty-sixth-floor conference room. Skilling sat at the head of the table, with most everyone else gathered in the informal pecking order that always seems to evolve in corporate meetings. When the time came for the finance department report, Skilling took the floor.

"Okay, Andy's back to heading the finance effort, and as of now they're the ones you turn to for capital for your deals. We're going to consolidate the banking relationships with them. They are going to be the primary contacts for the banks. If you want capital, you're going to have to deal with Andy's group. They're going to be a profit center now, not a cost center."

Skilling looked around the room of silent faces.

"That doesn't mean anything to you," he said. "We'll still have allocation of profits to your divisions. So don't worry about your staff and budgets."

Fastow handed out sheets showing how the commercial groups would be charged internally for capital. Each business unit would be assigned a representative from Fastow's group, working deals to ensure that every possible finance angle was explored. Sometimes that could mean offering new deal structures, complex financial alternatives that might otherwise have been overlooked.

None of the other executives spoke. There was nothing left to argue about. The decision had been made.

The group of children tumbled in the clear blue surf of the Cayman Islands. They looked healthy and vigorous, their skin toasted brown from days on the beach. Nearby on the sand, Skilling watched as tears filled his eyes.

"I've fucked up my life," he said. "I've fucked up my marriage. I've fucked up my kids."

More tears. "I've fucked up everything."

Beside him, Rebecca Mark listened with sympathy. Both knew everyone at Enron would be stunned to see them together; they were, by all accounts, avowed enemies.

But quietly, almost surreptitiously, they had become . . . not friends, exactly, more like confidants. They were both young and successful. They were both parents with failed or failing marriages. They could identify with each other, even as their pitched battle for dominance inside the company showed no sign of abating.

They were in the Caymans that day in June 1996 with the Young Presidents' Organization, an exclusive network for young business leaders. The idea of the getaways was to share strategies with colleagues in similar situations while having fun with the family in an exotic location.

But Skilling was a wreck. His divorce was just going through; he had hoped to set up a home a few blocks from Sue, so that the kids could come over whenever they wanted. But it wouldn't work. There was a visitation agreement, and Sue insisted he stick to the terms of the deal.

"If I had known the wedge this would drive between me and my kids . . . ," he said, the words trailing off.

"Jeff," Mark murmured, "you've just got to be sure to be there for them when they need you. It's never too late to fix things."

Skilling pinched the bridge of his nose as he closed his eyes. "I've just fucked everything up," he said. "How did it get like this? How did I get here?"

Mark looked at Skilling, feeling strong twinges of pity. How could he possibly be handling the demands of his life while falling apart?

Skilling exhaled slowly as his eyes glanced over another interminable report from retail. He was seated in a tiny conference room deep in the bowels of the Enron building, listening as Ray Bowen and his staff detailed problems facing the division. *Problems, always problems.*

It was mid-1996. Bowen had come to Skilling weeks before, saying he wanted to treat retail like a laboratory project, conducting internal reviews to figure out the business. Skilling approved the idea enthusiastically, but now the result was this. Problems.

As members of the retail staff listened, Bowen droned on, laying out a more developed version of Gustav Beerel's original calculations that showed the challenges of providing electricity to residential customers. Profit margins were razor thin, massive capital investments were required. Bowen was describing the cost of acquiring a customer when Skilling held up a hand.

"You're making me really nervous, guys," he said. "The fact that you're focused on the numbers, and not the underlying essence of the business, worries me. Working from the numbers is backward. I don't want to hear that."

"Well, Jeff, the numbers have to make sense," Bowen said. "And there are challenges here. We've got to be honest and ask ourselves realistically whether we can scale this to the point where we can actually make a profit."

Skilling bristled. "Then you guys must not be smart enough to come up with the good ideas, because we're going to make money in this business."

"I'm not drawing any final conclusions. These are just observations about things we have to consider."

"Well," Skilling replied, "you're making me very nervous with the way you're thinking about this business."

A heavy silence followed. "I'm just telling you what I think," Bowen said. "But we'll go through it again."

The meeting wrapped up, and Bowen led his team out the door. He was flabbergasted. Sure, ideas were important, but they had to be built around numbers. A business wasn't going to succeed just because Jeff Skilling thought it should. Bowen punched the button for the elevator. *This place I work for is a crazy company*, he thought.

Near the lobby of the Phoenician hotel in Scottsdale, Ken Rice glanced up at Camelback Mountain as he walked past a sparkling swimming pool tiled with mother-of-pearl. He headed inside and soon was passing through a palatial hallway toward a conference room reserved for Enron's talks on the possible Portland General merger.

It was July 16, 1996, a day when teams from both companies had traveled to the Phoenician for what everyone hoped would be the final negotiations. Most of the deal had been hammered out, and Enron had put an offer on the table that Rice considered pretty rich: a 25 percent premium over the trading price of Portland General's stock.

But Joe Hirko, Portland General's CFO, argued the company needed more. Rice and Baxter wouldn't budge. Hirko went off and phoned Ken Harrison, the company chairman who was golfing in Scotland. He returned after one in the morning; Baxter, Rice, and their team were playing hearts.

"Guys," Hirko said, "you have to get us more money."

Rice held up his hands. "All right, tell you what. We'll call Rich Kinder. I'm sure he's asleep, but we'll call him and wake him up. He'll decide."

"Great," Hirko replied. "Let me know."

Hirko headed out of the room. Rice glanced at Baxter.

"Hey," Baxter said. "*I'm* not waking up Kinder."

"I'm not gonna call him either," Rice said. "We don't need to. We're not going to raise the price."

He picked up his cards. "Let's keep playing."

Feet went up on the conference table. Baxter checked his watch. "How long do you think we should wait?"

"Aw, let's give it forty-five minutes," Rice replied. "Let's make them think we're really pushing Kinder hard."

Minutes later, in the middle of a hand, the conference room door swung open. Hirko rushed in and saw everyone looking relaxed.

"What are you guys doing?" he asked.

Rice didn't miss a beat. "We called Kinder, but couldn't get him. We're waiting for him to call back."

Hirko eyed everyone suspiciously. "Oh. Okay."

He left the room, and soon Rice and Baxter came out with the bad news—there would be no more money. Kinder, they lied, had said no. The negotiations collapsed.

The next day, Ken Harrison called Kinder at the office, asking to get the talks back on track. Within days a deal was struck. Kinder caved, giving

Portland General the huge premium it sought. The merger, worth more than three billion dollars, was approved by both boards.

In late July, Ken Lay flew to Portland to welcome a thousand new employees to the Enron family. He looked buoyant as he promised that they were part of a grand mission that would shake the industry to its core.

"We have started something today that everyone in the electricity industry, and everyone in the gas industry, is going to remember for a long time," he told the crowds.

Lay was right, but not for the reasons he imagined. With the merger announcement, events had been set in motion that, in time, would lead to Enron's first major crime.

CHAPTER 5

THE FALCON 900 DESCENDED through the clouds over New Jersey, gently touching down on runway 13-31 at the Morristown Municipal Airport. The jet taxied toward an array of small buildings, coming to a stop beside a corporate hangar. As the screaming of the turbofans died out, a pilot popped the door and unfolded the stair steps. Lay appeared, walking down to the tarmac.

His trip this Sunday evening, September 15, 1996, was a closely guarded secret. As far as anyone at Enron knew, he was in Indianapolis, attending a board meeting at Eli Lilly and Company. Not even his children were aware that he had instead spirited himself away to New Jersey for a covert meeting about taking the top job at AT&T, the telecommunications giant.

The opportunity had come up a week or so earlier, when an executive recruiter told Lay that AT&T was looking for a new leader and was interested in candidates outside the industry. His wife, Linda, had encouraged him to pursue the idea, and so here he was, on a clandestine trip to meet Bob Allen, AT&T's current chairman and chief executive.

The timing seemed perfect. He was in his eleventh year at Enron's helm and had been thinking of moving on. Two years before, Rich Kinder had been anticipating taking over, but Enron's directors had balked. Kinder was recognized as a great operator, a man who could squeeze the last dime of expense out of any business. But some directors worried he wouldn't be able to take Enron to the next level.

The rejection had infuriated Kinder, but he had agreed to continue in his job for two more years if his contract was changed. Under the new terms, if he wasn't selected for the top job by early 1997, he could walk away from Enron with millions of dollars. The deadline was just months away; if Kinder was going to take over, Lay thought, jumping to AT&T would be a brilliant career move.

Lay walked into the hangar. Just inside, he saw a large man with dark slicked-down hair. "Ken?" the man said. "Hal Burlingame, head of human resources for AT&T."

They shook hands. Burlingame asked about the flight, then escorted Lay upstairs, where Allen was waiting. For an hour and a half, they talked about

AT&T—its challenges, its possibilities—with Lay describing his own week-old vision for the company. Then Allen took him by surprise.

"What I've been thinking," Allen said, "is that we would have a transition period, a time where I would stay as chairman while everyone settled in. Two years or so."

Lay shifted in his seat uncomfortably. *Two years?*

"Well, Bob, that could be a problem," he said. "What would be your role versus my role if I took the job?"

Allen held up his hands. "There's nothing to worry about, Ken. You would have complete latitude to do whatever you needed to change the company."

Not enough, Lay thought. "If you're still there full-time, walking the halls every day, that could be a problem. It sets up a situation where there would be divided loyalties between the previous CEO and the current CEO."

"Ken, really, this is not something to worry about."

A short while later, Allen thanked Lay for coming. Lay headed back down and found his pilots, Kage Reese and Darvin Mitchell, and the three climbed onto the plane. Within minutes, they were winging their way back to Indiana.

Lay settled into one of the leather seats on the right, gazing out at the evening lights below as he pondered Allen's words. His desire to stick around left Lay uncomfortable, but still, this could be a dream job.

There was no question about it. Lay needed to inform his directors about what was happening; after all, in a few weeks Rich Kinder might need to take over the helm at Enron.

Shortly after six the next evening, Lay pulled into the garage of his house on Looscan Lane. At that point, he and Linda were in transition; they had recently sold their larger home and were living here until renovations were completed on their apartment at the Huntingdon.

Lay headed inside and greeted Linda with a kiss. After filling her in on the Allen meeting, he went to a small office to phone John Duncan, head of the board's executive committee. "Hi, Johnner," Lay said.

"Ken, how are you?"

Small talk. Then Lay shifted gears.

"John, I've got an interesting thing that happened to me," he began, "and I need to share it with you."

The story spilled out. The call from the headhunter. The invitation to New Jersey. The meeting with Bob Allen.

"I'm certainly still interested in this," Lay said. "And it just highlights that the board's got a decision to make on Rich Kinder before year-end."

"Yes," Duncan drawled.

"Well, assuming Rich is going to become CEO, the timing here has turned out to be pretty fortuitous."

Lay took a breath. "So in the next few days I'm probably going to have to let them know if I'm willing to continue considering this. And I didn't want to get to that point and surprise all of you."

A moment's hesitation. Duncan was having trouble digesting the news. The board wasn't ready for this.

"Ken," he finally said, "I can see where this opportunity would be certainly something to consider. But you made Enron. You're the person most closely identified with everything it has accomplished."

Duncan laid it on thick. The board loved Lay. Loved his strategies. Loved his demeanor. Just loved everything about him. "Now," he said, "even if we make a change, we had hoped you would continue with the company in some capacity, chairman emeritus or something like that."

Lay replied that he was grateful, but said the AT&T job might be an opportunity he couldn't pass up. The two agreed to speak again soon and got off the phone. Within seconds, Duncan was back on the line, spreading the news to his fellow directors. At the same time, Lay sat in his office, thinking about Duncan's words.

For months he had assumed Kinder would take over. But there was such reticence in Duncan's voice. Perhaps the board wanted him in its back pocket in case Kinder didn't work out. Perhaps. But there was another possibility. Could the directors be planning to pass over Kinder again?

In the days that followed, a flurry of secret calls and meetings took place between Lay and the directors.

Led by Duncan, the board repeatedly pushed the same message—stay. Enron needed his counsel even if Kinder took over, they said. That couldn't happen, Lay replied. There should be just one chief. Once someone else took over, he needed to leave.

The conversations evolved into a debate about Kinder. Some directors thought he was more than ready for the job; others weren't so sure. Yes, Kinder was a hell of an operations guy. But was that what Enron needed? Somebody who could keep the trains running on time? What about somebody with the vision to plan new routes instead?

Kinder, some directors argued, was not the type who would come up with the Next Big Idea, the lofty strategy that would keep Enron chugging ahead with growth of 15 to 20 percent a year. Lay, whose word could have swayed them, was tepid in defending his heir apparent.

Maybe it was the pressure from the board. Maybe it was the meeting with Allen. But as the days passed, Lay's infatuation with AT&T cooled. Then suddenly, on a weekend in late September, as he sat in his living room with Linda, he made his decision.

"Linda," he said, "this just doesn't feel right."

Lay telephoned Duncan that very day. He was pulling out of the AT&T search, he said, and wouldn't make any personal plans until after year-end.

"Thanks, Ken," Duncan sighed.

The small crowd gathered at the San Diego offices of Science Applications International Corporation, eager to witness a little history. It was September 23, 1996. Right on schedule, Pete Wilson, California's governor, emerged and took a seat at a table stacked with papers.

After years of debate and fighting, Wilson was about to sign Assembly Bill 1890, the opening salvo for deregulation of California's electricity markets. New players would be allowed into a power system that for years had been dominated by a small group of utilities.

This was a moment to remember, Wilson told the crowd.

"We're doing more than signing a new law; we are shifting the balance of power in California," he said. "We've pulled the plug on another outdated monopoly and replaced it with the promise of a new era of competition."

With that, Wilson picked up the pen and signed his name. California's brand of deregulation had become law; a new market would have to be ready to go within two years.

"How the fuck did we let this happen?"

Lou Pai was raging about the California law to his fellow Enron executives. This wasn't deregulation, he shouted, this was Rube Goldberg, some sort of freak hybrid—a bit of deregulation, a dash of regulation, with a dollop of centralized government on the side.

Skilling, Causey, and others in the room weren't about to argue. Enron had been pushing for a system where any company with power—from its own plants or from trading—could gain access to the transmission lines and compete for customers. Whoever came in with the best prices would win the day. But California had created a mishmash of rules based on market theories that only a politician could love.

The California utilities had, until then, purchased power through long-term contracts. Now they were required to sell their own generation plants and buy power every day, in the spot market, where prices fluctuated.

But the price most consumers paid was cut ten percent from their regulated price, then locked in place for five years. In other words, no matter how much it cost for the utilities to supply the power, the price to consumers wouldn't change. The approach was based on the idea that changing the rules would cause spot prices to drop dramatically. No escape hatch was written into the law in case the theory proved wrong.

The rules also created a new marketplace—one controlled by two quasi-governmental bodies—to set the wholesale prices for electricity and manage the state's transmission lines. This wasn't a setup where the best competitor won, Pai argued. It was all about the rules, figuring out how to best play the system.

Causey nodded his agreement. "These rules are really a disaster," he said.

Pai shot a look at Steve Kean, a government-relations specialist who had lobbied for Enron out in California. "Why didn't we get this damn thing changed?" he shouted.

Kean, a calm, professional sort in his thirties, set his hands on the table. "Lou, we did the best we could. This is a political process. We certainly can't dictate outcomes. All we can do is nudge it one way or the other."

Sure, Kean said, Enron contributed to California politicians, but so did the utilities, which fought deregulation tooth and nail. And they had the best advantage—large numbers of California employees, voters, living in every district. Campaign cash might buy Enron a seat at the table, but it wouldn't give the company the right to order the meal.

"Well," Causey said, "it's just going to be very hard to make our business work in California."

"Listen," Kean said. "I know it's certainly not optimal, but there should be some way we can get at it."

That grabbed the room's attention.

"The one thing you can count on is that if the government set up the market, there will be subsidies someplace," he said. "And if you can find the subsidies, and offer the people who aren't getting subsidized a better deal, you'd own that part of the market."

Nodding, Skilling jumped in. "That's right," he said. "If the government sets up the market, it's going to be done wrong. The only way it'll be right is by accident."

He looked down at the row of faces. "Just know the rules better than anybody else. Then you'll make money."

By October 1996, the merger agreement with Portland General was still generating plenty of work at Enron. The deal itself wasn't the issue; rather, its ramifications were keeping everyone busy. If Enron was really going to buy an electric utility, then federal rules made it essential for the company to sell other assets.

The first on the block were two co-generation plants—Texas City and Clear Lake—that were jointly owned by Enron and Dominion Resources, another energy company. Because such plants convert waste heat into power, they were designated as "qualifying facilities," requiring utilities not only to purchase their power but to pay higher rates. Problem was, plants owned by a utility didn't get the price boost. So buying Portland General meant the premium pricing for the co-generation plants would soon disappear, making them less valuable for Enron to own than to sell.

The task of putting together a sale was given to Amanda Martin; she and her team searched for bidders, but soon headaches emerged. The gas contracts for the plants had been struck with Enron at unreasonably high levels. No company would purchase the plants only to be gouged on fuel by the seller. The contracts had to be renegotiated.

That, of course, meant trouble. Using its aggressive accounting, Enron had long ago booked the total, lofty value of the gas contracts as profit. Renegotiating them to reflect more reasonable prices meant decreasing their total worth. What mark-to-market had given, it would take away; the previous profits would become losses—as much as $100 million.

Once she understood the dilemma, Martin reported her findings to Skilling. As she laid out the numbers, Skilling scowled. "I don't want to take a loss," he fumed.

It's not like there's a choice here. "We have to take a loss, Jeff," Martin replied.

"Well, it better be small."

Skilling thought for a moment. Maybe there were alternatives. "I want you to get Cliff involved," he said.

"Fine," Martin replied.

"Have you met with the accountants?" Skilling asked. "Get them involved. If we have to take a loss, we have to be very careful when we take it."

Another idea. "I want you also to work with Andy's group," Skilling added. "See what they can come up with."

"All right." Now Fastow was joining in; this deal would be like old-home week for Martin and her friends.

Ken Lay hung up the telephone and sat in his office for a moment, trying to keep calm.

Rumors had been circulating for weeks that Kinder had struck up a romantic relationship with Nancy McNeil, one of Lay's most trusted assistants.* McNeil had been with Lay since Transco and had become a power unto herself, knowing almost everything that happened at the company. Lay had paid no mind to the allegations, but now some directors were calling with word they were hearing the same stories.

The possibility infuriated Lay. This was just wrong for the company, he thought. Even though both Kinder and McNeil had filed to divorce their spouses, Lay believed it set a terrible example. Sure, Lay's current wife, Linda, had been his secretary at Florida Gas. But they hadn't started dating until months after he had moved on to Transco.

The only way to deal with this is to confront it. Lay walked out to the hallway, heading to Kinder's office. He nodded a greeting to Kinder's secretary before walking in. Kinder was at his desk. Lay shut the door.

"What can I do for you, Ken?"

Lay stood over Kinder's desk. "Rich, I'm getting word from people, including some directors, that you and Nancy are having an affair," he said bluntly. "I need to know. Are you or are you not?"

Kinder didn't miss a beat. "No."

Lay paused, eyeing Kinder. "All right, I know these are rumors, but I wanted to check whether they're true."

"They're not."

"Fine. So I can tell anybody else, including the directors, that this is not true, and I'll never have to worry later about finding out that it was."

"No, you won't."

A flicker of hesitation. Lay excused himself, heading back to his office. He had his answer; he would call his directors and let them know Kinder had denied everything.

Somehow, though, he feared it wasn't the truth.

Weeks later, Rosalee Fleming, one of Lay's secretaries, pushed the "hold" button on her phone, got up from her desk, and crossed over to the doorway.

"Ken, Sharon's on the phone. Can you take the call?"

Lay smiled. He loved hearing from his younger sister.

"Sure," he said. "I'll pick up."

He reached for the phone and punched the button for the flashing line. "Hi, Sharon Sue."

"Hey, Ken. How are you doing?"

---

*While Kinder and McNeil later married, there is no definitive evidence that they were in a romantic relationship at the time Lay began to suspect one existed.

The siblings chatted for a few minutes about their families. Then Sharon's tone turned serious.

"Listen, Ken, I just heard something last night that I thought I needed to share with you."

"All right. What did you hear?"

Sharon spelled out an unpleasant story: She had been out to dinner with a few friends, including Nancy McNeil, the subject of the Kinder rumors. They had all been talking and just having a good time. And then Nancy had dropped a bomb.

"Well, Nancy just starts telling us about what's been going on inside the company," Sharon said. "She said that the board was very unhappy with you. And she said they were kind of pushing you out so Rich could take over."

Lay listened to Sharon's words, floored. This couldn't be right. How could McNeil do something like that—in front of his *own sister*? Had she forgotten who Sharon was?

"Now, Sharon, are you sure you heard her right? Maybe you misunderstood what she was saying."

"No, I talked to another person who was there, and she heard the same thing. That's what she said."

Lay assured his sister that there was nothing to worry about. They talked for a few more minutes before saying their good-byes. Lay placed the phone back in its cradle.

For a moment, he glanced out the wall of windows lining his office, turning his sister's words over in his mind. He had heard rumors like this before—third-hand, fourth-hand. But there was no doubting Sharon.

It all made sense.

Kinder. It had to be Kinder. All the pieces fit. Rumors of the affair, McNeil talking down Lay and talking up Kinder. McNeil's comments had to be what she was hearing from none other than Kinder himself, Lay thought.

He had done so much for both Kinder and McNeil over the years, helping them with their careers, helping them find their way. And then *this*. This thankless thing.

Hurtful. That was the right word for it. And just untrue. Kinder and McNeil didn't know about the recent escapade with AT&T, or of the board's efforts to keep him connected with the company. Anyone who knew would have understood that the story Sharon had heard was nothing more than fanciful.

But nobody did. If he stepped down at year-end, Lay thought, rumors would devour him. People would think the board—*his board*—had kicked him out. No graceful exit, no dignity in departure. Just the stench of failure.

Well, the board was on the fence. And thanks to the AT&T discussions, they already knew Lay was willing to stay.

Maybe now he just might.

Among top managers of Enron, Lay's fury at Kinder was no secret, but few understood where it was coming from. Lay began quietly lobbying for the support of executives who had worked with him for years. He didn't believe Kinder had the skills to represent the company, he told them. Would they, he asked, support him in that point of view?

The managers agreed but weren't happy about it. Lay and Kinder had been an awesome team. They had brought the company through tough times. They couldn't help but wonder: would Lay, without Kinder, be as effective?

The Río Piedras shopping district in San Juan was just coming to life, with shoppers peeking through store windows that beckoned with jewelry and knick-knacks. It was 9:30 on the morning of November 14. Nearby, a van emblazoned with the name of the San Juan Gas Company, an Enron company, parked on the street. A technician climbed out, carrying a small gas detector with him, and walked to the shoe store on the first floor of the Humberto Vidal building.

A store employee greeted the man, taking him to the building's east side before heading down into the basement. The gas smell, the employee explained, was getting stronger each morning. Could there be a leak?

The technician examined the basement for five minutes and found no problems. Then he turned on his portable gas detector. He waited for a minute.

Nothing. No beep. No smell of gas in the basement. Everything was okay. The technician headed on his way, checking first with the office to give the all clear.

But the technician was wrong. A decade before, a consultant to Enron had identified problems with the training of the San Juan safety personnel, but little had been done in response. The gas company had been cited, year after year, for safety violations and was even sanctioned in 1994 for failing to fix the problem. The fine? Five hundred dollars.

Now all the problems were coming together. The technician had not been properly trained to use the gas meter. It could only read *changes* in the level of gas in the air; for it to work, it first had to be turned on in a place with no gas, then taken to where a leak was suspected. And unless the area was brimming with gas, it would be hard to smell. For safety reasons, companies add a chemical to natural gas to create its recognizable odor. But Enron's unit in San Juan long ago stopped using sizable amounts of the additive.

Gas was leaking into the basement. But no one knew.

The diagram in Michael Kopper's hand was one of hundreds churned out, month after month, by Fastow's finance group. Boxes and names, lines and numbers. All depicting structured deals that juggled around assets—power plants, cash, whatever—so Enron could present its prettiest financial face to the world.

This one, though, was something new. Fastow and Kopper had spent weeks on a deal to help Enron dispose of its co-generation plants, the ones Amanda Martin insisted would create a huge loss when they were sold.

But Fastow and Kopper had another idea. They were going to use the accounting rules and sell the plants to an entity created by Enron itself. Three percent of its capital would come from outside investors; the rest would be a loan from Enron. The entity would pay full price for the plants, with no renegotiation required for the inflated gas contracts. No renegotiation, no losses. It was the type of deal that no true independent buyer would accept; all the benefits went to the seller, all the problems to the buyer. The finance group was creating its own little world, where buyers worked hard to protect the interests of sellers.

Kopper arrived in a conference room for a meeting with Martin's deal team. They had already found a buyer, a company called Calpine, and weren't all that eager to hear what Kopper had to say.

He walked in looking little like a banker. His suit was dark and mod; his hair was spiky, a new style for him. Over a few minutes, he presented the proposal to Mark Miles, who worked with Amanda Martin. It struck Miles as strange; there were lots of moving parts, all somehow resulting in Enron's avoiding a loss. It didn't make sense.

Miles took the proposal to Martin; she stared at it, trying to understand what she was seeing. Finally, she did.

"That's bullshit," she said.

The deal might look good in the reported financials, Martin said, but it was ridiculous. Enron would still have the risks of owning the things outright. The deal didn't eliminate the loss; it just shoved it to the future, when falling gas prices might make it *bigger*. No matter what, at some point the high-priced gas contracts were going to have to be renegotiated. Fastow's plan would increase Enron's long-term exposure, all to avoid a quarterly loss.

Not only that, *the deal just smelled bad*. How could Enron sell troubled assets to some entity set up by the company, for a price no real buyer would pay? Irrationality usually doesn't fly with the legal and accounting rules. Worse, the whole purpose of Fastow's deal was to cheat the partnership that owned the plant. Sure, Enron owned half of it, but the other half was held by Dominion Resources. Legally, Martin had to act in the partnership's best interest. Doing Fastow's deal would cost it huge sums in unnecessary fuel payments. She could be sued herself. Enron couldn't just rip off its partners to avoid a loss.

"Mark, just let them know," Martin said, "I don't think this is the direction we should be going."

The message was delivered. And in no time, Kopper returned, eager to argue his case. Martin was civil but didn't trust Kopper. She considered him devious, somebody who would throw a fit if he didn't get what he wanted. And this, she thought, was going to be one of those times.

For several minutes Kopper walked through the deal, explaining it step-by-step. "The accountants are going to sign off on this. The lawyers will approve. It will work."

Martin didn't buy it. "Michael, this is silly. It's financial engineering versus a real deal."

"Everybody likes this," Kopper responded. "Andy took it to Skilling, and Skilling really likes this deal. Causey's fine with it. This is the deal we should do."

"Oh, come on, Michael," Martin responded, pointing to the diagram. "What you've got there is a shell game."

She tapped the page as she spoke. "What we're putting together is a real sale. We don't have to worry about what happens in the future. We've taken our lumps, and we're out of the picture. Versus your way, where we're half-pregnant."

As the two kept talking, Cliff Baxter, who often wandered Enron's hallways, walked in, returning from a cigarette break. He took a seat, listening to the debate.

"Remember our mandate here," Kopper said. "Skilling wants to avoid a loss, not renegotiate the gas contract. We've created a vehicle that lets him do that."

Baxter stuck out his chin. "Wait a minute," he said. A barrage of questions followed. What do the accountants say? What do the lawyers say? How can that be?

A pause. "I don't like this one fucking bit," he said. "It's not clean."

After another few minutes Kopper quit trying. He was going back to speak with Fastow, he said. They were having a meeting with banks tomorrow about this very deal, and they were going to move ahead on it. Then he left.

Martin and Baxter hung around for a few minutes. Martin argued her case, and Baxter agreed a real sale was the better deal; it was what was best for Enron. They felt confident that Fastow would come to accept that.

In late November 1996, Kinder sat among Enron's directors in the boardroom, trying to disguise his fury.

The decision about Lay's succession had come down to this—a private meeting with the directors. Kinder listened in disbelief as question after question signaled the board's unwillingness to trust him with the company.

Can you lead the development of new businesses? Can you attract talent? Any chance that we could talk you into staying put for one more year? Maybe two more years?

Kinder fenced as best he could, but he was seething. Lead business development? Attract talent? Hell, *he* was the one who had pushed the creation of Enron's trading and finance business. *He* had brought in Skilling and his bunch. All while Lay flew around the world, playing corporate ambassador with those mammoth international projects. *Kinder* was revenues; *Lay* was expenses.

Still, Kinder could tell he wasn't persuading the doubters on the board. *Lay's* board. Lay could make it happen if he wanted to. He had sandbagged Kinder two years earlier, promising to step aside—then nothing. And now he'd been double-crossed again. The meeting broke up, and Kinder, fuming, went to see Lay.

"How did it go?" Lay asked as Kinder walked in.

"Terrible, Ken! It was terrible."

Kinder paced the room. "It doesn't make any sense. Why are they having so much trouble signing off on me as CEO?"

Lay offered a few words of advice, and soon Kinder walked out. Not long after, Skilling came up and sat with Kinder, watching as his boss's wrath escalated.

"That SOB is going to fuck me again," Kinder growled.

Skilling didn't need more explanation. Kinder thought Lay had stabbed him in the back.

"Look," Skilling said. "What do you want me to do? I'm willing to go, if that'll help."

Kinder fixed Skilling with a look.

"I will absolutely support you," Skilling continued. "You can go to Ken and say, 'If you don't make me CEO, I'm leaving and taking Skilling with me.' "

The threat would be strong. But Skilling's idea wasn't Kinder's style. If the directors wouldn't give him what he wanted—*what he deserved*—so be it.

"No," Kinder said softly. "That's not necessary. Let's just see how this plays out."

The battle over the competing co-generation deals wouldn't end. Martin and her team couldn't understand. Why were Fastow and Kopper pushing so hard? Why did they care?

A summit meeting was held. Fastow and Kopper came downstairs, meeting with Martin and her deal makers. The two proposals were laid out.

"Your deal isn't any good," Fastow announced. "It doesn't avoid the loss. Skilling wants us to avoid the loss. Our deal does that. We should stop arguing and give Skilling what he wants."

With that, Fastow left. The meeting was over.

At 8:30 on the morning of November 21 in San Juan, the bell signaling the end of first period rang out at La Milagrosa School, across from the Río Piedras shopping district. Children gathered up their books and packs.

Across the street, next to the Humberto Vidal building, a technician with Enron's San Juan Gas Company held his combustible-gas indicator up to a small hole his crew had just drilled in the pavement. The technician pumped a bit of air into the device and checked the gauge.

Twenty percent. Way past the danger zone. The underground air was saturated with propane gas. He looked up at his crew and stepped forward onto a manhole cover.

That same second, five floors up in the Vidal building, an air-conditioning contractor conducting monthly maintenance touched a switch to start the cooling system. An electric circuit closed, and a five-ton air-conditioning unit in the gas-filled basement sparked to life.

The explosion was instantaneous and deafening. The first three floors of the building collapsed, falling into the basement. Store merchandise—underwear, sunglasses, a small doll smeared with blood—spewed into the street. The contractor was killed instantly. Outside, the gas technician was blown into the air. At the school, children screamed as shards of concrete and metal blasted through classroom windows. By the time the debris was cleared away, thirty-three people had died; sixty-nine had been injured.

Back in Houston, the Puerto Rican explosion sent Enron into crisis mode. Within a few hours Puerto Rican officials had zeroed in on a gas leak as the likely cause, and if they were correct, Enron's subsidiary could well be held accountable. The company set up a war room at the Houston head-quarters, filling it with insurance professionals, lawyers, public-relations specialists, and operations executives. Nobody knew at that point if Enron was responsible, and a decision was made for the company to start its own investigation.

Suddenly David Haug, a project developer with the international division, phoned into the room, demanding to speak to somebody.

"Look," Haug said. "I've got a deal under way to build a power plant in Puerto Rico. This thing is going to impact our ability to get it done. We just need to accept the blame and move on. We need to get my deal done."

The room descended into a screaming match. Enron's lawyers weren't going to allow the company to just blindly take the blame. Haug fought back, yelling about his deal.

Over at the conference table, Mark Palmer, a newly hired public-relations executive, listened to the back-and-forth as he manned the phones. Haug hung up, and a number of people began bad-mouthing him and his project. It was a lousy deal anyway, they said. The prices were crazy; there was no telling if Enron would ever get paid. One of the golfers in the room called the proposal "a long putt."

Palmer didn't get it. "So why don't we just not do the deal if it's lousy?"

One of his new colleagues looked at Palmer knowingly. He explained the compensation system for the international division, detailing how developers gained huge bonuses if the financing and other paperwork on a project was signed.

"So you're telling me," Palmer said, "it doesn't matter if it's a good deal, so long as it gets done?"

There were nods around the room.

On November 26, Enron's directors reached their decision about the succession. Lay and Kinder would be offered extensions of their contracts. No one was under the illusion that Kinder would accept. After being informed of the vote, Lay sought out Kinder, finding him in his office.

"Rich, the board has met, and they considered the issues related to future leadership," Lay began.

Enough. Kinder knew the result.

"They think you've done a fabulous job as COO," Lay went on. "And they'd like you to continue in that position. They're still not comfortable, at this point in time, with moving you up to the CEO's job."

Kinder looked calm and contemplative. "I'm disappointed. I think it's a mistake. So it's probably in everyone's best interest that I leave at year-end."

Lay watched Kinder carefully. He had expected that. "I'm sure the board will be disappointed," he said. "They'd love to keep the team together."

Kinder shrugged. "It's what I have to do."

"I'm sorry it's worked out this way, Rich," Lay said. "You'll be badly missed."

Later that day, the fiftieth-floor receptionist peered over her desk, watching as Amanda Martin dashed from the elevator banks toward the security door leading to the executive offices. She released the electronic lock just before Martin darted inside, headed to see Kinder.

She had just heard the news. She adored Kinder and thought he had one of the best minds in the building. But there he sat at his desk, looking calm and relaxed.

"Rich, how could this happen?" she gasped as she walked into the room. "You are getting screwed!"

Kinder didn't rise to the bait. "It's just time to move on. This is how things worked out."

"Oh, come on, Rich! This is wrong!"

"But this is how things are. It'll be for the best."

His serenity pushed Martin to the edge. "Rich, you can't just take this! You've got to do something!"

Kinder raised his index finger. "I'm going to tell you something, girl."

He paused. "The best revenge is always living well."

The simplicity of Kinder's words, the stillness of his demeanor, brought Martin up short. Kinder was going to stay above the fray. It was really over. He was gone.

Skilling could barely control his anxiety. With Kinder leaving, somebody else would be chief operating officer, would dictate Enron's future. If not Skilling, then who?

By that point the board had decided to turn Kinder's responsibilities over to Lay, but Skilling knew that couldn't last long. Lay was nice enough, but that was the problem. He was *too* nice. He wasn't the type to pound his hand on the table and kill a stupid proposal. Everybody who pitched an idea to Lay seemed to think they had his approval—even executives with contradictory ideas.

Unless he moved quickly, Skilling figured, somebody else would snag Kinder's job. He called Lay and made an appointment. The two got together two days later.

Lay welcomed Skilling warmly. This was his most talented executive, critical to Enron's future. He couldn't afford to lose him. The two sat at the conference table, and Skilling leaned his arms against the granite top.

"Ken, with everything that's going on, I want to tell you what I think about all of this," Skilling began.

"All right."

"Okay, well, at some point, somebody's going to be the new COO. And it strikes me there are three alternatives for that job: me, Rebecca Mark, or somebody from outside."

Lay's face revealed nothing. *Not true*, he thought.

So many people believed Mark was in line to succeed Kinder. Lay had heard lots of speculation about her favored status but considered it a corporate myth. He thought Mark showed talent in international. But operations weren't her strong point. Enron's backbone was still the pipelines, and she knew little about that. She wasn't deeply knowledgeable about domestic gas and electricity markets, either. In short, she didn't have a shot at number two.

Lay did have a fallback lined up: Forrest Hoglund, head of Enron's oil-and-gas division. A longtime Exxon executive, Hoglund impressed Lay, who had long ago told directors that if he was ever hit by a truck, Hoglund would be the best person to run the place.

But Skilling didn't know any of that. So Lay just listened as he ripped into his imagined rival.

"I just want you to know, Ken," Skilling said, "that if Rebecca's chosen, I'm leaving. And I guarantee you half of my people would leave, too. They don't respect her."

Lay said nothing.

"And if it's somebody from outside," Skilling continued, "I'm willing to work with somebody, but they're probably going to see things differently from me. My company is kind of my company. And if they want to change it, I'm not going to want to stick around for that."

Skilling took a breath. "I just want you to know that," he continued. "I'm not asking for any action now. I just want you to be aware of my thinking."

Lay nodded. "I understand," he said.

On a Monday night in downtown Houston, Enron's directors walked with their spouses through the chilly wind toward the Museum of Natural Science. Once inside, they made their way to the second floor, then down a long hallway decorated like a cave. Around them, a rainbow of crystals sparkled in the Gem Room, where Ken and Linda Lay were hosting their annual board Christmas party.

It was December 9, 1996, the night before the directors' final meeting for the year. As they arrived, guests were instructed to reach into small baskets for their seating assignments. This was a night of traditions, a celebration that never failed to delight. There would be carols around a piano—brought in specially—and Santa, loaded with presents for the directors and their spouses.

After all the guests had found their seats, tuxedo-clad waiters moved about the room serving dinner. Lay walked to the front, where he gave his traditional dinner blessing. Afterward, he smiled to the assembled crowd.

"I just wanted to thank all of you for joining us," he said, "and to wish you a Merry Christmas and express our hopes for a Happy New Year."

Before Lay finished, Kinder signaled he wanted to speak. It was his last company Christmas party, and the discomfort in the air was palpable. He stood at his table.

"I wanted to take this opportunity to let everyone know how much I've enjoyed Enron," he began. "It's been a great opportunity, and I've really grown over the years."

Kinder launched into an analysis of the company, describing its improvement in earnings, revenues, everything. The speech was nothing but gracious; still, the words left some directors uncomfortable. It sounded too much like Kinder was defending his tenure, sending the subtle message that his accomplishments hadn't been appreciated.

Kinder wrapped up his speech to polite applause. As the evening went on, Lay worked the room, mixing banalities with serious discussions about Kinder's successor.

As the hours rolled by, an unspoken understanding emerged. There was no hurry. Lay should take his time to get to know his division heads better. A slow, steady selection process was probably the best path. The candidates in the wings would just have to wait.

The next day, Lay called Skilling and asked him to drop by. He wanted to break the news personally of the directors' decision. Maybe, he thought, that would soften the blow.

"Jeff, I know you're eager to find out what we're doing regarding the COO spot," Lay said. "The board and I have decided that rather than rush to fill that position, we're going to leave it open for a while."

Skilling's face fell. "Why? Why can't we do it now?"

Such a change. Not long ago, Skilling had been uninterested in top management, wanted to work half-time. But now, moving up right away had become critical to him.

"The board and I think it would be better if I get time to deal with the

CEOs of each major profit center. We're going to wait a few months, then make a decision."

Skilling protested, dredging up one argument after another. But Lay wouldn't budge. Sullen, Skilling thanked Lay and left. On the elevator he hit the button for the lobby. He had to get out. He needed to think.

Skilling gripped the steering wheel as he veered around a curve on Loop 610, speeding toward Houston's Galleria area. It was about five o'clock that same day.

He had been driving for more than an hour on 610, the outer loop surrounding the city. He was angry, frustrated, scared. This could be a turning point for Enron. He had to make sure that Lay understood that. He had to take Kinder's job. His vision for the company might die if he didn't.

He glanced at the car-phone console and dialed Lay's office. A secretary patched him right through.

"Ken? It's Jeff. I'm out of the office, but I was wondering if you would be able to come over and meet with me. In the lobby of the Four Seasons."

The Four Seasons. Lay's favorite hotel.

"Sure, Jeff. I'll head over there right now."

Half an hour later, a uniformed employee held open the door of the Four Seasons. Lay nodded his thanks as he walked into the thirty-story hotel. Inside, Venetian chandeliers illuminated an assortment of antiques around the lobby. The place was quiet and luxurious, a comfortable combination of urban elegance and easy southern charm.

Lay spotted Skilling near a grand staircase. He crossed over and shook hands. Skilling led the way to the lobby lounge, and they took seats at a table against the wall. Anxiety creased Skilling's face. Lay waited.

"Ken, I know I reacted pretty badly in our meeting this afternoon, and I needed to get my head clear afterward. So for the last few hours I've just been out driving around 610 and thinking."

"All right."

"And basically, I just want to stress that I think it's a big mistake if you don't go ahead and make me chief operating officer now. It will send a very negative signal to my group. With no full-time replacement, it will be pretty obvious that succession is wide open."

He took a breath. "My whole group is going to feel that maybe we're not as important as in the past. And given their contribution to the bottom line, it just seems like a mistake to leave our people vulnerable to being picked off by other companies, simply because they're nervous. We don't need to do it. You need to name me to the job, just to ensure we can keep up our past performance."

The two men spoke for another hour and a half as the bar began to fill with evening customers. Skilling's words were calm but passionate, and Lay was impressed. This wasn't some "*I want the job*" argument; Skilling had thought through his position and was presenting a strong case.

Finally, shortly before seven, Skilling was spent. The men stood and headed to the lobby. Outside the doorway, Lay turned to Skilling.

"All right, Jeff," he said. "Let me think about it. I'll talk with some of the directors, and I'll get back to you probably in the next twenty-four hours."

Skilling nodded. "Okay. Thanks for hearing me out."

The valet pulled up in Lay's Mercedes 600. Lay handed the man a tip, climbed into his car, and drove away.

The next morning at dawn, Lay pushed his hands against a tree in his front yard. Wearing shorts and a sweatshirt, he leaned forward, stretching the muscles in his legs. After the short warm-up, he headed out for his morning jog. As he huffed down Looscan Lane, Skilling's words from the previous night echoed through his mind.

Skilling had certainly painted a bleak picture of Enron's future if the lines of power were left in limbo. What was really the downside of just going ahead and anointing Skilling as the heir apparent?

Probably the best thing to do is move him in now.

As the morning sun drifted past the horizon, Lay made his decision. Skilling could move up. But until everybody got comfortable with the new team, he would just be responsible for the marketing and trading groups while Lay handled everything else. It made a lot of sense.

By 6:30 Lay was back home. After getting ready, he telephoned John Duncan, chairman of the executive committee. Duncan was still at home when Lay reached him.

"John, after our meeting yesterday, I met with Jeff," Lay began.

Later that day, Skilling was holding his emotions in check when he reappeared in Lay's doorway.

"Ken, you wanted to see me?"

Lay smiled. "Sure, Jeff. Come on in and sit down."

The two took their usual spots at the table. Skilling already figured that this was it, all or nothing.

"I want you to know I listened to you very carefully last night," Lay said.

He pulled himself forward in his chair, smiling. "I've thought about it overnight, and I've decided we should move you into the position now," he said. "I've talked to the board, and they're delighted. They fully believe you are my likely successor. So we're just going to get on with it."

Skilling's face showed no reaction. "Thanks, Ken. I'll do everything I can to make sure it's the right decision."

Then Lay put down some ground rules and sounded a cautionary note. Skilling was going to be president of the whole company, not just trading. He needed to let employees in other divisions know that he appreciated their work. There should be no more feuding with the international division. Lay said he would meet with the management team, let them know his decision. Then, when everything was set, they would announce his elevation to the world.

By next morning, the necessary meetings had been held, all the important people informed. Skilling's power was finally beyond question.

Rebecca Mark stormed into Lay's office almost as soon as she heard the news.

"Ken, you've got to be kidding me!" she blurted out. "You cannot make Jeff Skilling the COO of this company!"

Mark was beside herself. Kinder had never been easy on her, but she always thought him fair. Then, when Lay and Kinder went into that weird breakup, she had cast her lot with Lay because of his commitment to turn over the number-two job to a team of managers. Almost any of those managers would have been fine with Mark. But Skilling?

"He has no respect for the other businesses," she railed. "He wants to tear us apart and throw us away. He has no respect for the pipelines. Why would you put someone like that in charge of the company?"

Lay gave her a placid look. "I had to make a decision that I felt was in Enron's best interest. Jeff has been—"

"Oh, come on, Ken," Mark interrupted. "He has no leadership experience, other than his trading business. He doesn't have a leader's psychology. Every other word is a profanity, everything is always chaos. Look, you may think he's brilliant, but his leadership skills just *suck*!"

"Now, Rebecca—"

"And, Ken, something I don't think you realize," she continued. "I don't think Jeff Skilling has the same ethical bearing as the rest of the company. He and his people march to a different drummer."

Mark stared Lay hard in the eyes.

"I think you're going to find that their way of viewing the world is very different from yours."

"I've talked to Jeff," Fastow said to Martin over the phone. "He says we're going to do my deal."

Months into the battles over the co-generation deals, Fastow showed no sign of backing off. Now he was saying that he had gone around Martin, undermined Baxter, and persuaded Skilling to sign off on his monstrous proposal.

Was Fastow bluffing? Had he even talked to Skilling? Did they understand this deal would cheat the partnership? She needed help. She scouted out Baxter and Rice.

"Guys, I'm in a pickle here," she said. The deal they thought they had killed had risen from the grave.

"All right, even if Andy's deal is good for Enron, it screws the partnership," she said. "We can't do that."

Baxter agreed to lead the charge against Fastow. He and Martin went up to Skilling's office to make their case.

"This is just bullshit, Jeff," Baxter raged. "We already have a reputation for screwing our partners. We're not going to do that here. We're doing Amanda's deal."

Skilling listened politely. He had a lot more on his plate to worry about. He didn't have time for this.

"Okay, okay," he said. "But damn it—do everything you can to minimize the loss."

The Martin deal went forward; Fastow's was shelved.

The rumblings inside Enron began almost immediately.

Fastow was furious. Martin and her team couldn't understand it. *What was this? Why did it matter so much?* Hundreds of deals came out of Enron every year. Why was Fastow taking this one so personally?

Then threats started. Kopper delivered the message to Mark Miles, who worked with Martin. Everyone on the Calpine deal would pay. Fastow was going to make sure of it.

"He's going to get everybody who worked on it," Kopper said. "He's going to nail you."

This was insane, but Fastow had the power to do it. Skilling's Performance Review Committee allowed for it. Every senior executive participated in the PRC; several days of ranking and debate decided everyone's bonuses and promotions. Skilling had pushed it on the theory that wide input meant an executive couldn't be held back by a single boss. But it didn't always work that way. Most members of the PRC didn't know employees in other divisions. If someone like Fastow came along, tearing down the people on the Calpine deal, he could have a real impact. Doing the right thing for Enron in the end could cost Martin's team in their wallets.

Miles hunted down Martin. "Fastow's fit to be tied," he told her, spelling out everything he had heard.

Martin was furious. "This is just bullshit."

It wasn't supposed to work like this. Skilling needed to know. She made an appointment to see him.

"Okay, Jeff," she said, "Andy's out of control. He's announcing that he's going to get the guys who worked on the Calpine deal. This is a great deal, it was the right deal for Enron. This shouldn't be happening."

Skilling listened impatiently. *Somebody said that somebody said that Andy said.* More rumors. Baxter was always in his office, hacking away at Fastow. Now Martin seemed to have joined in. He didn't think Fastow could hurt her team in the PRC even if he tried; Fastow rarely said much of anything there except about his own guys.

Skilling held up a hand. "Amanda, your work is great, and of course I'll cover for you. Andy's bright, but he's got a temper, and we need to get that under control. But trust me on this. I'll take care of you. I'll talk to him."

It sounded okay. Martin thanked Skilling and headed back to her office.

Two weeks later, Martin was in her office, feeling confused. She still had heard nothing directly from Fastow. But the rumors had gotten uglier; now he was supposedly attacking her directly, accusing her of purposely trying to discredit him with the banks involved in his deal.

How did things get to this point? Andy had been her friend for so long. Now all this fury over a deal. It was like she had gotten in the way of some big plan—but what? Maybe Fastow had painted himself into a corner and had too much pride to end the feud. One of them needed to take the first step and get their friendship back on track.

Martin reached for the phone and dialed Fastow.

"Andy," she said, "I need to talk to you."

"Fine. Come up." His voice was cold.

When she walked into his office a few minutes later, he stayed behind his desk, rigid and unsmiling.

"So," he said, "you wanted a meeting."

Martin took a breath. This was going to be bad.

"Andy, I've been hearing things that I'm really, really bothered about," she said.

Fastow stared at her, saying nothing.

"You know, I don't understand what it is about this," she said. "You worked on a deal. We worked on a deal. Cliff made a decision. Jeff made a decision—"

"Jeff never made a decision," Fastow snapped.

God. "Fine. A decision was made that ours was better for the partnership. It was approved, and we did it."

Martin paused. Fastow sat motionless.

"I don't understand where all this stuff is coming from about me trying to discredit you," she continued. "We go back a long way. It shouldn't be like this."

She kept at it for another minute or so, but he just stared at her. She fell silent. Fury twisted Fastow's face. He thrust his hand forward, jabbing a finger on his desk.

"We worked on this deal. I went out to the banks. They believed they were closing with us in three weeks. I promised them the deal. You made me look like a liar to them. You damaged Enron because these are Enron's banks."

He glared at Martin. "You sabotaged my deal."

Martin didn't know what to say.

"Andy, I don't have the authority to sabotage—"

Fastow interrupted again. "You sabotaged me. You went to Skilling and attacked me."

Martin closed her eyes. Her complaints to Skilling had gotten back to Fastow. "Andy . . ."

Fastow shook his head. "You undermined my deal," he said angrily.

He paused, leaning up in his chair.

"If I were you," he threatened, "I would be very, very careful."

BOOK TWO
RAPTORS

CHAPTER 6

A MARILYN MONROE LOOK-ALIKE, draped in a red dress with faux diamonds, giggled and cooed as she walked by the second-floor ballroom at the Hyatt Regency hotel in downtown Houston. Just inside, an Elvis impersonator in a white jumpsuit wandered near an actor decked out like Clark Gable. Music blared through speakers and colorful lights flashed, creating the illusion of a movie premiere for the hundreds of Enron employees milling about the room.

Despite the early hour—eight o'clock on the morning of January 14, 1997—the mood in the room was jubilant. The big announcement was at hand. The planning had been very hush-hush, but now the employees were about to see the unveiling of Enron's new image for the world.

On the far side of the room, Lay and Skilling walked across the stage, stopping beside a large object covered by a massive cloth. Lay held up his hands, making barely audible shushing noises until he had everyone's attention.

"Well," Lay said, "we've come a long way since 1985, when we were just a pipeline company with a vision—a vision of becoming the premier natural-gas company."

A smattering of applause.

"We have become much more," he said. "We're a force the world can be proud of, for everything we're doing. Deregulating markets. Providing alternative services. Making markets more efficient."

Applause again, louder this time.

"So we tried to develop a new logo that would reflect the dynamic company Enron has become," he said. "It will be recognized as the logo of a company leading the energy industry into the next century, into the next millennium."

The loudest applause yet.

"It's a logo we'll all be very proud of."

Lay gestured to the covered object. "And here it is!"

Recorded trumpets blared. Lights flashed. Smoke enveloped the stage. Someone pulled a rope, lifting the covering cloth. On the stage rested a giant sculpture—a single tilted *E*. Multicolored lights surrounded each prong of the letter. The crowd loved it.

They celebrated the logo's birth for an hour, then trickled back to the office, where delightful surprises awaited. The logo was posted in hallways; new letterhead and business cards were at their desks. It was official: Enron had a cool new icon to show the world.

Within hours, the world would laugh it off the stage. Houston faxed the logo to Enron's offices in Europe. But in transmission the middle, yellow prong disappeared, leaving the new design meant to celebrate Enron's triumphant ascension looking more like an electric plug. Worse, to the Italians it resembled an obscene hand gesture, one that meant about the same thing as shooting a middle finger at an American. The European executives roared with laughter: *now* they had a unique way to win Italian customers.

Back in Houston, dismay grew; the yellow prong also vanished when run through the copying machine. Somehow, Enron had spent millions of dollars on a new business logo without bothering to check if it worked in business. Soon the hallway signs went down, the new cards and letterheads were shredded. With no fanfare, another logo was introduced, replacing the yellow prong with a green one.

The symbol meant to carry Enron into the next millennium hadn't lasted a week.

They arrived at almost the same time: A new chief operating officer. A new logo. And then, a new accountant.

Since 1990, Stephen Goddard at Andersen had overseen Enron—meeting the board, reviewing deals, auditing financials. Goddard wasn't Hollywood's idea of an accountant; this was no boring technocrat with green eyeshades. He was a specialist in client services, a backslapper who maintained a close relationship with the managers whose numbers his team reviewed.

Thanks in part to that familiarity, Andersen and Enron developed an unusually close relationship. The firm was both its auditor and its consultant. Veterans of Andersen's Houston office jumped to Enron as internal auditors; even Rick Causey, Enron's top accounting guru, had been an Andersen manager. The relationship couldn't have been cozier.

But by February 1997, things had to change. Andersen rotated partners on accounts every seven years, and Goddard's time was up. Some partners lobbied to move up Tom Bauer, a top-notch accountant, who audited Enron's trading operations. But Goddard thought there was only one candidate— David Duncan, a thirty-six-year-old who had worked on Enron for years. With Goddard's support, Duncan got the nod.

Duncan rarely impressed anyone as a towering intellect, and his background was unremarkable. Born in Lake Charles, Louisiana, and raised in Beaumont, Texas, Duncan attended Texas A&M, where he studied accounting. In college he had been something of a party boy; he and a group of friends had formed what amounted to a co-op for illicit drugs, purchasing large quantities of marijuana that they divided among themselves. Often, Duncan and his pals could be found around campus laughing it up, stoned.

In 1981, straight out of college, Duncan joined Andersen's Houston office but didn't change his ways. For years, he and his friends kept up their mass drug buying. Several days a week he would leave the staid accounting world and head home to toke up; sometimes he branched out to cocaine. But a few years after starting on the Enron engagement, Duncan straightened up. He hadn't used illegal drugs since.

Enron seemed the ideal assignment. In his early days at Andersen, Duncan struck up a friendship with Causey, then just another accountant in the Houston office. The two became close, often lunching, golfing, or going out with their wives. Now his buddy was Enron's top accountant.

Clearly, Duncan was no accounting whiz, but nobody worried about that; like most partners, he would rely on the experts in the firm's Professional Standards Group to rule on tough issues. But he struck some partners as top-flight where it mattered—his familiarity with Enron and a close relationship with its executives. His good looks and disciplined organization didn't hurt, either.

In early February, Goddard and Duncan had an appointment with Lay, to notify him of the coming change. Lay was polite, if not particularly interested; he vaguely knew Duncan and thought he seemed competent enough.

"I'm very excited about the opportunity to work more closely with Enron," Duncan said. "It's really an honor."

Lay smiled. "We'll have a lot of fun," he said.

By any measure, Duncan seemed a man on the precipice of big things. But it was not to be; the great opportunity at Enron would be his last high-profile accounting job.

Steve Goddard pulled out a pen as a group of Andersen accountants took their seats. It was later that month, and the accountants were gathering for their annual client review. Andersen partners liked to think of themselves as selective, representing only the best, and this exercise was aimed at weeding out clients that fell short.

One at a time, the partners ranked their clients based on the risk in their accounting practices. Eventually, the discussion turned to Enron.

On one side of the room, Carl Bass listened skeptically. Unlike some colleagues, Bass didn't see his job as helping clients weave through the accounting requirements, twisting transactions for the desired result. His was a purer view: the client puts together a deal, the accountant figures out the financial effect. In his mind, accountants were referees; they weren't supposed to join the team huddle with ideas on how to run the ball.

His approach made Bass something of an eccentric among his flashier colleagues. He was never going to be a David Duncan, glad-handing clients over a game of golf. But what he lacked in kowtowing skills he made up for with intellectual firepower. Bass was a technician with an encyclopedic knowledge of the profession's rules. He even spent some years with the Financial Accounting Standards Board, or FASB, the primary rules setter for the profession.

Since returning from FASB in 1994, Bass had spent a lot of time on Enron and hadn't liked what he saw. Its executives struck him as sloppy, always seeking shortcuts, often pushing Bass to be "creative" in finding favorable results. Bass refused, usually because Enron wanted accounting results divorced from economics. If the company wanted to report revenue, the deals had to produce revenue. Simple as that.

Bass firmly believed he knew the source of Enron's unrealistic expectations: Rick Causey, who had spent his Andersen years handling straightforward pipeline accounting. Now he was making judgments on derivatives, structured deals—the tough stuff. Problem was, Bass never considered Causey to be all that sophisticated; he didn't even seem to understand basic concepts, like when revenue could be recorded. Enron was in the outer reaches of the accounting universe with a pilot who, in Bass's mind, didn't understand what all the knobs on the control panel were for. But as his fellow partners discussed Enron, it was clear few shared his doubts. Causey's lunch and golfing partners had a much higher opinion of his skills than Bass did.

Some partners mentioned Enron's complex accounting, stressing how close to the edge it flew.

Goddard held up a hand. "That's why I'm glad Rick Causey is in there. Without him, I might be more concerned. But Rick is a very strong player."

Bass couldn't help himself. "Steve, I disagree. I don't think Causey is as strong as you say he is. I think he's got some serious deficiencies as an accountant."

The room was silent. Goddard eyed Bass evenly. "Well, that's your opinion," he replied. "I don't agree."

That was it. No one asked Bass to explain, to find out whether representing Enron might be riskier than they imagined. Goddard moved on to the next topic on the agenda.

———

In Snowmass, Colorado, the Big Burn ski lift rumbled around a curve. Skilling and Fastow climbed aboard, lolling their skis in the air as the lift set off up the mountain.

The two were excited, almost giddy. They had come to Colorado for a public-pension-funds conference about investments beyond the bread-and-butter stocks and bonds that dominated their portfolios. Skilling felt sure Enron had a lot to offer. At that point Enron and Calpers, the California fund, had a four-year record with the JEDI partnership. The deal had been wildly successful; its only problem was that JEDI had pretty much committed all of its cash.

There were hundreds of other pension funds, but somehow, after JEDI, Fastow had largely ignored them. He preferred working with bankers, who practically begged to do his deals so they could win Enron's fees. For pension-fund money, Fastow would have to do the begging.

But banks make loans, pension funds make big investments. So Skilling and Fastow had come to Colorado hoping to whet their appetites. In a presentation at the conference, Skilling had laid out the workings of JEDI and Enron. He didn't expect to wow the crowd; by that point he considered JEDI pretty run-of-the-mill. But at the break, fund managers flocked to the two men, thrusting out business cards, almost pleading for a chance to invest.

As the lift glided up Big Burn, Skilling couldn't help but gloat about the moment. "I'm just stunned how well that went. You know, there was probably a trillion dollars of capital sitting in that room, looking for a place to go."

"Yeah, we need to pursue this," Fastow agreed.

Skilling thought for a moment. "We need to spend more time with these guys, find mutually agreeable deals."

Fastow promised to get right on it.

He knew the executive who could get the job done: Jim Timmins, a specialist in private equity who had been sniffing around Enron for a job. Fastow brought Timmins on board just a few weeks later, in February 1997.

The timing seemed fortuitous. A couple of deals were coming down the pike that needed outside investors. With Timmins's contacts, Enron would be able to tap into those pension funds and start building some new relationships.

But Fastow had no intention of seeking Timmins's help. Not on the next deal. He had another idea.

Amanda Martin settled into her office chair and flipped through some papers. It was March 1997, months after her run-in with Fastow over the cogeneration deals, but Martin still felt wounded by the experience. She knew she had lost her friend, and didn't understand why.

The Calpine sale was wrapping up. Causey had helped devise a way to do the deal without highlighting the loss. It would be announced March 31, the last day of the first quarter—by Calpine, not Enron. Enron investors who might notice would no doubt assume the deal's financial effect was going to hit that quarter's results. But sort of accidentally, Enron left a closing document unsigned until days later. That technically pushed the deal into the second quarter; the loss would be reported months later, buried where no one could find it. A mistake that could rightly call into question Enron's mark-to-market accounting would disappear in plain sight.

Now a new deal had come along. In January, Enron had acquired Zond Corporation, a wind-farm operator. But three of Zond's assets—Zond Windsystems, Victory Garden, and Sky River—raised the same problems as the co-generation plants. They were qualifying facilities, or QFs, meaning under law they could be paid higher rates, but those larger payments would disappear once Enron finished its acquisition of Portland General. The wind farms would be worth a lot less if Enron kept them; they needed to be sold.

Martin finished reviewing the records for the plants and assigned two deal makers, Mike Miller and Mark Miles, to look for a buyer. Not long after, Miles and Miller came back to Martin's office with news.

"Kopper's working on a wind deal," Miles said.

Again? Martin wasn't ready for another round of hand-to-hand combat with Fastow. She wanted out.

"Guys, we don't need to put up with this shit again," she said. She called Baxter, who oversaw asset sales.

"Cliff, I'm out of this wind project," she said. "Fastow's in it, and I'm not going through that again."

"Amanda," Baxter replied, "we already have interest from some buyers . . ."

"If there's somebody who's expressed interest, you do it. Let me and my guys out of this. You carry the water this time, so if there's a problem, you get tagged."

Baxter raised a few feeble arguments but ultimately gave up. He didn't have much interest in battling Fastow either. He hated the guy, but the tiny wind deal just wasn't worth the fight. He stepped aside.

Fastow's rages had worked. Now nothing could keep him from doing the deal the way he wanted.

The idea was so delicious, so simple it was breathtaking. Somebody was going to make money on the wind farms; why shouldn't it be Andy Fastow and his family?

The deal Fastow and Kopper were cobbling together was a structured transaction, where outside investors provide three percent of the deal's capital. A company could provide 97 percent of the capital to an off-books partnership, find 3 percent somewhere else, stir in some legal legerdemain, and—poof!—an "independent" buyer was created. The company could then legally "sell" an asset to the partnership—even if most of the payment originated from its own pockets. The round-trip of cash complete, the company had converted an asset on its balance sheet into revenue. When Andersen accountants first laid out the rules, Fastow had ridiculed them, saying the three percent could come from anybody—even his gardener or his family. Now he was ready to put that thought into action.

With Kopper's help, he constructed an entity called Alpine Investors to make the purchase. It would cost about $17 million, far more money than Fastow had in his bank account. But with the magic of structured finance, he didn't have to worry about that. Almost $16.5 million would come in a loan to Alpine from Enron. Then Fastow—along with his wife's wealthy family, the Weingartens, and friends like Patty Melcher, a wealthy Houstonian close to Lea—would kick in $510,000. Fastow would run the partnership, with Enron's friends as investors.

Fastow sang the praises of the deal to Kopper. "Enron keeps control, without the burdens of legal ownership," he said. "It's perfect."

Something about Alpine Investors made Jordan Mintz uncomfortable. A tax lawyer, Mintz had joined Enron a few months before, coming from Bracewell & Patterson, a Houston law firm. Abandoning a secure partner's position for an iffy chance at a gas company struck some in his family as crazy. But Mintz had represented Enron and now wanted the thrill and challenge that came with working there.

Then along came Alpine Investors. Mintz's job was to handle tax issues on the deal, but the whole thing just seemed weird. In a power-plant deal, he figured he would see heavy-hitting investors walking through the office. Pension funds. Maybe the capital investment unit of General Electric. Or some Wall Street private-equity fund.

Instead, he saw *Patty Melcher*. She was presented to Mintz as someone heading up the investment group providing equity for the deal. Melcher, a former investment banker whose husband was an heir to a fortune from Houston convenience stores, was pleasant enough. But this just wasn't the way corporations did deals. Some friend of Lea Fastow's? That felt like something put together by a backwoods county commissioner rather than by a cutting-edge Fortune 500 company.

Mintz sought out Larry Lawyer, who was working with Fastow on the deal. "Dude, this is so strange," he said. "How often do we bring in outside investors like this?"

Lawyer shrugged. "Not too often," he replied.

Trouble.

Alpine Investors wouldn't work. Fastow hadn't hidden his family's role in the deal from the accountants, and they decided the structure didn't meet the rules. If he or his relatives provided part of the three percent, they said, the magic disappeared. Enron would still own the wind farms, the plants would remain on the books, the qualifying-facility status would be lost.

The news was a disaster. It wasn't just Fastow losing an opportunity; there was no ready fallback. He didn't have other investors lined up to provide the three percent, and certainly not ones who would allow Enron to control the plants. If a deal wasn't done soon, the plants would lose their special status, and their value would crumple. Coming on the heels of the retail fiasco, the collapse of Alpine Investors could spell trouble for Fastow—and for Enron.

He sought out Kopper, and together they devised a solution—a dishonest one. They needed $510,000 but had raised only $91,000 from wealthy Houstonians they knew. The rest, $419,000, would be put up by Fastow but made to look as though it came from someone else. The cash went to Kopper from the Fastows' account, with Lea writing records showing it as a loan. Kopper then funneled the money to his domestic partner, Bill Dodson, and to Kathy Wetmore, the Fastows' real estate agent. Both agreed to act as fronts for Fastow, pretending the money was theirs.

With the "investors" in place, Fastow and Kopper created two entities for the deal, naming them RADR ZWS and RADR ZWS MM. The $91,000 in authentic investments came in, right alongside the $419,000 cash hoard that secretly belonged to Fastow. RADR closed in May 1997.

With a little money laundering, Fastow had pulled off the very deal that the accountants had said couldn't be done—at least not legally.

On the morning of May 14, an Enron corporate jet banked over the Sacramento River before landing at the Executive Airport, minutes from the California capital. Fastow unfastened his seat belt and stood as the pilot taxied to a stop. Four colleagues lined up behind him.

They had come to Sacramento for a meeting that could well reshape Enron's future. The company was preparing JEDI II, another fund to provide financing to energy producers. And again it wanted Calpers as a co-investor.

The executives headed to the front of the terminal and piled into a waiting private car. Arriving at Calpers's offices in downtown Sacramento, they were whisked upstairs to a second-floor conference room. Barry Gonder, Calpers's head of alternative investments, arrived, all smiles.

"Andy!" he said. "How you doing?"

"Great, Barry," Fastow said, pumping Gonder's hand.

A few Calpers staffers trickled in. Fastow pulled out a six-page presentation and laid it on the table.

"We wanted to come out here to give you an update on JEDI, talk to you about how the partnership is doing, and discuss some new opportunities we think will be particularly attractive to you," Fastow said.

Fastow glanced down at his presentation. The cover was emblazoned with a logo for JEDI. He turned to the first page, studying it. Down the table, Shirley Hudler sat stone-faced, trying not to wince.

He's going to wing it again. Hudler had put together the presentation for this meeting, but, as always, her work had been a waste of time. Fastow seemed to excel at being unprepared. She had watched him in previous meetings reviewing a presentation for the first time as he delivered it. He would get his facts wrong, flipping through the pages, trying to find his way as he spoke. Somehow, Fastow seemed to believe he was smarter off the cuff than executives who did their homework. He wasn't.

It didn't take long for his first mistake. He was boasting about Enron's accomplishments, its creativity. Why, he proclaimed, it had even figured out how to use its Transwestern pipeline, which had always moved gas out of California, to deliver fuel back into the state!

It's the other way around, Andy, Hudler thought.

Finally, Fastow reached his main point. "We're thinking about doing another private-equity partnership. Obviously, we'd like you to be our partner in it. And we'd really like to expand the box a little bit."

The original JEDI had made investments in the gas industry. But Enron wanted JEDI II to invest in anything energy-related. Wind, oil, coal—whatever was promising.

"This one's going to be bigger," Fastow said. "A billion dollars. And this time we're not going to be putting in stock as our contribution. We'll invest cash. So whatever the partnership puts its money into will be something Enron wanted a piece of, too."

Gonder looked uneasy. "That sounds good, Andy. But I'm not sure how the board would receive making another Enron investment. We've got $250 million in JEDI. I don't think they'd be happy tying up more with one company."

Fastow was ready with a response. "That's the beauty of our idea, Barry," he said. "Enron will take you out of JEDI. We will buy your interest in the partnership. Then you can roll the proceeds straight into JEDI II."

Under the plan, Fastow said, Calpers's half interest in JEDI would be purchased for almost $350 million, locking in its annual return at better than 20 percent. Then Calpers could use that money for JEDI II and participate in a much wider array of energy businesses.

Gonder looked intrigued. "It's an interesting idea, Andy. Why don't you guys put together a full proposal, and we'll see what everybody here thinks."

Mission accomplished. Everyone could tell that Gonder was eager to do the deal. Any fund manager would lick his chops at the chance to lock in returns—all while getting a chance to put money into a new, broader opportunity.

But some of the Enron executives who had listened to the pitch were bothered by its gaping holes. Enron *itself* couldn't purchase the Calpers interest in JEDI; if it did, all of its assets would come crashing onto the company's balance sheet. The whole purpose of JEDI was to provide financing to gas producers that would be off balance sheet.

So who in the world was really going to own the Calpers interest in JEDI once the deal was done?

Patty Melcher? Again?

Word had quickly swept through the finance division by June 1997. Enron was negotiating a deal worth more than $300 million with the largest, most respected public retirement fund in the country. And to get investors for the other side of the deal, Fastow was hitting up . . . *Patty Melcher*, a friend of his wife. It struck everyone as just so *scuzzy*, so wrong. Enron was the big leagues, not some charity fund-raiser.

But as time passed, the names of the outside investors who would purchase the Calpers interest became a deeper, darker secret. Melcher's name was still tossed around, but the identities of everyone else stayed under wraps.

Jim Timmins, now in charge of Enron's dealings with pension funds, was flummoxed. Here was the perfect opportunity to attract new investors; Enron could sell JEDI II to other funds, whether Calpers wanted in or not. Or it could arrange for another fund to buy Calpers's JEDI stake. It was the kind of thing the company should be talking up. The pension plans wanted to do business with Enron; why wouldn't Fastow jump at the chance?

Instead, Timmins was kept out of the deal on the purchase of Calpers's interest in JEDI, spending his time on the structure of JEDI II. But occasionally he would hear of others asking about the investors buying Calpers's interest. The answer was always the same.

Don't worry about it.

It was dubbed the "special-projects group."

By the middle of 1997, Fastow had decided that his favorites needed their own unit within finance. This would be an assemblage of the best, a financial SWAT team. Their work would be almost clandestine. As the elite, they would not only be trusted with sensitive deals, they would be given the opportunity to make special, personal investments alongside Enron, deals that could make them rich.

The head of special projects, of course, would be Michael Kopper, Fastow's most trusted ally. Bill Brown, another young deal maker who had worked for Enron only two years, was also named to the group in its earliest days. But its rising star was Ben Glisan, a highly skilled thirty-one-year-old accountant who had joined Enron just the year before. Glisan, another Andersen alum, was a native Texan from a blue-collar family. He seemed almost starstruck by Fastow, who eagerly took the young man under his wing.

Once special projects was assembled, Fastow met with each of its members individually to lay out their next big deal: they would buy out Calpers's interest in JEDI. And they'd do it in a very unusual way.

"I'm putting together my own investment partnership for the Calpers buyout," Fastow said.

Sitting nearby, Kristina Mordaunt, a lawyer and Fastow confidante, took notes. The name of the partnership would be Chewco Investments, a tongue-in-cheek continuation of the *Star Wars* theme begun with JEDI; Chewco's name was derived from Chewbacca, the film's fur-covered warrior.

As for investors, Patty Melcher was out. Calpers wanted the deal done quickly, Fastow said, and Melcher just wasn't jumping when he told her to. She wanted her advisers to review JEDI's records, to make sure she understood the investment. Enron couldn't wait for that. So, in Melcher's place, he said, he would bring in institutional investors. He didn't identify them or explain how he would persuade them to blindly invest in a deal they hadn't investigated.

Mordaunt finished her meeting with Fastow and telephoned Ronald Astin, a lawyer from Vinson & Elkins who was advising Enron on the dealings with Calpers.

"This is the proposal, Ron," Mordaunt said. "Tell me what you think."

The concept struck Astin as pretty out-there.

"Wait, Kristina," he interrupted. "If you've got institutional investors in Chewco, why does someone from Enron management need to be involved?"

"Well, the idea is that the deal will be more attractive if they know Chewco has a manager who understands the assets," she replied.

Astin thought about that. "All right, Kristina, but you do understand, the way this is structured, the Enron manager is going to end up with an interest in Chewco."

"Yeah," Mordaunt agreed. "We know that."

The projector clicked to the next slide. A chart appeared on the screen. "Okay," Lou Pai told the assembled group. "This lays out the challenge we have."

Pai, now head of retail, had been struggling for months to get the business off the ground. Today he had organized a presentation for Skilling and other executives, hoping to explain the difficulties the division faced.

The story on the slide was the same one Skilling had heard before. Because of high fixed costs, the potential profit margin for the business was low. Pai began explaining the numbers. Skilling didn't want to hear it.

"Lou, you're too fucking smart for this," he snapped. "I don't want to ever see this slide again."

Pai's face was hard. "Jeff, it's the truth."

"I just don't want to ever see that slide again."

Pai slammed a hand on the table. "It's the fucking facts, Jeff!"

"It may be the facts," Skilling shouted back. "But I don't want you to think about it that way!"

"Well, if you think it's going to be the retail provision of gas and power, that math suggests it's not!"

The angry back-and-forth continued for a few minutes, then both men fell into a sullen silence. The lights came up and, after failing in an effort to go forward with the meeting, the discussion ended and everyone left the room. As the retail executives headed to their offices, some couldn't help but wonder whether it was time to start looking for another job.

"Hey, Carl, can I talk to you for a second?"

Tom Bauer, the Andersen accountant for Enron's trading operation, walked into the office of Carl Bass, the resident accounting wonk in the Houston office. Bass turned from his computer.

"What's up, Tom?"

He was having a problem with an Enron accounting issue, Bauer said. As part of the Portland General merger, Enron had acquired a supply contract with Bonneville Power in Seattle. The contract was worth millions, and Enron wanted to book the value as income right away.

Bass shook his head and laughed. "They came to me with the same question last year, on another contract from Portland General," he said. "But that one would have been at a loss. So they wanted to know if they could avoid the loss by counting it against the purchase price."

The logic was simple. If a company acquired for ten million dollars had, say, a million dollars in immediate losses from an outstanding contract, then the real purchase price was eleven million. Of course, that's a two-way street: if the acquired company came with immediate profits, the purchase price should be reduced. Otherwise, Enron was simply using its cash to purchase instant income.

"I gave them a memo on this," Bass said. "I already answered the question."

Bauer looked uncomfortable. There was clearly a lot of pushback from Enron on this one. "We're going to need to make the case again," he said.

The group of accountants walked alongside the stainless-steel oyster bar at Tony Mandola's Gulf Coast Kitchen, a 120-seat seafood restaurant in Houston. Leading the way, Rick Causey headed to a table near the back. He sat, picking up a napkin and placing it on his lap. Bauer, Bass, and David Duncan took the remaining seats.

The Andersen accountants had invited Causey to lunch to let him know the bad news. They couldn't support booking the Bonneville contract as income. As the lead partner, it was Duncan's job to tell the client the decision.

Everyone ordered, and small talk soon dwindled out.

"Okay," Causey said, "so what's up?"

Duncan looked down at the table. It was about that Bonneville contract, he said. "Well, our thinking is—now, it's our advice at this time," Duncan stammered. "There are lots of really complicated issues here, and some of them are not real clear . . ."

Bass and Bauer glanced at each other. *What was Duncan talking about?* Why was he dithering? Bass tapped his palm against the tips of his fingers.

"Wait, time out," he said. "Rick, we can't support booking this as income."

They had consulted the firm's top accounting experts in the Professional Standards Group, Bass said, and consulted the Houston practice. All were in agreement.

Bass vaguely shrugged. "So that's the answer."

Wait a minute, Causey argued. It *was* income. He rolled out his arguments, but Bass and Bauer just shook their heads. Sorry, they said. Duncan sat at the table, silent.

Causey refused to give up. He hurried back to the office, placing calls to Andersen's Houston managers and making his case. But despite the protests, none of them would back down.

Well, *tough*. The financial statements were from Enron, not Andersen. Causey wasn't *required* to take their advice. If he thought they were wrong, he could take it to the mat and report the income. And he did.

Andersen, still certain the accounting was in error, put the item on what is known as the adjustment sheet. Under the rules, if the numbers on the sheet were high enough, the company had to report them. But Duncan, having lost the accounting issue, argued that the amount was not material when viewed a particular way. *That* was an audit judgment—the area where Duncan had far more control. His argument won out; the dispute was kept hidden.

In the end, Andersen ruled that a single transaction almost doubling Enron's annual profits—from $54 million to $105 million—would not strike investors as important.

Joe Hirko, the chief financial officer of Portland General, sauntered into Skilling's office in high spirits. After months of work, the merger was all done, and now Hirko was in Houston, eager to push his next great idea.

"I wanted to lay out some ideas we've got for telecom," Hirko said.

Skilling pulled a face. Portland General, he knew, had launched a tiny telecommunications business in late 1996 called FirstPoint Communications, with plans to lay fiber-optic cable encircling Portland for high-speed Internet communications. The whole idea made no sense to him; it just seemed like money spent for little reason. When calculating Portland General's value, Skilling had always assumed, at best, the telecom group was worth nothing—at worst, Enron would have to shoulder the expense of shutting it down.

Now Hirko was throwing out this grand vision of building a long-haul fiber-optic network, linking Portland and Los Angeles, ultimately spanning more than sixteen hundred miles.

"You've gotta be kidding me," Skilling sneered. "You want to get backhoes out there and start digging holes? We're not doing that. We're not putting money into it."

"Well, Jeff, what if we could presell something like thirty fibers? Because that will pay for the project."

Skilling laughed. Thirty fibers was less than one-third of what Hirko was talking about putting into the ground. It was like saying he would sell a tire to pay for the car. *No way in hell*, he thought.

"Okay, sure," Skilling said. "If you can presell a third of it and pay for the whole project, have at it."

Approval in hand, Hirko went on his way. Weeks later, he returned, stunning Skilling with the news. He had presold the fibers and raised all the money he needed.

"Come on!" Skilling said. "Businesses don't work that way. Why aren't people putting in their own fiber instead of buying it from you if the prices are this screwy?"

Hirko shrugged. "It's telecom."

The whole thing was goofy. But suddenly Skilling wasn't so negative about his energy company spending money to join the Internet mania.

Carl Bass skimmed through the details of the power-plant transaction, certain that Enron was pulling another fast one on the accounting. Only this time, it was following the rules. The results were just insane.

Somebody at Enron had fallen in love with obtaining financing by selling power plants to off-books partnerships. But these weren't sales any reasonable person might expect. Under the complex deals, Enron received cash from the partnership—all borrowed—in a "sale" of the plant. But even though the company lost control of the plant, it still retained the risks of ownership. Then, sometime in the future, Enron could swap everything around and pull back most of the ownership when it wanted.

It was nuts, a way of allowing Enron to report cash flow where none really existed. But Bass had a hard enough time fighting the company when it *abused* the rules. What was he supposed to do when it was following the literal rules to an irrational end?

Bass thought about it for a moment.

Change the rules.

What if, Bass wondered, he helped John Stewart, Andersen's top accounting guru, persuade the rule makers to write a couple of revisions? It would be tough, but there was a logic to the plan. Accounting for real estate tended to be more onerous than for other assets. If the rule makers deemed such financings couldn't be done with real estate, it would be a small step. Then, Bass figured, the big part. Power plants are attached to land. So shouldn't they be real estate?

It would take almost eighteen months for Bass and his colleague to execute their subterfuge. But they would be successful in shutting down—for one of the only times—an illogical Enron accounting practice.

Causey and Enron executives cursed the real-estate rules when they were finally changed. But no one ever learned—not even Arthur Andersen—that it was two of the firm's own accountants who had pulled it off.

On August 26, a wire operator at Bank One glanced at a single sheet and began typing numbers into the computer.

From Account #1883757583.

An account in the name of Michael Kopper.

Routing instructions. Several numbers, directing the electronic system to send the money to J. P. Morgan Chase.

To Account #054-06029219.

An account in the name of Andrew and Lea Fastow.

Total funds to be wired: $481,850.

In a flash, almost half a million dollars zipped into the federal banking system. Within seconds, it appeared at J. P. Morgan Chase, ready to be credited to the Fastows.

The loan to Kopper for the wind-plant purchase had been repaid. In just over three months, the Fastows had received back the money they had fronted to the bogus investors in RADR, plus almost sixty-three thousand dollars in profit.

It was just the first in a steady stream of cash they would receive from the deal for years to come.

Ron Astin stared at the inch-thick document on his desk. It was September 4, 1997, and Enron had just sent over its latest draft of the Chewco private-placement memorandum. The document, which would be used to solicit investors, was loaded with the required arcane information so potential investors could make informed choices.

Astin had reviewed most of the details before; the first draft had landed back in July. This would be another structured-finance deal, meaning Enron only had to raise three percent of the total capital—in this case, still a hefty chunk of change, about eleven million dollars.

Turning the pages, Astin studied portions of the document marked in the margin with a straight black line, a designation by the word-processing program of a revision. One new entry took him aback.

A group of Enron executives, including Fastow, would be investors in Chewco. The intertwining of Chewco and Enron had always made Astin uncomfortable, but he signed off on it. But now Fastow was trying to make it a vehicle for personal profit. That went too far.

Astin didn't know it, but Fastow thought he had finally found a way around the accounting problems that had killed Alpine Investors. Chewco wasn't buying anything from Enron; Calpers was on the other side of the table. With the Chewco structure, Fastow and a few select colleagues would post a little cash and gain control of a quarter of a billion dollars in JEDI assets. Enron knew exactly what reserves JEDI owned; at this point the partnership was just clipping coupons, receiving a reliable stream of cash. The investors would be rich, with almost no risk.

But Enron, not Fastow, was Astin's client. And this deal looked bad for the company. He reached for the phone.

Four days later, on September 8, Fastow scowled as he and Kopper led a small cadre of lawyers to a conference room. He closed the door and slumped into a seat. The new Chewco documents had set off alarm bells at Vinson & Elkins, and now three lawyers—Astin, Joe Dilg, and Bob Baird—had marched over to Enron to air their concerns.

Even before coming over, the lawyers had raised the same arguments Fastow had heard before: executives couldn't be investors in their own companies' structured deals. That left Fastow burning. He hadn't *invented* the concept of special investments for insiders. Wall Street did it all the time. And Chewco wasn't even buying anything from Enron, for heaven's sake! What was the problem?

This time Fastow wasn't going to give up the money without a fight. His staff had called around to Wall Street firms and gathered information about their investment deals. He had also made sure to bring a few Enron lawyers along to the meeting—Mordaunt, Carol St. Clair, and Rex Rogers.

Fastow's expression oozed contempt as Astin spoke.

"As we told you earlier," Astin began, "this new provision allowing Enron employees to be investors has raised some serious concerns for us."

Fastow listened impassively.

"Now, no matter what is ultimately done here, there is one absolute," Astin continued. "Chewco cannot proceed in its current form unless Enron's senior management specifically approves of the inclusion of this provision."

Shaking his head, Fastow tossed up a hand. "Oh, come on, Ron. What, we have to drag in Lay and Skilling? What in the world is the big deal here?"

"It's a business issue, Andy. The timing and the form of this are not sound from a business perspective."

"It's got nothing to do with Enron!" Fastow snapped. "We're not negotiating with the company."

"That's not the problem, Andy," Astin said. "Look, the business units in Enron have a lot of rivalries. With your group getting special investment opportunities, that's only going to make that problem worse."

Fastow said nothing.

"But the most important element here is the substance," Astin continued. "This may trigger Enron's conflict-of-interest policy. And if it does, the board

has to approve it. You are an executive officer, and there are serious legal issues raised by that."

Astin suggested that Fastow's involvement in Chewco might even have to
be disclosed in Enron's financial statements. After several minutes, he finished
up. Fastow sat silent for a second, then leaned forward in his chair.

"You done?" he asked.

Before Astin responded, Fastow launched his rebuttal.

"Look, Ron, you guys are getting worked up over nothing. I mean, take
a look at Wall Street. A lot of investment banks have compensation plans that
let their best executives take equity interests in deals."

He poked his finger onto the table. "And damn it, Enron is not just some
pipeline company. We're like an investment bank. We do the same things. And
if investment banks can do this, there isn't a damn reason Enron can't."

Astin sat for a moment in the ensuing silence. Fastow's eruption had surprised him. The man clearly wasn't weighing all the issues here.

"Andy," he said, "Enron isn't an investment bank. It's an energy company.
And even if at the end of the day we decide that it's fine from a legal and
policy perspective, that doesn't change the fact that the board and the senior
management have to approve this."

Fastow didn't miss the message. If he was in the deal, the board had to get
involved.

"Look, Andy," Astin continued, "you might not be CFO of this company,
but you've sure taken on a lot of those responsibilities. Given your position,
you really need to think about how this kind of arrangement is going to affect this whole company. I know Chewco seems like a great opportunity, but
you've got to consider Enron's interest."

There was a long silence.

"I'll think about it," Fastow mumbled.

The solution was obvious. *Michael Kopper.*

When Fastow got knocked out of an official role in the wind deal, Kopper
had stepped into his place. He had proven reliable and trustworthy. He wasn't
an executive officer—the thing that seemed to bother the lawyers so much.
If Fastow couldn't manage Chewco without triggering problems, Kopper
was the ideal substitute.

But Astin had raised other concerns. It was clear he wasn't going to endorse
the involvement of Enron employees in Chewco unless Skilling or Lay approved. But that didn't worry Fastow. He knew how to speak Skilling's language.

A few days later, Fastow walked down the wide fiftieth-floor hallway past
a line of cubicles. Since Skilling's appointment as chief operating officer, he

had moved up to the top-floor executive suites. Fastow had called ahead, telling Skilling he wanted to bounce an idea off him.

Fastow breezed into the office, and Skilling broke into a smile; he seemed more energized than he had in years. The two wandered to the seating area on one side of the room.

"Okay," Skilling said. "What's up?"

"We've got an idea for how we can really do some great stuff for Calpers on JEDI."

Skilling smiled again. God, he loved Fastow. The guy was always finding new ways to get an edge.

"I'm intrigued," Skilling said. "What's the idea?"

"You know, we could get Michael to do this. I've talked to him, and he's willing to put together a deal."

Skilling nodded.

"He's willing to do it at a higher price than we could get if we sold it to a third party," Fastow continued.

"Why?"

"Two reasons. First, he doesn't have to do any due diligence. He knows the assets. If we try to find investors like General Electric or someplace like that, they're going to have to go through every single one of the assets."

"Mm-hmm."

"The engineering would be very expensive, because they have to figure out the geology, that kind of stuff. But Michael trusts the geologists we've already used, so there wouldn't be any money spent on that."

Skilling liked that idea. Enron was going to pick up the sale costs; this meant lower expenses for the company.

"And because he's so familiar with the assets," Fastow said, "he's not going to give us as high a discount rate as an investor like GE might."

Even better. The discount rate would be used to calculate the present value of JEDI's future cash flows. If Kopper was willing to use a lower discount rate, that meant a higher present value—and so a higher purchase price.

"So," Fastow said, "would you consider that?"

Skilling laughed. "Hey, Andy, if we can make Calpers more money that way, you bet."

Fastow nodded, hesitating for a second. "Listen, also, what would you think of my family investing in this? You know, the Weingartens, Lea's family?"

Skilling sat back and crinkled his nose. *Enron putting together family investments?* That felt kind of low-rent.

"I don't think so, Andy," Skilling replied. "That doesn't sound like something I want to be messing with."

The small pushback was all Fastow needed. "Fine, we won't do that," he said quickly.

Finishing up, the two men stood. Skilling slapped Fastow on the shoulder. "Sounds great, Andy," he said.

Banks provide loans, money that has to be paid back, with interest. Chewco needed equity, a third-party investment at risk of being lost. But equity from an independent investor meant the profits would have to be divvied up. That's why Fastow and Kopper wanted to get the money for Chewco from banks.

So how to finagle it so that loans looked like investments?

A proposal was floated with Barclays Bank, which had been involved in the original financing of JEDI: The bank would "invest" several million dollars in Chewco. Then Chewco would hire Barclays as a consultant, at a cost of one million dollars a year. If the bank injected five million into Chewco, the consulting agreement would last five years; if six, then six. On October 20, Barclays's operations committee met to discuss the idea. Every dime it put in, Barclays would get back. With its maximum potential loss at zero, Barclays thought it could classify the "investment" as a loan on its own books.

Then the accountants nixed the advisory fee idea. Without that tit for tat, Enron lost interest in the bank's consulting expertise. After all, what good was Barclays's advice if it didn't help manipulate the accounting?

Jordan Mintz, Enron's newest tax lawyer, plastered a fake smile on his face, trying to mask his loathing of Kopper. He barely knew the guy and couldn't stand him.

The Chewco deal had grown endlessly complicated, and Mintz had been brought in to review its tax consequences. As best he could tell, Enron needed to provide a tax indemnification to Chewco. Often, an entity like Chewco will be deemed to have reportable income—and be required to pay tax on it—before it actually receives the cash. So Mintz was crafting a document requiring Enron, in the event of such a timing mismatch, to advance Chewco the money. Then, when Chewco got its cash, it would repay the loan.

While the concept was simple, the details were complex, and Mintz asked a series of questions to make sure he had everything right. "Michael," he said, "I need to understand more about the full structure, the investors—"

"I can't do that," Kopper interrupted. "Enron doesn't have a right to know more. We're negotiating for Chewco, but it's behind a black curtain. You're not supposed to know what's there. That's what all the parties have agreed to."

Mintz took a breath. This was ridiculous; he was being asked to write up a legal document without having access to the necessary information. It was like being told to fly an airplane with his eyes closed.

He gave up on Kopper, but for the next few days Mintz nosed around the office, seeking information. While he picked up scraps, no one would say anything about Chewco's investors. There were intimations that the money was coming from wealthy Middle Easterners, but nobody volunteered details.

The more the secret eluded him, the more Mintz wondered: what was really hidden behind that black curtain?

The Chewco negotiations took on a through-the-looking-glass feel. Everybody at the bargaining table was from Enron, but it wasn't clear whether *anyone* solely represented the company's interests.

Kopper kept musing about his concerns for the Chewco investors. Bill Brown, a chief negotiator on behalf of the company, had believed Fastow would give him a chance to *be* a Chewco investor. Everyone knew conflicts were rampant, but no one seemed to understand where they all were.

Despite Fastow's suggestions, Brown took a tough line on Enron's behalf. By his calculation, Kopper wanted terms that could cost Enron millions of dollars. He fought them.

One day, after some tough haggling, he heard from Fastow.

"How are the talks going on Chewco?" Fastow asked.

"We're making some progress. It looks pretty good."

That sounded great, Fastow said. "I hear you've been negotiating pretty hard on this thing," he added.

Maybe a compliment was coming. "Well," Brown said, "that's my job. I just want to get a good deal for Enron."

"Yeah, I understand that. But we really need to close this deal. I mean, how far apart are we?"

Well, Brown replied, if Kopper got his way, he said, it could cost Enron as much as thirteen million dollars.

Fastow scoffed. "Come on, Bill, that's pocket change to Enron," he said. "And it hardly seems unreasonable, given the risks Chewco's investors are taking."

Something's not right. Fastow wanted to leave money on the table? Fastow, who fought for every dime in a deal?

"So," Brown said tentatively, "you're okay with us walking away from the thirteen million?"

"Yeah. Let's just get the deal done."

The discussion over, Brown got back to work. His exuberance over his progress on the Chewco deal was replaced by a cold apprehension. He couldn't shake the feeling that he had just been warned by Fastow to back off—a warning he figured he probably better keep in mind.

In a wooded enclave outside of San Antonio, children wedged into inner tubes floated lazily in a man-made river at the Hyatt Regency Hill Country Resort. Throughout the onetime ranch, visitors basked in luxury—swimming, golfing, or enjoying a fancy meal beneath a huge chandelier made of interwoven deer antlers.

It was November 5, 1997. For the second day the Hyatt was packed with senior Enron executives, there for the company's annual management conference. Lay viewed it as an opportunity for his hardworking executives to take a breather, to think about their jobs in a relaxed atmosphere, and maybe to come up with new ideas.

Somehow, though, the tensions of the office weren't so easy to shake off, particularly a new dispute between Jeff Skilling and Rebecca Mark. For weeks, Mark had been negotiating what she thought would be a breakthrough deal, a sale of a 50 percent interest in Enron's international deals to Shell. A Shell executive had presented Lay with a three-billion-dollar bid, but Lay and Skilling shot it down. Lay thought the number too small, and Skilling didn't believe it was real. All Shell wanted, he argued, was the trading rights in the regions where Enron had plants. He wasn't about to let a competitor stick its nose into his tent, not on some bogus offer.

Then, weeks later, Skilling and Lay had come back with a proposal that had stunned Mark and her team: they wanted international, which now was responsible for development outside North America, to hand over their projects in most of Europe to the trading division.

Lay found the reasoning persuasive. Skilling and the traders were trying to move into Europe and set up trading arrangements with the utilities. But those potential customers still saw Enron as a competitor because of its international power plants. Turning those over to Skilling's group would allow Enron to gain entrée into those markets and eliminate a threat to potential customers' business.

After weeks of discussion, the final issues were hashed out at a meeting in the hotel's Bandera room. Skilling—along with Mark Frevert, head of trading in London, and his deputy, Dan McCarty—sat with Lay at the conference table. For about twenty minutes, they explained their plans for opening offices in places like Frankfurt.

As the discussion was wrapping up, Rebecca Mark and her deputy, Joe Sutton, were hustling down a hallway to the meeting. When they had first heard of the proposal from Lay two weeks before, they had mobilized the entire division to put together a report against the plan. Their argument was basic: Outside of a few pockets, the energy businesses in Europe and the United States were nothing alike. Enron could not easily secure supplies of gas or electricity. There were entrenched and government-protected utilities and pipelines, with few players there to buy from and trade with on any meaningful level. That, the report said, left plant development as the only reliable way into Europe.

Mark and Sutton reached the Bandera room and pushed inside. Lay, Skilling, and the two London executives looked up. The international executives stopped at the edge of the table and started passing out their report.

"Okay, let's go through our analysis," Mark said.

Skilling glanced through the bound report. "We don't need this," he said. "We've reached a decision."

She stared Lay in the eye. "Ken, you need to see this report. You need to understand what this market is about."

Lay had heard all the arguments before. "We already reviewed all this material," he replied.

"So what's the conclusion?" she snapped.

"Well," Lay replied, "it seems pretty obvious that we need to move the European assets into ECT."

The room exploded.

"That's ridiculous!" Sutton shouted.

Mark shot a look at Frevert. He was a short, overweight man, his face red. She looked back to Lay as she raised her arm to point at Frevert.

"You think that *that* can do a better job in this marketplace than me and my people?" she snapped.

Frevert said nothing. He glanced up at Mark, hatred in his eyes. Skilling sat back, taking silent delight in what was unfolding. He knew Mark was sinking herself.

"We've been in Europe for years," Sutton chimed in. "These people don't know what they're doing!"

This makes no sense, Mark thought. She knew the European markets; she knew there wasn't a lot of room for trading profits. She looked at Skilling and the traders.

"Where are your numbers from?" she asked sharply. "You say you've got trading profits. But we know you've been selling bits and pieces of assets. How much are you earning from trading and how much from just asset sales?"

The response was calm: virtually all from trading.

Mark leaned into the table. "Show us."

"We don't need to do that," Skilling said.

"There's no way that you're making money in trading," Mark snapped. "And without assets on the ground, there's no way you can keep making money in Europe."

The arguments came back fast. *The utilities. Competition with customers. The trading possibilities.*

Sutton turned and threw his briefing book down the table. It smashed against the wall with a thud.

"This is ridiculous!" he shouted.

He headed to the door. He turned before walking out.

"Rebecca, are you coming with me?"

Mark followed Sutton to the doorway. There, she turned and looked at the assembled executives with disgust.

"This is a complete waste of our time," she said, her voice icy. "You're going to run this business however you want, and there's no point in us talking about it."

She looked straight at Lay. "But if this is the way it's going to be, we've got to talk about the contract."

The contract. Lay knew instantly what she meant. The compensation agreement with international. If the developers lost Europe, it was a change in their contract; they would have to be paid a lot to get them to agree.

Mark followed Sutton out the door, furious. *First they shoot down Shell, now they take Europe away,* she thought. They just wanted her assets, so they could sell them and make it look like trading profits. She was certain of it.

Back in the Bandera room, Frevert was speaking to Lay.

"This is what we've been facing for the last two years, Ken," he said.

Skilling joined in. "It's what I've been saying, Ken. This is what we're dealing with."

Lay looked appalled at what he had witnessed.

"Guys, I apologize for what just happened," he said, looking contemplative. "We have got to get this fixed."

Ray Bowen was quitting. He was sick of Enron's retail division, sick of the mismanagement and silliness. Nobody wanted to consider the numbers, but the numbers never changed. The whole place was chaos, and he wanted out.

When word got around that Bowen was lining up another job, Skilling met with him. He heard him out on his concerns, then told him that Enron didn't want him to leave. If he wasn't happy in retail, they would find him something else. Fastow was going like gangbusters in finance—maybe Bowen might consider working there? Bowen agreed to meet with his old boss to see if there was a role for him.

Bowen went to Fastow's office, laying out his frustrations with retail.

"Ray, I'd really encourage you to stay," Fastow replied. "You can reinvent yourself here, start again in the same building. I mean, look at me. When I was leaving retail, I thought I had destroyed my career. But Skilling put me somewhere else, and things have been going great."

Wander through the division, Fastow suggested. Learn what people were doing. Bowen agreed and found the finance division an exciting place. Around the hallways he heard about its deals; in particular, one called RADR had almost a mythic reputation. Bowen didn't quite understand the deal; it had something to do with buying wind farms. But to hear the hallway chatter, it was brilliant.

"We're going to have lots of future opportunities to do deals using the RADR approach," Kopper told him.

Bowen's interest was piqued. In late November, Fastow got back to him with a proposal. He had this new group, Fastow said, that was doing a lot of great things, and he wanted Bowen to be the co-head, alongside Michael Kopper.

It was called portfolio management, he said. But around the office, most people knew it by another name: the special-projects group.

Barclays Bank thought it had finally found the answer, a way to provide a loan that Chewco could pretend was an investment. All that was needed was for Chewco to guarantee partial repayment.

On November 20, George McKean, an associate at Barclays, put together a letter to Kopper and Bill Brown spelling out the idea. The last bit of cash going into Chewco would be used to set up "reserve accounts." That would secure Barclays's money in the deal, regardless of the effect it might have on the accounting.

Enron didn't have much choice; because of demands from Calpers, Chewco had purchased its interest in JEDI on November 6, relying on short-term bank loans guaranteed by Enron. If Chewco didn't pull together final financing by year-end—without an Enron guarantee—then JEDI could no longer be off balance sheet. All its debt, financial performance, everything, would come onto Enron's books.

The job of drafting the new deal was shuttled to Vinson & Elkins. There, in mid-December, a young associate named Joel Ephross drafted a "side letter" establishing the reserve accounts. Then Enron and Chewco reached another agreement, providing that the accounts would be funded with an immediate six-million-dollar JEDI distribution from the sale of an asset. The letter, signed by an executive named Jeremy Blachman for Enron and by Michael Kopper for Chewco, was placed in a massive pile of closing documents.

But somehow, no one bothered to explicitly consult Andersen accountants about the reserve agreement. It would be years before they discovered the document.

High above Fannin Street, Kopper wandered from room to room in the plush offices of Vinson & Elkins—asking questions, barking orders, occasionally nibbling some of the food piled on side tables. His usual crisp appearance had wilted long ago. His eyes were glassy and red-rimmed, his hair wild. Around him, the rooms swarmed with people. Charcoal gray legions of lawyers and bankers dashed about, buzzing with their assignments, drinking in the excitement.

It was late on the evening of December 30, a Tuesday. Enron was proceeding with the closing for the deals related to JEDI and the creation of JEDI II. Conference tables in multiple rooms were stacked with documents undergoing one last review before the final signatures.

There were so many transactions being wrapped up that night nobody could completely keep up with everything. The financing of Chewco. Calpers's investment in JEDI II. Then a near-simultaneous sale of almost seven percent of retail—now known as Enron Energy Services—to JEDI II and the Ontario Teachers' Pension Plan, in exchange for commitments to eventually pay a combined total of $165 million.

Time and again, lawyers glanced at a document that laid out the side agreement between Chewco and Barclays. It seemed innocuous enough. Certainly, there were no typos. No red flags leaped out. Every reviewer flipped the page.

Kopper wandered into one of the conference rooms, watching the hordes of lawyers. "Okay, what's going on here?" he called out. "Where are we on the documents?"

Jordan Mintz glanced up at Kopper and was shocked. He looked like a zombie. Mintz walked over to him.

"Hey, Michael, you okay? You don't look so good."

Kopper glanced over Mintz's shoulder, watching the lawyers work with the documents.

"Yeah," he said. "I've been up for two days."

Two days without sleep? That seemed a little extreme.

"Well, don't worry, Michael," Mintz said. "Everybody's got this under control. We're getting it done."

Kopper stared at Mintz for a second. "Okay," he said.

Then he walked away.

Late that night, the documents were finally signed. And when all was said and done, most people in the room still didn't know the identities of the independent investors who had put up more than $11 million for Chewco.

No wonder. In truth, they didn't really exist.

Chewco was the financial equivalent of a stack of Russian nesting dolls, a hollow figurine hiding smaller and smaller versions of itself inside. As one by one they were cast away, only a single figure remained: Michael Kopper.

In its final structure, the largest figurine was Chewco, which, to be counted as separate from Enron, had to obtain three percent of its capital, or about $11.5 million, from independent sources. Inside Chewco, two entities supposedly provided the money, SONR 1 and Big River Funding. SONR injected $115,000—just one percent of required "equity"—with money from Kopper, who obtained it from his profits in RADR, the illegal wind deal.

The rest of the cash, $11.4 million, came from Big River—the next hollow figurine. Big River obtained north of eleven million dollars from Barclays Bank. Kopper treated the cash as an investment; Barclays recorded it as a loan. But Big River was another special-purpose entity, meaning it had to find three percent of its capital—more than $300,000—from outside sources.

That money came from the next, smaller figurine—Little River Funding, another special-purpose entity. Little River again borrowed 97 percent of its cash from Barclays but, to remain independent, also had to obtain 3 percent—now down to about $10,000—from an independent source. Kopper provided that cash.

Using the multiple special-purpose entities, Kopper had purchased three percent of one vehicle, which owned 3 percent of another, which owned three percent of another, which owned half of JEDI. All for $10,000, along with the $115,000 kicked in to SONR.

Before it was all over, Kopper decided that his ownership of Little River Funding might threaten Chewco's accounting. Because of Fastow's experience, Kopper already knew an investment from a relative wouldn't work. So instead, he transferred his holdings in Little River to Bill Dodson, a man he knew well. Dodson wasn't family; he wasn't a spouse. He was Kopper's live-in lover.

Every element of the deal was hardwired; Kopper and Dodson couldn't possibly lose. Not even their relatively paltry $125,000 investment was at risk.

Within seconds of making the investment, they received a management fee from Chewco of more than $140,000—an immediate return of all of their capital, plus a ten percent profit. And they still retained ownership of the entity.

But the Chewco deal created an issue for Kopper and Fastow. With RADR, Fastow had been the big financial winner. Kopper had come out in the best position on Chewco. There were going to be plenty of future deals, plenty of opportunities to even up the books. But somebody needed to keep score, to make sure things eventually balanced out.

The job went to Kopper. Fastow instructed him to start a running tally of who had earned what off of their side deals—and keep it on his personal laptop. This wasn't the kind of data that should appear on Enron's computer system.

After the holiday financial rush, everyone could finally relax. Work at Enron was always a fire drill at year-end as deals to help the company make its numbers raced through. But, still, 1997—with Chewco, JEDI II, and the sale of seven percent of EES—was a standout.

Staffers sent around jokes, congratulating themselves on their achievement. "Top 10 Reasons Why We Thought It Was a Good Idea for You to Spend Your Christmas Holidays and Year End with Us," one parody read. Number nine: "Making sure that Enron hits its earnings targets."

Over the weeks that followed, Enron assembled its final numbers for the year, and executives liked what they saw. More than half a billion in profits—*half a billion*.

But there were some problems. First, there was this international deal called J-Block. Despite its bad experience with take-or-pay contracts, Enron had entered into one early in the decade to buy gas for its power plant in Teesside, England. The international team was sure gas prices would rise; they fell, leaving Enron in the hole for billions. Skilling had settled that problem earlier in the year, costing the company $450 million after taxes.

Then there was MTBE. After years of trying, Enron had pushed MTBE onto mark-to-market accounting. But then the government changed the rules on the fuel additive. Enron shut down the business, costing another $74 million after taxes.

That left $105 million. But there were more squirrelly numbers. Enron had included the $51 million in profits from the Bonneville Power contract, even though Andersen said it shouldn't. Without it, the annual profits would have been just $49 million.

That amount contained the sale of the seven percent stake in EES. And *that* deal was done in exchange for a *commitment* to pay, not for cash up front.

Still, Enron reported the whole thing—$61 million. Under proper accounting, only $20 million should have been reported.

With all the errors, omissions, and bad business decisions excluded, Enron's total earnings for 1997 should have been $8 million, on $20 billion in reported revenue.

The evidence of trouble at Enron was there for anyone to see—anyone, that is, who could figure out the real numbers.

Kopper bent his knees as he glanced at the golf ball resting on a tee near his feet. He shot a look down the fairway for the fifteenth hole on a course at Sugar Creek Country Club. In a single effortless motion, he brought his arms back and swung. The ball soared away.

Behind him, Ray Bowen, his colleague from Enron, watched with envy as the ball sailed into an ideal position. Bowen wasn't much of a golfer and had been whacking the ball all over the place that day. But he could appreciate athletic skill when he saw it.

"Very nice," he said.

Kopper looked at him, his face confident. "Thanks."

It was January 1998, and the two men were taking time to get to know each other. Now that they were the co-heads of special projects, they needed to establish a rapport.

They climbed into the golf cart, heading after their balls. In the driver's seat Kopper looked relaxed, dressed in slacks and a sweater. The two rode in silence until they had the course to themselves.

"You know, Ray," Kopper said suddenly, "you can make a lot of money at Enron working for Andy."

Bowen glanced over at Kopper. He had already heard the rumors swirling around the office, something about Kopper snagging a piece of Chewco with Fastow's permission.

"Yeah?" Bowen said.

"Yeah. Andy will really take care of you. He's done that with me."

Bowen's expression didn't change. "Yeah, I'm kind of aware of that. I've heard the rumors."

Kopper kept his eyes on the fairway. "Yeah, there's stuff available. Stuff on the side. You can make money a lot of ways. You just have to ask for it."

Was this some kind of test? If Kopper was fishing, Bowen didn't want to take the bait.

"I'm just not sure that's the right kind of thing for me," he said. "I don't want to be too beholden to one person, even Andy. I'm not too interested in doing the kind of things I think you just did in Chewco."

Kopper went silent, driving the cart forward.

"Okay," he said finally. "Where's your ball?"

On Monday they were back at Enron as co-heads of special projects, but not much work was sent Bowen's way. Weeks later, word came down from Fastow. Maybe special projects wasn't right for Bowen. He was moved out to work somewhere else.

Whatever the test at golf had been, Bowen had failed. Now the hunt was on for others willing to pass.

CHAPTER 7

THE SIXTH FLOOR OF the SEC's Washington headquarters had a leaden, functional air, just anonymous office space in an uninviting government building. Elevators on either side of the H-shaped complex led to hallways of somber disposition; when office doors were closed, not a single window to the outside world could be seen.

But here, amid the austere decor, American capitalism was regulated and restrained by a cadre of government officials whose judgments could mean wealth or ruin. Every day, top lawyers and accountants bustled in and out, hoping to catch the ear of the man who ruled this realm: Arthur Levitt, the SEC chairman.

Levitt—tall and white-haired, with a talent for making those who met him feel privy to a special secret—was in his sixth year as chairman. A mix of Wall Street and Main Street, he was a wealthy former stockbroker who hobnobbed with the financial industry's leaders but never lost sight of his modest Brooklyn roots.

In earlier years, Levitt had struck colleagues as happy-go-lucky, maybe at times a bit facile. But as SEC chairman, he had emerged as an articulate advocate for small investors. To some in business, his style was too hard-charging, too confrontational. But among the mom-and-pop investors with trillions in the markets, his was a singular dedication to their interests—championing investor education while checking some of Wall Street's abuses.

Now, in early 1998, Levitt's next battle was looming. The Internet boom had created a casino marketplace for stocks—frothy, exuberant, unreasonable. Signs of decay were evident. Reported profits were getting squishy, twisted, perhaps meaningless. Companies were playing games, manipulating the rules to present numbers that had little basis in reality. With easy money rolling in, investors were more than willing to turn a blind eye to the shenanigans spreading through corporate boardrooms.

It all began before Levitt took the SEC job, as a stratagem for corporations to lavish riches on top executives without reporting the costs. Corporate America had discovered the magic of a new currency—stock options, which gave their owners the right to buy shares at a preset price. The accounting rule setters wanted the options to reflect reality. After all, the argument went, they had value and involved costs to shareholders; when an executive used the option to buy—and then sell—stock, investors lost part of their ownership in the company. But executives knew expensing options meant lower profits, possibly jeopardizing the carefully constructed gravy train.

So corporate America fought back, recruiting members of Congress to take on the SEC and the standard setters at the Financial Accounting Standards Board. Charging options as expenses would drive down stock prices, they said—a point Levitt found bizarre, since any cost would do that. But in the face of congressional wrath, Levitt, to his lasting regret, told FASB to back off. He'd had some success since then, but was losing the accounting wars—and knew it. His accounting experts wanted him to launch a new front, but he wasn't quite sure how to do it.

Levitt stepped off the north elevator onto the sixth floor. He passed photographs of outdoor adventures—river rafting, mountain climbing—shot on Outward Bound trips he sponsored. He stepped into his office. Outside, he could see the red facade of the National Building Museum; to the right, the Capitol dome gleamed in the distance.

Levitt noticed the two large computer screens on the credenza behind his desk. Something was different; the familiar screen saver was gone. In its place, words of varying sizes bounced back and forth. Levitt moved closer, squinting until the words came into focus. He smiled.

ACCOUNTING. ACCOUNTING. ACCOUNTING.

His staff was lobbying him again. Grab the accounting issue, they were urging, get ahead of it. Out there, right now, were companies on the path to destruction, because accounting standards had collapsed. They knew it. *He* knew it. But for now Levitt had no idea which companies they might be.

At Andersen's Chicago headquarters, John Stewart sat at his desk, preparing to do battle over Enron. As the top member of the firm's Professional Standards Group, or PSG, Stewart was Andersen's star analyst on generally accepted accounting principles, or GAAP, the rules applied by every American corporation in reporting financial performance.

Now, having read Enron's latest filings, Stewart believed the company was violating the rules—with Andersen's knowledge. He had noticed one of the games pumping up the numbers: the sale of seven percent of retail had created sixty-one million dollars in profits over three years. But Andersen was allowing it all to be booked as 1997 income, even though only twenty million dollars had been paid. It was wrong.

Stewart fired up his computer. He popped open a new e-mail, typing in the address for Patty Grutzmacher, who worked on the Enron account in Houston. He typed the issues that had been raised, then gave his opinion.

"I do not agree that Enron can book all the gain up front," Stewart typed. "The SEC is clear on this point." He hit the "send" button.

Nothing would change. Enron had already told the public about the income. Andersen certainly wasn't going to force the company to turn around and tell the world that its reported profits were nothing more than phantoms.

The public image of Enron and the reality of its operations were diverging more each day—and not just because of accounting gimmicks.

Enron was becoming a virtual cult of creativity, often placing swagger over substance. New ideas were celebrated for their newness, for their potential; tried-and-true businesses like the pipelines were almost derided. This was a company where a thousand flowers bloomed, where the only impediment to pursuing a new project was initiative. The usual controls—expense limits, financing constraints—vanished. First-class travel became a standard, except for those who relied on the growing fleet of corporate jets. Everything—flat-screen monitors, computers, pads of paper—was purchased with no centralized control.

Worse, Enron was diversifying into business after business with no unifying strategy. By 1998, it was operating pipelines and international power plants. It was trading gas and electricity. It was managing energy needs of commercial customers and providing electricity to small consumers through retail. It was starting to dabble in the water business. Portland was building its Internet network, while London was secretly constructing an automated energy-trading system. Houston was creating and trading financial derivatives to protect customers from the business effects of bad weather. Enron was becoming anything and everything.

At the same time, it was beginning to operate like an investment fund, purchasing stakes in companies on the public and the private markets. These "merchant investments" were often in fields far from Enron's expertise, like high-tech. Executives who found investments—particularly deals that brought quick profits—were virtually guaranteed fat bonuses. There were no rewards for holding down costs.

Enron's buying spree mirrored events in the marketplace. The dot-com boom was pushing stock prices beyond reason. The eye-glazing basics were no longer the backbone of investing; if a stock price climbed because other investors believed, that was good enough.

So began the twisted interplay between Enron and the market. As prices rose, so did asset values, including for many of the company's merchant investments. With mark-to-market accounting, those increases translated into reported profits. So long as markets kept climbing, Enron could do no wrong. It was bathed in an aura of infallibility.

Still, with so much of the reported profits tied to mark-to-market accounting, Enron brought in comparatively little actual cash, the commodity desperately needed to pay for all of the spending and new businesses. Fastow's group filled the gap. Ever more complex ways of borrowing were assembled. Bank loans were structured to look like gas trades, known as prepays, and were reported as operating cash flow. Off-books deals were assembled to funnel in other money from banks and outside lenders. Even the tax department got involved, structuring deals that created future tax benefits, which Enron claimed all up front.

The setup was unsustainable. Enron's heavy spending for everything—fat salaries and bonuses, new businesses, parties at Planet Hollywood—came, in large part, from borrowed cash. Enron was getting deeper into a hole, betting on a conviction that the marketplace would keep rising. And then, when it did, going double or nothing.

Blocks from the White House, Skilling hustled down I Street. It was January 29, 1998, and he had been in Washington since the night before, schmoozing with members of Congress and energy regulators. But the most important meeting was coming up: he was about to interview a person who might be Enron's next chief financial officer.

In Kinder's last months, he had served as his own CFO, but now Enron had no one in the position. The CFO managed the balance sheet, made sure the credit rating stayed high, lined up cash for operations, and dealt with accounting. Fastow had picked up most of those responsibilities, with Causey taking the accounting role. But truthfully, Fastow was a deal guy. Neither Lay nor Skilling thought he had the chops to be CFO. So Enron had hired a headhunting firm, Spencer Stuart, to find someone qualified.

So far, none of the candidates had wowed Skilling. But Denise Boutross McGlone, the woman he was meeting today, was supposed to be something special. She was CFO at Sallie Mae, the quasi-governmental body in the education-loan business. McGlone knew complex financings and could oversee a multibillion-dollar portfolio, all talents Enron needed.

Skilling reached 1775 I Street and went up to suite 800, Enron's Washington headquarters. After greeting everyone, he was escorted to an office. Soon after, McGlone arrived. She was all energy, with a direct, self-confident manner.

"I really appreciate you coming here," Skilling said. "Were you surprised by the call?"

"No, not surprised," McGlone said as she sat. "I've heard of Enron and what it does. Seems pretty impressive."

They spoke for forty-five minutes. McGlone hit Skilling with rapid-fire, insightful questions. Skilling was impressed; she had clearly done her homework.

Gee, this is fun, Skilling thought. "All right," he said. "Do you think you have an interest in Enron?"

McGlone nodded. "Yes. I'm not sure Houston is a good fit, but the company sounds very interesting."

"Well, listen, I'm going to talk to Ken Lay. We'll get back to you and let you know how we're going to proceed."

"Fine," she said, standing. "Thank you very much for meeting with me."

Skilling watched McGlone make her exit. In a flash he was on the phone, dialing Lay's number. He wanted to let him know that Enron may have found its next CFO.

Fastow was stunned. *Enron's credit rating was about to be downgraded.*

This was the worst possible timing. He knew Skilling and Lay were hunting for a CFO, and he desperately wanted the job. If Enron's credit rating dropped from investment grade to near junk—if it was deemed less worthy of lenders' trust—that hope would die. Enron would be charged more for loans, its profits would fall, other traders would be less likely to do business. Fastow was sure to be blamed.

"Holy shit," he told a colleague. "I'm about to be CFO and we're about to be downgraded. *That* doesn't work."

Fastow fumed, blaming the problem on Bill Gathmann, Enron's treasurer. That work, he thought, was the boring stuff—managing cash, maintaining bank relations, visiting rating agencies. Careers were made on high-flying deals, not by babysitting bean counters. So he left those details to Gathmann. Now that decision could cost him the promotion.

Fastow found out that Gathmann had taken numbers to New York before they had been prettied up. All the tweaks—the deals that made things look better—were missing. Looking at the raw numbers, Moody's Investors Service had gone berserk; Enron, they concluded, wasn't generating enough cash to pay the interest on its debt.

Enron had just twenty-four hours, then Moody's would announce its downgrade. Fastow called an emergency meeting of his best credit people, trying to forestall disaster. He looked around the room desperately.

"Listen," he said, "I'm not a good credit guy. I don't know how to do this."

Pages of raw financial data were brought in and passed around; it was the first time most people in the room had seen the numbers. Enron had a lot more debt than it reported. Masking borrowings could be done legally, but Enron seemed reckless in its use of those methods. It was almost as if Fastow believed off-balance-sheet debt didn't exist. But it did, and there was too much of it, more than Enron's cash flow could comfortably support. Now that the numbers had been laid out so clearly for Moody's, the problem had to be fixed.

Ray Bowen went to the whiteboard and gave Fastow a quick lesson on credit. At each step, Fastow asked questions about fundamental issues. *Is this guy for real?* Bowen wondered. How could someone making a play for the CFO job have such a fuzzy understanding of the basics? It was like teaching introductory swimming to the new lifeguard.

Bowen cut to the chase.

"Andy," he said, "it probably wouldn't hurt to put in more equity." Enron needed to sell stock and use the money raised to pay down debt. This wasn't rocket science.

Still, Fastow reacted as if some deep secret had been revealed. "Yeah," he said. "But Skilling's never going to issue equity at this point."

Bowen laughed. "He will if he wants to keep this company's credit rating at investment grade."

Fastow hatched a plan. Gathmann would be blamed. Enron would commit to bringing in a new treasurer and raising more equity. That day, Fastow made the pitch, and Moody's bought it. With some fast work, he had sidestepped the event that should have wrecked his career.

The half-dozen executives and accountants from Andersen and Enron laughed and joked as they played a round of golf on a private Arizona course. Every year they put together a game at some of the better Arizona courses when Enron held its management conference there. But during this round there was more than usual on the agenda.

"Listen," Rick Causey told the assembled Andersen accountants, "we need to talk about Carl Bass."

Days later, Bass looked up at his colleague Tom Bauer, disbelief etched on his face. "They think I'm too *rule-oriented*?" he repeated. "Tom, I'm an accountant!"

Bauer was sympathetic. None of this was his idea. Causey and the accountants in Enron's trading group wanted Bass gone. Bauer had been selected to let him know.

"I understand, Carl," he said. "But they've got this perception." Enron thought Bass didn't try hard to come up with creative answers, Bauer said. So Andersen was going to move him out of trading and over to international.

Bass's face was tight. Not long ago, he had fought to stop Enron from booking fifty-one million dollars in bogus earnings, and they'd run him over. Now they were pushing him aside.

"This is wrong," he muttered.

Fastow's eyes narrowed as he stared at Skilling.

"Are you fucking kidding me?" he barked.

"Now, Andy—"

"No!" Fastow said, holding up his hands. "No."

He shook his head. "I can't fucking believe this."

It was 1:30 in the afternoon on March 2. The front-runner for the CFO job, Denise McGlone, was flying to Houston the next day to meet with senior management. Among them was Fastow, and Skilling had just let him know.

"Listen, Andy—" Skilling began.

"Why wouldn't I be CFO?" Fastow interrupted. "Is there anything I haven't achieved that I should have?"

"Andy, look, it's the obligation of the board to turn over every stone. I think you have a good shot at being CFO, but we need to look at the alternatives."

Fastow looked away. "Goddamn it."

His jaw clenched. "Fine," he said. "I'll do what you want."

Then he walked out.

The next morning at eight, Skilling turned his gray Mercedes 500 SE onto the drive of the Four Seasons Hotel downtown. McGlone, waiting just outside, climbed in.

"Hey, Denise, good morning!" Skilling said.

"Morning, Jeff," McGlone responded.

Skilling turned left onto Lamar Street, heading toward Enron's offices. Already something didn't feel right. McGlone was reserved, almost pensive. Maybe, Skilling thought, she was just nervous about the day's meetings.

"Have a good trip down?" Skilling asked.

"Oh yes, it was fine."

Silence. "Okay, well, you'll be starting out the morning meeting with Rick Causey," Skilling began.

The rest of the day would be busy, with McGlone visiting a new department about every hour. Then, for dinner, Skilling and Lay planned to take her and her husband to a Houston hot spot called Café Annie.

Skilling parked at the Allen Center Garage and escorted McGlone over to the Enron building.

"How can you do this, Jeff?" Fastow demanded. "I trusted you. I thought we were in this business together!"

It was ten o'clock that morning. Fastow had made a last-minute appointment with Skilling and now was almost pleading for the CFO job. This was a personal betrayal of Andy Fastow by Jeff Skilling, he said. How, he asked, could Skilling do it? Skilling listened, surprised at the desperation. Fastow didn't seem the type to beg for a job.

After Fastow said his piece, Skilling went to find Lay. Weeks before, he had told Lay that Fastow would never leave Enron if he was passed over. Now he wasn't so sure.

Word came back fast on Denise McGlone: *huh?*

Somehow, the dynamo that Skilling—and, after him, Lay—had met on the East Coast had become a milquetoast in Houston. Causey and Fastow came away believing Enron intimidated her—or at least they told Skilling that.

By early afternoon, when Skilling met with her again, McGlone had already fallen back in the pack as far as he was concerned. She seemed subdued; clearly, something about Enron was bothering her. After she left for her next meeting, he went for another visit with Lay.

"Boy," Skilling said, dropping in a chair, "that was just a totally different Denise than I saw in Washington."

Lay nodded. "Yeah, me, too. Totally different."

This wasn't going to work, they agreed. They needed somebody dynamic. There was still their number-two candidate—Ron Hulme, a McKinsey consultant. But if Hulme said no, Fastow was the only choice left.

Two days later, March 5, Skilling was leafing through a document on his desk. It was a deal-approval sheet—or DASH—seeking authorization for executives in Portland to make a relatively small, ten-million-dollar investment in an Internet start-up called Rhythms NetConnections.

For its money, Enron would own ten percent of Rhythms, a high-speed Internet data-transport company. The return was estimated at about 19 percent per year, with Enron holding the stake until 2003. Skilling flipped to the back. A sticker marked where he needed to sign. His subordinates had already given approvals. Not a lot at risk here. Skilling signed his name and wrote in the date.

The next bomb was ticking.

By early the next week, things had gotten tight. Fastow was grumbling about quitting. Skilling was preparing to take his kids on a vacation. He wanted the CFO search resolved. He talked it over with Lay and put together a plan. Skilling called up Hulme and asked him to come over.

Hulme arrived that afternoon in Skilling's office. The time had come for an answer, Skilling said.

"Look, I'm leaving soon for spring break with the kids, and Andy's about to quit," Skilling said. "If you want the CFO job, it's yours. If not, I've gotta give it to Andy or else I'm gonna lose the guy."

"Well, Jeff," Hulme said, "I appreciate the offer . . ."

That was all Skilling needed to hear. Hulme didn't want it. Fastow would be Enron's CFO. The decision was made.

That evening, Fastow picked up the receiver on his home phone. "Hello?"

"Andy," he heard Skilling say. "Ken, I, and the board would like to offer you the job as CFO of Enron."

Fastow sighed in relief as the news sank in.

"Jeff," he said, "I'd be proud to accept the job."

The next morning, Lay was in his office, getting ready to leave for a ten o'clock flight. Fastow appeared, tapping on the door. Lay broke into a smile and walked toward him.

"Andy!" he said.

Fastow beamed, shaking Lay's hand. "Ken," he said, "I just wanted to thank you and the board for placing so much confidence in me. I'm not going to disappoint you."

"Well, Andy, we became convinced after looking at the other candidates that you were the best choice. I'm sure you'll do a great job, and I'm delighted it worked out."

Lay promised that he would put out an announcement the following day, making everything official. Causey, of course, would continue handling the accounting side. And Skilling had decided to name Rick Buy as chief risk officer. All three announcements, Lay said, would be issued at the same time. Fastow thanked Lay again and left.

With that, the top financial job at one of the nation's largest companies was in the hands of a criminal.

The e-mail hit the system at 5:30 the next afternoon.

"As Enron's finance and capital related activities increase in complexity," it began. Around the building, eyes zipped down computer screens. Fastow, CFO. Causey, top accounting guy. Buy, chief risk officer.

Back in finance, there were congratulations for Fastow. But when he wasn't within earshot, the gossip took a sharp turn. *Andy Fastow? As CFO? What was up with that?*

Shirley Hudler, who worked on the JEDI partnership, was stunned. She had worked with CFOs at other companies, and Fastow was no CFO. He was a terrible manager. He wasn't particularly smart. He didn't know accounting, treasury operations, nothing. He had done some fancy structured transactions, but that made him a deal guy, not a CFO.

Then Hudler had a thought. Was this some sort of salvage operation to undo the damage to Fastow's reputation from his retail flameout? Nothing else made any sense.

How else could they name someone so unqualified to such an important job?

Vince Kaminski stared at the e-mail on his computer screen. What were they thinking? Selecting Andy Fastow—*Andy Fastow!*—was bad enough. Still, there was only so much damage an incompetent CFO could inflict. But *Rick Buy as Enron's new chief risk officer?*

How could they name someone so unqualified to such an important job?

Kaminski, Enron's top risk analyst, considered Buy a nice enough guy—but that was the problem. The chief risk officer had to go to the mat to stop bad ideas. That wasn't Buy. He wasn't confrontational, wouldn't get in people's faces. He'd already let a lot of lousy merchant investments slide by. He sure wasn't going to grow a backbone now.

He didn't even have the background for the job. An engineer by training, Buy was all about systems and organization. That was fine when he ran Enron's credit analysis, assessing the finances of business partners. But that was arithmetic; risk analysis was calculus. Kaminski was sure this was a disaster in the making.

Not much later, Kaminski was at his desk in his twenty-ninth-floor office when Buy wandered in.

"Hey, Vince."

Kaminski smiled. "Rick, congratulations on your promotion," he said in a thick Polish accent. Whatever his thoughts, Kaminski was a model of civility.

"Thanks," Buy replied. "But now that I'm chief risk officer, I think I need to buck up my understanding of options. Could someone go over option pricing with me?"

Buy didn't understand options pricing? In the complex world of derivatives where Enron did business, options were rudimentary. A chief risk officer was supposed to be at the top of his field, the guy everyone turned to for the answers, not someone who required on-the-job training.

Kaminski hid his horror behind a smile. "No problem," he said. "I'll arrange a few sessions for you."

For the tutoring, Kaminski recruited Stinson Gibner, one of his best risk analysts. A day later, Kaminski and Gibner headed to the conference room near Buy's office for the first lesson. Buy's questions were surprisingly basic, so Gibner kept dialing back the sophistication. Finally, Gibner was reduced to scribbling down the definitions for the general lingo of options trading on a whiteboard.

A "put" is . . . A "call" is . . .

After about half an hour, Buy stood. "This has been helpful," he said. "But I've got another appointment. Can we get together another time?"

Some time later, they gathered for the next lesson. Gibner picked up where he left off. After a moment, Buy held up a hand. "I'm sorry, I know we talked about this already," he said. "But I need to go over it again."

Gibner glanced at Kaminski, who showed no reaction. He turned back to the whiteboard and started writing.

A "put" is . . . A "call" is . . .

It was, by any standard, an unusual first date.

They went to a friend's wedding, arriving separately so their colleagues from Enron attending the event wouldn't gossip. At the wedding's end, Skilling and Rebecca Carter each slipped out alone, agreeing to meet later over dinner.

Skilling's divorce had gone through, and he had been feeling lonely. With most of his time spent at the office, it was unlikely he would find romance outside of Enron. Soon he began focusing attention on Carter, an Enron veteran who had held a range of positions at the company.

She grew up Rebecca Comeau in a strict Catholic home of five children and had worked ever since she was fourteen. She started as a waitress before moving on to other jobs, using the money to buy her own car, a Toyota. But in her first year of college, she had a terrible accident and was thrown through the car windshield, tearing up her face and her knees. As soon as she was able, she went back to college; the onetime cheerleader now wandered the campus with huge red scars on her face, and found people taking her more seriously than they once had. Years of reconstructive surgery followed, but she never forgot the lesson.

After obtaining a degree in psychology, she married and pursued a master's degree in accounting. By 1990, she had begun working at Enron, first on its financial filings, then in investor relations. When her marriage started falling apart, she asked for a less time-consuming job to give her more time for her young son. She was assigned to control risk in wholesale trading and gained a reputation for toughness that won her the nickname the Dragon Lady. Work again impeded on time with her son, so she moved on to dealing with the credit agencies. By then, she had attracted Skilling's attention, and the two decided to have their first date at his secretary's wedding.

Afterward, they went to dinner at Café Annie and over the meal found they enjoyed each other's company. Perhaps, they both thought, this could be a relationship that would have some staying power.

As the end of the first quarter rolled around, the finance division was scrambling again. If nothing was done, Enron was going to miss its earnings projections. A little extra creativity was needed to close the gap.

Special projects took on the task. Ben Glisan, the accounting superstar who was a Fastow favorite, hit on the perfect idea—Chewco. The partnership had pulled Enron over the hump before, maybe it could again.

Under the original deal, Chewco had agreed to pay Enron an annual management fee of about two million dollars. Under the accounting rules, that fee could only be reported by Enron after it provided the services.

But what if . . .

What if, Glisan wondered, Enron and Chewco took, say, 80 percent of that fee and called it a "required payment"? Meaning Chewco had to pay, no matter what. Rapidly, the contracts with Chewco were rewritten to change "management fee" to "required payment."

The amount Chewco owed Enron stayed the same. The terms of the transaction were identical. But since it was now *required*, Glisan argued, Enron could count the present value of the whole amount it would be paid over five years as a corporate asset. Then, thanks to mark-to-market accounting, most of that could be booked as income.

Glisan had found almost twenty-six million dollars in new profits, all by changing two words. Everyone celebrated his genius. But the accounting again was wrong. And nobody noticed.

It felt good to be back in America.

Jeff McMahon—onetime Andersen accountant, longtime Enron executive—wandered through the finance division, leaning into various offices to greet old friends. He had worked in the London office for almost three years and was back in Houston for a visit with the bosses.

Blond and boyish, McMahon had been sent to Britain to handle accounting issues for Enron's merchant and trading business there. At first he reported to Causey but soon found himself involved in finance, reporting to Fastow. He liked the setup; his résumé had lacked finance experience, and now he was qualified for a more high-powered job.

McMahon dropped by Fastow's twenty-seventh-floor office. The two men, standing on either side of Fastow's desk, discussed London and the challenges back home.

Fastow's tone grew serious. "Listen, I haven't been real happy with Bill Gathmann's performance as treasurer," he said. "There've been some screwups. I just don't think he's the guy for that position. I'm replacing him."

McMahon just listened.

"So I was wondering," Fastow continued. "Do you know anybody who might be interested in the job?"

McMahon's eyes went wide. *Excuse me?*

"Well, yeah," he replied. "What about me?"

Fastow raised his eyebrows, as if the thought had never entered his mind. Why would somebody like McMahon want a job that was so, well, dull?

"Oh," Fastow said, pausing for a moment. "I didn't know you'd be interested."

"Treasurer of a Fortune 100 company?" McMahon laughed. "I'd be very interested in that."

Fastow turned the idea over in his head. "Well, okay. Let me bounce this off Skilling, and if it's okay with him, yeah, let's go ahead and do it."

Shortly before noon in Houston, the gold-colored elevator doors opened, and John Ashcroft stepped onto the second floor of the Four Seasons Hotel. Ashcroft, a Missouri senator and future United States Attorney General, walked down the softly lit hallway toward the Livingston Room, one of the hotel's larger meeting areas. Outside the room, he saw a smallish, balding man standing beside a reception table. Ashcroft smiled. It was Ken Lay.

"John, welcome to Houston," Lay said as he approached Ashcroft. "I think we've got a good group of people here."

Ashcroft thrust out a hand. "Well, Ken, I appreciate you doing this, getting this group together."

It was April 7, and Lay was hosting a luncheon to raise money for Ashcroft's anticipated 2000 presidential bid. The men met in 1992, when Ashcroft was Missouri's governor and Lay was chairing the host committee for that year's Republican Convention. They quickly found that they had a lot in common—roots in Missouri, sons of ministers, similar values. It only seemed right that when Ashcroft began exploring a presidential bid, he would turn to Lay to gain entrée to Houston's big-money men.

At first, Ashcroft's request had presented Lay with a quandary. He remained close with the Bush family, and now the former President's son—George W., the Texas governor—was rapidly becoming the Republican Party's perceived front-runner. Lay feared that if he hosted an Ashcroft fundraiser, he risked alienating the Bush team.

So once Ashcroft approached him for help, Lay had asked for a few days to consider the situation. He had sent a message to Bush's top political adviser, Karl Rove, explaining what Ashcroft wanted and asking if his participation would set anyone's nose out of joint.

The reply came back quickly. The Bush team would love for Lay to host an Ashcroft fund-raiser. At that point, Ashcroft was attracting support among the Christian right. But of the most conservative politicians who might launch a campaign, Ashcroft seemed the least likely to catch fire. Sending money and support his way would only serve to keep it away from other—and potentially stronger—candidates. So with the secret go-ahead from the Bush campaign, Lay informed Ashcroft that he would be delighted to help out.

As the two men chatted, guests for lunch arrived, and Lay took a moment to introduce them to Ashcroft. Finally they headed inside and found their seats. After giving the guests some time with their food, Lay stood. He picked up a knife and tapped on a glass until everyone was quiet.

"We're delighted to have John Ashcroft here with us," Lay began. He told the crowd of their shared backgrounds, and detailed Ashcroft's political history.

"So let's give a warm welcome to Houston to Senator John Ashcroft," Lay concluded as the crowd clapped.

Ashcroft walked to the podium. "I'm delighted that Ken agreed to host this event today." He glanced toward Lay. "Like he said, we've known each other for years."

The early-morning sky on April 17 was dark with a low cloud cover, creating an eerie vista through the windows of the fiftieth-floor boardroom. It was seven in the morning, and the finance committee of Enron's board had gathered to hear the first presentation from the new CFO, Andy Fastow.

From a central position at the great table, a white-haired man surveyed the room. He was Herbert Winokur, known universally as Pug, the Enron director widely considered the savant on finance issues. For most directors, Winokur was a lifeline who could translate Enron's complex financial dealings. Enamored with esoteric deals, Winokur naturally emerged a huge Fastow fan. He was seen as something of a mentor for Fastow; now Winokur couldn't help but feel pride as he watched the young, newly minted CFO preparing to go through his paces.

Winokur brought the meeting to order and glanced over at Skilling. "All right, Jeff, why don't you get started?"

"Thanks, Pug," Skilling said. "Well, as you know, this meeting has been called to consider the sale of a new issue of Enron common stock."

Skilling outlined the basics, then turned the floor over to Fastow. "Thank you, Jeff," Fastow began. "There is a strong rationale to pursue this offering at this time."

Fastow was delivering on the promise he had made to Moody's to preserve Enron's credit rating—but made no mention of that. Instead, he hailed the equity offering as an opportunity to give Enron more financial flexibility.

"The management is recommending Donaldson, Lufkin & Jenrette as lead underwriter," Fastow said.

One director, Norm Blake, was surprised. Merrill Lynch handled much of Enron's underwriting business.

"Why DLJ?" he asked.

Mark Koenig, the head of investor relations, broke in. "I can explain that."

The directors liked the justification. Enron was getting tough. Fastow's request to issue stock passed unanimously. Half an hour later, the whole performance was repeated for the full board. Again approval came easily. The meeting ended, Winokur stepped over to Fastow.

"Very nice job, Andy," he said.

That evening, Fastow sat in the desk chair in his brand-new fiftieth-floor office. The place dripped of extravagance—mahogany paneling, a curved wall of windows, a private bathroom with black fixtures. Everything screamed that Fastow had arrived. And now, with the board behind him, he was ready to start playing hardball.

He reached for the phone and dialed the Houston office of Merrill Lynch. He was feeling comfortable and cocky. He was about to let the world know that Enron was changing the way it did business; it would reward its supporters and punish its detractors. Everybody needed to choose sides.

A few blocks away, Schuyler Tilney, a young investment banker who was one of the managers Merrill's banking relationship with Enron, reached for the phone.

"Schuyler, it's Andy Fastow."

"Andy, how are you?"

Fastow was in no mood for chitchat. He wanted to strike hard. "Schuyler, I'm calling to let you know the board has approved going forward with the stock offering."

"Great."

"But Merrill's not going to be lead manager," Fastow continued. "In fact, you aren't going to be co-managers."

Tilney's heart sank. Merrill was going to be shut out by Enron, his top client? He could scarcely believe it. Tilney was particularly close to Enron; his wife, Beth, had run corporate communications at Enron and was close to Lay. Weeks before, after telling Moody's that Enron would do a stock offering, Fastow had consulted Merrill. The firm's bankers had done preliminary work on the offer, even providing information Fastow had used in meeting with the board. The bankers had expected to get the plum—and lucrative— assignment of bringing the offering to market. But now Fastow was saying no dice.

Tilney kept a calm tone. "Well, Andy, you certainly have my attention. Can I ask why?"

"It's John Olson, Schuyler."

Olson—*again*. Olson was Merrill's stock analyst on Enron. The previous July, he had cut his rating on the company, angering top executives. His past dozen reports had been neutral—or at best vaguely positive. *And he was proud of it.* He liked to boast that his main recommendation, Williams Company, delivered better returns than Enron. But investment bankers care more about fees than investor returns, and Enron was the cash cow, not Williams.

"We have been undeniably clear in our concerns about your research effort," Fastow continued. "Our decision here is intended to send you guys a message about how viscerally we feel."

Speaking calmly, Fastow railed about how allowing Merrill a role would effectively endorse Olson's judgments.

"Are there any concerns about the quality of our investment-banking effort?" Tilney asked.

"Not at all. We don't want to harm our investment-banking relationship with Merrill, and we'll be directing some future business your way."

He paused. "This decision has been made solely on the basis of our concerns about the research coverage."

Tilney let that sink in. "All right. I hear you."

Two days later, at 8:30 in the morning, Ken Lay was at his desk when the phone rang. His secretary answered, then put the call on hold.

"Herb Allison from Merrill Lynch is on the line."

Lay smiled as he reached for the phone. Allison was president of Merrill Lynch in New York. Apparently, Enron's shot across the bow had hit its target.

"Herb," Lay said jovially, "good to hear from you."

And the dance began.

On a Monday in April, Jeff McMahon arrived at Enron to start his new job as treasurer. Right off, something seemed wrong. His new colleagues looked on him with suspicion. They were evasive when he asked about their duties. Nobody seemed to want to explain anything.

After a few hours of getting the runaround, McMahon was flummoxed. He had assumed he would get a quick handle on the operation's structure, but none of it was clear. Everybody did everything; it was all sharp elbows and jockeying for a place on the latest deal. From what he could tell, banks were barraged with deal proposals, with no one coordinating the contacts. The commercial units had no finance executives; Fastow had taken them all, without establishing lines of authority. No one was in charge.

McMahon cornered Ray Bowen. The two men went into a conference room, and McMahon handed Bowen a marker.

"Listen, I'm trying to understand the organization," McMahon said. "Can you just draw it for me? Who's in what box, who reports to who, like that."

Bowen laughed.

"Sorry, Jeff," he said. "I don't think there are boxes where people fit in. It's pretty much catch-as-catch-can. Everybody's just trying to get in on the next deal."

After reviewing the chaos, McMahon sought out Fastow.

"Andy, you've got to organize this thing," McMahon said. "People are all fighting. You've got a lot of animosity between the commercial divisions and the corporate guys, and, really, you've got to shift people back into the divisions to make things work better."

Fastow considered that for a moment. "Okay, fine, whatever. Just leave me out of it as much as possible. I really don't like dealing with organizational issues."

McMahon started reorganizing finance, shifting executives back to the commercial units. At the same time, he created strong definitions for everyone's job. But he also came away with an important lesson. Enron's new CFO wasn't much interested in managing. He was just a deal guy.

The faxes from Schuyler Tilney of Merrill Lynch started arriving in the late afternoon of April 28.

The firm had begged its way back onto Enron's stock offering and had reached an unspoken understanding about the future of John Olson, the analyst whose muted enthusiasm for the company had started all the trouble.

For now, Olson was flogging Enron stock, calling institutional investors—dozens of them—about the stock offering. Whatever happened in each call—a message left, an interest expressed—Olson wrote it down. Then Tilney faxed the information to Fastow and Mark Koenig, Enron's investor-relations chief. The message was clear. Merrill had reined in Olson. The firm was trying to be good.

At 11:15 on the morning of May 7, Rebecca Mark was standing in the doorway to Skilling's office. He glanced up and smiled, inviting her in.

Skilling studied Mark as they spoke. As usual, she looked fabulous, in a blue suit with stiletto-heeled pumps. But now their odd relationship—locking horns in strategic battles while at times privately confiding in each other—was taking a new turn. The previous day, Enron had announced that Mark was no longer chief executive of Enron International. Instead, she was being kicked upstairs, to be vice chairman of Enron, and was turning over international to her longtime deputy, Joe Sutton.

No one—not even Mark—had any illusions about the authority in her new job; there was none. Enron already had another vice chairman, Ken Harrison, whose role was pretty much nonexistent. But Mark didn't mind. She had no intention of remaining vice chairman for long.

As she spoke with Skilling, Mark couldn't help but see the man who had confided his fears to her in the past. In truth, she worried about him. The people Skilling trusted, the ones he rewarded with outsize salaries and bonuses, were not looking out for him. Fastow, Causey, Rice—none would protect him from his own worst impulses.

Mark decided to say so. "You know, Jeff, if you're going to run Enron, you need to move Joe Sutton to chief operating officer. You could trust Joe."

Skilling listened in silence.

"Truthfully, Jeff," Mark continued, "you can't do that with the guys you've got around you. They're a bunch of prima donnas. They're all off doing their own thing and grandstanding, trying to get your attention."

She paused. "Jeff, they're not your friends. You need to protect yourself from them."

Skilling blinked. "Well, those are the people I depend on. Those are the people who got me where I am."

The conversation ended. Mark could tell that Skilling hadn't heard a word she'd said. He was going to continue holding his lieutenants in his trust.

In London, Michael Kopper stepped into the lobby of the Metropolitan hotel, making his way past its pear-wood interiors. Young staffers clad in Armani suits ambled about, lending the place the chic aura it cultivated.

After a few minutes in the lobby, Kopper met up with Fastow, and the two headed outside. Across the street, Hyde Park was in bloom, while to the southeast the springtime splendor of the Buckingham Palace Gardens was emerging. They climbed into the back of a car, telling the driver to take them to an address near the House of Parliament.

It was May 19, just after eight o'clock in the morning. Fastow and Kopper had arrived the previous morning in London as part of a wide-ranging world tour to meet Enron's bankers. But in London they would be getting together with executives from only one bank, Greenwich NatWest, a unit of National Westminster.

Fastow already had plenty of reason to feel good about the bank. It was rated by Enron as Tier 1, signaling that these bankers would go the extra mile. Two months earlier, when Fastow was struggling to find thirty million dollars to finance an expansion of Enron's Bammel gas storage field, Greenwich NatWest stepped up; its bankers made clear that they were only doing the deal as a favor.

The car pulled up to 4 Millbank. Kopper and Fastow hopped out, heading upstairs to Enron's London offices. About an hour later, five bankers from Greenwich NatWest arrived. No introductions were necessary; they had all met the night before over drinks.

One executive they had known awhile—Kevin Howard, who handled the bank's relationship with Enron. For this meeting, Howard had brought along the big guns, including the co–chief executive, to drive home the bank's interest in doing business with Enron. But it was two other bankers at the meeting who most intrigued Fastow and Kopper.

One, Gary Mulgrew, had grown up in a middle-class Scottish home but was now renowned as the hard-charging director of the bank's structured-finance business. The other, Giles Darby, was lower-key but struck colleagues as the smarter of the pair, a man who often hid his intelligence behind the demeanor of an English country boy. They were almost the mirror image of Fastow and Kopper—an aggressive boss, a smarter colleague, and both on the lookout for the edge to make them rich.

"You recover from last night?" Mulgrew said with a laugh.

Fastow smiled. "More jet lag than anything else."

The group settled in. As the meeting wore on, Fastow and Kopper felt increasingly comfortable with Mulgrew and Darby. They knew how the corporate-finance game was played. Maybe, in time, they could do some special deals together.

John Olson was stunned.

Fired. He was being fired.

It was the next day, May 20. As Fastow flew around Europe, Merrill was taking its final action to appease him back in America. Andrew Melnick, from Merrill's research division, let Olson know the news. He was too negative on Enron, Melnick said. He had made snide remarks that had offended Lay. He was hurting the firm. He had to go. Merrill would be good to him, though, and pay him $400,000—more than twice his annual salary—to leave quietly.

Olson scarcely knew what to do. He had never been snide about Enron in front of Lay or anybody else. His stock picks outperformed Enron. What was he doing wrong?

The timing couldn't have been worse. Olson and his wife had just closed on a house a few days before. They could never afford it now. This was a financial disaster.

Maybe, he thought, there was still a chance. Maybe if Lay told Melnick that there were no snide remarks, maybe he could stay. Olson reached for the phone to call Lay.

Everyone at Enron was feeling flush.

The company's stock offering had been a hit. More than seventeen million shares sold at fifty dollars each, bringing in $800 million in new cash. Enron now had the chance to cut back its debt. But the rating-agency concerns that had inspired the offering seemed forgotten.

If Enron could raise so much money so easily, what was the problem? Surely the company could do it again, whenever it wanted. Thoughts of any concerted effort to clean up the balance sheet were shelved. Instead, Enron set out on its biggest spending spree ever.

Rebecca Mark and Cliff Baxter set down a thick report on the circular conference table in Ken Lay's office. For months, the two had been working on an idea, something so radical they felt it could redefine Enron's future.

Water. Enron would do for water what it had done for energy. Under Mark's prodding, it had already tossed $300 million into a water company. Now it was time to go for broke, by starting a whole water division.

"Water is going to be huge, Ken," Mark said.

Lay sat back. "All right. Tell me about it."

Baxter took it from there. The market was worth some $300 billion and would grow to $400 billion by 2000. "It's largely government-owned," he said. "But it's going through privatization. We'd be using a lot of the same skill sets we used in energy, just with a lot less competition."

There was a global shortage of usable water, Mark said. As world economies improved, demand would grow. International markets were opening *now*; Enron had to get in fast. Opportunities were everywhere—Britain, Germany, Brazil, even the United States. There were synergies with energy and lots of opportunities for the kinds of creative financial engineering Fastow did so well.

What did Skilling think of the idea? Lay asked. Baxter replied that he had spoken with Skilling and received, if not a green light, then at least a yellow.

Lay was impressed; the two made a strong case. And Enron *had* been so successful at its other gambles, it certainly seemed like water was something to consider.

"Well, Rebecca, Cliff, this was an excellent presentation," Lay said. "And based on what you've shown me, I would be happy to take it to the board."

Mark smiled. "Wonderful."

On June 3 at about 7:45 in the morning, Amanda Martin walked through the lobby of the Warwick Hotel in Houston. The place was stodgy but elegant, with the decor of a European château. She made her way to the Hunt Room, walking beneath chandeliers in the shape of hunting horns.

By then Martin was struggling. Over the past year, everything had come off track. Her romantic relationship with Ken Rice had fallen apart. One underling she had passed over for promotion had sued, claiming Rice backed the decision because of the affair. Their poor judgment had left Enron vulnerable, but only Martin paid a price. She was the subject of vicious gossip, mostly by traders.

She wanted distance from Rice, wanted out of the brutal environment inside Enron. Now Skilling had an idea and wanted to discuss it over breakfast. The two met at a table. After ordering, Skilling leaned toward her.

"I want you to do me a favor," he said.

Rebecca Mark was launching a water business, he said. This wasn't going to be just another division; it would eventually be a public company, with Mark in charge.

"I need somebody there I trust," he said evenly. "Somebody who understands how Enron works, somebody with a track record in building businesses and fixing problems. And I want somebody I'm comfortable communicating with."

To Martin, it sounded like salvation.

"I'm interested, Jeff," Martin said.

"We're going to take the best of Enron and leave the worst behind."

Martin listened, enthralled, as Mark laid out her vision of a water business that would be a kinder, gentler version of Enron. No more competitive backstabbing. No quarter-to-quarter battles. The Performance Review Committee, or PRC, where everyone fought for promotions and bonuses, would be gone. No benefits for politicking; the water business would be a meritocracy.

"We're going to build a business," Mark said, "where you can be rewarded for being nice, too."

The vision captivated Martin. She was on board.

Over time, she and Mark discussed the business. First thing, it needed a name. Martin pulled a face at Mark's first idea—WaterMark. A little too egocentric. But eventually a name was found, a name that they knew could change the nature of business: Azurix.

His chin in one hand, Skilling flipped to the second page of a report on another proposed international deal, this one in Brazil. He sat at the circular conference table in his office, his back to his desk, as he listened to Joe Sutton, the new division head, make the pitch.

It was just past one o'clock on June 30. Skilling was silent—every motion, every breath exuding boredom. He turned to the third page. Then he saw it. *A map.*

A map of Brazil and its neighbors. It showed the asset—Elektro Eletricidade e Serviços S.A., Brazil's sixth-largest electricity distributor—and flows of electricity from power generators moving out onto the grid. Suddenly, Skilling understood. This wasn't some tired power plant. This was an access point to the grid. An asset that would allow Enron to build a South American trading operation.

As Sutton droned on, Skilling looked up with a smile. "I like this deal," he said. "I want to do this deal."

Sutton barely noticed. He turned to the next page. Ray Bowen, who was working on the financing for the deal, raised a hand, trying to make Sutton stop.

One thing I learned as a banker: once the guy says yes, you stop talking, he thought.

Sutton looked up, realization sinking in. Skilling was ready to go.

"Okay," Skilling said. "How do we get this done?"

"This is a very sensitive project we're about to discuss. So I'd prefer if only people directly involved remained in the room."

Joe Sutton glanced around the fiftieth-floor boardroom. Most of the people attending the board's executive committee meeting didn't need to be there.

"I agree," Skilling chimed in. "People who aren't needed should leave."

It was past seven on the morning of July 14. Sutton watched silently as half a dozen executives stood to leave. Once the room settled down, he began his pitch for Elektro.

Under Mark, he said, Enron had already invested some $700 million in Brazil, mostly for the construction of a gas power plant in Cuiabá. Now that country was beginning to sell government-controlled energy assets. A large stake in Elektro—90 percent of the voting shares and more than 40 percent of the economic interest—was coming on the market. An aggressive bid would give Enron a strategic leg up in Brazil.

To finance the purchase, Sutton said, international would rely on Fastow's group. Then, Fastow explained how he planned to have banks lend the total amount for the closing, after which parts of the financing would be sold off.

"This is a fabulous project," Lay said. "It's really going to bring some significant value to the company."

The directors turned to Skilling; if anyone would oppose the transaction, it would be him.

"I agree with Ken and Joe," Skilling said. "This is a great opportunity to apply our strategies from wholesale trading in North America to Brazil."

The directors watched Skilling with expressions of awe. He was holding out the prospects of repeating his domestic success in Latin America.

"This is different from asset development," Skilling said. "This is a core position. Much like we used Portland General in North America, we can use Elektro in Brazil."

Still, a few problems emerged. Sutton acknowledged that Enron hadn't reviewed all of Elektro's financial and operational data; his team just hadn't had the time. But he had confidence, he said, in their analysis.

No one asked, wasn't Enron taking a huge flier? International had always been power plants and pipelines. Electricity distribution was a lesser known beast, and a heavily regulated one at that. Worse, Enron would be using billions in borrowed dollars to purchase a company with cash flow in the *real*, Brazil's currency. If the *real* collapsed, Elektro's flow of currency would be unchanged, but the value of the cash in dollars—needed to pay lenders— would drop. With this deal Enron would be making a billion-dollar bet on the currency of a Latin American government.

There wasn't time for much discussion, Sutton cautioned. Enron had to enter its bid in just forty-eight hours. After thirty minutes of discussion, the vote was unanimous. Enron would bid for Elektro.

Two days later at nine o'clock, a silence descended over the crowd gathered in a small auditorium at Bovespa, the São Paulo stock exchange. As everyone watched, four envelopes were brought to the stage. This was the moment of truth. The high bidder would own a huge stake in Elektro.

One at a time, an official sitting at a long table tore open the envelopes. The first contained a bid for just over $700 million. The Brazilian government officials were delighted; they had set a minimum price of about $640 million. This was a good sign.

The second envelope. The official sliced one end with a letter opener, removing the slip inside. The bid from Terraco Participacoes, the entity formed by Enron.

"*De Terraco Participacoes*," the official began. He then recited the number. The crowd exploded in cheers.

Just under $1.3 billion. Enron had bid almost twice the government's asking price. In the jubilance that followed, it took several more minutes to open the other bids, but that was a formality. The auction was over.

Enron had wildly overpaid for a stake in a company with risks its executives only vaguely understood.

The Enron directors who gathered in the thirtieth-floor video conference room on July 21 were a surly, short-tempered bunch. It wasn't just all the chatter about the embarrassing price Enron had coughed up for Elektro. Now, only five days after committing more than a billion dollars to Brazil, the managers were back again, this time for two billion dollars—for the water business.

The water business! Why? Sure, a few weeks back, the board had agreed to Rebecca Mark's request to see if there were opportunities there. But none of them ever imagined she would be coming back so quickly, asking to spend almost as much as Enron had committed to its India power plant.

The video conference system was turned on, and the meeting began. The images of Rebecca Mark and Cliff Baxter filled the screen, broadcast from London. They had been there for weeks, negotiating to purchase a British water company called Wessex Water Services.

The idea was called Project Trident, Mark said, and it would be the heart of their water strategy. Enron would set up a new, stand-alone company to purchase and manage Wessex. With that company, Enron could get its foot in the door of the growing market. All for just $2.25 billion.

The directors glanced at Fastow.

"The price shouldn't be a problem," he said. "We can pay that without hurting our balance sheet."

The finance team had constructed a device for raising the money, he said. It involved a labyrinth of financing that created risks most of the directors— and Fastow himself—failed to understand. In its simplest form, Enron would set up a couple of off-books entities—the Marlin Water Trust and the Atlantic Water Trust. Enron owned half of Atlantic, which in turn owned the company that would purchase Wessex. The result was that a lot of the acquisition and its related costs could be kept off Enron's books.

The co-owner of Atlantic was Marlin, which would borrow more than a billion dollars from institutional investors. To attract them, Fastow sweetened the deal, committing Enron to repay whatever Marlin couldn't—in company stock, if necessary. Enron would be like a parent co-signing the world's biggest car loan for a teenager. But the nettle was in the details. If Enron's credit rating fell below investment grade when its stock price dropped beneath $37.84, Marlin debt holders could demand repayment.

Fastow wrapped up his pitch. Lay, sitting in the center seat, glanced around. "Any questions?" he asked.

Not a second passed. Norm Blake, a director, slammed a hand on the table. "I don't know what the *hell* we're doing," he blurted out. "What's the Street going to think when Enron puts a couple of billion into water companies?"

Pug Winokur, the head of the finance committee, joined in. "I agree with Norm. This isn't our area of expertise."

Other directors sat still; Enron's boardroom was rarely a place of confrontation. All eyes turned to Lay.

"Norm, Pug," he began, his voice soothing, "it's a good deal. It looks and smells just like an energy development, except it's water. Buying this company would give us the expertise in water that we need."

"I hear that, Ken," Winokur replied. "But if you believe you have limited capital in an organization, you've got to be careful where you put it. And I don't want to do some big water project and forgo something in energy."

"That's not a problem," Fastow responded. "Capital is not an issue for Enron."

Skilling took the floor. "Right," he said. "By doing this deal, we're not forgoing some other transaction."

"Come on, Jeff!" Blake spluttered. "You don't have anything else on the table today. But tomorrow, next month, next year, there will be opportunities."

As the argument heated up, John Duncan, head of the executive committee, tried playing peacemaker.

"You know," he said gently. "These are all good questions, but I think we need to side with the chairman on this one. Ken's done the due diligence here."

Crossing his arms in disapproval, Winokur stared at Fastow. "We really have enough capital for this?"

"Yes," Fastow responded. "This structure works."

"But this can result in Enron issuing equity," Winokur said. "And the question I have is, should we issue a billion in equity for water? Or for energy?"

"Well," Lay began, "it makes sense as—"

"I don't care," Blake interrupted. "It doesn't make sense to *me*."

Lay paused. "Well, Norm, if you would let me finish, I could explain to you why it does make sense."

After allowing Lay to speak for a minute, Duncan rejoined the fray. "All right," he said. "Well, I suggest we side with the chairman."

From one end of the table, Ken Harrison, the former chairman of Portland General and a man who had been listening quietly throughout the meeting, spoke up. "Well, my opinion is . . ."

A stunned silence. Lay's face seemed to register a wide look of surprise that Harrison was even speaking.

"There's a lot of opportunity in energy, and we shouldn't turn away from our core business," Harrison continued. "Ken, I think this idea is wrong."

A pause. "All right," Lay said. "Thanks, Ken."

He turned his attention back to Winokur and Blake.

"I think we need to go into executive session," Duncan said suddenly. "Outside directors only."

Lay, Skilling, and Harrison left the room, waiting outside the door. Other executives, including Fastow, McMahon, Rice, and Causey, headed back to their offices. They got on the elevator, and the snickering began. The board's pecking order had been established, and for some reason Ken Harrison was at the bottom.

"Hey," Rice said. "Anybody want to take the bet how much longer Harrison is with the company?"

The executives were reduced to helpless giggles.

Back in the conference room, Duncan waited until everyone was gone. He glanced around the table.

"Listen," he began. "I understand your concerns. But we need to support the chairman."

Less than twenty minutes later, the directors called Lay, Skilling, and Harrison into the room.

"Mr. Chairman," Duncan said, "we're ready to consider the question on Project Trident."

Lay took his seat and picked up his gavel. "We're now going to consider the resolution," he began.

In ten minutes it was over. One director abstained. Two others, Blake and John Urquhart, voted no. But the others approved sending Enron into a new multibillion-dollar business, using financing they wouldn't fully understand until years later, when it helped to destroy the company.

This can't be right.

Jeff McMahon, Enron's new treasurer, pored through the Elektro paperwork again. *Nothing.* It wasn't there.

He called Ray Bowen, who had handled the financing.

"Ray, listen, I'm looking through Elektro," McMahon began. "Did you know we didn't hedge the currency risk?"

Hedge the currency risk. In the lingo of finance, McMahon was highlighting the critical risk of Elektro: Enron had done nothing to protect itself from a decline in the value of Brazilian currency.

"Yeah, Jeff, I know," Bowen replied. "That is absolutely the front-and-center issue on this deal."

This was nuts. "Well, why did we do the deal then?"

Bowen chuckled. "Go ask Sutton, Skilling, everybody. The risk was right up there. In every discussion I talked about how we were taking a big bet on the *real.*"

"Well, why did we do that?" McMahon asked sharply.

"Hey, Jeff, I don't know, I'm just the funding guy. This was the commercial guys' call."

Bowen wasn't going to take the blame here.

"Come on, Jeff," he said. "You had to have known."

McMahon thought a moment. "God, yeah, probably. I must have known at some point. It just went by me."

John Olson's career at Merrill Lynch ended in August 1998. His protests and calls to Lay proved fruitless. He was officially let go for failing to forge strong relationships with the firm's bankers. His replacement, Donato Eassey, didn't have that problem. Early on, he upgraded Enron's rating.

The three percent. Enron seemed to always be hunting for the equity slice for its structured deals. Maybe, McMahon thought, there was a better way. What if Enron started its own equity funds, raising cash that would be available when needed? That would speed up deal making.

In his first months as treasurer, McMahon was working to expand the universe of Enron investors. Its debt was triple-B, not great. More investors were available for A-rated companies. But equity investors took higher risks; Enron just had to find them. Setting up its own private-equity fund was the answer. He took the idea to Fastow.

"Hey, Andy, listen, I've been thinking about how we could make it easier and faster to raise our equity tranches, how to expand our investor base."

He wanted to look into hiring someone with expertise to put together and manage an equity fund, McMahon said.

"And I've already figured out who I want to hire," he said. "Mike Jakubik at Bankers Trust in London."

"Jakubik?"

"Yeah, I think he'd be perfect."

Fastow considered it. He'd been thinking about creating some captive equity fund for months, even talked about it with some Enron bankers. If McMahon knew somebody to run such an effort, Fastow said, all the better.

A month later in a London restaurant, McMahon handed his menu to the waiter after ordering dinner. Across the table, Mike Jakubik sipped his drink and waited.

"Anyway," McMahon said, "I've been in this new job for only a few months. And it's already clear this company rides it right to the edge on liquidity every month."

Liquidity. McMahon was talking about the lifeblood of business. Enron, he was saying, was cutting it close on the cash it needed to pay for its daily business operations.

"Basically," McMahon continued, "Enron is really good at spending money and not very good at selling anything."

Jakubik smiled. "Okay."

"A lot of our problem comes from our investment portfolio," McMahon said. "We're investing six or seven billion dollars, but we're not earning cash."

"Okay," Jakubik said. "So where would I come in?"

"We need to hire someone who will be responsible for financing this big position. We've just been basically writing checks, and we need to stop that."

The job would be investment czar for Enron, McMahon said, responsible for managing the portfolio. Lots needed to be sold. There would need to be equity funds to purchase company assets. Other assets might go elsewhere. But in the end Enron's investments would be used to bring in cash.

"Jeff," Jakubik replied, "that sounds interesting."

As dinner wrapped up, Jakubik felt excited. Effectively, he would be an investment banker with one client. This was the type of creative idea that gave Enron such a market aura. Who wouldn't want a job like that?

The crowd gathered for dinner at New York University applauded warmly as Arthur Levitt, the SEC chairman, walked across the dais toward a podium.

It was September 28, 1998. For Levitt, this was the moment; he was ready to throw down the gauntlet. Corporate America was out of control, relying too much on gimmicks and games to keep the music going.

The evidence was everywhere. In the past nine months, scores of corporations—including investor favorites like Waste Management and Sunbeam—had restated previous financial filings, revealing that profits from prior periods had relied on bad accounting. The SEC was already investigating one accounting firm, Arthur Andersen, which represented both Waste Management and Sunbeam, to determine how things had gone astray. Among regulators, it was already an article of faith that Andersen's fast-growing clients should face tough questions. But the market simply zoomed on.

So Levitt decided to come out with guns blazing.

"Increasingly," he said, "I have become concerned that the motivation to meet Wall Street earnings expectations may be overriding commonsense business practices. Too many corporate managers, auditors, and analysts are participants in a game of nods and winks."

Levitt paused, then continued.

"Wishful thinking may be winning the day over faithful representation," he said. "I fear that we are witnessing an erosion in the quality of earnings, and therefore the quality of financial reporting. Managing may be giving way to manipulation. Integrity may be losing out to illusion."

This was no secret, Levitt implied. Regulators knew, executives knew. The market was punishing companies with real numbers, while competitors were rewarded for playing games.

The honest executives "know how difficult it is to hold the line on good practices when their competitors operate in the gray area between legitimacy and outright fraud," Levitt said. "A gray area where the accounting is being perverted; where managers are cutting corners; and where earnings reports reflect the desires of management rather than the underlying financial performance."

It was a moment virtually unparalleled in the sixty-five-year history of the SEC. A chairman for the agency was announcing that the success of untold numbers of corporations was the result of dreams, not dollars. But the warning went unheard. The day after the speech, the Dow Jones Industrial Average closed above 8,000. Over the next two years, it would climb almost another four thousand points—the unprecedented price increase later derided as the bubble.

And the stock price of Enron, Andersen's biggest client, went right along for the ride. Without question.

CHAPTER 8

MORNING IN HOUSTON BROUGHT only darkness and flooding. Ominous pitch-black clouds of Tropical Storm Frances had rolled in overnight from the Gulf of Mexico, dumping sheets of water. Swollen bayous around the city spilled into the streets, trapping cars and buses in swirling torrents.

Just past eight that Friday morning in September 1998, Michael Jakubik, the Bankers Trust deal maker from London, walked out of the St. Regis hotel and into the deluge. *Not a good start.* Not today, when he was interviewing with Jeff Skilling and Andy Fastow about joining Enron.

It had been more than a month since McMahon pitched the idea of making him Enron's investment czar, responsible for managing billions of dollars in holdings—setting up equity funds, selling assets, everything. Even though it meant moving his family from London, the opportunity seemed too enticing, one that could lead to even bigger things in the private-equity business. That is, if Enron hired him.

Jakubik approached a couple of taxis before finding a driver willing to brave the weather. About twenty minutes later, the cab pulled up to corporate headquarters. Jakubik hustled in through the pelting rain and was directed to the fiftieth floor. Upstairs, it was empty and dark, with rain drumming on the floor-to-ceiling windows. Lightning flashed outside, and a sharp clap of thunder shook the room. A door opened, and a small man emerged, making his way through the shadows toward his visitor.

"Mike?" the man said.

"Yeah?"

A few steps closer. A hand thrust out.

"Jeff Skilling."

They sat on either side of Skilling's desk, talking. Jakubik was awed. Here was *the* guy, the oracle of corporate strategy, speaking to him like a peer.

"So of course, in this job, you'll come to my weekly staff meetings," Skilling said.

Wow. "All right."

Skilling turned on the charm, jabbering about Houston and his family. But he asked nothing. It struck Jakubik as an oddly nonchalant stance toward a candidate for what would be one of the most powerful positions at the company.

"I leave it up to the guys to judge brainpower and whether you're appropriate for the job," Skilling said. "If they're fine with you, I'm fine with you."

He leaned in. "But I am eager for your questions."

"Okay. Why do you think this job's important?"

Skilling shrugged. "I trust Jeff and Andy, and they tell me this is important. That's good enough for me."

The telephone rang. Skilling grabbed it. "Hello?"

A pause. "No, let me pass you to the operator."

Jakubik stifled a smile. With no one else on the floor, the oracle was now the receptionist.

For fifteen minutes, Jakubik tossed questions at Skilling, but the answers were perfunctory. His would-be boss seemed distracted, even indifferent. Whenever the phone rang, he snatched it up. Not one call was for him.

Okay, Jakubik said. This job will involve stepping on a lot of toes. Every asset, every business that needs to be sold was purchased or built by somebody in the building.

"Everybody's going to claim I'm selling the company's crown jewel," Jakubik continued. "So I'm worried about coming here, only to find nothing can be sold."

Skilling shook his head. "That's not how Enron works," he said. "If Andy and Jeff say we need liquidity, then we'll do it. They tell me to do it, I'll do it."

Jakubik nodded. *Okay, good enough.*

Suddenly Skilling stood, signaling an end to the interview. The two walked back to reception and said their goodbyes.

"Stay dry," Skilling said.

About that time, Fastow was in his office, hanging up his raincoat in a hidden closet. He walked to his desk, rubber duck boots still sloshing, and told his secretary to send Jakubik back whenever Skilling was done.

Jakubik arrived minutes later. Fastow spun toward him on his desk chair. "Sorry about the water," Fastow said wryly. "So how'd it go with Skilling?"

I have no idea. Why didn't the guy ask me anything?

"I think it went fine," Jakubik said.

Fastow nodded. "Okay, good." He paused. "So what's it gonna take to get you here?"

"Well, I'd like to hear how you see the job."

Fastow leaned back. "This company has to do a better job of financing our merchant investments. They're a drag on the balance sheet." He laid out the same concerns McMahon had described weeks before. Enron needed to set up equity funds, sell assets, create new sources of cash.

"I haven't worked with you," Fastow said. "But everyone who has says you're the right guy. We need someone with your talents who understands private equity."

Jakubik said nothing. This was flattering.

"We're going to be looking to you," Fastow continued. "You're empowered. You'll be the guy to make these calls. You're going to be running this thing."

He paused. "So, what's it gonna take to get you here?"

"This is a copy of an address given a few weeks ago by Arthur Levitt from the SEC," David Duncan said.

Duncan passed a pile of stapled printouts down the boardroom table to the directors on Enron's audit committee. It was about 4:30 on the afternoon of October 12, a day of scheduled board meetings. Duncan had just finished discussing Andersen's view of Enron's accounting practices. It seemed the right time to bring the Levitt accounting speech to the attention of the directors.

"This speech is really the official notice of an SEC initiative to take a tougher view of corporate accounting practices," Duncan said. "It is very detailed, and everyone would be well served to read it."

Causey, sitting nearby, motioned for a slide to go up on the screen. "Levitt Speech: Five Popular Earnings Management Practices," it read. Underneath the heading was a list of five abusive tactics Levitt had criticized.

"I would like to address each one of these," Causey said. Levitt's tough talk wasn't aimed at anything Enron was doing, he said. The company had no giant restructuring charges, and it didn't use creative acquisition accounting—two of the biggest sins Levitt had singled out.

On the other hand, Levitt had also attacked accounting abuses that Enron would have to guard against. One was the premature booking of revenue—a temptation that, happily, Enron had not succumbed to, Causey said.

"We do recognize a good portion of our revenue quickly, under mark-to-market accounting," Causey said. "But, as you remember, the SEC approved our approach a number of years ago. So that is not a concern."

Last, materiality. Levitt had warned companies not to abuse the practice that allowed them to avoid reporting accounting errors that affect less than a defined percentage of income. Causey glanced at Duncan.

"Now, we have had a dispute with Andersen about the proper account-ing for a contract that we acquired as part of Portland General," Causey said. "We've disagreed on the accounting, and that disagreement has not been re-solved."

However, the net effect was not reported to investors, Causey said, because Andersen had made the determination that the numbers were not material.

Duncan jumped in. "I think that judgment is valid."

The directors listened, content with what they heard. Whomever Levitt was criticizing, they certainly weren't like Enron.

Later that night, at 8:15, the board gathered in the fiftieth-floor conference room for its regular meeting. They still had not recovered from their heated debate over the water business. Some directors worried there was no over-arching strategy for the decisions being made at Enron. Lay had heard the grumbling and decided to address it head-on.

About forty minutes into the meeting, Lay glanced around the circular table. "There have been a lot of concerns, expressed by a number of you in recent meetings, about the state of the company," he said.

He nodded toward Skilling. "Jeff has prepared a presentation to lay out where we've been, where we are, and where we're going."

"Thank you, Ken," Skilling said. A slide, showing the Enron logo, clicked up on the screen. "At our last board meeting, a number of you expressed some concerns about a number of areas," he began.

Click. The concerns. A loss of focus. Too rapid an expansion in interna-tional. Too many acquisitions of regulated businesses. Worries about the bal-ance sheet and liquidity. Too many diverse activities in individual business units—what Skilling called "conglomeration."

But Enron's performance had been stellar, Skilling said, rushing through the slides. By diversifying its business interests, the company had seen its stock dramatically outperform other energy companies. The trading business in particular was in a unique position to generate profits.

Another slide. "For our international effort, we have developed an excel-lent platform network in both the Southern Cone in Latin America and in India," he said. "We are going to have strong earnings and cash flow as these projects move toward completion."

The new business would make things even better. The company had a lot of upside—potentially increasing its stock price by twenty dollars a share—because of its strong entry in the telecom and water businesses.

"Our key concern, of course, is of a liquidity meltdown, and the impact that would have both on our balance sheet and on our trading capabilities," he said.

That concern, he said, was mitigated by unexpected strengths—momentum in retail, a shakeout in power trading, and general stability in the wholesale business.

The presentation was impressive. The directors asked questions; Skilling and Lay fielded them deftly. It sure sounded like management knew what it was doing and where it was headed. Maybe those worries had been for nothing.

After going late into the evening, the directors reconvened at eight the next morning. After the first hour, Pug Winokur, the finance chairman, took the floor. His committee had approved a range of issues, he said.

Fifteen pages of resolutions were distributed. They included authorizations for Enron to sell debt, preferred stock, and other securities and changes to policies on corporate guarantees. The resolutions ranged over so many issues there wasn't time to discuss every detail. Nothing was mentioned about a paragraph on page 14, giving authority to Enron's CFO to issue guarantees of up to ten million dollars without approval.

No one knew that for years, Enron had struggled in its structured deals, trying to find investors willing to cough up far less than that amount. If Fastow could use an Enron guarantee—assuring potential investors who provided the three percent that they would get their money back—that hunt might not be so difficult anymore.

The directors had just handed Fastow a loaded pistol. It would not be long before he pulled the trigger.

Just past 2:15 on the afternoon of October 27, a yellow cab snaked through Park Avenue traffic in midtown Manhattan. In the back, Skilling sat beside Fastow, gazing through the car window at pedestrians. To his agitated mind, their faces were frozen in fear, dark circles defining their eyes. The elite of the financial world worked here, and Skilling thought they had good reason to be terrified.

A global economic depression was on the way; Skilling was sure of it. Russia had defaulted. The Asian financial crisis was still digging into world economies. The Fed had been forced to engineer a bailout of Long-Term Capital Management LP, a hedge fund, on concern its collapse would trigger a market meltdown. Skilling feared the gathering financial storm would swamp Enron itself. Banks were ruthlessly tightening credit. If they shut off the spigot to Enron, the consequences could be dire.

So he had ordered Fastow to fly to Paris, Düsseldorf, Brussels, and London, seeking reassurances from the banks. Now the time had come for meetings with Enron's New York lenders, and Skilling wanted to attend these himself; any banks planning to call Enron's loans would be more likely to listen to the company's number two than to its CFO.

The taxi pulled in front of the fifty-three-story headquarters of Chase Manhattan Bank. Within minutes, Skilling and Fastow were upstairs, in an office near a trading floor. A short man with gray hair and a chunky gold ring on one finger bounded toward them. It was Jimmy Lee, Chase's colorful chief of global investment banking.

"Gentlemen, good to see you," he boomed.

After the pleasantries, Skilling got to the point.

"Listen, guys, I've got no illusions," he said. "There's probably a liquidity crunch on the way, and you might have to start making choices among your borrowers."

Skilling braced himself, then asked the question. "So I need to know, if you have a problem, where does Enron stand? Will you continue to support us?"

Lee smiled. "Jeff, we like Enron," he said. "This is exactly the kind of business we want to do long term."

Skilling listened as other bankers in the room praised the company—and Fastow. He always kept them up on events, always gave them plenty of feedback. He made the bank comfortable.

Afterward, as the two Enron executives left the building, walking to Park Avenue, Skilling was exultant. *This* was how it was supposed to be; any doubts he had harbored about appointing Fastow as CFO evaporated.

"You know, Andy," he said, "they could be putting the screws to us right now, and instead they're telling us how much they want to work with us."

Fastow nodded, smiling broadly.

"This is what makes the difference, Andy," Skilling continued. "When times are tough, if we're doing a good job with our bankers, that makes all the difference."

Skilling slapped Fastow on the back. "Keep up the good work, man," he said.

A week later, a group of Chase bankers held a lengthy meeting about Enron. There was a lot to talk about. The bank had committed $750 million in two credit lines to different Enron-related entities. They had made large commitments for the Elektro acquisition.

But some of the best deals weren't quite so straightforward. For example, in the past year, Chase had arranged what looked like $650 million in gas trades involving Enron and a Jersey company called Mahonia. But in reality, Mahonia was a front for Chase itself. No gas changed hands; money simply circled from Chase to Mahonia to Enron, then back again, with the equivalent of interest. The transactions were effectively loans dressed up to look like energy trades. That let Enron report the borrowings as cash flow and trading liabilities. Chase bankers knew Enron loved the deals, because they could use them to hide debt.

With all this business, Enron was at the top of the heap at Chase. The bank ranked corporate customers based on a color code, with "blue" clients having the richest potential for bringing in future fees. And Enron, the bankers agreed, was the bluest of the blue.

After the meeting wrapped up, one banker, Matt Lyness, approached George Serice, a colleague. Lyness was stunned by the numbers he just saw— in "Enron shock," Serice joked. Chase couldn't be the only bank putting together off-balance-sheet deals with Enron, Lyness mused to Serice.

"Just how much in off-balance-sheet commitments do these guys have?" he wondered.

Serice was coy. "You don't want to know," he replied.

Should Enron try to raise its triple-B-plus credit rating to an A level?

Skilling had pushed the question for years. For most companies the answer would be obvious: yes. An A rating was insurance against defections by trading partners in wobbly markets. Trading was Enron's profit center. There was good reason to go all-out and protect the crown jewel.

But, somehow, nobody on the board seemed to worry much about Enron's credit rating. The complacency rested on the assumption that Enron had grown so powerful in the energy markets that trading partners would have nowhere else to turn. Besides, raising the rating would have a price. Enron would have to cut billions in its debt levels and limit its financing choices. Its light-speed growth would slow. All to ward off some unseen, theoretical future threat. It was, some directors and managers thought, like spending millions of dollars for insurance against being hit by an asteroid.

Skilling raised the question with Pug Winokur.

"Tell me, Jeff," Winokur responded, "what business are we losing because of our credit rating?"

Skilling shrugged. "None."

"So what business would an A rating bring in?"

"None."

Winokur smiled. "So why do we need it?"

The logic seemed strong. It wasn't like Enron was in danger. Skilling dropped the idea.

Ken Rice walked briskly into a conference room down from his office. Kevin Hannon, his co–chief executive in Enron's wholesale-trading division, was there waiting.

The two men were getting together for the task that everybody hated—putting together their budget for the coming year, reporting not only current performance but projected profits for 1999. And there was no doubt that whatever numbers they wrote down, they had to be larger than the ones reported this year. That's what Enron told Wall Street was coming, and that's what wholesale trading had to deliver.

The past year's performance was not an issue. By any measure, it had been spectacular—almost 50 percent higher, before interest and taxes, than in 1997. The problem, as always: what to do for an encore?

Rice sighed. "Man, this is gonna be hard. How the hell are we gonna make earnings next year?"

Both Rice and Hannon were already familiar with the tyranny of Enron's mark-to-market accounting. They called it "the treadmill," and each year it just got steeper and steeper. No matter the division's performance, once January rolled around, the earnings cupboard would be empty. All the cash coming in for the next several decades on energy contracts had already been eaten up, reported as current profits.

Maybe it was time to break out the idea they had been tooling around with for months: using the fledgling Portland telecom business—now called Enron Communications—to trade Internet bandwidth like a commodity. The idea was simple: Couldn't Enron's West Coast network swap broadband time and access with a network in the East? Then it could transform a regional network into a national business. New markets meant big profits. And no potential market was bigger than the one for the Internet.

Rice looked up from the paperwork. "Kevin, it's time for us to get serious with what we're going to do next."

Hannon stared at Rice evenly. "Bandwidth trading?"

"Yup. Gotta get serious."

Thirty million dollars.

For Rex Shelby, the number seemed beyond comprehension. Enron Communications wanted to pay thirty million for his tiny, eight-person Houston company, Modulus Technologies, and its cutting-edge software called InterAgent—sort of a tool kit that programmers used to link computers and operating systems.

Modulus had attracted interest from an industry giant, Sun Microsystems. Then a friend, Scott Yeager from Enron, had dangled greater opportunities before Shelby: not just the thirty million, but the prospect of going public, making Shelby and other shareholders millions more. Sun executives were stunned; they were offering less than fifteen million dollars and thought *that* was a stretch. They walked away.

Even so, Shelby wasn't dazzled by the prospect of vast riches. He drove an old Toyota. He ignored friends' advice on how to minimize his income taxes. What enthralled him was the chance that Enron would allow him to make his mark on the high-tech world by letting him pursue a dream.

Joe Hirko and Yeager, both with Enron Communications, had told him they wanted to build an advanced, software-driven "intelligent" network, providing more options and features than were usually available on the Internet. It would be a bandwidth-on-demand method for delivering data, video, whatever could be carried over the network. InterAgent, they said, would be key to the vision.

Building the network, of course, would involve a lot of cash. But at the same time, a separate part of Enron was pursuing another strategy—bandwidth trading. Shelby had no idea that even before he started, Enron Communications was already going in two different directions.

At noon on November 20, a Friday, executives swarmed about a conference room on the forty-ninth floor of the Enron building. On one side of the giant table sat executives from international; on the other were corporate officers, including Skilling and Causey. The meeting had been called for international to lay out its performance for the past year and its expectations for the future.

Skilling reviewed the bound report in front of him with growing anger. Despite his enthusiastic comments to the board about Enron's inroads overseas, the results were disappointing. Something had to change.

This, he knew, would be his last battle with Rebecca Mark—at least over international. Now that she was in charge of Azurix, this meeting would be her swan song with her old division. It wasn't going to be pleasant.

Skilling tossed the latest report on the table.

"We've got to get these returns up," he snapped.

"Our returns are excellent," Mark shot back.

Skilling gaped at her. *Is she on the same planet?*

"What are you talking about, Rebecca? We've got billions invested, and you guys are pulling in like sixty million dollars for the quarter, and even that's a stretch."

"All our projects make money," Mark replied simply.

Skilling tossed up his hands. "Come on, Rebecca! What are you talking about! Look at the Dominican Republic!"

There wasn't, he figured, much argument there. That project destroyed a hotel. The Dominicans stopped paying. On any level, the Dominican Republic was a disaster.

Mark didn't bend. The returns there were strong.

Skilling blinked. "How the hell do you figure that?"

"Cash in, cash out, we got all our money out. We got millions of dollars in cash out from fees."

"Rebecca," Skilling said, "we still have to pay back the financing. We can't just count money we put in and money we took out. We've gotta pay it all back!"

This is beyond ridiculous, Skilling thought. Here they were, the chief operating officer and the vice chairman of Enron, and they didn't have anything close to the same idea about how to calculate investment returns.

McMahon glanced up from his desk when he heard the tapping on his open door. It was Bill Brown, one of the division's better deal guys. McMahon invited him in.

Brown hesitated. "Uh, no. Can we go to your conference room? I've got a problem I need to discuss."

McMahon pushed back from his desk, following Brown next door. The conference room was one of the few spaces on the floor without a glass wall. Apparently, Brown didn't want anyone to see this meeting taking place.

McMahon flopped into a chair. "Okay, what's up?"

"We need to make a change in JEDI," Brown started.

McMahon couldn't take it all in. Something about changing the division of cash flow out of JEDI. There were going to be some fees paid to Enron's partner in JEDI.

"So you know Calpers was bought out by Chewco—"

McMahon interrupted. "No, I don't know anything about that. Remember, I've been in London."

"Oh, okay," Brown replied, walking over to the whiteboard. "Let me draw the structure for you."

McMahon watched, mesmerized, as Brown sketched boxes within boxes and lines. *What the hell is that?* he wondered.

Brown pointed at the boxes, explaining how each fit in the deal. Then he tapped a small box at the bottom. "This is where the equity ownership of Chewco is," he said. "That's Bill Dodson."

McMahon said nothing for a second. "Okay."

"You know who Bill Dodson is?"

Some wealthy investor? "Never heard of him."

Brown set down the marker, fixing McMahon with a look.

"He's Michael Kopper's domestic partner."

It was as if all the air had been sucked out of the room. McMahon couldn't have heard that right.

"Michael Kopper?" he asked.

"Yeah."

A pause. "*Our* Michael Kopper?"

Brown nodded.

McMahon was an accountant. He knew the equity portion of Chewco had to be independent. "That works?" he asked. "I mean, that doesn't make it an affiliate?"

"No, the lawyers all signed off," Brown replied.

McMahon brought his hand up to his head and laughed. "Okay. That seems kind of crazy. I mean, if there was an officer of the company in that box, or even an officer's wife, that would raise a lot of accounting questions."

Brown shrugged. "Yeah, well, Kopper's not an officer. And Dodson's not a wife."

Boy. That seemed an awfully thin string to hang such a huge accounting question on. Why did Enron do it this way?

"All right, so what's your question?" McMahon asked.

"Okay, here's the issue. Michael is representing Bill in this negotiation."

McMahon sank in his chair. "Oh, Christ. Why is he doing *that*?"

That was the way that Dodson set it up, Brown said.

McMahon was flabbergasted. "All right, well, I guess you negotiate with Michael. Just get a reasonable deal."

"That's the problem," Brown said. "Michael is being a real prick about negotiating Chewco's fees, and he's close to Andy. So all this is likely to go to Andy."

"So?" McMahon said. "Bring it on. Get a reasonable fee, and if he doesn't agree to it, we'll go to Andy and tell him that Michael's harming the company."

He smiled. "Remind Michael who signs his paychecks. It says Enron on the bottom of those things, and if he's trying to get a few extra hundred thousand for his domestic partner, let's tell Andy he's screwing the company."

"Okay," Brown said. "So I'm going to go ahead and negotiate this as hard as I would with anybody else?"

McMahon leaned in. "Yeah, Bill. That's how it works."

Joe Sutton stepped into the Enron boardroom, eager to share the good news with the finance committee. The government in São Paulo, Brazil, needed cash. Another stake in Elektro was up for sale. Enron had the inside track.

"This is a fabulous opportunity," Sutton declared. "By making an additional investment, Enron International will enjoy either a substantial increase in recurring earnings from Elektro or a substantial gain by selling the equity when market conditions improve."

Of course, there were risks, Sutton said, such as the chance of a currency devaluation. But a sharp drop was unlikely. The government was working to get its finances in order, he said, and the International Monetary Fund had put a plan in place to stabilize the country's economy.

After a brief discussion, the committee authorized a bid of as much as $700 million for an increased stake in Elektro at the auction scheduled for January 15. The next morning, the full board signed on to the idea.

Everyone was excited. It seemed like a smart move.

Ben Glisan swiveled his chair, pulling up to his desk. His twenty-seventh-floor office was piled high with accounting and financial files—cluttered testimony to the esteem he had won at Enron. All the best deals, all the challenging transactions, were coming his way. His accounting acumen made him irreplaceable in special projects, and both Fastow and Kopper were making sure to take good care of him.

Reaching onto his desk, Glisan picked up a form authorizing an electronic funds transfer. A bank wire.

Here was graphic proof of his new standing. Glisan, just thirty-two years old, could sign his name, and that same day corporate funds would move out of Enron's bank account to whatever account he designated. He reviewed the form.

$400,000. For Chewco. Payment of a fee from Enron.

Glisan scribbled his name on the authorization line.

This was the fee that Brown had been negotiating and that McMahon suggested taking to Fastow. In the end, Kopper got what he wanted. Under the new deal, the percentage of cash distributions going to Chewco was moving *up.* And Fastow ordered that Chewco get its fat fee for being willing to revise the agreement. In essence, Chewco was being paid a fee for agreeing to take more money.

The illogic was staggering. But in secret, events were taking place that made the reasons for the payment clear. After receiving his fee, on December 30, Kopper wrote a series of checks—to Andy, Lea, and their two sons—each for ten thousand dollars or less. Just below the level that had to be reported to the IRS. Just below the amount that would force the bank to issue a currency-transaction report to the government, as a guard against money laundering. Then, in January, as a new tax year rolled around, Kopper wrote checks again. All told, Fastow received more than sixty-seven thousand dollars of the fee, tax-free.

Kopper then dutifully entered the transactions into the file on his laptop, keeping score of how he and Fastow were doing on their secret deals.

Mike Jakubik reached for the telephone in his London home and dialed Houston. For weeks, he had been parrying with Enron over the job offer and making only minor progress. The compensation package, while unspectacular, was all right, but the company was shortchanging him on his title. He was a managing director at Bankers Trust, but Enron wanted him to come in one step back, as a vice president. Still, he was uncertain about his future at Bankers Trust and plowed ahead on the Enron offer.

The Jakubiks entered into contracts to sell their London house and buy another in Houston. Mike's wife, Nancy, shopped for schools in Houston for their sons. One boy was autistic, and arrangements proved difficult. But the Jakubiks decided that the Enron opportunity was worth all the effort.

Then, a stumbling block. Out of the blue, Bankers Trust paid Jakubik a huge bonus and promised to make him a key player in its future. McMahon bristled at the news; he refused to sweeten Enron's offer. It was take it or leave it.

Now, twenty-four hours later, Jakubik had made his decision and called McMahon. "Jeff, it's Mike."

"Hey, how you doing?" McMahon said coldly.

"I'm going to take the job, Jeff."

"Ahh, great!" McMahon replied, his tone warming instantly. "Fantastic!"

The next morning, Jakubik gave notice to Bankers Trust. He and his wife took the final steps for selling their house and pulling the kids out of school. They had cast their lot with Enron. There was no turning back now.

Why the hell did Enron need Mike Jakubik anyway?

Fastow had been thinking about it. He didn't really know Jakubik. He didn't know whose interests he would represent. The guy seemed pretty independent. There was a better idea. A better alternative.

Michael Kopper. If Kopper was running the investment fund, Fastow could have a piece of it. Maybe it would be his ticket out of Enron, his route to big money. Kopper would be there for him, would let him play a role. Jakubik might not be so accommodating.

It was settled. The fund would be Kopper's job. Jakubik could do something else.

Few corporate start-ups spend their early lives in a palace. That is because, with huge initial expenses and little hopes for massive revenue, hoarding cash to pay only for the essentials is often necessary for survival.

Azurix, Enron's new water company, was an exception.

The new Rebecca Mark division was set up in Allen Center, across the street from the Enron building. Mark's own office was built with a private bathroom, gorgeous fixtures, deep woods. Nearby, an extravagant circular staircase was constructed between two floors, lending the place an air of elegance.

The free-spending attitude spread. In one of her early days at Azurix, Amanda Martin was in Mark's office when she glanced at the floor. No carpeting or polished wood here; instead, limestone had been installed.

"Rebecca, this is *good*," Martin said, admiring the floor. "*I* want limestone in my office, too."

She got it. And then so did one of her colleagues.

"I ought to be CFO of the Year."

Fastow was perched on the edge of his chair in his expansive fiftieth-floor office, one arm resting on the circular conference table. Across from him sat Mark Palmer, Enron's head of corporate communications, whom he had just summoned for a special assignment.

"I've seen it in *CFO* magazine," Fastow said. "Each year they name CFO of the Year. I want it to be me. Could you do that, get them to write a nice article about me?"

Palmer smiled, then laughed. Fastow was CFO of Enron, a Fortune 100 company. Why worry about such silliness?

"Are you joking?" Palmer asked.

Fastow squinched his face, shutting his eyes tight for a second before jerking up his eyebrows. Another tic.

"No, no, I'm serious," he replied. "Do you realize what a great job I've done at this company?"

He rattled off his achievements. He was using Enron's stock in creative ways—sticking it in partnerships as capital, all sorts of things. And the Elektro and Wessex financings—strokes of genius, Fastow said. He had persuaded investors to buy debt from off-balance-sheet entities just on the *promise* that Enron would issue new stock to pay them back if they ever got stiffed. For nothing but a future commitment, Enron got billions—*billions!* All thanks to Fastow and his innovative thinking.

As Fastow boasted, Palmer occasionally glanced off to his left at a long buffet-type table. It was built from wavy strips of blond wood, with bumpy, impractical surfaces. It was furniture as art, a triumph of form over substance, much like Fastow himself these days. After landing the CFO's job, he had stuffed his office with expensive knickknacks, with the seeming purpose of displaying an elevated taste worthy of Houston's moneyed class. His wife, Lea, had even begun decorating him, hiring a fashion consultant to make sure he dressed the part.

Fastow fiddled with a pen. This thing with *CFO* magazine was important, he said. It would be useful for him to have before the time of Performance Review Committee—the PRC—where bonuses and promotions at Enron were awarded.

"Every year I schedule time with Jeff Skilling and go tell him how great I am," Fastow said. "It's right before the PRC, and it's all about Andy."

Fastow squinched his face again. "I do it because I want to keep my profile up with Jeff, let him know the great things I'm doing."

Palmer tried not to recoil. He had heard of businesspeople with huge egos, but he had never actually encountered one whose conceit matched his reputation.

"If *CFO* magazine writes a nice article, names me CFO of the Year, I can use that," Fastow continued. "I can show Jeff I'm being recognized. It'll help with the PRC."

Now Palmer got it. Fastow wanted to be recognized by the magazine so he could make more money.

"Well, okay," Palmer began. "But understand, Andy, I don't know how to proceed on this. No guarantees."

Fastow nodded and stood. "Keep me updated," he said.

Palmer headed down to his division on the forty-ninth floor. Maybe, he thought, if he assigned the task to a top lieutenant like Karen Denne, there would be a chance of pulling something off. He found Denne at her desk.

"Hey, Karen," he said, "I've got an opportunity for you to hit a home run with the CFO."

Just after lunch on January 8, 1999, much of Enron's senior management made their way to the Highland Room on the second floor of the Four

Seasons Hotel. They were there for the PRC, the ranking system advanced by Skilling as the best method to reward Enron's top talent.

The competition was intense. Rankings were one through five—ones being worthy of fat bonuses and big promotions, fives needing to get their act together or move on. Skilling believed the PRC prevented a single boss from impeding a subordinate's career; and indeed, in the early days of the trading business, the process worked well, since everyone knew everyone. But as the concept expanded throughout the company, the PRC became all horse-trading and lobbying. In such an atmosphere, any employee without a boss's strong support was guaranteed a substandard ranking, the very result Skilling had hoped to avoid.

Executives gathered at a U-shaped table surrounding another table that was divided into five sections, one for each of the rankings. As the day wore on, small cardboard placards with employee names were placed in the sections, based on the recommendations of supervisors. Once the table was full, negotiations would begin. Only a set percentage could be at each level, usually meaning that some had to be moved down.

The moderator, Rocky Jones from human resources, stood in the center of the room, calling out employee names for discussion. Jones picked up the next placard.

"Jim Bouillion," Jones said. "Who's his sponsor?"

Jeff McMahon, flipping through a three-ring binder, raised his hand. "That's me," he said.

McMahon found his materials on Bouillion, although this was one case he could make by heart. Bouillion didn't have a glamorous job, just an essential one. He purchased Enron's insurance, making sure coverage was complete, negotiating the best rates, handling disasters. If a pipeline exploded, Bouillion was there. If the directors or senior managers were ever sued, it was Bouillion who protected them with liability insurance. McMahon thought he was top-rate.

But the PRC didn't. Bouillion had been at Enron for years, but time and again was passed over for promotion and never received much bonus. When McMahon started as treasurer, Bouillion had dropped by, explaining his situation. McMahon had promised to watch Bouillion's work and—come January, if he was impressed—to go to bat for him at the PRC. Bouillion hadn't let him down.

McMahon found his one-page summary in the binder.

"Okay," he said. "He runs the risk-management group, basically his job is insurance coverage."

Citing statistics and other details, McMahon made the case for Bouillion but was soon losing his audience. Some yawned. There were no splashy deals here, no accounting maneuvers that created profits. Just insurance. No one cared. After two minutes McMahon wrapped up his spiel.

"Okay," Rocky Jones said, holding the cardboard placard. "Where would you put him, Jeff?"

The key to the PRC. Don't go too high, don't start too low. "I would put Jim in the two category," McMahon replied.

Jones set the placard on the table's second section.

Hours later, all of the names for this session were on the table. As always, there were too many ones and twos.

"Okay," Jones said. "Some people have to move down."

McMahon knew this would be tough; there were plenty of names on that table of employees who had worked on fancy, eye-catching deals. They always got the attention. And sure enough, Kevin Hannon from wholesale soon went after Bouillion.

"Now, that guy could move down," Hannon said. "Look, I've got a guy there who did a trade that brought in millions. And what did Bouillion do? Buy insurance?"

He glanced at McMahon. "I mean, I don't know this guy, Jeff. But just listening, I'm sorry. He's got to go down."

"Well," McMahon said, "I disagree—"

"Oh, come on, Jeff!" Cliff Baxter interrupted. "Would you take any of these other guys in this category and put them in that job?"

"That's apples and oranges, Cliff," McMahon replied. "These guys can't do Jim's job. They don't understand the industry; they have no expertise in it."

"But they can learn! These other guys are better because they're flexible. They might even change it."

Other executives jumped in, voicing agreement. *Buy insurance?* A monkey could do that!

Skilling took the floor. "I agree. I think we can be doing a lot more with insurance." Maybe, he was suggesting, there were ways to make insurance a profit center. Possibly underwrite policies to other companies.

"Well, Jeff," McMahon responded, "this is a guy who has been there for the company, does a great job, and has been passed over time and again."

Skilling sighed. "Come on, Jeff. It's insurance. This isn't rocket science. This is not a top performer."

Done. Bouillion's name was moved down to level three.

By day's end, Enron had chosen its priorities. Employees on the big deals—like the Wessex and Elektro financings—got promotions and bonuses. *They* were the ones who brought value to the company; they were the ones who defined Enron. Not some guy who just purchased insurance.

It started in the most unlikely of places, the tiny Brazilian state of Minas Gerais, an area so little known that probably few at Enron had ever heard of it.

On January 13, 1999, Itamar Franco, the governor of Minas Gerais, abruptly announced his state could not pay the fifteen billion dollars it owed the national government. Reporters pressed Franco: Brazil's finances are so shaky, what about the impact this might have on world markets?

"I am very worried," he sneered, "about my shares in Hong Kong, New York, and Tokyo."

Others certainly were. Around the globe, currency traders scrambled to cash out of Brazil, dumping the *real*. Within twenty-four hours, the Brazilian government threw in the towel, announcing a devaluation of the currency. Sell orders flooded the floor of the São Paulo stock exchange. Twelve minutes after the opening bell, stock prices there had fallen ten percent.

The collapse of the *real*—one day before the scheduled auction of the new stake in Elektro—saved Enron from wasting another $700 million. But its original gamble on Brazil could not be salvaged. In no time, Enron had lost more than half of its investment.

Throughout the company, sheer terror. It seemed almost certain that Enron was going to have to restate the value of Elektro, knocking down reported earnings. Enron would look stupid—first it overpaid, then lost its shirt.

The accounting team got to work. The rules were on their side here, they decided. They didn't have to tell investors how much had just been lost through foolishness.

Chandeliers of glittering pink glass loomed over the ballroom at Houston's Four Seasons Hotel. It was approaching noon on January 21, and the Wall Street analysts in the room were getting hungry. For almost four and a half hours, they had been listening to presentations about Enron—and they had been impressive. Sure, there were some bumps in the road, like Elektro. But that was brushed off as one of those wrinkles to be expected from Enron's daring strategy of expansion in the developing world.

Finally, executives from the retail division wrapped up the last presentation. Skilling took the floor.

"All right, I think we're all about ready for lunch," he said. "Now, this morning you've heard a lot about our energy divisions, but during lunch you're going to see presentations about some exciting new businesses."

Skilling encouraged everyone to move to the ballroom foyer. There, china and glassware sparkled as light spilled from old-fashioned sconces on the walls. The analysts found their seats, and soon waiters began serving the first-course salads. Every sight, every sound spoke to the financial success of a company just drowning in profits.

Rebecca Mark stepped to the front. There were exhilirating developments at Azurix, Enron's water effort, she told the assembled crowd. The company was in a perfect position to profit handsomely from the rapidly changing international water business.

"This is a logical extension of Enron's expertise developed in the worldwide energy business," she said. "And with the acquisition of Wessex, we have the credibility and experience we need to move forward."

Half an hour later, it was time for Enron Communications to strut its stuff. Joe Hirko, now the unit's chief executive, revealed that on that very day his division was introducing the Enron Intelligent Network, the dedicated delivery platform envisioned months before, using the InterAgent software from Modulus. With this network, he said, customers could select the quality of service they wanted based on the type of content they needed to transmit.

Few of the analysts knew what the Enron executives talking about. *Water? Delivery platforms?* These people were energy analysts. They covered pipelines and power plants, not water utilities or the Internet. Mark and Hirko could be touting recipes for disaster, and most everyone in the room would be hard-pressed to know. But none saw that as a sign that Enron's executives might be past their own level of expertise as well.

After all, why should water and broadband be any different from their other businesses? Didn't everything Enron touch turn to profit?

A trio of Bell helicopters cut southward along the shoreline of the Arabian Sea. Inside the aircraft, Enron's directors watched as the streets of Mumbai gave way to tiny huts and villages, almost as if they had been transported from the modern era to the Middle Ages.

It was February 10, just before 10:30. For the first time, Enron's directors were headed for Dabhol to view construction at the giant power project approved so many years before. As the last vestiges of civilization disappeared, the muddy waters of Mumbai cleared; finally, there was nothing to see but overgrown landscape melting into the white sandy beaches that trailed the sea.

Then—*there it was.* Steel and concrete merged in a vast entanglement of buildings, towers, and wires. The greens and browns of India's countryside were overwhelmed by the blues, reds, and whites of the massive site. The helicopters circled before landing, giving a view of a housing area, crops of mango trees, a mobile medical unit, a hospital under construction. A man ran to a helicopter as the turning blades slowed, and threw open the door.

"Welcome to Dabhol!" he shouted.

The group was escorted to the on-site cafeteria and served a buffet lunch. After that, a plant manager arrived to give the directors a tour. They were dazzled.

"I just can't believe the size of this place," mumbled Pug Winokur.

Two hours later, they were back on the helicopters, returning to Mumbai. On board, they chatted excitedly about what they had seen. It was simply magnificent.

That night in central Mumbai, the first evening stars were coming into view from the seventh-floor patio at Hotel Oberoi. There, Enron's directors and managers mingled with crowds of Indian officials and businessmen beside an outdoor pool. As they chatted, darkness slowly transformed the gritty urban landscape into a sea of twinkling lights.

Wandering through the crowd, Ken Lay, dressed in an open-collared shirt and slacks, exuded a robust energy. In recent weeks, he had been jetting around the globe but showed no signs of strain. It was as if hitting the road had infused him with the drive to tackle the next challenge. Lay ventured toward a microphone. The patio fell silent.

"I just wanted to thank everyone for coming," he began. "This evening is really in honor of the Enron board, and it's a real treat for them to be here and to see what we and our business partners have accomplished."

Lay smiled. "So everybody enjoy yourselves, stay as long as you like, there's plenty of food."

He walked back into the crowd amid a smattering of applause. Over the next few hours, directors buttonholed him, expressing awe at what Enron had accomplished. Who would have thought such a top-of-the-line plant could be plunked down in the middle of nowhere? It was, they told him, worth every penny of the billions Enron had spent.

In his office, Jeff McMahon grabbed the phone as soon as his secretary told him Fastow was on the line.

"Hey, Andy, what's up?"

There were no pleasantries.

"I've decided to make Michael Kopper responsible for the private-equity fund we discussed," Fastow said.

McMahon sucked in a breath, speechless. Jakubik was on his way to Houston. He had already sold his London house, was moving his family. He had made the complex arrangements for his autistic son. What the hell was Fastow up to?

"Andy, what are you talking about? We've just spent months getting Jakubik. What's he supposed to do?"

"Well, you'll find some other thing for him to do in finance, won't you?"

McMahon struggled to collect his thoughts.

"Andy, that's not what we hired the guy for. He's leaving investment banking for this. He doesn't want to come here and issue bonds. He was going to create a fund, raise a bunch of capital, sell assets. That was the job!"

"Well, I've decided to give the job to Michael."

McMahon held the phone tight. "I'm coming up."

He slammed down the phone.

Five minutes and two elevator rides later, McMahon was charging down the fiftieth-floor hallway to Fastow's office. He walked in without knocking.

"Andy, I need to talk to you about this."

Fastow sat back. "Talk."

"You've got to reconsider. Jakubik has already quit his job; he's in the middle of moving."

McMahon sat. Fastow stayed behind his desk.

"This just doesn't make sense," McMahon continued. "Why Michael Kopper? Jakubik does this for a living. He's raised lots of equity for structured finance. Michael has never done this. Why is he qualified?"

"I've made my decision," Fastow said. "This is what we're going to do, and you just have to deal with it."

"Andy . . ."

"Call Jakubik and take care of it. Blame it on me if you want."

McMahon laughed. "Damn right, I'll blame it on you!"

The meeting ended, and McMahon left. Fastow went back to work, irritation gnawing at him. He didn't like his decisions to be questioned, certainly not by his own team.

In River Oaks, Fastow parked in the lot at Tony Mandola's Gulf Coast Kitchen. He popped open the door, waiting until Mike Jakubik emerged from the passenger side. Inside, the hostess escorted them to a table.

It was February 15, Jakubik's first day on the job, and he was eager to get going. McMahon had already told him something about Fastow asking Michael Kopper to start an equity fund, but the whole thing sounded vague.

Jakubik wasn't too worried; no company would recruit someone for a job, then hand it to somebody else.

Once the orders were in, Jakubik cleared his throat. "Okay, Andy, I'm ready to get going. What first? Do we go meet with the business heads to talk about what we're doing? Do I start with Skilling? What are your thoughts?"

Fastow mumbled a few suggestions, nothing definitive. The guy's demeanor struck Jakubik as odd—cool, distant. Not somebody he would enjoy working with. But Jakubik had dealt with lousy bosses in the past; he could live with Andy Fastow.

He remembered McMahon's cautionary words about Kopper.

"Listen, I also need to know, what's Michael Kopper's group doing? McMahon told me about it, and I'm a little worried this is similar to what I'm doing."

Fastow shook his head. "Oh no, no, no. What Michael's doing is totally different. Nothing like your job."

A fleeting smile passed over Fastow's face. "You own the institutional investors," he said. "They're yours. Anything going on with those guys, you own."

What the hell are you talking about? Jakubik felt like he'd had the wind knocked out of him. That wasn't the job they'd been discussing. Enron had already brought in somebody, Jim Timmins, to deal with institutional investors. Jakubik was supposed to be the equity-syndications guy. Was Fastow changing his job—*on his first day?*

"Andy, that's not what you hired me for. I'm supposed to be the equity-syndications czar. My group is named Equity Syndications! I'm supposed to get old investments off the balance sheet and make room for new ones."

Fastow sipped his water. He said nothing.

"What does it mean, I own the institutional investors?" Jakubik asked sharply.

Fastow pulled his collar. "Well, anytime we want to bring in the institutional investors, you're the guy."

Dear God. Jakubik was beginning to understand. He wouldn't be structuring deals; he would be managing relationships with pension funds. Talking up fund managers, getting them information, holding their hands. That wasn't what he did; he was an investment banker. And Enron waits to tell him until his job was gone, his house was gone, his kids were out of school?

"Andy, hold on. Who's doing triage up front? Who's going to work with the business side, decide what to sell, decide what goes where?"

Fastow looked at Jakubik evenly. "I'm not answering that. I'm telling you, you're responsible for managing the institutional investors."

There was a moment of silence. "So you're making me an investor-relations guy," Jakubik said simply.

Fastow reached for his water. "No, no," he chuckled. "Don't be ridiculous."

An hour later, Jakubik stomped back into his new office. He grabbed the phone to call his wife, Nancy, who was still packing the family in London.

"Hello?" she said.

"Holy shit!"

Nancy immediately recognized her husband's voice.

"Mike, what's wrong? What happened?"

Jakubik spoke slowly. "I have moved *five-fucking-thousand* miles to be an investor-relations *jerk!*"

"Rebecca, there is no *fucking* way we are doing that!"

Skilling, in a foul mood, glared at Rebecca Mark. It was about eleven on the morning of March 8, and Enron was days away from announcing plans to sell a huge chunk of Azurix to the public. For weeks, Mark had been pushing for every benefit and now wanted Enron's commitment to send every opportunity it found in the water business to Azurix.

Skilling refused.

"That just opens us up for lawsuits, Rebecca," he snapped. "If somebody in the bowels of Enron hears about some water opportunity and we don't bring it to you, we're liable for it. There's no way I'm setting that up."

Mark was furious. "But if the corporate-opportunity language isn't there, then anytime you want, you could go into the water business and compete against us!"

Skilling opened his eyes wide and smiled. "That's right. We could. We won't. But we could."

It was a delicious moment for Skilling. Everything at Enron was about to change. With Mark gone, there would be no more battles where she could go around his back to Lay. She would be off at Azurix. And he could run Enron the way he wanted, without interference.

Two days later, just before three o'clock, a woman tapped lightly on the large wooden door to Skilling's office. Skilling stood, delight on his face.

"Hey, Mary," he said. "Come on in."

Mary Joyce, who managed executive-compensation issues at Enron, stepped inside and took a seat. Soon they were joined by Rick Causey, Joe Sutton, and a few other executives. Skilling's face grew serious. He had waited for this moment for years. He wanted to enjoy it.

"Okay, we're making some big changes in the compensation for international," he said. "We're doing away with the old contracts. No more big bonuses on closing."

Sutton seemed to have anticipated what was coming. Mark wasn't even out the door yet, and Skilling was tearing up her business. "Jeff," he began.

Skilling didn't wait for the objection.

"We're going to a single, standardized compensation plan. Everybody goes through the PRC, everybody gets ranked, everybody gets paid according to their rank."

There were some protests, but they all knew it was pointless. The bonuses that Skilling and his team had railed against for almost a decade were dead.

Late on March 16, Fastow reached for the phone. The Azurix stock offering was another great opportunity, a chance to punish a Wall Street firm that wasn't cheering loudly enough for Enron. Fastow was looking forward to it.

This time his target was Don Dufresne with Salomon Smith Barney, part of Citigroup. As a stock analyst, Dufresne had always been too cautious in his ratings for Fastow's taste. He told investors that Enron had potential, but also sizable risk. That wasn't the kind of analysis Enron's management wanted to hear—or to be told to investors. Dufresne, they were convinced, just didn't get it.

But they wanted to be sure his firm did. Enron had just announced plans for the Azurix offering. Merrill, which had ingratiated itself to Enron by firing Olson, was lead underwriter. Salomon was allowed only a trivial role.

On the call, Fastow spoke with Robert Holloman, head of Salomon's investment banking group for energy. His message was identical with the one conveyed the year before to Merrill.

"Don Dufresne is just not constructive in his views about Enron," Fastow complained. "He wasn't supportive in our stock offering. And I think that showed up in the fact that you guys sold fewer shares than any other manager."

Holloman pressed Fastow. Were there problems with his company's investment-banking services?

"Nothing like that," he said. "Dufresne is the one reason you guys don't have a big role in Azurix. We want to see progress in your equity-research view of us before our relationship can really progress."

Within months, Dufresne was gone, giving Fastow another notch in his belt. In his place, Citi installed a new analyst, one recommended by Enron itself. Salomon Smith Barney's rating on Enron stock went up.

Wall Street got the message. Questioning Enron cost business. So questioners lost jobs.

Fastow's approach was subtle, almost seductive. With Mike Jakubik shoved aside, Fastow and Kopper were ready to start on this new equity-fund idea. But McMahon had been right: neither of them knew much about raising private equity. So they needed help from someone who did. The answer was obvious: Jim Timmins, the executive hired to handle relationships with the pension funds.

One afternoon Fastow spoke to Timmins. "We need to come up with ways to attract passive equity to our deals," he said. "Come back to me with any ideas you've got."

Timmins was excited. "Sure, Andy. Sounds great."

Timmins went off to work on the project. Fastow was eager to hear his ideas, particularly on which institutional funds to contact. Then he could steal them for himself and Kopper.

A group of Azurix executives watched as a Learjet pulled up to the Enron hangar. The aircraft stopped beside an Enron jet being prepared to fly the group to Hamilton, Ontario, for a business meeting. It took a moment for them to realize the Lear had been chartered for a specific trip.

When the Enron plane was ready, the executives walked out to the tarmac. One executive, Amanda Martin, saw a car approach, ferrying Rebecca Mark. It took a moment for Martin to add up the pieces; the chartered jet was for her boss.

Mark stepped out of the car and approached her team.

"Where are you going?" she asked.

"Hamilton," Martin responded. Azurix was negotiating to purchase some assets from Philip Services, based there. "Where are you going?"

"New York," Mark said. "Well, have a good trip."

Everyone flew away. On the crowded Enron plane, the Mark trip was the only topic of conversation. Finding a flight to Hamilton was difficult, and time was of the essence for this deal. But *New York*? There was a flight there almost every hour out of Houston. But rather than just buy a ticket, Mark had *chartered a Learjet*.

It gave the executives on board a very bad feeling.

The draft document was fifteen pages long, too skimpy to attract much attention from anyone. But Fastow and Kopper were sure this idea, at long last, would be the one that made them rich.

With Jakubik out of the way, and Timmins devising ideas Fastow was eager to take, the special-projects group was assembling an investment fund.

Fastow had toyed with the idea for months, raising it with bankers from Merrill Lynch. Now, by March 1999, the pieces were coming together.

They had drafted an offering memorandum for a fund called Enron Merchant Partners LP. The draft still had typos, and Merrill was nitpicking aspects of the deal. But the broad outlines were all there. Kopper would run it, reporting to Fastow. Both would be investors. The fund would raise a billion dollars. If Enron needed to sell something, Merchant Partners could be there. No more hunting for investors. Enron wouldn't have to worry about the market; it would *be* the market. Deals like RADR and Chewco would become part of the way Enron did business.

It was the perfect solution just looking for a problem.

CHAPTER 9

BEDLAM REIGNED AT ENRON on the morning of April 7, 1999, a Wednesday. Around the building, televisions and computers blared reports about Wall Street's hottest new stock. Traders wanting real-time information watched their quote monitors, awed by the rapidly rising numbers.

Rhythms NetConnections—the Internet start-up that had sold a chunk of itself to Enron thirteen months before—had just gone public and, on a day that powered the Dow Jones Industrial Average past 10,000, was swept up in the get-rich-quick mania. Even by the irrational standards of the bubble market, Rhythms stood out, nearly tripling in its first trade on the NASDAQ market to fifty-six dollars. With mark-to-market accounting, Enron had just earned a fortune.

As the market's euphoria spread throughout the building, Jeff Skilling was in a conference room presiding over another interminable planning session, this one with the merchant-investment committee of the wholesale division. Skilling was pushing the executives to find a way to protect Enron's gains in its high-flying merchant investments with "hedges"—related investments that would go up in value if Enron's holdings went down. Without hedges, every dollar of profit from merchant investments could turn into a loss when the market soured.

As the meeting droned on, Kevin Garland, from Enron's private-equity group, glanced at his alpha pager to check something.

"Hey, Jeff," he interrupted. "Remember that Rhythms investment we made?"

"Yeah."

"Well, it just went public today. You know how much money we've made?"

A ten-million-dollar private investment, held for one year? Maybe ten million in profit? "What?" Skilling asked.

"Last I checked, we're up around ninety million dollars."

Stunned silence. "*What?*" Skilling barked.

And the price just kept going. By afternoon, the value of Enron's investment in Rhythms had climbed to nearly $400 million, up from around $28 million. Under mark-to-market accounting, each one of those dollars could be recognized by Enron as profit.

But there was a hitch. Under its deal with Rhythms, Enron could not sell its shares until six months after the public offering. The condition was standard fare for an IPO; no start-up wanted big shareholders dumping stock just as trading began. If Rhythms' stock price collapsed while Enron was still required to hold on to the shares, the huge, unanticipated windfall in the second quarter could transform into a huge, unexpected loss in the third.

"*This* is what I'm talking about," Skilling told the assembled executives. "This is why we need to figure out how to put together some good hedges."

A good hedge on Rhythms would avoid the black eye of a loss down the road, he said. It was a serious problem. They had to find a solution.

Setting up a hedge is a bit like taking a photograph. The idea is to capture a moment in time, freezing it in place. But as blurs and dark streaks can distort a snapshot, unanticipated imperfections can sabotage a hedge.

The reasons for wanting to lock things in place vary. With Rhythms, it was simple financial management: The price run-up brought in profits that Enron didn't want to lose. Setting up a hedge at the high price—snapping the picture at that moment—would theoretically allow Enron to halt everything at the best possible point for the company.

But what sounds easy in theory is difficult in practice. A perfect hedge would move up in value the exact amount that the investment moves down—the posed professional portrait of the financial world. Owning a stock, for instance, is usually a bet that its price will go up; investors can also bet that the price will go *down*—by borrowing shares and selling them, in what is known as a short position. So a perfect hedge for a stock would be to short the same stock. But that would be the same as selling, so for Enron that wasn't an option.

There were messier alternatives. The most obvious was to set up a different short position, betting that prices would fall in the stocks of an array of companies similar to Rhythms. That would protect Enron from a price collapse in high tech, but not from problems limited only to Rhythms.

There was, in theory, one more possibility. Enron could pay a third party to assume the risk that Rhythms' price would fall. Wall Street often sells what are known as put options on a stock—in effect, agreeing to purchase the stock at a set price in the future. If Enron could find an investment bank to sell it a put option—and agree, for a fee, to purchase Rhythms at its high-flying price six months in the future—then its profits would be locked in.

Unfortunately, that was impossible. Such a deal would likely violate Enron's agreement with Rhythms. Worse, no investment bank would sell a put option on a volatile, thinly traded stock like Rhythms without receiving a gargantuan fee—cutting into the profits Enron wanted. This was business, not love. No one would take on the risk of an almost-inevitable price decline just because Enron needed them to. Certainly not without some sort of inside deal.

Later that same day, April 7, reporters and photographers watched as Ken Lay shook hands with Drayton McLane, owner of the Houston Astros. They were on the northeast side of downtown, ready to make the formal announcement: Enron had agreed to pay $100 million for the right to name the new ballpark being built for the team. From now on, the Astros would play in Enron Field.

Lay thought it was a great arrangement. The money would be owed over thirty years, but during that time the retail business would manage the energy contracts at the baseball stadium, hopefully bringing in as much as $200 million. It was win-win all around.

Lay and McLane made a few statements for the reporters. Enron was excited to be part of the ball club, Lay said, and looked forward to opening day in 2000, when the ballpark would be ready for use.

"We'll do what we do best, which is manage energy and facilities," Lay said. "And we'll let the Astros do what they do best, which is winning baseball games."

"Isn't there another way to look at this?" David Duncan implored. "It's really important to Causey."

Duncan was on the phone with Carl Bass, haggling over some international deal designed to defer taxes Enron owed. But Bass had come back and said no, it couldn't be done. Now Duncan was pleading with him to try again, to find a way to let the tax expense go unrecognized that year.

"Not a lot I can do, Dave," Bass said.

Duncan pushed back one more time.

"Okay, tell you what," Bass said. He would call Andersen's top accounting experts in Chicago and ask them to review the deal one more time to see if he had missed anything.

He hadn't, they reported back. Bass figured it wasn't a big deal. The taxes owed were less than fifteen million dollars. Enron couldn't possibly need profits that badly.

Bass stood uncomfortably in the anteroom outside Causey's office. It was April 10, and in recent days Causey and Duncan had been down in Augusta, Georgia, watching the Masters Tournament. But they flew back early to meet Bass and hash through the tax issue one more time.

Causey called Bass into his office, where Duncan was already waiting. The three men wandered to the formal sitting area.

"All right, we all know why we're here," Causey said. "I'm going to lay out Enron's position."

Causey spoke for several minutes. He said nothing about the rules; instead, he talked about the financial outcome Enron wanted. Bass was unmoved.

"Sorry, Rick," Bass said. "I've looked at this, Chicago's looked at this. It is what it is."

"Wait," Duncan said. "Rick, I hear your point. So, Carl, what if you moved your position a little bit?"

Duncan explained how he thought Bass could compromise. Bass gaped at him. Duncan was supposed to represent the firm's opinion, not try to broker a compromise.

This isn't a negotiation, Dave. There's an answer. I gave it. We're done.

"So what if you did that? Do you think we could find a middle ground?" Duncan asked.

Did they not understand what accountants did? "No, Dave, there's no middle ground. There's an answer. The firm has put in its best people. And we have given the answer."

Causey sighed, looking furious. "Okay, fine."

The meeting broke up. As Bass left, anxiety welled in his mind.

God knows what these two are going to do now.

The stock analysts covering Enron were excited by the numbers coming in from Rhythms. This, they knew, could mean big income. So during a conference call on April 13, one analyst asked Skilling if Enron was booking any profits from its Rhythms investment.

"You got us," he replied. "No, we're carrying that on our books right now at a value of about twenty-eight million dollars."

But if Enron hadn't yet recorded the stock's full value, he said, it hadn't lost sight of the profit. "Just do the math. It's worth, at close yesterday, about $406 million, and again it's on the books at $28 million."

Someone mumbled a price update in Skilling's ear.

"Oh, it's up another fifteen dollars," he said, chuckling. "We're trying to figure out how we deal with this thing."

The next day, at the governor's office in the Austin Capitol building, George W. Bush took out a small white postcard embossed with his name. He picked up a felt-tip pen to write a quick note to his friend Ken Lay.

Lay and Bush had taken a few years to get to know each other, but the relationship had finally begun to bloom around 1994. That year Bush was battling then-governor Ann Richards for her job. Lay was also close to Richards but sided with Bush, shoveling almost thirty-eight thousand dollars into his campaign—three times what he gave Richards.

Since Bush had become Governor, his friendship with Lay had strengthened. Lay had been appointed by Richards to the Governor's Business Council, and Bush had reappointed him in 1995. When Bush started testing the waters for a presidential bid, Lay stepped up early with campaign contributions. Bush often sent Lay small Christmas gifts and frequently received reading material and letters from him.

Recently, Lay had forwarded a *New York Times Magazine* article written by Thomas Friedman, the Pulitzer Prize–winning writer, about the importance and challenges of globalization.

Bush dated the note and started scribbling: "Dear Ken, Thanks for the Friedman article—I too found it very interesting. All is well."

He signed the note "GW."

At about 10:15 on April 19, Skilling wrapped up with Fastow and his team, reviewing the agenda for the next meeting of the board's finance committee.

"Okay, guys, this looks fine," Skilling said as everyone stood.

Fastow lingered behind. He had asked Skilling's secretary to squeeze in a few minutes for a quick discussion. Skilling turned to him once everyone was gone.

"Andy, what's up?"

"I've got an idea," he said. "Anytime we do a complex transaction around here, we incur an incredible cost from all the investment-banking fees."

That Skilling knew; the fees were just killers.

"So what if I set up something, an independent investment fund where I was the general partner," Fastow continued. "To the extent you guys want to, you could offer me assets, and I would probably be able to give you a better price, because I understand the assets."

Skilling didn't know it, but this was the third version of the equity fund. Jakubik, someone who would have far less of a conflict than the CFO, had already been sandbagged and pushed aside in favor of Kopper. Now Fastow was supplanting Kopper. With Chewco, Kopper was already way ahead on the financial rewards from secret side deals. The numbers Kopper kept in the file on his laptop left no doubt this fund should go Fastow's way.

With the fund, Fastow told Skilling, there wouldn't be a need for investment bankers. That meant a higher purchase price and lower transaction costs.

"Well, yeah," Skilling said. "But it's got a conflict-of-interest issue."

Fastow nodded eagerly. "Yeah, that's true," he said. "But the whole issue is, is it cheaper, are we getting more benefit to shareholders by doing it this way."

Skilling thought about that. "Yeah, that's right," he said. "All right, go ahead. Look into it."

The discussion lasted a minute or so; neither man even bothered to sit down. Ever so nonchalantly, the most destructive move in Enron's history was under way.

"How the hell could you give away ten percent of the fucking company?"

Skilling glared across the table in the thirty-sixth-floor conference room at Ken Harrison and Joe Hirko, the Portland General executives now running Enron Communications. They stared back, unbending.

It was the morning of April 29, and Skilling had just discovered the unit's dirty secret: its managers had been giving out large chunks of itself to new employees. Private stock options—essentially bestowing ownership in the division—had been distributed like paper. Such a move was commonplace in privately held high-tech start-ups, to attract top talent. But this was different; Enron, a public company, was paying for everything. Now a bunch of untested new employees owned a large part of an Enron division and had been lobbying to sell it to the public.

"So this is what all that IPO talk was about, so your guys can each make a quick fifteen or twenty million bucks!" Skilling railed. "This is nuts!"

"We think it makes sense," Harrison continued. "You have to understand the way this business works—"

"It's not gonna happen, Ken! You want to fight about this, I'll fight it all the way to the board."

Skilling leaned in, glowering. "We are not doing an IPO of this business. It can't stand on its own."

"We think—" Harrison began.

"You want our money, but you want separate governance so you can pass out stock options?" Skilling roared. "It ain't gonna happen! It is *not* gonna happen!"

"Fine," Harrison said. "We'll take it to the board."

But Skilling would win his battle in a matter of weeks. The directors decided to keep Enron Communications as a core division and repurchase the stock options that had been distributed so casually.

It was going to cost Enron hundreds of millions of dollars to recover from this blunder. Now Skilling knew how he would use all those earnings magically created by Rhythms. If only they could figure out how to hedge them.

Fastow and a small band of supporters were already hard at work on figuring out how to safeguard the Rhythms treasure chest. The key would be Fastow's new equity fund.

The outside fund could be the third party that provided Enron with a hedge against a price decline in Rhythms. It would offer what no rational investor could: an agreement to assume the risk of owning Rhythms. No financial firm would do that without being paid a fortune.

Of course, neither would Fastow.

Azurix needed a win.

Rebecca Mark's water company was weeks from going public but still hadn't done a big deal since Wessex the year before. Mark was already promising Enron-style profits—annual returns of 20 percent, twice as much as competitors. To pull that off, Azurix needed transactions. And now Mark thought she had found one.

It was called AGOSBA, an acronym for Administración General de Obras Sanitarias de Buenos Aires. A governmental body in Argentina was selling the rights to operate water services for six areas around Buenos Aires. In running the numbers, financial analysts at Azurix had calculated that the present value of the cash flows came in at about $333 million. Initially Mark and her team planned to bid between $321 million and $353 million for the deal, a range that almost guaranteed a healthy return.

But as the date of the Azurix IPO approached, their eagerness to trumpet a big acquisition prompted them to revise their offer up to more than $400 million. They justified the increase among themselves by extolling the virtues of the Wessex managers now at Azurix; they had no doubt that those executives could work magic in Argentina.

Mark and other Azurix executives took the matter to their board of directors, a group that included Lay, Skilling, Pug Winokur, John Duncan, and Joe Sutton. Amanda Martin, head of the Azurix division for the Americas, laid out the proposal. When she finished, Lay spoke up.

"We really need to win this one," he said.

Winokur agreed. "It would be very important for the IPO pricing," he said.

"You're right, it is critical that we win this in order to have a good IPO," Mark said. "So we would really like to see the board approve this number for our bid."

Lay looked at Martin. "Amanda, will this number win?"

Martin turned up her hands in a feigned shrug. "They're sealed bids, we don't know. But we've put as much juice into this as we can."

"Where's RAC on this?"

It was Skilling, pushing to know what Risk Assessment and Control—the group run by Rick Buy, the chief risk officer—thought of the planned bid.

"We're at the edge of RAC's tolerance," Martin said.

Skilling pushed harder. "Have they approved this number?"

"This is the highest number they'll approve."

"What does Buy say?"

"He's got warnings all over this," Martin replied. "But he's okay."

Mark picked it up from there. "Again, it's important that we win this. It's important this is approved."

Hard to argue that point. In fact . . .

"Does it make any sense to push the bid price higher?" Lay asked.

They took every precaution to maintain total secrecy.

The Azurix bid for the Argentina project was not put on paper. Instead, it was loaded onto a laptop computer; no one could access the file without the password. Their phones in Buenos Aires were checked for listening devices. Azurix executives felt sure their big French competitors, Vivendi and Suez Lyonnaise des Eaux, would do anything to knock an American upstart out of the running.

On May 17, the night before the bid, an executive carrying the laptop was put on an overnight flight from Houston aboard an Enron corporate plane. The next morning, the computer was brought to the Azurix team working on the Argentina deal. The data were downloaded and examined.

$438.6 million.

Under pressure from the Azurix board, the bid had been kicked up by about thirty million dollars at the last minute. The bid was placed in an envelope and hand-carried over to a government building in Buenos Aires, where bids were scheduled to be unsealed.

José Luis Vittor, a lawyer working with Azurix, watched as the officials opened up the envelopes and read the results. The process was complex; different companies were bidding for different portions of the water services. Vittor listened as the numbers were called out, calculating the differences between what others were willing to pay and the Azurix offer. A horrible re-alization settled in.

Azurix had overbid—by twice the amount that anyone else in the indus-try was willing to pay. If profits were there to be found at such a lofty price, only Azurix could see them.

It was Brazil all over again. Only worse.

Rebecca Mark tracked down Ken Lay with the news.

"We won in Argentina," she said. "We left some money on the table. But we'll make it work."

Lay nodded, smiling.

"Congratulations," he said.

Jim Timmins was back with his proposal for an equity fund. No one had told him yet that Fastow was already putting his own together, but that was the point. Fastow just wanted to take the best of whatever Timmins suggested.

Timmins called it Enron Equity Syndication Program, or Enron ESP. The company would raise about $400 million from five or six pension funds. Then Enron would put together deals and present them to the investors. Each would be allowed to pass on three opportunities before being replaced by another institution that wanted the chance to invest.

Jeremy Blachman, a finance executive, came back to Timmins with Fastow's verdict. "Andy doesn't like it. It gives the investors too much voting power."

That was the point, Timmins said. The fund would be attractive because investors would have control over what investments were made.

"Andy doesn't want to do that," Blachman said. "He said come back with something else."

Busy murals of blue and purple dominated the walls of La Griglia, an Italian grill in River Oaks popular among the city's power elite. In a secluded cor-ner on May 21, a Friday, Amanda Martin was eating lunch with Jeff Skilling. The food was good, but the conversation was unnerving.

Martin was terrified. Azurix was in trouble. It wasn't just the ridiculous Argentina bid; the company wasn't ready to go public. It had spent lots of money setting up offices around the world. It had signed a five-million-dol-lar lease on space in London, not to mention the hugely expensive Houston offices. The costs of circular staircases and limestone floors stacked up fast.

Worse, Martin thought, Rebecca Mark still seemed to have no idea how

Azurix would bring in her promised hefty returns. Skilling, she thought, had to stop the IPO. Azurix needed to stay under Enron's skirts a little longer.

"I am really concerned about the IPO," Martin said.

Skilling watched her, chewing his food.

"I'm afraid that Azurix just isn't ready," she said. "Once we're out there, we're going to be running naked. And I'm really nervous about that."

Skilling set down his fork.

"I want my money back," he said. "I fell on my sword for this one with the board. We didn't have a unanimous vote. I promised them I would get our money back and that we wouldn't make any more investments in this business."

"But, Jeff . . ."

"Just get out there and do the best IPO you can. I know you can do it. Market the shit out of it. And it's going to work. Make it happen."

Martin took a deep breath. "Well, okay," she said. "But I'm also concerned about Rebecca."

Skilling cut her off. "She's a smart woman."

There was a pause. "You don't want to talk about it, do you?" Martin asked.

Skilling's face was expressionless. "No, I don't."

Fastow had been hitting the hustings, speaking to bankers about his fund. This was not going to be a splashy deal like the planned Enron Merchant Partners. This was smaller, for only $15 million of outside investments.

He approached Kevin Howard, the prime banker for Enron at Greenwich NatWest. "I have a deal to discuss," Fastow said. "But I have to insist on total secrecy."

He would be setting up a fund, tentatively called Martin, Fastow said. It would be like any special-purpose entity, with a small sliver of capital from outside, independent parties like Greenwich NatWest. Fastow would be investing himself, maybe Kopper, too. Enron would kick in more than $220 million in the form of company stock. That would back up the fund's commitment to provide the hedge for Enron's investment in Rhythms.

Howard listened attentively and agreed to forward the idea to bankers in structured finance. The response was uniform: what the hell was Fastow talking about?

The thing sounded like nonsense. Enron would give $220 million to its CFO, and then get that money back if its Rhythms investment lost value? Wouldn't it get the stock back anyway, or at least be paid for it?

On May 28, David Bermingham, a structured-finance banker with

Greenwich, reviewed Howard's e-mail about the proposal. He couldn't shake the feeling that this whole thing sounded like some sort of scam being perpetrated by Fastow. He hit "reply" and began banging out a response.

"The fact is that a two-bit LLC called Martin, owned by a couple of Enron employees, will all of a sudden be *gifted* $220 million of Enron stock," Bermingham typed.

In fact, the way the deal was structured, Martin would never have to do anything for Fastow to get rich, he wrote.

Fastow and Kopper could "sell the stock in the market, pack up their bag and disappear off to Rio," he wrote. "If you owned it, wouldn't you? Now I'm beginning to understand why these guys are so keen to get in on it."

Bermingham hit "return" on his keyboard.

"What am I missing???????" he typed.

"Why would any director in his or her right mind ever approve such a scheme?"

That same day, Ben Neuhausen—a partner with Andersen's top accounting division, the Professional Standards Group—was at his computer in the firm's Chicago office. David Duncan, the lead partner on Enron, had consulted him about some harebrained idea from the company to have its CFO manage an outside fund, one set up to do business with Enron itself.

Neuhausen was floored. The idea made no business sense, and it screamed of conflicts. So on May 28, Neuhausen began typing his response to Duncan, expressing disbelief that any company would ever try something like this.

"Even if all the accounting obstacles below are overcome, it's a related party," Neuhausen typed. "Would Enron want these transactions disclosed every year as related party transactions in their financial statements?"

But that wasn't the main thing bothering Neuhausen. The way this fund was being set up, it looked like Enron hoped to use it as its own little marketplace, available to purchase assets. That was fine, but Enron couldn't then turn around and book profits from those sales to its captive fund, Neuhausen wrote. That would be going too far.

Early the following Tuesday morning, June 1, David Duncan logged on to his computer and read the e-mail message from Neuhausen that had arrived after he left on Friday. He clicked "reply" and started typing.

"On your point (i.e. the whole thing is a bad idea) I really couldn't agree more," he wrote.

But, he pointed out, this was far from a done deal. After all, it would have to be approved by the board, the general counsel, everybody. Once the directors realized what Fastow was up to, Duncan felt confident that they might kill the proposal outright.

"This thing is still very much in the brainstorming stage, but Andy wants to move through it very quickly to get all this done, if possible, this quarter," Duncan typed. "Andy is convinced that this is such a win-win that everyone will buy in. We'll see."

If it did go through, Duncan wrote, he would need Neuhausen's help to stop Enron from trying to book profits through sales of its assets to the fund. "I'll need all the ammo I can get to take that issue on," he typed.

The dark BMW 740i pulled out of the garage at Allen Center before turning onto Smith Street. Inside, Cliff Baxter gripped the steering wheel lovingly, enjoying the engine's finely tuned growl as he drove toward Dong Ting, a favorite Chinese restaurant. Beside him, Ray Bowen glanced around, admiring the fine leather and fancy trimmings.

"Nice car, Cliff," Bowen said.

"Thanks," Baxter responded. "I thought about getting the 750iL, but it would have been a bit too flashy."

Bowen nodded.

"You know, Ray, I don't live in River Oaks," Baxter said. "I could, but I didn't want to. I live in Sugar Land, outside of town, and I wanted a nice car for the commute."

"Well, it's a nice car," Bowen responded.

Baxter, who worked as the top deal maker with wholesale, had invited Bowen to lunch that day in hopes of persuading him to take a new job. The merchant-investing effort was a mess; deals were being done for all the wrong reasons, largely by executives who wanted accomplishments to brag about when bonus time came around. But the follow-through was terrible; for every successful investment like Rhythms, there were untold numbers of disasters costing Enron plenty. Baxter wanted to set up a division of sharp-eyed finance guys like Bowen to serve as a check on the unfettered enthusiasm of the company's deal makers.

This, Baxter said, would be real quality control, digging through the deals' numbers and assumptions. Supposedly, this was the job Rick Buy was doing with RAC, but Baxter wasn't impressed with their performance. They seemed to have neither the time nor the spine to root out the bad deals and stop them. Those were decisions, Baxter said, that should be made inside the wholesale family. Bowen found the idea intriguing and told Baxter it sounded like a challenge he would be eager to take on.

Baxter kept his eyes on the road.

"Well, part of that, you know, is you'll be leaving finance," he said. "What do you think of that?"

"I have no issues with leaving Fastow," Bowen said. "I don't want to be in that organization anymore."

Baxter smiled. This was music to his ears. "Good. I'm not surprised. I'd heard you were ripe to move on."

The two began gossiping about Fastow. Baxter clearly detested the man and his ideas. Both of them had heard about this fund that Fastow was putting together. Bowen asked Baxter what he thought of it.

"Ray, I don't understand why we'd do that. Don't you think there are better ways to set up a pool of capital?"

"Yeah, there are better ways."

"Yeah, I don't understand Skilling and Fastow. I don't understand why Skilling sees Andy as a great CFO. I don't think this advice is the best for the company."

The restaurant was just ahead, at the Stuart Street intersection.

"Skilling sees Andy as a problem solver," Baxter continued. "He's got a blind spot when it comes to Andy. I've talked to him more than once about it. But he won't listen to me about Andy. He's just got a blind spot."

Signaling with the blinker, Baxter turned the car in to the lot for Dong Ting and pulled up to the valet on duty.

Lay reviewed the three-paragraph letter that had been composed for him. It was short and to the point. An attachment that ran five pages laid out the details. They were impressive, Lay thought with satisfaction, ample evidence to persuade *CFO* magazine that it should recognize Fastow as one of America's best chief financial officers.

The project to win Fastow the accolades had been under way for six months. Skilling had put in the nomination. Ben Glisan, the young accountant down in special projects, had written a letter from the employee's perspective, raining praise on Fastow. Now the crowning touch—Ken Lay's glowing endorsement.

His eyes darted over the last paragraph: "Andy's innovative and creative approach to financing is exemplary of the caliber of talent we employ at Enron. Andy is a true example of Enron's intellectual capital, which we consider to be Enron's greatest asset."

Everything seemed in order.

Four days later, Fastow was in Skilling's office, practically gloating. "We've got it, Jeff. We've worked out a hedge for Rhythms. You're going to love it."

Fastow described the broad plan, hammered out with the help of Kopper, Glisan, and Causey. Enron would contribute the bulk of his new fund's capital by turning over some of its stock. Outside investors would contribute about fifteen million dollars, enough to keep the fund off Enron's balance sheet. Fastow himself would put in a million.

There were a lot of complexities, featuring entities within entities. But in the end, a vehicle called Swap Sub, backed by capital from Fastow's fund, would sell Enron a put option on Rhythms stock. Then it wouldn't matter if the Rhythms stock price fell; Swap Sub would be required to purchase the shares from Enron six months in the future at its current price. The value of Rhythms would be locked in place, allowing Enron to hold on to its gains.

Skilling was impressed. The idea was complicated and creative, just what he liked. He wanted to talk to Causey about it, but on first listen it sounded pretty good.

"Keep plugging away," he said.

Ken Rice roamed through the lobby of the Houstonian hotel, looking for the Olivette restaurant. It was about 8:00 A.M. on June 8, and Rice was headed for a breakfast meeting with Skilling—about what, he wasn't sure.

Rice had plenty *he* wanted to discuss. Since November, he and Kevin Hannon, his co-head at wholesale, had been secretly working on their idea to start trading broadband. But now a turf war had begun: Portland wanted the new business to be part of Enron Communications, while Rice wanted it to be in his wholesale group, now called Enron Capital & Trade.

To resolve the issue, Rice had hired McKinsey to recommend the best organizational structure for the new business. McKinsey split the difference: it recommended that Enron Communications staff up in Houston while bringing in a wholesale manager to run the place. Rice liked the idea.

Rice and Skilling met up just outside the restaurant. The place was woody and bright, with chandeliers and sconces everywhere. At the table they ordered and were served quickly. As Rice munched on a piece of toast, Skilling started laying out what was on his mind.

"Ken, I've been thinking about creating a trading capability within Enron Communications," he began. "And I know you and Kevin have been talking about whether that should be with ECT."

Rice studied Skilling evenly. "Mm-hmm."

"But," Skilling continued, "I think the best approach would be to take a senior person out of ECT and put them in Enron Communications and build the capability there."

That's so typical. Rice always suspected McKinsey acted as Skilling's spy, revealing its conclusions to him, which he then passed off as his own ideas.

"I think you're the perfect guy for the job," Skilling said. "Would you be interested?"

"Yeah," Rice said. "I would be."

Skilling nodded. "Okay," he said slowly. "But here's the thing. I can't afford to lose Joe."

Joe. Joe Hirko, the former CFO of Portland General. Rice knew he had been running Enron Communications for a little more than a year.

Rice shrugged. "That's okay. Joe and I get along."

"Well, I'm afraid if we don't make the two of you co-CEOs, Joe is going to get pissed off and leave."

Rice was stunned. "I am not going to be co-CEO at Enron Communications," he said.

"Come on, Ken. We've got hundreds of high-tech people in Portland. We can't replace them all in Houston. If Hirko leaves, then they're all going to leave."

"I don't think they're all going to leave, Jeff. I don't even think Joe's going to leave."

"I don't want to risk it."

Skilling fixed him with a pleading expression. "Come on, Ken. Work with me. We've been together a long time. I promise it will work out. Just work with me on this."

Rice took a breath. "Let me think about it. I don't like it. But let me think about it."

A couple of days later, Rice came back with his answer: he would do as Skilling asked. Skilling was delighted.

Enron's latest venture, one that was supposed to be the cutting edge of the complex and ever-changing high-tech world, would be in the hands of Rice and Hirko, two guys from the gas and electricity business.

In Portland, Rex Shelby wandered past anonymous legions of casually dressed techies clattering at their keyboards. He headed to his desk and slumped in his chair.

Enron Communications was a mess. After selling his company, Modulus, to Enron the previous November, Shelby had hoped to see it aggressively pursue the vision of building a top-of-the-line, software-driven intelligent network. Instead, Enron was all over the place, talking about the network in one breath, veering off into discussions of broadband trading the next. A lot of high-tech companies had trouble doing *one* thing well; Enron seemed unwilling to limit itself to three or four.

And the arrogance of the place. Shelby didn't understand the swagger. Enron executives clearly considered themselves brilliant because of their success in energy. But why did they think that made them tops in high tech? It was like arguing that a skilled brain surgeon would, by extension, be a brilliant rocket scientist.

They were all so puffed up that they hadn't noticed how badly managed the broadband unit was. It was having trouble hiring people because it wasn't competitive on software. At the same time, it was still growing too fast as executives pursued every idea that popped into their heads. Now, Shelby heard, some trading guy was coming to co-head the division with Hirko, himself a technology neophyte.

Maybe I ought to resign, he thought. Go back to the techie world. There were plenty of jobs; the high-tech and Internet industries were booming. There was no reason to hang around Enron.

Shelby went to see Hirko to talk about it. But Hirko told him to bide his time. Things were getting better, he said. The pieces were coming together. Just wait and see.

Robert Jeffe, a banker with Credit Suisse First Boston, couldn't help but feel suspicious.

It was June 8, and Enron's chief financial officer had just come to him with a bizarre proposal: Enron was forming an equity fund and wanted Fastow to run it. And now he was hitting up CSFB to make an eight-million-dollar investment in it.

Jeffe didn't like the idea. Why would Enron's board, its lawyers, its accountants ever consider such a thing? The conflicts were overwhelming; Enron's CFO would be selling assets to himself. What was everyone thinking?

"You know, Andy, you really need to be careful here," Jeffe said. "If this transaction ever comes to light, you will look very, very bad."

Fastow pushed the idea, proclaiming the fund as a wonderful opportunity. It didn't take long for Jeffe to understand Fastow's enthusiasm. If the deal went through the way Fastow envisioned, Jeffe realized, Enron's CFO stood to rake in north of twenty million dollars.

On June 10, three pairs of fifty-five-foot legs, decked out with giant shoes, dangled down the front of the New York Stock Exchange. Inside, mannequins draped with custom-made clothes jammed a balcony overlooking the trading floor.

As 9:30 approached, nine men and women—salespeople from Nordstrom, the department-store chain whose stock was beginning to trade on the exchange that morning—appeared on the balcony alongside the mannequins. At the half hour, they pressed a button, sounding the opening bell.

While Nordstrom grabbed the limelight, another company was quietly making its Big Board debut—Azurix. And in history's hottest market for new stock issues, investors greeted it with indifference. Azurix executives had hoped to issue shares for twenty-two dollars each; investor demand only supported nineteen dollars. There was no massive price run-up; Azurix shares just drifted, closing the first day up thirty-seven cents.

The outcome didn't ruffle Rebecca Mark. Azurix had raised almost $700 million, enough to launch some big deals. She seemed to forget the fact that Azurix had some debts to pay.

Jeff McMahon, Enron's corporate treasurer, was at his desk when he heard that Rebecca Mark was holding for him. He picked up the phone.

"Morning, Jeff. How are you?"

As always, McMahon found Mark unerringly pleasant.

"I'm fine, Rebecca. Congratulations on the offering."

"Thanks. But that's why I'm calling. Our proceeds have been swept into the corporate account. I want my money."

McMahon paused. "I don't understand it to be your money, Rebecca," he said.

"No, no. The IPO funds are mine. They're supposed to go to the Azurix accounts."

"That wasn't my understanding. My understanding is that money from the IPO issuance came back to satisfy Marlin obligations and other debts."

Marlin—the water trust set up by Fastow to finance the original acquisition of Wessex, the British water company—had sold certificates to investors, who were now owed money. Some of the IPO funds were meant for them.

"That wasn't the deal," Mark objected.

"Rebecca, read the Marlin certificates. The funds are pretty much earmarked."

"That's not the deal I had with Ken."

"You need to talk to Skilling," McMahon said. "Because Skilling told me that was the deal."

"You misunderstand the deal."

"Rebecca, the deal wasn't with *me*," McMahon said, an edge to his voice. "I'm just telling you what I'm being told. So if you have an issue, you have to talk to Jeff."

The call ended, and McMahon dialed Fastow.

"Hey, Andy, I just had a call from Rebecca Mark," he began. He recounted the conversation.

"Let me talk to Skilling about it," Fastow said.

A minute later, McMahon's phone rang. The caller ID displayed Skilling's name. McMahon grabbed the receiver. Skilling skipped the pleasantries.

"You are absolutely right," he said. "We're getting our money back. I've told them this a lot of times. That is not her money, and under no circumstances are you to release funds to Azurix without my okay."

McMahon agreed and hung up. He never heard back from Rebecca Mark about the issue.

That same day, the phone rang in the twenty-ninth-floor office of Vince Kaminski, Enron's top risk analyst.* It was Rick Buy, calling from his office one floor down.

"Hey, Vince, Jeff Skilling and I have been down here talking," Buy began. "He wants you and the guys to start working on a put option on Rhythms stock."

Skilling had just gone through his final briefing on this fund idea of Fastow's with Causey. Skilling considered the idea a godsend; with it, Enron could use the Rhythms profits to repurchase employee stakes in Enron Communications, without worrying about future price falls.

"This has to be a top priority," Buy continued. "It's really urgent. Skilling wants your best guys on it."

"Okay," Kaminski said. "We'll get on it."

Kaminski dialed his top options-pricing expert, Stinson Gibner, and asked him to come by. As Kaminski hung up, Skilling dashed in. The man had just bounded up the staircase from the twenty-eighth floor. Kaminski thought he looked like somebody who had partied too hard the night before.

"I want to talk to you about this Rhythms put option," Skilling said as he walked in.

Gibner arrived, glancing at Kaminski with a look of surprise. What was Skilling doing here?

Kaminski stood. "Okay. Let's go to the conference room and talk about it."

The three men traipsed out the door, turning right toward the nearby conference room. Skilling started jabbering about . . . *something*. Neither

*Several official reports have identified the events in this section as occurring on June 2, 1999. However, in arriving at that date, each report relied on the same source document. Additional reporting shows that the source document is incorrect and that the actual date is June 10. See *Notes and Sources* for details.

Kaminski nor Gibner could make heads or tails of it. The words all seemed to run together. Hedging Rhythms. Some outside fund. Transferring a couple of hundred million dollars in stock.

Kaminski held up a hand. "Umm, Jeff, I'm not sure we're getting all of this."

"Okay," Skilling said.

He walked to the conference room whiteboard, picked up a marker, and began drawing boxes and arrows. He hesitated. It looked like a mess. "I'm not gonna draw it," he said. "Hold on, just hear me out."

Back to the monologue. This was going no place fast.

"Jeff, I think we have enough information," Kaminski interrupted. "Who can we call if we have other questions?"

Skilling set down the marker.

"Call Rick Causey," he said.

Skilling thanked the men for their time and traipsed out of the room. Kaminski and Gibner stayed behind for a moment, then glanced at each other.

"You know what he was talking about?" Kaminski asked.

Gibner shook his head. "No."

Kaminski shrugged, standing to head back to his office. "Well," he said, "let's call Causey."

A minute later, he had Causey on the line.

"We were just talking to Jeff about Rhythms," Kaminski began on his speakerphone. With his thick Polish accent, the company name came out sounding like "RITH-Ma."

"Oh yes, yes," Causey said excitedly. The two should make sure the option was as expensive as possible, he said.

What? The more expensive the option, the more Enron would have to pay. Why would Causey want that? Kaminski asked a few questions, but Causey didn't seem to know much of the deal's intricacies either.

"Just in case," Kaminski said. "Who has all the details of the transaction? Who do I call if I have questions?"

"Bob Butts." The company controller.

Kaminski thanked Causey and hung up. Maybe the third time would be the charm.

It was.

Butts laid out the deal structure, explaining how Enron would contribute its own stock—now with a value of about $250 million—to some outside fund, which would then sell a put option on Rhythms stock to Enron.

Kaminski still struggled with the idea. "One problem. Who's writing the option? Because I don't understand how they're going to protect themselves from a price decline."

Butts's response was matter-of-fact. "The option's being written by a partnership set up by the finance group."

The finance group? *Fastow's* finance group? A thought shot into Kaminski's head—a few years back, Fastow running retail, asking him to come up with a way to hedge against operating losses. The man was *an idiot!* He didn't understand hedging. People in Kaminski's group were always laughing about the silliness coming out of Fastow's group. One analyst, Rick Murphy, even suggested Fastow would destroy Enron with his ridiculous financial ideas.

Those guys, Kaminski thought, *have no idea what they're doing.*

Kaminski went back to his office, deeply distressed. This deal was nonsense, gibberish, the product of foolish minds. It couldn't work, and no one seemed to know that.

The evidence was there for anyone to see. Ordinarily, if Enron needed a put option on a stock, it could just buy one from some investment bank. But in this case, no institution would ever offer to sell one because of the enormous risk involved.

Ah, but here the hicks of the financial world think they're smarter than Wall Street.

If the market won't provide something, Kaminski thought, there's usually a darned good reason. And there was. No one—*no one*—would sell a put option on a volatile stock without taking precautions against a possible price fall. Essentially, that would mean setting up *another* hedge by establishing a short position—borrowing shares and selling them in a bet that the share price would go down. But for the stock to be shorted, it had to be heavily traded. There would have to be plenty of shares available for borrowing, and with Rhythms there weren't.

That wasn't the worst of it. The very stock sales required to create the short position could drive down the price, triggering the financial obligations of the option writer. And Rhythms was so thinly traded, Kaminski was fairly sure that was exactly what would happen.

Plus, the economics of the deal were laughable. Enron was taking $250 million in stock out of its own pocket and putting it into the fund's pocket. Then the fund would give the money back if Rhythms' price went down. *But the fund owed the money either way!* Enron would receive nothing that the fund wasn't already obligated to surrender.

Suddenly it hit him. A moment of clarity.

Fastow put this together assuming Enron's stock price would go up, no matter what. Such an increase would give this fund the ability to pay Enron for any losses in Rhythms and ultimately pay back the $250 million.

Kaminski shook his head. This was just a massive bet on Enron's stock price. The company's top managers might as well have gone to Las Vegas and placed a few hundred million dollars on black.

Minutes later, Kaminski stuck his head into one of the analysts' offices. "We need to have a meeting," he said. "Could you come down to the conference room."

He wasn't going to fight this until he and his team worked it through. He still needed to give his bosses the pricing answers—no matter how foolish the idea. But he had already decided to do his best to kill this thing.

After gathering a few more people, Kaminski walked with them down to the conference room. "Listen," he said. "We have to price a put option on Rhythms NetConnections."

No purpose in sugarcoating this.

"We have to price an option on a large number of shares. But this is a stock with a small trading volume, so it's basically impossible to hedge."

He paused. "The option will be written by a partnership formed by our finance group."

Silence for a second as his words sank in. Then the room exploded in laughter. Loud, sidesplitting laughter.

Kaminski brought a hand to his eye, until he, too, began chortling. "Okay, I know. But first things first. Let's figure out a fair value for this option."

At eight the next morning, June 11, Causey put down the phone and looked toward his doorway. Vince Kaminski and Stinson Gibner were there waiting.

"Rick, hello," Kaminski said. "We've put together the pricing model you wanted for Rhythms."

"Wonderful," Causey said. "Come in. Take a seat."

The two sat down at the conference table. Kaminski handed over a copy of a PowerPoint presentation he had written up. Causey quickly riffled through the pages.

"As I'm sure you know, this is a very difficult option to price," Kaminski began.

There was no way to make it affordable without incorporating some mechanism for the fund to hedge its position by shorting Rhythms stock, Kaminski said. That could only be done by building up a position slowly, so that the short sales didn't bring down the stock price. He and his team had calculated it would take about a year until a fully protected position could be set up. During that time, the fund would be exposed to a collapse in the value of Rhythms' stock. That risk left the cost of the option very high, Kaminski said.

Causey seemed unpersuaded.

"Okay, thanks, Vince. We might try some other ideas."

Kaminski headed to the twenty-eighth floor, where he wandered over to the office of Rick Buy, Enron's chief risk officer.

"Vince," Buy said, "what can I do for you?"

"My group has finished pricing this Rhythms option."

"Great."

"But I have some things I wanted to say," Kaminski continued. "I am very uncomfortable with this whole thing. This is a cockamamy idea."

The word came out "coke-a-memmy." Buy stared at Kaminski, not quite sure what he was saying. Kaminski realized that Buy hadn't understood him.

"This idea is so stupid," he said, "only Andy Fastow could have come up with it."

Buy smiled. "Yeah, it's Andy's idea. He's going to be the guy who runs the partnership."

What? They weren't just going to set it up—Fastow *himself* was going to run it?

"Enron should never go forward with such a thing," Kaminski said. "It is a terrible conflict of interest."

Buy held up a hand. "Wait a minute, Vince. Don't just jump to a conclusion. Look at the entire transaction. Analyze the whole thing, then tell me what you think."

Kaminski nodded.

"But get Stinson Gibner involved," Buy said. "I want to hear what he thinks, too."

They agreed that Buy would poke around for more information about the planned deal. After that, the three of them could take up the issue again the following week.

Kaminski would be out of town for a few days after that, but he promised Buy that he would have the full analysis wrapped up by Monday, June 21. He figured there wasn't a rush.

Exactly one week later, on June 18, Lay walked into his personal conference room at 10:00 A.M. and found the place packed. Skilling was there waiting, along with Fastow, Causey, and a couple of Enron lawyers. The air inside the room was electric.

"Okay, what's this about?" Lay asked.

Skilling spoke first. "As you may remember, Ken, we made an investment in Rhythms NetConnections, and it's gone up quite a bit in value," he said. "Now, it's very volatile, and we've been looking for some way to lock in the gains."

He nodded toward Fastow. "Andy and his people have looked at alternatives. And I think they've come up with a creative way to accomplish what we need."

Fastow pulled himself up straight. "Thanks, Jeff."

He brought out a PowerPoint presentation and passed it around. Skilling was right, there were a number of ways to lock in the gains, Fastow said. But none offered Enron strong protection against future losses in Rhythms.

"So," Fastow said, "we've come up with a better idea, a structure that gives us a pretty clean hedge."

He explained it in broad terms—the off-balance-sheet fund, the stock from Enron, the put option. "Now, we've concluded that the best way of structuring this would be for me to be the general partner of the fund," Fastow said. "That would give us more control over it."

Lay nodded. *Interesting.*

They had already approached two large investors, CSFB and Greenwich NatWest, and they seemed interested, Fastow said.

"Now," he said, "I have to admit, I'm concerned about doing this. I wouldn't want to damage my career at Enron or damage my compensation possibilities here."

He smiled. "Because, clearly, Enron's going to continue to be a far more important source of income for me."

Fastow was lying. Already bankers looking at the deal understood that he could rapidly make in excess of twenty million dollars from the fund, far more than his Enron pay.

"Despite my reservations, I'll be willing to invest money in it, raise some capital for it, and serve as the general partner," Fastow said. "It's the best way to get the deal done quickly. It's the right thing for Enron."

Lay nodded, intrigued by the idea. Not only did Fastow do a good job; here he was, taking on personal risk to benefit Enron. Lay couldn't have been more impressed.

He pressed his hand on the table and stood. "All right," Lay said. "I'll take this to the board, and tell them I support it."

The chairman had spoken. Lay headed out the door. Then Skilling stood and looked at the others in the room.

"Get it done," he ordered them.

"This deal should not be done," Kaminski said. "It is terrible for the company."

It was three days later, Monday, June 21. Kaminski and Gibner had spent the weekend working on their analysis, with each of them relying on different mathematical models. But both calculations had reached the same conclusion: this idea was a disaster waiting to happen.

"Explain," Buy said.

First, the conflicts. No company had ever put its chief financial officer in such a position, and for a very good reason. The CFO needed to be on the company's side, not his own.

"You can already see why, the way the partnership is structured," Kaminski said. "The payout of the structure is completely skewed against Enron shareholders."

"What do you mean?"

Kaminski looked somber. "It's heads, the partnership wins, tails Enron loses."

Fastow would receive money early in the partnership's life, largely from huge management fees. But Enron's payout, if it ever came, would be very late in the deal—meaning that it was betting this fund would hold together.

"But the structure is simply unstable," Kaminski said. "It's a partnership funded with Enron stock, and if Enron stock drops at the same time Rhythms stock drops, the partnership will be unable to meet its obligations."

The probability of such a dual decline was uncomfortably large, Kaminski said. He stood at the whiteboard, capturing the cold, mathematical reality. The deal would make Fastow rich but could leave Enron's shareholders holding the bag.

Buy held his chin. "This really surprises me," he said, staring at a graph of the profit distributions. He chuckled. "Now I understand why Andy's doing this. Next time he's running a racket, I want to be part of it."

Kaminski stood still. "What are you going to do?"

"What can I do? I'll try to stop it."

"Would you like me to write up my analysis in a report? Would that help?"

Buy shook his head. He picked up a single chart Gibner had produced. "Don't worry about it. I'll handle it."

The e-mail that David Bermigham clicked open was nothing if not effusive. It was from a Greenwich NatWest colleague, Mike Ellison, and was all about the Fastow fund deal.

Ellison had figured out that if Greenwich NatWest invested in it, the bank would do well. It could recognize profits from the recent climb in Enron's stock value almost immediately, profits that would count toward the bankers' bonus pool.

"This is a GREAT deal, I love it (greed and avarice)," the e-mail read. "And the year-end bonuses raise their ugly heads!"

Officials from Greenwich NatWest checked things out a few more times—meeting with Skilling and Fastow, making sure this deal wasn't a symptom of some hidden financial trauma at Enron. They concluded it wasn't and tossed up their hands. It was crazy; it was reckless, but it would be profitable. Greenwich NatWest signed on as an investor.

Over at CSFB, Robert Jeffe was still wrestling with his discomfort about the Fastow proposal. It struck him as more than just reckless. It seemed downright sleazy.

Jeffe and his colleagues decided to play it safe. Adebayo Ogunlesi, the head of CSFB's energy group, called Skilling to see if Enron was really behind this off-the-wall idea. Skilling assured him that management knew everything Fastow was doing and backed him 100 percent.

The bankers were in a corner. They knew Fastow had the ability to decide what business went to which bank, and that he had been more than willing in the past to retaliate against institutions that didn't play ball. If they followed their ethical instincts and turned away, the fund would never get put together by the end of the quarter. Fastow would punish CSFB. They knew it. They personally would pay a price for trying to uphold integrity at Enron.

CSFB approved the investment.

In a government office in the Cayman Islands, Cindy Jefferson pulled together a stack of papers faxed from the United States. It was the afternoon of June 21. Jefferson, the deputy registrar of exempted limited partnerships, thumbed through the sixteen pages. They concerned three partnerships, managed by some fellow named Andy Fastow.

Nothing unusual. Americans were always registering partnerships in the Caymans, where bank secrecy laws were strict and tax codes lax. Fastow, through lawyers at Kirkland & Ellis, was applying for his partnerships to be exempt from tax in the Caymans. Such applications were so common that Jefferson's entire day was spent approving them.

She reached for her stamp, pressing it onto the first page of each application. Then she filled out a certificate declaring the partnerships registered.

Fastow's fund—and the related entities—could now open for business. But he had dispensed with the original name, Martin, replacing it with the initials of his wife, Lea, and his two boys, Jeffrey and Matthew.

From now on, the fund would be known as LJM.

Enron needed to get rid of one of its international projects, a power plant in Cuiabá, Brazil. The company had a high-priced gas-supply contract with the plant but couldn't use mark-to-market accounting to recognize all the earnings. After all, the fuel was being sold to Enron itself.

But if someone else purchased part of the plant, not only could Enron shuck some $200 million of debt from its books, it could transform the gas contract into $65 million in profits. Still, finding a buyer would be tough. Cuiabá was a debacle, with construction delays and financing problems.

Then, in June, an answer. Ben Glisan searched out Kent Castleman, an executive working on the Cuiabá deals, to speak with him.

"Kent, I wanted to talk with you about Cuiabá. Global finance may have found a buyer."

This was good news. "Great. Who is it?"

"It's called LJM," Glisan replied.

Kaminski needed an answer. He had heard nothing from Buy about the fate of this terrible Fastow idea for almost two weeks. So now, on June 25, he strode into Buy's office.

"What happened with Rhythms?" Kaminski asked.

Buy gave him a sheepish look. "I couldn't stop it," he said. "The momentum was too strong."

Kaminski's face hardened.

"It will be fine," Buy said. "It's just temporary."

"That's fine, Rick," Kaminski replied. "But it is still a terrible conflict of interest."

Kaminski turned to leave, furious. Buy had faced a choice, he thought, between confrontation now or shame later. And he had chosen shame.

Wendy Gramm pulled off to the side of a road in northern Virginia, parking near a pay phone. Gramm—former chair of the Commodity Futures Trading Commission, wife of Texas Senator Phil Gramm, and current director of Enron—needed to hurry if she was going to call in time for the meeting of the board scheduled for today, June 28.

She pushed open her car door and hustled to the phone, carrying a sheaf of papers faxed to her for today's meeting. As she dialed in, the wind picked up, rustling her papers. She couldn't hear all that clearly, either. Well, no big deal.

"Wendy!" Lay intoned. "Glad you could join us."

Gramm's voice echoed over the speakerphone, along with the sounds of passing cars. "Wouldn't miss it, Ken."

The meeting began. "Let's come to order," Lay said. "We have a number of issues to deal with today."

The first, Lay said, was a vote on whether Enron should split its stock, two for one. Doubling the number of shares, but halving the price, would send an upbeat signal to the marketplace. It would be a testament to the directors' faith in the stock's future, and keep the cost in the reach of small investors.

"Do I have a motion?" Lay asked.

Gramm's voice came over the speakerphone, moving to adopt the stock-split resolution. The vote was unanimous.

"Next issue," Lay said. He recognized Skilling, who explained that Fastow was there with a proposal.

A slide clicked up onto the screen, with the words "Project LJM Board Presentation." Fastow gave the same run-through he had provided to Lay days before.

"The benefits from LJM are enormous," Fastow said. "It immediately shifts the mark-to-market risk in Rhythms in our merchant-equity portfolio."

This might also be a precursor, Fastow said, the first step toward setting up a larger equity fund that could be available for Enron. This first fund could also be used for other transactions, he said—perhaps capturing the value of Enron's investments in Brazil, like Cuiabá.

"Now, even though LJM will be capitalized with Enron stock and I will be an investor in LJM, I will not receive any current or future financial benefit from the appreciation of the Enron stock it holds."

But there were issues for him, Fastow said. "I do have serious concerns about me being general partner," he said. "But if the board and the company want me to do this, I'll be happy to do it."

"Andy, so long as this is a small part of your activities," Pug Winokur said, "there's no reason this should interfere."

The board asked a series of questions—nothing complicated. For most of the directors, what Fastow was describing was going past them. They quickly approved the resolution to allow for Fastow's participation in LJM.

The next day, Jim Timmins stood before Fastow and Kopper, making his big pitch for an Enron equity fund. Neither told him that the board had just approved one, although it was far smaller than what Timmins had in mind.

"Okay, so here's the idea," Timmins said. "We raise money for the fund under the Enron name. But we let it become more independent over time. The perception will still be that it has access to Enron deal flow."

In essence, the manager would ultimately run a fund that was separate from Enron but that had the credibility of the company name. Fastow was intrigued. He was already planning another fund something bigger and more lucrative in the future. Maybe Timmins had laid out the perfect structure for it.

"Okay," Fastow said. "Let me give it some thought."

Vince Kaminski was at his desk late on a Friday afternoon when the telephone rang. Skilling's name flashed on the caller ID. Kaminski reached for the handset.

"Hi, Vince. This is Jeff Skilling."

Kaminski froze. Skilling almost never called him. And why now, on a Friday afternoon? Everyone in the building knew to stay away from Skilling by that point in the week, when he was invariably tired, frustrated, and abrasive.

"Yes, Jeff," Kaminski said. "What can I do for you?"

There were going to be some changes, Skilling said. Kaminski's group was moving out of RAC. They would no longer review transactions from throughout the corporation. Instead, they were being shifted into wholesale trading.

Kaminski was stunned. "All right. Can I ask why?"

"There have been some complaints, Vince, that you're not helping people to do transactions," Skilling said. "Instead, you're spending all your time acting like cops."

A pause. "We don't need cops, Vince."

CHAPTER 10

"IT'S FUCKING RIDICULOUS!"

Cliff Baxter fumed as he sat in the back of Tony Mandola's, staring across the table at Ken Rice and Amanda Martin. The three had gone out for lunch on this day in July 1999, hoping to rekindle the close friendship damaged by the now-ended affair between Rice and Martin. But since taking their seats at the restaurant, Baxter and Rice had been raging almost nonstop about some terrible happening at Enron.

Martin set down the menu. "What's going on?"

"Haven't you heard?" Baxter asked earnestly.

Martin held up her hands. "Hey, I work on the other side of the street now. No one talks to me anymore."

Baxter shook his head. "Skilling has lost his fucking mind," he grumbled.

Martin waited expectantly, but Baxter said nothing.

Try again. "What's going on?" she asked insistently.

Baxter leaned back, flashing a fake smile. "Well, looks like Andy's going to be general partner of his own partnership so Enron can take things off balance sheet."

That was a surprise. Fastow was giving up the CFO job, after a little more than a year? Not a problem for Martin; she'd avoided Fastow since he threatened her a few years back. But a job change hardly seemed worth all the teeth gnashing.

"Great," Martin replied. "When does he go?"

Baxter's eyes narrowed, and Rice laughed.

"Oh, and *you're* so smart," Baxter said.

Rice just kept laughing. Martin was perplexed.

"Uh, okay," she said. "Am I missing something?"

Baxter leaned in on the table. "He's going to be the partnership's general partner, *and* he's going to be CFO."

Martin looked from one man to the other. They were both staring at her expectantly. This had to be a joke.

"Oh, bullshit," she said. "You can't do that. It's a conflict of interest."

"Fucking ridiculous!" Baxter barked.

Rice laughed. "Yeah, you'd think."

"Oh, come on, Ken," Martin said. "It's a conflict."

Rice and Baxter answered together. "No, it's not."

"Says who?"

"The board approved it," Rice said. "Skilling took it to the board, and the lawyers have signed off on it."

"It's just bullshit!" Baxter snapped.

Martin's bewilderment deepened. The CFO of Enron was going to represent a partnership that was negotiating *with Enron*? The whole idea was just loony.

"Amanda, you're an attorney," Rice said. "Isn't this a problem?"

"Well, I haven't practiced in a while, but this is sort of Corporate Law 101."

Baxter was in a rage. "This is the *worst* fucking decision that Skilling's ever made! I don't know what the fuck is wrong with him these days!"

"Are you sure they're doing this?" Martin asked.

Baxter lowered his voice to a growl. "I went to Skilling and I told him he was making a fucking mistake. And he tells me he's gone to the board and they've approved it. It's a done deal."

Martin brought a hand to her face. "This is frightening," she said.

Baxter nodded. "Frightening," he said softly.

"No," Rice interrupted. "This is dangerous."

Across town in Andersen's Houston offices, Carl Bass was trying to absorb what he had just heard from his colleague Tom Bauer. "Oh, come on," he said, a tone of bewilderment in his voice.

Bauer nodded. "Yup. They've set up this partnership to do business with Enron, and the CFO is running it."

Bass could only shake his head. "That's unbelievable."

"I told Dave we should just tell them no and say we won't do it," Bauer said. "But I got overruled."

This was going to be one hell of a Pandora's box, Bass thought. It was Andersen's job to audit transactions between clients and third parties, making sure that everything was arm's-length, with no wink-and-nod agreements designed to pump up the value of low-grade assets. But with Fastow on both sides of the table, how could Andersen judge whether anything was arm's-length? It was the same arm!

"You can't audit this," Bass said. "You can't get inside Andy Fastow's head and figure out if he's doing an honest deal. It's impossible! He's on both sides of the equation. That should have stopped this idea right there."

Bass quickly set to work digging for more information. One partner told him that it had been run to the top of the firm and approved.

The top of the firm. That had to mean John Stewart, head of the Professional Standards Group. Bass called Stewart in Chicago to ask if he had endorsed it.

"Well," Stewart said, "I wouldn't say we approved. We raised a bunch of issues on certain transactions. But we never looked at the entire thing and signed off on it."

Bass finished the call, lost in reflection. He didn't have the authority to do anything about this. But he couldn't help wondering, what kind of business executives would entertain, much less champion, such a terrible idea?

In Buenos Aires, a team of Azurix executives walked toward the administrative building for AGOSBA, its new water service. It had been weeks since Azurix won the company, bidding about twice the nearest competitor. But now, with the contracts signed, Azurix and its executives were firmly in charge. The team, led by John Garrison, head of South American operations, arrived at the door and strode inside.

Everything was a shambles. Computers had been pulled out of the wall and stolen. Filing cabinets were open, documents missing. The building had been looted.

In the days since taking control, no one at Azurix had thought to secure the offices. Argentine workers, fearful of losing the security of government employment, had rebelled against the privatization by wrecking the place.

After about an hour of assessing the damage, the executives realized that things were far worse than they had imagined when they first arrived. Stunned, Garrison headed over to the phone. He had to call Rebecca Mark in Houston right away.

"You're never going to believe this."

Mark, sitting in her office in Houston, could hear the panic in Garrison's voice. "What's the matter?"

Garrison answered slowly. "We don't have a billing office," he said.

"What do you mean, we don't have a billing office?"

"We don't have the computer system. We don't have computerized records. We don't have anything."

This couldn't be true. "You've got to be kidding me."

"No, I'm not kidding," Garrison replied. "Everything's gone! We're providing water to two million people and don't know who they are. We can't bill them!"

The numbers didn't lie. Huge sums of money had flown out Enron's doors since January, far more than had been budgeted. All for a hodgepodge of merchant investments, slapped together by deal makers in wholesale who were looking for something to tout come bonus time.

Cliff Baxter, who on July 1 had been appointed chief executive of Enron North America, the wholesale division, was still assembling a unit to stop bad merchant deals. And there were plenty that needed stopping—investments in paper companies, a Thailand steel mill, a fiberboard plant, an environmental services company—all businesses Enron knew next to nothing about.

On July 7, Enron's top managers met in the Evergreen 1 Room at the Houstonian hotel. Sitting at one of three tables assembled into an open-ended rectangle, Fastow and McMahon laid out the sorry statistics. Enron had budgeted $1.1 billion for merchant investments in the first six months of 1999. But the company had blasted through $3.6 billion—or $2.5 billion more than planned.

Something had to be done with all those investments, particularly the bad ones. Fastow already had an inkling that the solution might lie in the special-projects group.

In the research unit, Stinson Gibner walked into Vince Kaminski's office, a self-satisfied expression in his face.

"Guess what," Gibner said flatly. "There's a problem with the Rhythms hedge."

Kaminksi looked up from his desk. "*Already?* They were just put in place a week ago!"

Gibner nodded knowingly.

"What's the problem?" Kaminski asked.

The finance group didn't know what it was doing, Gibner said. In the best scenario, the value of the put option in the hedge would move up by a dollar for every dollar lost in Rhythms' share price. But Fastow and his colleagues had used a long-term put option. None of them seemed to be aware that the short-term prices of such puts moved less than the prices of the stocks that they hedged. So now, every time Rhythms' stock fell a dollar, the put went up by only fifty or sixty cents. And the difference would have to be reported by Enron as a loss.

Kaminski chuckled. "Just confirms what we said. People who don't know anything about hedging shouldn't hedge."

The two analysts knew that there weren't many people at Enron who could fix the problem. Pretty much only the research unit.

"What do we do?" Gibner asked.

Kaminski sighed. "Well, I suppose we should be good corporate citizens and try to fix it for them."

If nothing else, lunch was sure to be uncomfortable.

The four Andersen accountants took seats around the restaurant table. Three—Debra Cash, Tom Bauer, and Carl Bass—worked on the Enron account. The last was Gary Goolsby, a global risk partner from the Houston office. The three had asked Goolsby to lunch that day so they could lay out their concerns about their lead partner, David Duncan.

"I don't know how else to say it, Gary," Cash said. "Dave is just too close to the client."

Enron already pushed hard for fast answers, Bauer said, and didn't like to hear no. But none of the accountants had the sense that Duncan was conveying the risk of this assignment to the Enron audit committee.

"In that kind of environment, you can't get too close to the client," Cash said. "But Dave is out socializing with Rick Causey, playing golf with him. They go out together with their wives. He's too close."

Duncan seemed wrapped up in keeping Enron happy, the accountants said. They didn't necessarily think his independence had been compromised, but feared that it could be.

Goolsby listened politely and told them to keep him posted. But he wasn't all that worried. Keeping clients happy was Duncan's job. To Goolsby, it sounded like he was handling things just right.

McMahon and Kopper waited in the mahogany-paneled alcove outside Fastow's office. The next meeting of the Performance Review Committee was coming, and the three wanted to prepare. The idea was, by reviewing each employee at a pre-PRC meeting, they could present a united front at the real thing.

Fastow led everyone to a conference room, where they paged through notebooks stuffed with information about their teams. One at a time, they rattled off each executive's accomplishments, working out what ratings they planned to recommend.

When Glisan's name came up, Kopper ticked off five deals he had worked on in the last six months, including LJM. "These are deals only Ben could have done because of his accounting and finance background," he said.

They all agreed that Glisan deserved a high rating. McMahon flipped a page and mentioned Bill Brown, who had been handling some of the company's treasury operations. McMahon said Brown was involved in a number of very important deals.

Kopper huffed. "Oh, come on, Jeff, an associate could have done those."

"Yeah, I have to agree," Fastow said. "Those aren't even close to the kind of things Ben is doing."

This is ridiculous. These two steered all the best deals to the darlings like Glisan, then complained when others didn't do them. Maybe it was time to throw that out on the table.

"That's part of the problem," McMahon said. "Michael, you steal all the structured deals, anything that is the slightest bit flashy. But Bill could do those."

"Oh no," Kopper said. "He's nowhere close to Ben."

For several minutes, Kopper and McMahon debated the merits of Brown versus Glisan. The argument was resolved with Glisan rated category one, Brown category two. Another McMahon recommendation, Barry Schnapper, was also placed at two. Later they turned to Cheryl Lipshutz, another Kopper favorite. Kopper reviewed her work for the year so far.

"Cheryl should be rated with Ben as a one," he said.

"No way," McMahon shot back. "Bill and Barry are every bit as good as Cheryl. If you put her as a one, Bill and Barry should be up there, too."

More back-and-forth. Fastow held up a hand. There had to be a compromise here, he said. The three hammered out an idea.

"Fine, that's it," Fastow said. "Ben's our top guy. Then Cheryl, Bill, and Barry are close behind as twos."

McMahon and Kopper voiced agreement. They had a deal.

The next day at the PRC, everything was playing out as planned. Kopper held up Glisan as the cream of the crop, recommending him as a one; Lipshutz was also excellent, he said, but placed her as a two. McMahon presented Brown and Schnapper—both category two.

Once all the names were on the table, the lobbying began. One executive went after Bill Brown, suggesting that he should be pushed down to make room for one of his own guys.

McMahon felt pretty good. This was the benefit of the pre-meeting, so finance could beat back these kinds of attacks. McMahon tossed out some more details about Brown's work to justify his ranking. He glanced over at Fastow, waiting for him to voice his support.

Fastow cleared his throat. "Well, you know," he said slowly, "I think there's a big difference between Cheryl compared with Bill and Barry."

McMahon's jaw dropped. *That wasn't the deal.*

"So," Fastow continued, "I would keep Cheryl at two and bump Bill and Barry back to three."

"*What?*" McMahon blurted out.

Fastow glanced at him, looking smug. "You know, Jeff, we've got to make something happen here."

McMahon stared at Fastow in a cold fury. *You son of a bitch.* McMahon had fallen for a setup. He had been conned into putting his guys behind Glisan. Now that he'd already pushed them as twos rather than ones, he couldn't start all over, lobbying for them as ones but settling on twos. It all became clear. Their little tête-à-tête the day before hadn't been called to manage the PRC; Fastow had used it to manage McMahon.

Minutes later, as the debate moved on, McMahon stormed across the room and cornered Fastow.

"You fucked me!" he whispered in a fury. "Not only did you fuck me, you fucked these two people!"

Fastow shrugged. "Well, we've got to move forward."

Kopper noticed the commotion. He wandered over.

"Why did we have yesterday's meeting if we're going to do this?" McMahon pressed.

"Well," Fastow said, "I think Cheryl is above them."

"Yeah," Kopper interjected. "I think that's right."

McMahon shot Kopper a look. "Thank you very much, Michael. You *would* think so. She works for you!"

He turned back to Fastow. "You screwed me, Andy. They're at the same level. We agreed."

"We had to move on, Jeff," Fastow said simply.

McMahon clenched his jaw. He threatened to refuse to vote for the results, blocking the required unanimous approval. But Fastow knew it was all just bluster. McMahon wasn't going to keep everyone locked up in a room, trying to get them to overrule the CFO. Maybe if he had recommended his guys for category one to begin with. But of course, he hadn't.

Fastow had played the corporate chess game all too well and had checkmated McMahon. He had co-opted the PRC process, shown it for the political sham it could be. All to reward Kopper and his favorites.

On July 27 in Birmingham, England, a room at the Centre City Tower filled with the chattering of reporters waiting for a press conference. A door opened and a group of British officials walked in. A thin man stepped to the front—Ian Byatt, the government's top water regulator. He was flanked by John Prescott, the Deputy Prime Minister. The signal was clear: whatever Byatt was going to say in the next few minutes had the full backing of the government's senior ranks.

"I've got good news for customers," Byatt began.

Regulators had completed their review of rates charged by British water companies, he said, and prices would be cut. Wessex Water, for example, would have to drop prices by 14 percent. At the same time, he said, companies would be required to spend more money to improve water quality.

Questions came quickly. Many water utilities had recently been privatized, a reporter said. What will this mean for the companies that bought them?

"There is no doubt that profits will be lower," Byatt said. "They will come down, and they will stay down."

At Azurix, shell shock.

The company had been public less than seven weeks—*seven weeks!*—and now Wessex, its revenue machine, had been kneecapped by this new ruling. They had known something was coming, but hadn't really believed that it would be *this* bad. Coupled with Buenos Aires, the Wessex situation brought Azurix dangerously close to disaster.

Rebecca Mark called an emergency meeting. Looming over the conference table was a painting of two cowboys on horseback, deep in conversation. It was titled *True Lies*; Mark had hung it as an unspoken barb at Enron's culture of mendacity. Mark glared at the speakerphone, connected to Colin Skellett, the top executive at Wessex.

"How the hell did this happen?" she snapped. "Why didn't the utilities get together, negotiate against it? What can we do about it?"

"It's a done deal, Rebecca," Skellett replied. "There never was much we could do."

Mark closed her eyes, trying to control her fury.

"I want you to file a protest," she said.

"No, no. You don't want to make them angry."

"Well, what's our recourse? We don't just have to live with it. Can we appeal?"

"Rebecca, it's done. We have to live with it."

Mark sank into her chair.

Seven weeks.

The glow from his television and computer screens bathed Ray Bowen in flickering light. He was in his home office, his chair pulled up to the credenza, typing at his computer as his eyes darted occasionally to the TV screen. The phone rang, and Bowen's wife answered in another room.

"Ray!" she called. "It's Andy Fastow."

Bowen grabbed the receiver. Fastow's voice was stern.

"Ray, you and I need to talk. I hear you've been making a lot of noise that you don't like LJM."

LJM. This wouldn't be pleasant. Ever since he had heard of the deal, Bowen had bad-mouthed it to anyone who would listen. Now apparently his words had gotten back to Fastow.

"After all the things I've done for you, I can't believe you would go around behind my back!" Fastow raged.

He raised his voice, his anger snowballing. Bowen had heard it before. They were headed for a blowup.

"I'm doing this because it's good for Enron, not for me!" Fastow shouted. "Goddamn it! I am sick and tired of people attacking this! It's good for you, it's good for your business! So fuck you guys!"

Bowen hadn't said a word.

"I'll tell you what!" Fastow yelled, careening out of control. "We'll shut it down! And you *fucking* guys won't be able to get your *fucking* deals done because you won't have the *fucking* capital. So just figure it out on your own!"

Bowen held the phone away from his ear as the screaming escalated. Finally, a break in the tirade.

"Andy," Bowen said, "I'm not going to deny I've had issues with this. But my big failure here is not being man enough to talk about it to your face. Talking behind your back was unfair, I grant you. And I apologize for that."

Fastow deflated. "Look," he said, calming down. "Come by and I'll explain it for you. Maybe you'll be okay with it."

Bowen agreed, but the conversation gnawed at him. In bed, he tossed and turned, replaying the diatribe in his head. It seemed so out of proportion, almost as though Fastow had more at stake in LJM than it appeared. Bowen pushed the thought aside. He must be reading too much into things.

Kopper and Glisan strode into the London offices of Greenwich NatWest on the afternoon of August 5. They were there ostensibly on business for Enron, which was paying for their airfare and hotel. But in truth, they had come to discuss a deal to help Fastow earn more money from LJM.

They were greeted by David Bermingham and taken to a conference room filled with bankers from Greenwich and Credit Suisse First Boston, LJM's outside investors. Before getting started, the group telephoned Houston, bringing Anne Yeager, another Fastow favorite, into the meeting.

CSFB made the presentation. The bankers noted that Enron had restricted LJM from hedging the stock it had contributed to the fund; after all, hedging ultimately requires short sales, which can drive down the price. But CSFB had come up with a complex transaction, called Sails, which would allow the fund to hedge the Enron stock anyway.

With Sails, LJM would lock in a guaranteed minimum return on the Enron stock while still getting a ten percent cut of any future increase. Better for Fastow, LJM would receive a payment of tens of millions of dollars. Even though the outcome was exactly like a sale, there were plenty of bells and whistles attached, all to give everyone the ability to argue that something else had happened. While Enron stock would be converted to cash, CSFB and Greenwich agreed that they would deem it a new capital contribution, not a sale.

The semantic game didn't affect the fundamentals, but it opened up a world of opportunity for Fastow. Since he was prohibited by the board from benefiting from LJM's Enron stock, he could only profit from the sixteen million dollars in cash contributed by the fund's investors. But with Sails, Fastow would have a kitty of tens of millions in new cash for personal profits. All they needed to do was spend a few months putting the deal together.

Everyone laughed. "Boy," Glisan said. "*This* is a great day at the office."

After months of effort, Karen Denne from Enron's public relations office landed the big fish: *CFO* magazine had selected Fastow as one of the year's best chief financial officers. Now the final push. The magazine was writing an article about Fastow, and Enron's top executives needed to participate in interviews. Skilling and Lay readily agreed.

But first, Fastow. Denne stopped by his office on August 11 to brief him about the interview, explaining that it would be conducted by Russ Banham, a freelance writer.

Fastow laid a sheet of paper on his desk. "I've got several points I want to discuss on this," he said.

Minutes later, they were on the phone with Banham from his home office in Missoula, Montana. After some initial discussion, Banham asked something specific about Fastow's work.

"Let me take a step back and raise a few points to explain that," Fastow replied.

Point one . . . Point two . . .

"Well," Banham said, "that raises another question."

Fastow listened for a moment as Banham spoke.

"Point three," he began, ignoring the question.

The next morning, Denne stopped by Skilling's office to prepare him for the Banham interview. He was in high spirits, obviously happy that his guy was being recognized by his peers. By the time Banham was on the line, Skilling was in a jolly mood.

"Hey, Russ, how ya doing?" he said. "Glad you're taking the time to talk to us."

Banham, who had interviewed plenty of corporate CEOs, was struck by Skilling's warm banter. Most corporate types were standoffish; Skilling treated him almost like a drinking buddy. And he was effusive in his praise of Fastow.

"Andy has the intelligence and youthful exuberance to think in new ways," Skilling said. "He deserves every accolade tossed his way."

That day, a letter from Fastow went out to his LJM investors, informing them that he had just paid himself $550,000 from LJM in a semiannual management fee.

His million-dollar commitment to the fund had been in place forty-two days; now more than half the money was back in his bank account. He'd get the rest in six months, with the payment of his next fee. And he would still own a million dollars' worth of LJM. It was a no-lose deal.

Wearing shorts and a T-shirt, Fastow jogged toward the Enron building. He pushed through the door and began walking across the lobby. Suddenly he noticed Jim Timmins coming toward him. He had been avoiding Timmins for weeks, ever since hearing his ideas for a huge investment fund. Nothing he could do to put him off now.

Timmins wasted no time in getting to the point. "Andy," he said, stopping Fastow, "I've been trying to reach you. Do you like this equity-fund idea at all?"

"Yeah," Fastow said. "We're going to do it."

"Really?" Timmins asked. "Who's going to run it?"

Fastow shrugged. "I am."

Was this a joke? "Really. Now, how do you do that?"

"The board has given me a code-of-ethics waiver to set up these kinds of partnerships."

Timmins scarcely knew what to say. "Are you *kidding* me? You're the CFO!"

"Well, yeah, there it is."

Fastow thought for a second. Now was the time to start snagging what he could from Timmins.

"So I'll tell you what I want from you," he said. "I want your top-ten institutional contacts."

Too few. That wasn't the way it was done. "I'll give you twenty-five," Timmins said.

Fastow shook his head. "Nah. Just boil it down to the top ten."

On an afternoon in September, Dave Duncan dropped by to visit Carl Bass. Enron had reorganized the international division, with the result that Bass had little accounting work to do there. Duncan wanted to redeploy him and believed he had come up with the perfect solution.

"So here's my thought, Carl," he said. "Why don't you come work with me on Enron's structured-finance deals?"

A warning light went off in Bass's head. He knew structured finance was where Enron played the loosest on the accounting rules. No matter what objections Bass might raise, Dave Duncan was driving the bus and was going to do pretty much whatever Causey wanted.

Fortunately, he had a way out. John Stewart, Andersen's top accounting guru, had been trying to recruit him for the Professional Standards Group. He promised Bass he could stay in Houston and could even continue working with Enron—advising the Andersen accountants rather than directly dealing with the client. Until now, Bass hadn't made up his mind whether to accept. But Duncan's suggestion made his choice easier.

"I don't know, Dave," Bass said. "I've got this opportunity to work with the PSG."

Duncan shrugged. "Well, if that doesn't work out, let me know. Then you can work with me on structured finance."

Before the week was out, Bass called Stewart to say he would love to come aboard.

Kent Castleman was puzzled.

He had recently moved to Brazil for Enron but was still involved in selling a stake in its Cuiabá plant to LJM. He now knew the fund was Fastow's and had called the office to find out who was handling the deal. Cheryl Lipshutz, a Kopper and Fastow favorite, got on the phone.

Castleman paused. "You're negotiating for LJM?"

"That's the assignment," Lipshutz responded.

Strange. An Enron executive was negotiating with an Enron executive—to sell something from Enron?

Not his place to question.

Enron was selling part of Cuiabá? *To LJM?* That Fastow partnership? Carl Bass was thunderstruck. This Rhythms hedge was bad enough, but now Andersen was letting Enron sell assets in a deal that couldn't be audited. Andersen must not have thought this through. He hunted down Duncan.

"Dave, about Cuiabá. Are we certain they can do transactions like this with this partnership?"

"Oh yeah," Duncan responded. "I've run it up the flagpole. It's a legitimate deal."

Legitimate? Bass seethed. Andersen was compromising itself for fat fees from an out-of-control client. Well, Bass hadn't left for the PSG yet. He was still responsible for international accounting. And, by God, he was going to do everything he could to stop this one.

The deal terms were more outrageous than Bass had imagined. LJM didn't even plan to put in any cash up front for its Cuiabá stake. Fastow just wanted to commit to pay in the future and receive ownership based on that.

Bass put his foot down. There could not be a sale here unless LJM ponied up the money. Enron squawked, pleaded, argued. But Bass held firm. Enron and Fastow backed down.

But Bass's biggest impact on the Cuiabá negotiations derived from something he had done years before with John Stewart from the Professional Standards Group. Something no one at Enron knew anything about.

The accounting was the big problem. As Castleman and Lipshutz struggled through their bizarre transnational discussions, they kept tripping up on new rules.

Recently, the accounting rule setters had issued a revised policy for power plants; now they were considered real estate. Under the old rules, Enron had been able to enter into "sales" of plants to off-books entities, structuring the deals to retain the future risks—and benefits—of ownership. It was a sale in name only, but the rules allowed it. That's why the change stung; real-estate rules were tougher. A "sale" was a sale.

No one knew the change had been driven by someone who worked in the building. Carl Bass had quietly lobbied for more than a year on the reformulation, all to block some of Enron's irrational transactions.

But Fastow liked things the way they used to be. Even with the new rules, he wasn't interested in letting his fund take the risk of owning a stake in some lousy foreign power plant. Fastow boasted to Kopper and others that he and Causey had struck a verbal deal. LJM would not be a true owner of Cuiabá, just a temporary warehouse for it. Under the agreement, Fastow said, Enron would be responsible for finding another buyer—and if it couldn't, the company would buy the stake back from LJM, at a profit to the fund.

The deal Fastow was describing was hard to believe. Was it even legal? He had managed to avoid the consequences of the change in accounting rules, and structure another "sale" where Enron held on to all the risks of ownership. With this deal, Enron's profits would soar. Fastow's fund would look smart. Everybody would be happy.

Ken Lay walked down a richly appointed hallway in a Manhattan office building. The place was elegant, with expensive artwork and rich, lustrous paneled walls. These were the offices of a business that clearly spent to impress, to show off its financial prowess with every meticulous—and expensive—detail. That was a good sign; today Lay hoped to persuade his counterpart here to do business with Enron's retail division.

Lay approached the reception desk.

"Ken Lay to see Dennis Kozlowski, please."

Kozlowski headed Tyco International, a global conglomerate that dabbled in everything from fire alarms to disposable surgical devices. He was a corporate dynamo, a man whose name was whispered in comparison to Jack Welch, the General Electric chairman and renowned management guru. Kozlowski and Tyco were exactly the kind of clients Enron wanted—visionary, innovative, aggressive.

Moments later, a door opened. A hulking man with a large, bald head bounded in. "Ken," he said, thrusting out a beefy hand. "Dennis Kozlowski."

The two wandered back to a conference room, where Lay was introduced to Mark Swartz, Tyco's CFO. The conversation was pleasant enough. They parted amicably, with the gears in motion for a final deal. Lay liked the men; they struck him as smart and honest.

None of them could have imagined that in less than three years, they all would be indicted—Lay for his role in the Enron debacle, Kozlowski and Swartz for taking hundreds of millions of dollars out of Tyco for themselves.

Fastow was almost giddy.

A 300 percent rate of return. The way he and Kopper figured it, LJM was already hitting those numbers in a little over ten weeks. Not all of that could go Fastow's way; the board had specifically restricted him from taking personal profits from increases in the price of Enron stock turned over to LJM by the company. But they were well on their way to finagling around that.

And now Fastow was ready to move to his biggest project of all. In his LJM presentation to the board, he had suggested it would be a precursor to an even larger fund. None of the directors gave the idea much thought, but Fastow brought it up again to Skilling in August, describing the fund as a way to manage risk and improve its balance sheet. Skilling thought the idea sounded good.

Fastow had the plan laid out. He had hired Merrill Lynch to sell the fund; he had snagged Jim Timmins's top-ten institutional investors. And he was set to use Timmins's idea of creating an Enron fund that became independent from the company. It would be his way out, his step toward becoming a fund manager full-time. No more begging for bonuses. He would be wealthy. He would be a player in Houston society.

Fastow had no doubt: LJM2 would transform his life.

"LJM2 will have a lot of unique features," Fastow said. "It will have access to massive deal flow from Enron. It will, in truth, be a virtual Enron."

It was 9:15 on the morning of September 16. Fastow had traveled to New York to present his big proposal to Enron's bankers. His first visit was with Chase Capital Partners, an investment arm of Chase Manhattan bank. He had described his vision weeks before to Rick Walker, Chase's banker in charge of Enron, and had won him over. Walker pushed Chase for the investment; it would make Fastow wealthy, he wrote his bosses, and buy the bank a lot of business from Enron.

But in the meeting this day, as Fastow described LJM2, the Chase executives seemed perplexed. Why would a CFO do this? Why would the company want him to?

"This pool of capital is viewed as a good thing by the board," Fastow said. "LJM2 will be the best bid on lowball deals by virtue of having better information."

And despite the demands of his CFO job, there was no danger he would neglect the fund. "Half my time will be effectively spent on LJM2's business because of the overlap with Enron," Fastow said.

The rewards would be ample. Look at the first LJM, he said. Its returns were hitting 300 percent. There was plenty of reason to expect that LJM2 would do even better.

Just before lunch that day, Fastow headed to Merrill Lynch's offices at the World Financial Center to visit with its private-equity group. Already Merrill had a special relationship to LJM2; it had agreed to raise money from institutional and wealthy investors. Now Fastow was asking Merrill's principals to kick in a few million of their own.

"This is what I want to be my next step," Fastow told the group. "I want an investment business, and this is a unique opportunity to set it up with unique access to deals and to develop that track record I need to develop."

The story he spun now differed from what he had told the board. No more breast-beating about his sacrifice. No words of concern about his position at Enron. Instead, just the bald truth: he wanted a more lucrative career. But why should they believe he could deliver stellar performance?

"Let me simply say I can do twice better than anyone else because I will have better information than anyone else," Fastow said.

The bankers laughed. The idea was just audacious.

Fastow displayed a chart headlined "Involvement of Principals in Price Funds." Listed on it were the names of LJM2's professional staff: Fastow, Kopper, Glisan, and Anne Yeager.

For nearly an hour, Fastow wove his tale of riches to come, opportunities to seize, deals to be done. The bankers ate it up. He was so pleased with the reaction, Fastow couldn't help taking a dig at his outside advisers.

"The only thing that's amazing to me," he said, "is that our really smart investment bankers didn't figure this out first."

Four days later, on September 20, Jimmy Lee, chief of global investment banking at Chase, sat at his rosewood desk, glancing over the pages of Fastow's presentation.

This is just stupid. Fastow was clearly out of his league and didn't understand much about private investments. But Enron was a big client. Chase couldn't blow this off. He reached for a pen and scribbled the name of a banker, Rod Reed, across the cover sheet. He asked Reed to review the proposal with Rick Walker, along with Arnie Chavkin, a principal of Chase Capital Partners.

"I am skeptical because the guy running it is inexperienced and sounds very naïve," Lee wrote. "However, the relationship is very big and important. We 'may' have to do a little."

Lee sent the material on its way. His message was clear: The corporate client was a player. If Chase needed to invest in the CFO's silly pet project, so be it.

The bankers who received Lee's instructions didn't feel any better about Fastow's proposal than he did. A lot of it struck them as wrongheaded.

Chavkin couldn't make sense of the fund's fee structure. Fastow said LJM2 would receive two percent of its total capital, but at the same time Enron was paying for finding and structuring deals. Fastow's information came from his work at Enron, work he was paid to do. Even the cost of LJM2's staff was being picked up by Enron. What was the management fee for? Shouldn't a portion go to Enron? What about all the oversight needed to monitor the conflicts, would Enron be reimbursed? And generally, why would this fund be considered independent of Enron at all?

He directed his questions to Rick Walker. On the morning of September 27, Walker contacted Fastow with the concerns. Fastow had plenty of answers. Not *all* the deals would come from Enron, he said; that's why there was a management fee. And Enron would be reimbursed for expenses.

Walker had one more question Chavkin wanted asked.

"Andy," Walker said, "can I call Skilling?"

At Merrill Lynch, they were wondering the same thing. Had Skilling thought this through? Had Enron put in place the mechanics to deal with conflicts?

Two Merrill bankers in charge of the Enron relationship—Schuyler Tilney and Robert Furst—e-mailed Fastow with their questions. It was clear they needed to speak with Skilling. Their chance would come days later—on the morning that the Enron board gave LJM2 its full blessing.

A pattern was quickly established. If a bank or brokerage had a financial interest in Enron's fees, it was hit up for Fastow's new venture. Starting at 1:30 on the afternoon of September 27, multiple forty-two-page documents went out—to Bankers Trust, CIBC Oppenheimer, Lehman Brothers, and many others. Included was a short note from Fastow himself along with his lengthy slide presentation boasting of the benefits of LJM2.

Nothing came on LJM2 stationery; there were no fund offices to contact. Instead, everything arrived on Fastow's letterhead from Enron. The document had been faxed from the machine he shared with Causey. Even the fax cover sheet came with the Enron logo.

The unspoken message was hard to miss. No matter what was said about the fund's independence, this was an Enron appeal. For a venture operated by the man who awarded many of the company's fees.

Sitting in an antique armchair in his family room, Lay opened his briefcase and pulled out the latest issue of *CFO* magazine, glancing at the cover. *The Finest in Finance.* Lay smiled to himself.

He found the table of contents, looking for Fastow's name. Beneath it were the words "How Enron financed its amazing transformation from pipelines to piping hot."

Lay turned to the article. "When Andrew S. Fastow, the 37-year-old CFO of Enron Corp., boasts that 'our story is one of a kind,' he's not kidding," it began.

Lay liked the piece. This fellow Banham, who wrote it, captured everything pretty well: asset securitization, special-purpose entities, the reduction of balance-sheet debt. Fastow was obviously as creative and sharp as Lay and Enron's directors had come to believe.

"So," Skilling said, "what do you need to know?"

It was October 11, and Skilling was speaking with Schuyler Tilney and Robert Furst from Merrill.

"Well, Jeff," Tilney began. "First, thanks for taking the time to speak with us."

"No problem."

"We've got just a few questions regarding LJM2. I'm sure they're issues you've already considered."

Had Skilling thought about the time Fastow would spend with LJM2? Was he comfortable with the controls for the conflicts? Had the board reviewed those? Skilling's answers were detailed and knowledgeable. He had obviously spent time on the workings of LJM2. The bankers were impressed.

"And really, on conflicts, I am very, very comfortable," Skilling said. "It's under control."

"What will be the mechanisms for that?" Furst asked.

"Well, first of all, Andy has no control over our decision to sell an asset. So if we sell something to LJM2, it's because *we* want to sell it. If LJM2 gets it, it's because LJM2 gave the best offer."

"Okay."

"And because Andy will know more about the assets, we're not going to be forced to leave money on the table because of bad bids. If LJM2 wins, it's because they had the best bid, probably because they knew the most."

"All right."

"Plus, none of this is taking place in a vacuum," Skilling continued. "Rick Causey is going to review every transaction with LJM2 to make sure it's in Enron's interest. And the audit committee of the board will receive LJM2's financial statements."

Besides, Skilling said, the only way this arrangement would work is if everyone focused on disclosure. There weren't going to be any secrets. With everything about LJM2, Skilling said, Enron would have an open kimono.

That same morning at 11:45, Lay was in a conference room reviewing the agenda for that night's meeting of the Enron board of directors. He had received his briefing materials days before, but this was the first time he'd had the chance to read them through.

When he came to the agenda for the finance committee, a name jumped off the page: LJM2. He turned to the text of a Fastow presentation about what appeared to be a new fund.

Nobody had mentioned this to him. Apparently, Fastow's first fund had been so successful he was back for more. Lay skimmed the presentation. It sounded pretty good.

Just after 4:30 that same day, Fastow sat before the finance committee in the boardroom, radiating confidence.

"This is a follow-on fund for LJM," he told the directors. "It will give us a lot of advantages."

With LJM2, he said, Enron would have a fund available for quick transactions, without the cost of investment-banking fees. The company would be better able to manage risk and have greater financial flexibility.

"The limited partners will be traditional pension funds," Fastow said. Nothing about the Enron bankers who would be kicking in the largest portion of the fund.

To protect against conflicts of interest, Fastow said, both Causey and Buy would review transactions between Enron and LJM2. Even so, Fastow said, the board would have to waive its code of conduct to allow him to serve both as CFO of Enron and as the general partner of LJM2.

That bothered Norm Blake. "Has Arthur Andersen reviewed this?" he asked.

Causey answered. "Yes, they're fine with it."

Blake paused. "I'm still concerned about the conflict of interest," he said.

"We've addressed that lots of ways," Causey replied. "We've given the limited partners enough authority to keep Andy from having too much power. The limited partners can remove the general partner without cause."

Skilling broke in. "No one has to do a transaction with LJM. We will only do a transaction if it's better than the alternative, which means it's no-lose for Enron."

Fastow assured the board his time on LJM2 would be minimal—a few hours a week, tops. After all, he said, Enron was providing the lion's share of his annual income.

The committee was satisfied. On a voice vote, they waived the code of conduct.

The full board gathered that night in the Whitney Room of the Four Seasons Hotel. Just past 8:30, Pug Winokur gave the rundown on LJM2, explaining why his committee had okayed Fastow's participation. The floor was opened for questions.

It was late. The directors were tired. They had a full agenda. Besides, Winokur always knew what he was doing. With no debate, the board approved the recommendation. It just didn't seem that important.

About a week later, Kelly Boots was walking down the hallway, bracing herself for her meeting with Jeff McMahon. Boots, the Enron executive charged with managing banking relationships, had been hearing a lot of disturbing noise in recent days. Bankers had been calling incessantly, muttering darkly about their dealings with Enron.

The issue had become so high-profile that Boots felt obligated to take it to the company treasurer. She knew McMahon well and trusted him. Still, the idea of suggesting that Fastow may have acted unethically wasn't comfortable. Boots arrived at McMahon's office, and he invited her in. She took a seat, pausing for a second to gather her thoughts.

"Jeff, I've got an issue, and I need to know how to respond to these questions."

"What questions?"

"Banks are calling me, saying Andy has stopped by on the road show, asking them to invest in LJM2," she said. "And they're not sure what will happen if they don't invest. They're worried that they'll be put in the penalty box and won't get business from us. How do I respond to that?"

McMahon blinked. "Are you telling me that Andy's trying to sell this deal to our banks? *Enron* banks?"

"That's what I hear."

McMahon slapped his desk with his hands. "I can't *believe* he's pitching this stuff to them. He told me he was going to raise his money from wealthy investors."

This was so sleazy. What was Fastow thinking?

"Kelly, how would you react if you're at some major bank and the CFO of one of your biggest clients comes in and asks you to invest in some fund he's running?"

"I know. That's the problem."

"I think I'd have the same reaction they're having."

The two were silent for a moment.

"This is unbelievable," McMahon said. "I'm going to go talk to Andy."

He leaned toward the doorway. "Sue!" he yelled out to his secretary. "Get me in to see Andy today."

McMahon was in Fastow's office, sitting across from him. He worked hard to keep his tone calm.

"I understand you've been calling on Enron's Tier 1 banks to invest in your new deal."

"Yeah, they're on our list."

"Well, that's a surprise to me, Andy. So I'm going to need to know what you're doing for this LJM2, who you're calling on, and who your investors are going to be."

Fastow squinched his face. "Why do you need to know *that*?" he asked sharply.

"Because I'm responsible for Enron's banking relationships."

"This has nothing to do with Enron," Fastow snapped.

"Well, these banks are calling up, saying they believe the deal you're pitching is, if they don't pay LJM2, they don't get to play at the Enron level."

Fastow snorted. "Oh, that's just not true."

"That's what their perception is."

"Well, they're wrong."

"Look, Andy," McMahon said. "We're dealing with perceptions, and I'm going to have to manage those. So I need a list of who you're calling, and who's making a commitment. That way, when they call me, I'll be prepared. And I can tell them that there's no connection between their decisions on LJM2 and their future Enron business."

Fastow thought about it for a second. "Yeah, you're right, " he said. "I'll get you the list."

The sky over Scottsdale was clear, with a breeze off the desert. Skilling had just parted ways with some Enron executives who had joined him for dinner. Now, the day over, he unwound as he strolled down a sidewalk at the Phoenician hotel toward his room in the Canyon Building.

That day, November 1, he had met with members of Enron Communications in hopes of hammering out a cohesive business strategy. He thought the meetings had gone well; there had been an agreement that broadband trading should be the primary business, with the intelligent network and video streaming taking a back seat. That was progress.

Skilling arrived at his room. Through the glass door in the back, he could see the pool, lined on one side by yellow-topped cabanas. He walked over to the desk and reached for the phone; he wanted to check the messages on his office voicemail. He dialed an 800 number, then punched in an extension—6894. After he entered a password, the messages began. He took notes on a pad of hotel paper.

"Message number twelve," the recorded voice said. "Diane Bazelides."

Skilling knew the name. The Azurix public-relations person.

"Jeff, this is Diane," the message began. "We have an urgent press release for Azurix that needs to go out, and we need you to sign off on it. We've faxed it to the front desk, and they're holding it for you."

Skilling closed his eyes and slumped on the desk.

Oh, great. The front desk. Back in the main building. He wasn't surprised Azurix wanted his approval; Enron was still its largest shareholder, and he was a director. He didn't want to hike back where he just came from. He groaned as he pushed himself up and trudged toward the door.

What a pain. I hope this is worth it.

Fifteen minutes later, Skilling returned with the fax still in a sealed manila envelope. He tossed it onto a table just inside the door. He didn't feel like looking at it. Instead, he walked to the minibar and grabbed a soda.

He futzed around the room—pulling things out of his briefcase, checking other work. Finally, he walked back to the table and tore open the envelope. He saw the words "For Immediate Release." He reviewed the page quickly.

And his mouth dropped. "What the *fuck?*"

Azurix was announcing that its fourth-quarter earnings were going to collapse. *The fourth quarter? The fourth quarter had just started!* Wall Street was expecting seventeen cents a share, and now Azurix was announcing it would bring in as little as nine. It had been public for—what?—less than five months. It had only reported one full quarter of results. And now the management team was planning to drop this bomb. No warnings, no explanations. Just—*We blew it. Bye!*

Skilling flipped over the page, looking on the other side. Suddenly, a thought. He smiled. *Of course.* This wasn't real. It was a joke. *Cliff.* It was Cliff Baxter. Sure. Baxter was messing with him. Ha-ha. Very funny.

But wait a minute. The Bazelides call. She wouldn't be part of a joke like this, making fun of her own company.

Skilling covered his face with one hand.

Oh, my God, he thought. *This is real.*

Skilling hit the phones. He ordered the press release held back until he could get more information and brief the Azurix board. Then he called Rebecca Mark at home.

"What's going on?" he barked. "Where did this come from?"

Her CFO, Rod Gray, had been running the numbers, she said. "This is what they're projecting for the quarter, so they wanted us to release this."

She sounded calm. Too calm for Skilling's taste.

"Rebecca, do you understand what's going to happen? When you put this out, all hell is gonna break loose. Your phone is gonna ring off the hook, your stock is gonna get slammed. I mean, any first-year analyst would be out there asking if this is a long-term or short-term problem."

Mark didn't respond.

"Rebecca, which is it?"

"We feel very confident in the future of Azurix."

"I don't *care* if you feel confident," Skilling snapped. They needed precise data, full projections for the following year. They needed to explain what happened. Fuzzy happy-talk wasn't going to cut it.

The longer he spoke, the more frenzied he became. Finally, Mark broke in and said she would get on the case. They hung up. Then Skilling picked up a small executive directory he carried. He knew the next call he had to make.

The ringing phone echoed through Lay's home. Paul Stokes, a member of his house staff, answered.

"Lay residence."

"Is Ken there?"

An urgent, angry-sounding man. "I'm sorry. This is?"

"Jeff Skilling."

"Oh. All right, Mr. Skilling. Please hold a moment."

Skilling, sitting at the desk in his hotel room, rubbed his face as he waited for Lay to come on the line.

"Jeff?"

"We've got a problem, Ken."

He spilled out the whole dismal story. The news release. His call to Mark. Her odd indifference. The potential for disaster that now hung over Enron.

"Ken," Skilling said, "this is really, really bad."

"We better get the board together tomorrow."

"Yeah."

A pause. Neither man knew what to say.

"Okay," Lay said. "I'll get Rosie to pull the board together."

The call ended.

Skilling just sat, staring at nothing. The air was still, quiet. The silence felt oppressive. *My God.*

He stood and snapped up his key. There was a bar in the main building. He needed a drink.

"This is Rebecca. I'm calling the meeting to order."

It was one the next afternoon, and the Azurix directors had called from around the world to meet by conference call. Mark was in the boardroom down the hall from her office. They spent a minute taking the roll, and then reviewed the press release, line by line.

Pug Winokur broke in. "The release is fine. But what's going on? How did this happen?"

"Well, we misjudged the pace of privatizations," Mark responded. "It's been a lot slower than we anticipated."

"Why are we finding this out now?" Skilling asked. "A week ago, you told me everything was fine. How did everything fall apart in a week?"

After much back-and-forth, the board made a decision. They wanted a review of every company asset. And they wanted Mark to propose three strategic alternatives—staying the course, ramping up, and cutting back.

"All right," Mark said. "I'll do that."

But first Azurix had to scramble to get out its press release. It would take two more days.

Exhausted from travel, Skilling dropped in to Lay's office at ten the next morning. He was jumpy, anxious; Azurix haunted him. He sank into a chair.

"Ken, this Azurix thing is a big problem."

Lay nodded. "Yeah, I know it's a problem."

His tone struck Skilling as almost blasé. "Ken, the repercussions are huge," he said, his voice rising. "They're gonna get sued, we're probably gonna get sued."

Lay nodded. "I know that."

"This isn't just their stock price going down," Skilling continued. "They just went public! If they get beat up by the rating agencies over this, their cost of capital is going to go up. Then they won't be able to compete to buy other companies. I don't know if their business plan is even feasible anymore."

He shook his head. "We've gotta cut costs there, Ken. I mean radical surgery, because the shortfalls are huge. You've got to let her know how serious this is."

Lay's face was grave now. "You're right, Jeff," he said. "I need to talk to Rebecca."

A silent agreement was reached. The Azurix dream of fast growth was dead. Its future was in massive downsizing.

Just past noon the next day, a group of Enron traders were watching Kitty Pilgrim, an anchor with CNNfn, on a television near the trading floor.

"Let's see what other stocks are moving on Wall Street. For that, we head down to the New York Stock Exchange. Rhonda Schaffler is there, tracking the action."

The camera cut to a brunet woman. "Hi, Kitty," Schaffler began. "Once again, a broad-based rally."

But not all the news was good. "Azurix is down sharply," Schaffler said. "It reported earnings in line with what the Street was looking for, but warned its fourth quarter and year 2000 results would be below expectations. Merrill Lynch downgraded the stock today."

A stock that went public at $19 a share was now floundering at $7.75. In just 105 trading days, more than 60 percent of Azurix's value had been wiped out. The traders roared. Azurix—"the chick company," as they called it—was a miserable failure. It was fun to watch.

None of them worried what that meant for *their* jobs. After all, Azurix had a different management team. Whatever their incompetence, they had nothing to do with Enron.

About an hour later in Antioch Park, across the street from the Enron building, members of the Houston Astros baseball team walked down an outdoor runway, modeling new uniforms for their top corporate sponsor.

Thousands of Enron employees cheered while eating a lunch served in what the company called the Big E Café. On a dais, Lay and Skilling watched as players appeared wearing multiple versions of the uniforms, including a pinstripe ensemble—an homage, the club's owner said, to the business community surrounding Enron Field.

By two the event had broken up. Lay and Skilling made their way across the street. Around them, employees jabbered excitedly. There was enthusiasm for the uniforms, but it was more than that. There was exhilaration about their place in the city. The Astros had become *their* team, with Enron emerging as part of the very fabric of Houston.

Skilling headed to the top floor, then changed elevators for the mezzanine level. He was scheduled to meet with Joe Sutton and part of the international group to review next year's budgets for projects in Asia, the Pacific, Africa, and China.

Even with Azurix's chaos in the marketplace, the baseball lunch had been a refreshing break and Skilling was in a good mood. He arrived at conference room 50M, then took a moment to chat with Sutton, who a few months earlier had been named vice chairman, taking Rebecca Mark's place.

"Okay," Skilling said, pulling in his chair. "Asia and Africa. Joe, want to kick it off?"

Sutton stayed in his seat. "All right. We have the regional team here. But we'd like to start with a review of the entire division, to show where this fits in."

An accountant with international rattled off the numbers. Skilling listened with growing alarm. He and Causey had sized up international recently, figuring it would chip in about $500 million in profits next year. But the more the accountant spoke, the smaller the numbers seemed. A slide went up, showing a region-by-region breakdown. Skilling's eyes drifted to the bottom line.

About $100 million. "Whoa, wait a minute," Skilling interrupted. "Is this for all of international?"

Sutton nodded. "Yeah."

Skilling looked at the faces around the table.

"Guys, we've got seven billion dollars invested in this business. *Seven. Billion. Dollars.* And you're telling me we're going to make $100 million next year? I came in here expecting a $500 million number."

Skilling had been around the block enough to recognize what was going on. *A sandbag.* Sutton was coming in with ridiculous projections so that next year, when he blew through those levels, his performance would look great.

"Joe, should we just stop meeting now, and you guys go out and come back with a different set of numbers?" he asked sharply. "Maybe something a little more realistic?"

"Jeff, those are the numbers."

"Oh, come on!" Skilling snapped.

Sutton stared back at him.

"Fine," Skilling said. "Let's go through it."

Region by region, the executives reviewed the performance. Asia. Africa. The Caribbean. South America. India—profits in India were *going down!* There were asset sales built into the numbers, so some of the results weren't even from operations.

Skilling worked his jaw. *Seven billion dollars.* Seven billion dollars invested to earn $100 million in profits. Hell, if they had stuck the money in a bank account earning 3 percent, the earnings would have been higher!

Numbers whirred through his mind. Two billion dollars in Azurix, flushed away in the morning. Seven billion in international, flushed away in the afternoon.

He held up his hands. "We've got seven billion of book value on this stuff. What's it worth if we sell it?"

The question hit the room like a percussive explosion. "Oh, it's worth a lot more than that," Sutton said.

Skilling slapped the table. "Fine," he snapped. "Then that's what we'll do."

He looked around the room.

"I want this stuff fucking sold!" he snapped.

Skilling was panicked. The shortfall in international was huge; it would be Azurix II, only this time *Enron* would be the laughingstock. He scurried to find Baxter. International needed to be sold, he said, and he wanted Baxter to handle the deal. Baxter was enthralled; a multibillion-dollar sale was just the thing to get his juices going.

The next afternoon, executives from Enron North America, the most recent name for wholesale, came in for the same budget exercise. Greg Whalley, newly appointed to run the trading desk, laid out his projections. Skilling could smell a sandbag. They could do a lot better.

"Listen," he interrupted. "Stop. I need another $400 million, pretax."

Whalley thought about it. "Okay," he said. "We'll get you another $400 million."

McMahon saw Fastow in the hallway. Weeks had passed since they spoke about LJM2 and the banks, but McMahon had never heard which banks Fastow was visiting and which had invested. McMahon flagged him down.

"You still haven't gotten me that investor list."

Fastow nodded solemnly. "Yeah, you're right," he said. "I've got to get that for you."

Then he continued on his way.

Lay and Skilling could not stop ruminating about the week's events. How could it have happened? How could so many billions of dollars have been invested so badly?

Skilling blamed Rebecca Mark, viciously attacking her to Lay as incompetent. But Lay wouldn't buy it. She almost single-handedly pulled together Dabhol—well, yes, that was having troubles. But it was a challenging project. Things could still turn out well. Lay believed in her.

The two decided to speak with Mark, to stress how Azurix's strategy needed to be rethought. Mark and her people were already talking about new bids, showing estimates of returns of less than ten percent. That just wouldn't work; when the cost of the capital needed for the acquisition was factored in, Azurix would *lose* money on the deal. The three set up a meeting to thrash things out.

Once they all got together, Lay was the first to speak.

"Rebecca," he said, "obviously, things aren't as much on track as we thought, so you're going to have to impose some more discipline on your investments and costs."

Like this new deal she was talking about, Skilling said. Azurix had to pay more than ten percent interest on its debt. So the company would be borrowing cash at, say, eleven percent for returns of nine percent. It was a money loser.

"That's not the point," Mark replied. "We need to keep investing to grow as fast as possible. Merrill Lynch says our valuation is all about EBITDA, not earnings."

EBITDA. A fancy Wall Street term for profits, with all of the financial expenses removed. It stood for "earnings before interest, taxes, depreciation, and amortization." Steady growth in EBITDA could be a sign of future strong profits, but not if it was being accomplished by manufacturing full, after-tax losses.

Lay couldn't believe what he was hearing. Was Mark really arguing that the deeper into a hole she got, the better off her company would be?

"Rebecca, that doesn't make any sense," he said. "Surely you understand that if you put capital into projects with returns that are below the cost of that capital, ultimately you're going to go bankrupt."

"This is what Merrill tells me is the way things are around this industry," Mark replied. "We have to grow EBITDA. That's all that matters."

This is ludicrous! "So the more money you lose, the more valuable you are?" Skilling said. "That's nuts!"

Mark stuck to her guns. Investors wanted EBITDA growth, she insisted. That would make the stock price go up. Azurix needed to keep buying water assets so that it could grow EBITDA.

Skilling wanted to pull out his hair. "Rebecca, Merrill doesn't mean grow EBITDA by creating losses! They assume nobody would do that! I mean, why not sell junk debt at 12 percent and use the cash to buy government bonds? You'll get plenty of EBITDA, but you'll lose big money for every dollar of EBITDA you get!"

Mark didn't give an inch. "Our bankers tell us we have to grow EBITDA. That's what investors are looking for."

Lay almost staggered out of the room. His faith was shaken, but not gone. He still believed Mark was smart. But suddenly he knew that he had entrusted billions of Enron's dollars to someone who could get locked into an illogical position. And he only realized it now. Years too late.

He and Skilling climbed onto the elevator. The doors closed, and Skilling seized the moment. He faced his boss.

"Do you understand, Ken?" he asked plaintively. "Do you see what I've been trying to tell you?"

Lay watched the numbers move over the door.

"Yes," he said, "I do."

Another week had passed, and still McMahon had received nothing from Fastow about LJM2 and the banks. At the end of the next meeting they both attended, he stopped Fastow as they headed out the door.

"Andy, I still need that investor information about the banks," McMahon said.

Fastow made a face. "Oh yeah, you're right," he said. "I'll make sure to get right on that."

Fastow headed down the hall. As McMahon watched him, realization settled in. That list was never coming.

This was no time for a breather. Enron couldn't slow down. Not if it was going to propel its stock price to the next level. Of that, Lay and Skilling were sure.

The growing tower of miscalculations—international, Azurix, a lot of merchant investments—none of that called for a reassessment of strategy. Lay and Skilling didn't even view all of them as mistakes. And they felt sure management would work through it—with asset sales, restructurings, whatever. The billions of dollars in debts associated with those deals were mostly off balance sheet. That was the past. Enron had to move to the future.

And they had a plan. Ramp up Enron Communications. The Internet was hot, the new economy was everything. Push hard, hire employees, invest plenty. That would catapult Enron ahead. But they needed somebody to take charge, to lead the troops onto the next battlefield.

They knew exactly who it should be.

At three on November 18, Enron's directors gathered for a special meeting. Their mood was sharp with anticipation. Enron, they knew, was about to propel itself in a new direction.

Lay called everyone to order. "The purpose of this meeting is to discuss opportunities the company is seeing for Enron Communications," he began. "We are more optimistic about the growth potential at ECI than any other division."

There had been a two-day session in Scottsdale, Lay said, where Skilling and the ECI team had reviewed everything. Now they were ready to put a plan in action.

"We're concerned whether the team is focused enough," Lay said. "And so this is our idea."

He looked around the table. "We want to have Jeff Skilling spend more time with the team," he said. "That would take him away from his corporate duties, so Joe Sutton and I would pick up the slack."

Skilling took the floor. This was a great opportunity to affect the future stock price, he said. Enron was now trading at forty dollars. With business as usual, it should end the year at fifty-one dollars. But pushing hard into broadband could be worth an additional ten to fifteen dollars a share, he said.

"I would like to have a significant role in this business," he said. "I'd like to continue my role at Enron but spend significant time at ECI as we ramp up."

The best outcome, Lay said, would be if Skilling remained chief operating officer at Enron but was also formally appointed chairman of Enron Communications.

John Duncan spoke. "I'm not sure. There is a chance of misinterpretation by the investment community."

Others differed. "What makes Enron great is *management flexibility*," Norm Blake said. "I applaud the decision."

The directors asked for the chance to discuss the decision alone, and Skilling left the room. Once the door closed, Lay spoke.

"This is the right decision," he said. "Jeff has the skills needed here. But doing this is riskier than just staying COO. We need a safety net for him."

Lay had thought it all through. He was ready to truly anoint a successor. The moment had finally arrived.

"We need to extend Jeff's contract through 2003," Lay said. "And we should make it official that he can consider himself constructively terminated by the end of next year if he is not offered the position as CEO of Enron."

Several directors were stunned. That meant if Skilling wasn't named CEO by December 2000, he could collect an entire three-year contract and go home. What about Lay?

"I will step down as CEO at year-end 2000, with the option to extend that if either ECI or Jeff isn't ready," he said. "I would also stay one year as chairman."

There was a pause. "Do I have a motion?" Lay asked.

Robert Jaedicke raised a hand, putting the proposal to the board. It passed unanimously. "Thank you," Lay said, smiling.

It was done. Enron had launched its last huge investment in a business that, again, no one in the room fully understood. But this time it would be led by the executive designated as the man to take Enron into the twenty-first century.

CHAPTER 11

EARLY ON A THURSDAY afternoon, Ken Lay escorted a man through crowds of Enron executives who were milling about the main floor at the Hyatt Regency Hill Country Resort. Several gaped as the two passed by, recognizing Lay's guest. The ill-fitting toupee was gone, and the years had softened his sharp, angular features. Even so, no executive was likely to forget Michael Milken, the former junk-bond king who had once been at the epicenter of Wall Street's crime wave in the 1980s.

Weeks before, Lay had invited Milken to attend Enron's annual San Antonio management conference out of a mounting sense of anxiety. In meetings, in hallways, in every discussion at the office, Lay had detected a growing swagger, an unrestrained boastfulness in the executive ranks. A culture of arrogance had emerged, a sense of infallibility bestowed by Enron's seemingly boundless ability to hit profit targets. With even faster growth sure to come, Lay wanted to teach his executives the value of humility.

And who better than Milken to warn about the perils of hubris? From his bond-trading desk in the 1980s, Milken had transformed the investment firm Drexel Burnham Lambert from a Wall Street also-ran to a powerhouse. Lots of struggling companies—Enron included—had turned to Milken and his financing machine. But as they went from triumph to triumph, Milken and his acolytes had grown arrogant. They had displayed a ruthlessness toward rivals, a belief that they were above it all. And when prosecutors came down on the firm, pushing Milken out, his followers committed the sin of doing bad deals. After the marketplace refused some Drexel junk bonds, the firm bought them itself. As the junk market tumbled, so did the debt-laden Drexel—straight into bankruptcy.

To Lay, the similarities between Drexel and Enron were too stark for comfort. Both had burst almost overnight from obscurity to world fame. Both were populated by young, well-paid, aggressive executives pumped up with their own self-importance. A sermon from Milken on the evils of overconfidence might strike fear in their hearts. How could anyone miss the connection? They were virtually the same story, just without the crimes and bankruptcy, of course.

The two men walked past Charlie's Long Bar on their way to the Brady room. Management committee executives already crowded the conference table; a buffet lunch was laid out along counters on the wall. After a few minutes of quiet chatting, Lay tapped his glass with a knife.

"All right, everyone," Lay began. "All of you are aware of at least some of Mike Milken's background, and he certainly has had the experience of growing a very, very successful finance-trading organization."

Milken was the master of analyzing risk, Lay said, a man who focused on seeing where a company would be in a year rather than on where it had been in the prior quarter.

"I thought there were some things we could learn from Mike as to his experiences at Drexel, both from the good times and the bad," Lay said. "And he's been kind enough to come out and share that with us today."

The executives applauded politely.

"Thank you, Ken," Milken said. "It's an honor to be here among the executives behind this dynamic and creative company. The people of Enron have plenty to be proud of."

But success could breed carelessness, Milken said. For twenty minutes he laid out a brief history of Drexel and its demise. His audience listened politely, and afterward asked plenty of questions. Lay thought the event went well.

He was wrong. That night several executives crammed Charlie's bar, tossing back drinks as they laughed about Lay and his guest. What was he thinking? Why bring that *criminal* to talk to them? The jokes flew, many at Milken's expense, and quite a few at Lay's. One executive laughed that it was a pity Fastow wasn't joining in the fun. His famously nasty wit would have certainly livened things up that night.

But Fastow had other priorities. During Milken's speech, he was in London, raising money from Enron's European banks for LJM2.

After months of work, struggling with the labyrinths of securities laws, the restructuring of LJM1 was finished.

The Sails proposal—first raised by CSFB at an August meeting in London—had locked in LJM1's profits on its Enron stock. Now CSFB and Greenwich NatWest were guaranteed huge returns from LJM1's holdings in Enron. And by transforming Enron stock into cash, Fastow obtained access to an additional twenty-five million dollars, money that the company's directors had prohibited him from ever receiving.

Now the ugly part—taking credit. Sure, Fastow made out like a bandit. But the bankers wanted to trumpet *their* success as well. After all, bonus time was rolling around in their shops, too.

In early December, David Bermingham, a banker on the deal with Greenwich NatWest, typed an e-mail to a colleague, Gary Mulgrew, touting the deal as a Greenwich brainchild. What they had done, he wrote, "is to strip out 94% of the value remaining in the vehicle after Fastow put his grubby little fingers in the till." And that money, he typed, went straight to profits for Greenwich NatWest.

"What we have executed was not Enron's idea, or Fastow's idea, or CSFB's idea, it was OUR idea," he typed.

At CSFB, bankers took a broader view: Not only had the firm made fat profits, it also had stuffed cash into Fastow's pocket. He was sure to ship more Enron deals their way now.

That same week, Mary Beth Mandanas, a CSFB banker, typed a report to her bosses. If LJM1 was liquidated now, she wrote, CSFB and Greenwich NatWest would walk away with almost $13 million, almost double the $7.5 million they had contributed five months before. But Fastow was the biggest winner: his one-million-dollar investment was now worth $17 million, not including $5.3 million in management fees.

This transaction, Mandanas typed, "provided a significant return to CSFB and has further enhanced our relationship with Andy Fastow, CFO of Enron Corp."

Paul Riddle, a banker from First Union, was on the phone with McMahon, and he sounded annoyed. "I understand from Kelly Boots that you guys are doing a bond deal."

"Yup, that's right," McMahon replied. Here it came, he thought, a pitch for a piece of the action.

Instead, he got a second of silence.

Then Riddle spoke. "I'm a little confused about the process. Kelly tells me it's going to be competitive."

Huh? Of course it was competitive; almost every bond offering was. Banks and investment houses bid for the lead role, with the cheapest proposal usually winning.

"Would you expect anything different from us, Paul?"

"Well, yeah. I was pretty much told by Fastow that by investing in LJM2, we would get the next bond deal."

LJM2. Again.

"I gotta tell you, Paul," McMahon said, "I was not told that by Andy, ever.

I think you misunderstood. We've talked about it, and I've been telling everyone that LJM investment and Enron business are completely different."

Riddle's voice hardened. "Jeff, I didn't misunderstand Andy. I know what he told me. And he told me I would get the next bond deal if we invested in LJM2."

McMahon wanted nothing to do with this. "Tell you what. Call Andy, because if you cut a deal with Andy, then you should talk to Andy and get that deal done."

"But . . ."

"Paul, did *I* tell you that you had a deal?"

"No."

"Then talk to the person who did."

The moment the call ended, McMahon dialed Fastow.

"Andy, this is Jeff. I just got a very disturbing phone call from Paul Riddle," he said. "He says he was promised the next bond deal for investing in LJM2."

Fastow answered fast. "Oh, that's just not true."

"Well, he said that's what you promised him."

"It's not *true*. Tell him no."

"Okay. I just wanted to make sure that's the deal. None of this stuff is tied."

"None of this stuff is tied. That's correct."

The call finished quickly, and McMahon hung up. He brought his hand to his face as he stared at the phone console.

Bullshit. Riddle hadn't been the first banker to call. McMahon had already heard the same thing—less bluntly—out of Merrill. *Everybody* hadn't misunderstood.

McMahon had no doubt. Andy Fastow was lying.

Anxiety permeated the room. Enron's stock had been falling—it was now in the high thirties—and the employees at the December 1 company-wide meeting weren't happy about it. When the time came for questions, the first to be asked was what they planned to do to get the price back up.

"I don't ever want us to be satisfied with a stock price," Lay replied. "I think there's no reason to think that over the next two years we can't double it again."

Later, the head of human resources, Cindy Olson, stepped up to answer questions. She received one anonymously, written on a card. She glanced it over.

"Should we invest all our 401(k) money in Enron stock?" she read out loud. She looked up. "Absolutely!"

She turned and smiled at Lay and Skilling.

"Don't you guys agree?"

Skilling smiled back. "You're doing good," he said.

After weeks of work, Rebecca Mark and the financial team from Azurix were ready to present their plan to save the company. A special board meeting was called at Allen Center. Mark's message was blunt: to move forward, Azurix had to step on the gas and buy more water companies.

"We've considered alternatives," Mark said, "and we believe going for aggressive growth is the best approach."

The status quo would not bring the dynamic shock to the marketplace that Azurix needed. And cutting back—well, that would just pull the company out of the competition. It would be an admission of failure.

Rod Gray, the company's CFO, explained the numbers. Skilling could feel his temper getting the best of him as he listened. He wasn't going to stand for another gamble based on Mark's cocky prognostications.

"Wait, Rod. How can you keep raising money for acquisitions without putting your credit rating at risk?"

"There's quite a bit of capital available out there," Gray responded. "It would be closer to junk rates, but I've been assured by our bankers that it's available."

With that, Skilling lost it. *Junk rates!* That would leave Azurix paying through the nose for borrowed cash. How could it bid against competitors who borrowed for less?

"Rod!" Skilling snapped. "How are we going to finance competitive bidding with junk?"

"That's not the question I was answering. I was answering if the money is out there, and it is."

Skilling shot a glance at Mark.

"All right. Rod doesn't want to answer the question. Rebecca, can you answer it? How are you going to compete?"

"It will be hard," she replied calmly. "The bids we see from other companies are aggressive. They are absolutely bidding to knock Azurix out of the business."

Skilling sat back. He looked at the other directors and asked if management could leave the room. He wanted to speak with the board privately. Mark and the rest of the Azurix team left. The door closed behind them.

Skilling started in, furious. "This is wrong! We do this, we're just throwing more money away," he said. "The only strategy that makes sense now is to significantly cut back. Cut overhead. Cut staff."

He stopped. The room was silent for a second. Lay broke the tension of the moment. "I agree," he said.

The directors all signed on. Mark had to be told she was not thinking radically enough. Cutting back on everything was the only choice. And Lay was given the job of telling her.

The numbers at Enron for 1999 were a mess. The company had spent too much money on deals that were producing lousy returns. If it revealed its actual performance, the stock was sure to get hammered.

But all those years of throwing together structured deals had created an answer. Enron had pockets everywhere, pockets that, under the accounting rules, it could treat as independent third parties. It had created its own fanciful marketplace, one where every participant only wanted what was best for Enron. There was a trust called Whitewing, with a related entity called Condor, which had plenty of cash. Of course, there was LJM1. And now there was the granddaddy of them all, LJM2, with $250 million in cash already available to hand Enron whenever it was needed.

Still, the LJM funds wouldn't take just anything; Fastow had already made that clear in the Cuiabá transaction, when he demanded a commitment for a future buyout. And one thing that needed to be cleared off the books—certificates in a trust called Yosemite—was the kind of low-return investment that Fastow didn't like.

So Enron executives turned to the Condor pocket. They began working on a deal to have Condor fork over thirty-five million dollars in its cash to Enron in exchange for Yosemite certificates. With that, the certificates would disappear from the books, and Enron would get to report tens of millions of dollars in new profits—from itself.

Then, a problem. A junior Andersen accountant in London nixed the deal. Condor was simply too intertwined with Enron to be treated as a third party. Putting the certificates in *that* pocket wouldn't change the financial reporting. Desperate, executives on the deal tracked down Fastow, begging him to let LJM2 buy the certificates—just temporarily. Fastow agreed, so long as Enron paid LJM2 a fat fee. The two sides started negotiating.

There was plenty of grumbling. Why was this junior Andersen accountant getting in the way? On December 6, Joel Ephross, now a lawyer at Enron, e-mailed Fernando Tovar, a lawyer at Vinson & Elkins, explaining the original Condor proposal and how the accountant from Andersen—AA, as he called it—had stopped the deal.

"So, now we have LJM, which is not in any way related to Enron (except that one of its investors is an executive, but we will not talk about that) making the equity investment," he typed. "That will satisfy AA."

But that probably wouldn't be the story's end, Ephross wrote. "We will see if the junior person who has made this trouble is employed with AA after January 1st," he typed. "However, very few people here are betting on that."

A giant American flag hung in the twelve-story atrium lobby of the Grand Hyatt Washington hotel, just steps from the capital's convention center. It was December 7, and the hotel was packed with accountants, all in town to hear presentations from the Securities and Exchange Commission about what their profession should be doing.

Just past eleven, Richard Walker, head of SEC enforcement, stepped up to the dais in the Constitution Ballroom. It had been a busy year for Walker. Since his boss, Arthur Levitt, had given his "numbers game" speech the year before, Walker had been working to give the words teeth. The agency had brought civil-fraud charges against officers at an array of big public companies, and then capped it off with a flourish—an accounting-fraud sweep against sixty-eight people and companies, all filed on September 28, 1999, the first anniversary of the speech.

Those actions, Walker said, communicated the lesson. "Our message deploring the practice of earnings management has been forcefully delivered and is being embraced, I believe, by responsible practitioners and issuers."

Still, Walker said, some companies were continuing to pump up their numbers—crafting bogus sales with secret side agreements, overvaluing assets, hiding important facts from accountants. Auditors themselves were falling down on the job, allowing their independence to be compromised out of fear of losing fees. But the SEC was stepping up enforcement, Walker said. No longer were regulatory investigations going to be genteel matters, resolved with fines and promises to be good. Instead, the SEC was working more closely with federal prosecutors.

"We are moving toward turning the 'numbers game' into a game of Monopoly," Walker said. "Cook the books, and you will go directly to jail without passing go."

Three days later, at 9:35, Andersen's offices in New Orleans, San Antonio, and Houston received an e-mail from the firm. It included a copy of an article describing Walker's speech to the accountants. In the Houston office, someone printed out the e-mail and stuck it in a file.

———

Jeff McMahon clicked up a slide.

"These are the 1999 investments by Enron to date," he said. "As you can see, there is a significant gap between the original estimates and actual performance."

It was the afternoon of December 13. The board's finance committee was holding its last meeting of the year to hear details of Enron's financial condition. Fastow had just given his spiel, and now it was McMahon's turn.

The news McMahon delivered was disturbing. Enron executives had originally estimated they would make somewhat more than one billion dollars in investments in 1999. Instead, they had exceeded that budgeted amount by almost four billion dollars.

Fastow broke in. "Anything we did that was in excess of the approved plan required my group to find additional financing," he said.

A minute later, a new slide clicked up. It was headed "Year End Transactions." There were a number of planned deals listed, worth $2.8 billion, all involving sales of assets to entities put together by Enron itself. All to help fix up the numbers before the company issued its financials.

Bob Belfer, one of Enron's largest shareholders, followed the flurry of financings with unease. "I find it disturbing that we're so close to the end of the year and we have to do all of these transactions," he said.

Heads nodded around the room. The directors conferred, then issued instructions. Enron should never get into this kind of situation again. Not if it could be avoided.

Three hours later, a cavalcade of black limousines moved through Houston's post-rush-hour traffic, pulling up to the front of Saks Fifth Avenue. The Enron directors and their spouses emerged and headed inside up to Ruggles Grill 5115, an elegant Houston restaurant closed to the public that evening for Enron's annual Christmas party.

Inside, festive lights and holiday decorations reflected off of a wall of mirrors. A pianist added ambience, playing holiday songs. Lay greeted the guests, congratulating them for helping Enron achieve so much.

"I'd like to commence dinner with a blessing," he said. Everyone bowed their heads.

"Dear God, we thank you for all the blessings you have bestowed on us," Lay said. "And we thank you for this group of leaders, both directors and their spouses, that indeed have led Enron to another great year."

The prayer ended, and the guests dug in to their meals. Later, as dinner was cleared away, a voice boomed out.

"Ho, ho, ho! Merry Christmas!"

A man dressed as Santa Claus, loaded down with a sack, moved through the room. He called the directors to the front, asking if they had worked hard to help Enron that year. Satisfied with their answers, he presented each with a Sony digital video camera. Once Santa departed, the directors sang Christmas carols, beginning with "The Twelve Days of Christmas." Each director played a part; Lord Wakeham, a former British Cabinet minister, was the natural to belt out "ten lords a-leaping."

The joviality was the perfect tonic for the directors on the finance committee. The presentations from that day had shocked some of them, but now they heard only laughter and singing and the clinking of glasses. The top executives there seemed so self-assured, high-spirited even. Maybe these numbers were just a hiccup. With Enron's profits so strong, there really couldn't be much reason for concern.

"Changing the accounting on this is going to cause Enron to take a charge of thirty million to fifty million dollars," David Duncan said. "We can't do that."

He was on the phone with Carl Bass, now a member of Andersen's Professional Standards Group. Duncan had called with a question about the restructuring of LJM1; apparently, he had misunderstood the accounting rules that applied to the options in the transaction. The restructuring had changed the nature of the Rhythms hedge, Bass told him, requiring Enron to recognize losses. But Duncan wouldn't hear of it. The amount was too big.

"I can't go back to them on this now," he said. "This deal is already signed or it's about to be signed."

"Dave, our advice has been consistent on this and timely," Bass replied.

It didn't matter, Duncan replied. He wasn't reversing course now. Enron would keep its unearned windfall, generated solely because David Duncan didn't know what he was doing.

As far as Fastow and Causey were concerned, the LJM1 hedge for Rhythms had been a blazing success. And it set them to wondering: if Enron could use its own stock to lock in profits from one investment, why not for dozens?

The money sunk into merchant investments was a hidden threat to Enron's profitability. The market had been booming for years, but now momentum had changed. If it tanked, Enron's losses could be horrendous. But if the company could lock in the values of its investments—if it could hedge them using Enron stock again—that danger would dissolve.

Fastow and Causey talked over the idea with Glisan. Getting the Enron stock was the easy part, they all agreed. Maybe shares already contributed to the Whitewing fund could be drained off and assigned to another entity, which could then follow the LJM1 example in providing the hedge.

The concept was bounced off Skilling, and he liked what he heard. Causey approached Wes Colwell, an accountant who headed the division known as transaction support, who in turn assigned the job to two accounting whiz kids, Ryan Siurek and Kevin Jordan.

Glisan and the other accountants began brainstorming, taking turns sketching models for the hedge. It would require a lot of effort, but almost from the moment they started, the accountants knew—just *knew*—that this would work. They could protect Enron from future losses.

Rupert Murdoch, the international media mogul and chairman of News Corporation, was at his desk in his New York office. It was ten on the morning of December 16, and Murdoch had just heard that his visitor had arrived. A secretary escorted Ken Lay in, and Murdoch stood.

"Ken, good to see you," Murdoch said.

Lay nodded. "Thank you, Rupert. How have you been?"

Lay and Murdoch had bumped into each other in the past, usually at the annual World Economic Forum in Davos, Switzerland. But this meeting was all business. The two men walked over to a conference table and sat.

"So, Ken, what brings you to New York?" Murdoch said.

"Well, Rupert, we've got some exciting projects under way, and I wanted to discuss them with you, because I think there's a good chance we could work together."

Enron was moving fast to expand its broadband division, Lay said, and was looking at streaming video across a cutting-edge network. Murdoch—through his Fox network and movie studio—had plenty of video content. The two companies were a natural to work together, Lay said.

"We've developed some top-notch technology," he said. "Head and shoulders above anything else out there."

The two companies, he continued, should see what they could do for each other. After forty-five minutes, Murdoch promised to have his staff check into what Enron was up to. This broadband effort, he said, really sounded top-rate.

Bill Collins, an executive in Enron Communications, was sick of the hype, the lies. All around him, executives babbled about their technology, their strategies, the importance of broadband for Enron's future. There was a time when Collins, as director of business development, was a believer; now he thought the whole thing was a crock.

The division was a mess. The people running it had no technology background. No one was making tough choices about how to target resources. Worst of all, nobody was being honest about the troubles they faced. What worked in small demos was proving a lot tougher in the real world.

On December 20, Collins was ready to throw in the towel. He was weeks from quitting in frustration, but before he did, he wanted somebody to hear the truth. He banged out an e-mail to one of his supervisors. Enron's ballyhooed effort to develop a software-driven network was fizzling, he wrote, with no market share, no purchasers, and no users. Enron talked a good game but wasn't playing one.

"I don't care what lipstick and rouge you paint that bitch up with," he typed. "She's still just dead meat lying on the sofa."

LJM2 had only been around for weeks but was already driving Bill Brown crazy. Brown, who worked with McMahon, had started negotiating with Kopper over some deals—if it could be called negotiating. Kopper had attended Enron's strategy sessions; he knew the prices it would accept and wasn't willing to discuss paying a penny more.

After a particularly infuriating morning, Brown headed to McMahon's office. Through the glass wall he could see McMahon at his desk and hurried in.

"Man, Jeff, this thing with Andy and LJM really sucks," he said. "It's crazy. We walk in, and before we make our pitch, they're telling us they know what we'll take. It's like selling a house when the buyer knows your bottom line. There's not a lot of negotiating going on."

McMahon sighed. *More trouble.* "Yeah, you're right, that's a problem."

The solution was obvious. "I'll take care of it," McMahon said. "I'll talk to Andy."

"Look, this whole LJM thing is starting to become a problem internally," McMahon said.

Sitting across from Fastow in his fiftieth-floor office, McMahon recounted his conversation with Brown.

"That's not right, Andy," McMahon said. "And how do you think the guys negotiating for Enron feel, knowing you own a piece of this thing? You're also the guy who's going to compensate them. So if they cut too good a deal for Enron, you're going to find out about it."

Fastow waved a hand dismissively. He wouldn't punish anyone for acting on Enron's behalf, he said.

"You're missing the point, Andy. It's the perception. If they perceive that by negotiating too hard they're costing you money, they can't help but wonder about the effect it will have on their bonus, on promotions."

Fastow didn't like the direction of this conversation.

"I would never do that," he repeated.

"That's not enough," McMahon replied. "It's just 'Trust me, I'm Andy Fastow.' That's not going to do it. You've got to fix the problems this thing creates."

"By doing what?"

Plenty. Get people committed either to Enron or LJM—no more straddling the fence. Then take them out of the building, to LJM's own offices, like any real third party.

"I don't know," Fastow said. "That might cost me some money."

Like a normal business. "All right, even if that doesn't work, at least get them off the floor so they can't just walk into strategy meetings," McMahon said.

Fastow didn't answer.

"But the one thing I'm adamant on is the weekly staff meeting," McMahon said. "Kopper shouldn't attend."

"I won't do that," Fastow snapped. "Michael is a key player here. He needs to know what's going on."

"But he's the guy leading the LJM charge, and by attending the staff meeting, he knows everything."

"He *needs* to know everything," Fastow responded.

They both were silent for a moment.

"Look," Fastow said. "Maybe if there is sensitive information we need to discuss, we just won't talk about it in the staff meeting. We'll arrange another meeting."

Companies didn't do that. What was Fastow thinking? "I don't see how that's going to work, Andy."

"Well," Fastow replied, "let me think about it."

As McMahon headed back to his office, his mind was churning. Fastow had never even put together an investor list for him. Why should he believe he would restructure the operations of his precious fund, just to help Enron?

Eleven days left in the year. Eleven days until Enron's books for 1999 would close. Eleven days left to make everything look better.

The flurry of planned deals weren't going well. Enron had a pool of loans to unload but couldn't find buyers for the riskiest portion. Same with a stake it wanted to sell in a group of Nigerian electricity barges. And with Nowa Sarzyna, a power project in Poland. And again for MEGS, a natural-gas-gathering system in the Gulf of Mexico. The marketplace was sending a message: nobody was interested, not at the prices Enron was asking.

Eleven days. Something had to be done fast. And it would. After all, that's why LJM2 was there.

The first to go was the Polish power plant. On December 21, LJM2 bought a 75 percent interest in the Enron-formed company that owned the plant. The fund paid thirty million dollars—part loan, part investment.

But the deal had a serious flaw. Enron was bound by its credit agreement for the plant to own almost 50 percent of the project until construction was completed. The LJM2 deal would violate that agreement. Enron persuaded lenders to waive that requirement for three months. By March 31, Enron would have to own its stake again.

That didn't matter. By then, Enron would have made its profit numbers for 1999. LJM2's rescue mission allowed Enron to book sixteen million dollars in earnings.

Kopper hung up the phone and headed out the door of his office. Fastow had just called, telling him that they needed to get together right away.

Minutes later, Kopper was on the fiftieth floor, heading down the hallway to Fastow's office. He ambled in and took his usual seat on the couch. Fastow came over.

"What would you think of LJM providing capital in order to buy some Nigerian power barges from Enron at year-end?" Fastow asked.

He laid out the details. It would only entail a few million dollars, he said, and there wouldn't be much risk; there would be a letter of credit from Citibank protecting the investment. Doing the deal would help the Africa group meet its year-end financial goals. But there was even more of a reason to step up to the plate at the last minute.

"If LJM could do this deal," he said, "I'd look like a real hero to Jeff Skilling."

Soon after, Fastow sent the paperwork for the barge deal down to Kopper, who was dismayed by what he saw. The letter of credit was long and complicated, with too many outs for the bank. The power purchase agreement with Nigeria wasn't even signed. All in all, the deal looked like a loser. He went upstairs to Fastow and let him know.

Fastow took it in stride. "Don't worry if we can't get it done through LJM," he said. "McMahon's working on another deal."

McMahon picked up the phone and dialed Merrill Lynch. The firm had already proven it would be there when Enron needed it; on that very day its capital-investment group was putting together a five-million-dollar check for a piece of LJM2. Maybe the firm would be willing to help Enron out of its current jam. McMahon, as the chief contact with the financial institutions, had been asked to make the call.

He reached Robert Furst, one of the Merrill bankers in charge of the Enron relationship. "Rob, we need help," McMahon said. "We've been negotiating to sell some power barges in Nigeria, but the deal's not coming together."

It was imperative for the deal to get done by year's end, McMahon said; otherwise, Enron could miss its numbers.

"So what we'd like to do is sell the interest to Merrill Lynch, just as a bridge to permanent equity," he said.

With that, McMahon said, Enron would be able to book an additional ten million dollars in profits.* While the total price would be twenty-eight million dollars, Merrill would only have to put up seven million of its own cash; Enron itself would lend the rest. Merrill would only hold the barges six months, no more. By that point, Enron would find a way to take the firm out of its investment. And for doing the deal, McMahon promised, Merrill would get a substantial return—more than 22 percent.

This wasn't the kind of thing Merrill did; investing in power barges was a little out of its field. But Furst liked the idea. He had reached similar arrangements with clients when he worked at Credit Suisse First Boston. He didn't see why Merrill couldn't step up to the plate.

"I'll run it past everybody," Furst said.

Merrill already had good reason to be nervous about its Enron relationship. That same day, it was hard at work on a transaction with another Enron division, designed to manufacture more than fifty million dollars in earnings for the company by year-end.

The idea had originated earlier that month in a telephone call from Cliff Baxter—first to the relationship bankers Rob Furst and Schuyler Tilney, then to Daniel Gordon, the firm's twenty-three-year-old whiz kid who had built its energy-trading business from scratch.

At first, Gordon was dubious. Baxter's plan was economically irrational. He wanted Merrill to enter into back-to-back long-term electricity trades with Enron, each the mirror image of the other. They would be structured to cancel each other out to the penny. If the first trade eventually forced

---

*McMahon was incorrect. The actual anticipated profit from the barge deal was twelve million dollars. The figure was corrected in all subsequent conversations.

Merrill to pay Enron a dollar, the second trade would require Enron to give it back. By any reasonable expectation, the whole thing would be a wash. And Baxter wanted to put it together in a few days, in a deal that would normally take months to negotiate.

Still, Gordon was intrigued by the accounting sleight-of-hand that Enron had devised for the deal. One transaction would require physical settlement—meaning that months in the future, Enron would have to deliver electricity to Merrill. But the other trade would require financial settlement—meaning that at the same time, Merrill would have to deliver the cash value of that electricity. And, Causey believed, a financially settled transaction could be marked to market; a physically settled one could not. So Enron could recognize tens of millions of dollars in profits that, in truth, were a mirage.

It was an ingenious scheme to allow Enron to dig itself out of a hole— Gordon understood that. But he also saw a potential windfall for himself and his firm. Enron was desperate. If it didn't hit its numbers, its executives wouldn't get their bonuses. For a transaction with no real economic impact, Merrill could charge fees that would make a loan shark blush.

"Let's see what we can do," Gordon said.

Baxter started working closely with Tilney and Furst, trying to put together the deal. The structure was designed so that the financial settlement would not even begin until September 2000, more than nine months away. Still, Baxter suggested the deal would never reach that point.

Enron, he said, would probably cancel the whole thing before September. But not until after it reported earnings from trades that everyone already knew would never be settled.

December 22. Ten days to go.

The riskiest portion of an Enron pool of poorly performing financings— doled out mostly by the merchant-investing effort—was sold. They went to LJM2 and an affiliate of Whitewing. For its piece, LJM2 paid Enron more than thirty-two million dollars, money it borrowed from the affiliate.

The transaction didn't bring profits to Enron; the loans were sold for the value listed on the books. But now Enron was able to avoid revealing how risky they were. Their value was collapsing; under accounting rules, Enron might have been required to recognize its low likelihood of being repaid, and taken a hit to earnings. Now it didn't have to.

That same day, Merrill convened a meeting in New York to formally consider the Nigerian barge proposal. Furst, the relationship banker, stressed that the deal was crucial to staying on Enron's good side. But at least one executive—James Brown, head of the project and lease finance group—just as emphatically urged the firm to walk away.

"We really have to think about the propriety of what Enron is suggesting here," Brown said. "I seriously question their proposed accounting. I don't think the transaction can be counted as a sale."

That wasn't all. Even after the investment, Brown noted, Merrill wouldn't have any real control over the barges themselves. And what was this about Merrill holding the investment for just six months? That didn't sound right, and there wasn't anything in writing. Worst of all, Brown said, the economics smelled bad.

"They plan to book a twelve-million-dollar gain," he said. "But we're only investing seven million dollars. How can that be?"

To Brown, the proposal had all the earmarks of profit manipulation. "Play out a scenario," he said. "What if sometime in the future, Enron has some credit meltdown and falls apart, and it comes out that we were involved in this, with all our concerns about the accounting? Would that damage our reputation?"

But Brown found himself with few supporters. This wasn't an earnings manipulation, some of the bankers said. Clearly, twelve million dollars wasn't going to be material for Enron, not when the rest of its earnings were so strong. And of course, Enron almost certainly was consulting Andersen to make sure the accounting was appropriate. And as for that fantasy about the collapse of Enron—*of Enron*? Ridiculous.

Brown had raised one good point, the group decided. Merrill was going into this without enough protection. It wouldn't mind buying the stake so long as it was assured that it wouldn't actually have to *own* it. So before the committee approved anything, they issued one requirement. Daniel Bayly, the head of investment banking, had to get Fastow's assurance the buyout would take place. They wouldn't go as far as demanding that the agreement be in writing; Fastow's word would be enough.

About that moment, in Santa Clara, California, Lay and Skilling were walking into the headquarters of Sun Microsystems. Behind them were a handful of executives from Enron Communications, including Hirko and Rex Shelby. The mood was one of nervous excitement. In a few minutes, they would be meeting Scott McNealy, Sun's CEO and an industry legend, in hopes of persuading him to join forces with Enron.

The men headed to reception. A baby-faced executive with a broad smile and a ponytail appeared. He was Jonathan Schwartz, vice president of Sun's strategic investments. After being introduced to Lay, Schwartz escorted everyone back to a conference room next to McNealy's office.

McNealy arrived in jeans and a golf shirt, accompanied by Sun's president, Ed Zander, and a few sales executives. There were greetings all around, and everyone took a seat.

"I really appreciate you taking the time to meet with us," Lay began. He gave a quick description of Enron's intelligent network, then turned the meeting over to Skilling.

"Our people believe your servers will work best for us," Skilling said. "But we want to see if we can do more and create a relationship beyond just buying servers."

The key would be Enron Communications' latest initiative, he said. It was trying to create a software interface to allow outside programmers access to the special functions in its network, to be used in the writing of other computer applications. It would be called the Broadband Operating System, or BOS. And Sun could help.

"We need programming assistance," Skilling said. "We need your help to pull this together and get it out."

McNealy held his chin in his hand. He glanced over at Schwartz. "What do you think, Jonathan?"

The two companies would be a perfect match, Schwartz said. Enron was doing big things. The company was willing to use Sun's Java programming language for its network. Yes, Sun had plenty of reasons to be interested.

Zander jumped in. "How many people are we talking about?"

"Twenty or thirty," Schwartz said.

Zander looked almost ill. "*Twenty or thirty?* Are you kidding me? You know the load those guys have right now."

Everybody had been prepared for this to be a tough sell. It was the end of the 1990s. Software programmers were in hot demand and hard to find. But Schwartz held his ground.

"This could be very, very important," he said. "The first mover on this will have the big advantage."

The Enron executives watched as McNealy, Schwartz, and Zander laid out their positions. But there was no mistaking their enthusiasm for putting together an alliance. Before he left, Lay wanted to raise one other issue. He turned to McNealy.

"Scott, I think our people have been talking a bit about this," he said. "But we would be delighted if you could come to our annual analysts' conference in Houston, and maybe make a few comments to the analysts about our relationship. And more importantly, about what you think about some of our technology."

McNealy shrugged. "If it works with my schedule, I'd be happy to."

Lay beamed. He had thought McNealy would be tough to convince. This was almost too easy.

McNealy pushed his hands on the table and stood. "Listen, Ken, come on out here again when you have more time," he said, shaking Lay's hand. "You and I can go out and play a couple of rounds of golf."

"I'd like that," Lay replied.

Schwartz escorted everyone out. The group headed through security to a courtyard outside the building.

Skilling nudged Lay. "So, Ken, what do you think?"

Lay smiled. "Boy, this could really be great," he said. "This could really be a turning point."

The next day, the conference call about the Nigerian barges was arranged between Fastow and Bayly from Merrill. Joining on the line was a group that included Robert Furst, as well as McMahon and Schuyler Tilney—both of whom were on vacation.

"Okay," Bayly began. "Well, Andy, thanks for taking the time. We just want to nail down a few items."

Fastow knew the words to use. He wanted to steer away from terms like "promise"; *that* would guarantee Merrill its money back, meaning the sale wouldn't be real. But that was exactly the assurance he wanted to give.

A transcript of the call, he knew, would look like Enron had committed that Merrill would lose no money; LJM2, he promised, would be available to take the firm out. He felt sure Bayly heard the implicit message. Fastow was proud of himself. He thought he was being awfully clever.

The call lasted a matter of minutes. When it was over, Bayly called Jim Brown at Merrill. He had just gotten off the line with Fastow, Bayly explained. "I'm satisfied," he said. "Go ahead and close the deal with Enron."

Three days. Wednesday, December 29.

The ringing phone woke Jeff McMahon first, before his wife. He glanced at the time—7:30 in the morning, during his vacation. He leaned up in bed and reached over for the phone, noticing the caller ID read "Enron Corp."

He picked up. "Hey, come on, I'm on vacation."

Bill Brown was on the line. "Sorry to bother you so early on vacation. But we've got a problem with Yosemite."

Yosemite. McMahon remembered. Enron wanted to sell some certificates issued by the Yosemite trust—originally to some entity called Condor. After Andersen nixed that idea, the decision was made to do the deal with LJM2.

"What's the problem?" McMahon asked.

"Kopper wants a fee for LJM2 that's way outside market rates, and this thing is supposed to be arm's-length."

"Well, tell him it's not going to work."

They had, Brown replied. Doug McDowell, the executive handling the deal, was holding tough. But Kopper was arguing such deals paid a certain number of basis points, each worth one-one-hundredth of a percent of the total. He was messing up the math, saying LJM2 was owed one-tenth of a percent for each basis point. At most, Brown said, Enron should pay $100,000, but Kopper wanted a million.

"Now Kopper's saying he's going to go to Fastow unless we agree to the fee," Brown said.

"That's bullshit," McMahon shot back. "I'll take care of it." He hung up and dialed Fastow at the office. The secretary answered; she and Fastow were often in early. She put McMahon right through.

"Andy, it's Jeff. Look, we've got a problem with the Yosemite deal."

Fastow snorted. "Yeah, apparently you guys are being real jerks about the fee."

"I don't think you have all your facts straight, Andy," McMahon replied. He explained how Kopper was making a mistake on the basis points.

"Look, your guys are negotiating way too hard on this deal," Fastow responded.

My guys? Don't we all work for you?

"This deal needs to get done," Fastow continued. "Tell them to stop pushing so hard. Just get it done."

McMahon sat up straight. "Now, hold on!" he said. "We are not just going to get this deal done and pay ten times the market rate for fees. We're supposed to do this stuff at arm's length, and this is not arm's length."

"Well, Michael tells me that you're just being outrageous. So talk to Michael. I just need a deal."

"No, I will not talk to Michael!" McMahon shot back.

He took a deep breath. "Look, Andy," he said. "*This* is the whole problem. You're the referee, and you're conflicted. It sucks that it's set up this way, but that's where we are. You're going to have to deal with this."

McMahon ran through the numbers one more time. "I'm going to sup-port my guys on this," he said. "We won't close this deal if you want a mil-lion dollars."

He paused. "Then I'm going to go to Skilling and tell him that we're not closing this deal because of this, and we'll have to find somebody else to buy the certificates."

Fastow was silent for a moment. "I'll call back," he finally said. The line disconnected.

Twenty minutes later, McMahon, dressed in shorts and a T-shirt, was in his kitchen in bare feet, pouring a cup of coffee. The phone rang. It was Fastow. His words were short and clipped; he made no attempt to mask his fury.

"We'll do it at $100,000, just to get this deal done," he said. "But get it done today."

Fastow insisted that McDowell be told that the negotiations were finished, no question. McMahon agreed and called Brown.

"Okay, I've talked to Andy, and it's all sorted out," he said. "Tell Doug we need to get this closed today."

Brown thanked McMahon, asking how Fastow had taken it.

"He was pissed," McMahon said.

The Yosemite deal wrapped up in a matter of hours. LJM2 agreed to pay $35 million for the certificates; no cash would trade hands for months. It would receive $100,000 for replacing Condor so quickly.

But Fastow still didn't want to own the certificates. He wanted to be paid a fee and to help Enron pretty up its books. He had no plans of hanging on to his new purchase for long. After all, LJM2's reporting year was about to end. And the Yosemite certificates weren't the kinds of things Fastow wanted his investors to see.

For LJM2, there were two and a half days left.

The rest of that Wednesday was a blur of deal making.

That same day, LJM2 purchased twenty-four million dollars' worth of notes and equity of MEGS, the natural-gas-gathering system in the Gulf of Mexico. Again, the structure was another short-term sale. Enron agreed to resell the MEGS securities to a permanent buyer within ninety days.

The deals were producing lots of benefits for Enron, creating new earn-ings and pulling weak assets off the books. Still, there was a problem. As al-ways, Enron's mark-to-market accounting was generating lower cash flow than profits. That kind of statistic would be the perfect tip-off that Enron was swimming in much choppier waters than it appeared. But how could Enron get cash if it wasn't flowing out of its businesses?

Borrow it. Using an innovation developed by Citibank, Enron launched Project Nahanni, named for a Canadian national park known for its wolves. As always, an array of entities with cryptic names was involved. But the outcome was simple: Enron, in effect, borrowed almost half a billion dollars and used the money to buy Treasury bonds—calling that a merchant investment. Then it immediately sold the bonds, with Enron's accountants arguing the proceeds could now be presented as cash flow from operations.

In a few hours on the last day of 1999, in a borrow-buy-and-sell frenzy that a child could understand, Enron generated more than 40 percent of the $1.2 billion in operating cash flow it would report for the year, almost all of it in money that would be returned to Citibank in a couple of weeks. With interest.

Thursday. Two days left.

LJM2 had owned its Yosemite certificates less than twenty-four hours, so now it was time to sell. And Fastow had the perfect buyer: Condor, the entity Andersen ruled couldn't purchase the certificates from Enron. But Andersen never said anything about LJM2 and didn't audit the fund. If LJM2 wanted to make the sale, nobody was around to stop it.

Months after the sale, when LJM2 finally had to pay Enron for the certificates, Condor was there with a thirty-five-million-dollar loan for the fund. Once the cash was passed to Enron, Condor forgave the loan. It accepted the certificates as payment in full. LJM2 never had a dime at risk; it had simply been a front for Condor, to escape the accountants' prying eyes. And it had been paid $100,000 for its trouble. Fastow was still peeved it wasn't a million.

That same day in New York, executives with Merrill Lynch gathered for an urgent meeting. On the table were the back-to-back electricity trades that Enron had proposed weeks before. It was a riskless deal; Merrill couldn't lose a dime. And Enron had agreed to pay through the nose—a fee with a present value of seventeen million dollars.

But there was a lot of uneasiness in the room. Fifty million dollars in profits from trades that cancel each other out? Trades that, far from enriching Enron, would cost it seventeen million dollars? This gimmick was going too far.

No, the participants agreed, they couldn't just approve the deal, not without an assurance that Andersen signed off. The meeting broke up; Schuyler Tilney and Robert Furst phoned Causey to say they needed him on the line answering questions if this idea was going to have any chance.

Hours later, the Merrill group reconvened. Causey joined the meeting from Houston. His voice crackled over the speakerphone. "I've heard about your concerns," Causey said. "I want to assure you that I'm aware of the accounting for these transactions and that Arthur Andersen has approved what we are planning to do."

That wasn't good enough, not for a scheme this bizarre. The Merrill executives weren't prepared to just take Causey's word.

"Can we speak to the accountants at Arthur Andersen ourselves?" one Merrill executive asked.

"No," Causey replied. "I have to oppose that."

There had to be some sort of compromise. What about, one Merrill executive asked, giving the firm a warranty? Causey could write a letter affirming Andersen's approval, stating explicitly that Merrill never provided accounting advice on the deal. It wouldn't change the issues; Enron would still report huge profits that weren't really there. But at least Merrill would be protected if Enron's game ever became public.

"I think we can do that," Causey said.

New Year's Eve. Last day.

The Causey letter was faxed to Merrill, and the trades went forward. Enron booked its last fifty million dollars in profits.

The company had hit the earnings projections. The fire drill of the last few weeks brought in not only almost $500 million in cash flow but also around $125 million in profits—about half what Wall Street hoped the business would generate in the fourth quarter.

All it took was paper shuffling, accounting errors, and some sweetheart deals. That, and a few crimes.

Ben Glisan was feeling uncomfortable.

He had heard about the barge deal—and about the commitments made to Merrill to get it done quickly. The whole idea struck him as just too desperate. Why would Enron want to rush out, doing backflips to lure Merrill into such a deal? What would Wall Street think if word got out about Enron's desperation for a mere twelve million dollars in profits?

Glisan tracked down McMahon at his office. For a minute, Glisan explained his worries about how the transaction—coupled with all the efforts Enron made to get it done—would be perceived by company bankers.

McMahon was unruffled as he listened, slipping on his suit jacket in preparation for his next meeting.

"I have no problem with a handshake deal," he said.

Then he headed out.

About two weeks later in Scottsdale, spirits were high among the Enron executives gathered at the Phoenician hotel for their annual management-committee retreat. Enron looked as though it was running on all cylinders, cranking out great numbers. Sure, there were those crazy end-of-the-quarter periods, but no one could argue with success.

They met in the boardroom of the hotel's Canyon Building on January 13, a Thursday. With Lay chairing, the heads of each division spelled out their expectations for the coming year. That was followed by discussions of their plans for the annual meeting with Wall Street analysts, scheduled for the next week in Houston.

Happy days. Wholesale was blowing the doors off the barn. Retail eked out a small profit. The pipelines—well, the pipelines always made money. There were problems of course, but solutions were in the offing. Finance was working on those hedges for the merchant investments. A lot of international was on the block. So was Portland General. Lots of cash could come in soon.

Ken Rice made the presentation for Enron Communications. The division was about to become a core business—renamed Enron Broadband Services—to draw attention to its advanced Internet work. That was just the first surprise planned for the analysts' meeting. The second would be its alliance with Sun. Discussions between the two companies were winding up, and it looked like Scott McNealy himself would indeed be there to bestow the seal of approval on Enron's technologies and strategies.

Excitement flooded the room. *Scott McNealy!* He was a legend. Enron had been in this business just a couple of years, and already had hit the jackpot. Nothing was hotter than tech stocks right now. And the company was about to tell the world that it was seizing a place at the high-tech table for the twenty-first century. No doubt, Enron's share price was going to go through the roof in a week.

The day was not without tensions. Bonuses for 1999 had been calculated, and the management retreat seemed the perfect time to let executives know the results. Skilling and Joe Sutton, Enron's new vice chairman, were taking people aside, delivering the financial verdicts.

As the day wore on, McMahon grew anxious. Others were already boasting—or sobbing—about their bonuses. But no one had told him anything. He tracked down Sutton.

"Listen, Jeff," Sutton said. "In case you're wondering why I haven't gotten to you, it's because Andy wants to give it to you. So find Andy and talk to him."

Sutton went on his way. McMahon stewed; this wasn't good news.

The Grayhawk Golf Club rests at the base of the McDowell Mountains, thirty minutes from the Phoenician hotel down Highway 101. By 2000, it had been in operation for less than six years, but its two elegant courses, Raptor and Talon, had already won the reputation as among the finest. So when Enron came to Scottsdale, Causey was adamant: he would not leave until he golfed Grayhawk.

The formal meetings wrapped up Thursday, but Causey, Fastow, McMahon, and a few others stayed behind for a day on the links. On Friday, January 14, they drove to Grayhawk, parking near the lush lawns and brilliant red flowers by the clubhouse. Inside, they headed to the pro shop. McMahon was at the register when Fastow sidled up. He still hadn't heard about his bonus. Now seemed a good time to find out.

"Hey, Andy," McMahon said, "are you going to tell me my bonus?"

Fastow looked surprised.

"Everyone got their review and was told their bonus," McMahon continued. "Except me."

Fastow shrugged. "I didn't know that," he said.

Lying again. "Well, Andy, were you told yours?"

"Yeah."

McMahon turned up his hands. "Well, there you go. So let me have it."

"I was waiting for the board to approve it first."

Causey wandered over. McMahon and Fastow dropped the conversation. Everyone trooped outside, where scores of golf carts waited. Causey and Fastow rode together, one cart behind McMahon. They drove out to the Raptor course; a game on Talon would have to wait for another time.

As their golf cart moved along vast stretches of green, Causey and Fastow were deep in conversation. They talked through details of Enron's new hedging program for its merchant investments; there was still a lot of work to go, but things looked good. Everything had been so busy in December, they had never even given this project a name.

There was one quick answer. What about Project Raptor, in honor of this glorious golf course? And this deal would need a named entity set up to provide the hedge, just like LJM1 did. Luckily, there was a second golf course here. It was decided: the hedging entity for Project Raptor would be called Talon.

Hit a few balls, back in the cart. The conversation continued. The news about Enron Communications—or Enron Broadband Services—was pretty exciting. And McNealy coming to Houston? That was unbelievable. The analysts would go nuts. That was sure to be a day for the record books on Enron's stock price. They rode on.

Then the idea was born.

The JEDI partnership was loaded with Enron stock from the company's original capital contribution to the deal. The previous September, Enron had put a hedge in place on the stock, locking the price in place. The value of Enron's contribution to JEDI couldn't go down and couldn't go up.

But what if part of that hedge were removed temporarily? What if, before the conference, Enron replaced the hedge with one that didn't limit any gains JEDI could recognize from increases in the stock price? The hedge could open up, the stock price would pop when McNealy walked in, the hedge could go back on. And Enron, which reported its share of any increased value in JEDI as earnings, would see that run-up translate into profits.

Fastow loved the idea. Enron would make millions—trading in its own stock! But they would have to hurry. They had less than a week to get it all done. They sure weren't going to waste time coming up with a name.

It would be Project Grayhawk.

The golf carts pulled back up to the clubhouse. Fastow clambered out and saw McMahon nearby. He headed over.

"Listen, Jeff, I've been thinking about it a little bit longer," he said. "Come by my office on Monday. I'll give you your review and your bonus then."

McMahon agreed.

The bonus number was good. McMahon had feared he might pay a price for his run-ins over LJM2. But in his review on January 17, Fastow lavished him with praise, promising a hefty check in a week or so. McMahon left feeling sheepish. Apparently, he'd been worried for nothing.

By mid-afternoon on January 20, the scores of Wall Street analysts were starting to wilt. They had been in an auditorium at the Four Seasons Hotel in Houston for Enron's annual conference since 7:30 that morning, with few breaks. The company's news was good, but it was all starting to blur together.

Showtime. Skilling stood on a stage before the crowd. "I have an interesting announcement. We have renamed Enron Communications. As of today, Enron Communications Inc. is now Enron Broadband Services."

The rechristening was just the outward sign of an inner transformation, he declared. Already the unit was far down the high-tech path, and greater glories lay ahead.

"We intend to be the world's largest provider of premium broadband delivery services," he said. "And we have a range of products for streaming of broadband services and data management."

More speeches followed, accompanied by plenty of videos. Hirko, Rice, and the others described what the newly empowered division was up to— the intelligent network, video streaming, bandwidth trading.

More than an hour into the presentation, Mark Palmer, Enron's public-relations chief, was standing in the back, watching the crowd. Almost every head was down, looking through materials as Skilling took the stage again. The door beside Palmer opened. A man dressed in blue jeans, a casual shirt, and a sports coat came inside, followed by a few other executives. It was Scott McNealy and his entourage.

Skilling was still speaking. "We are announcing today an agreement with Sun Microsystems that's intended to accelerate the adoption of broadband Internet services."

Sun would help Enron build out the Enron Intelligent Network, he said. Enron would purchase thousands of Sun servers to drive the network. And the companies would work together in marketing the network's services.

He motioned toward the back. "I would like to introduce Scott McNealy, the chairman and chief executive of Sun Microsystems, to provide his perspective."

All heads in the room popped up and craned around in unison. Palmer stifled a laugh; the analysts looked like a covey of quail reacting to a shotgun blast. The crowd burst into applause. As McNealy approached, Skilling commented that his new partner had come from his sickbed.

McNealy climbed onto the stage and faced the crowd. "Actually, I'm feeling pretty good," he said. "Eighteen thousand servers tend to snap me right out of it."

The analysts roared.

"I even put a jacket on for this event," McNealy said. "I almost went out and rented a tux."

As expected, details of the Sun relationship and other positive news sent Enron's stock price into the stratosphere. That day it shot up $13.75, closing at a new high of $67.25 a share. And that was before McNealy even appeared. The *next* day was sure to be another blowout.

In the evening, senior managers headed out to a bar in downtown Houston to celebrate. They all were there—Lay, Skilling, Rice, Pai, everybody. There were cheers and laughs as they knocked back drinks. All of them had made a fortune that day—at least on paper.

As the night wore on, one executive approached Ken Rice, who was nursing a beer at the bar. "Wow, Ken, what a day!" the executive said. "What are you going to buy?"

Rice just looked at the man and laughed.

The executives were not the only ones who made money that day. Project Grayhawk had come off without a hitch; the hedge on JEDI's Enron stock had been removed in time, then quickly slapped back on. Enron brought in eighty-five million dollars in profits, just from the increased value of its own stock. It was, by any measure, a great start for the year.

Bonus-check day finally arrived. Sutton called McMahon up to his office to hand over the envelope. McMahon traipsed to the fiftieth floor, where Sutton had moved after becoming vice chairman. His office door was closed.

McMahon waited several minutes, occasionally chatting with the secretary. Finally Sutton emerged, looking harried.

"I'm sorry. I'm really, really busy," he said. "But I wanted to give you your bonus check."

There were people in his office; Sutton waved for McMahon to follow him. They huddled in an oversize closet, where Sutton held out an envelope. McMahon looked inside.

Wait a minute. A quarter of the bonus was missing.

"Joe, this isn't what Andy told me I was getting."

Sutton shrugged, raising his hands. "Well, you're going to have to talk to Andy about that. I'm very busy."

Sutton left the closet, heading back into his office. McMahon headed straight down the corridor to see Fastow.

"Andy," he said as he walked in, "there's a huge discrepancy in my bonus numbers."

Fastow looked up from his desk. "Well, I told you early on I wasn't comfortable telling you the number before the board approved it. We had to move around some of the numbers. But it's still a good bonus for you."

Next year would be better, Fastow said. McMahon stopped listening. Not much later, he saw a list with bonus figures on it. He knew what Michael Kopper was supposed to have received; Kopper had been ranked, and the rank came with a bonus range. But Kopper's number on the bonus list was much higher than what he had been slated to get.

It didn't take McMahon a lot of guesswork to figure out what had happened. Fastow had wanted more money for his boy, the one who had pushed through the lucrative LJM2 deals. So he had taken it from the guy who kept causing trouble for the fund.

Fastow had manipulated him every step of the way, putting him off until the board had acted and nothing could be changed. All for Kopper; all for LJM2. McMahon understood. Fighting against LJM2 was going to cost him.

That was it, McMahon decided. He was going to have to leave this job. But not before he went head-on at Fastow and his precious LJM2.

CHAPTER 12

VINCE KAMINSKI WATCHED THE gathering storm clouds through the gray-tinted glass of the Dallas Street sky bridge. His footsteps clicked on the flamed granite floors as he approached the entrance of the DoubleTree Hotel, just blocks from Enron. He made his way down a hallway to the Milam room, a meeting area on the hotel's second floor.

The first to arrive, Kaminski sat down and pulled out a pile of reports he had been putting together. For weeks, he had been pressing Rick Buy for this meeting; the topic was so sensitive that Buy insisted the meeting take place at the DoubleTree, away from any curious eavesdropping.

Kaminski was deeply troubled; in fact, he feared for Enron's future. He had not been taken in by the giddy sense of invincibility that permeated the company; instead, he harbored an inner disquiet. Did anyone really understand all of the financial dangers Enron faced? Risk was analyzed deal by deal, as if the sum of those pieces composed the total potential hazard confronting the company. But that was myopic. They needed to analyze risk across the business, to discover hidden dangers that might be festering in Enron's books.

Both Buy and Kaminski knew that the idea was politically treacherous. An enterprise-wide analysis would step on lots of toes; no one would want to be accused of ignoring risks. If Buy was going to give the go-ahead, Kaminski's course of action had to be planned carefully.

The other participants arrived: Buy, another member of the Risk Assessment and Control Department, and a couple of Kaminski's analysts, including a young financial whiz named Kevin Kindall. After making small talk over sandwiches and cookies, Buy looked over at Kaminski.

"All right, Vince," he said. "Let's get started."

Kaminski passed around the ten-page report he had completed over the weekend. "What I want to discuss today is defining and implementing guidelines for enterprise-wide risk management for Enron," he said.

One big issue the company had to face, Kaminski said, was the mismatch between its debts and its assets. It was borrowing huge sums of money—often billions at a time—frequently for terms of just weeks or months. But then the cash was used in long-term projects, like power plants. Using short-term loans for long-term investments was a classic financial blunder that had crippled the savings-and-loan industry, and it could wreak havoc on Enron, too.

"We have to estimate the possibility Enron could face a liquidity crisis," Kaminski said. "Even a large trading loss—or a news report suggesting such a loss—could deny us access to short-term loans and set off such a crisis."

A liquidity crunch would leave Enron short of the cash it needed to stay in business. To ensure every defense against that outcome, Kaminski wanted a team analyzing everything—trading risks, merchant investments, debt management. And perhaps most important, *all* of the company's assets and liabilities, on and off the books.

"Now, asset/liability management is sensitive because it typically belongs to the CFO's office," Kaminski said. "We may be trespassing, but as far as I know, it is not being done by Andy or anyone in his department."

Buy shifted uncomfortably in his seat. He didn't like the politics. "I don't know, Vince. I'm not happy about this part of the project. I'm not sure you should do it."

Kaminski didn't bend. "It's too important *not* to do it," he said. "It's an essential part of this analysis."

He had already put together a team, Kaminski said, with Kindall hired to lead the project. But his group had no mandate to collect information around Enron; only Risk Assessment and Control did. If RAC joined, it could request the data, and Kaminski's analysts could pore through it.

Buy agreed to assign a RAC member to the project. But he again voiced reservations about casting so wide a net. Maybe, he said, they should just forget about assets and liabilities. Kaminski nodded, as if in agreement. In reality, he had no intention of narrowing the analysis.

The project would take almost a year to complete. It would prove to be Enron's last, best chance to avert the debacle that was now just twenty-two months away.

Kopper dug in his heels. "I just don't think Doug's a smart guy. He's not as good as a lot of other people."

Around him, an array of executives listened. They were gathered in a windowless conference room, attending the latest PRC session. Kopper was on one side of a table already littered with paper and pencils. In the center of the room stood Rocky Jones from human resources, holding a nameplate labeled "Doug McDowell."

Kopper was vehement in his criticism, treating the junior executive as if he were Enron's worst mistake. McDowell's supervisors, Bill Brown and Jeff McMahon, knew exactly what was going on. McDowell had fought hard against LJM2, refusing to pay the million-dollar fee Kopper demanded for the Yosemite deal. Now it was payback time.

"McDowell is just not on the scale of talent that Enron should expect," Kopper said.

"Wait a minute, Michael," McMahon said. "When did you work with him that gave you a problem?"

Kopper raised his chin. "We worked on Yosemite."

McMahon and Brown both laughed. "Michael, that's an LJM deal," McMahon said.

Recognition swept across every face in the room. *That's* what this was all about. McMahon fixed his eyes on Kopper. "Michael, was the problem that LJM was paid a lower fee than you wanted?"

Kopper's response came fast. "No, no, nothing like that. It was the way the deal was negotiated."

That was enough. The other executives in the room sided with McMahon and Brown. On one side of the table, Andy Fastow watched the event unfold. Throughout the verbal sparring, he didn't utter a single word.

The room commandeered by Glisan was a hive of commotion as Project Raptor went into high gear. Glisan stood at the whiteboard, scribbling boxes and arrows. Ryan Siurek and Kevin Jordan, now working as Glisan's assistants, analyzed reams of documents and data. Causey and Fastow dropped by frequently for updates.

The plan was numbingly complex. But Glisan was sure Raptor would allow Enron to avoid future losses in its merchant investments. It would be like some elixir; with mark-to-market, Enron reported profits from investments as their values increased. With Raptor, it could avoid reporting losses if those values collapsed. What mark-to-market gave, Raptor would keep from being taken away.

In essence, Raptor would be the Rhythms hedge writ large. It would set up an entity, Talon, to provide Enron with a commitment to make up losses in its investments, again by depending on Enron stock. The company would transfer stock to Talon, with restrictions against selling or shorting it—terms that would diminish the shares' worth by 35 percent. In other words, if Enron gave Talon stock worth $500 million at market price, Talon would only owe Enron $325 million for it.

For Talon to be treated as a true independent entity, it needed three percent of its capital from a third party—the perfect job for LJM2. The Fastow fund would contribute thirty million dollars to Talon, enough to treat it as separate from Enron.

Then things got tricky. While Fastow was happy to kick in the cash, he didn't want his investors exposed to losses. So the team devised a simplistic—and absurd—solution. Before hedging anything, Talon was first required to give forty-one million dollars—the original thirty, plus an eleven-million-dollar profit—back to LJM2. Fastow's fund was guaranteed a massive profit before Talon took on any new risks. A baboon could make money under those terms.

But the forty-one million dollars couldn't be deemed as a return of the original investment; otherwise, there would be no independent cash in the deal. So Glisan had to find a way to argue that LJM2 still had thirty million dollars at risk in Talon. Semantics provided the answer. The forty-one million would be deemed a distribution of pure profit to LJM2. That would arguably still leave the fund with thirty million in Talon.

It was all smoke and mirrors. The requirement for an independent three percent investment was designed to make sure *somebody* cared about the financial performance of an entity like Talon. Otherwise, the company that set it up could just dump all its low-quality assets into a special-purpose entity, making its own performance look superb. But once Fastow had locked in his profit, he couldn't care less what deals Talon did. LJM2's investors would still see a stellar performance, guaranteed by the forty-one-million-dollar payout.

But the Enron shares couldn't be sold to make the payment; Talon needed cash from someplace else. So the team went to the only source available: Enron itself. Under this last leg of the plan, Enron would pay Talon forty-one million dollars. In exchange, Talon would commit to pay Enron a sum of cash if the company's own stock dropped in price.

Even for a transaction that had already soared past the outer reaches of common sense, this final step was a mass of contradictions. Talon was dependent on the value of Enron stock to make good on the hedge. In other words, by setting up Talon, Enron was betting its stock price would hold steady or go *up*. But now it was paying Talon millions of dollars in a bet that the price would go *down*. And of course, Talon would be hard-pressed to honor its commitment; if Enron's stock went down, the entity would lose its primary source of capital to compensate the company for the decline.

Talon was nothing more than Enron itself. Enron had handed it some assets; in the event that the merchant investment lost value, Talon would hand the assets back. Enron would be better off economically by doing nothing at all—at least then it would save forty-one million dollars.

––––––––––

As Glisan's explanations about Raptor droned on, Ron Astin and Mark Spradling, lawyers from Vinson & Elkins advising on the deal, grew uncomfortable. In particular, it seemed this forty-one-million-dollar distribution to LJM2 would eliminate all of the independent equity in the deal.

"Ben, wait," Astin said. "Doesn't that leave Talon with insufficient outside equity?"

"Not at all," Glisan responded. "It's a return *on* capital, not a return *of* capital. LJM2 keeps its interest in Talon. The three percent is still satisfied."

Astin wasn't convinced. Glisan's word game just sounded too cute. Still, the lawyers had time to mull it over, maybe talk it through with Andersen. After all, they were the accountants. Not Vinson & Elkins.

Chewco had become nothing but a headache. The entity formed years before—and now secretly owned by Michael Kopper and his domestic partner—for the purpose of buying half of the JEDI partnership had emerged as a source of endless trouble at Enron.

Both Enron and Chewco had to prepare valuations of JEDI's assets for establishing Enron's profits and figuring out if Chewco was owed any money. But their conclusions were sharply at odds; Kopper argued that the Chewco assets were worth double what Enron's analysts calculated. The disagreement broke down into bickering.

McMahon was sick of it. Why did Chewco even exist? He still didn't know. Maybe it would be better, he thought, to buy out Chewco and make JEDI wholly owned by Enron. He asked Bill Brown what he thought of that idea.

"Well," Brown replied, "buying out Chewco would mean negotiating a deal with Kopper."

That wasn't a fun prospect. "Does that mean Fastow will be involved?" McMahon asked.

Brown said yes. So McMahon cut out the middleman and went straight to Fastow with the proposal.

A million-dollar profit seemed fair. From what McMahon could figure, the Chewco investors put up $125,000 for an investment just over a year old. They couldn't possibly object to an annual return approaching 800 percent.

But Fastow didn't like the number. "I'll take it to Michael, but he's never going to accept that."

Soon after, Fastow called McMahon and Brown in for a discussion. He had been right; Kopper had refused. He proposed another deal, one that would give Chewco a ten-million-dollar profit.

McMahon gaped at him. An *8,000 percent return.* "You've gotta be kidding," he said. "Ten million?"

Fastow nodded.

"Ten million *dollars*? Why don't you just tell Michael to check what company is on his paychecks. He works for Enron. Ten million is unconscionable."

"I think it sounds fair," Fastow said with a shrug.

No way, McMahon said. This money would go to Kopper's domestic partner or Kopper himself. It was extortion.

"I will not allow this company to pay ten million dollars for this," McMahon said. "Tell Michael there's no deal."

At his home on the evening of Friday, January 28, David Bermingham of Greenwich NatWest sat in front of his computer, crunching some LJM1 numbers. He hit the "return" button and up popped a figure he was happy to see.

Bermingham was analyzing the value of Swap Sub, set up by LJM1. That entity held a huge slug of the Enron shares gifted to LJM1 and was legally responsible for making good on the Rhythms hedge. In essence, for the Rhythms hedge, LJM1 collected cash from investors, Swap Sub did the business. For a long time Swap Sub wasn't exciting. Weeks before, on January 5, Bermingham had reviewed an analysis showing Swap Sub had a value of *negative* twenty-five million dollars.

Then, it happened. Scott McNealy walked into a room. Analysts went nuts, and so did Enron's stock price. Now it wasn't just the usual lot of shareholders who had a paper fortune—so did Swap Sub. Bermingham's calculations showed that if the Rhythms hedge was shut down and the value of Swap Sub distributed, the LJM1 investors would make millions.

That got Bermingham thinking. His office was in turmoil. National Westminster, the parent of Greenwich NatWest, looked like it would soon be acquired by Royal Bank of Scotland. Greenwich was sure to be sold. Bermingham and his pals—who had brought LJM1 to the bank—could be out on the street. Then this windfall of profits would go to—whom? RBS? That, Bermingham decided, just wasn't right.

Not when there was another choice: the guys who worked on the deal. Bermingham, Giles Darby, Gary Mulgrew. *They* should make the profits. They might be able to pull it off, with help—from Fastow, probably Kopper, too. Then it could work. The next day, Bermingham typed an e-mail to Darby, explaining his analysis of LJM1 and Swap Sub.

"There is quite some value there now," Bermingham typed. "The trick will be in capturing it. I have a couple of ideas but it may be good if I don't share them with anyone until we know our fate!!!"

The next conspiracy had begun.

The conference call between Houston and Chicago had been dragging on for more than thirty minutes. The Andersen accountants had been intensely reviewing Project Raptor for days; now, on February 3, they were trying to decide whether the deal could be done under the accounting rules.

Calling from Houston with the Enron engagement team were David Duncan and Deb Cash, along with Carl Bass, now with the Professional Standards Group. On the line in Chicago were John Stewart and Jim Green, both from the PSG.

The whole idea, as described by Duncan and Cash, struck Bass as ludicrous. Enron was just shifting around assets and pretending to set up a hedge—with itself.

"This whole deal has no substance," Bass said. "All the money at risk comes from Enron. How is this a hedge?"

Duncan countered with a monologue on the three percent rule. But the accountants in Chicago were unconvinced.

"Why not bring in a real third party, like Goldman Sachs, to do a straight hedge?" Bass asked.

"They don't want to do that," Duncan said. "It would be too expensive."

That spoke volumes. If the market won't provide the hedge at a low price, there was probably a good reason.

"Look, David, the way it is put together is just not going to work," Green said.

"Well, wait a minute," Duncan responded. "Listen to this. What if we make these changes?"

A nip here, a tuck there, and everybody started signing on. It made Bass's head ache. Whether Raptor could be twisted to meet some tortured interpretation of the rules wasn't the point. *The deal did nothing*. It didn't protect against losses. Apparently, the client didn't *care*. Enron just wanted protection from having to *report* losses.

The next morning, Bass arrived early in the office. He had been thinking a lot about Raptor since the previous day, and his doubts had hardened into conviction. Nobody should be doing this deal. He logged on to the Andersen system and addressed an e-mail to Stewart and Green.

"I am still bothered by the transaction we discussed yesterday," Bass typed.

Essentially, he wrote, Enron was jury-rigging a contraption to hedge with itself. "I have to ask myself, why not do a straight deal with Goldman?" Bass typed. "They said so themselves. It will be too expensive."

And why was Enron providing the capital Talon would use for hedging? "Because," Bass wrote, "no bank is dumb enough to loan money whose payment is dependent on changes in the value of an Internet stock."

At 6:38 A.M., Bass hit the "send" button.

The response came back in just over an hour. Stewart wrote that it sounded like Bass was arguing Talon would have to be consolidated into Enron. "We should discuss it some more," he wrote. "You have some good points."

Three days later, Azurix was ready with its latest plan to save the company. At a board meeting, Rebecca Mark explained that the company was on the verge of a big announcement: it was about to plunge into the dot-com mania, a surefire way to drive up the stock price.

The idea was to create a sort of Enron Lite, a trading business designed not for gas and electricity, but for water. Not long ago, Enron had introduced an operation called Enron Online that allowed it to serve as a principal for energy trades over the Internet, and it had grown like gangbusters. Well, this new idea—water2water.com—would do the same thing, Mark said. It would be a huge business.

The directors listened, skeptical. Online trading for electricity and gas made sense, since those commodities were pretty much the same all over. But *water*? Upstate New York wouldn't trade with downstate. Different localities had different qualities; it simply wasn't standardized. Of course, there were industrial uses for water, like applications for farms. But why would potential customers turn to the Internet when they could just turn on the spigot?

As Mark rambled on about the latest brainstorm, the directors grew restless. They had made it clear to her repeatedly that they wanted to see belt-tightening in the company. Yet here she was, proposing more spending. All told, she still planned to burn through in excess of $100 million a year.

And Mark thought even that was tight. "Again," she said, "I would advise that the best option is to pursue an aggressive growth strategy rather than cutting back."

The directors jumped on her. "Rebecca, that is not going to happen," Pug Winokur said. "We have turned aside that idea, and we are not going back to it."

Skilling picked it up from there. "Rebecca, this is just not enough. I mean, look at this. You've got something like thirty million dollars here for computer-system development."

"That's for the Internet water exchange," she said. "That will give us a significant growth in market cap."

Skilling sucked in a breath. Spending millions just so Azurix could bandy about the word "Internet"? Did she really think that would make investors clamor for Azurix stock? Was there *any* real business plan here?

"Rebecca, you need to cut the burn rate way back," one of the directors said. "Down to forty million."

Mark's face fell. "Wait a minute—"

"Forty million, Rebecca," Skilling interrupted. "That's all you've got. Figure out how to make it work."

Mark was stunned. There was no way she could pursue her vision with just forty million dollars. She wouldn't be able to make acquisitions. No bidding, no public relations. Forget the corporate jets. Azurix would be reduced to managing the water assets it already owned. It was a dreadful prospect.

"I can't in good conscience do this," she said. "We would have to cut the water2water site, which is going to be gigantic. It would mean abandoning it."

Lay spoke up. "Rebecca, we need to see this alternative. Run the scenario, and show us what it means."

After the meeting broke up, Mark, Lay, and Skilling stayed behind. It was time for another talk.

Lay was the first to speak. "Rebecca, I want to stress that this is very serious. And to tell you the truth, I don't think the board has confidence in the case you're making."

He eyed her, seeing if this was getting through.

"I think we need to see something that is a much more significant effort to ratchet this back," he said. "I want you to know that's what the board wants."

Mark nodded. "I got that loud and clear," she said.

All right, Lay replied. He and Skilling left the room and climbed onto the elevator.

"She hasn't thought this through," Lay said suddenly. "She doesn't understand the severity of it."

Skilling felt a wave of relief. *Lay got it.*

That same afternoon, directors from Enron's audit committee clustered around the circular table in the boardroom to hear the final wrap-up for 1999, checking for accounting problems that might need attention. Robert Jaedicke, the Stanford Business School dean who chaired the committee, recognized David Duncan for Andersen's annual audit review. As usual, everything sounded great.

"Arthur Andersen's financial statement opinion for 1999 will be unqualified," Duncan said. "There were no significant audit adjustments, or disagreements with management, or other significant difficulties."

Later in the meeting, Jaedicke introduced a new topic. "As you know, we have approved the participation by Andy Fastow in certain investment vehicles called LJM1 and LJM2," he said. "It is our committee's responsibility to review Enron's participation in transactions with those vehicles, to ensure they were done at arm's length."

Jaedicke recognized Causey, who proceeded for several minutes to rattle off deals, including the flood from year-end. He left out a few, but no one noticed.

"It is my opinion," Causey said, "that all of these deals have been conducted on an arm's-length basis."

There were no questions. The presentation had taken less than ten minutes. The committee moved on.

Having two chief executives in Enron Broadband just wasn't working. Rice and Hirko kept stumbling over each other, and they both knew it. Someone had to step aside, and they agreed it should be Rice.

The job had become a bore. Rice didn't want to manage people anymore and would rather do deals. They made up a title, chief commercial officer. The agreement reached, they went to Skilling with the news. He was delighted that the two had solved the problem on their own. Later that day, Skilling dropped by Rice's office.

"I really appreciate you guys working this out," he said. "It's a pretty good solution."

"Yeah, I think it'll work out well."

"So what's it going to cost me?" Skilling asked.

Rice didn't flinch. It had never occurred to him that Skilling would *pay* him to leave a job he didn't want. It looked as though the first deal he would negotiate in his new position would be one for himself.

"Dunno," he said casually. "Let me think about it."

The price tag was big. His years at Enron had made Rice wealthy, so he asked to have his entire salary and bonus converted into stock options from then on. Skilling agreed without hesitation.

McMahon was losing hope of ever falling asleep. LJM2 was eating at him; he knew that he had to do something. He just didn't know what. About two in the morning, he reached for the television remote and clicked on the set. Beside him, his wife, Margaret, stirred.

"What's the matter?" she mumbled.

McMahon's eyes stayed locked on the television. "I'm stressed about this Andy thing. I don't know what to do."

"If you're that troubled, talk to him again."

McMahon said nothing for a moment. "Maybe I should leave the company," he said.

"Then leave. No job is worth this. Get another one."

She smiled. "Just stop waking me up in the middle of the night."

A while later, McMahon shut off the television. Things couldn't continue like this. Something had to give.

It was over. He was quitting. Everything he had seen about LJM2 was just too over the top, too unethical. Jim Timmins couldn't put up with it anymore.

Timmins, Enron's contact with the pension funds, had at one point been eager about the company setting up its own equity fund. But then Fastow took the idea and bastardized it, putting himself in control, creating conflicts of interest that Timmins found grotesque.

Plus, he was already hearing plenty from his contacts in the institutional-investor world to make him worried. Pension-fund managers were uncomfortable with the whole thing, couldn't understand what Enron was doing, and told Timmins about their concerns.

Originally, Fastow had wanted Timmins along on the road show for LJM2. But as his discomfort with the deal became evident, Timmins was cut out. He eventually told Kopper that he wanted nothing to do with LJM2, that he feared bad things would come from it. He quickly saw the results: his bonus that year was his worst ever.

Finally, by February, Timmins realized that he couldn't continue at a company that would do such a thing. He went to see Fastow. His message was blunt. "I don't agree with what you're doing with LJM," he said. "I don't want any part of it. I want to leave Enron."

Fastow argued, saying that the fund was good for Enron, but Timmins would have none of it. Still, Fastow wasn't eager to see Timmins storm out in a huff. He offered to let the executive continue working at Enron for months, so he could use the office to look for another job. Then, when something good came along, he could move on.

Timmins thought the offer was fair. He didn't realize that Fastow had just set up a situation that made sure no one would have cause to ask the real reason Timmins was leaving.

_____

Somehow, Andy Fastow had to get twenty-five million dollars. If that could happen, the bankers at Greenwich NatWest were certain they could persuade him to help rip off their employer.

The three bankers—Bermingham, Darby, and Mulgrew—had been perfecting their plan for weeks. The idea was simple. Nobody at Greenwich NatWest, other than the bankers themselves, knew that Swap Sub, the partnership controlled by LJM1, was now worth millions. Everyone assumed it was valued at nothing. There was no need for the hedge anymore; the restriction against selling the stock was gone. So if the hedge was shut down, there would be tens of millions of dollars in Enron stock locked up inside Swap Sub. Whoever owned it owned the profits.

If all of them worked together—the bankers, Fastow, Kopper—they could pull off the perfect con. Fastow and Kopper could make some lowball offer of their own for NatWest's stake in Swap Sub, and the three bankers could tell their superiors it was a good price. Then, once they owned Swap Sub, they could turn around and sell its shares for tens of millions of dollars—and divvy up the loot.

Bermingham had been working hard on a presentation for Fastow and Kopper, showing how much money could be made. There had already been some preliminary discussions, and the two seemed amenable. But Mulgrew didn't like what he saw in Bermingham's analysis; Fastow might not be getting enough. The more available for him, the greater the chance the bankers would get their millions, too. Mulgrew e-mailed Bermingham with his concerns about Fastow.

"If I knew there was a realistic way to lock in the $40m, and give him $25m, we would jump all over it I guess, since it would give us $15m," he typed. "I will be the first to be delighted if he has found a way to lock it in and steal a large portion for himself."

But with all the cash sloshing around, Mulgrew felt sure there was a way to bring Fastow on board. "We should be able," he typed, "to appeal to his greed."

Two days later, on February 22, the bankers flew to Houston to meet with Fastow and Kopper. Normally, the Greenwich banker in charge of the Enron relationship, Kevin Howard, would be there. But Darby asked him not to attend, with a cryptic comment about becoming rich.

Once they were all in a room, Bermingham made the presentation. "We've put together several alternatives for this transaction," he explained. "Any one of them will lead to the result we're trying to achieve."

The different proposals had the same objective: cheating NatWest. But there were challenges. Under the rules originally issued by Enron's board, Fastow couldn't profit from the company's shares in LJM1. And that was exactly what would happen here.

There was a way around that, Bermingham said. Once the Rhythms hedge was unwound, perhaps LJM1 could do some sort of transaction converting the Enron stock into another asset, which could then be sold.

But, Bermingham warned, that involved a lot of moving parts and might raise suspicions among NatWest and CSFB.

"It might be too obvious," he said. "There's a bigger chance they'll figure out they're getting robbed."

That wasn't the only problem. "Also," Bermingham said, "that way, there's no certainty we'll make money."

Cliff Baxter's effort to sell the international power plants was going full force. He had hired Morgan Stanley Dean Witter to help and quickly concluded that there weren't buyers around who wanted the whole thing. Probably, Baxter decided, it was best to try and unload them one region at a time.

The first planned sale was called Project California, and it bunched together Enron's energy assets in Latin America. Any buyer would gain entrée to Guatemala, Brazil, El Salvador, Venezuela—a cross section of the region. Skilling liked the idea and asked Causey to run numbers on each regional slice of the international assets. That way, they would know what to expect as the sales effort moved forward.

It was an exciting prospect, but still it made Skilling a little nervous. What, after all, was Enron going to do with all those billions in cash?

Fastow wanted to know: what was everybody else paid at Enron? The information was locked up pretty tight. About the only person who knew—outside of Skilling and Lay—was Mary Joyce, a human-resources executive in charge of compensation. Maybe she would tell him.

One afternoon, Fastow dropped by Joyce's office. He needed to see the compensation information for members of Enron's top management committee, he told her.

Joyce looked at him skeptically. "I'm sorry, Andy. I'm not allowed to give that out."

"Jeff said it's okay. I need it for something I'm working on."

Skilling approved this? That didn't sound right. Joyce reached for the phone. "Well, let me call him and ask."

She got through right away. "Jeff, I've got a question," she said. "Should I release compensation for members of the executive committee to anyone?"

Skilling laughed. "No! Why would you ask that?"

"I was just checking," Joyce replied.

She hung up and looked at Fastow. "Sorry, Andy."

Outside a terminal at Houston Intercontinental Airport, Ken Rice tossed a suitcase in his car, ready for the trip home. It was March 1, a Wednesday, and Rice was just back from the opening of Enron's new London office. In minutes, he was out of the lot, driving onto Interstate 45.

His car phone rang. "Ken Rice."

"Ken, hey, it's David Cox."

More business. Cox was one of Rice's favorite deal makers in Broadband. If a transaction needed doing, Cox was the guy. His calls always meant something big was up.

"Yeah, what's going on?"

"I'm in Dallas, been negotiating with Blockbuster Entertainment. I'm on the verge of closing a twenty-year exclusive deal with them for video on demand."

What? Rice didn't know what Cox was talking about. No one had mentioned a Blockbuster deal before. How fast had Cox put together this two-decade commitment?

"Think you better explain this to me," Rice said.

The idea was simple. Enron and Blockbuster would form a venture to provide videos over a broadband network. Customers could choose from a library of films, place an order, and watch the video at home. No returns, no leaving the house. Enron would provide the network, and Blockbuster would secure the films through its studio connections.

It sounded promising. But, still, Rice was on Interstate 45. Couldn't this wait? "You're not ready to close this today, are you?"

"Yeah," Cox replied, "we are."

"Surely this can wait for a few days."

"No, we want to sign right away."

Rice understood. When somebody was ready to do a deal, dithering was always a bad idea.

Well, we can clean up things later if we have to. "Okay," Rice said. "Let's go for it."

Later that week, two Greenwich NatWest bankers, Bermingham and Darby, flew to the Cayman Islands for the next step in their plan. The directors of Campsie Limited, a Caymans entity set up by NatWest to invest in LJM1, were meeting to consider the proposal to sell Swap Sub to a partnership controlled by Fastow and Kopper.

Darby made the presentation to Campsie directors on March 3. This new partnership—at this point called NewCo—had offered one million dollars for Campsie's interest, which Darby called a fair offer. Bermingham, a director, urged the board to authorize formal talks.

The board approved the plan. And why not? Selling an asset for its value certainly wasn't controversial.

The next evening in the Caymans, the soft rays of the setting sun lit up the horizon in streaks of gold and crimson. Bermingham was in a local restaurant, enjoying his dinner. With him was Fastow, there to keep tabs on the Campsie vote. It was a complicated deal, and lots could go wrong. Bermingham, Fastow said, needed to move quickly.

Skilling learned the basics from Greg Whalley, the executive now in charge of the wholesale-trading desk.

West Coast rainfall was down. The amount of hydroelectric power, generated by the flow of water, would decline. California imported hydro from Canada and Washington, and had not built new power plants in years.

In the meantime, temperatures were rising even as California was in the midst of an Internet-fueled economic boom. Demand for energy to keep its factories humming—and to cool the homes and offices of its residents—was about to explode, even as supplies shrank. And under the state's two-year-old electricity program, rising costs wouldn't dampen demand; most customers' rates were locked in place.

"It's a classic supply-and-demand mismatch," Whalley said. "California is going to hit a wall sometime soon."

"Okay," Skilling said. "So what's your plan?"

"We're setting up a long position, a big one."

A long position. Enron was setting up some trades that would allow the company to profit from rising electricity costs.

It sounded solid. "Great," Skilling said.

The Swap Sub purchase was looking like a blowout winner. Maybe, Fastow and Kopper decided, it would be a good idea to let others have a taste.

Glisan was an obvious candidate. He'd spent plenty of time on LJM matters; his work had already enriched Fastow. Then there were people like Anne Yeager, who had helped negotiate the Sails deal. And Kristina Mordaunt, a lawyer who had worked on LJM1 and was now general counsel for Enron Broadband Services. Why not spread around the wealth?

Fastow sounded out Glisan, who quickly agreed to invest. Kopper headed over to Mordaunt's office to talk. He went inside and closed the door behind him.

"An interesting opportunity has come up," he said.

The Royal Bank of Scotland was taking over NatWest, and some of the bank's managers were leaving, Kopper said. A few of them, including Gary Mulgrew, had approached them about buying part of the NatWest interest in LJM.

"So Andy and I came up with the idea of forming a partnership to purchase their interest," Kopper said, "and were wondering if you might want to participate."

Mordaunt was intrigued. "What kind of investment do you have in mind?"

"Under ten thousand dollars."

Sounded reasonable. "Sure. I'd be interested."

Kopper looked satisfied. "Great," he said. "I'll get back to you in a couple of weeks."

He stood and left. The conversation that would destroy Mordaunt's career had lasted all of two minutes.

What the hell is this? McMahon stared at the multipage deal-approval sheet in disbelief. The document, known internally as a DASH, had been sent to him for a sign-off, authorizing Enron to spend money for the transaction. But this was unlike any DASH that McMahon had ever seen; Enron was repurchasing something it had just sold to LJM2.

Under the proposal, Enron would buy back its stake in MEGS, the gas-distribution system that it had sold to LJM2 in December. Scarcely ninety days had passed; why buy it back? It would just cram another asset onto the bloated balance sheet—and of course give LJM2 a quick profit.

No one had done an analysis to demonstrate that this would be a good investment for Enron. It had all the earmarks of a sweetheart deal. Enron had booked cash flow and profits from the MEGS sale and now wanted to undo the deal? McMahon wasn't signing.

But soon the pressure began—from Causey, from Fastow. The deal needed to get done, they told him. He finally relented but made sure to register his distaste. After signing the DASH, he jotted an addendum.

"There were no economics run to demonstrate that this investment makes sense," McMahon wrote.

That same night at the Compaq Center arena in Houston, Neil Young, the rock icon, sat at a pump organ warbling "After the Gold Rush" slightly off-key. Nearby, his partners—David Crosby, Stephen Stills, and Graham Nash—

listened to the solo as they stood among candles, Tiffany lamps, and palm trees scattered about the stage.

High above, McMahon and Baxter watched with their wives. This was the reunion tour for Crosby, Stills, Nash & Young, and neither McMahon nor Baxter had wanted to miss it. But they didn't feel young enough to battle crowds on the floor. Listening to some sixties songs from a well-appointed skybox seemed a suitable, if ironic, compromise.

Baxter and McMahon stood in the back of the skybox, drinking as they peered down at the musicians' bald spots.

"Guess we're all getting kind of old," McMahon said.

As they chatted, McMahon got to thinking about the MEGS deal and the other oddities of the last few months. Baxter was wise in the ways of Enron and was close to Skilling. Maybe he would have an answer.

"Cliff, I want to ask you a question," McMahon said. "How much do you know about LJM?"

Baxter gave a derisive snort. "Probably more than you think. What's up?"

"Why did the board waive this conflict?"

"Andy convinced them that in the long run, the company is better off to have these. Why? What's your problem?"

"You can't run a finance department this way. You have Enron people negotiating against other Enron people. And Andy is their supervisor, controls all the promotions and raises and bonuses, *and* he has an interest in the company Enron's negotiating against. It's just a mess."

Baxter nodded. "I've got similar problems with it."

"I've talked to Andy about fixing things, and nothing happens," McMahon said. "So I'm thinking of just moving to another post internally."

Baxter took a sip. "I'll talk to Skilling. And before you do anything, you should talk to him, too."

McMahon thought about it. Maybe that was a good idea.

The next day, March 9, the formal, written offer for Swap Sub was ready to go. Kopper sent it to Giles Darby at the Greenwich NatWest office in London. The terms were the same as those described days before in the Caymans; this entity, still called NewCo, would pay one million dollars for the share of Swap Sub owned by Campsie on behalf of NatWest.

"The principals are committed to working with you to rapidly conclude a transaction," Kopper wrote.

The job offer to McMahon came out of nowhere.

Greg Whalley, Enron's chief trader, called with news that they were starting another business. The idea was to apply Enron's business model to a range of commodities—metals, paper, anything. Whalley would be chief executive of the new division and wanted McMahon to join him.

"It'll be fun," Whalley said. "Come work for me."

McMahon was unimpressed. The business didn't have a name yet, this job had no title. He had already figured he was probably leaving Enron, maybe to take a job as CFO at some other company. But *this*? It didn't sound right.

"I don't know if it's a good move for me," McMahon said. "Maybe if I could be president."

"I can't make you president," Whalley said. "But trust me, things will work out."

McMahon thought about it. "Well, I guess I'm not happy where I am."

Whalley laughed; McMahon had made it clear long ago that he wasn't comfortable working for Fastow. "I *know*," Whalley said. "That's why I thought you'd be easy pickings."

That same week, on March 15, Fastow was alone in his office when McMahon showed up for a scheduled appointment. Since speaking with Baxter, McMahon had agonized about what to do. Going to Skilling would be a virtual declaration of war. Before taking such a drastic step, he had to give Fastow one last chance to do the right thing.

"Andy, you've been promising for four months that you would take care of the LJM problems," McMahon began.

He recounted the commitments Fastow had made—forcing employees to work for Enron or LJM2, finding office space, pulling LJM2 people out of Enron strategy meetings.

"You've done none of them," McMahon said. "Not one."

Not only that, McMahon said, but he was sure his bonus had been affected because of his battles against LJM2.

"That's not true," Fastow shot back.

"I'm just telling you how I feel, given my number."

"I told you what happened there."

McMahon decided not to mention that he knew about Kopper's pay. "I know what you told me, Andy," he said. "I'm just telling you my perspective."

He took a breath. "Look, Andy, something's got to happen here. Something's got to change."

Fastow scowled. "Well, I'm doing everything I can do. You just need to be patient. Just trust me."

The meeting dwindled to an end, and McMahon headed to the elevator.

By the time he got back to his office, he had worked himself into a fury. He walked over to his secretary.

"Get me on Skilling's calendar for thirty minutes as fast as possible," he said. "Just say it's personal."

That night, McMahon mentioned nothing to his wife, Margaret, until they were in bed, watching television.

"I'm doing it tomorrow," he said. "I've got an appointment with Jeff."

"Good. It's about time."

McMahon glanced over at her. "He may fire me."

"Are you going to give him an ultimatum?"

"No. But I am going to say I have to leave my job. And he might not have another job for me."

Margaret gave him a hug. "We'll survive," she said.

The next morning just after ten, Skilling stood beside Lay as a photographer snapped their pictures for an article in *Fortune*. They were more than happy to participate; already that year, in its annual rankings, *Fortune* had hailed Enron as America's best-managed company, knocking General Electric from the number-one perch. This new article, one that would again be singing the company's praises, would no doubt be the icing on the cake.

About that same moment, McMahon was at his desk, staring at a pad of lined paper. His meeting with Skilling was soon, and he was gathering his thoughts.

"Discussion Points," he wrote near the top of the page. He thought for a moment. "Untenable situation."

The notes just flowed, point by point, the months of anger finally finding release. At the bottom of the first page, McMahon listed possible alternatives to deal with the LJM situation. One point he wrote in capital letters: "WILL NOT COMPROMISE MY INTEGRITY."

He underlined the words before flipping the page.

Skilling was at his desk when McMahon arrived just before 11:30, his pad of notes in hand.

"Hey, Jeff, come on in," Skilling said. McMahon started to take a seat in front of the desk.

"Oh, come on!" Skilling said. "Let's go sit at the conference table."

Skilling brought a notepad with him and wrote down the name "Jeff McMahon." He placed an elbow on the table and rested his chin in his hand.

"Okay," Skilling said. "What's up?"

McMahon glanced down at his notes. "I want to talk to you about this whole LJM thing," he began. "I've got some real concerns about the conflicts of interest."

Skilling didn't nod, didn't react. He seemed focused on every word McMahon was saying.

"I understand the notion, and I know the board approved Andy being the general partner. I'm not questioning that. My issue is how it's being managed. It's at the point where I can no longer manage the conflicts."

The setup was affecting people's behavior, McMahon said. LJM2 staffers were allowed to attend strategy meetings within Enron. People were feeling pressured to do deals that weren't in Enron's interest.

He alluded to Yosemite, when Fastow tried to get a million-dollar fee. There was pressure to accept terms that were wrong for Enron, and Fastow wouldn't back down.

"Here's the CFO of the company, a few weeks before bonuses are paid, telling me to close the deal under bad terms," McMahon said. "I didn't do it, we got it fixed and done right. But, man, that was major pressure."

And there was no doubt in his mind that he had paid a price for his efforts to look out for Enron. "I think my compensation's been affected because of that," he said.

Skilling listened but didn't take a single note.

"I didn't ask to be in this position," McMahon said. "But now here I am, stuck in the middle."

There had to be a solution, McMahon said. Either all the conflicts had to be fixed, or he needed to change jobs. "Those are the two options," he said. "And I need something to happen pretty quickly."

There was a second of silence. "Is that it?" Skilling asked. McMahon nodded.

Skilling stood, and McMahon followed. "Listen, thanks for coming up," Skilling said. "It's important for me to know that. And I'm glad you told me."

They reached the doorway. Skilling opened the door.

"I've heard you loud and clear," he said. "Trust me, I'm going to fix this. I'm going to fix this for you."

In no time, McMahon was back in his office. He sighed; he hadn't been fired yet.

Andy's going to blow a friggin' gasket.

———

Skilling walked back to his desk. He understood what McMahon's concerns were; this was about compensation, about ensuring Fastow didn't target him for doing right by Enron.

He knew McMahon had no reason to worry. *That* was the beauty of the PRC. Fastow was one voice out of twenty-three; if McMahon stood up for Enron, everyone would see it. He knew the PRC system was pristine; this was just a matter of appearances. Skilling was annoyed Fastow had allowed bad perceptions to fester, but he'd take care of that, too.

As for McMahon's other worries, Skilling wasn't worried. Where people worked, what meetings they attended—those were administrative issues. It would probably take a few days to work it out. But Skilling's schedule was packed that day, and he was leaving the next morning for vacation with his kids. He didn't have time to fix this.

Maybe Joe Sutton. He was vice chairman. He was supposed to help out on operations issues. Skilling would talk to him about it later that day.*

The same day, Darby and Bermingham from Greenwich NatWest were back in the Caymans for a Campsie board meeting. Darby provided an update about the formal offer and recommended accepting. The suggestion was approved.

The paperwork was finalized the next morning. Campsie, for NatWest, agreed to sell its share of Swap Sub to the Fastow partnership for one million dollars. About that same time, the other LJM1 partner, CSFB, also signed its contract to sell Swap Sub to the partnership—for ten million dollars. But even at that price, it was being cheated.

The crowd of partygoers leaped out of their hiding places as soon as Mike McConnell walked into his house.

"*Surprise!*" they yelled.

McConnell, a top technology executive at Enron, looked stunned. It was the night of his fortieth birthday party, and his house was filled with friends. As the beer and fun flowed, Whalley spotted McMahon and sidled over.

"Jeff!" he said enthusiastically. "What do you think? You gonna come work with me? You want to do this?"

---

*In a nonpublic affidavit from 2002, Sutton said he believed his meeting with Skilling took place the following Monday, March 20. His recollection is incorrect; contemporaneous records from the time show Skilling was in Brazil on that day and did not return to the office until March 29. See *Notes and Sources.*

McMahon made a face. "Well, I've thought about it a lot, Greg. And I just don't think it's right for me."

Whalley urged him to reconsider, but McMahon seemed steadfast. He wasn't going to jump at the first opportunity that came along.

But Whalley wasn't ready to give up.

At 3:45 the following Monday, March 20, McMahon was up in Sutton's office, again spelling out his concerns on LJM2. Sutton, who was scheduled to leave the country the next day, was eager to get the matter resolved.

"Now, of course, I know this was approved by the board . . . ," McMahon said.

"Yes, it was approved by the board!" Sutton interrupted. "They approved the whole conflict of interest. Is that your issue, Jeff? Come on!"

"No, that is not my issue, Joe. My issue is now we have to manage that since it's . . ."

"Well, we're not going to change. It's been approved. It's not like we can get rid of LJM at this point."

This wasn't going well. "I'm not proposing that either, Joe," McMahon said. "All I am proposing is that the way Andy works in the organization has to be managed."

Sutton picked up a pen, ready to take notes. "Give me an example," he said.

"Well, first off, we should get the LJM guys out of the building."

Sutton wrote it down. "That makes sense," he said. "Did you tell that to Andy?"

Many times.

"And what did he say?"

"He said he'd fix it."

Sutton's tone was blunt. "Okay, he said he'd fix it. So what's the problem?"

"He's been saying that for four months."

Well, that was different, Sutton said. What else?

"Andy being part of the compensation system is flawed," McMahon said. "People believe they're going to get screwed if they cut too good a deal for Enron."

Sutton made a face. "Come on. Do you know how much money Fastow makes off of LJM?"

McMahon shook his head.

"Well," Sutton continued, "whatever he's making off LJM is not enough so that he'll screw somebody who's doing right by Enron."

"Okay," McMahon said. "So do *you* know how much he's making off LJM?"

Sutton shrugged. "No, but it can't be close to what he's making from Enron. And I know *that* number."

Well, McMahon said, LJM was private equity, and those funds all worked pretty much the same way. Fastow would receive a two percent management fee. While he didn't know LJM's size, McMahon said, he'd heard it had raised about $400 million.

"So that's eight million annually, off the top."

Sutton considered that. "Well, he has expenses."

"He does? As near as I can tell, the employees are free—they're Enron people. He's using our office space, our phones. What are his expenses?"

Sutton waved a hand. "That can't be right."

McMahon smiled. "Wait a minute, Joe. That's just part of it. The eight million is just for showing up."

On top of that, the general partner gets a percentage of the profits past a target level. McMahon ran some quick numbers by Sutton, possibilities of outcomes. All told, he said, Fastow could be pulling in about twenty-four million dollars a year.

Sutton's eyes went wide. "That can't possibly be right!" he said. "That's more than *I* make!"

Later that day, Sutton walked down the hall to Fastow's office. Since his days as an officer in the Army, Sutton had never been one to beat around the bush. He wanted to hear Fastow's reaction to McMahon's concerns.

After taking a seat in Fastow's office, Sutton mentioned that McMahon had dropped by and raised some worries; he summarized everything McMahon had said.

Fastow dismissed the issue out of hand. "I don't think there's any problem at all. This is overseen by Buy and Causey. They have to sign off on every deal. And I don't have any control over them. They report to Skilling."

"All right," Sutton said. "That's what I understood."

But there was also another LJM matter, Sutton said. "Are you going to make a lot of money from this?"

Fastow laughed. "Joe, come on," he said. "I'm not going to make a lot of money here. At best, I'm just going to get a small return on the cash I have at risk."

He pressed a finger against the desktop.

"And, Joe," he said, "any money I do make will be insignificant compared to my compensation as Enron's CFO."

At about that same time, Kopper was preparing the final paperwork for the Swap Sub buyout. NewCo had been formally named Southampton Place, after the well-heeled neighborhood where Fastow and Kopper both lived. Now the partnership agreement for investors was ready to go.

Kopper brought the document around for everyone to sign and collected checks. Mordaunt and Glisan invested $5,816 each; the others put up far less.

Among the investors was another partnership, called Southampton K, which retained a sizable percentage of Southampton. It was the secret front company for the Greenwich NatWest bankers. Under their agreement, the bankers would get an option to own all of Southampton K for $250,000; they had until May to decide if they wanted to make the purchase. It seemed like a clever subterfuge; the bankers could argue that they were not actual owners of the entity buying Swap Sub until weeks after it was purchased.

The deal was all but finished two days later.

Southampton now owned Swap Sub, which held the Rhythms hedge, Enron stock, and a few million in cash. Under a letter signed by Causey, Enron agreed to cancel the hedge and pay Southampton thirty million dollars for the stock. Ten million would go to CSFB. One million to Greenwich NatWest. And the lion's share—nineteen million dollars—to the Southampton owners. The LJM1 investors, and Enron itself, would be cheated.

Still, the damage was worse than it appeared. Since the stock was never supposed to be hedged, LJM1 had purchased it at a discount to the market price, a discount that was still in place. But in figuring what he was owed, Fastow calculated the value of the shares at full market price. Causey and his staff didn't blink before agreeing to cough up the clearly inflated amount.

After his vacation, Skilling returned to the office on the morning of Wednesday, March 29. There was plenty to catch up on, and soon he had an update from Joe Sutton about his conversations with McMahon and Fastow.

Sutton considered the relationship between the two irreparable. Beyond that, he thought there were some issues regarding the LJM deals. Skilling needed to take a more active role in overseeing the negotiation process with LJM, Sutton said. Skilling said that was a fine idea.

There was another thing, Sutton said, on this issue of compensation. McMahon seemed certain Fastow was making a killing, but Fastow insisted that he wasn't. If McMahon was right, the conflict could be larger than Enron imagined.

"You know," Skilling replied, "Andy's assured me, too, that he's not making a lot of money here."

He thought about it for a second. "Tell you what," Skilling said. "I'll look into that, too. I'll find out."

Sutton headed back to his office. As far as he was concerned, his role in this squabble was over.

That same afternoon, the three months were almost up. Almost ninety days before, in the end-of-the-year rush, LJM2 had invested thirty million dollars to purchase an interest in the Polish power plant. The company had reported sixteen million dollars in profits from the sale, but under terms that would only allow LJM2 to keep the investment until the end of March. Now the day of reversals had arrived.

Enron and an affiliated entity bought out LJM2's interest in the Polish plant for $31.9 million. Fastow's fund had received a rate of return on its short-term investment of almost 25 percent.

The sixteen million dollars in profits, in economic truth, did not exist.

The next day, March 30, Skilling approached Fastow's secretary for an un-scheduled appointment. Fastow was at his desk, reviewing a spreadsheet. Skilling knocked.

"Hey, Jeff," Fastow said. "Come on in."

Skilling sat in front of Fastow's desk. The two talked about Skilling's vacation and a few business matters.

"Listen, Andy," Skilling finally said. "I've got a problem. I need to talk to you."

"Yeah?"

"Jeff McMahon came to see me the other day. And he's kind of concerned about his compensation."

"I don't know why."

"He's worried about his dealing with you. He says he's been feeling pres-sured on deals with LJM. He's concerned how he'll be dealt with by the PRC."

"He shouldn't be."

"I know. The PRC is fair. But if there's anything going on that makes him feel concerned, that's not right. Because that's not the way the system works."

Fastow's face was blank. "Okay, well, I'll talk to him about that and straighten that out."

A lot of the concern seemed to center on Fastow's LJM profits, Skilling said. Fastow agreed to give Skilling the details, just to reassure him.

"Thanks," Skilling said. "One other thing."

McMahon had raised some issues about getting LJM2 off the finance floor, things like that. That needed to be handled somehow. No problem, Fastow said. He'd been planning to do something about that soon, anyway.

"Great," Skilling said. "So you'll talk to McMahon, make sure everything's okay?"

Fastow nodded. "I'll talk to him."

Hours later, just past 1:30, a black sedan from Avanti Limousines & Transportation sped down the Hardy Toll Road in Houston. In the back, McMahon was relaxing. He had just returned from Austin, where he had hosted a golf game at the Barton Creek resort with Enron's second-tier banks. Exhausted, he was debating whether to head home or drop by the office.

His cell phone rang. It was his secretary.

"Andy wants to speak with you right away," she said. "Let me put you through to Bridget."

The phone clicked onto hold, and music began to play.

Guess Skilling and Fastow finally talked.

"Jeff?" It was Fastow's secretary.

"Yeah, Bridget."

"Andy wants to see you right away."

"Can you tell me what it's about?"

"No, but he needs to see you ASAP."

McMahon sighed. Getting fired could wait. "Bridget, I've been out of town for two days, and I'm almost home," he lied. In fact, he was ten minutes from the office.

"So," he continued, "I'm going to have to turn around and go back through rush hour to get back downtown. Any chance we can do this tomorrow?"

"I'll check." Hold music again.

McMahon glanced at the driver. "You probably ought to slow down. I don't know where I'm going yet."

The music stopped. "Can you do tomorrow at 7:30?"

McMahon sighed. "Yeah," he said. "I'll be there."

At about that moment, Greg Whalley was in Skilling's office, making his pitch. Skilling listened to the proposal with growing interest. Maybe this was a way to solve this stupid battle between Enron's top financial officers.

The next morning, Fastow templed his fingers beneath his chin as he stared across his desk at McMahon.

"I'm not sure you and I can work together anymore," he said calmly.

"Sorry to hear that, Andy," McMahon replied. "Why?"

Fastow's eyes grew intense. "First thing you should understand, Jeff," he snapped. "You say something to Skilling, you might as well be saying it to me."

"That's exactly what I did assume, Andy."

Fastow ignored him. "Skilling told me everything. He told me about the conversation you had with him."

McMahon nodded. Okay.

"I *never* put pressure on you to do a deal that wasn't in Enron's best interest," Fastow railed. "Never!"

Wow. Fastow's information *was* good. "That's not true, Andy," he said. "You and I had conversations many times about paying you excessive fees that we pushed back on."

Fastow waved a hand. "That's just business."

"Well, I feel it's pressure," McMahon said.

"Come on," Fastow shot back. "Any time I didn't do something that was right, you could go right to Skilling."

McMahon blinked. *Was this guy delusional?*

"Yeah, exactly," he said. "And this is what happens when I go to Skilling. We're having this conversation. I mean, that was a great avenue to take."

McMahon raised the issue of LJM2's location on the finance floor. "I told you," Fastow replied, "I'm going to fix those things. You just have to trust me."

Fastow was like a little boy, pushing off some chore with promises to do it later. "All I can tell you, Andy," McMahon said, "is that I'm extremely unhappy. This whole thing is affecting my work and my personal life."

Fastow said nothing.

"There are ways to fix it," McMahon said. "I've told them to you; I've told them to Jeff. But it doesn't appear that anything's moving toward that end."

A pause. "I just don't know if we can work together anymore," Fastow finally said. "I just don't know."

The two stared at each other in silence.

Hours later, Causey—followed by Glisan and Fastow—walked into Skilling's office to talk about Project Raptor, the effort to hedge Enron's merchant investments. Causey's smile said it all; they had reached a breakthrough.

"We've really been working on this hedging idea," Causey said. "And I think we've got something that works."

Glisan took over. With charts and graphs, he laid out the premise of Project Raptor. Skilling recognized it as a variation on the Rhythms hedge. It sounded pretty clever to him.

Skilling nodded and stood. "This is looking good," he said. "Keep me up to date."

Everyone left the room, and Skilling checked his schedule. He had a meeting set up with McMahon in a few minutes; with luck, they'd sort out that quarrel between McMahon and Fastow. He walked out into the hall.

McMahon glanced at his watch. Three minutes until his meeting with Skilling. Suddenly, out of the blue, Whalley popped into his office.

"Hey," Whalley said, "I'm here to hit you up again. I really want you to think about this job."

McMahon shook his head. *This guy just won't let up.*

"Look, Greg, I can't right now. I've got a meeting with Skilling in a couple of minutes, and I've got to go."

As if on cue, Skilling strode in. "Okay," he said. "Are we meeting here?"

Huh? McMahon looked from Skilling to Whalley. Wasn't this going to be about Fastow and LJM? "We can meet here if you want," McMahon said tentatively.

Whalley sat. "I set up this meeting, and I want to have it here."

"You set up this meeting?" McMahon asked.

"Yup. With you, me, and Skilling, so I can tell you why you should take this job."

The discussion went down the familiar path, with Whalley lobbying hard and McMahon voicing reservations.

Skilling jumped in. "Look, this is going to work out. Greg'll do a great job, you'll do a great job."

He stood. "Jeff, look, I really need you to do this," he said. "But I've got to go. You guys work it out."

With that, Skilling hurried out the door.

McMahon thought about it over a sleepless weekend. By Monday, he had decided. The new job would get him out of the Fastow mess. Maybe it would open up new opportunities. He told Whalley he would start as soon as possible.

Then, the best part. McMahon visited with Fastow and let him know he was stepping down as treasurer.

Fastow was delighted. "Sounds like a good idea. You should take it. It's a more important job than treasurer."

McMahon nodded. "Look, I don't want to leave you in the lurch," he said. "So I've got three names for you, any one of whom is ready to step in to fill my role."

The top choices, McMahon said, were the three with the strongest knowledge of banks and finance: Bill Brown, Ray Bowen, and Mike Jakubik. Fastow listened, his face blank.

"Thanks," he said. "I'll think about it."

News of McMahon's reassignment quickly hit the rumor mill. Among the first to hear was Bowen, a McMahon friend. He was surprised; moving from treasurer to an undefined job seemed like a big step down. He dialed McMahon's office right away.

"What the hell's going on?" he asked when McMahon picked up the line. "You've gotta tell me."

"Come up," McMahon said. "I'll tell you about it."

McMahon was leaning back in his chair, his feet on the desk, when Bowen arrived. "I don't really know what just happened," he said. "But it's true. I'm leaving the treasurer's job, and I'm going to go work with Whalley."

Bowen was about to ask a question when McMahon sat up.

"You know, Ray, you'd be the perfect guy to be treasurer," he said. "I gave Andy a few names, but you need to make a play for it. You'd be great."

McMahon laughed. "Thank God I don't have to put up with that shit anymore. The pressure's off. I don't have to deal with negotiating against my own boss."

He shook his head. "But really, you ought to try for treasurer. We need somebody who knows what they're doing."

Bowen smiled. "Not a very good sales job, Jeff."

Fastow's call to Bowen came days later from the Caribbean. People were lining up for a shot at being treasurer, Fastow said, but he hadn't heard from Bowen. How about coming by when he got back, so they could talk? When the appointment rolled around, Fastow seemed relaxed.

"I guess everybody's coming up here, begging for the job," Bowen said softly.

"Yeah, I've got a tough decision," Fastow replied. "What about you, Ray? Why haven't you called me?"

It just wasn't his style to plead for a job, Bowen replied. And he was pretty happy with the seat he was in.

Fastow listened politely. Apparently, he wasn't too keen on pressing Bowen to change his mind. "What do you think I should do, Ray?" he asked.

Bowen mentioned a few people. Bill Brown, maybe.

Fastow shook his head. "I think Bill's okay. But I don't think he's the guy to take us to the next level."

There was a pause. "What about Ben?" Fastow asked.

Ben Glisan? The guy who was an accountant a year ago?

"Well," Bowen said, "Ben's got the gray matter. But he doesn't have the experience. He's got a ways to go."

Fastow responded quickly. "I think he's smart enough. Ben's done a lot since you've been out of finance, Ray."

With that, Fastow started talking up Glisan as though he were the solution to every challenge Enron faced. "Ben has become a real leader here," Fastow said. "After McMahon, he's the best guy in the department."

Bowen nodded. "Great."

He didn't know what else to say. Fastow's praise went far beyond the reality of Ben Glisan. No one who looked at Glisan's résumé would consider him qualified for the job. Bowen, by contrast, would be an ideal candidate, but Fastow wasn't even sounding him out. Clearly, he had summoned Bowen not to gauge his interest, but to make sure he wouldn't impede Glisan's anointment.

It didn't take much guesswork for Bowen to figure out why. McMahon, whatever his flaws, was tough and gave Fastow grief. Bowen wouldn't be a pushover, either. But in Glisan, Bowen thought, Fastow had found someone trusting and pliable.

Fastow wanted a puppet, Bowen concluded, and he already controlled Ben Glisan's strings. Now almost nothing could stand in his way.

CHAPTER 13

FOUR BLACK-CLAD SOLDIERS plummeted from the sky above Houston. One after another, they pulled rip cords, releasing yellow-and-black parachutes that billowed above them. The men—members of the Army's Golden Knights parachute team—gently guided themselves toward second base on Enron Field as the crowd of more than forty-one thousand fans cheered wildly.

It was 7:02 on April 7, the night of the Houston Astros' first regular-season game in their glistening new ballpark, a modern-day temple celebrating Houston, baseball, and, most spectacularly, Enron. A sign proclaiming "Welcome to Enron Field" spun on the video board beneath a giant company logo. Enron had placed its imprint not only on the Astros but on Houston itself, granting the city the gift of outdoor baseball. The fans roared their approval.

The parachutists gathered their equipment and headed off as the announcer's voice echoed through the stadium.

"Ladies and gentlemen, throwing out tonight's first pitch, please welcome Ken Lay, chairman and CEO of Enron!"

Lay, dressed in dark slacks and a button-down shirt, hustled out to the pitcher's mound and waved to the crowd. He went into a windup, keeping in mind the instructions he'd received to throw high. The ball sailed across the plate, into the mitt of Astros catcher Paul Bako.

Amid more applause, Lay headed to his seat behind home plate. Striding up the steps, he passed former President George Bush and his wife, Barbara; a few rows away, he saw Governor George W. Bush and his wife, Laura. Lay arrived at his seat alongside Nolan Ryan, the former Texas Ranger pitcher, and Don Sanders, a prominent Houston stockbroker.

"Hey, you know," Sanders joked, "Nolan was betting me you wouldn't get it across the plate."

Lay glanced over at Ryan. "O ye of little faith, Nolan," he laughed.

The first inning began, but the Astros didn't live up to the occasion. By late in the game, it became clear the Phillies would win. Governor Bush and his wife left early; Lay would hear from him a few days later with some gentle ribbing about his pitch. As the last innings played out, former President Bush and Barbara dropped by to speak with Lay.

Lay stood. "Mr. President, Barbara, nice to see both of you. Looks like you're enjoying the game."

"You did a nice job getting across the plate, Ken," Bush said. "I've hit the ground more than once."

The three chatted for another moment, then the Bushes headed out. Lay settled back to watch the rest of the game. He couldn't have been more delighted. He was friends with presidents and governors. Houston, his town, was saluting his company. There was no denying that he had reached a pinnacle of professional and personal success. This had to be one of the happiest days of his life.

Wanda Curry's career had been sidetracked. The young Enron accountant had worked with wholesale for some time, until the back-to-back electricity trades with Merrill Lynch came along. She objected to the structure, slowing the project down. Not long afterward, she was transferred.

Still, Curry remained a Causey favorite. So that month—after Andersen raised concerns about the financial controls at Enron Energy Services, the retail division—Causey appointed Curry to head a team to investigate.

It would take months of analysis before Curry realized that retail, one of Enron's glowing businesses for the future, was in fact another growing problem.

The young waiter balanced a tray of drinks as he pushed into a room on the executive floor of the Enron building. Inside, Joe Sutton and his guest, Dr. Amin Badr El-Din, stood beside a table decked out with three place settings of fine bone china and silverware. The waiter glided between them, delivering their drinks.

Badr El-Din was a short man, a few inches past five feet, and exuded sophistication. He wore a crisp Saville Row suit and displayed impeccable manners; his conversation was laced with references to life's finer things—expensive cars, a hard-played game of polo. But Badr El-Din was not just another cultured Arab businessman. For American companies, he could literally be a key to the kingdom. He had deep ties with Jordan's royal family and now served as a special adviser to Sheikh Zayed bin Sultan al Nahyan, President of the United Arab Emirates.

As head of the UAE Offset Group, Badr El-Din—known as Dr. Amin—had for years generated deals to help the Emirates. He was a man with money to burn—potentially as much as eight billion dollars—and that made him very popular with American corporations.

Sutton had come to know Badr El-Din over months of working with him on a huge pipeline project. During one meeting, the two discussed the impending sale of Enron's international division; Badr El-Din was intrigued. His enterprise put together a proposal, and he came to Enron today to spell out the details to Skilling.

As the two men chatted, Skilling arrived. The waiter reappeared, catching him off guard; Skilling had never seen one on the executive floor before. He ordered a tonic water. Later, as they ate, Sutton explained how he and Badr El-Din had begun talking about the sale of the international assets while working in the Emirates together.

Badr El-Din nodded. "Yes, we are very interested."

Skilling smiled politely. *Bullshit.* The price was going to be some seven billion dollars. As soon as Badr El-Din heard that, Skilling figured, this deal would die.

"Well, you know, this is a very large operation," Skilling cautioned. "We're interested in selling, and obviously we'd prefer to sell it as one package."

"That is our interest," Badr El-Din said.

"Hmm," Skilling said. "Who's your adviser on this?"

The acid test; the quality of the adviser would signal the seriousness of the potential offer. So Skilling was impressed when Badr El-Din replied that he was represented by UBS, the global financial firm.

"All right," Skilling said. "Probably the next step would be to have your bankers talk to Cliff Baxter, who's working on the sale. Whatever information you need will be made available to you."

They returned to their food, but Skilling couldn't shake his skepticism. After all, how likely was it that Enron could dump its overseas blunders in one fell swoop?

The Enron trading room in Portland was a hodgepodge of cubicles and workstations, nothing like the sleek, high-tech setup in Houston. It had been pulled together from the offices of Portland General Electric to serve as Enron's main West Coast trading artery. On one side, near big plasma screens that tracked power flows, about one hundred traders barked orders over telephones. It was just the sort of chaos that traders thrived on.

The top trader, Tim Belden, had been an academic researcher before testing his mettle in the marketplace. He loved the study of market minutiae, and in California he had found his ideal subject. What the state had described as deregulation was in fact a labyrinth of complex—and often contradictory—rules, combining the worst features of both government bureaucracy and unbridled capitalism. Power was delivered to the state through an arcane system involving two bodies called the Power Exchange and the Independent System Operator, which conducted auctions to buy or deliver power to the state.

From the beginning, traders had been poking and prodding at the rules, looking for loopholes. And they found plenty: Power from out of state was allotted a higher price than electricity generated within California. If lines were congested, the ISO would compensate any company that agreed to cancel a transmission of electricity or move electrons the other way. And companies would be paid for committing to provide backup power, even if the electricity ended up never being needed.

The rules struck Belden and his team as open invitations for gaming the system. Just playing with the rules, they could force California to pay more for power. The easy money was just too tempting to pass up.

At 9:41 on the morning of April 15, a Saturday, John Forney, one of Belden's top traders, hit a button on his phone console. The line rang through to a power-scheduling desk at Portland General Electric.

"Portland. This is Robert."

"Hey, Robert. Good morning. John Forney at Enron."

The call from Forney should have been surprising. Enron and Portland General were related—one a marketer, the other a power generator—and weren't supposed to deal directly with each other on transactions in the state. Working together, they could drive up prices.

But Forney had developed an idea: using Portland General to transform lower-priced power from California into higher-priced out-of-state electricity. All that was required was a loop—buying electricity in California, passing it around through out-of-state trading companies and then to Portland General, which would deliver it back. The transactions were all on paper, but so much the better; traders could mark up the price at each stage, making a tidy profit courtesy of California consumers.

As Forney described the details of the plan to the scheduler, he chuckled. "I can't hand off directly," he said. "What I'm trying to do is give it to LA."

"Yeah?"

"But I can't. I've got to involve a northwest utility, and I just can't deal with you because of our arm's-length rules. I can't transact directly with you."

The scheduler at Portland General was confused. "Hang on a second," he said.

He called to someone else. "Hey, Bob, have you ever done this deal with Enron where they loop it around?"

A new scheduler got on the line. "Hey, man," Forney said. "I know this is kind of a nasty deal, but we kind of worked this out with our pre-schedulers."

Forney described the transaction again. He commented that he hoped this deal wouldn't cause him trouble.

"Hopefully not," the scheduler said. "It probably will, but—"

"It probably will," Forney interrupted. "Because it's basically just a loop."

The scheduler asked some more details, quickly realizing the true purpose of the proposed trades.

"Okay," the scheduler said. "Are you going to do it just for one hour, then, or—"

"No," Forney interrupted. "I'd like to get it going on. I may do it all day, if I can."

"Okay, okay."

"Since I don't come in on the weekends very often, I'm going to come make a big mess for everybody."

The scheduler laughed.

The Forney Perpetual Loop, as the in-and-out trades came to be known, was only one of the schemes cooked up by Enron's traders to exploit the California power market.

They all had cute names. One, Death Star, involved submitting fake transmission schedules that showed lines would be overloaded; Enron would then be paid for "reducing" congestion by removing scheduled power it never meant to send. Another, Fat Boy, was a variation on that theme but allowed prices to drive up in anticipation of the coming fake congestion. With Get Shorty, Enron pledged to line up backup reserves while in fact doing nothing, under the assumption that the reserves would never be needed. And Ricochet was another variation of the Forney Loop.

Together, the schemes were methods of collecting money from California for services that would never be provided. But there were clear benefits to Enron, which still held a large position that would gain millions if California prices rose. Coupled with the deep structural flaws in the California electricity system—one that allowed for a massive mismatch between demand and available supplies—the market was in perfect position for utter disaster.

The first day of calamity was only weeks away.

The unofficial word was finally out: Glisan was in line to be Enron's new treasurer. Fastow had pushed his candidacy hard, and both Skilling and Lay had endorsed it. If the board approved, Glisan would have the job.

The prospect left Ray Bowen anxious. Glisan was so young; Bowen worried he might unwittingly become Fastow's dupe. It only seemed appropriate to warn him. Glisan was working in his small office when Bowen tapped on the door. Bowen ventured inside, offering his congratulations.

"You'll do a great job," he said, hoping the words were true. "But I've got some advice for you. Be your own man. Don't let people define you as Andy Fastow's boy."

Glisan pondered that. "Yeah, well, I realize I'm not so well known around the company, so I've got to get to know people better," he said finally.

Bowen just listened. *Was I speaking in tongues?* Glisan seemed not to have understood his fairly blunt message.

"Well," Bowen said, "then go around the building, do a little road show for yourself. Go see everybody."

Let's try again. "But be your own guy. Don't let them think you're just somebody who does what Andy says."

Bowen's tone was serious. "Ben, you've got to know, Andy's not the most popular guy here. I don't think he's somebody you want to completely hitch your wagon to."

Glisan blinked, looking bewildered. "Gee, you know, Ray," he said, "Andy's been really good to me."

"Fine. But the guy plays hardball. So you're going to want to watch your head."

"I don't know, Ray," Glisan replied. "I haven't seen any of that."

He shrugged. "Andy's just been really good to me."

On April 28, wire transfers for more than twenty million dollars arrived in Citibank account 4079-8061, in the name of a Fastow partnership, LJM Swap Sub. Much of the cash—from Enron and Swap Sub—was then transferred to an account at Chase, this one in the name of the Southampton partnership.

The Southampton scheme was finally paying off. With those transactions, Fastow and his selected friends—Kopper, Glisan, Mordaunt, and a few others—had gained the cash that had been conned out of the investors in LJM1. But they weren't alone. Days earlier, Fastow's British co-conspirators—the Greenwich NatWest bankers—had invoked their rights to become partial owners of Southampton. Almost $7.4 million was wired that day to the bankers' Bermuda account.

After confirming the wire transfer, Fastow telephoned a number in Toronto, where Gary Mulgrew, one of the three bankers, was waiting. "Congratulations," Fastow said. "You guys just made seven million dollars."

His hand resting on the boardroom table, Fastow took a read of the directors on Enron's finance committee. Their meeting had been droning on for a while as McMahon took them through his last presentation as treasurer. Then Pug Winokur called on Fastow to present his report.

"Before I do," Fastow began, "I'd like to take a moment to introduce Ben Glisan."

He glanced over at Glisan, who nodded a greeting to the committee. "The management of Enron is recommending Ben to succeed Jeff McMahon as company treasurer," Fastow continued. "Ben has demonstrated himself to be a brilliant and exceedingly valuable member of our team."

Fastow laid it on thick, and afterward the committee gave its unanimous approval. Glisan thanked the directors and promised to do the best job he could. Fastow took the floor again and began his official report. Several minutes in, he looked at the directors. "That leads us to an update on the transactions conducted with LJM2," he said.

The fund, he said, had been an all-out win for Enron. Combined with LJM1, he said, it had contributed almost $230 million in profits and more than $2 billion in cash flow, not to mention the investment-banking fees that were saved.

A director asked how much the LJM deals were distracting Fastow from his duties as CFO. "The time I am committing is negligible," he replied. "I am personally devoting no more than three hours a week to them."

Three hours, and all those profits! The directors beamed with delight. "Now," Fastow said, "we've been working for months on a project involving LJM2 that we believe will take us to the next level. We call it Project Raptor, and Ben Glisan has been the point man on that."

Using a four-page PowerPoint presentation, Glisan launched into his pitch. This would be a variation of the Rhythms hedge, Glisan said, only this time to protect Enron against future losses from an array of merchant investments. He spelled out the terms: Enron stock shifted into Talon, outside cash coming from LJM2.

"Under the deal, LJM2 will be entitled to a 30 percent annualized return, plus fees," Glisan said. "Enron will receive 100 percent of any returns beyond that."

Glisan said nothing about the forty-one million dollars that LJM2 would receive before hedging began, guaranteeing a blockbuster return. Still, he was frank about Raptor's limitations.

"Raptor does not transfer economic risk," he said. Instead, it simply moved any big swings in the value of Enron's investments off the books.

While the directors seemed to be listening, few grasped the full import of what Glisan was saying. A handful of questions later, they unanimously approved Raptor.

That same day, final instructions went through to distribute the cash from Southampton. At about the time that Glisan was meeting with the board, a clerk at Chase entered wire instructions into the computer. In an instant, $1,040,744 moved from Southampton's Chase account to account number 3714-9242 at Charles Schwab, owned by Glisan. An identical sum was wired to an account held by his co-investor Kristina Mordaunt.

Fastow had transformed two Enron executives—including his new treasurer, a man with power to block his wheeling and dealing—into millionaires.

A bell sounded in Saugus High School in California at noon on May 22, but students were not changing classes. School officials were being notified that, under their agreement with state utilities, the power had to be shut off. Lights and air-conditioning went dead. Students kept working in their dim, sweltering classrooms.

For days, California had been roasting in an unseasonable heat wave, with temperatures blasting past one hundred degrees in many areas. Demand for air-conditioning had drained power reserves dangerously low. On this day, the California Independent System Operator, which managed the grid, declared a stage-two emergency, forcing customers like Saugus to shut off power or pay massive fines.

The California energy crisis had begun.

Antiques and portraits from another era decorated the corner suite at the Ritz-Carlton Montreal, where Robert McCullough was working. It was the next morning, May 23, and McCullough, head of his own energy-consulting firm in Portland, was on his cell phone, trying to learn details of the strange power crisis hitting the West Coast.

McCullough was in Montreal for an international symposium of electrical utilities but knew the real industry epicenter that day was in California. Much of the world seemed to be taking the state's emergency in stride; the news hadn't even made the front page in Los Angeles. But to McCullough, the previous day's events were the chest pains that foreshadowed a massive heart attack.

It was May, for heaven's sake; summer hadn't even begun. McCullough had always believed that the new system in California was rickety, but this was worse than he had imagined. Prices were already spiking; this was going to damage a lot of his clients, not to mention the state's economy.

As the morning wore on, McCullough learned enough to fuel his suspicions that something was drastically wrong. Somebody, he decided, had to be manipulating the market, driving up prices for profit. He was sure of it.

Later that day, McCullough was on a conference call with Paula Green and Mike Sinowitz, both with Seattle City Light. Washington State had shared in California's problems the previous day, although no emergency had been declared. What was going on? McCullough asked them.

"Well," Sinowitz said, "if the prices are high, that just means there's a lot of demand."

Not good enough. "Mike, what's your demand?"

"Not very high."

"So therein lies the question," McCullough replied. "Why are prices so high if there's not a lot of demand?"

He could almost hear Sinowitz's brow furrowing.

June 1. Only thirty days left until Enron had to take Merrill Lynch out of its investment in the Nigerian barges—the deal that had helped Enron hit earnings at year-end.

But there was a problem. The accountants at Andersen had never been told about Fastow's guarantee, and there was nothing about it in any of the paperwork. After all, the guarantee might have led Andersen to nix the original deal as not a real sale at all. So if Enron bought the barge interest back now, would Andersen get suspicious?

One executive on the deal, Alan Quaintance, was wrestling with that problem and sent an e-mail to other executives asking for help. He explained Enron had convinced Andersen that Merrill was making a long-term investment in the barges, and now had to come up with a reason why the company was working to take Merrill out of the deal.

"I need help formulating this story," Quaintance typed, "if it is even possible."

Boxes and lines filled the whiteboard in a conference room over in the offices of Azurix. Rebecca Mark was at the board, delivering a lecture to two McKinsey consultants, Ron Hulme and Suzanne Nimocks. *This* was the idea, the one that would salvage the company, the story that would turn Wall Street around on its opinion of the company.

The door opened, and Amanda Martin walked in; Mark had just called and asked her to join the meeting. For several minutes, Mark continued her lecture, laying out the vision.

Mark checked the time. "Okay, I need to catch a plane to New York. Amanda, can you explain these boxes?"

She looked at the McKinsey consultants. "Then you guys think about it and get back to me in a week on how we can present this to the analysts and get them fired up."

With that, Mark swept out of the room. Everyone who remained behind looked at each other. And then smiled.

"So," Nimocks said to Martin. "Can you tell us how this works?"

Martin opened her eyes wide and took a deep breath. "Why don't you tell me first what she told you?" she said.

Ron Hulme laid his head down on the table and started laughing. The other two joined in for five minutes.

"Okay," Martin finally said. "We need help."

Glisan had barely settled into his new office when an old deal reared its head: the proposed Chewco buyout.

Months before, McMahon had suggested that Enron purchase Chewco—the half-owner of JEDI that was controlled by Kopper—to minimize the administrative difficulties. But he had proposed a deal that would have given Chewco no more than one million dollars in profit. When Kopper and Fastow pushed for ten times that, McMahon had pulled the plug.

Now McMahon was gone, and his replacement—just enriched by Fastow and Kopper—wasn't likely to make the same kind of waves. The buyout went through. It would take a year to close, but Kopper would receive his ten million dollars. And then the cash would go to Fastow.

Skilling studied the draft report regarding the possible sale of the international projects. The numbers were terrible, worse than he had imagined. Could this stuff even be sold? He had no idea what to do.

Amanda Martin was with a few friends at La Griglia when her cell phone rang. She spoke for a minute, then started to stand. "Sorry, I have to go," she said.

Skilling, she explained, wanted to see her right away.

Later that evening, Martin waved her hand, brushing away the swarming mosquitoes outside Skilling's house. It was past 9:30, and she had arrived minutes before to find Skilling outside, on the telephone and surrounded by wine bottles. He held a finger to his lips, telling Martin to be quiet. His demeanor on the call was smooth, debonair. He gestured, offering her a glass of wine.

Skilling hung up. His calm facade vanished. Tears welled up. He looked like a frightened little boy.

"You're my friend," he said suddenly. "You've always been my friend. I miss you. I really miss you."

Martin was taken aback. She had been pushing Skilling for months to get her out of the mess at Azurix. He could have brought her back to Enron, but didn't. She'd told him before that she didn't think he knew how to be a friend. But now that he was drunk and rambling, he was trying to be.

"You look good," he said suddenly. "Have you been working out?"

"No, Jeff," she replied. "I've just been running around with the kids."

"I've been working out. Can you tell?"

Sure, Martin said. Skilling blinked, and the tears emerged again. "You've got to make Azurix work, Amanda," he said. "Promise me you'll take care of that problem."

Martin slapped at a mosquito. "I can't, Jeff," she said. "There are real problems."

Skilling listened, still clearly unnerved by some unspoken fear. "Promise me," he said. "I'll take care of you. Just promise me you'll take care of it."

He drained his glass. "You want more wine?" he asked.

Martin declined, and he considered that for a second.

"I'm going to get another glass," he said finally.

Skilling disappeared into the house. Martin was perplexed; she knew he was emotional, but she had never seen him this far gone. What had happened? What was eating at him? A short time later, he wandered back.

"I'm going to show you something," he said.

He brought out his briefcase and removed some papers, apparently a report of some kind. "Swear to me that you won't tell anybody you saw this," he said.

Martin agreed. Skilling thrust the report toward her. It was an accounting analysis on the international assets, he said, put together for the sales effort.

"Look at those fucking numbers," he said.

Martin studied them. If what she was seeing was true, the entire division might be worth a lot less than anyone at the company had ever believed. Enron might not be able to sell them.

Skilling stared down at his lap. "I don't know what I'm going to do," he said, his voice distant. "What do I do with these numbers?"

He shook his head, tearing up again. "I don't know what I'm going to do. I don't know what I'm going to do."

Martin didn't keep count. But Skilling must have repeated himself at least a dozen times.

In Avon, Colorado, green hills from the Gore mountain range eased down to a patio behind the Park Hyatt Beaver Creek Resort. Dick Cheney and his wife, Lynne, appeared at the patio entrance, carrying their buffet lunches, and found seats at a table covered by a large gray umbrella.

Cheney—chief executive of Halliburton, the energy-services company—was in Colorado to attend the World Forum chaired by former President Gerald Ford. Despite his close ties with the Republican White House—having served as Ford's Chief of Staff and as Secretary of Defense under Bush—few would have been surprised if he hadn't shown up. He had recently been selected by George W. Bush, the presumptive Republican candidate for President, to vet possible running mates. It was the kind of task that could easily push a policy forum onto the back burner.

As the Cheneys settled in, Ken Lay emerged from the hotel with his lunch. He had noticed the Cheneys ahead of him in line and now scanned the patio looking for them. He made his way over. "Mind if I join you?" he asked.

The Cheneys looked up and smiled. "Ken, not at all," Lynne said. "We'd be delighted."

Lay sat, removing his lunch from the tray. "Well, Dick, it seems like you have your hands full these days."

"Quite a bit going on," Cheney agreed. "It's been very exciting."

"I haven't spoken to George in a few weeks. He set for the fall?"

"It's going to be a tough campaign," Cheney replied. "Particularly with the economy as strong as it's been."

Lay understood. Bush's expected opponent, Al Gore, was the sitting Vice President. Strong economic performance usually gave the party in power a leg up.

A voice interrupted. "All right if I sit here?"

Lay glanced up. It was Karl Rove, Bush's chief political strategist. By all means, he was told. The discussion ramped back to politics. Yes, Rove acknowledged, the economy presented a challenge. Still, there was the wild card of the sexual scandals involving Clinton; there was no telling if that might hurt Gore come November.

The free-flowing discussion lasted throughout lunch. Anyone spotting the group would easily have understood that Lay had secured a place in the inner circle of the next Republican presidential nominee.

Off the boardroom in the Manhattan offices of Deloitte & Touche, Arthur Levitt was loading up a plate with food. It was June 20, just past noon. Levitt, the SEC chairman, was at the firm's headquarters with a few members of his staff, hoping to avert an ugly public battle.

Levitt's efforts to stop the flow of fluffed-up numbers coming out of corporate America had led him on this pilgrimage to the accounting firms, the private sectors' independent policemen. The firms were supposed to stop games playing, but somewhere along the line, Levitt believed, they had lost their way. Now they relied on their corporate clients to pay huge fees for consulting—helping put together deals, reviewing systems and technologies.

Consulting was an honorable trade, of course. It was just that Levitt believed it shouldn't mix with accounting. How could a firm receiving millions from a company for providing strategic advice fight management over bad accounting? Auditors were supposed to resign if managers reported misleading numbers; Levitt was convinced that fear of losing consulting work would dissuade them. Auditor independence was being compromised for the worst of reasons: money.

So Levitt planned to issue new rules that month, requiring accounting and consulting to be separate. He hoped to avoid a political battle by persuading the firms to join in the effort. He had invited the three firms he found most uncompromising on the issue—Deloitte, Andersen, and KPMG Peat Marwick—to meet in Washington. They had refused, agreeing to get together only on their own turf.

The mood in the room was frosty. As he spooned food onto his plate, Levitt chatted up one executive, hoping to drive a wedge between members of the group. No luck. He wandered out of the kitchen and set his lunch on the conference table. His chief accountant, Lynn Turner, and legal counsel, Harvey Goldschmidt, joined him. The accounting firm honchos—Robert Grafton, Andersen's chief executive; Stephen Butler, chairman of KPMG; and James Copeland, chief executive of Deloitte—sat across from them, stony-faced and curt. This was not a receptive crowd.

"I'm glad we're meeting on this issue," Levitt began. "It will be much better if we were together on it, with something we can all agree on."

The faces across the table registered nothing.

"We don't want to have this become a public cause," Levitt continued. "Both sides here have everything to gain by coming to an agreement here."

Levitt laid out his plan, explaining how the goal was to ensure firms did not consult for clients that they audited. There would be plenty of time for a transition, Levitt said, but the ultimate goal would be nonnegotiable. He finished. Copeland from Deloitte was the first to speak.

"Arthur," he said, "we might as well shut down the firms if this is what you're going to do."

The accountants couldn't perform good audits without consulting, he said, and would certainly be hard-pressed to generate the income they needed to stay in business.

"There is absolutely no evidence that consulting for accounting clients causes any problems," Copeland said.

Levitt and his staff tried to explain how, in the long run, ensuring auditor independence would be in the firms' best interest. But the executives would hear none of it.

"Arthur," Grafton from Arthur Andersen interjected, "if you go ahead with this, it'll be war."

The meeting lasted ninety minutes, with the firms holding fast—a huge miscalculation, Levitt thought. The world thought of accountants as benign, boring defenders of the public interest. But here they were, grubbing for cash like any greedy Wall Streeter. Their image protected them for now, but in the end, Levitt wanted the truth to do them in. He had already decided to hold public hearings to force the accountants to show their hand.

He walked onto the elevator with Turner and Goldschmidt. "Okay," he said. "Now we go to war."

Andersen was working hard to guide Enron through its growing thicket of deals. LJM2 proved a lifesaver time and again, allowing the company to sell assets when no real buyer could be found. But each time, Andersen had to structure the deals to meet a literal reading of the rules. A few times, Enron executives held back on some details—like secret guarantees and buyback agreements—out of a fear that even a compliant accountant might balk.

Much of the work centered on Raptor. Talon hadn't hedged anything yet, but already Enron executives were rushing in, brandishing wish lists of assets with values they wanted locked in place. Stock prices were getting more volatile; they could start falling anytime.

Still, Talon could only hedge so much before running out of capital. So on June 22, Fastow and Glisan went back to the directors, seeking authorization for Raptor II. The board approved it readily. LJM2 would be the investor again, with the same lucrative terms.

But Raptor was only one of many deals cooking. After all, it was late June. The quarter was about to end, and Enron needed to make its numbers.

Broadband Services had to unload something fast. Its profits weren't strong enough, and a quick sale was the only option to push them up.

Fortunately, there were assets it could market. For example, the division had laid far more network fiber than it needed, believing it could sell what it didn't use. But now fiber prices were slipping, and EBS wanted to find a buyer for some quickly before values dropped further. So far, no luck.

So the division turned to LJM2. One of its primary negotiators on the deal was Larry Lawyer, who had worked years before on Fastow's first attempted crime, the Alpine deal which later evolved into RADR. Lawyer had secretly been given part of the return from RADR for his Alpine work. In fact, months before, he had received his last check, for more than thirty-nine thousand dollars—all tax-free, since he had decided long ago not to declare the cash as income.

The top lawyer for EBS was Kristina Mordaunt, who had just received more than one million dollars for her secret Southampton investment. Fastow and Kopper had the satisfaction of knowing that two key people on the other side of the table were financially beholden to them.

After the final terms were negotiated, the deal-approval sheet, or DASH, went around for everyone to sign. There was a line for Skilling's signature, but he was on vacation in Africa. So the sheet instead was shipped over to Lay.

He studied the document. Four people had already signed, including Mordaunt, Lawyer, and Glisan, all secret participants in Fastow's schemes.

Lay didn't know how to run the numbers or how to assess the valuation. But he knew he could trust his people. He signed with a flourish.

Kopper answered the phone in his office. Andy Fastow was on the line, giggling.

"What would you think," Fastow said, "about the Nigerian barges coming back to LJM?"

Enron's commitment to take Merrill Lynch out of its investment in the Nigerian barges by June 30 was starting to look like a disastrous miscalculation. Merrill executives were banging on Enron's door, demanding their money back. But the company could find no takers.

So Enron turned again to Fastow and LJM2. There were no negotiations. LJM2 simply paid Merrill more than $7.5 million, giving it the 22 percent return that had been promised so many months before.

Now Merrill's problem was Fastow's; he didn't want an interest in a bunch of Nigerian barges either. He persuaded Enron to shift its guarantee to LJM2; it would find another buyer and take the Fastow fund out of the deal with a profit. The obligations and risk of ownership remained with Enron six months after it reported the profits from the "sale."

The rolling commitment left some Enron executives queasy. Sales were supposed to be clean, not weighed down with secret side agreements. One Enron accountant, Alan Quaintance, heard rumors about what was going on and approached the lead finance executive on the deal, Dan Boyle.

Quaintance mentioned what he had heard about secret guarantees and said he considered it inappropriate.

Boyle seemed surprised. "I don't see why," he said.

Enron's trading business was going great guns, but not enough to offset the huge expenditures—and investment losses—piling up all over the company. Even with the LJM2 shenanigans, Enron would miss Wall Street's predicted earnings of thirty-two cents a share for the second quarter.

Fortunately, it had some airplanes to sell—airplanes that, according to the company's books, were worthless. The planes had been part of a deal begun in 1997, called Cochise. In essence, Enron had shuffled a bunch of paper to create expected future tax deductions. Then—for lack of a better term—it "marked to market" those expectations, reporting the future deductions as current income. Using the tax credit the deal created reduced the book value of the planes from $46.7 million to zero.

So in the final days of the quarter, Enron sold the planes for $36.5 million to an entity controlled by Bankers Trust. Now the energy company could report every penny of its airplane sale as income. But the bank wouldn't be stuck with the planes for long. There was already an agreement that a few weeks later, one of Enron's innumerable entities would buy them back. For the same price.

Fax machines were starting to annoy Rick Buy.

The company's chief risk officer had purchased a new summer house in New Hampshire, a bucolic retreat from the hurly-burly of his job. But as the end of the quarter approached, deal-approval sheets, particularly for LJM2 deals, kept scrolling out of the fax machine.

It was, after all, near the end of the quarter, and it remained Buy's responsibility to review such deals. No one had ever formally told him that the directors wanted him to handle the job; instead, Skilling and Fastow had just let him know informally about his new duties. But they didn't instruct him specifically on what he was supposed to be looking for.

Pages from a new approval sheet churned out of the fax machine. Buy eyeballed the terms to make sure they struck him as reasonable. It looked fine. He signed it.

It was 3:45 on the afternoon of June 26. In some parts of California, temperatures exceeded a hundred degrees. Air conditioners were going full throttle. The electricity grid was approaching a danger point. Another stage-two alert. Customers voluntarily shut off their electricity.

The evening stars pierced the African sky above a forest belt surrounding Mount Kenya. There, Skilling, his younger brother, Mark, and his oldest son were vacationing, spending that night in early July in one of a series of rustic cabins. Skilling was relaxing on the back porch with Mark. He dragged on his cigarette as he watched the sky.

This is the life. Just mountains and trees and sky. No international projects. No water companies. No complaints. Nobody picking at him to give them, do for them, fix for them.

Why was he at Enron anymore? What the hell was he trying to prove? He took another puff. The smoke pleasantly burned his lungs before he exhaled it into the still air.

He glanced at his brother. "How would you like to come work for me?" he said.

Mark was taken aback. "What are you talking about?"

"I'm really thinking about what I'm going to do after Enron," Jeff said calmly. "I need to start getting stuff in place. Would you have any interest in helping me?"

The idea wasn't fully formed. Mark was a lawyer; maybe, Jeff suggested, he could manage his money, handle tax issues. But Mark had just moved to Turkey and was happy with his new life. Houston had little appeal for him.

"I don't know. Right now I'm enjoying Istanbul."

"Look, there are some neat lofts downtown. I can invest in one, you could stay there. I could set you up in an office, have a secretary available for you."

"I don't think so, Jeff," Mark said. "I mean, right now, I've got some things I still want to do."

Jeff wasn't going to be so easily put off. "Why don't you take to the end of the year and think about it."

That long? Mark was surprised. But some things about the proposal still bothered him. "Well, I'm a little concerned about being fired by my own brother," he said.

Jeff stayed quiet. "Yeah, that would be an unfortunate thing," he said finally.

Andy Fastow was rolling in cash. While Glisan and Mordaunt had reaped just over a million dollars each from Southampton, Fastow and Kopper each raked in $4.5 million. Fastow, who aspired to a place in Houston's wealthy philanthropy circuit, stuffed the cash in the newly formed Fastow Family Foundation. It was a great way to stave off taxes and still have the money available for vacations and other expenses that he could declare as foundation business.

Besides, Fastow didn't need the money. Still sitting in LJM1 was more than twenty-five million dollars from the Sails deal, which converted a huge slice of the Enron shares into other assets. And Fastow had the sole power to decide when he would receive his share.

On July 14, the time came. Fastow declared a cash distribution from LJM1 to its investors. He filled out three wire-transfer requests, authorizing the movement of money from the LJM bank account in the Cayman Islands. The signed documents were faxed to the bank, and in the blink of an eye the funds were wired.

The two largest investors in LJM1—CSFB and Greenwich NatWest— each received $5.9 million. But Fastow made out the best: he transferred $17.9 million to himself.

After three weeks in Africa, Skilling returned to the office on July 17, feeling despondent. He had tasted life without Enron and liked it.

Early that morning, Lay dropped by. Weeks before, he had seen that Skilling was burning out and had hoped an extended vacation would recharge his batteries.

"Welcome back," Lay thundered as he strolled into Skilling's office. "Did you have a good time?"

Skilling looked up from his desk, his face sagging.

"I had a great time," he said. He blinked and swallowed. "And, Ken, I didn't want to come back."

Lay made a joke, laughing it off. But he could tell his young president was serious. Skilling needed a new challenge. He needed to know that he would be running Enron by year's end. Lay had to figure out some subtle way to let him know: the CEO spot was his to lose.

In Manhattan, Lay strolled past statues of Chinese lions as he climbed up the steps to the Peninsula hotel. Inside, he headed to the lobby lounge. He spotted Kelly Kimberly, an Enron public-relations executive who had been sent ahead to explain Lay's holdup. Beside her was Dr. Amin Badr El-Din, whose proposal to purchase all of Enron's international assets seemed to be picking up steam.

It was July 18, 2000. Lay was in New York for multiple meetings that day, but this could be the most important. He shook Badr El-Din's hand. "Dr. Amin, sorry I'm late. We were delayed in landing."

"Not a problem, Dr. Lay. It's good to see you."

Lay thanked Kimberly, and the two men repaired to the Adrienne restaurant upstairs.

"I wanted to let you know this is a very serious project for us," Badr El-Din said. "We are convinced we can add a lot of strategic value to many of these assets."

"Well, Dr. Amin, that is very good to hear."

"The money is basically already committed," Badr El-Din continued. "Now it is just a matter of finishing up the due diligence and trying to get the deal done."

Sweet words, but Lay was not quite seduced by them. At that point, there was no way to know if Badr El-Din would bail Enron out from its billions of misspent dollars or simply prove to be another false hope.

High above Times Square that same day, Sumner Redstone was in his fifty-second-floor office, oblivious to its breathtaking views of the Hudson River and New York City skyline.

Redstone, the billionaire chairman of Viacom, had heard minutes before that his next visitor, Ken Lay, was in the building meeting with Mel Karmazin, the company president. Redstone had good feelings about the upcoming meeting. A few months back, Viacom's publicly traded subsidiary, Blockbuster, had struck a deal with Enron to provide video-on-demand to retail consumers. The twenty-year exclusive contract hadn't been disclosed yet, allowing Blockbuster to wrap up other negotiations with the movie studios. Now everything was ready to go, and Lay was in town to help with the big announcement.

When Lay arrived, Redstone escorted him to the office.

"Ken, this is wonderful," he said. "I've been worried about Blockbuster. The returns haven't been what we hoped. But this could really provide some excitement and give them a strategy that'll help protect the franchise."

Lay was just as enthusiastic. "Well, if Blockbuster needs excitement, this will bring it," he said. "It's a wonderful setup, a winner for both of us."

Neither man knew that, even as they spoke excitedly of their future together, the twenty-year contract was months from collapse.

Enron would hit Wall Street's earnings estimates for the quarter. But that was it. Nothing special.

So the week before the earnings release, some Enron executives got together to scour the books for more profits to squeeze out. They soon found their quarry—the prudency reserves. Enron held back on reporting millions in income from its energy trading to ensure the bottom line only included profits that it actually expected to make once all the trades closed. There was certainly some money there.

Millions of dollars were released from the reserves into income. Now Enron could report thirty-four cents a share for the quarter, beating the Street's estimate by two pennies.

"Welcome to the Enron Corporation second-quarter earnings-release conference call."

Sitting at a table surrounded by top executives, Skilling listened as the operator finished the introductions for the quarterly phone call with Wall Street analysts. He was still feeling demoralized, but knew that he had better mask his mood. No one would understand why he felt so tortured on a day the company's earnings seemed so good.

"Thank you very much and good morning to everyone," Skilling began. "We had another outstanding quarter in each of our business units and continue to be very excited about the developments across the company."

He described how each business line was meeting or exceeding expectations. "I've been with the company, in one form or another, for eighteen years, and I've never seen the company in better shape," he said. "Our core markets are just absolutely moving from strength to strength."

With that, Skilling opened up the call for questions. David Fleischer, the analyst who covered Enron from Goldman Sachs, was the first up.

"Great quarter, Jeff," he began. "Don't slow up."

The furnace in California showed no signs of cooling. With temperatures soaring, the power shortage had grown from a temporary nuisance into a full-blown crisis.

Throughout July, prices in the wholesale market bumped up against the state's price caps of $750 a megawatt hour; in response, the state reduced the caps. Still, utilities were paying more for power than they could charge retail customers, most of whom paid fixed rates. Most, but not all. Some cities, like San Diego, let their rates float with the market, and the only direction was up. Electricity bills soared; some residents burned them publicly.

The turmoil forced California's governor, Gray Davis, to act. On August 2—a day of another stage-two emergency—he received a report from the Public Utilities Commission that Californians had paid one billion dollars more in June and July than in the comparable months the year before. Power-plant construction needed to be fast-tracked, the report said, and that same day Davis ordered faster approvals.

Another section of the report also caught Davis's attention. It concluded that there was "enough evidence" of questionable trading behavior to warrant an investigation. Davis forwarded the information to the state's attorney general, Bill Lockyer, whose staff was already on the case. Weeks before, they had opened the first investigation into possible manipulation in the California electricity markets.

That day, rows of Mercedeses, Lexuses, and other pricey cars jammed the streets outside of the Four Seasons Hotel in Philadelphia. A frustrated doorman shouted at a driver to make room for the luxury autos boxed in by the traffic.

The Republican National Convention had come to town, and the excitement was palpable. The party faithful were there to nominate George W. Bush as their candidate for President, and to ratify his recent choice for Vice President, Dick Cheney. Like most political conventions, the event was wall-to-wall parties, celebrating the Republicans themselves and the big-ticket donors whose money had made the campaign and the convention possible.

Just before 10:30, Ken and Linda Lay emerged from the lobby. Outside, they stood beside an eight-foot fiberglass elephant, its trunk raised in a salute. The statue was a replica of the image on a gold-and-black badge pinned to Lay's suit coat. It was the logo of the Regents, the 137 Republicans who had each contributed or raised at least $250,000 for the Bush campaign.

An official shuttle picked up the Lays and a handful of the other Regents, whisking them to the Philadelphia Convention and Visitors Center for an audience with Bush, Cheney, and their wives. The shuttle stopped at an entrance on Twelfth Street, and the Regents were escorted to room 102A. The Bushes and Cheneys were waiting in a receiving line.

The Lays walked down the line, shaking hands. Governor Bush smiled when he saw them, taking Linda's hand and giving her a light kiss on the cheek. Ken Lay did the same with Laura Bush. Lay shook the governor's hand eagerly.

"Congratulations, George. We're all very proud of all the success of your campaign."

Bush smiled warmly. "Well, Ken, we couldn't have done it without all the help from people like you and Linda. You've really made the difference for us."

After about thirty seconds, the Lays moved on to the Cheneys. The couples greeted each other like old friends.

"The rising generations of this country have our own appointment with greatness. It does not rise or fall with the stock market. It cannot be bought with our wealth."

From behind a large lectern on the main stage at the Republican National

Convention, George W. Bush was giving his acceptance speech. His delivery was almost deadpan, with few smiles or gestures. But every applause line left the party faithful enthralled.

Above the stage, Ken Lay listened attentively, sharing in the excitement of the crowd. Around him sat family and work associates, gathered in what was being called the Enron box. Their seating spoke to their influence; the box was dead center in the auditorium, with Lay in the front row, one of the best seats in the house.

Bush's speech ended, setting off bedlam. Confetti and balloons rained down as the stage filled with politicians and Bush family members. Lay stood, applauding.

If Bush pulled this off, Enron's voice in Washington was sure to be even stronger. Lay couldn't help but feel that the next few years would truly be a golden era.

By all appearances, Project Summer, the sale of Enron's overseas assets, was moving toward success. But Skilling's mood was heading noticeably lower.

The problem, as far as Skilling was concerned, was Joe Sutton. Under the terms of the emerging deal, Sutton would head the new company and take the division's employees with him. That left Sutton hopelessly conflicted; he was pushing for every advantage. He wanted Enron to inject more cash into the new entity; he wanted Badr El-Din to leave it relatively debt-free.

By August, the outlines of a deal had been prepared. The Middle Eastern investors would assign the assets a value of $7.1 billion and purchase an 80 percent interest, with the rest staying with Enron. Expenses included, it translated into a loss from book value, but Skilling was ready to take the lumps. Now, he thought, it was time to teach Enron's directors a lesson about their mistakes. Maybe then he could drive every remnant of Rebecca Mark's businesses out of Enron once and for all.

Skilling's voice was calm as he addressed the Enron board about the status of Project Summer. But his words were slashing.

"What is very clear is that the international assets are not worth as much as most members of the board thought they were," Skilling intoned, glancing at the accounting report he had first seen months before. "We have invested a disproportionate amount of resources for what are clearly inadequate returns."

The numbers he disclosed were stunning. Enron's total cumulative investment in international amounted to billions. For that kind of money, the company should have enjoyed *at least* a fifteen percent return. In reality, though,

Skilling said, it had reaped somewhere between three and six percent, leaving Enron some $1.3 billion short of normal expectations.

"We are just barely able to sell these assets at book value," Skilling said. "But when the transaction expenses are added in, we will have a net loss from this investment in excess of $300 million."

Skilling looked directly at Sutton and Rebecca Mark, who were sitting at the boardroom table. "I believe we have been misled about the values of these assets by the management of the international division," he said, anger in his voice. "If Project Summer does not close, we need to very aggressively start selling them off piece by piece and shutting down the development business."

Mark boiled. She had heard rumors that Skilling was up to something like this, so she had run her own numbers. All told, *her* calculations showed a 12 percent after-tax return. She had laid out her numbers for Lay days before, but now he was sitting there, saying nothing.

She spoke up. "I just want everyone to know that I disagree with Jeff's presentation. I disagree with the numbers, and I think the returns are substantially higher than he's presented."

She wasn't arguing against the sale of the power projects, she said; if they had better places to invest their capital, then they should go ahead and do it.

"I just want you to know that they are performing better than what you've been shown," she said sternly. "But I'll take that up separately with Jeff and Ken."

She stopped speaking. The room was absolutely silent. No one asked her a single question.

Mark stood. "Unfortunately, you'll have to excuse me," she said. "I have another appointment."

She strode out of the room. Sutton blinked, a look of shock in his face. He picked up the gauntlet. "Jeff, I truly believe you are overstating the situation," he said.

Skilling's face registered nothing but contempt. "These are the numbers, Joe."

"Those are *not* the numbers. You are making a lot of extremely negative assumptions. Cash on cash, the returns on the international assets have been tremendous. Rebecca's right, in the neighborhood of 18 percent, pretax."

Cash on cash? Again? "Joe, you've got to be kidding me!" Skilling snapped. "That's not how return on investment is calculated! This is Finance 101!"

"Oh no," Sutton said. "Those are the numbers."

Finally, the fireworks ended. As everyone left, a few directors gathered with Lay. Pug Winokur expressed dismay, not at Skilling's analysis, but at the tone and tenor of his presentation.

"I am just stunned that Jeff made those comments in front of the international group's leadership and made them so personal," Winokur said. "He was attacking their integrity and their competence."

Lay agreed. The episode was out of character for Skilling, and that made them question the quality of his analysis.

"I think the real truth," Lay said, "lies somewhere in the middle between what Joe and Jeff said."

By August 11, Project Summer seemed all but finished. Cliff Baxter signed the agreement with the Badr El-Din group. A team of Enron's executives began hammering out the press release. A list of 154 potential questions—and answers—was drawn up for the inevitable calls from analysts and reporters.

Ninety days, and the deal would close. When all was said and done, Enron would have four billion dollars in new cash. Skilling could almost taste it.

As the sale of the international assets came together, Azurix continued to fall apart. Rebecca Mark's efforts at assembling a new strategy were a bust; repeatedly she had failed to deliver an effective plan for cutting back. The Azurix directors were tired of the battles, tired of the excuses. A new direction seemed necessary. Skilling dropped by to speak with Lay, to see if he was ready to accept the inevitable.

"We've got to call it quits, Ken," Skilling said. "We're not making the progress we need to make."

Lay nodded solemnly. "I agree," he said.

Lay steeled himself as he neared Rebecca Mark's office on the tenth floor of Allen Center. He arrived in her doorway, looking somber. Mark had been expecting him.

"Ken, good to see you," she said breezily.

He stepped across the limestone floor and took a chair. Mark sat directly across from him.

It was best to get right to the point. "Rebecca, you must know that things aren't going very well here." A beat. "I think that it's time for you to resign."

Mark said nothing as Lay rambled on about the contribution she had made to the company, about how she had raised the international stature of both Enron and Azurix.

"We really thank you for what you've accomplished," he said. "But now it's time for you to leave."

Mark blinked, showing no reaction.

Eighteen years. That was all she could think. Mark gave eighteen years to

Enron, gave Lay his international stature with her division. Now, she thought, he was making a bad decision, based on Skilling's numbers. Skilling had made her look incompetent, and apparently it had worked.

"Ken, if that's what you and the board want, then I accept that," she began. "But I really think you need to take a look at the numbers we put together. Our performance in international has been better than Jeff says. Our performance here is very promising."

Lay's anger swelled. He had seen too much evidence of shaky financial analysis coming out of her teams. So much money had been wasted. He just wanted this to be over.

"Rebecca, that is not the issue here," he said.

"Ken, I really think you need to take a look at our numbers," Mark pressed.

Lay's patience vanished. "Rebecca!" he snapped. "I don't give a *fuck* about your numbers!"

Days later, just after eight on the morning of August 24, Rebecca Mark sat for the last time with the Azurix board. The summit was being held at Enron in a room on the fiftieth-floor mezzanine; Azurix couldn't even host its own board meetings anymore.

Mark was the first to speak. "I disagree with your decision. I think it's the wrong thing to do."

No one responded.

"But the decision's been made," Mark said. "Before I agree to this, though, there are three things I require."

Mark listed her demands quickly. Her bonus for the year, prorated. Input in the press release announcing her departure. And, if she ever returned to buy Azurix assets, a commitment that she would be taken seriously.

Skilling leaned in. "Tell me about this bonus."

When another senior Azurix executive was terminated, Mark said, the company had given him a prorated bonus, based on the amount he had received the prior year.

Skilling snorted. "Yeah, but when he left, Azurix was still on budget."

"I should be paid for the time I worked."

"Okay," Skilling retorted. "And this thing about buying assets. Are you asking for preferential treatment?"

"Of course not," Mark said.

Pug Winokur, who was acting as chairman, glanced around the room. No more questions. "All right, Rebecca," he said. "If you give us a moment, we'll discuss it."

Mark left the room. Skilling started right in.

"Paying her a bonus is absolutely incomprehensible!" he said. "We pay for performance. She should get nothing."

The debate went on for several minutes. Winokur brought it to an end. "Look, Rebecca is not a wilting flower. This is a small amount of money, just to get this over with and make sure that she leaves quietly and that we can get back to business."

Winokur's argument won. The directors decided to pay Mark several hundred thousand dollars and send her on her way.

The day began by pushing out one executive. It would end with Skilling inviting hundreds more to join her. At ten, Skilling gathered executives from the international group to formally notify them that they would soon have a new owner.

"We intend to sell the international division," he said. "The sale is basically complete."

Until this moment, Skilling said, the international executives were bound by their agreements to Enron. But no more. Now they could negotiate with their new owner, and Enron would raise no objections, he said.

Skilling took some questions and described the outlines of the deal. After that, there wasn't much more to say. He left the room and headed downstairs to his office.

Skilling felt almost giddy. Mark was out. And all the international executives, the ones always bugging him to crack open Enron's wallet to pay for new projects, were all but gone, too.

Cliff Baxter dropped by with an update on Project Summer, and the two men went outside for a smoke.

Skilling kept smiling and shaking his head. "Man, I'm feeling good," he said. "Feeling real good."

Baxter took a drag on his cigarette. "Yeah," he chuckled. "It all seems almost too good to be true."

It was.

BOOK THREE

THE PROBABILITY OF RUIN

CHAPTER 14

EARLY ON THE MORNING of August 28, a team of transplant specialists wheeled an empty stretcher down a deserted hallway at the Cleveland Clinic. No patients were visible in the rooms as the doctors passed; instead, an entourage of Middle Eastern officials, there to attend the needs of one man, had taken over the floor. The medical specialists were cleared through security and ushered into an elegant suite where an elderly man lay surrounded by a virtual garden of fresh orchids and other expensive blooms.

The patient was Sheikh Zayed bin Sultan al Nahyan, President of the United Arab Emirates, ruler of Abu Dhabi, and the sixth-richest man on earth. As best as anyone knew, he was somewhere between seventy-nine and ninety-one years old; birth certificates weren't in wide usage in the Arab world when Sheikh Zayed was born. Whatever his age, this day he would become one of the oldest kidney-transplant recipients ever.

The team wheeled Sheikh Zayed toward the operating room. The doctors could scarcely guess at the outcome; the sheikh was in decent physical condition, but there was no telling how, at his age, he would bear up under the ordeal.

One thing was clear. Sheikh Zayed, the man whose authorization was required for the investment of billions of dollars in Project Summer, would be out of commission for weeks, if not months, to come.

Three days later, Stuart Zisman, a lawyer in Enron's wholesale division, was finishing a draft memo. He had been asked weeks before to examine Project Raptor and analyze the legal risks of the transaction for Enron. To do the job, Zisman had obtained data about the various assets that were going to be hedged with Raptor I.

Zisman didn't like what he had seen. Most of the hedged assets were truly dreadful, the holdings most likely to lose value over time. In essence, Enron was entering into terrible merchant investments, then locking in marked-up values to avoid admitting the consequences of the company's monstrous business decisions.

So Zisman pulled no punches. On the first page of his memo, he wrote the heading "Overall Book Manipulation." He mentioned that at first he had believed Raptor would hedge investments of varying quality. "As it turns out," he wrote, "we have discovered that a majority of the investments being introduced into the Raptor structure are bad ones."

That, he wrote, "might lead one to believe that the financial books at Enron are being manipulated in order to eliminate the drag on earnings that would otherwise occur." Zisman finished the memo and sent it to his bosses. He wouldn't get the response he expected.

Even as Zisman prepared his memo, the hedging scheme had become far broader than most anyone knew. Raptor I and Raptor II were already up and running. Another vehicle had been presented to the board as Raptor III in August, and again the directors approved it. Despite the name, Raptor III wasn't the third Raptor, it was the fourth. The real Raptor III had been created without board approval. And it was the most irrational structure of all.

The third Raptor was designed to help Enron hedge one asset—its investment in the New Power Company, a business Enron set up to sell electricity and natural gas to residential customers, both directly and over the Internet. New Power was about to go public, and executives feared its potentially volatile stock price would whipsaw Enron's bottom line. So the third Raptor was used to lock in the New Power share price. Of course, to hedge, the third Raptor needed capital it could arguably use to repay Enron if the New Power shares fell in price.

The finance group found the capital they needed in the most unexpected of places: the New Power shares themselves. The stock being hedged was contributed to the third Raptor; again LJM2 was the outside investor, putting in thirty million dollars and getting back just under forty million dollars one week later, before any hedging took place.

Still, hedges are supposed to go *up* in value as the price of the stock being protected goes *down*. But here, Enron had taken the irrational Raptor structure to its absurd extreme. New Power shares were backing the hedge of New Power shares. There wasn't even a pretense at economic sense.

But the Raptors would get still worse.

Negotiations between Enron and Joe Sutton were bogging down. If Project Summer went forward, Sutton wanted, at a minimum, his full severance, plus an extended contract in case the new company didn't pay as much as Enron. Lay called the demands unreasonable. Sutton insisted he deserved to be rewarded for taking a chance on new owners who, he contended, would walk away from the deal if he refused to join.

Frustrated, Lay finally called Badr El-Din personally. He opened by asking about the Emir's transplant and the progress of the deal. Then he shifted topics.

"Dr. Amin, I need to know what the deal's breaking points are," he said. "We're having a little difficulty negotiating Joe's severance arrangement, and I guess I need to know if Joe is essential to this deal."

"No," Badr El-Din replied. "All things being equal, we'd probably rather have him than not have him. But other people are essential to the deal. Joe's not."

Then Badr El-Din mentioned something else. While Sutton was lobbying for an Enron severance, he was pushing Badr El-Din for a huge pay package, too. Lay thanked Badr El-Din and hung up. These shenanigans were the last straw. He discussed it with Skilling, and they agreed. If Sutton didn't leave through Project Summer, Enron would force him out.

The anonymous letter from India had been making its way around the Enron building for days. Somebody, probably an employee, claimed an Enron executive was operating his own business out of the company's India offices, using company copiers and computers, even its business contacts.

The letter was routed to the general counsel, Jim Derrick, and a copy was then forwarded to Skilling. Most of the allegations struck Skilling as penny-ante. But one, deep in the letter, made him sit up and take notice.

The Maharashtra State Electricity Board, the body contractually obligated to purchase power from Enron's Dabhol plant, couldn't pay its bill. And Enron's office in India, the letter said, was helping the board finagle the numbers to hide the problem.

This couldn't be right. Dabhol was still only generating power from stage one, the least expensive part. Stage two, the piece that would drive Dabhol's costs into the billions, hadn't begun. If Maharashtra couldn't afford to pay for the available electricity *now*, how could Enron start generating even more?

Skilling dashed out of the office. Causey had been looking at the Dabhol numbers for Project Summer. Maybe he could shed some light on this.

"It's not possible," Causey said. "Their numbers don't show that."

A failure to pay bills, he said, would show up in the books from India as accounts receivable—essentially, money owed the plant. But these numbers weren't building up.

Skilling sighed in relief. "Okay," he said. "Maybe there isn't a problem here."

He headed back to his office, but his reprieve didn't last. He couldn't quite shake the suspicion that something was seriously wrong in Dabhol.

Ken Lay loved Enron stock. For years he had invested in almost nothing but the company's shares, watching happily as his net worth multiplied with the rising stock price. But by 2000, things had begun to change.

Beau Herrold, Lay's stepson, had been brought in months before to join the team managing the family investments, and soon he and the other advisers were pushing Lay to expand his portfolio by selling Enron shares and buying other stocks. Lay always refused.

"Why sell a stock when you feel strongly it's going to continue on up?" Lay asked Herrold.

Herrold and the other advisers didn't give up, and Lay eventually relented a little. He wouldn't *sell* his Enron shares, but he would pledge them as collateral for bank loans. Then Herrold could use the borrowed money to purchase other investments. Lay saw no real risk; he felt confident that the banks could be repaid in the future with the growth in value from Enron shares. The borrowing started in earnest.

On the evening of September 2, the Saturday of Labor Day weekend, Andy and Lea Fastow were dining at Tony's with two friends, Michael Metz and his wife, Clare Casademont. Other diners shot furtive glances at the four attractive young professionals; Casademont was well known in town, a former local news anchor who had left the station when she moved to London with Metz, an international oil trader.

As the four chatted over drinks, Fastow noticed a group of people making their way to a second, smaller dining room. It was Jordan Mintz, an Enron tax lawyer, accompanied by his wife, Lauren, and her family, all there celebrating the eightieth birthday of Lauren's father.

Fastow caught Mintz's eye and signaled for him to come over. After settling the rest of the family, Mintz and his wife walked to Fastow's table. The three couples made some small talk.

"Listen, Jordan," Fastow said. "When you're back in the office on Tuesday, make an appointment to see me. I have something important I want to discuss with you."

Mintz knew not to ask details. "Okay, I will."

As the Mintzes headed back to their table, Lauren tilted her head toward her husband. "What was that about?" she whispered.

Mintz was sure he knew. The previous year, Fastow had approached him about becoming the finance division's top lawyer, only to snatch the offer away when Enron's general counsel, Jim Derrick, pushed another candidate, Scott Sefton. But word was out that Fastow was unhappy with Sefton. This couldn't be a coincidence.

"I think," Mintz replied, "it's about the global-finance job again."

The following Tuesday, Fastow was sitting behind his desk, sipping on a bottled water as he spoke to Mintz.

"Derrick sold me down the river on Sefton," he said. "I'm getting rid of him. And I think you're the right person for this job."

"Well, Andy, what's Jim going to say?"

"Derrick's out of the loop on this," Fastow replied casually. The task had been delegated to the deputy general counsel, Rob Walls, a lawyer Mintz knew well.

Fastow told Mintz to speak with Walls, and wished him luck. This time everything worked out. Walls called days later with the news that Mintz had been selected as the finance group's new general counsel, starting October. Mintz was ecstatic. This was a dream opportunity.

His enthusiasm wouldn't last through his first day.

The next morning, Fastow and Causey got together at nine. It was, Fastow told Kopper, a meeting to discuss an agreement dubbed Global Galactic.

If LJM2 was going to keep buying Enron's assets—helping ensure its ability to meet its earnings—then Fastow wanted the company committed to repurchasing the ones he really didn't want, at a preset profit.

There were plenty of assets to discuss: the investment in the Nigerian barges, now owned by LJM2 since its purchase of the stake from Merrill Lynch; the stake in Cuiabá; deal after deal. As far as Fastow was concerned, with an agreement in place, he would be guaranteed not to suffer any losses.

Fastow put it all in writing, listing each asset, the repurchase price, and the predetermined profit that LJM2 stood to make. It was an agreement that, Fastow knew, proved Enron's "sales" to LJM2 were a sham. The company bore the risk of ownership; no matter what happened to the asset values, LJM2 would profit. Any losses would be Enron's. The "equity investments" from LJM2 were nothing more than disguised loans.

The document would prove to be what the government considered the smoking gun, the proof LJM2 was at the center of a web of illegal schemes. It would remain undiscovered by investigators until years after the company's collapse.

The news coverage of the California energy crisis was relentlessly bad. Mutterings about market manipulations by out-of-state energy companies were growing louder. That was enough for Richard Sanders, chief litigation manager for Enron's wholesale division; he could almost smell the lawsuits coming. In early September, Sanders visited his boss, Mark Haedicke, the division's general counsel.

"I think it might be a good idea for us to go see what's going on out there," Sanders said. "To see what we can do to head off the litigation."

Haedicke agreed. He authorized hiring an array of specialists from several firms. If there was anything to worry about, an army of lawyers would find it.

That same day in Portland, Christian Yoder, Enron's top lawyer on the trading desk, received a call from Haedicke in Houston to fill him in on the decision. "Do you know any attorneys who are really expert and up-to-date on California trading and California issues?" Haedicke asked.

"No," Yoder replied. "It's kind of an unknown area."

Yoder agreed to look around. He thought of Stoel Rives, a renowned Portland firm, which suggested Stephen Hall, a bright third-year associate. Yoder interviewed Hall and agreed he was the right man for the job. The two lawyers became friendly, which helped in future years, when they both emerged as key witnesses in the storm of scandal.

Mark Haedicke sat down with Stuart Zisman not long after receiving his letter on the legal perils of Raptor I.

"I want to thank you for your candor," Haedicke began. "But I do have some issues."

Zisman's language, he continued, was inflammatory and opinionated. Not what Haedicke wanted to see. For example, he said, Zisman had described Raptor as "cleverly designed." That seemed almost snide and really had no place in this kind of legal memo, Haedicke said.

The meeting lasted less than fifteen minutes. Haedicke never mentioned Zisman's warnings about possible earnings manipulation. Word choice—that was the problem.

Cliff Baxter was on the phone with Badr El-Din, hearing more about kidney failure than he wanted to know. Sheikh Zayed needed to give the final sign-off before Project Summer could be closed, Badr El-Din said. But the sheikh had experienced complications and was in no condition to consider such a complex deal.

"I don't dare go in while his family is there, tending to his care," Badr El-Din said. "We will have to wait."

Anxiety gnawed at Baxter. Delay on a transaction this large was a bad omen. And sure enough, efforts to jump-start the process faltered. UBS tracked down one of the sheikh's family members in Spain and asked him to fly to the Emirates to get *somebody* to sign. Endless other calls were placed—to Spain, to the UAE, to Cleveland. Repeatedly, there were promises signatures were coming. They never did.

On September 8, Baxter dropped by Skilling's office and slumped into a chair. "This isn't working, Jeff," Baxter said. "Every day that goes by, this starts receding. There's going to be second thoughts."

Skilling nodded. This was bad.

The SEC's proposal to split accounting and consulting had stirred up a hornet's nest on Capitol Hill. Day after day, outraged letters and phone calls arrived at Arthur Levitt's office from Congress. When pressed on the problem, though, many objectors displayed an unfamiliarity with the issues bordering on ignorance; some seemed not to know the difference between a balance sheet and a balance beam.

Still, Levitt respected a handful of the staunchest opponents—like Phil Gramm, a Republican senator from Texas. Gramm, whose wife, Wendy, served as an Enron director, believed the rigors of the marketplace, not the dictates of the government, should guide American business. That left him philosophically opposed to the Levitt plan. But Gramm was also infused with an abiding sense of fair play and wanted the proposal to die on the merits, not political gamesmanship. He secretly appointed himself Levitt's congressional spy, monitoring his colleagues' intrigues.

Levitt was in his office one day when Gramm called with news. "Arthur," he said, "thought you'd like to know that Shelby is after you."

Shelby. Richard Shelby, a Republican senator from Alabama. "How so?" Levitt asked.

"He's putting together an appropriations rider. Something to bar the SEC from spending any of its budget implementing this proposed rule of yours."

Levitt thanked Gramm and hung up furious. It was a typical Washington power play. If politicians couldn't win on the issues, they'd attack the budget. Levitt decided to fight back, finding the home number for Senator Trent Lott, the majority leader. Lott had the power to squelch Shelby's shenanigans; Levitt hoped to appeal to the senator's sense of fairness. Lott was gracious when he came on the line.

"Trent, this is too important an issue to be sabotaged in the dead of night with some appropriations rider," Levitt pleaded. "No matter what you think about the issue, the process should be aboveboard."

There was plenty of support for what he was proposing, Levitt said. A number of newspapers and magazines, including *The New York Times, The Washington Post,* and *Business Week,* had endorsed adoption of the rule.

"Well, Arthur," Lott drawled, "I'm not familiar with what you're proposing to do, but if those liberal publications are in favor of it, then I'm against it."

Levitt hung up, shaken. Political power was aligning against his proposal. Somehow, ensuring that *public* accountants represented the interests of the *public* was too controversial for Congress. The members' ties to the industry, Levitt figured, were too strong. If he continued down this path, Congress could cripple the SEC's budget. He had no choice. He had to compromise.

Cliff Baxter spoke to Skilling shortly after noon on September 14. His voice was calm, his manner decisive. Still no progress on Project Summer, he said. Just more promises that soon signatures would arrive.

"I don't like this," Baxter said. "It feels wrong."

"What do you want to do?" Skilling replied.

Baxter showed no emotion. "I think we ought to terminate the offer."

What? "Why do that, Cliff?" Skilling asked sharply.

"We've got to do something," Baxter replied. "We've got to make them focused. We'll give them a period of time to sign, or tell them we're going to terminate the deal. If something's going to happen, that'll make it happen."

Skilling took a deep breath. It sounded like an all-or-nothing bet. Still, he trusted Baxter's instincts.

"Okay," Skilling said. "Do it."

The deadline passed the following Monday, September 18. No response. Baxter, looking worn down, dropped by Skilling's office with the news. "Got nothing, Jeff," he said. "Looks like Project Summer is dead."

Oh, God. Skilling had invested so much emotional energy in this deal, hoping it would solve all of his problems. He rubbed a hand over his face, then looked at Baxter.

"Okay, so that's that," he said. "We've got to gear up again. Start over. Sell it in pieces if we have to."

Baxter nodded. Skilling headed down to talk to Lay. There were a lot of things to do. And one of the first was to sit down with Joe Sutton and tell him to get out of Enron.

That same day in Dallas, Causey led an entourage of Enron executives down a fiftieth-floor hallway in Renaissance Tower. They found room 5050, the Dallas bureau of *The Wall Street Journal*, and stopped at a receptionist's desk, asking to see a reporter named Jonathan Weil.

A lawyer by training, Weil was a self-taught financial sleuth who, months before, had received a tip about the accounting at some energy-trading companies, including Enron and its top rival, Dynegy. Weil, a reporter for the regional section called Texas Journal, had dug into the records, realizing that the companies depended on mark-to-market accounting—loaded with plenty of assumptions—to report spectacular earnings. He had called to get responses, then suddenly today, two days before publication, someone at Enron phoned back to say Causey was on the way to Dallas to speak with him.

The Enron team made their way into the bureau's newsroom. Weil was at his desk and heard someone asking for him. He gathered his notes and stood. After introducing himself, he led the group to a nearby conference room.

They dispensed with the niceties quickly, and Weil let Causey take the floor. The calculations of its mark-to-market earnings weren't just wild guesses, Causey said, but conservative estimates based on quoted market prices. If market prices weren't available, then Enron relied on long-term pricing trends to calculate the proper values.

Weil listened quietly, rapidly writing Causey's words into his notebook. Causey struck him as incredibly cocksure of Enron's abilities. After Causey began to wrap things up, Weil was ready with some questions.

"So did the models last year tell you that California electricity prices would be going berserk this year?"

"Of course not," Causey replied.

"Then how can you be so sure of your abilities to predict future trends?"

The conversation went on a while longer, until finally Causey had had his say. Later, Weil was back at his desk, typing the information. If nothing else, he was certain of one thing. If Enron was willing to fly top officers up to Dallas for this, he thought, he must be hitting a sore spot.

David Duncan reviewed the two-page draft letter. With one more go-through, it would be ready for Lay's stationery and signature. Then off to Arthur Levitt at the SEC.

Duncan, on Andersen's behalf, had written the letter objecting to the SEC's proposed rule on consulting. Lay had agreed to sign, making it appear he had been so outraged by the proposal that he had banged out his objections—rather than just signing something written by the very accountants who stood to lose money if the idea was approved.

The tone of the letter struck Duncan as just right. It described Enron's close relationship with Andersen, and its reliance on its consulting, as mechanisms that helped keep tabs on the company's far-flung businesses. In essence, the letter argued that much of Enron's success, and its skill in controlling its operations, were attributable to Andersen's ability to provide both auditing and consulting services.

The letter was sent up to Lay, and he signed it on September 20. The irony seemed lost on everyone. By persuading its largest client to lobby the government on its behalf, Andersen had compromised the very independence that the letter claimed was holding strong.

The bulls for a company's stock are the supporters, the ones who cheer every time the price rises another point. But the market also has its bears, short sellers who scour for overvalued stocks and put together trades betting on an eventual collapse in share price.

In New York, Jim Chanos was a market professional who had made his career rooting out the bad news about high-flying stocks. That fall, Chanos, the president of Kynikos Associates, was looking for his next big idea. A call from a friend alerted him to an article by Jonathan Weil that appeared on September 20 in the Texas regional section of *The Wall Street Journal*. Chanos was intrigued; it sounded as if Enron and other energy-trading companies could use their accounting to manufacture earnings just by adopting aggressive assumptions about the future of the marketplace.

Maybe it wouldn't lead anywhere, but Chanos wanted to take a closer look at Enron. And the first thing he needed to do was review some of the company's financial filings.

When managers from India came to Houston to work on the next plans for selling the international assets, Skilling dropped by for a chat. The letter about troubles in Dabhol still ate at him. He figured he'd ask about the Maharashtra State Electricity Board and see what happened.

"Listen, guys," Skilling said after he entered the room. "What's going on with the bills to the MSEB?"

Not a problem, one manager responded. "They're having trouble paying. But we're working it out."

Trouble paying? "What do you mean?" Skilling asked.

"The bills are really big," the manager responded. "And they're really straining under it."

Skilling left the room more disturbed than ever. He began poking around and soon hit pay dirt. He discovered that Enron managers in India were helping the electricity board stay out of hock. Whenever it ran out of cash, they simply shut the Dabhol plant "for maintenance." That way, they limited the flow of electricity to whatever Maharashtra could afford. That was why there were no accounts receivable; Enron only turned on the juice when its primary customer had cash.

Skilling was furious. He wanted the top executives from India to fly to Houston immediately.

The meeting took place days later in conference room 50M03 at Enron headquarters. Sanjay Bhatnagar, head of Enron India, was joined by Wade Cline, the second in command. Across the table sat Skilling and Lay, looking impatient.

"All right, Sanjay, straight out," Skilling said. "Is there a problem with MSEB paying?"

Bhatnagar raised his hands in a dismissive motion. "This is what it's like doing business in India. We just stay on top of them and keep pushing to get it done."

He had been keeping up the pressure, Bhatnagar said, just as he had always expected he would have to. "So there's no problem. No problem."

Skilling turned toward Cline. "What do you think?"

Cline glanced at Bhatnagar, then answered. "We have a problem."

Bhatnagar smiled. "Wade is always worrying. This is India. This is how things happen in India. Not a problem."

Skilling ignored him. "Wade, what are you thinking?"

The cash wasn't there, Cline said. Under phase one, Enron should be billing about $30 million a month, but the energy board didn't have it. They could only afford $15 to $20 million. When phase two began, Cline said, the monthly billings should climb to about $110 million. But the board would still have only about $20 million available.

Bhatnagar turned to Cline, looking livid. "Wade," he said sharply, "you're thinking about this all wrong. That's not the way things are done in India."

The Indian government had guaranteed payment, Bhatnagar said. The government would make good. They wanted foreign investment; they would never default on this.

Skilling held up his hands. "Fine. We understand the problem. They have $20 million; they need more than $100 million. Let's start working on that."

The executives needed to speak with Indian officials to find out if they would write a check. But whatever happened, Enron's plant would not operate without payment.

The meeting broke up, and Bhatnagar headed downstairs, where executives in Broadband were waiting for him. Cline lingered behind for a moment. Skilling approached.

"Okay, Wade," he said. "What's your assessment?"

Cline looked Skilling in the eye.

"It's bad," he said. "We've got a big problem here."

Arthur Levitt needed an ally in the accounting industry. And he found one at Arthur Andersen in a soft-spoken yet scrappy managing partner named Joseph Berardino.

After spending his full career at Andersen, Berardino was a favorite to be the firm's new chief executive. But even as his star was rising at Andersen, Berardino was becoming Levitt's secret weapon. Quietly, he broke ranks with other accounting firms, working with Levitt to hammer out a compromise on the auditor-independence rules.

The presidential elections were a little more than a month away. Levitt knew he didn't have a lot of time.

Fall's arrival broke the California heat wave, but anxieties about the marketplace and trader gaming made the state's energy crisis only grow worse.

Gray Davis, the state's governor, became desperate. Things were out of control. The system seemed on the verge of collapse. Davis was ready to turn anywhere for help. So on October 2 at nine o'clock, he was in his office with two aides, preparing for a conference call. A secretary let Davis know everyone was on the line. He hit the button on his speakerphone. "This is Gray Davis," he announced.

"Governor, good morning. Jeff Skilling at Enron."

They spent more than half an hour brainstorming. From Enron's side, Greg Whalley, the company's top energy trader, and Steve Kean, its senior government-relations executive, helped out. But for the most part, the conversation was all Skilling and Davis.

The state couldn't afford to pay hundreds of dollars for every megawatt hour, which last year cost less than twenty dollars, Davis said.

"It's easy to fix," Skilling said. The problem, he said, was that California bought most of its power shortly before it was needed, in the spot market. That left the state subject to the vagaries of market fluctuations. Instead, it should strike long-term contracts, locking in prices for years. Such deals could probably be purchased for less than fifty dollars a megawatt hour right now.

"That's interesting," Davis replied. "Give me some of the numbers on that."

Skilling sketched out the details. The best way to handle it was through an online auction, he said. That would prove to suppliers that there was a market at a lower price. Davis said he would look into it.

The call ended, and Skilling felt pumped. Enron might have its foot in the door in helping put together a huge set of power contracts. Maybe the California mess could be fixed soon—and all to Enron's advantage. After all, the contracts could be marked to market. Daily sales couldn't.

The next day, Richard Sanders and his newly assembled team of lawyers and economists arrived in Portland, ready to hear from the Enron traders about California. The two primary lawyers working on the trading floor, Christian Yoder and Stephen Hall, joined the group.

Legally, things had worsened. The California Public Utilities Commission had served Enron with a subpoena seeking voluminous records. Sanders's suspicions of oncoming litigation were already starting to look prescient. The team was taken to a conference room, where they met Tim Belden, the head of the trading desk, along with other traders, including John Forney, father of the Forney Perpetual Loop.

Sanders opened things up. "Just to make sure everyone is clear. We are here as representatives of the company. We are not your lawyers. We do not represent you."

That was fine with Belden, but not Forney. He worried about his job, he said, and declined to speak with the lawyers. With Forney gone, Belden launched into a lecture about the California market. It dragged on for hours, until Belden said he was ready to discuss his traders' specific strategies. The economists were booted out of the room; this was for lawyers only. Belden approached a whiteboard and wrote the names that his traders had given to their various ploys. Death Star. Fat Boy. Ricochet.

Sanders looked at the list with dismay. It almost didn't matter whether the methods Enron employed in these schemes were legitimate, not with these kinds of names. Such in-your-face flamboyance would be enough to sway a jury. Topping it off, they were *juvenile*. Sanders couldn't understand how someone like Belden would tolerate something so sophomoric.

Gary Fergus, another lawyer in the room, spoke up. "Why would you use names like that?" he asked.

Everybody laughed. "Yeah," Sanders said. "Why didn't you use names like 'Mama's Cooking' or 'Baby's Baby'?"

As the meeting wore on, the lawyers knew they had their hands full. The strategies may have violated state anti-gouging laws, maybe even antitrust laws.

Some practices looked terrible but could probably be defended—like exporting power generated in California, where price caps were in place, and selling it out of state for more. Belden argued that the trading was just a mechanism to pull different markets into alignment. But of course, Californians plagued by brownouts and power shortages wouldn't care much for an academic argument about why Enron was sucking electricity out of state.

Other tactics posed more than public-relations headaches. There were transactions where Enron traders had submitted false records to California or were paid for making commitments that they didn't plan to keep.

The most egregious scam had just started. The traders discovered that if they submitted a schedule ending in a fraction—say, to sell 22.49 megawatts—they could make more money. When power flowed, California rounded the amount delivered down to 22, but at payment time it was rounded up to 23. That meant Enron was paid for a megawatt it never delivered. Multiplied by enough transactions, that could rake in serious money. So far, though, the traders had only done it twice, bringing in about fifteen thousand dollars.

Sanders was horrified. "Not only do you have to stop that, you have to send the money back immediately."

"But if we send the money back," one trader argued, "they'll figure out what we did."

Sanders stood firm. "I don't care," he said. "Send it back anyway."

The next morning, Christian Yoder was at his desk. He glanced up and saw John Forney in his doorway, a troubled look on his face. "Hey," Yoder said. "What's up?"

Forney seemed reluctant to speak. He glanced at the floor for a moment, then looked Yoder in the eye.

"I've got a concern," he said. He took a second. "Am I going to be implicated in anything serious?"

Yoder eyed him evenly. The man seemed terrified.

"I don't know, John," Yoder replied. "If you are, the people in the company that you need to talk to about handling it are Richard Sanders and Mark Haedicke."

Forney glanced at the floor again, nodding. He was silent for a second. "Okay," he finally said. "Thanks."

He turned to leave.

In Palm Beach, a crew from Florida Power & Light was at work just before 5:30 on the morning of October 6. The backhoe operator digging in the ground didn't see that he had hit an electric cable. A second later, it sliced in two; all the power was cut to the Breakers, the oceanfront hotel where Enron's directors and managers were mostly still sleeping, resting up for their meetings that day.

The Flagler boardroom was illuminated by candlelight. It was four hours later, and the directors from Enron's Compensation and Management Development Committee were holding the day's first meeting. They had awoken in near darkness. Now, they were sweating and uncomfortable, straining to read the agenda. Lay's plans to take his directors on a fun Florida trip had been dashed.

The directors, led by Charles LeMaistre, had finished approving changes to Enron's compensation plans when they invited Lay into the room to make a presentation. And a momentous one. He was there to announce that he was ready to start the handover of Enron to Skilling.

"Jeff has made it very clear that if we don't make a decision about this by year's end, then it will be time for him to seriously think about something else," Lay said. "I don't believe that is an idle comment."

Lay glanced around the table. "I think he's ready for the job, and I am ready to step down."

The directors made all the right noises. They were disappointed, wished Lay would stay, but could understand his desire to move on. They knew that, at his age, Skilling would not wait around much longer.

"I would like your approval," Lay said, "to speak with the full board about this tomorrow."

There was no formal vote, but the directors agreed.

"At this time," Fastow said, "Enron's management is recommending the company begin transacting with a new private-equity fund called LJM3."

It was an hour later, and the finance committee was gathered in the Ponce de León III ballroom, listening to Fastow's latest report. LJM1 and LJM2 had done their jobs, Fastow said, with the second fund having invested some $500 million in more than twenty transactions.

"Of course, my role in the LJM funds could create a conflict of interest," Fastow said. "Still, we have put in place important mechanisms to mitigate those conflicts."

Fastow listed the controls: he still maintained a fiduciary responsibility to Enron, and the board could ask him to resign at any time. "As you know," Fastow added, "Rick Buy, Rick Causey, and Jeff Skilling approve all transactions between Enron and the LJM funds."

Nobody seemed to notice the problem. The board had never asked for Skilling to review the LJM deals. And Skilling never had; there was a place for him to sign on the approval sheets, but it was almost invariably left blank. Still, Fastow's statement was no slip of the tongue. He had included it in his formal report submitted to the board.

Causey and Skilling joined in on the discussion. The LJM funds had brought plenty of benefits, they said. They recommended that the transactions be allowed to continue.

One director, Norm Blake, had concerns. "There are a lot of deals here, far more than we could properly review just once a year," he said. "I would propose that the finance committee should review these quarterly."

Pug Winokur, the chairman, had another issue. He wondered how the board was supposed to be alert for signs of conflicts when no one knew Fastow's compensation from LJM.

"I would propose," Winokur said, "that the compensation committee review the amounts Andy is receiving both from the LJM funds and from the company."

The committee unanimously agreed to the two proposals. That meant once the full board gave its nod, Fastow would be required to provide details of his dealings every three months, along with a breakdown of the money he made—from every source.

The power would not come back on, so the board changed hotels, moving down the beach to the Four Seasons. The next morning, Skilling was sitting in the lobby, waiting for his breakfast companion, when he spotted John Duncan, chairman of the executive committee, walking past some lush greenery. Duncan smiled and came over.

The two sat beside each other, chatting about their relief at staying in a hotel with the electricity still on.

Duncan changed the subject abruptly.

"Jeff, I know you're angry about everything we've done on the international side," he said. "But don't you think with all the investments we made, we've really created an international company?"

Duncan looked him in the eye. "Don't you think it was worth it?"

A dozen thoughts shot through Skilling's mind. Duncan was talking about *seven billion dollars*. For that amount, Enron could have taken out ads on every Super Bowl for the next fifty years and simply announced that it was an international company. It could have sent direct mail to everyone on the planet. So much money producing so little cash, dragging down the company's overall performance. *And Duncan thought it was worth it?* Skilling was speechless.

Another director walked by. "Oh, there's my breakfast meeting," Duncan said. "See you later, Jeff."

Duncan walked away. Skilling had never responded.

Later that day, the full board approved Fastow's participation in LJM3. At the meeting's end, after Skilling and other executives had left, Lay announced his plans to step down. This wasn't the formal handover; that would happen at the end-of-the-year meeting. Even so, some directors had not expected Lay's announcement. They pressed him to stay on as chairman, to give Skilling time to get his footing.

Lay knew Skilling would be agreeable; whenever the topic of succession came up, Skilling made the same request. It was almost as if the man were afraid of running the show alone. Lay didn't mind keeping the title for a while. After all, what difference could another year make?

Their own annual meeting. That, Fastow thought, was what the LJM2 investors needed. A nice one in Florida, with ample golf and spa treatments. With LJM3 in the works, it would also be the perfect time to let investors know that Enron still had important deals in the pipeline that could bring fat profits to another fund.

And Skilling could be Exhibit A. He had achieved the status of a corporate rock star. If *he* showed up, the investors would get the message: Enron just loved the LJM funds. Fastow dropped by Skilling's office to sound him out on the idea.

"Hey, look," he said. "We're getting the LJM investors together. I'd really like you to come make a presentation, to let them know Enron is still growing."

Skilling shrugged. No big deal. "Sure."

Jordan Mintz arrived in the finance division on October 16 as the new general counsel—but with trepidations. He was a tax specialist, not a securities lawyer, and this new job involved a lot of securities work. That day, he met with Fastow to review his duties. After going down the list, his new boss added one more item.

"Oh," he said, "and one of the responsibilities will be to maintain the files for LJM."

Standing at a row of metal filing cabinets, Mintz pulled open a drawer and ran his finger across the green hanging folders. Finally, he saw the label he wanted.

LJM. There were no subcategories, just a large brown folder inside stuffed with paper. Mintz carried it to his desk and pulled out the scores of documents and printed e-mails inside. Before long, his eyes were bulging.

This is unbelievable. Deal upon deal, totaling hundreds of millions of dollars. All done with an entity controlled by the CFO. How could Enron tolerate this?

There was a lot for Mintz to learn, fast. Enron was not the kind of place where somebody struggling to master a problem would be thrown a rope. More likely an anchor. He didn't want people to see him trying to get his arms around all this, and end up thinking he was stupid.

Mintz set his course. He would have to educate himself on everything about the LJM deals from the beginning. Review the board minutes, examine the deal documents, talk to everybody involved. Then he'd know the whole story.

It didn't take long for Mintz to figure out that the LJM acolytes formed their own cult inside Enron. Strange doings caught his attention from the beginning. For one, Kopper was running legal meetings, discussing how Enron could avoid disclosing information about the LJM funds. Then Mintz came under pressure from Kopper and Glisan to fire a lawyer they accused of not being responsive enough during an LJM deal. And throughout the department, Mintz detected an unmistakable odor of anxiety among executives about the conflicts involving their boss that Enron tolerated.

He needed to speak with Fastow again, this time solely about the deals with LJM.

The Raptors didn't work. After all the careful planning, all the consulting from Andersen, all the confident boasting about the finance group's genius, the supposedly brilliant hedges were failing just weeks after their creation.

The problem was exactly what Stuart Zisman had detected: executives had used the vehicles as a dumping ground for financial toxic waste. Some investments in Raptor I collapsed in value so quickly that they couldn't even be hedged before losses piled up. Fastow and his colleagues dealt with that easily—backdating the documents, making it appear the hedges were in place when values of the merchant investments were at their peak. But that immediately locked in huge losses for the Raptors.

Worse, the third Raptor was hit by a double whammy: After a week of trading, New Power's stock price began deteriorating. Those shares, of course, were hedged by the third Raptor and were its only significant asset. So it owed Enron more money even as its capital dried up.

If something wasn't changed, the Raptors might be deemed "impaired"—

a five-dollar accounting word meaning that they couldn't pay their debts. That would leave Enron having to report the losses from its merchant investments.

Fastow and Causey acted quickly. On October 20, they created a "costless collar," obligating Enron to pay Raptor I for any losses it suffered if Enron shares fell below eighty-one dollars. The idea was to make sure that Raptor I would not suddenly become impaired because of a drop in Enron stock.

Raptor I had become an absurd circle. If Enron's stock price fell below the target, the company owed Raptor I money, which Raptor I would then have to pass back to Enron to make up for the losses in merchant investments. Enron, by any definition, was hedging with itself.

Fastow made room on his calendar for Mintz on October 23. The two men, both carrying pads of paper to take notes, sat at the office conference table. Mintz asked what Fastow expected from him regarding LJM. Fastow spoke about all the paperwork to be handled—deal sheets, closing documents, and the rest. Mintz listened uncomfortably.

"Let me give you my overview of why LJM exists, and why Skilling and the board approved it," Fastow began.

LJM could move quickly, he said, and be available for any crisis when Enron needed to sell fast. "LJM is close to the company, we understand the deals. There won't be weeks of negotiations, with lawyers dragging everything out."

Mintz scribbled notes, trying to hide his revulsion. What Fastow was describing was simply perverse, like justifying incest because the brother really knew the sister well.

Or was it? He thought of all those gold-plated names he had seen on LJM documents: Arthur Andersen, Vinson & Elkins. Their experience was much broader than his, and they had pronounced LJM squeaky-clean. Maybe there was something he didn't understand.

Fastow launched into the history of his funds, lauding his own work on the Rhythms hedge as a stroke of genius.

"Because LJM1 was so successful with Rhythms, we started LJM2," Fastow continued. "And LJM2 allowed us to hedge even more investments, through the Raptors."

The lawyers and accountants were always filled in on every detail, he said. "Nobody's hiding anything from anybody," he said. "Everything is just an open kimono."

Open kimono. Mintz hated that phrase. Too many people at Enron said it. He had never heard it anyplace else.

"That's why Enron's comfortable," Fastow said. "They're comfortable it's me and Michael. They know we wouldn't do anything that wasn't in Enron's interest."

But, he went on, Enron didn't have to rely on their integrity alone. Plenty of controls were in place, from Enron's right to refuse to do a deal, to the requirements for a sign-off from Causey and Buy. Plus, Fastow said, the company disclosed everything in its annual proxy sent to shareholders. It was all there, in the section on related-party transactions. Mintz nodded silently; these were the disclosures he knew Kopper was working to *remove*.

Fastow looked at Mintz sternly. "Now, the money I make from LJM doesn't have to be disclosed," he said.

In case Mintz wanted to know more, he named the lawyers who had worked on the LJM disclosures the prior year. "Our approach in the past," Fastow said, "has been to try to keep our disclosures as innocuous as possible."

Mintz wrote down the words "keep innocuous."

The meeting ended after forty-five minutes. Mintz headed to the elevator, eager to put together a plan of how to substantiate everything Fastow had just told him. He didn't want to leave anything to chance.

Rick Buy was behind his desk, acting aloof. It was two days later, October 25, and Mintz was questioning him about LJM. Buy struck Mintz as torn: convinced the deals were good for Enron while plagued by doubts about the wisdom of using the funds.

Buy explained that a lot of the analysis on the LJM deals was handled by Dave Gorte, in Risk Assessment and Control. For a few minutes, he discussed the economics of the transactions. He paused, glancing away.

"I don't know," he said. "What a great deal Andy's got for himself here." He looked back at Mintz. "In fact, he's sort of talked to me about going over there, joining LJM. I may do it. I don't know."

Mintz sat motionless. Buy, one of the people charged with reviewing the fairness of LJM deals, *had been approached about working there*? Just *making* the offer deepened the conflict. Wasn't anybody bothered by all of this?

Jeff McMahon couldn't stop laughing.

It was the next morning at 10:30. Mintz had just walked into McMahon's office for a briefing about his experiences with LJM during his time as treasurer. McMahon communicated his thoughts fast, breaking into laughter before Mintz said a word. Mintz understood immediately. McMahon hadn't joined the cult. He could skip the political niceties.

"Jeff," Mintz said, "what the fuck is this LJM stuff all about?"

McMahon broke up again. "Well, you've got your hands full now that you've gone over to the dark side."

"What do you mean?"

"Fastow, Kopper, and that group. Never a dull moment." McMahon sighed. "It's a real conflict. And fucking Andy is so blind he doesn't even recognize he's got a problem. People are afraid to talk about it."

He paused. He wasn't laughing anymore. "Andy knows he's got everybody by the balls," he said. "Buy just rubber-stamps those deals, and Andy rolls right over him. Andy's trying to get our bankers to invest with him and holding out a threat that they might lose Enron business if they don't. And Causey's in a big dilemma because, at the end of the day, he's responsible for the financial statements, and LJM helps make the numbers."

It was, in short, a disaster waiting to happen. And McMahon blamed Skilling for the whole problem.

"I think Skilling's just afraid to get rid of assets," he said. "He wants it both ways. So here we have LJM, and it's the perfect situation. We can sell it to them and later, if we want, maybe buy those assets back."

McMahon gave Mintz a brief course on the intricacies of the relevant accounting rules. "What you've got to understand here is, with these deals, now Enron is just a holding company," McMahon said. "We're not an operating company anymore. We just take investments and sell them."

In just thirty minutes, Mintz's worst fears had been validated. He had been in his new job for ten days.

Later that day, outside a meeting room at the Ritz-Carlton in Palm Beach, Florida, Skilling was shouting. He was in town for the LJM2 investor conference and was set to be introduced for his presentation in a few minutes.

He had arrived about an hour before and had found an executive from New Power there to make his own presentation. Enron and New Power were in the middle of a dispute, and Skilling decided to take care of it right there and then. After the initial blowup, things calmed down as the two men began negotiating an agreement.

In the midst of the bargaining, the door opened. Time for Skilling's talk. He walked to the front of the room and for twenty minutes described Enron's accomplishments and expectations. After a few questions, he headed out the door and returned to the airport. He missed hearing Fastow brag about LJM2's stellar performance over the past year.

The numbers were staggering. LJM2 projected returns of 69 percent, exclusively from transactions tied to Enron. If any real third party had cut deals with Enron that generated profits like that, company executives would have hung their heads. But Fastow beamed as he reviewed the results. After all, the third party walking away with the cash was his fund.

The breakdown of investments showed that big payoffs came from a handful of deals. For most of the others, the returns were almost run-of-the-mill. The fiber purchase from Broadband, for example, was expected to yield 18 percent. But the Raptors were off the charts. Projected returns for Raptor I were 193 percent. Raptor II, 278 percent. And Raptor III? A nice, round 2,500 percent.

His investors had put up $437 million. They could expect profits of almost $345 million. Soon.

The next day, October 27, Mintz saw Dave Gorte, the analyst who examined the LJM2 deals. Gorte seemed almost laid-back about the process.

"When things go into LJM, the prices aren't wildly out of line with the market or anything," Gorte said. "But these are tough transactions to review, because we're moving so many assets off the balance sheet."

"Do we care about whether a particular sale is the best option?" Mintz asked.

Gorte shook his head. "No. We probably should. But we just look at whether the deal is fair on its own. We don't necessarily compare it with other deals."

Mintz took a mental note. Gorte was unknowingly contradicting Fastow's assurances that LJM2 was never anything other than the buyer of last resort.

"But a third party would take too long," Gorte continued. "We just want to get comfortable that the deal passes the smell test."

Mintz asked how the assumptions from finance that were used to justify the deals were reviewed. "We don't usually test the assumptions," Gorte said. "But we need to."

Mintz left the meeting convinced that McMahon was right. The vaunted review of LJM2 deals was a rubber stamp.

What did the accountants think about this?

In his interviews, Mintz was hearing lots of things that made him question how the numbers were being counted; Enron, he had heard, was even buying back assets it had sold to LJM2. That alone might suggest the sales should never have been counted as revenue. Still, he couldn't shake the notion that his lack of accounting experience was creating unnecessary doubt. Maybe the accountants could explain why LJM made sense.

So he visited Causey on October 30. For a few minutes, Mintz ran down the list of people he had spoken with in his efforts to understand LJM. "Now, obviously, you're a very important person in this process," Mintz said. "But I want a better understanding of your role."

Causey described briefly how he reviewed the transactions. Then he gave them a ringing endorsement.

"This is a win-win for the company," he said. "We sell assets to LJM; we're not going to buy the assets back. So we get them off our balance sheet."

Not buy assets back? But Mintz had just learned that assets *were* repurchased. He mentioned what he heard.

"I don't know anything about that," Causey replied.

A eureka moment. It suddenly struck Mintz as so obvious. The executives entrusted with reviewing all of the LJM transactions—Causey, Buy, the board—approached their duties casually, giving everything just the once-over. They seemed to figure that somebody else was doing the tough analysis. But no one was.

"Where does Andersen stand on this?" Mintz asked.

"We've got to manage Arthur Andersen in the process," Causey said. "They don't love it, but they don't see anything wrong with it."

He shrugged. "So long as we keep making the disclosures they require, they'll sign off on it."

The lawyers working with the trading group returned to Portland on November 3, ready for more interviews. Sanders surveyed the traders assembled in a conference room.

"Now, about those strategies we discussed," he said to the traders. "We're not doing those anymore, right, guys?"

Belden looked sheepish. "Yeah, we're not."

The calming air of twilight had arrived, and Skilling watched as the woods darkened behind Rebecca Carter's house. The two were on the back deck, enjoying cigarettes while Skilling talked about his desire to get out of Enron.

"Why can't I leave now?" he asked.

There were plenty of good people who could take over. The biggest problems were under control, he said. Azurix, International—even California. But Carter disagreed.

"You can't leave now, Jeff," she said. "The company needs you too much. Ken is getting ready to leave, there's nobody to step into your shoes. You have to stay."

Skilling puffed on his cigarette. All right, he wouldn't leave. Not yet.

"What the hell happened? I thought we had everything worked out!"

It was November 5, and Joe Berardino, the Andersen managing partner who had been working with Levitt on the industry compromise on consulting, was calling the SEC from Europe. He had played diplomat for weeks and thought an agreement had been struck. But at the last minute, Levitt had gambled badly, telling the other firms that the compromise was not open for debate, take it or leave it. They left it.

The proposal had been pretty much half a loaf for everybody. Some of the most lucrative consulting deals would still be allowed, but the size of the payments for non-audit services would have to be disclosed. The firms could even continue handling internal audits, so long as no company used them for more than forty percent of the work.

The sticking point proved to be the part Levitt considered the most important. The compromise required accounting firms to be independent, both in fact and in appearance. Three of the five big firms weren't willing to accept the "appearance" standard, believing it was too vague.

With word of the breakdown, Berardino started his diplomacy again, pushing until a majority of the industry accepted the appearance provision. Meanwhile, Levitt hit the phones. Eventually everyone agreed to a deal except Philip Laskaway, chairman of Ernst & Young.

Levitt called Laskaway, urging him to join his colleagues. The Ernst & Young general counsel, who was also on the line, argued against the proposal.

Tired and frustrated, Levitt lost his patience. "Be quiet!" he shouted at the general counsel. The call went silent.

"Philip, do I have your support or not?" he asked.

There was a pause of several seconds. "I think it's in the best interest of the profession to get a deal done," Laskaway said. "You have our support."

On November 15, Levitt stood in his conference room surrounded by agency staff. The final rules on auditor independence had just been adopted by the commission. He raised a plastic glass filled with champagne.

"This is a great achievement," he told the troops. "Everyone here has so much to be proud of."

He went around the room, singling out people for their contributions to the effort. Levitt felt happy, but not fully content. The rules were not as good as he had hoped. They didn't completely fix the problem. But the accounting industry's argument that the SEC hadn't been able to produce a smoking gun—a case that showed unequivocally that a firm's lack of independence had allowed a client to go too far—had won the day.

As he sipped his champagne, Levitt was torn. He believed the markets had just been made better. But in his heart he knew the era of accounting scandals was not over. Not by a long shot.

There was something wrong at Enron. Jim Chanos, the New York short seller, was willing to bet money on it.

Over a little more than a month, Chanos and his analysts had examined Enron's filings and discovered plenty. Despite its aggressive accounting, Enron had only a seven percent return on its invested capital—a sign of lots of bad business decisions. That was so low that, given what he calculated as Enron's cost of capital, Chanos wasn't even sure if Enron was earning money at all.

But the truly bizarre mother lode turned up in Enron's third-quarter filing. The company was doing deals with entities that Enron said were run by some senior officer it didn't identify. Chanos and his staff reviewed everything they could about the deals but couldn't decipher the impact that they had on Enron's reported financials.

Still, Chanos saw enough. In November, his firm began making its big bet that Enron's stock price would fall.

In Portland, Christian Yoder visited Stephen Hall, the lawyer he hired from Stoel Rives. Yoder was beginning to fear Enron's top management had no idea about the trading problems in California. Something needed to be done to get their attention. Hall had been assigned to understand the trading strategies; that was the opening he seized.

"Steve, I want you to write down everything you've got," he said. "I need it for upper management."

The examination of Enron Energy Services, or EES, that was begun the previous April by Wanda Curry and her team of accountants had turned up a financial house of horrors. The division had a small trading desk to hedge price risks on the long-term contracts it offered customers, but Lou Pai had allowed the desk to take a speculative bet on power prices. While wholesale set up positions to profit if prices rose, retail was betting they would fall. And retail was wrong, leaving it with huge losses.

But the troubles in EES weren't limited to trading. Customer deals were a disaster, too. The full values of contracts were reported under mark-to-market accounting, using what the accountants found to be wildly optimistic assumptions. An analysis of just thirteen contracts showed a discrepancy of $200 million between the reported earnings and what Curry believed were their actual value.

Chaos and disorganization ruled the day in EES. That fall, an employee discovered trays full of envelopes under a desk. Inside were checks—hundreds and hundreds of checks—from utility companies trying to pay their bills to Enron. All told, the slips of paper being treated like EES garbage had a value of about ten million dollars.

The division couldn't even cash its checks properly.

Jim Derrick, Enron's general counsel, templed his fingers in front of his mouth, contemplating the words he was hearing. It was November 20, and the lawyers from the wholesale division—Richard Sanders and Mark Haedicke—were in Derrick's office, spelling out everything they had learned about the California trading schemes.

Sanders listed the sophomoric names that the traders gave the strategies, without detailing the nitty-gritty of how they worked. Derrick listened silently until Sanders finished.

"What sort of causes of action do you think people can bring against us because of these?" he asked.

"Potentially antitrust violations," Sanders said. "Some of the strategies I'm not too worried about. But I am worried about the congestion-management strategies."

Derrick thought about that for a moment. "Do we have the right lawyers to defend us in the lawsuits?" he asked.

The first complaint would be filed nine days later. But even then, Derrick never mentioned anything to Lay or Skilling about what he had learned.

On the afternoon of November 27, Mintz was at his desk when the phone rang. Fastow's name flashed on caller ID.

"Hey, Andy."

"Jordan, hey. Just wanted to let you know the board approved LJM3."

Mintz scribbled "LJM3" in his schedule. *Another one?* He didn't know that board approval had come weeks ago.

"Kirkland & Ellis is working on the private-placement memorandum," Fastow continued. "Call them, they'll give you a copy to look at. But basically, it's out the door."

Mintz drew an asterisk next to the name "LJM3." He would have to move fast.

Later that day, Mintz was leaning on his desk, his eyes gliding across the words in the LJM3 offering documents. On page 2, he stopped. *That can't be right.*

He read the sentence again. Fastow was telling investors that they would profit from his access to proprietary deal-flow data from Enron. In effect, he was putting Enron's inside information up for sale. Mintz grabbed a copy of the LJM2 memorandum and discovered the same bold claim. Any Enron investors who saw this would go nuts; it was *their* confidential corporate information that Fastow was selling.

Mintz rubbed his face. Plenty of lawyers had reviewed this. It *must* be okay. After all, it was all being disclosed, right up front. But, still . . .

How are we getting away with this? How can they ever be comfortable saying it?

At five on the afternoon of December 5, Governor Gray Davis stood beside a fifty-six-foot Christmas tree towering above the Capitol's rotunda floor. He looked out at the eager faces of the festive holiday crowd. The First Lady, Sharon Davis, took the hand of seven-year-old David Almberg and helped him push a small button. Power flowed to the four thousand lights strung around the white fir tree.

The seventieth annual lighting of the California Christmas tree was a welcome reprieve from the sense of emergency that permeated the state, but it was only temporary. At 5:35, the electrical grid was under renewed strain. The Governor quietly pressed the "off" button, and the tree went dark. The crowd wandered away in silence.

Mintz finished his full review of the LJM3 offering documents on December 6. This, he decided, was the means to bring the LJM problems to everyone's attention. He would write a memo to Causey and Buy. And to some of the other lawyers, too—Rex Rogers in the general counsel's office, Ron Astin over at Vinson & Elkins.

It wouldn't be hysterical, just a sober rendering of the facts. But that should be enough. The powers that be at Enron, he had concluded, just hadn't focused on what Fastow was doing. His memo would change that. The simple facts would set off a panic at the top. He was certain of it.

That same day in Portland, Stephen Hall was in the offices of Stoel Rives, heading for the office of his boss, Marcus Wood. He had finished his memo about the Enron trading strategies and wanted to run it by Wood, the firm's top energy specialist. Wood reviewed the document and decided it needed to be tougher. By the time the two finished, each sentence had been made more devastating than the last:

"The new effect of these transactions is that Enron gets paid for moving energy to relieve congestion without actually moving any energy or relieving any congestion . . . By knowingly increasing the congestion costs, Enron is effectively increasing the costs to all market participants . . . This strategy has produced profits of approximately $30 million."

The message couldn't be missed. Enron had big trouble.

Once they printed out the memo on Stoel Rives letterhead, Hall and Wood walked the three blocks to Enron's Portland office to meet with Yoder. The Enron lawyer's name was included on the document as one of the writers, and they wanted him to review it before sending it out.

Yoder studied the document, a bit uncomfortable. *It's on Stoel Rives letterhead, and I'm listed as an author?* He thought about it for a moment. He was involved in this. His name would give the memo more force.

"Okay," Yoder said. "Let my name be on there."

Later that day, Richard Sanders read the memo, scarcely able to contain his anger. No one had consulted him, or had even told him this was coming. Here was this document, laying out suggestions that Enron had violated the rules—written while the company was being sued!

He went to see Haedicke, who was even more furious. He thought the analysis was wrong and the memo dangerous.

"Collect every copy," he told Sanders.

Yoder held the phone to his ear, listening as Haedicke shouted. "What the hell were you thinking, Christian? Why put this on paper without consulting anyone first?"

The whole idea had been to brief everyone, Yoder replied, so they could understand the situation.

"Look, I accept that," Haedicke replied. "We always need to develop a factual understanding of the issues. But not like this! I'm really upset this memo was produced."

"Well . . ."

"Plus, I think there are some factual inaccuracies here. And it sure might be dangerous to our strategy to have something in writing that might not be right!"

After the call ended, Yoder was still glad he had sent the memo up the line to Houston; at least now everyone was sure to know what had happened in California. But he would never hear anything about it from top officers again. It was as if no one in senior management even knew that the memo existed.

The next day, December 7, Jordan Mintz sat in front of his computer screen, reading the final draft of his memo on LJM3. No one, he felt sure, could miss his message.

He opened by describing how documents for LJM3 were about to go out, with wording that closely mimicked those from the LJM2 offering. But certain elements deserved particular attention, Mintz wrote. The discussion of LJM3 as an attractive investment because of its access to Enron's proprietary deal flow. The inside knowledge that allowed Fastow and Kopper to evaluate assets. The board's waiver of the code of conduct.

After a final read through, Mintz e-mailed the draft to Rex Rogers in the general counsel's office and Ron Astin at Vinson & Elkins, hoping for their input before he sent the memo to Causey and Buy. He figured the lawyers would come running, eager to fix all of the issues he had found.

They didn't. So Mintz arranged a conference call. The three got on the phone that day. "So, about my memo," Mintz said. "Did you take a look at it?"

Rogers replied. "Yeah, the description about the board waiving the code of conduct isn't wholly accurate," he said. "Actually, the board just found that Enron's interests wouldn't be harmed by the conflict. But the private-placement memorandum is already out, so we'll just issue a supplement correcting that."

Mintz paused. "Well," he said, "aren't we concerned about this other language, and what it says?"

"It's not a problem," Astin replied. "It's no different than what was in LJM2, and that was approved."

Mintz couldn't get out of his chair. Were these two afraid to get in front of a political train? Was he crazy? He typed Rogers's comments into the memo, then printed it out for Causey and Buy, sending it to them that day.

He never heard back from either of them.

Five days later, on December 12, Lay looked around the packed Enron boardroom, taking in the moment. The directors had been meeting for hours, and now, at 12:30, everybody was ready for lunch. There was one thing left to do.

"All right," Lay said. "I'm calling for an executive session. So if everybody else could please head on out."

Skilling, Fastow, Causey, and nine other executives left the room. Lay waited until the door closed behind them. He took a moment to glance around the conference table at his directors. His friends.

"I think we should formally discuss the issue of succession and have a final vote," he began.

Fifteen minutes later, Skilling arrived in a dining room on the fiftieth floor mezzanine, where the Enron directors were enjoying a light lunch. As he stepped in, the directors stood and applauded. Lay approached and shook his hand.

"Well, Jeff," Lay said, "I'd like to let you know the board has unanimously decided that they want you to be the next CEO of the company, effective in February."

Lay turned to face the directors. "And I think we're all looking forward to the excitement that you're going to be able to create around here," he said.

Everyone clapped again.

The next night, Skilling was in Dallas, alone on a business trip and consumed by depression.

Wow, he thought. *I just made CEO.*

He was exhausted. Feeling lousy, sorry for himself.

Is this what he wanted? There just wasn't really any magic to it. He had basically been running the place for years. Now he had to keep doing it, just hanging on, handling the same old complaints, the same old problems.

He wandered into the hotel bar. He needed a drink.

CHAPTER 15

JORDAN MINTZ SAT AT his desk in shirtsleeves, his sports jacket hanging nearby on a coat rack. It was the morning of December 15, 2000, and he had just ended a call about Fishtail, a new LJM2 deal designed to create about $100 million in profits. The transaction struck Mintz as aggressive, and he was checking to make sure proper procedures were being followed. He opened the files to check the deal-approval sheet. It wasn't there.

From his examination of the old files, Mintz already knew the approval sheets were a big problem. They were supposed to contain loads of information to allow reviewers to decide whether an LJM deal was good for the company. But often the details in them were skimpy at best.

Mintz wandered out of his office, over to Nicole Alvino, a lower-level staffer who had been given responsibility for managing the approval-sheet process. Standing by her cubicle wall, he asked her to come to his office for a moment. There, the two sat down on either side of his desk.

He threw out a series of questions. Who told her how to prepare the sheets? Why were they put together so late in the process? Was there some other way that the necessary data were communicated? Alvino didn't have a lot of answers.

"I've been reviewing some of the old sheets," Mintz said. "Some of them have lots of detail, some don't."

"Well," Alvino replied, "people are always sensitive when they prepare these."

"What do you mean?"

"About how much detail to put in, because of the awkwardness from the related-parties issue."

Mintz sat back. So now the LJM deals, the ones that should have the *most* review, were getting the least.

"The way it's been done," Alvino continued, "is we include enough information to answer the checklist attached to the approval sheet. That's been the general practice, to keep the information to the minimum necessary."

The minimum necessary. Mintz remembered Fastow's telling him how important it was that the public disclosure of the facts about LJM deals be as innocuous as possible. Everything was secretive. The worst approach imaginable.

Mintz wrote a memo about his conversation with Alvino and sent it around. But he knew it would barely register in Enron's collective consciousness. He needed to do something more dramatic, to marshal all the evidence into a single document that would startle management out of its lethargy.

It would take almost three months to complete.

Andersen's accounting team was flummoxed by Fishtail, the latest LJM2 deal. A J. P. Morgan Chase entity would be listed as an "investor," even though it wasn't putting up any cash; the only up-front money would come from LJM2. This one went past the edge of the envelope.

Needing help, the accountants turned to the Professional Standards Group. The questions landed on the desk of Carl Bass, who had joined the PSG months before.

Bass plunged into the documents, getting progressively more disturbed. With only LJM2 ponying up the money, nobody had enough skin in the game for Fishtail to be counted as a true off-balance-sheet entity. If nothing else, LJM2 had to put up more cash, eight million dollars.

He called Duncan and let him know. And unknowingly upended his career.

Eight million dollars! The verdict came as a shock to the Enron executives involved in the deal. Somehow, they had gotten the idea that Andersen had signed off on Fishtail and already closed the deal. Now everyone had to restart negotiations and extract more money out of Fastow's fund.

Fastow was furious. He complained to Causey, who told him not to worry. He would take care of everything.

Carl Bass closed his eyes as he pinched the bridge of his nose. He was on the telephone with Deb Cash, an Andersen partner on the Enron account, venting about the company's latest accounting horror.

It involved another off-books deal, this one called Braveheart. Enron had decided that its video-on-demand agreement with Blockbuster could be partially sold to a partnership. But the Enron-Blockbuster relationship was struggling. Each side bickered that the other wasn't living up to its end of the agreement. They held everything together by striking a deal in December that prevented the arrangement from being terminated until March 2001.

All of that made Braveheart shaky enough. Worse, Bass thought, there wasn't a real business here, just a test market. But Enron wanted to use that as the basis of a sale to bring in more than $100 million in revenues. The only way that could be done, Bass ruled, was by getting an independent appraisal, showing that the value was there.

As Bass complained about the Braveheart deal, he mentioned that one of the outside investors in the off-books partnership was Canadian Imperial Bank of Commerce.

"You know," Cash said, "we found a side agreement on another Enron deal with CIBC. They gave them a letter protecting the bank's equity interest."

Bass sat up. "Really?" he said.

This was big. If Enron guaranteed the investment by CIBC, then *Enron* was at risk in the deal, not the bank. In truth, there were no outside investors, just a bank willing to be a front for Enron itself. This violated every rule.

"What did you do about it?" Bass asked.

"Well, they fixed it."

Bass snickered. "How do you fix that? They made the offer. How do you make sure they took it away?"

"It shouldn't have happened," Cash said. "They just made a mistake."

That same week, Bass was on a conference call with Duncan and some other Andersen partners, thrashing through Project Braveheart one more time.

"Listen, I want to ask," Bass said. "I understand from Deb that there was some side agreement in another CIBC deal protecting their equity. Are we sure we don't have that happening here, too?"

Duncan bristled. "You've got your facts wrong, Carl. That wasn't the case."

Bass was about to speak.

"Anyway," Duncan said, "it got fixed."

Bass hardly knew what to say. *It hadn't happened, but it was fixed.*

In fact, it wasn't. The original side deal survived Andersen's discovery. And Bass was right: Fastow had provided the same guarantee to CIBC in Braveheart.

On a morning in December, Skilling looked up from a report as Causey walked into his office. He placed the document on his desk and headed over to his conference table, ready to review the problems in California.

For the last couple of days, Skilling had been hearing lots of bad news about the state. He had learned about how EES had taken a position in the California markets and been clobbered. Worse, he had been told Enron was facing growing financial exposure to Pacific Gas and Electric or Southern California Edison—two giant utilities in the state—which his executives were sure would soon implode.

The utilities not only were slow in paying their bills; the wild market had triggered a quirk in the rules, transforming a fee that Enron was supposed to pay into something the *utilities* were supposed to pay to *Enron*. And the amounts owed just kept growing as Enron did business with its own retail customers in the state.

"This is ridiculous," Skilling said. "We've got to take care of this." They took two steps quickly. First, Enron put its electricity customers back on the California grid, essentially handing them over to the utilities. That would eliminate payments owed by the utilities to Enron.

Still, that didn't eliminate the danger from the utilities' all-but-certain bankruptcy. If that happened with them owing Enron huge sums, all of those earnings would be put in limbo. Skilling wanted to be able to say that, no matter what, California would not affect the company. He and Causey made a decision. They would squirrel away Enron's California profits in an accounting reserve. More than one billion dollars, never reported as income. If everything worked out, they could dip into the reserve later and report the earnings then. Enron not only would be protected from the possible bankruptcies but would be well on its way to meeting budget targets for next year.

Besides, the way Skilling figured it, Enron didn't need the earnings now. It wasn't like there were huge losses in the company that needed to be offset.

The hundreds of millions of dollars in losses hidden by the Raptors just kept climbing. The temporary fix from two months before—the costless collar—hadn't solved the problem. Enron's share price had fallen below eighty-one dollars, so now the company was funneling cash into Raptor I. Even so, the two troubled Raptors—the first and the third—were underwater, with less capital than they owed. But the other two—Raptor II and Raptor IV—were still in decent shape.

Causey and the accountants pondered the problem. If two were fine and two weren't, could the healthy ones support the sickly ones? Fastow hated the idea. After all, profits from the strong Raptors might be available later for LJM2. But there was no time to argue. If the problem wasn't solved, even temporarily, by December 31, Enron would have to report losses from the two sickly Raptors.

The accountants cobbled together a plan. They would allow the strong Raptors to guarantee the obligations of the weak ones—but only for forty-five days. That would carry Enron past December 31 and allow them to avoid disclosing the festering problems. Then they would have until the end of the next quarter to find a permanent solution. But just to make sure Fastow went along with the idea, Enron paid fifty thousand dollars to LJM2 for letting the arrangement go through.

All they needed now was the go-ahead from Andersen.

"Dave, that doesn't work at all," Carl Bass said. "It doesn't even make sense."

Bass was flanked by David Duncan and Michael Odom, the practice director for Andersen's Houston office. They had gathered in Odom's office to discuss Enron's request to place its forty-five-day Band-Aid on the Raptors. All three were frustrated. Duncan and Odom wanted to give the okay; Bass could barely keep from shouting at them.

An assistant walked in. "Rodney Faldyn's on the phone. He wants to know if you've made any progress on this."

Bass knew the name. Faldyn was an Enron accountant. They were really pushing hard. "I'm still talking to Carl about it," Duncan replied. "We'll have an answer soon."

Bass stared at him. *We have an answer.*

"I don't see why this can't work, Carl," Duncan said.

Bass set his jaw as he started to speak. "Dave, it's just a silly gimmick," he replied.

"But . . ."

"Look, suppose I default on the mortgage on my house," Bass said. "Even if I convince the bank not to call my note for forty-five days, I can't go tell everybody I'm okay on my mortgage. I'm not. I'm in default."

Duncan sighed. "That's not the same thing, Carl."

"It *is* the same thing. They want to push off reality for forty-five days. But they can't. It's still reality."

"Then what can they do?"

Bass closed his eyes, irritated. He had already been through all this with another member of the accounting team. He had been planning to cut out early this day, to take his kids ice-skating. Instead, he had to keep going over the same ground because Enron didn't like the answers.

"The only option they have is a true cross-collateralization," he said. "Turn the Raptors from four pools of capital into one. But that means having a substantive, binding legal agreement among the four entities, combining their obligations."

Bass knew Enron would hate this answer, but he didn't care. He was tired of these accounting perversions. Enron wanted to report profits it didn't deserve, and make real losses vanish. That just couldn't be done.

He finished his explanation of a cross-collateralization. "But who's going to do that?" Bass asked. "Why would one Raptor give up its value to another?"

The assistant returned. "Dave, Rodney Faldyn's on the phone again."

Days later, Duncan printed out a draft memo for the files about Raptor. He reviewed its three pages carefully. The second-to-last paragraph was the most important. It described a negotiated agreement allowing the forty-five-day cross-guarantee among the Raptors. Andersen, the memo said, concluded that the arrangement worked.

"We discussed this conclusion with the Professional Standards Group (PSG)," the memo read, "who concurred with our conclusion."

It wasn't true. Carl Bass and other members of the PSG had told the Enron team in no uncertain terms that the arrangement couldn't be done. But Duncan and the practice directors in Houston had simply overruled them.

In a meeting room down from his Washington office, Alan Greenspan, the Federal Reserve chairman, took a seat at the head of the conference table. To his left sat Lawrence Summers, the Treasury Secretary, and a few staffers. On the right was Gray Davis, the California Governor who had flown in that day, December 26, to discuss his state's power crisis with the country's two most influential economists.

"Mr. Chairman, Mr. Secretary, thank you for meeting with me. I'm hoping that we can find some solutions to the troubles facing my state. The thing is, if deregulation fails in California, it will fail in the United States."

Greenspan placed his hand on a thick briefing book in front of him. He and Summers had met privately minutes before and decided to throw a splash of cold water on Davis. The man needed to understand there were limited answers to California's problems, all of them unpleasant.

"Truthfully, Governor, California hasn't deregulated," Greenspan said. "The state simply replaced one form of regulation with another. It's become a system of central planning run amok."

Summers joined in. "You have a fixed price set by the state for selling electricity to the public. But you have a variable, floating price when you buy electricity."

"That's not sustainable," Greenspan said. "The problem is your regulatory system. And there are a very limited number of solutions. But the first step is that prices for consumers are going to have to go up."

Davis showed no emotion. "I really feel the problem is the energy producers," he said. "They're manipulating the markets and forcing up prices."

"They may be," Greenspan said. "But that's beside the point. That's not *causing* the problem; that's making it worse. The real problem is a supply-and-demand imbalance."

Davis objected. There was plenty evidence, he said, that energy producers were withholding power from the market. Greenspan and Summers didn't argue the point, stressing that it made economic sense for power to be withheld. The utilities weren't making good on their bills already. With the utilities now careening toward bankruptcy, it would be folly for power companies to keep pumping electricity into the state without limits. It would just increase their exposure to the likely bankruptcies.

Gently, the two economists suggested that the state government hadn't helped matters. By attacking power companies, accusing them of crimes and refusing to meet with them, Davis and other politicians had signaled an unwillingness to deal with the structural problems. In a market, perceptions could be as important as reality. Until California took a more realistic approach, power companies would continue to be reluctant to do business with the state.

"Governor," Summers said, "this is classic supply and demand. The only way to fix this is ultimately by allowing retail prices to go wherever they have to go."

Davis's face hardened. He didn't like being lectured from the ivory tower. "Fine," he said. "You two live in your world of economics, supply and demand and pricing."

He leaned in. "Let me tell you about my world," he said. "About California politics. About referendums, where anybody with enough signatures can take a ballot initiative to the voters and overrule anything that we're doing."

Greenspan and Summers listened as Davis laid out his political dilemma. The words made it obvious that the power problems in California would become much worse. Economics and politics were in conflict. And for now, politics would rule.

Two days later, a black sedan pulled to the front of the Ronald Reagan State Office Building in downtown Los Angeles. Ken Lay emerged from the back, followed by Steve Kean, his chief of staff and Enron's government-relations specialist. They had interrupted their vacations for this quick trip to California to meet with Gray Davis.

Lay and Kean headed to the fifteenth floor and were taken to the Governor's conference room. After a couple of minutes, Davis came in and walked to Lay, who put out a hand.

"Governor, I'm Ken Lay."

"Good to meet you, Ken."

Davis sat at the head of the table, while Lay and Kean took seats on one side, across from a member of the Governor's staff. "Governor," Lay began, "as you know, Enron is a major participant in the California market. And clearly the state has some serious problems."

Lay broached the next subject cautiously. He understood the politics and—Republican though he was—suggested that Davis shift the blame for all the troubles onto his Republican predecessor.

"Governor, you didn't cause this problem; you inherited it," he said. "But you can solve it by giving the state true competition and consumer choice."

The advice he gave could have come out of the mouths of Greenspan and Summers. Supply had to be increased and demand cut, he said. The market had to see the state was serious. Announce plans to build power plants, with temporary waivers from environmental regulations. Allow for pricing models that would result in lower costs during nonpeak hours. Then let the consumers feel the effects of higher prices, in order to change behaviors.

"I can't do that," Davis said sharply. "I'm not going to raise rates."

"Governor," Lay said, "it's going to be very difficult to get consumers acting rationally if they're paying five cents a kilowatt hour for electricity that costs twenty-five cents."

If Davis took those steps, Lay said, prices would ultimately drop. Then the state could enter into long-term fixed contracts and never face this problem again.

Couldn't happen, Davis said. And he couldn't suspend the environmental rules. Voters wouldn't stand for it.

The conversation dragged on. Davis tossed out a few ideas he was considering—orchestrating state takeovers of power plants, invoking emergency powers. Lay cautioned the market would react terribly to such moves, and again stressed that he had to address supply-and-demand issues. At the meeting's end, Lay left confident Davis was ready to act decisively, one way or the other.

Enron wanted to close the chapter on the Azurix mess. It went to the market and offered to repurchase the public shares, making Azurix an Enron division again. It was the best way to lessen the damage from shareholder lawsuits.

The company had arranged to recognize its losses in Azurix and report them in the quarter just ended. But that question got kicked up to Carl Bass, and from what he could tell, the losses should have been reported almost a year earlier. He spoke with David Duncan, reminding him that he had been told many months before that losses had to be taken if the value of an investment fell and stayed low for two or three fiscal quarters. Now eight quarters had passed, without Enron reporting the Azurix disaster. There might be a need for a restatement of prior earnings.

That wouldn't happen. "I never told them the original advice," Duncan said. "I can't go back and do it now."

Cash flow. That was always Enron's Achilles' heel.

No matter how much it stitched together in mark-to-market earnings, it simply couldn't force cash to appear. Sure, it borrowed plenty of money through the complex transactions known as prepays and reported those billions of dollars as cash from operations. But that just pumped up debt without taking care of the real shortfall.

This year, though, would be different. With energy prices in California so high, Enron's trading partners were forced to put up huge amounts of cash as collateral—some two billion dollars by late December. The cash wasn't really Enron's to use; it was more like a security deposit, which the company would probably have to hand back in a few months.

Still, to the untrained eye, the collateral allowed Enron to appear flush. The company reported the two billion dollars as cash flow from operations. If Enron had to return the money when prices dropped, so be it. Its finance team would deal with that later.

In early January 2001, Skilling and Baxter stood on the ground level of an Enron parking garage, smoking. Baxter dropped the butt to the ground, crushing it with his foot. He was cranky and frustrated, like he'd been most days in the months since the end of Project Summer. Every other sales effort had bombed out.

"This is like pushing on a string, Jeff," he said. "I'm not getting anywhere."

"We're going to have to keep plugging," Skilling replied. The international projects had to be sold.

Baxter shook his head. "You don't need *me* to do this," he said. "I'm not having any fun doing this."

He breathed deeply. "Jeff, I think it's probably time for me to go," he said. "I want to spend more time with my family, just do something new."

This can't be, Skilling thought. Baxter was his go-to guy, his smoking buddy, the person he most trusted on deals.

"Cliff, look, I need you," Skilling said. "Don't do this to me now. Go back and rethink this thing."

"I'll think about it," Baxter said. "But I doubt I'm going to change my mind."

Days later, he returned with the news. He would leave in a couple of months. Skilling was devastated.

Appearing stiff, Gray Davis stood in the Assembly chambers at the state Capitol, delivering his third State of the State address.

"We will regain control over the power that's generated in California and commit it to the public good," he said. "Never again can we allow out-of-state profiteers to hold California hostage."

Davis listed a series of hard-nosed solutions: forbidding generators from conducting unscheduled maintenance, making it illegal to withhold power from the grid, expanding his emergency authority, prosecuting evildoers.

"The remedies I am proposing tonight are reasonable and necessary," Davis said. "There are other, more drastic measures I am prepared to take if I have to."

After all the advice from the free-market evangelists, Davis had chosen another path—all-out war.

Rick Causey's voice was icy.

"Enron does not want Carl Bass consulting on anything involving the company anymore," he said.

Steve Goddard, the Andersen partner who had run the Enron accounting team before Duncan, tried to sound conciliatory. "Well, Rick, why don't you tell me what the problem is," he said.

The *problem*? Bass had been an impediment in several deals. He had forced LJM2 to put more cash into Fishtail. He had argued that the video-on-demand venture wasn't a real business yet, and then tried to use that position to stop Braveheart. The man had no creativity, Causey said.

Goddard asked for some time to think about the request. Maybe there was something they could do. Andersen had a new chief executive, Joe Berardino, the man who had forged the rules compromise with Arthur Levitt. He'd be down in Houston in a few weeks. Maybe Andersen's new top diplomat could negotiate a solution with Causey, too.

But if Causey was insistent, there was little doubt what would have to be done. Enron was Andersen's biggest client, paying more than forty-nine million dollars in fees that year, with thirty-five million dollars of those payments from consulting. Clients like that could expect to be kept happy. So if Enron didn't want Carl Bass anymore, Carl Bass would have to go.

In Washington, Dick Cheney, the Vice President–elect, was on the telephone with Ken Lay.

Months of uncertainty had followed the November presidential elections, with the Bush and Gore campaigns fighting it out in court over the razor-thin margins of victory in Florida. Now, with Bush declared the victor, the Administration was assembling its Cabinet.

A number of candidates had already been selected—including Don Evans, the campaign's national finance chairman and an old friend of Lay's, to serve as Commerce Secretary. Lay himself had interest in one particular job, which was why Cheney was on the phone to Houston this day.

"Ken," Cheney said, "I'm sure you know, we've been seriously considering you for Treasury Secretary."

Lay could already tell the news wasn't good.

"The President has decided that with he and Don Evans and I all from Texas, all from the energy business, things were getting too top-heavy. Nominating a fourth person that was in the energy business and from Houston would probably just create too many problems."

"Well, I certainly understand, Dick," Lay replied.

Lay wasn't all that disappointed, though. He didn't lust for Washington. He was happy staying Enron's chairman.

Vince Kaminski, Enron's top risk analyst, examined the data on the latest request out of the finance division with amusement. It was just another bit of foolishness.

For more than a year—since the troubles related to their opposition to LJM—Kaminski's group had basically been ignored by finance. But now that Fastow and his crowd were struggling, they were coming back, trying to get somebody to bail them out of one of the messes they had created.

These silly Raptor structures were the problem. This was LJM all over again, a hedge in name only that offered no real economic protection. And now, with losses from the hedges piling up, the Raptors couldn't cover them. Finance had asked Kaminski's group to analyze what would happen if all of the Raptors were pooled together permanently.

The answer was pretty simple—nothing. Kaminski's analysts concluded that the Raptors were so far underwater that combining them wouldn't help. Plus, because three of them were capitalized with Enron stock, they all had exposure to the same risk. Kaminski contacted finance and let them know their idea wouldn't work. Then he forgot about the Raptors. Surely the losses would just have to be recognized. There was no other logical alternative.

Usually, the final weeks of a presidential Administration are like the last days of high school. Nothing much gets accomplished as years of belongings are packed and people prepare for the next stage of life.

So by early January, with George Bush preparing to move into the White House, members of the Clinton Administration might have been expected to be kicking back. Instead, Treasury officials decided to take one last shot at fixing the California electricity mess. They tried to bring everybody together—the energy producers, the Secretary of the Treasury, the governor—for a final bargaining session.

But Davis refused to return to Washington and rejected efforts to meet halfway in Kansas City or St. Louis. Everyone, Davis said, needed to come to California, but the Clinton Administration officials declined.

Instead, this crucial meeting—the last chance for the Democratic governor to obtain help from a Democratic Administration—would be handled by conference call.

On January 13, a series of officials made their way down a hallway deep in the Energy Department. They were all dressed casually, not surprising for a Saturday. Summers, the Treasury Secretary, led the pack, followed by members of his department. Clinton's National Economic Adviser, Gene Sperling, joined the group, along with an assortment of executives from some of the nation's leading energy companies.

They arrived in a secure room filled with flashing monitors and high-tech communications devices designed for use in a national energy emergency. The government's conference call with Gray Davis was about to begin.

About that same time, Ken Lay, Steve Kean, and Rick Shapiro, a company lobbyist, found seats around a conference table in Davis's Los Angeles office. Lay greeted the other industry executives in the room, including Steve Bergstrom, the president of Dynegy, a top Enron competitor.

The video hookup with Washington was switched on. Larry Summers appeared, sitting at the head of the conference table in the Energy Department's secure room. They could see Sperling from the White House, as well as the rest of the officials, staffers, and executives.

Everyone on the call was ready to get started, but the sound was left on mute. Governor Davis hadn't arrived.

Minutes passed.

In Washington, Summers fumed. He didn't want to sacrifice the weekend with his family waiting around for Davis to show up. He switched on the sound.

"Do we know where the Governor is?" he asked.

A voice responded. "No, but he's expected soon."

Lay watched Summers on the video screen. The answer from the Governor's aide had clearly annoyed him.

He turned to chat with some of the others at the table, then glanced back at the video screen.

Summers was gone.

After five minutes out of the room, Summers walked back in and switched on the sound. "Okay, anybody know where the Governor is?" he asked.

Again, no real answer.

Back in Los Angeles, Lay leaned toward Steve Bergstrom from Dynegy. "If the Governor doesn't show up soon," he said softly, "no matter what we talk about, this isn't going to be a good meeting."

After thirty minutes Davis walked into his conference room. Aides scurried to be sure that the sound was on.

"Okay," Davis said. "Let's go."

He offered no apologies or explanations.

Summers kicked things off, reviewing a series of recent recommendations. Long-term electricity prices needed to be stabilized, the market calmed, so California could enter into long-term power contracts. Announcing plans to temporarily suspend the environmental studies required to build a power plant would be a big step forward.

Some analysis had already been conducted, one industry executive said. The companies agreed that long-term prices could be locked in at just under seven cents per kilowatt hour. That was a little more than a penny above the current mandated retail price. A small rate hike, and the utilities could be back in financial health.

Davis looked straight into the monitor.

"That's all very interesting," he said. "But as I said in Washington, I cannot agree to any rate increase. And no environmental waivers for the power plants."

The energy executives spoke up. They had gone as far as they could. Lay suggested that they dig through the numbers to show how closely everything had been shaved.

On the television screen in Los Angeles, Larry Summers looked like he was about to jump out of his skin.

"Governor," Summers said, fixing his eyes on the screen in front of him, "it appears to me that these guys have done a pretty good job figuring out what the markets will do if the political leaders in California make the tough decisions to get things stabilized."

The numbers were close, and certainly would help circumvent disaster. "We have to do what's doable," he said, "and not just what we want politically."

Lay watched Davis stiffen. *This isn't working.*

"The political reality is that I cannot agree to any rate increase or any environmental waivers," Davis said. "We've got to find some other way to solve the problem."

The answer should be price caps, Davis said. Just knock down the amount that the energy companies could charge. Some of the other state officials in the room agreed.

Summers's voice rang through the room. "Price caps are just something temporary while we put together a bigger packet of reforms. It would distort the market."

The Clinton Administration had allowed California to impose temporary caps, but it would be up to the Bush Administration to decide if those continued. And in the long term, Summers said, they were destructive, because they would push energy producers out of the California market.

The discussion meandered around the table. Neither side would budge. The attitude of some energy-industry executives was almost detached, as if they were indifferent to the prospect of a financial collapse in California.

About thirty minutes had passed. Then, without explanation, Davis abruptly left the room.

With Davis gone, the conversation continued for several minutes. Finally Summers spoke.

"I see the governor hasn't returned," he said. "I think we should suspend the conversation until he does."

Everyone sat in silence for ten minutes. Finally Summers stood, signaling for some of the industry executives to follow him to a nearby anteroom. Sperling from the White House and several Treasury aides followed.

Away from the camera, Summers lectured the energy executives. They couldn't just shrug the crisis off as California's problem. They needed to bend over backward to find a way out. Their business was on the line.

"Do you guys understand the political reality?" Summers asked. "If you don't agree to something that works for California, they are going to come at you with every political and legal gun blazing."

Sperling agreed. "Without some arrangement, they have to come after you. You may think you've done nothing wrong legally. We don't know. But they have to come after you."

The executives objected. They had worked hard to make a deal work, they said, but the Governor refused to budge.

"It doesn't matter!" Summers snapped. "Regardless of whether it's a bad system, or whether they need a price increase. They are going to dig into your companies, upward, left, and right. You're going to be the demons."

In fact, Summers said, if this was handled badly, the prospects for deregulation were going to dim. "The whole trend could go the other way," he said.

One executive started to argue that California's system wasn't real deregulation.

"You're missing the point!" Summers shot back. "What state legislature is ever going to consider deregulation again if this problem isn't solved?"

Davis hadn't returned. Lay caught the eye of Bergstrom from Dynegy and signaled they should head out into the hall. They huddled outside the doorway.

"This is really strange," Bergstrom said.

Lay agreed. "You can't make any progress when one of your principals keeps leaving the meeting."

"I'm not even sure it was worth coming." Bergstrom shook his head. Maybe Davis just wasn't serious. There was all this talk about him as a top contender for the Democratic presidential nomination in 2004; maybe he was just setting up a showdown with the Bush Administration.

"Well, one thing's for sure," Lay said. "He's got a better chance of solving this with these guys than he will with the Bush Administration."

Davis returned about thirty minutes after he had left. Someone told Washington to find Summers, who was still lecturing energy executives off camera. A minute later, Summers returned. He took his seat, furious.

"Governor," he said sharply, "a lot of us here have given up our Saturday afternoon to make progress on this problem. Some of us have commitments tonight. We're willing to keep working if we can make some progress."

He pressed his hands against the table. "But if we can't make any progress, we really shouldn't waste time," he said. "Let's just decide now we're not going to get this solved, certainly not in this Administration's lifetime."

Davis looked unruffled. "Larry, I really appreciate what everybody's trying to do," he said. "But I have made it clear from the beginning that I cannot and will not agree to any solution that increases rates to consumers in California or requires any type of environmental waiver."

He glanced around the room. "And if all of you think that's the only way we can solve this, then we might as well go in a different direction," he said.

The solution was price caps, Davis said again.

In Washington, Summers launched into one final lecture about the evils of price controls. Then he threw in the towel.

"I wonder if, in fact, it's not best to decide that we are not going to solve this problem today, and let everybody go home to be with their families," he said.

On the video screen, Davis appeared calm.

"I think that's right," he said.

The meeting ended, and the video was shut off. Several officials gathered in the anteroom, frustrated and angry. They complained that Davis was too big a stumbling block, seemingly focused on just saving his political skin.

"So if we get to the 2004 Democratic convention and this guy is a serious contender for President," one Treasury official said, "which one of us is going to lead the 'Anybody but Davis' crowd?"

Fastow turned from the two connected computer monitors on the credenza behind his desk and waved his new general counsel, Jordan Mintz, into the office.

"Jordan, hey, thanks for coming up," he said.

It was three days later, January 16. The two men took seats at the conference table. Fastow explained that a board meeting was coming up in a few weeks, and there needed to be a presentation on the LJM funds. Mintz's predecessor used to handle them, Fastow said, recommending that he just follow the established format. Mintz agreed.

Fastow sat back. "We starting work on the proxy?"

Yes, Mintz said. The document sent to shareholders before the annual meeting was about half done. That was a filing that contained many of the disclosures about the LJM deals.

"Okay, good," Fastow said. "Do you know the basis for why my compensation from LJM wasn't disclosed last year?"

He did, Mintz said. The lawyers had concluded that enough transactions were still open that it wasn't practical to reveal Fastow's financial rewards until later.

"That's right," Fastow said. "And I think we can make the same argument this year."

Mintz shifted in his seat. "I don't know if we're going to be able to, Andy," he said. "I've been through the files, and there have been a number of transactions that have already settled."

Fastow argued the point, and Mintz promised to check everything with Ron Astin at Vinson & Elkins and Rex Rogers, the assistant general counsel, who both had extensive knowledge of securities law.

"Okay, fine," Fastow said. "Just get back to me."

Fastow walked over to his desk, checking the markets on his computer screen. After a moment, he turned and headed back toward Mintz, chuckling softly to himself.

"If Skilling ever found out how much I've made," he laughed, "he'd have no choice but to shut down LJM."

Mintz hesitantly joined in the laughter. "Oh, come on, Andy."

Fastow chuckled again and nodded. "No, no. Really."

Minutes later, Mintz was back in his office, typing an e-mail to Rogers and Astin. He explained what Fastow had just said, including the part about Skilling's predicted reaction to the LJM payouts. Then he forwarded the message to Rob Walls in the general counsel's office. Walls, in turn, sent the message to Derrick, Enron's general counsel.

The lawyers all debated the meaning among themselves. Rogers and Astin were skeptical that Fastow's compensation could be calculated. Still, no one tipped off Skilling that Fastow was afraid of what he might learn.

Finally, Astin came in with the final word. He was very comfortable with the previous year's limited disclosure. Fastow's compensation—an amount unknown to the lawyers—could stay secret.

Shortly after that decision, Walls bumped into Astin in the lobby of the Enron building and pushed him again on whether the company was going too far in keeping the information under wraps.

"Look, Ron, I'm not going to stick my neck out for Andy Fastow," Walls said.

"I'm not sticking my neck out," Astin replied. "I am playing it right down the middle."

On January 19, few of Enron's top executives could be found anywhere near the company headquarters. Instead, they were getting ready for the big event that weekend—the inauguration of George W. Bush as forty-third President of the United States. By early that Friday, much of the senior management team was headed out to Houston Intercontinental, ready to stamp Enron's imprint on the new Administration.

That morning, Lay stood beside his wife, Linda, outside the Enron hangar, watching a few black sedans approach. Lay stepped forward as one pulled up nearby. Former President George Bush and his wife, Barbara, got out of the car.

"Mr. President, Barbara," Lay said, "I'm so delighted this worked out. We're just incredibly pleased you're willing to share this time with us."

Bush smiled. "Well, we're pleased that you're going to give us a ride up there."

The Lays and the Bushes climbed aboard the Enron corporate jet and found their seats. Lay felt the moment; here he was, a onetime Missouri farm boy, with a front-row seat to history. This weekend, a former President would be watching his son assume the same high office, and Lay would be witnessing the events through the family's eyes. He commented to the Bushes how incredible it all was to him.

"Well, it's an honor for us to be able to do this, Ken," Bush replied.

"Absolutely, Ken, Linda," Barbara Bush added. "We're just honored you could share this time with us."

The plane taxied out to the runway and was aloft in seconds. Lay chuckled; apparently planes carrying former presidents were cleared more quickly for takeoff.

Corporate planes clogged the skies over Washington, but the Enron jet landed immediately. The Lays and the Bushes stepped off. A stretch limo, complete with police escort, waited on the tarmac. Bush walked to the passenger door. The Lays looked around for their car.

Bush signaled to them. "Linda, Ken, come on, get in here. We've got to go."

The Lays hesitated, then climbed in, figuring they would get a lift to their hotel. As the car moved through Washington, the Bushes chatted about the first event, a Kennedy Center reception hosted by General Motors and its onetime top Washington representative, Andrew Card, who tomorrow would become White House Chief of Staff.

The car pulled up to the front of the arts center. Bush tugged on Lay's arm. "Come in with us," he said.

The Lays hadn't been invited to the party, but they weren't about to turn down a former President. Inside, Card rushed over to greet the Bushes, who gestured toward the Lays. Card thrust out his hand.

"Nice to have you here," he said. "Delighted you brought the President and Barbara here with you."

About that moment, Jeff Skilling and Rebecca Carter stepped out of a black Lincoln Town Car in front of the Library of Congress. Carter's taupe evening gown fluttered in the breeze as Skilling, in black tie, escorted her inside. They handed their invitations to security guards and passed through metal detectors.

The two milled about, chatting with industry executives. Suddenly, a staff person appeared, setting up a thin rope to hold back the crowds. Skilling and Carter were right against it.

The President-elect and his wife appeared in the entryway. Bush walked down the line of supporters, shaking everyone's hand. He reached Rebecca Carter and smiled.

"Mr. President," she said.

"Hey, how are you?" Bush replied, shaking her hand.

A woman shoved her way between Skilling and Carter, and Bush released Carter's hand as he turned to greet the new arrival. Skilling glanced down and raised his eyebrows. Bush was on automatic pilot, his hand still drifting up and down beside Carter. Bush moved on, taking Skilling's hand.

"Mr. President-elect," Skilling said. "Jeff Skilling from Enron."

Bush's smile widened. "Hey!" he exclaimed. "That's a great company!"

The next day, a chilly rain soaked Washington, transforming large portions of the inaugural grounds into slicks of mud. As a biting wind blew, George Bush took the oath of office, then stepped up to the podium.

"I am honored and humbled to stand here," Bush said, "where so many of America's leaders have come before me."

On the great lawn in front of the inaugural platform, Skilling sat in a chair sinking into the ground. He was cold and uncomfortable. His clothes were wet, his cashmere overcoat ruined. Just before the inaugural, he had been in the office of Tom DeLay, the Republican congressman from Texas. He wished he had stayed there, and stayed dry.

He glanced at Carter, who was shivering beside him.

"Isn't this cool?" he said softly. "Aren't you glad we gave money to the Bush campaign?"

Well, he figured, at least he wasn't the only Enron executive who was miserable right now.

Nearby, Ken Lay brought a steaming cup of coffee to his lips, blowing on it lightly. He was sitting with his daughter Elizabeth Vittor in the warmth of Bistro Bis, the restaurant at the Hotel George in downtown Washington. From their linen-covered table, the two stared at the restaurant television, watching Bush deliver his inaugural address.

They had considered attending the inaugural, even had VIP tickets, but it was just too cold. Besides, Lay would see Bush at the White House soon anyway.

Minutes before ten o'clock the next morning, a driver from Carey car service stopped in front of the east gate of the White House. He lowered his sedan window as a guard approached. "Mr. and Mrs. Kenneth Lay," he said.

From the back, the Lays watched as the guard first checked a list, then conducted a quick security inspection of the car. The gate opened, and the sedan pulled around the driveway. Staffers opened both passenger doors, and the Lays stepped out, holding hands as they walked inside. Leaving their coats with a checker, they walked down a hallway into the expansive first floor of the White House.

There was a huge brunch buffet, with eggs, sweet rolls, and muffins for the select group invited to share the new President's first morning meal at the White House. Lay glanced to one side and saw former President Bush at a table with Barbara, enjoying brunch as some of their grandchildren ran along the floor nearby.

The new President's selections for his Cabinet secretaries were scattered about the room: Donald Rumsfeld from Defense, Colin Powell from State, Tommy Thompson from Health and Human Services. Nearby, Lay saw Don Evans, his longtime friend who had just been elevated from the Bush campaign's national finance chairman to the post of Commerce Secretary. He and Linda walked over.

"Don," Lay said, "congratulations on your selection. I know you're going to do a great job."

Evans smiled. "Thank you, Ken. And I want to thank you and Linda for all the strong support you gave George."

Lay basked in the praise.

Minutes later, George and Laura Bush made their way through the hectic swirl of supporters on the main floor of the White House. They wandered into the West Room, shaking hands and accepting congratulations, then moved on to an adjacent parlor. Bush was chatting with some well-wishers when he noticed Ken and Linda Lay walking toward him. He excused himself and moved through the crowds.

"Kenny boy!" Bush exclaimed. "Welcome to the White House!"

Bush shook Lay's hand and gave Linda a hug and a kiss.

"I'm so glad you and Linda are here," Bush said. "I really appreciate everything you've done for Laura and me, and for all the support you've given my campaigns."

"Well, Mr. President, we were proud to play a role."

Mr. President? For Lay, it was such a strange thing to say. This was just good old George.

By noon, the White House brunch had begun to wind down, with most of the guests preparing to return to their lives. A White House staffer found the Lays, with word that former President and Barbara Bush were ready to leave. The Lays walked to an exit where they had agreed to meet before heading back to the airport together. The Bushes arrived, accompanied by the new President and Laura.

All the members of the Bush family hugged, making jokes about the hard part now beginning. The Bush parents headed out the door. The new President shook Lay's hand.

"Take good care of them, Ken," he said gently.

The next afternoon, Jeff Skilling was on a conference call, reviewing Enron's quarterly performance with Wall Street analysts, when suddenly he gagged. He reached for a Diet Coke and took a sip, trying to clear his throat.

"I really apologize," he told the listeners. "I sat outside in the rain in Washington, D.C., watching the inauguration, and I'm really paying for it."

A moment later, Skilling broke into a coughing fit and hit the phone's mute button. He returned, apologizing again. All in all, he said, Enron had experienced another fantastic quarter and was looking forward to a great 2001. "Let me comment for just a minute on California," he said. "The situation in California had little impact on fourth-quarter results. Let me repeat that. For Enron, the situation in California had little impact on fourth-quarter results."

There were several reasons, Skilling said. Enron was not a power generator in California and didn't have significant investments in the state. He mentioned nothing about the billion dollars in California trading profits that Enron had stashed away in accounting reserves.

Later that same week, Linda Lay sat beside her husband on the Enron corporate plane as they traveled to Davos, Switzerland, for the World Economic
Forum. On her lap she held the latest report on the family finances.

"Ken," she said, "I'm really uncomfortable that we have so much debt."

Lay smiled. All the borrowed money didn't matter. They owned plenty of
assets, particularly Enron stock. This was all part of the strategy to diversify
their investments while still holding on to the company's shares.

"Honey, it's really all right," he said. With a net worth upwards of $400
million, he added, having $70 million in debt really wasn't a big deal.

It was to her, Linda retorted. The number bothered her a lot, she said. She
had fretted about the debt before, but this time she seemed more disturbed
by it than usual. Lay thought about his options.

Enron offered Lay and a few other executives short-term lines of credit,
which allowed them to borrow as much as four million dollars at a time. Lay's
stepson and financial adviser, Beau Herrold, had told him that he could use
it to pay some of the bank loans. If necessary, he could repay the company
with Enron stock. When the stock price went up, he could repay his debt
without trouble.

He promised to call Beau and get it taken care of.

After months of betting on the collapse of Enron's stock price, Jim Chanos,
the New York investment manager, was ready to share his research with the
world. Soon a group of other short sellers would gather in Florida for their
first annual "Bears in Hibernation" meeting to swap ideas, and Chanos was
planning to lay out his case against Enron. The more people who knew about
what he had discovered, the faster the stock price would drop and the
quicker his bet would make money.

Of course, there was a better way to get the word out: take the story to
some enterprising journalist. Bethany McLean, a reporter at *Fortune*, seemed
a perfect choice. She would understand the problems Chanos saw.

In several phone calls, Chanos and his chief operating officer, Doug
Millett, pitched her the Enron story. The company, they said, was nothing
more than a hedge fund sitting on top of a pipeline. But despite having the
risks of a high-stakes trader, it had the returns on investment of a car company.

"Would you put your money in a hedge fund earning a seven percent return?" Chanos asked.

Their barbs intrigued McLean. She set to work.

At three on the afternoon of February 2, Mintz appeared in Causey's doorway. For weeks he had watched the finance division do cartwheels to avoid disclosing Fastow's LJM compensation. The time had come to short-circuit the whole effort. Causey was the way to get it done.

The next directors' meeting was ten days away, and some committees had asked for details of Fastow's LJM compensation. Mintz figured that no one could object to making sure the board got what it wanted—from Causey.

Mintz sat across from Causey and explained the work he had been doing on the question of disclosing Fastow's compensation. "I think it's a big number, but Andy's never told me," he said. "From reading the board minutes, it seems the directors want to know what it is."

He watched Causey for a second, then took the plunge.

"So I think it's important for you to make sure it gets before the board how much Andy is making from LJM."

Mintz stopped. He was uneasy telling somebody higher up the corporate ladder how to do his job. Causey nodded.

"Yeah, I understand that's important," he said.

At about that same moment, Fastow was carrying a single sheet of lined paper down a hall on the fiftieth floor. He tapped on the door to Skilling's office and walked inside.

Skilling had been thinking about the compensation issue and had suggested that Fastow review the LJM numbers with him, to be sure they were ready if the board asked about them.

"Okay," Skilling said as he joined Fastow at the conference table, "let's take a look at this."

Fastow showed him the sheet of paper. On one side, it showed his interest in Enron stock and options, assuming a 15 percent return each of the next five years. All told, Fastow's Enron stake would bring in about seventy million dollars in profits. That struck Skilling as reasonable.

On the other side, Fastow had performed the same analysis for LJM. He showed about ten million dollars in profits, assuming a 25 percent annual return over the same period.

Oh, come on. Skilling was skeptical.

"Andy, you're not going to get a 25 percent annual return," he said. "That's ridiculous. It's way too high."

Fastow shrugged. "I don't think we'll make 25 percent either. I'm just trying to be conservative."

Well, Skilling said, there was conservative and there was silly. This number couldn't possibly include expenses. Those had to be subtracted. Skilling ran numbers through his head.

"So what we're talking about, horseshoes and hand grenades, is like two million dollars?" Skilling asked.

Fastow nodded. "Yeah, probably."

Skilling sat back. Two million versus seventy million over five years? Well, nobody could possibly question where Fastow's strongest financial interest lay.

By that point, Fastow's records for the previous tax year had been submitted to his accountant. And the results were nothing like what he had just shown Skilling.

His 2000 income was more than forty-eight million dollars, almost 90 percent of it rolling from the LJM funds. And even that wasn't all of his earnings. The Kopper kickbacks from the RADR deal were still coming in. Of course, no one would be so foolish as to declare blatantly illegal income.

"This will be the easiest year ever," Causey boasted. "We've got 2001 in the bag."

Causey glanced around the boardroom at the dozen or so top accountants from each of Enron's main divisions. He was happy and confident. The huge, billion-dollar-plus reserve Enron had set aside in the fourth quarter was going to be the gift that kept on giving in 2001. The utilities in California were spiraling toward bankruptcy, state politicians seemed incapable of taking decisive action—yet for all that, the impact couldn't possibly hurt Enron.

One accountant, Wanda Curry, wasn't buying into the high spirits. It had been almost ten months since she and her team had been appointed to examine Enron Energy Services, and she had found a breeding ground for overvalued contracts and bad trading bets. By her calculations, EES, a Skilling baby, far from being in the black as it claimed, was losing as much as $500 million.

The meeting ended. Curry waited for the other accountants to leave the room, then approached Causey. "Rick," she began, "we've got some serious problems at EES."

Skilling was infuriated. The losses at EES were intolerable. Lou Pai, the EES chairman, argued that they weren't real losses. The California market had just gone berserk, he said; things would return to normal if they just held on.

The argument was silly. Enron used mark-to-market accounting. These losses would appear in EES's books when the quarter closed. There needed to be drastic action. Pai was shoved aside, given a million-dollar bonus, and put in charge of a new division to oversee the creation of new businesses. To run retail, Skilling brought in a favorite from wholesale, a Canadian trader named Dave Delainey.

Delainey, working with Skilling and Causey, arranged to shift the EES trading book into wholesale. The losses would show up, but only as reduced profits of Enron's most successful division. An announcement of huge EES losses could be avoided. Besides, wholesale was better at trading. They would disclose the change and describe it as an efficiency move. They wouldn't have to mention the losses, they decided.

On the afternoon of February 12, Mintz sat near a giant jar of M&M's in the Enron boardroom, watching as the directors arrived. Fastow had instructed him only hours before to attend the meeting, and he had since rushed home to put on one of his best suits. Now he worried that the corporate bigwigs might wonder why he was here.

The board meetings over the next two days were important. By the end, Skilling would officially take over as Enron's chief executive, and Lay would be just chairman. But Mintz was less interested in corporate succession than in seeing how Causey and the board dealt with the swarming issues about Fastow's LJM compensation.

The outcome was disappointing. Causey made an almost rote presentation about LJM2 to the audit committee. He listed the same controls that had been touted countless times before. He gave a rundown of all the great deals that the fund had made possible. And that was pretty much it.

What about the compensation? Mintz thought. Hadn't he agreed to bring it up? Maybe it would come out in the question-and-answer period. Mintz took a breath and waited.

"All right, thank you, Rick," said Robert Jaedicke, the head of the committee. "Now Mark Koenig is going to review our policies on communicating with analysts."

Nothing about compensation. No questions at all.

The meeting broke, and everyone began to head out. Mintz wandered over to Derrick, Enron's general counsel.

"You know, Jim," he said, "I was really surprised there weren't more questions about LJM."

Derrick smiled. "Our directors have a lot of confidence in senior management," he said.

On the sixteenth floor of the Time & Life building in midtown Manhattan, Bethany McLean, the *Fortune* magazine reporter, was sitting at a desk piled high with spreadsheets and other papers. It was February 13, and she was almost ready to go with her big Enron story. She had spent weeks analyzing the company's financial data and interviewing investment professionals. Now all she needed was a comment from Enron.

That day, Karen Denne from Enron's public-relations office spoke with her boss, Mark Palmer. She had taken the call from McLean but quickly realized this was a topic that needed to be handled higher up the line.

"Mark," Denne said, "you need to give a call to Bethany McLean at *Fortune*."

Palmer sat back in his chair. "What's up?"

"She's doing a story that people think our stock is overvalued. You need to talk to her."

Palmer thanked Denne, getting the number for McLean. He dialed her right away. "Bethany, Mark Palmer from Enron. I understand you wanted to check a story with us. Have you talked with anyone at Enron about this yet?"

No, McLean said. So far, she had relied on Enron's filings and had interviewed an array of people who dealt with the company. Point by point, she described her findings. Palmer didn't like what he was hearing.

Enron, McLean said, was a mind-numbingly complex operation that seemed to gush earnings—but from where, no one knew. The company was a black box, its financial statements impenetrable. Its earnings multiple—the ratio of its stock price to every dollar it earned annually—was more in line with a high-tech star like Cisco Systems than with other trading companies. And, of course, there was that anemic return on invested capital.

This was a tough article. Already Palmer knew that he was going to have to bring Skilling into this.

"Tell you what, Bethany . . ." Palmer began.

The next morning, Skilling stared down at a triangular Polycom speakerphone, anger rising in his voice.

"Enron is *not* a black box," he growled. "It's very simple to model."

As Palmer watched, Skilling delivered his personal treatise on Enron as a moneymaker. It was a logistics company, he said, moving commodities through the infrastructure to customers for the lowest possible price. Mark-to-market accounting created more earnings than cash, he said, but Enron just sold slices of its trading position in prepay transactions. And the off-balance-sheet debt was meaningless, since it mostly related to international and was not money Enron was obligated to repay.

As she listened, McLean grew concerned. Skilling's response was so vehement, she feared she might be mistaken. Was there something she was missing?

Finally, Skilling had enough. "I see where you're going with this," he said.

Writing this article was unethical, he said; McLean didn't understand Enron. She needed to sit down with its accounting and finance experts, he said, and learn about the reality of the company.

"Anyone who is successful, people would like to take them down based on ignorance," Skilling snapped.

With that, the interview ended.

Off the line, Skilling looked at Palmer. He wasn't going to take this. "You get Andy Fastow and Mark Koenig and get up there as fast as you can," he said.

Palmer nodded. Fastow and Koenig, the CFO and the head of investor relations. Skilling was going all out to fight back against the article.

Skilling seethed. "I see what's going on here," he said. "They're trying to take our multiple away."

The next afternoon, Palmer bit into a thick sandwich, scraping the roof of his mouth on a sharp piece of bread crust. He was with Fastow and Koenig at an Au Bon Pain restaurant near the offices of *Fortune*, grabbing lunch and plotting strategy before the showdown with the journalists.

They had flown up that morning on Continental Airlines. But they had been seated in different parts of the plane, making this the first opportunity to discuss their plans for the meeting.

Fastow swallowed a bite of his sandwich.

"The approach I want to take is to just keep going over that Enron is a logistics company," Fastow said. It was exactly like Toyota, he said. Until the rise of the Japanese carmaker, Detroit owned every step of the process in manufacturing cars. But, Fastow said, Toyota just wanted to assemble the best car, so it outsourced all the different pieces, buying the radios, the transmissions, and all the other components from whatever manufacturers made the best ones at the best price.

"We're like that," Fastow said. "We find the best."

Enron was more than a trading firm, he said. The Toyota analogy would get that point across.

After lunch, the three Enron executives arrived at *Fortune*'s sixteenth-floor offices. They were escorted to a windowless, dark conference room normally used for reviewing the magazine's photos. Joining them were McLean and two editors, Joe Nocera and Jim Impoco.

Palmer handled the introductions, then turned things over to Fastow, who expounded on how Enron was diverse and dynamic, providing customers with "optionality." He largely ignored McLean at first, making his pitch directly to her editors.

He looked at them confidently. "The way to understand Enron," he began, "is to think of Toyota."

Toyota? What is this guy talking about?

The discussion had been dragging on and wasn't making a lot of sense. Jim Impoco was getting annoyed. Fastow kept coming back to his analogy. *Toyota, Toyota, Toyota.* But everything he said was *wrong*. An old Japan hand, Impoco had covered Toyota for years. It didn't negotiate with suppliers; it had long-running feudal relationships with them. It told them what to charge. If Fastow wanted to trumpet this analogy, he should at least know what he was talking about.

Fastow circled around again. "Just like with Toyota—"

Impoco couldn't take any more. "I'm sorry," he interrupted. "You've got to drop the Toyota analogy. It doesn't make sense and shows a lack of understanding about the company. It's making it hard for me to figure out what you're trying to say about Enron."

Fastow laughed nervously.

Then he moved on. He stopped mentioning Toyota.

Gradually, McLean forced Fastow to deal with her. His answers were all generalities, loaded with business-school buzzwords that might dazzle the local bridge club but weren't going to sway sophisticated financial journalists.

As the story unfolded, the editors relaxed. Enron had been so insistent on meeting, they and McLean had feared she had missed something, some silver bullet that would kill the article's thesis. But the more Fastow spoke, the less they worried. He didn't marshal evidence to counter McLean's point. He just argued that she was wrong. He wasn't accomplishing anything. In fact, he was damaging his cause. To fly to New York to make such a feeble assault sure signaled a company desperate to keep its stock price up.

This story was going to run in the next issue. No doubt.

After a round of questions, McLean glanced at her notes. She had something else to ask.

"I read about the related-party transactions involving LJM Cayman," she began. It was as if the quality of the air in the room changed. Fastow stiffened. The editors weren't sure what this was about; McLean's draft said nothing about any entity from the Caymans.

"One of our senior executives runs that fund," Fastow replied. "It's confidential who it is."

Some photo editors came by and commandeered the conference room. The two sides moved the discussion to Impoco's office. After two hours they were done; the mood lightened as the executives turned on some Texas charm.

The visitors gathered their things. Palmer and Koenig said their good-byes and headed toward the elevator. Fastow dawdled for a moment, then turned to look at McLean.

"I don't care what you say about the company," he said. "Just don't make me look bad."

CHAPTER 16

CARL BASS SHIFTED HIS feet nervously as he waited for an elevator on the ground floor of a Houston office building. It was March 2, a Friday, just weeks after he had been offered a new job to manage Andersen's relationship with the SEC, a post that would have meant relocating to Chicago. Days before, he had finally declined, saying that he wanted to stay in Houston, handling accounting issues.

Then yesterday, another call. Gary Goolsby, a top partner in Houston, asked him to drop by. As Bass rode up, he couldn't shake the feeling he was about to be ordered to Chicago. He stepped off on the thirteenth floor. Goolsby welcomed him warmly and whisked him to his office. There, his demeanor hardened, like a doctor about to deliver bad news.

"Carl, I'm going to tell you something, and I'm going to tell you straight up," he said. "Enron has a big problem with you consulting on their engagement."

Bass's mouth fell. He wasn't *on* the Enron engagement. He was with the Professional Standards Group, work that in theory made him anonymous to the outside world. How did Enron even know what he was doing?

"Who has a problem?" he asked.

"Causey in particular thinks you're caustic and cynical toward their transactions. It's a big client-relationship issue, and, long story short, we're not going to let you consult on Enron transactions anymore."

The demands to sideline Bass had been swirling for weeks, and Andersen had tried, timidly, to fight them. But even the appeal to Causey from Joseph Berardino, Andersen's new chief executive, had been to no avail. So Andersen caved. Standing up to Enron wasn't considered a plausible option; the deep-pocketed client could shift its consulting business at the drop of a hat, leaving Andersen only the low-paying audit work. That was a risk that the Andersen partners were simply unwilling to take.

Bass, however, was flabbergasted. To his way of thinking, clients couldn't boss accountants around like this. Accounting judgments were based on the rules, not the person. Bending to Enron's demands was sure to have a chilling effect, maybe nudge Andersen partners to loosen up their interpretations. Then again, Bass figured that was what Enron wanted to achieve.

"Gary, I'm stunned," Bass said. "If they don't want me involved, that's their call, I guess. But I can't believe the firm is going along with this."

"We've attempted to talk to them—"

"Gary, it shouldn't be their call!" Bass retorted. "Them, of *all* clients. A high-risk, maximum-exposure client! And we're letting them dictate to us what our quality-control procedures should be!"

Goolsby held up a hand. "Carl, I'm not telling you to quit. Maybe consider that SEC opportunity in Chicago."

Bass said he would think about it. Then he left.

The next morning in Galveston, music filled the Moody Gardens coliseum as a group of young girls broke into a competitive dance routine. Two of Bass's daughters were performing that day, and he had driven the family down the previous afternoon for what was supposed to be a time of fun.

But as he sat in the auditorium, Bass could only stew. Something had shattered for him. Andersen had a storied history, a tradition, and central to that was its unwavering integrity. *That* Andersen would never have allowed Enron to have its way like this. That Andersen was gone. The tradition was dead. It tore at Bass.

So be it. He would not be party to the collapse of values. He would not let a client decide his fate. *I'm just going to leave the group*, he thought. *Maybe leave the firm.*

One way or another, he had to do something.

In his home office the next afternoon, a Sunday, Bass switched on his laptop and connected to the Andersen network. He was scheduled to speak the next day with John Stewart, a top partner in the OSG, about Enron's demand. But first Bass wanted to tell his side of the story.

He opened an e-mail, addressing it to Stewart. "I know you did not ask me for this," he typed. "But I believe you should at least have a version of what I know about this Enron 'thing' with me."

He recounted all of Enron's questionable deals in December—Braveheart, Fishtail, and of course the absurd forty-five-day Raptor guarantees. His involvement in these had been limited to communications with the Andersen partners, who were obviously blaming the accounting judgments on *him* rather than presenting the decisions as the firm's opinion.

"Once we conclude something, or render some advice, the engagement team should deliver that advice or conclusion as if it were their own," Bass wrote. "It is after all the engagement team's responsibility to sign the opinion—not ours."

He typed for almost an hour. He hit the "send" button shortly before seven that evening.

John Stewart was a gentle man, not easily prone to anger. But the Bass affair had thrown him into a fury—at Enron, to be sure, but also at Andersen. He arranged a meeting with a number of senior partners in Chicago.

"The behavior of the client in this instance has been unprofessional," Stewart declared. "This should not have been allowed to happen."

One senior partner, Larry Rieger, agreed to speak with David Duncan, but that went nowhere. Soon Stewart reached a new resolve. If Enron didn't like what Carl Bass had to say, too bad. His was too fine a mind to ignore; Stewart was still going to consult him. But he'd do so on the sly, so that nobody at the company would know.

After months of work, Jordan Mintz had almost completed the memo summarizing his concerns about LJM. With a little more work, it would be ready for Causey and Buy.

First, he wanted to be sure his bosses knew what he was up to, so he forwarded a draft copy to Fastow. Then he briefed Derrick, the general counsel, as well as other Enron lawyers, telling them about his findings and promising to send them a copy of the final memo.

The writing was a measured, almost dry account of the LJM funds and the shortcomings Mintz had detected. Some dated back to problems McMahon had protested years before, like the fact that Enron allowed LJM staffers to work alongside the company's own finance employees.

To fix the system, Mintz proposed an array of actions. More requirements that analysts explain *why* a deal was in the company's interest. Better involvement by Skilling in reviewing transactions. And coordinated approval of deals by an in-house legal, accounting, and commercial staff.

On March 7, the day before Mintz planned to send out the final memo, he was working at his desk, trying to get out early for his son's seventh birthday. Kopper appeared in his doorway. Before Mintz could say a word, Kopper stepped in, throwing Fastow's copy of the memo at his desk.

"What are you trying to do?" Kopper snarled. "Shut us down?"

Kopper stormed away, leaving Mintz behind, feeling a shiver of self-satisfaction. His little missive had apparently drawn some blood.

That same day, Vince Kaminski sat in his office, reviewing a stunning document. It left no doubt that Enron's finance division could well be spinning out of control.

The decision the previous year to have a team analyze Enron's company-wide risk was paying off. This document—written by the team leaders, Kevin Kindall and Li Sun—established a strong case that Fastow's off-books partnerships had created an uncontrolled, unseen threat to Enron's survival. The work was based on limited information, and more research was needed. But this effort had been undertaken without any real budget. Pushing it to the next level required money—and cooperation from the finance group.

Kaminski needed to get this in front of the right people and win their support so Kindall could finish the job. He had little concern about whether his team would get what it needed. Anyone could see that their findings so far were just a preliminary sign of a very large, very ugly problem.

On March 9, Kaminski and his analytic team dropped by Ben Glisan's office for their scheduled presentation. Glisan led the group down the hall, where everyone took a seat at a conference table. Kaminski launched the discussion with the history of the analytic team and the rationale behind conducting a company-wide risk analysis. Then he turned the floor over to Kevin Kindall.

Glancing down at his report, Kindall went through his analysis. It was calm and reasoned, but painted a graphic picture of a finance division out of its depth, taking risks it did not fully comprehend.

Global Finance—through its structured deals—had entered into repeated arrangements where purchasers of assets could force Enron to take them back through what were known as total-return swaps. But nobody had any idea what potential damage these arrangements might cause in the future. No one kept a book on the swaps; basically, Fastow and his crew had no clear idea of how many there were or of the terms that had been created for them.

Then there were guarantees to purchasers that were issued by the finance division; again, no one kept track of them. The best estimate was that the finance group had put out some twenty-seven hundred corporate guarantees, without assessing the associated risks. It was like a bad housekeeper sweeping dust under the rug and forgetting about it.

There was another problem spelled out by Kindall, one Kaminski considered an emergency issue: Enron, a Fortune 50 corporation, had no idea of its cash position on any given day. No system was in place to track daily inflows and outflows for the whole company. What did exist, Kindall said, resulted in untimely reports from divisions, forcing Enron to borrow money unnecessarily, simply because no one knew if the cash was available. Disorganization was needlessly increasing Enron's debt levels.

Still, the biggest risks were in the special-purpose vehicles, Kindall said, the off-books partnerships that had been the key to Fastow's work.

"We weren't able to gain access to a lot of information," Kindall said. "But what we could review pointed to the existence of huge risk exposures that Enron simply hasn't fully analyzed and does not understand."

Just two off-books entities, Whitewing and Marlin, created enormous hazards. Because of their structure, underperforming assets that the entities had purchased could lead to future liabilities for Enron, Kindall said.

Plus, the deals had been structured with "trigger events" involving Enron's share price and credit rating. Basically, to make the entities more attractive to outside investors, Fastow and his team had made commitments on behalf of the company—to issue stock, assume debt, or otherwise take on new obligations—if Enron's stock price or credit rating sank.

Of course, that was exactly the time that Enron *shouldn't* be taking on such commitments. Issuing more stock when the stock price was falling meant that the price could fall even *faster*. It was like striking an agreement to hose down a house with gasoline if a fire started. To make the original deal sweeter for outside investors, Fastow had created a structure that could push the company toward collapse as soon as trouble started.

Glisan listened silently. He wasn't all that concerned about the triggers in Whitewing and Marlin. Finance used them all the time; even the Raptors had stock-price triggers. He knew all about them.

Kindall flipped the page of his presentation. "We've assessed the likelihood of hitting one of those triggers. For example, we have a five percent chance of a credit downgrade in the next twelve months."

Five percent. That struck Glisan as high.

"But you have to understand, these are just the triggers we have located," Kindall said. "There appear to be other triggers embedded in other vehicles as well."

Those were hidden in documents that Kindall's team hadn't been allowed to review. The triggers appeared to have been assembled without regard to each other. Ultimately, they could all be activated in tandem, since they were all based on the same two factors.

"It's likely the occurrence of one trigger will push down the share price so far that we hit another one embedded in some other vehicle," Kindall said.

He cleared his throat. Presenting doomsday scenarios was never easy. "In truth, it's conceivable we could hit a cascading series of triggers, setting off a domino effect, where each trigger pushes down our stock price even more," he said. "That would result in a massive decrease in the share price and lower our bonds to a junk rating."

Everyone knew what that meant. Enron, as a massive trader, could not survive if its credit rating fell below investment grade to junk status. Other traders would shut the company out of the market, fearing it lacked the financial wherewithal to stand behind its commitments.

The Raptors only increased the danger level, Kindall said. He focused on Raptor I. "Already there are unrealized losses totaling hundreds of millions of dollars in Raptor. It's conceivable that just the disclosure of those kinds of unrealized losses may force our stock price and credit rating down to an extent that we hit one of the trigger events and set off the domino effect."

Kaminski spoke up. His group needed a budget to finish its project, to identify the full scale of the threat. Much work remained to be done: assembling a complete list of *all* the off-books entities, calculating the risks they contained, and creating a forecast of expected liabilities.

Kindall agreed. "We need to take each off-book vehicle and closely examine all of the assets in them."

He paused. "Once we have that information, we would then be able to estimate the probability of ruin."

It was all there.

In a single stroke, Kevin Kindall—an inconspicuous mid-level analyst relying on scraps of data—had exposed the financial rot eating away at Enron.

It had come to this: Enron, the supposed corporate success story of the last decade, had ignored—no, *disdained*—the basics of business, allowing them to slip away in its single-minded pursuit of profit. To executives richly rewarded for each newfangled deal, cash management was boring, not the cutting-edge stuff that let Enron be *Enron*. Closely tracking exposures was seen as an expense, not a moneymaker. The workaday business of business just didn't have the kind of sizzle that won plaudits and praise. Buying insurance? A monkey could do that.

That was the culture that had flared in the high-money days of the 1990s and had since spread through Enron like wildfire. Now, with eerie precision, Kindall had predicted the scenario that would ravage the company in just seven short months. The disclosure of the Raptor losses. A market shock. A cascading collapse as Enron's stock price blew through one trigger after another, pushing the company toward its ultimate demise.

It was as if an unknown engineer at the White Star Line had laid out the dangers of icebergs to the *Titanic* months before the great ship's ill-fated voyage. There was still time. Changes could be made, disaster averted. The survival of Enron depended on the response of Ben Glisan, a man whose se-cret million-dollar profit from a partnership gave him plenty of reason to op-pose letting anyone look too closely at Fastow's dealings.

As Kindall wrapped up his presentation, Glisan skimmed the last two pages of the written report. The analyst was explaining how the recent *Fortune* magazine article had spelled out a series of dismal statistics for the company, which would be even worse if the "hidden Enron" in all of the off-books partnerships were included.

Glisan flipped the pages closed. "Well, I appreciate all the work that went into this," he said. "But there really isn't anything to worry about."

Nothing to worry about? Kaminski bridled at the brush-off. Kindall's analy-sis portrayed a company that could be on the precipice, and simply not have the data to be aware of it. This might be a matter of life and death.

"Ben," Kaminski said, "we can't know that without conducting a full analysis."

Glisan smiled. "Vince, I was involved in designing almost all of these ve-hicles," he said. "We know what the risks are. It's not an issue."

Kaminski pressed his point; more study was needed, he insisted. Glisan raised his hands, relenting a bit.

"All right, Vince, I hear you," he said. "I'll go through this again and get back to you."

The next morning at eleven, Glisan—now Enron's only senior executive with the knowledge of the potential debacle the company faced—boarded a Continental Airlines flight with his family for a weeklong ski trip to Beaver Creek, Colorado, where they would be staying at the luxurious Villa Montane Townhomes. There he could relax, hit the slopes, maybe forget about work for a while.

Glisan never bothered to get back to Kaminski and Kindall about their analysis. And he also neglected to tell Lay, Skilling, or any of Enron's direc-tors about the terrifying warning he had just received.

Enron's deal with Blockbuster was dead.

The skirmishes of the last few months had escalated into all-out warfare. Blockbuster complained that Enron had failed to provide the technology and access to customers that it had promised; Enron countered that Blockbuster wasn't delivering quality content. By March, the recent contractual agreement forbidding either side from walking away had expired, and both were ready to call it quits.

In the days before the deal was called off, Lay was briefed on the troubled arrangement by David Cox, the primary negotiator. The movies secured by Blockbuster had been terrible, he said—lowbrow teen sex romps like *Porky's 3* and a bunch of how-to videos. As Cox described it, the celebrated Blockbuster relationship with movie studios was a bust. As the biggest player in video rentals, it had used its leverage to extract big studio concessions for its retail stores. The studios weren't about to help Blockbuster build another business using their content, and several studio executives had quietly let Enron know that.

Lay listened with dismay. After all, the entire basis of the agreement with Blockbuster had been its supposed Hollywood contacts. But apparently no one from Enron had bothered to check by calling the studios. It was as if this twenty-year contract had been entered into on the fly.

Still, Cox was quick to assure Lay that all was not lost. Enron, he said, was developing its own Hollywood contacts. It would all work out in the end.

Perhaps. But that prospect didn't change the fact that Enron's twenty-year contract with Blockbuster would soon be terminated, just eight months after it was signed. Now its video-on-demand business would have no business partner, little content, and few customers. Yet, because of Project Braveheart, Enron would still have what really mattered to its executives: more than $111 million in reported revenues, enough for the broadband division to reach its financial targets.

The morning after the Blockbuster deal was canceled, Carl Bass was at his home office, surfing the Internet. He noticed a Reuters report on a news Web page.

"Blockbuster, Enron Broadband End Video-on-Demand Deal," it read. He clicked on the story.

This could be bad. Bass knew that Enron had reported huge revenues from Braveheart, already a shaky deal. Not even Enron could argue a business with a name-brand partner was worth the same once the joint venture ended. Bass opened an e-mail and addressed it to John Stewart. He pasted a copy of the Reuters article in it, then typed a message: "I do not know if you knew of this yet."

Stewart was on his computer at that moment and opened Bass's e-mail. The Reuters report was disturbing, given the revenues Enron reported from Braveheart. In his reply, he typed that this was news to him.

"So what happens to the joint venture and the part that was securitized through an SPE to produce a material gain?" he typed.

That's the sixty-four-dollar question, Bass thought.

He hit the "reply" button. "One would think (no direct knowledge since my phone no longer takes their calls) that there should be a loss reported," he typed. "The 'venture' has now lost its value."

A loss would never be taken. The collapse of the Blockbuster relationship, Enron executives argued, was a good thing. Its partner's dicey relationship with movie studios had impeded the joint venture's success. With Blockbuster out of the way, Enron was sure to sign the studios up even faster. Why, executives enthused, with Enron now fully in charge, Braveheart might even be worth *more*, not less, than was originally projected.

A week had passed, and Mintz still hadn't heard back about his LJM memo. He asked his secretary to set up a meeting with Causey and Buy, and they agreed to get together a few days later. At the appointed time, Mintz arrived at Causey's office. Buy showed up soon after, and the three took seats at the circular conference table. Mintz placed a copy of his memo on the table in front of him.

"Okay, Jordan," Causey said, "it's your meeting. What's up?"

"Well, I wanted to find out what you guys are thinking about the memo," Mintz said.

Blank stares. "What memo?" Causey asked.

Mintz felt himself deflating. They never read it.

"I wrote a memo about the policies and procedures on LJM and how they weren't being followed," Mintz said. "I included recommendations on how to fix the problems."

Causey closed his eyes and nodded. "Oh, yeah."

He stood and walked over to his desk, riffling through piles of papers. Buy looked evenly at Mintz.

"I didn't bring my copy with me," he said.

Causey started walking back to the table. "I can't lay my hands on it right now," he said.

Keeping up a tough front, Mintz suggested that he have Causey's secretary run the copy he had brought through the Xerox machine. A fine idea, Causey and Buy agreed. Minutes later, everyone had a copy of the memo. Causey and Buy leafed through it. Their faces gave no sign of recognition.

"How do you want me to proceed?" Mintz asked, trying to end the awkwardness of the moment. "Should I just go through it page by page?"

Absolutely, they replied. Slowly, Mintz reviewed his concerns and recommendations. Causey and Buy repeatedly muttered words of approval, then encouraged Mintz to move on to the next topic. Mintz reached the last page.

"Now we have this screwed-up situation where these LJM people are on the twentieth floor," he said. "And I want to be sure I have your support in getting them moved out."

No question, they said. Mintz should get it started. They were behind him all the way.

Mintz was back in his office about ten minutes later. He slowly closed the door and walked to his credenza. He placed his copy of the memo there and just stared at it.

They hadn't read the memo. Even when they heard about it, they could barely disguise their indifference. He had hoped they would be so outraged that they would set things straight. Instead, they had just patted him on the back, wishing him good luck in taking on his boss.

What a bunch of pussies, Mintz thought. *I can't believe these guys are senior executives with this company.*

Riding an Enron elevator, Skilling glanced at one of the television screens embedded in the wall. The stock price flashed by and he almost winced. Below fifty-six dollars a share.

Just last August, Enron's stock had hit an all-time high of more than ninety dollars a share. It had fallen steadily since. And today, March 21, it would hit a new fifty-two-week low.

No doubt, the 1990s were over. In just the last eight weeks, the value of telecommunications stocks had plunged—Level 3, Global Crossing, all of them—and a vicious cycle had begun. Many of those high-tech companies had financed their operations by selling stock; now, with no takers, the prospect of their collapse loomed large.

Enron was being hit every which way. The market knew about its India troubles, making investors skittish. That *Fortune* article—*that* Fortune *article!*—had started raising questions about the quality of its earnings.

Now the high-tech debacle was draining its shares of the value from Broadband. But as storm clouds gathered, Skilling put on a happy face. The shakeout was a good thing, he insisted, since less competition meant lower prices for network access. It also meant fewer businesses to trade with, but Skilling expressed no worries about that.

Still, there was another element to the stock-price collapse in Skilling's mind. The real troubles had started about the same time that Lay was announcing his plans to leave. Each day's new drubbing struck Skilling as the market's vote on his elevation. Investors apparently wanted Lay, not him. They were giving him almost daily criticism of his performance. And Skilling hated criticism.

As the elevator whooshed along, an Enron employee interrupted Skilling's thoughts. "Jeff," the employee said, "what's happening to the stock price?"

Skilling glanced over at the employee, then looked back at the television screen. "I don't know," he said.

How did things get to this point? By March 22, Fastow and the other executives in finance were struggling to answer that question and avert disaster.

The problem again was the Raptors. When they had been created, everyone pronounced them a stroke of genius. With Enron's shares trading at close to ninety dollars at the time—and climbing—no one expected they would so quickly reverse course, so there were no concerns about the price trigger built into the structure. In essence, if Enron's share price fell below fifty dollars, the stock meant to provide the Raptors with capital would effectively disappear. Back then, the trigger point seemed laughably low—*fifty dollars a share?*

But today, the price was at fifty-five and falling. Worse, losses were still piling up from the collapse of values in the merchant investments hedged by the Raptors. Now there was a good chance that in a week or so, the Raptors could arguably have no capital. The hedges would vanish, and all those merchant-investment losses would come back.

To fix the problem, Fastow and Causey brought in some top accounting minds. They came up with what they viewed as the perfect solution: if the Raptors needed more capital to hedge Enron's investments, Enron would give it to them.

The two best Raptors would continue to be harnessed to support the worst. Then Enron would pump another twelve million shares of stock into the stronger ones. The deal was done on credit, with the two stronger Raptors pledging to pay Enron another $568 million sometime in the future. In essence, the finance group was doubling down, *again*, in its bet that Enron's share price would rise. A price run-up would bail out the entire structure and allow the Raptors to make good on their obligations, eventually.

But this time the finance group sweetened the deal. They priced the new shares for the Raptors at forty-seven dollars each, a significant discount, since under the sale agreement the shares could not be hedged. The discount was run past Kaminski, who agreed on the valuation.

The price cut was standard fare, but the next step wasn't. Once the deal terms were signed, Enron waived the requirement forbidding hedging. The shares—worth less because they could not be hedged—could now be hedged. And no one told Kaminski, whose pricing was used to justify the numbers in the deal.

Of course, to hedge, the Raptors needed a third party to take on the risk that Enron's stock price would fall. They turned to Enron itself. Now, if the share price dropped, the company was obligated to make up the loss for the Raptors, which in turn were pledging to give Enron back its own money to make up for losses in the merchant investments. By any measure, the Raptors were a meaningless, laughable fraud.

After 3:30 on the afternoon of March 26, Ryan Siurek was in his office speaking with a colleague, Gordon McKillop. He had been working night and day on the Raptor restructuring, and the deal documents had finally been signed. He was exhausted and ready for a break.

The telephone rang. "Ryan. Jeff Skilling."

Siurek was shocked. He hadn't expected Skilling's call; he didn't even think Skilling knew who he was. Unknown to Siurek, Causey had asked Skilling to send an "attaboy" the young accountant's way.

"Listen," Skilling said, "I just want to tell you how much we appreciate your hard work on the Raptor restructuring. It's a really great transaction for Enron."

Siurek muttered his thanks, and the two talked for a minute. From what Siurek could tell, Skilling had a working understanding of the deal.

In Washington, the heavyset, bearded man crossed Pennsylvania Avenue to the security booth at the northwest gate of the White House. A guard inside asked for his name.

"Harvey Pitt," he responded.

Pitt, one of Washington's most celebrated securities lawyers, was on the verge of achieving a career-long dream. Some time before, he had been contacted by the White House personnel office, inquiring if he would have any interest in serving as the new chairman of the SEC.

The son of a grocer and a seamstress, Pitt first attracted the attention of SEC officials during a moot competition in law school, and soon was working in the general counsel's office at the agency. He stayed ten years, becoming the agency's youngest general counsel, before moving on to become a top partner at Fried, Frank, Harris, Shriver & Jacobson. But he never lost interest in returning to the SEC—this time as chairman. Pitt wasn't close to Bush; in fact, he'd never met him. But he knew this new President might grant him the post he coveted.

Security issued him an identification tag, and Pitt slipped it on. Minutes later, he was in the West Wing, being escorted to the Oval Office. Bush was waiting for him at the doorway. The two men shook hands.

"Mr. President, it's an honor to meet you."

Bush smiled. "Well, Mr. Pitt, delighted to meet *you*."

A White House cameraman snapped a picture, then Bush showed Pitt to the sitting area. Cheney was there, along with a handful of other staffers. Pitt greeted them, but Bush quickly made clear this meeting was his.

"All right, Mr. Pitt," Bush began. "Why do you want to be the chairman of the SEC?"

They spoke for half an hour. Pitt had prepared for this moment for years and had an array of ideas ready to go. The SEC could become more than what it was, he said, and he was the person to drive the agency toward that goal.

For one thing, he said, the SEC should become a real-time enforcer of the securities laws; too often, investigations languished for years. Moving faster would give investors confidence that the cop was on the beat. Disclosure was inadequate, too, he said. Investors mostly received historical information, with little explanation of where companies would be down the road.

Bush nodded, occasionally asking a question. Finally, he had heard enough. "Well, Mr. Pitt, thank you for coming," he said. "We'll get back to you."

Again, handshakes all around. Minutes later, Pitt was on the street, walking back to his office. He felt good about the interview. This job could very well be his.

Late on the afternoon of April 2, Amanda Martin was in Skilling's office, again asking to be pulled out of Azurix. There were other things she could do, she said. She had fixed the troubled North American power plants; she could take on the same responsibilities for the India project, she argued.

Skilling's tone was distant. "I'm not sure it will work, Amanda. I'm getting a lot of resistance from Andy about you coming back."

Fastow. It had been so many years since their battles began over that silly wind deal. Martin could scarcely believe Fastow was still carrying a grudge.

"But, Jeff, I don't want to stay in Azurix," she said.

"I need you there," Skilling replied.

Everything about Skilling's demeanor struck Martin as wrong. He seemed unsure of what he was doing. "Jeff," she asked, "what's going on here?"

Skilling didn't answer.

"You know, Jeff," she continued, "every time I leave late at night, I go out to the parking lot and that whole row of cars of your lieutenants are gone. But your car is there. And I come in early in the morning, and no one's arrived yet. But your car is there then, too."

She leaned forward in her seat. "So what does it say right now about your organization that you're working harder than the people who report to you?"

Martin waited to be shouted down. That would show her that Skilling still had the old fire in the belly. But he just sat there.

"The problem is, Rice, Pai, all your lieutenants, they've checked out; they're not doing their jobs anymore," Martin said. "You've made them too rich. They've got too much money. They don't need to be here."

Still no response. Martin plowed ahead. "And the next layer of people—Whalley, Delainey, and the rest—they'll cut your throat if they thought it would get them to the feeding trough sooner. So what are you going to do?"

Skilling just looked at her with a sad expression, then silently glanced out the window. Finally, he looked her in the eye. "One thing about you, Amanda," he said. "You always tell it the way you see it."

He paused. "You're most likely right," he said.

What? Skilling *never* conceded a mistake. *Never.* He was so quiet, so resigned. He looked lost.

"I don't know what I'm going to do," he said softly.

A week later, on April 9, Skilling finished wandering around the building, dropping in on traders and deal makers. Now he was headed to a conference room to meet with his CFO.

Fastow was getting anxious. LJM's deals with Enron had slowed to a trickle. With stock prices sliding, there was little available that promised good returns, even in a rigged deal. With one exception: Enron Wind, a renewable-energy division. Enron was already negotiating to sell it to a unit of UBS, the global financial firm, but Fastow wanted in, with LJM2.

In the conference room, Fastow explained all the benefits LJM2 could bring by bidding for Wind. Skilling was unimpressed. He was tired of LJM, tired of Fastow jabbering about it. They never spoke about Enron anymore, he thought gloomily. It's *always LJM, LJM, LJM.*

"I don't want a structured deal," Skilling replied. "You want to make a bid as a stalking horse, that's fine."

A stalking horse? That meant LJM2 would be used just to force up the UBS offer. There was nothing in that for Fastow and his investors. "Wait, Jeff," Fastow protested. "I think LJM can really bring some value to the table."

They spoke for another twenty minutes. Skilling left the meeting confident he had gotten his point across.

Days later, on April 13, Mintz was at his desk, embarrassed as he worked on his latest trivial assignment. Fastow's nanny had purchased a new car—a lemon—and now his boss had asked him to write a threatening legal letter to the car dealer. Head buried in paperwork, Mintz sensed someone's presence. He looked up and saw Michael Kopper.

"Jordan," Kopper said brusquely, "LJM2 is bidding on the wind deal. Do you know where things stand with UBS?"

What? In just two short sentences, Mintz's worst fears about LJM emerged. The fund was elbowing its way in on Enron's sale of an entire business? Not only that, but Kopper wanted to know what UBS was doing with its bid? No third party would *ever* get that kind of information.

"Michael, I don't know," he replied. "But I work for Enron. I don't think that it's right to be telling you how things are going with a potential competitor."

Kopper started to speak. Mintz kept going.

"If you want to talk to somebody on the deal, call Lance Schuler, because he's working on it," Mintz said, doing nothing to hide his contempt.

Kopper's eyes narrowed in anger. Mintz was pushing him off to Schuler, another lawyer? Giving him the brush-off?

"You know, Jordan, Lance was on the short list to get your job," he hissed. "And he didn't get it, because he didn't know how to play well in the gray areas."

Kopper stormed out.

This was out of control. Mintz needed to roll up his sleeves and figure out some way to get attention directed to the LJM problems, and get them fixed once and for all.

The following Monday, April 16, Fastow muttered curses as he read an e-mail. It was from Adam Umanoff, an executive with the wind company, canceling an appointment. The Enron deal maker in charge of the transaction, Mark Metts, had ruled that a meeting between the two would give LJM2 favored treatment over other bidders.

Fastow clicked the "forward" button on the e-mail, typed in Skilling's address, and began composing a message:

"Jeff, I'm sure this is just a 'misunderstanding,' but I know that UBS Capital has spent innumerable hours with management. While Mark says that he doesn't want LJM to have an advantage, it looks like LJM is being put at a disadvantage."

As Fastow banged the keyboard, a group from finance—Glisan, Mintz, Tim Despain, and Barry Schnapper—walked in for a 2:30 meeting. Fastow didn't even look up.

"Until this is resolved, I'll assume that LJM is out of the bidding and will not do any further work. Enron is back to one bidder (the lower one)—better for our company???"

"Great!" Fastow laughed. "That's great!"

He hit the "send" button and stood.

"Goddamn Metts," Fastow said as he turned to the assembled group. "I told Skilling that LJM could buy Enron Wind and get it off the balance sheet, and Metts is being an impediment. He's not letting us do any due diligence."

He smiled. "Well, Skilling's aware of it now, and I'll just let him speak to Metts about it."

Fastow sat at the table, smirking with self-satisfaction. They went around, discussing the matter at hand. When the meeting ended, Mintz lingered behind.

"Andy," he said hesitantly, "why does LJM want to buy Enron Wind?"

The sale, Mintz thought, would be too large to keep quiet. It would almost certainly require full disclosure, thrusting LJM front and center as a major issue for investors. All for a business that was really just expensive advertising, to project an environmentally friendly image.

But Fastow saw only dollar signs. "It's a great asset," he said. "*We've* screwed it up, but if somebody incubated it, you could double your money in two years."

He smiled. "I'll tell you, we're going to invest like $600 million and turn it into more than a billion!"

Skilling looked at the e-mail he had just received, annoyed. What the hell was Fastow talking about?

A stalking horse! LJM was a stalking horse. He didn't want a structured deal. He wanted Enron Wind gone. He thought he had been very clear on that point. Apparently Fastow wasn't listening.

Just before ten the next morning, Lay sat on an upholstered seat in the waiting area outside Vice President Dick Cheney's White House office. He was there with Enron's top government-relations executives, Steve Kean and Linda Robertson, for what was supposed to be a confidential meeting to spell out Enron's vision for the Administration's national energy policy.

Nine days into his presidency, Bush had named Cheney to chair the National Energy Policy Development Group, known as the Energy Task Force. Unlike many federal advisory committees, this one was staffed exclusively with government employees, meaning no public hearings would be required. This way Cheney and others in the Administration could hold meetings—like the one today with Lay—behind closed doors, setting the agenda without public scrutiny.

An assistant stepped into the room. "The Vice President will see you now," she said.

Cheney was sitting at his desk when the Enron contingent walked in. He stood, walking toward Lay.

"Mr. Vice President," Lay said, "delighted you could give us some of your time today."

Cheney nodded. "We're looking forward to hearing your ideas," he said. He gestured toward an upholstered chair, and Lay took a seat. Cheney sat in the chair beside him, while the others found seats on a nearby couch. Lay held some talking points on his lap.

"Dick," he began, "primarily what we hope is that any energy program by the Administration is market-driven, something that reflects economics and not just the government trying to pick the best technologies itself. The marketplace should make those choices."

Cheney said nothing. Lay was preaching to the choir.

"But at Enron," Lay continued, "we are primarily interested that natural gas and electricity are able to continue to be deregulated, in a way that will in fact give the maximum benefits to the customers."

Things were all right in natural gas, Lay said, but a lot of work was needed in electricity. The California debacle showed how bad things could become. Regulators had to bring competition to all electricity markets, he said, to avoid another California.

"One of the biggest problems in electricity today is the grid system," Lay said, sounding the main message he had come to deliver. "Regulated utilities and the state regulators still control the interstate transmission grid, even though it is clearly interstate commerce."

That, Lay said, meant that the oversight of the grid ought to go to federal regulators. "And we ought to have larger regional transmission grids, not so many chopped up transmission grids making coordination so difficult. Those chopped-up grids are used to give monopoly utilities first shot at their own markets and keep out competitors."

"Well," Cheney interrupted, "what part of the country are you getting the most opposition from?"

At about the same moment, "hold" music played as Wall Street analysts waited for Enron's quarterly conference call to begin. An operator came on and introduced Skilling.

"I hope you all heard that music that was on before," he said. "We're all dancing here; it's pretty good stuff."

The numbers were sure to pump up the analysts—an 18 percent increase in earnings, a 281 percent increase in revenues. Skilling announced them with excitement in his voice. A number of other Enron executives were in the room, listening in. Causey was just one seat away. No one mentioned anything about the Raptor losses.

As Skilling spoke, Ray Bowen was down in his office, playing to the conference call over his computer.

"So in conclusion, first-quarter results were great," he heard Skilling say. "We are very optimistic about our new businesses and are confident that our record of growth is sustainable for many years to come."

Great. Great. Everything was great. The claim left Bowen uneasy. He was hearing rumblings in the company about troubles in Broadband, about the India project possibly being worthless. But everything was great.

In a conference room in another part of the building, Mark Palmer, the head of corporate communications, was also listening in on the call along with members of his department. Just in case something important came up.

Lay's conversation with Cheney weaved through an array of issues, from supply questions to concerns about price caps in California. After thirty minutes, an aide reminded the Vice President of his next appointment.

Lay took the hint. "Dick, we appreciate your time," he said, standing. "We wanted to be sure you heard firsthand what we're thinking should be the priorities for your energy plan. And obviously, we want to keep in touch."

Cheney shook his hand. "Well, we want you to," he said. Before leaving, the Enron executives turned over a lengthy position paper. Then Cheney excused himself.

As Lay and his colleagues walked out of the White House, Colin Powell, the Secretary of State, was just arriving. Spotting Lay, Powell broke into a smile. The two had known each other since the first Bush Administration.

"Hi, Ken," Powell said. "Good to see you."

Lay offered his greetings, and Powell mentioned that he was heading inside for a Cabinet meeting.

"Well," Lay joked, "maybe I'll stand here for a few minutes and talk to the whole Cabinet."

But he wasn't going to let this opportunity slip away with nothing more than a wisecrack to show for it.

"Listen, Colin," Lay said. "I may need to come see you or one of your senior people about the power project we have in India. We're having some real problems there."

Powell already knew about it. India had agreed to make good on any obligations owed under the power contract but was trying to wriggle out of the deal. Powell urged Lay to contact one of his deputy secretaries, Alan Larsen. "I'll let Alan know that you're going to call," Powell said.

The short discussion gave Lay comfort. The Administration was foursquare behind Enron in its showdown with the government of India.

The conference call was dragging on, with Skilling still trumpeting the quarter's performance. After that came the question period. It started predictably enough, with requests for information about run-of-the-mill operating matters. Then the operator called on the next questioner.

"Richard Grubman, of Highfield Capital."

As Skilling stared at the speakerphone, Mark Koenig, the investor-relations chief, began scrawling a note. Grubman asked what the balances of assets and liabilities were in the trading business at quarter's end.

"We do not have the balance sheet completed," Skilling replied. "We will have that done shortly."

No sooner had he spoken than Koenig slipped him the note. Grubman, it said, was a short seller, one of the money managers betting that Enron's share price would fall.

"I'm trying to understand why that would appear to be an unreasonable request," Grubman responded, "in light of your comments about daily control of all your credits."

Yeah, Ray Bowen thought. *Good question.*

Whoever this guy Grubman was, he was asking a key question. The balance sheet—and its lesser-known cousin, the statement of cash flows—would let investors know if Enron had enough money on hand to finance growth. It might give hints about how much of Enron's earnings came from fancy accounting rather than the true generation of cash.

He hoped Skilling was ready with a good answer.

"I'm not saying we can't tell you what the balances are," Skilling replied. "We clearly have all those positions on a daily basis, but at this point we will wait to disclose those until all the netting and the right accounting is put together."

The nonanswer annoyed Grubman. "You're the only financial institution that cannot produce a balance sheet or a cash-flow statement with their earnings," he said.

Skilling was furious. This guy was stirring up controversy, trying to talk down his company. "Thank you very much," he said. "We appreciate that."

"You appreciate that?"

Skilling glanced up, looking around at the others with him in the room. He wanted the last word.

"Asshole."

Palmer almost fell over. Did he hear that right? Enron's chief executive had just called someone an asshole? On an open line? *On an analysts' call?*

He jumped out of his chair. He needed to get upstairs.

Bowen stiffened. *Asshole?* He called the guy an asshole? His phone rang. It was Billy Lemmons, a friend from Enron.

"Did you hear that?" Lemmons asked, laughing. "What do you think *that* means?"

"I don't know," Bowen said. "But I thought it was a good question."

Upstairs, the conference call continued, with everyone in the room now jolted wide awake. Palmer rushed in while Skilling was taking a question from the analyst from First Boston. He slipped Skilling a note on a piece of yellow legal paper, saying he should apologize before getting off the line. Skilling read the note, then slid it under a pile of papers on the table.

Lay was still making the rounds in Washington when his phone rang. It was Steve Kean, who had just heard from Palmer. Lay was perplexed. He had just parted ways with Kean. What was the problem?

"Ken, since you're meeting with a lot of people today, we thought you should know about the analysts' call this morning," Kean said. "Jeff, well, I don't know if it was inadvertent or if he just said it."

Kean was stumbling over his words, sounding uneasy. That wasn't like him. "But Jeff, in response to a comment, called one of the analysts an asshole," Kean said.

Lay was silent for a moment.

"Well, that's not very nice," he said finally.

The "asshole" comment hit the newswires and soon was all over Wall Street. Outside of Enron, reaction was bad. This just wasn't appropriate behavior for a Fortune 50 company. Executives of Skilling's rank had to deal with verbal potshots from short sellers all the time. Besides, Grubman's sally barely qualified as harsh. How would Skilling hold up if the fire really turned hostile?

When Lay came back to Houston two days later, Skilling appeared in his office, hanging his head. Lay let him know that he could not lose control like that again. But the controversy didn't end there. Some directors complained to Lay about the episode. Skilling acknowledged to friends that he had over-reacted but defended the name-calling, saying that Grubman was trying to drive down Enron's stock price.

Even so, the tempest he had created bothered Skilling.

He was being criticized. Again.

Wildly swinging, but ever increasing, prices of electricity in California were taking a toll on Enron's trading desk. The traders were restricted by a com-plex formula that determined the maximum possible losses they could risk. The result was, if the possible loss grew, the traders might have to sell posi-tions for cash even if they were making money. Now, the fluctuations in California were playing havoc with the formula, known as value at risk, or VAR. One perverse effect was that even if the traders stopped trading, they still might hit the risk limits.

Whalley called Skilling to let him know the dilemma. The directors would need to kick up the VAR limit by about 30 percent to maintain current po-sitions, he said.

"No problem," Skilling said. "I'll take care of it."

This was just administrative, Skilling figured. He telephoned Pug Winokur, the head of the finance committee.

"We're going to need to make a request to the board for additional VAR," Skilling said, giving the 30 percent estimate.

"Well," Winokur said, "we'll have to talk about this at the board meeting."

Skilling paused. "What's to talk about?"

"This is a significant increase," Winokur replied.

"It's just mathematical, Pug. It's not a big deal."

"Well, you'll have to make the case for the board."

Skilling didn't argue and called Whalley to let him know what was up. Whalley was furious about the demands but said he would get a presentation put together.

Not long after, Lay appeared in Skilling's office.

"I just got a call from John Duncan about you wanting to get a VAR in-crease," he said. "What's going on?"

John Duncan? Why was the head of the board's executive committee call-ing Lay? "I don't know what's going on, Ken," Skilling said. "I told Pug we were going to ask for an increase in VAR. It's just a mathematical function, because of the increase in volatility."

Lay sat down. "Well, there's something else going on. I mean, the directors are all talking among themselves."

This is ridiculous. "Ken, the position we have in VAR is just one-tenth of the risk we were taking in India. We've gone through hoops to tell them how VAR works. But they can approve a project in India in a twenty-two-minute phone call. There's something *wrong* here."

Skilling set his jaw. He knew what this was about. It wasn't VAR. It wasn't risk. It was *him*. The board was taking out its unhappiness on him, probably for that "asshole" comment. They were dinging him.

Billows of cigarette smoke wafted over the deck behind Rebecca Carter's house. Night after night, she and Skilling had come out here as he griped about his new job. He hated it—putting out fires while everyone scrutinized his every move. This wasn't building a business, it was babysitting.

The market obviously didn't like him. The stock price had been falling ever since he took over. And now—*and now!*—the board was coming after him. Maybe, Skilling thought, Lay was getting ready to stab him in the back and take over again. Hell, maybe *Winokur* had designs on coming in. He was spending lots of time with Fastow. And John Duncan! Skilling and Duncan had never hit it off.

"I don't know," Skilling said. "What's Winokur's objective? What's Duncan's? Where are they all coming from? And I think I see a shift in Ken's attitude."

Carter nodded. "Yeah, I kind of think so, too."

That stopped Skilling short. "Why?"

"Well, the 'asshole' comment didn't help you."

As they talked late into the night, Skilling sank deeper into depression. "I don't need this," he said. "I really don't need this. I've got plenty of money. I've got lots of things I'd rather be doing. Why am I here?"

Carter felt terrible. Skilling had wanted out in November, said so right on this porch, and she had pushed him to take over the chief executive's job.

Skilling puffed his cigarette. He was sure his enemies at Enron were mounting a coup against him. It was obvious. The directors and Lay were planning to push him out. Well, he wouldn't let them. He'd get them before they got him.

On April 30, Skilling sat on a stool in Carter's kitchen, a pad of paper on the counter in front of him. He had come to a decision. He wasn't having fun, the board was undermining him, his family was suffering. He was quitting.

Pen in hand, he considered how to write his resignation letter. Maybe something flowery, listing his grievances and complaints. No, that would look bad. Why kick them on the way out the door?

Maybe . . . maybe . . .

Dear Ken and the board of directors, Because you guys are a bunch of idiots and assholes . . .

No, no. He started writing. He scratched out a few words. Start again. "I hereby resign my position as Chief Executive Officer of Enron Corp.," he wrote.

Good. Right to the point. He scribbled a couple of more sentences, saying nothing much. His resignation, he wrote, was effective immediately.

Carter came inside. Skilling handed her the note. "I need you to type this up," he said.

She read it, then looked up. "Don't show this to anyone until you've thought about it some more, until you spend some time with Ken."

Skilling reflected for a moment.

"Okay," he said. "I'll see Ken first."

Skilling left the letter inside his briefcase. When he was ready to see Lay, he wandered down the hall. Lay greeted him cheerily, and Skilling took a seat.

"Ken, I don't know what's happening, but something weird's going on," he said. "I don't like being second-guessed by Pug, and he's calling Duncan? If they have a problem, why don't they call me? What are they doing?"

Lay listened impassively, masking his alarm. Skilling was reacting far too strongly to something of little real consequence. He sounded . . . well, almost paranoid.

"I don't know where you come out on this," Skilling continued. "But I'm not happy. I am not happy."

Lay didn't know what to say. He made a mental note; he needed to speak to the directors about his protégé's emotional reaction. But this wasn't the time to go into that.

"All right," he said soothingly. "I'll find out what's going on."

Minutes later, Skilling was back in his office, on the phone with Rebecca Carter. He was bowled over by Lay's reaction. He had seemed genuinely astonished by Skilling's complaints about the board being out to undermine him.

"I don't think Ken was involved in anything," Skilling said. "He seemed surprised, like he didn't know there was anything going on."

Maybe the resignation could wait.

———

Lay got back to Skilling that same day, coming down to his office with the news. "Look," he said, "I've called Pug, I've called John. I can tell you that there is no lack of confidence whatever in you."

"What about this VAR stuff?"

Lay shrugged. "It didn't seem to be a big issue."

Skilling considered that. "Okay," he said.

Skilling and Carter were back on the deck again that night. Lay might be talented at putting a good face on things, Skilling said, but he really seemed to be telling the truth. Maybe, he told Carter, he could figure out a way to hang on. At least for a little longer.

In a small office on a side street in Cambridge, Massachusetts, Mark Roberts was reviewing a confidential financial report he had prepared. Roberts ran his own independent investment-research firm called the Off Wall Street Consulting Group, which scouted out investment opportunities for his sophisticated clients. And the idea in this next report, he thought, was close to a sure thing: Enron's stock price was headed for an even bigger fall.

To Roberts, the stock market was a fashion show, with Enron just the latest supermodel parading around. Analysts were taken in by the glamour and the lights, but weren't doing the hard digging. Until now. Roberts and his staff had pored through financial statements, and what they found wasn't pretty. Cash flow in particular was a problem. Roberts had found two billion dollars in collateral posted by California traders that Enron had counted as cash from operations in 2000—money that was beginning to flow out of the door as energy prices stabilized.

Then there were those related-party transactions. Enron was doing business with funds managed by a senior officer—a huge red flag. No Wall Street analyst seemed to know the details. But Roberts thought it was clear that a lot of questionable transactions had been conducted with these funds, all to manage and boost Enron's earnings.

Roberts finished his review. The report was scathing but deserved. In a few days, this would go out to his clients. Then, he knew, plenty of people would finally start questioning Enron about these bizarre LJM deals.

Cliff Baxter was gone. He had packed up his things, bid his colleagues farewell, and walked out of Enron for the last time. Now somebody needed to take over the job of selling Enron assets. Looking around the company, Skilling could think of only one person for the task—Andy Fastow. Skilling summoned him to his office to let him know the news.

"Look, somebody needs to take over for Cliff," he said. "You're the guy. It's your job over the next few years to get rid of these assets we want to sell."

Fastow was thrilled. "That's great, Jeff," he said. "Cliff's done a real shitty job at this. We should've gotten rid of some of this stuff a long time ago. I'm really going to do a much better job at it."

This again. Fastow seemed to never stop selling himself.

Ken Lay was in Austin on May 2 to chair a meeting of the Governor's Business Council when he received word that his stepson, Beau Herrold, needed to speak with him.

Calls from Herrold were coming at a fast clip. With Enron's stock price falling, banks that lent Lay tens of millions of dollars against the value of his shares were getting itchy. They wanted him to pay down the debt, either by selling shares or by coming up with cash. For a while, they had been doing that by borrowing from Enron's short-term loan program, often pulling out the maximum of four million dollars at a time. Then Lay would hold on to the stock, hoping the price would go up. If it didn't, he would pay back the Enron loan with stock, then borrow again when needed.

Today was no different. Bank of America this time, Herrold said. "The credit line is running real tight, and the bankers need us to pay some of it down," he said.

"Okay," Lay said. "How much?"

Herrold laid out the amount that was owed.

"Fine," Lay said. "Let's use the revolver and pull down that amount." Herrold promised to take care of it.

Holy shit.

Jordan Mintz was at his desk, thumbing through copies of the old approval sheets required for LJM transactions. It had taken six months to locate all of them, and what he saw was as bad as he had feared. The board had been told by Fastow the year before that Skilling was approving the deals. That was never formally required, but *that's what they were told was happening.* And it wasn't. Not once.

Mintz scheduled an emergency meeting with Causey and Buy. He wasn't prepared to confront Enron's chief executive without some advice. At ten on May 7, he went upstairs to Causey's office to tell them what he had found.

"We need to get Jeff's signature on these," Mintz said. "But how do I do that? I've never really worked with Jeff before. Do I send a bunch at a time?"

There was another possibility, Mintz suggested. With all the issues surrounding LJM, maybe he could just sit down with Skilling and talk. Buy hated that idea.

"Send Jeff a memo about getting his signature," he said. "But remember, Jeff is very fond of Andy Fastow."

He looked Mintz in the eye. "Don't stick your neck out on this," he said.

The call from the White House personnel office came the next day to Harvey Pitt at the Fried, Frank law firm.

"Congratulations, we have good news for you," the White House official said. "The President has decided to nominate you to serve as the next chairman of the Securities and Exchange Commission."

The formal announcement would come, the official said, at the regular White House press briefing. Pitt thanked the caller and hung up. He was never asked if he would accept the job. Everyone knew that he would.

The next morning, Jordan Mintz stood in line at a Starbucks on West Gray Street with a folded copy of *The New York Times* under his arm. He ordered a tall red-eye, then carried the steaming drink to one of the tables outside. Sitting down, he unfolded the paper and skimmed the front page. His eyes drifted to an article on the left side.

"White House Picks Chairman of S.E.C.," the headline read. Mintz set the paper down, studying the article.

"The Bush Administration has chosen Harvey L. Pitt, a prominent corporate lawyer, to be the next chairman of the Securities and Exchange Commission."

Harvey Pitt. Mintz knew the name—a well-respected, top-flight securities lawyer. Worked at Fried, Frank.

Suddenly an epiphany. *Fried, Frank.* If it was good enough to have Harvey Pitt, it was sure to have other experienced securities specialists. Mintz even knew somebody there, a buddy from college. Fried, Frank was sure to give an unbiased view of the whole LJM situation.

Mintz stood, carrying his coffee to the car. He needed to get to Enron and call Fried, Frank's Washington office. By day's end, Fried, Frank would be putting the formalities in motion to finalize its retention to launch an examination of LJM. It would take about a month, but then Mintz would have an independent analysis of whether the sloppy, halfhearted procedures designed to deal with the conflicts in Enron were as bad as he thought.

Why are they doing this? It's just inappropriate.

Lay read those words with irritation. He had been flipping through news articles about Enron, provided to him each week by a clipping service, when he came across something from May 9 by TheStreet.com, a news Web site.

The article was all about a new research report by some outfit in Cambridge called Off Wall Street. Apparently, the recent report, which Lay had never seen, attacked Enron for declining profitability and rising debt.

But according to this article, the sharpest criticism was reserved for the dealings with Fastow's funds. The piece quoted some Wall Street analyst—anonymously, Lay noted—slamming the propriety of the arrangement. Lay set down the clipping. How could anyone criticize LJM?

This was scrubbed and reviewed by the accountants, the lawyers, everybody. And they're trying to make it look like we're doing something shady.

Lay's annoyance grew. If only everyone knew about all the top-notch protections built into the process, they would never criticize LJM. Enron's managers had thought of everything. There was no reason to worry.

Fastow was ready to tell his staff about his new responsibilities. This was the big time, a chance to push more deals and make a whole lot more money. People like Mark Metts, the deal maker on the wind-company sale, had blocked him in the past. Back then, Metts worked for Baxter. Now he would work for Fastow. It was all too delicious.

Fastow summoned a few close advisers to his office and almost danced a jig as he let them in on the big secret.

"There will be an announcement coming out about me becoming head of corporate development," he began. "This is exactly what Jeff wants because we're just gonna move assets off our balance sheet."

Mintz was horrified. With all the conflicts that already existed, now Skilling was making Fastow the top asset seller—*when he was already a top asset buyer?*

Fastow broke into a wide grin. "We're just gonna sell a *shitload* of assets to LJM," he beamed.

Everyone listened, tight-lipped. None of them had imagined that Enron could actually find a way to make such a horrible situation so much worse. But unknown to any of the executives in that room, Fastow was wrong. There would be no flood of sales. The once-impregnable walls that surrounded and protected the LJM funds at Enron were about to come crashing down.

CHAPTER 17

AS NIGHT FELL IN Miami Beach, the seventeen-story tower of the Loews Hotel glowed a brilliant white, illuminated by an array of spotlights. On the sidewalk at the tower's base stood Andy Fastow, clad in jeans and a light sweater and wearing a mobile-phone headset. He looked distracted as he listened to a harangue from Jeff Skilling.

It was May 17, 2001, the day that President Bush announced the release of the final report of Cheney's Energy Task Force. The proposed policies—from electricity deregulation to streamlining rules for building power plants—struck investors as a boon for industry, driving up stock prices for almost every energy company.

But not for Enron. On a day that the company should have been preening, its stock was the industry laggard, dropping almost three dollars to close at $52.20. Skilling heard the news while on a couples retreat with Rebecca Carter in Napa Valley, and since then, he had been calling around, trying to figure out what was going wrong. His director of investor relations, Mark Koenig, told him that the market was buzzing with fears about Enron. Some had to do with concerns that India planned to cancel the Dabhol power contract. But there was something else, Koenig said: in the wake of the Off Wall Street report, a growing skittishness about Enron's dealings with the LJM funds.

Skilling hunted down Fastow, who was in Florida meeting with executives from Enron's top banks. When Fastow's phone rang, he was outside the hotel, waiting for a chartered bus that was taking everyone to dinner.

"Andy, do you know our stock lost more than $2.80 today?" Skilling asked icily the moment Fastow answered. "Worst performance in the industry."

Fastow was stunned. He already knew about the release of the task-force plan. "I don't understand that," he said. "That is just really frustrating."

Jordan Mintz emerged from the hotel, looking for the bus. He saw Fastow and sidled up to him. Fastow shook his head. "On the phone with Skilling," he said softly.

Skilling's voice droned on through the headset. "Listen, Andy," he said,

"I've been hearing a lot of concern from the investment community about the company and about LJM. There's just a lot of noise about this."

Not quite true; he'd heard it from Koenig. But Fastow couldn't blow it off as just something Koenig made up if Skilling took the credit for divining this bit of market gossip.

Fastow shifted his feet. "Well, I don't understand why," he said. "There's nothing wrong with it."

"Andy," Skilling said, "perception is reality. If it's having a bad impact on the stock, it's not worth it."

A minute later, Fastow hung up, looking troubled.

"Everything okay?" Mintz asked.

Fastow nodded. "Yeah, Skilling's upset about the stock price. Says he's hearing a lot of noise about LJM."

As he spoke, the bus arrived. The two executives climbed on board, followed by a troupe of bankers.

At about that same time in Beverly Hills, Ken Lay was sitting in the Magnolia Room at the Peninsula hotel. A wall of French doors coaxed in the late-afternoon sun, spilling shimmers of light across the crowded conference table.

Some of the most influential members of Los Angeles's political and financial community were there. To one side was Richard Riordan, the city's mayor. Across the table sat Michael Milken, the disgraced financier turned philanthropist. And on one end was Arnold Schwarzenegger, the movie star who had recently begun dipping his toe in California's political waters.

The group was there to discuss the continuing crisis in the state's energy markets. Lay, who was the primary speaker, explained that Enron and Southern California Edison were working together on devising a solution that would require some action by the legislature.

Milken asked a question. "How much progress are you making up in Sacramento?"

"We're beginning to get support on both sides of the aisle," Lay replied. "I think if we can get something passed, the Governor will sign it."

After the meeting broke up, Lay lingered. In a moment, he saw Schwarzenegger approaching. During the meeting, the actor had asked no questions, but now seemed eager for a conversation. The two were introduced and shook hands.

"I thought your ideas were very interesting," Schwarzenegger said. "I'm delighted at least to see that *somebody* is thinking about how to solve this problem."

Lay nodded. He understood. Everyone, Schwarzenegger included, was tired of the dithering by Gray Davis. "At least we're trying," Lay replied.

"Well, I look forward to following your success," Schwarzenegger said. "I'll mention a few of your ideas to my friends in Sacramento."

Back at his home in Houston that weekend, Lay settled down on a couch with a copy of the report from the Cheney task force. Right away, he saw it strongly supported electricity deregulation. Well, no surprise there.

Still, as he dug into the details, Lay felt disappointed. His big push had been for regional transmission organizations, to take the place of the system of state-by-state electric grids. But it just wasn't there. Lay closed the report. Well, he had known the utilities would fight that issue, and they were always a formidable opponent in Washington. This time they had won.

In a cramped office in the back of the Los Angeles bureau of *The Wall Street Journal*, a fifty-one-year-old reporter named John Emshwiller was on the phone with California's attorney general, Bill Lockyer. Emshwiller was working on an article about the state's investigations of power marketers and their lack of success in turning up evidence of wrongdoing.

Tethered to his headset, Emshwiller took notes as Lockyer made clear his frustration in the lack of progress in the inquiries. Emshwiller asked if Lockyer believed there would be criminal prosecutions.

"I don't have any doubt that there will be civil lawsuits prosecuted by the state," Lockyer said.

A pause. Lockyer hadn't answered. "There is nothing I would rather do than nail a high executive," he continued.

Silence again. "You know what I'd really like to do?" Lockyer asked.

"What?"

"I'm not sure I should really say this."

Words that have led to breath holding by countless reporters.

"Why not?" Lockyer finally said. "I'd love to personally escort Lay to an eight-by-ten cell that he could share with a tattooed dude who says, 'Hi, my name is Spike, honey.'"

Emshwiller took it all down, almost in disbelief. This was one of those too-good-to-be-true quotes that was automatically guaranteed to be printed in the paper.

Skilling showed no expression as he walked over to his office conference table, where Fastow waited. In recent days, he had taken to cleaning messes he saw at the company: he had told Lou Pai that it was time to leave; he had shut down a tiny investment business. Rice had already told Skilling his days at Enron were coming to an end, and Baxter was gone. Enron's old guard was checking out.

Now the only unfinished business of consequence was getting rid of LJM. If Skilling left, he knew Lay would need a full-time CFO. That, coupled with market jitters, made the choice clear: Fastow had to choose—LJM or Enron.

"Andy, I want to tell you something," Skilling began. "I've been growing increasingly uncomfortable with the content of our conversations."

Fastow blinked. "What do you mean?"

"Our last ten phone calls, all of them in one way or another dealt with LJM. And to be quite honest, I don't give a shit about LJM. I care about the company."

It couldn't continue that way, Skilling said. There was too much noise about LJM. It was hurting Enron.

"Andy, you have to make the call," he said. "If you want to spend your time working for LJM, you can. Or you can spend your time being the CFO of Enron. But I'd like you to make a decision between the two."

Fastow had listened intently, watching his boss's face. There were no emotional clues; his tone had not been combative, just blunt. "I can't just say I want out, because I'm the managing partner," Fastow said. "Can you give me a couple of days to think about it?"

Skilling leaned back. "Sure," he said.

Ken Lay hurried past the large red sculpture of a number 9 in front of the midtown Manhattan office building. He had just come in from Teterboro Airport and was rushing for his eleven o'clock appointment on Fifty-seventh Street with Kohlberg Kravis Roberts & Company—a meeting, he knew, that could well decide his next career.

KKR was tops in leveraged buyouts and owned an array of companies through its investment funds. It won national fame in its successful battle for RJR Nabisco. Now its principals, Henry Kravis and George Roberts, wanted to speak to Lay about taking a role at the firm.

Lay rode to the forty-second floor and was escorted to see Kravis. The two chatted until the arrival of Roberts, who had been discussing the new opportunity with Lay for weeks.

Kravis took the lead. "I know you and George have been talking about our plans," he began. What KKR wanted, Kravis said, was a council of five or so wise men—corporate chiefs who had proven their mettle on the business battlefield—to advise on strategy.

"You can be as active as you want to be," he said. "You can give us a little bit of time, you can give us a lot of time, you can give us all of your time."

A flexible commitment. That sounded good.

"And," Kravis continued, "we'll certainly set it up to be very rewarding for you financially."

Work as much or as little as he wanted and be paid well either way? Why, Lay could be involved in an array of KKR companies, doing different things every day. He would have responsibility, but none of the administrative duties that were part and parcel of being chief executive.

Only six months remained until Skilling took over as Enron's chairman. Lay had been trying to find his next act, but nothing had grabbed him. This place did. KKR, he thought, would be a great place to hang his hat.

"*. . . who says, 'Hi, my name is Spike, honey.' *"

Tim Belden, Enron's top energy trader in Portland, reread Lockyer's quote in that morning's *Journal*, dumbstruck. The state attorney general was boasting that he wanted Ken Lay *raped in prison*? This was crazy.

Worse, it was scary. Belden knew there was something out there for investigators to find—the secret trading strategies. Already the firm had been hit with subpoenas from California, and an investigating committee in the legislature was demanding reams of documents. About the only thing keeping the dirty details secret was the legal wall that Enron had erected around its trading operations.

But how long could that last? For the first time Belden wondered if he might need to hire his own criminal lawyer, just to protect himself.

It had taken a few weeks, but Mintz finally completed his memo for Skilling about the missing signatures on the LJM approval sheets. He had written it in longhand, being cautious in his wording to make sure that he showed appropriate deference to the top boss.

The memo, only three paragraphs long, laid out the sheets' purpose, mentioning that there was a line for Skilling's signature that had apparently been missed. The sheets from 2000 had all been collected, he said, and were ready for him to officially give his approval for the deals.

"To that end," Mintz wrote, "I will arrange to get on your schedule to assist you in this regard; alternatively, I can send such approval sheets to you as a package and you can sign them at your convenience."

Once the memo was typed up, Mintz signed it and carried it back out to his secretary. "Darlene, can you put this in a P&C envelope and take it up to Jeff's office?"

She fetched one of Enron's "personal and confidential" envelopes and slid in the document. Neither knew that in hours, Skilling would leave the office for days. At best, he wouldn't pick up the memo for a week.*

Fastow was out of options. He couldn't back partly out of LJM and keep Skilling happy. It had to be all or nothing.

He had asked the lawyers to examine whether he could hold a *small* interest—say, less than ten percent—in the general partners of the LJM funds and avoid disclosure. The answer was no. In fact, their position was changing. Even if he held only a small interest, the market probably should know his compensation, they now said.

It was obvious what he had to do. He needed Kopper to come to the rescue once again. They had been working together on their side deals for almost four years. Kopper knew everything; he was the one keeping track of their comparative financial winnings on his laptop. He had bailed Fastow out before, on RADR. There was nobody else Fastow would trust to take over LJM2, and certainly nobody else likely to quietly cut him in on profits in the future.

That was decided. Fastow would sell his interest in the LJM funds to his buddy Kopper.

At 3:30 on May 24, Mintz breezed into Fastow's office. That day, he had gotten word Fastow needed to talk, and this was the first time their schedules had both been open.

"Hey, Andy," Mintz said cheerily. "How's it going?"

Fastow, standing at his desk, nodded in the direction of the small conference table. "Sit down," he said.

Mintz took a chair as Fastow picked up a small pad of paper and joined him. Then the words rushed out.

"I'm gonna sell LJM," Fastow said.

What? Had Mintz heard correctly?

"Really?" he replied calmly.

Fastow nodded. "Yeah, I've got to get out," he said. He explained how everyone had ruled he would have to disclose his stake in the funds, no matter how small it was.

"Well, is that right?" Mintz replied. What, he wanted to know, were the lawyers saying?

*In later sworn testimony to Congress, Skilling said he never saw Mintz's memo.

"I don't care," Fastow replied. "Skilling thinks the time has come for me to move on. So fine."

He took a deep breath. "Talk to Ron Astin. Find out what types of disclosures we'll have to make if I sell."

He'd take care of it, Mintz promised.

The meeting ended, and Mintz headed to the elevators. He climbed on alone, and the doors closed behind him. A second passed. Mintz clenched his fists and thrust them up in the air.

"Yes!"

Back in his office, Mintz grabbed the phone. He dialed the Fried, Frank firm and asked to be put through to the lawyers working on the analysis of the LJM conflicts.

"Guys," he said happily, "I've got some good news."

Skilling was at his desk, his face stern. It was 10:30 on the morning of May 29, his first full day after a week out of the office. Fastow sat before him.

"You've asked me to think about this issue regarding LJM, and I've come to an absolutely clear-cut decision," Fastow said. "I unequivocally want to be the chief financial officer of Enron."

Skilling was surprised.

"That's what I've always wanted to be," Fastow continued. "And from now on, that's my dream job."

The transition would take time, he said. He would probably have to travel, to sell the funds' investors on the idea.

"I talked to Michael Kopper about taking over for me, and I think the investors will be okay with that," he said. "But one way or the other I've made my decision. Within a month, I think I can do it."

"Okay, Andy," Skilling said. "Let me know if there's anything I can do to help."

They talked for another minute. Fastow sounded almost relieved with the outcome.

For good reason.

That week, Enron was in the final stages of repurchasing the interest in the Cuiabá power plant from LJM1. The agreement to buy back the investment—at a profit to LJM1, of course—had been struck long before.

But this repurchase *had* to be disclosed. LJM1 was a related party, already identified in the filings. Its transactions with Enron couldn't, under any interpretation, be kept secret. Anyone looking closely at Enron's disclosures—and now, it seemed, many investors were—would spot the repurchase. It was going to be awfully hard to explain why assets were moving from Enron to LJM and back again, all at a loss to the company.

Now, maybe no one would have to. The agreement in principle for the Cuiabá buyback had just been signed, with an expectation of closing on May 30, the day after Fastow told Skilling of his intention to sell the LJM funds. Kopper wasn't a senior Enron officer; LJM technically wouldn't be a related party once ownership changed hands.

So why not just postpone the buyback? As for the money—well, Fastow could get it by adding his share of the Cuiabá repurchase to the LJM2 sales price. No one—not investors, not directors—would ever have to know about it.

Enron had committed the cash, the deal was ready to go. But now, just for a while, they were going to pretend no deal existed, all so Enron could avoid revealing the truth.

Lunch hour had arrived, and Sherron Watkins—the married name of the former Sherron Smith, the sometimes-salty-tongued executive who formerly oversaw the operations of the JEDI partnership—was heading out. After emerging from the elevator bank, she bumped into her former boss, Andy Fastow, in the lobby. She had long considered Fastow something of a snake, but she was smart enough to know when to make nice.

"How're you doing, Sherron?" Fastow asked.

Watkins shrugged. Not good, she replied. She had been working in Broadband, and it was in a meltdown. Watkins had recently learned her job was being eliminated, and she was scrambling. She didn't mention it, but she had reached out to a friend at Reliant Energy, hoping for a lead. The only opportunity she found inside Enron was investor relations, but she had a two-year-old and wasn't looking forward to the hours that job demanded.

Fastow's eyes lit up. "Come talk to me," he said. "I think I've got something for you."

She smiled. "Okay, I'll do that."

The two parted ways, and Watkins's smile vanished. Work for Fastow again? She could almost feel her stomach sinking.

Days later, Watkins met with Fastow to discuss his plans. It hadn't been announced yet, he told her, but he was slated to take over corporate development now that Cliff Baxter was gone. And he needed help.

"You can be my eyes and ears around the building," he said. "You can even put your name on any deal you find."

Watkins tried to sound pleased with the offer, but she wasn't. It was just a new version of the chief-of-staff position he had come up with years before for Shirley Hudler—essentially making her his glorified spy, partly so she could find out what other Enron deal makers were up to.

She mumbled a few comments, then headed out. She called her friend at Reliant; nothing was available for at least a month. That left her with either investor relations or spying for Fastow. Unpleasant as the second option might be, at least it would allow her time with her toddler.

Looked like she was heading back to Fastow's stable.

Near Cannes on the French Riviera, Ken Lay walked out of the exercise room at the Hotel du Cap-Eden-Roc, the internationally acclaimed hot spot for the heavyweights of the corporate and entertainment worlds.

It was the morning of June 2, and Lay had just finished putting in time on the treadmill. As he headed toward the sidewalk, he saw two friends he had brought along on the trip—John Duncan, chairman of the board's executive committee, and Harry Reasoner, the managing partner of Vinson & Elkins. The two apparently had just finished their morning walk and were sipping juice.

"Well, good morning, you two," Lay called out.

The men lingered. After fifteen minutes, Lay thought of something. The night before, he had received a message from Skilling. It reminded him of the evidence he had seen of Skilling's apparent depression. He had been meaning to inform the directors. This was as good a time as any.

"On another matter, John, there's something I think you ought to know," Lay said.

"What's that, Ken?"

"Jeff Skilling really isn't a happy camper," he said. "There's a lot of frustration and stress."

Reasoner stood by, listening to the conversation. Duncan considered Lay's words for a moment.

"What do you think he might do?" he asked finally.

"I don't know," Lay said. "I probably ought to call Pug on this, too. But I just wanted you to know that he's not enjoying his job. I'm trying to help, but he's just having a tough time right now."

"Do you think everything will be okay?"

Lay shrugged. "When somebody gets unhappy, sometimes they do weird things," he said.

The negotiations, if they could be called that, to sell LJM2 to Kopper went along swimmingly.

Already Kopper was flush with cash—thanks to Fastow. Just weeks before, Enron's thirty-five-million-dollar buyout of Chewco finally closed, giving Kopper a ten-million-dollar profit, the payment once blocked by McMahon. Now all Fastow and Kopper needed was a swap. Fastow would give Kopper control of LJM2. In turn, Kopper would hand over the millions that Fastow had secured for him. Plus the $7.3 million distribution from LJM1 that Kopper would receive in a few weeks from selling the Cuiabá stake back to Enron. Oh, and some property he owned in Houston, too. It would take a few weeks, but when the dust cleared, Fastow would be able to pocket another $16.4 million.

The price was a bit on the excessive side, Fastow knew. But if he was going to be forced to walk away from his moneymaker, he wanted cash.

Lots of it.

Vince Kaminski was furious.

Once again he was being forced to put his analysts through the wringer of the Performance Review Committee, the PRC, and the outcomes were inane. These were top minds in their field, but now Kaminski was almost required to designate a portion of them as average or below.

They called it forced rankings. Skilling had sent out an e-mail announcing new requirements for the allowed percentages in each ranking level—just five percent at level one, thirty percent at two, and so on. While he mentioned flexibility, human resources treated the numbers as inviolate. The system was not only unfair, it was illogical. Even if his entire staff consisted of modern-day Einsteins, Kaminski would be forced to brand the performance of most of them as average or worse.

Not surprisingly, the analysts were in open revolt. In written evaluations, they told Kaminski that forced ranking was destroying the company. If everyone did a good job, the only way to move ahead was by undermining a colleague, but analysts needed to work as a team to get the best answers. Rather than sabotaging each other, they verbally attacked Enron and Skilling for pushing an idea without understanding the consequences.

Kaminski sided with them completely and made a stand at the PRC.

"I will not do the forced ranking," he said. "It's not in the best interest of the company."

His defiance was short-lived. If he wouldn't rank his troops, he was told, somebody else would. And Kaminski had no doubt that in the white-hot competition that was the PRC, his analysts would be given short shrift as rival executives jostled to elevate their own people.

He buckled, and ranked his staff. He did try to cheat by stuffing too many of them into categories one and two. But he was just ordered to try again, until he hit the preset percentages.

One victim of the process was Kevin Kindall, whose yearlong inquiry had uncovered the threats posed by the Fastow partnerships. Vital work, but other, more senior analysts had been involved in pricing splashy, moneymaking deals. No matter how important Kindall's effort, the truth was, it couldn't even get a budget. His rank was forced down.

Kindall didn't take the news well. "Vince, I did not deserve this," he said. "My work did not deserve this."

"I tried, Kevin," Kaminski replied. "I know this is unfair. But there was nothing I could do."

Wearily, he described how the process worked, recounting his attempts to thwart it. But Kindall wasn't interested in the system's mechanics, only its results.

"If Enron doesn't operate in a way that can recognize my contribution," he said, "then I need to move on."

Kaminski tried to persuade his young charge to change his mind, but to no avail. Kindall resigned.

The person who had discovered the true nature of the financial threats that would ultimately destroy Enron was gone, his contribution dismissed as irrelevant to the company's continued success.

The mood was electric on June 12 among the technology executives gathered in a Las Vegas auditorium. Vivek Ranadivé, CEO of Tibco Software, approached the stage to introduce the day's featured speaker, Jeff Skilling.

The company was honored to have Skilling there, Ranadivé said. "Enron is being hailed as America's most innovative company," he said, "And Jeff Skilling has been declared the number-one CEO in the entire country."

Skilling bounded onto the stage, dressed in an open shirt and a sports coat. He launched into a lengthy speech, telling his audience that the Internet had only begun to show its usefulness for business. It would transform industry, he said, and Enron's future would be found there.

"We couldn't do what we're doing now without the technology of the Internet," he said.

The questions after his speech touched mostly on technology matters. But one broached a different subject.

"Can you give us your thoughts about the power crisis in California?" an audience member asked. "And tell us what you think the state could have done differently?"

Skilling smiled. He thought of the attorney general's comment a few weeks before about taking Lay to a prison cell to be raped. Maybe it was time to shove back. "Oh, I can't help myself," he said. "You know what the difference is between the state of California and the *Titanic?*"

The crowd laughed. Skilling glanced away. "I know I'm going to regret this," he said, almost to himself.

He looked back at the crowd. "At least when the *Titanic* went down, the lights were on," he said.

The crowd roared.

The SEC reached its final decision: the quality of Andersen's accounting violated the fundamental principles of the profession. Despite protests from Andersen's top lawyers, the firm would have to be sanctioned and charged with civil fraud. At least that way, SEC investigators hoped, Andersen would learn its lesson, and other accounting firms would know that they had to straighten up. The nation's securities regulators never wanted to see another case like Waste Management again.

The violations at Waste Management, an Andersen client whose financial restatement years earlier helped spur Arthur Levitt's "numbers game" speech, had horrified agency investigators. Andersen accountants had known about violations, but year after year failed to stop them. Now the SEC told Andersen it could settle the case or fight it out in court. Andersen, after much grumbling, took the deal.

On June 16, Gary Goolsby, a senior Andersen partner in Houston, reviewed a two-page consent form, essentially the firm's agreement to settle. Goolsby, the partner who months before informed Carl Bass of his removal from Enron accounting issues, had been chosen to sign the documents.

In recent days, Goolsby had spoken repeatedly with Tom Newkirk, the SEC lawyer handling the Waste Mangement case, assuring him that Andersen had learned its lesson. The firm would mend its ways, Goolsby promised.

He glanced through a second document, called the final judgment. On the second page he saw that the firm was forbidden, by a permanent injunction, to deceive anyone in the future. It all seemed pretty boilerplate. Goolsby signed the consent. Andersen was now on notice. If it played fast and loose with the rules again, the consequences would be stiff.

That same week, federal energy regulators bowed to political reality. The California electricity shortage was not going to end on its own, not as long as traders could go state to state around the West playing games with prices. So price caps were extended to all western states. That clampdown, coupled with rising supplies, finally ended the crisis, more than a year after it began.

That might have delighted electricity customers, but it troubled Enron investors, who saw California as an opportunity for almost unlimited profits. Now that bonanza was slipping away. Enron's stock price the day of the announcement hit $43.07 a share, a new fifty-two-week low.

Vince Kaminski could almost feel his heart tearing out. His best analyst, Stinson Gibner, had just come in to let him know that he was leaving Enron, too. It wasn't a matter of pay or title. It wasn't the PRC. It wasn't that there was a better job offer. It was the Raptors.

"I can't have pride in a company that can do something like Raptor," Gibner said. "I can't keep working here."

Kaminski tried to argue, but his efforts were feeble. It was hard for him to disagree.

The lawyers arrived in Skilling's office at 9:15 on the morning of June 20 to talk about the continuing ripple effects from the California electricity crisis.

Days earlier, Skilling had received a call from Pacific Gas and Electric, a California utility that had filed for bankruptcy months before. PG&E was reaching out to creditors like Enron, asking for meetings to discuss a proposal to help get it back on its feet. After the call, Skilling had asked Mark Haedicke and Richard Sanders, the two senior Enron lawyers handling the California mess, to come discuss the utility's request.

Once the lawyers arrived, Skilling decided to raise another issue. He was heading out to California the next day to deliver another speech. Before he left, he wanted to check his facts again. He mentioned his plans and said that his speech was again going to underscore that everything happening in California was a market-driven phenomenon.

He looked from one lawyer to the next. "Enron has got to be clean as the driven snow. So one more time. Are we as clean as the driven snow on this?"

Haedicke nodded. "Yeah. There was some stuff going on last year, but we shut that down."

What kind of stuff? Skilling asked.

Sanders was surprised. By now—so many months after they had discovered Death Star, Fat Boy, and the other trading strategies—he thought that Haedicke would have *told* Skilling about this.

"Well, there are some allegations of unfair competition and antitrust allegations," he replied.

Skilling seemed taken aback. "What are the kinds of things we're being accused of doing?"

Sanders paused. Did Skilling really want to know details? He mentioned the names and described each one. Some, he said, were problematic because they involved false documents. Others, like one looping power out of state and back in, smelled bad, but legally were probably okay. Still, Sanders said, the lawyers had ordered the tactics stopped as soon as they were discovered.

"Okay," Skilling said. "So we're as pure as the driven snow?"

Beau Herrold was desperate. As one of Lay's investment advisers, he had been scrambling for months to get the family's finances in order. But every time he felt he was on solid footing, Enron's stock price dropped, decreasing the value of the assets securing Lay's loans and triggering more demands for cash from the banks. It was like trying to build a sandcastle at high tide, with new waves coming in every so often, knocking down the latest fortifications.

And Lay wasn't making things any easier. His belief that Enron's share price would pop back up was unshakable. As much as possible, Herrold had been tapping everything else—dumping some of Lay's few other easy-to-sell investments, trying to negotiate better terms with the banks. But still the destructive waves kept coming.

So, on June 20, Herrold decided to check out a more aggressive strategy he had been contemplating. Until now, he had used Lay's revolving credit line with Enron only occasionally, pulling down four million dollars in cash at a time, then waiting before repaying it with Enron stock in hopes the price would recover in the interim. Instead of doing that every so often, Herrold thought, what if he did it again and again and again, to really pay down some of the debt? Get the sandcastle out of the tide's reach?

He spoke with lawyers and compensation experts at Enron, asking about limits on the credit line. Scribbling notes as they spoke, Herrold learned he could draw down four million dollars every business day—up to twenty million dollars a week. The only restrictions were that he had to give the company notice, and if Enron stock was used to pay back the loan, Lay had to have held the shares for at least six months.

What about disclosure? Usually when corporate executives sold stock in their own company, they were required to file a document known as a Form 4 to let investors know. Would Lay have to do that each time he paid back the loans with Enron shares? Herrold telephoned Rex Rogers in the general counsel's office to find out. Rogers assured him that the disclosure requirements on selling shares to the company were far less stringent.

"It only has to be reported in the proxy for the year that you're in," Rogers said. "There's no need for a formal Form 4, because it's a private transaction between Ken and the company."

Satisfied he understood, Herrold consulted his stepfather about the idea.

Getting his approval, he set to work using the revolving credit line to pay down some debt.

The next day, June 21, protesters in pig masks shouted and marched outside the Commonwealth Club in San Francisco, eager to show their contempt for the afternoon's featured speaker, Jeff Skilling. On the street, a black sedan pulled by. Behind tinted windows, Skilling and two other executives watched as the protesters raged about Enron and corporate greed. It infuriated Skilling; *they* hadn't created the mess in the state, the politicians did.

He clenched his jaw. "I wish we didn't have to do business in the state of California," he muttered.

Minutes later, Skilling was on a platform in the club's main room. The place was already packed with ticket holders awaiting the discussion about the energy crisis.

From the back of the room, a blond woman in her early thirties walked up to the third row. Skilling noticed her; she seemed to be staring at him. He figured she knew him from somewhere, but he couldn't place her face.

After several more minutes, the time of the speech finally arrived, and an officer of the club stood up to deliver the introduction.

In the third row, Francine Cavanaugh tried to move slowly. She had just sneaked past security without anyone detecting the item she had smuggled in.

Asking permission, she moved up to an empty seat in the front row. Then she reached inside her black book bag, pushing aside a brown paper bag she had put there as camouflage. She drooped her shoulders a bit to mask what she was doing; she didn't want anyone to alert security before she had the chance to take her shot at Skilling.

The club official droned on as Cavanaugh watched Skilling; he crossed his legs, seeming distracted, then took a breath. Cavanaugh stood and started running toward him.

Skilling was annoyed. He thought the introduction was a little obnoxious, with all sorts of innuendo that Enron had something to hide. He didn't like it.

Suddenly, at the edge of his field of vision, he detected something. A blur. A commotion. He turned to look.

A woman was running toward him, screaming something. She brought her arm back. Then, he felt a sharp pain in his head.

———

"Jeff, that could have been a gun."

It was a couple hours later. Rebecca Carter was standing in Skilling's house back in Houston, hearing about the protester at the Commonwealth Club who had hit him in the face with a pie. The attack had left his head bleeding slightly, but Skilling brushed off the incident as just one of those things. Carter wouldn't have it.

"I thought they had all these security people there."

"They did," he replied.

"But this woman got close enough to put a pie in your face?" Carter said sharply. "You could've gotten shot."

Skilling put up a feeble argument but realized she was right. It could have been a gun. Nothing was worth this.

About that same time, in Islamorada, Florida, Lea Fastow took a seat in a spa chair at Paul Joseph's Tiki Salon and slipped off her shoes. She placed her bare feet on the towel in front of an older woman, who proceeded to soak, trim, and shape her toenails.

Lea and Andy had just arrived in the Florida Keys on Enron's Hawker 800XP. It was a personal trip, but their use of the plane had been approved by Skilling, so long as they each paid a fourteen-hundred-dollar round-trip fare. That would come on top of the cost of a few days at the Cheeca Lodge and Spa, an oceanfront resort. But Fastow didn't mind the expense. After all, it was being picked up by the Fastow Family Foundation, the charitable group set up with the $4.5 million he stole from NatWest in the Southampton deal.

Lea and Andy weren't the only ones relaxing on the foundation's dime. It was also paying to fly in two other couples—Andy's brother Peter and his wife, Jana, along with Lea's brother Michael and his wife, Lilly. Together, they would enjoy a weekend of spa treatments, personal massages, fly-fishing, and tennis lessons—all on the foundation's tab.

The siblings had been appointed trustees of the foundation, and this luxury trip was dubbed their first annual meeting. But, legally, the couples couldn't just party and relax, not if the foundation was going to pay the bill. So over dinner on the evening of Friday, June 22, the official meeting was held—for all of thirty minutes.

They reviewed the foundation's "investments"; almost all of the cash was sitting in a money-market account. Still, with so much on deposit, the foundation had earned interest of almost $280,000. The amount going to charity was far less. In 2000, the foundation had made grants—many for as little as a few hundred dollars—of less than $63,000. By far the largest went to the Fastows' place of worship and to local museums—just at a time when Lea was striving to reach an elite rung among Houston's art patrons. So far in 2001, just over $34,000 of the interest on the money had gone to charity, again mostly to museums.

The patterns seemed to belie a true purpose of the foundation: to avoid paying taxes on the stolen money by taking advantage of the exemptions for charitable groups. And the money the Fastows did give away advanced their position in the most exclusive reaches of Houston society.

But this slush fund of cash had other uses, and not just financing tax-free vacations to posh resorts. On the night of the official meeting, the family members voted to hire a fund administrator, who would receive both a salary and relocation costs. The perfect candidate? Andy Fastow's dad Carl, who would soon be flown down with his wife at foundation expense to live in the Houston house Kopper turned over when he purchased the LJM funds. The stolen money could help keep Fastow's parents comfortable in old age.

Life was good.

Hoisting a carry-on bag over his shoulder, Skilling, along with his teenage son Jeffrey, bounded down a ramp at Houston Intercontinental Airport. Their flight to Madrid was scheduled to leave in just a few minutes, and Skilling could hardly wait; another three-week vacation about to begin.

As they approached the plane the morning of June 27, Skilling's cell phone rang. He pulled it out of his pocket.

"Jeff, it's Joe Nacchio."

Skilling sighed. Nacchio, the chief executive of Qwest Communications International, and several of his executives had been riding his tail for days. Qwest had its own broadband division and was struggling like the rest of the industry. Weeks before, Qwest and Enron had begun negotiating a fiber-swap deal; essentially, Enron hoped to sell much of its network to Qwest, which in turn would sell back rights on the system. Skilling liked the idea; Enron could dump its network and all the associated costs while still having the capacity available that it needed to serve customers.

But the terms Qwest wanted made no sense. If Enron was going to keep its customers, it would need to schedule capacity instantaneously. Qwest said it couldn't provide that service but still wanted a deal. Skilling refused; why sell the network if Enron would have to find another one?

Qwest kept pushing, and soon it became obvious to Skilling why. They wanted to pay what Skilling considered a ridiculous price for the network, Enron would in turn pay a ridiculous price for the rights to use it, and everybody would book revenues. Nothing much would really change hands; the entire transaction looked to Skilling like an accounting gimmick.

Skilling made his lack of interest clear innumerable times. Nothing could be done, he told them. But still Nacchio kept calling. Skilling was sick of it. "Joe," he said, "I'm heading down the ramp for my plane to Madrid."

"You're going on vacation?" Nacchio asked.

"Yeah." Skilling reached the door of the plane.

Nacchio didn't relent. Skilling should call back as soon as he reached Madrid, he said. The two sides resumed negotiations, but nothing came of it. For that quarter, Qwest and Enron weren't able to report the revenues that, in truth, would have brought both companies nothing but trouble.

What the hell is this?

Sherron Watkins looked through the Enron assets listed on an Excel spreadsheet, trying to comprehend what she was seeing. She had recently started working for Fastow on the corporate-development side and now was spending her days on work she considered demeaning.

Watkins had been digging through Enron's records, looking for assets that could be readily sold. Plenty had lost value, like Elektro in Brazil, but could bring in cash. Then there were other investments—in companies with names like New Power, Avici, and Hanover Compressor—that were hedged by entities called the Raptors.

What Watkins saw made little sense. The losses in the Raptors were gargantuan, totaling hundreds of millions of dollars. A lot, if not all, of that money was owed to Enron. How could any company make good on a commitment that was so huge?

Stumped, Watkins decided that to do her job, she needed to understand these entities. She called Causey's office and asked for someone to teach her about the Raptors.

In Spain, Skilling gripped the steering wheel of his rented car, passing vineyards on both sides of the road. It was his second day of vacation, and he and his son were driving southward on the first leg of a trip from Madrid to Morocco. Their conversation was free-flowing, and Skilling was grateful to be alone at last with the boy.

There was a pause in the conversation. Skilling decided to broach a new topic. "Jeffrey," he began slowly, "would it bother you if I weren't CEO of Enron?"

This was Skilling's last fear, that leaving Enron would cost him his children's respect. But Jeffrey had no idea what his father was talking about. "No," he replied.

"It wouldn't make you think any less of me?"

"No, it would be good, because then I'd get to see more of you."

Skilling thought about that. "Well, I've decided—don't tell anyone, don't tell your mother or brother—but I've decided to leave Enron."

Jeffrey glanced at his father. "Oh, good."

As June rolled to an end, it was clear that cutting costs and redeploying staff wouldn't hold back the tide of red ink at Enron Broadband Services. The division, which had been introduced with such fanfare just two years before, couldn't stand on its own. Senior managers decided to fold it into energy trading. The glory and the hope were dead, the plans for an intelligent network shelved, the push to build a broadband-trading effort scaled down dramatically.

But Fastow saw the division's collapse as just another opportunity. The general counsel of Broadband, Kristina Mordaunt, had long been a favorite. Plus, she had shown her ability to play in the gray zone; she had invested fifty-eight hundred dollars in Southampton and hadn't said a word when Kopper surprised her with a million-dollar payday weeks later. If Fastow was going to handle corporate development, he wanted somebody like Mordaunt as his general counsel.

Mordaunt was game. She spoke with Jim Derrick about the idea and was persuaded. This was a great opportunity.

Even as Fastow was giving Mordaunt a push up the career ladder, he was moving her further into his illegal conspiracies. The RADR deal—where Fastow, through Kopper, had set up bogus "investors" as fronts in the purchase of some wind farms—was still producing cash. One front investor, Kathy Wetmore, was holding $750,000 generated from the fraud scheme. Fastow instructed Kopper on the next move.

Kopper called Wetmore with the details: the money was to be wired to account HS-75406-EJ at UBS Paine Webber. On July 2, the money was sent on its way. Mordaunt, Fastow's new lawyer, had been gifted another $750,000.

Kaminski couldn't let it rest. Kevin Kindall might be gone, but his former underling's report about the dangers Enron faced was still there and as damning as ever. Glisan apparently didn't care, so Kaminski decided to try again, this time with somebody else.

Nobody knew more about trading, or the risks it faced, than Greg Whalley, who had worked in wholesale for years. Kaminski dropped in to see him. Point by point, he laid out Kindall's findings.

"Greg, we have huge exposures that we don't understand," Kaminski said after several minutes of explanation. "We have to analyze them and understand them."

Kaminski looked Whalley in the eye. He could tell he wasn't getting through. The trader seemed to be treating his exposé as some sort of academic exercise.

Whalley stood up. "Let me think about it," he said. "I'll get back to you."

It was the same answer Glisan had given. Kaminski didn't expect things to turn out any better this time.

It was a sultry evening in Houston, with the sounds of chirping crickets filling the screened-in porch behind Skilling's new mansion. It was July 9. Skilling had just returned from Spain and was now relaxing over cigarettes with Rebecca Carter, talking about life after Enron.

He would tell Lay that week, he said. After that, travel for months at a time. He had no money worries; between compensation and stock sales, he had socked away more than fifty million dollars. There was no need to rush a new job. He could take his time.

Carter listened to the plans with alarm. His plans for world travel and adventure didn't seem to hold a place for her. Maybe, she feared, she wasn't part of his grand strategy.

"So where does all this leave me?" she asked.

Skilling glanced at Carter and saw the torment on her face. *Uh-oh.* He had hoped to wait a while. Her birthday was just nine days away; that had been the date he had selected to tell her. Obviously, he couldn't wait that long.

"Okay," he said, standing. "I better do this now."

He walked inside the house, through the kitchen toward a study in the back. There, he picked up the small box he had hidden away weeks ago, then headed back to the porch.

He stood in front of her. "Okay, so you wanted to know where this leaves you. Here's how I'm thinking about it."

He opened the box, pulling out an engagement ring. He got down on one knee. "Will you marry me?" he asked.

Tears welled in Carter's eyes, and she wiped them with her hand. Then she smiled. "Yes," she said. "I will."

Skilling had a few days left and wanted Enron's directors braced for everything. What if a disaster hit the world economy, something that shook companies around the globe? He needed analysis, numbers, something to show the board the company's ability to withstand a shock.

He met with Rick Buy and one of his analysts, David Port, at 10:30 on the morning of July 11. They came in with a report showing the effects of various market disruptions. Skilling thought the assumptions too timid.

"Put some real liquidity stress on the portfolio," Skilling said. "Take it much further than you ever have."

Consider a global calamity, he instructed them. A huge nuclear meltdown, one that caused massive casualties. Imagine that, in the aftermath, public fears forced the overnight shutdown of the global nuclear industry.

"I want to know what kind of effect that would have on prices," Skilling said.

Port laughed. "It would be *huge*."

"I know. But tell me what would happen here, how much liquidity we would need to ride it out."

Buy and Port left Skilling's office, eager to get started on this intriguing project. When they returned one week later, the news was good. Enron would only need a couple of billion dollars to survive, they reported.

Skilling was relieved. He had heard the reports from Fastow and Glisan showing that Enron had much more cash at the ready than that. So there was nothing to worry about. No war, no earthquake, no external threat could do Enron in.

No one thought to consider what might happen if, instead of a global calamity, Enron faced a far more plausible disaster. Like a credit downgrade, or the forced disclosure of the Raptor losses. Kaminski and Kindall had already done that analysis. And the terrifying results had been ignored by everyone who heard them.

Just before 1:30 on the afternoon of Friday, July 13, Ken Lay was working at his desk. It was his first day back in the office after a tough trip to Spain, Italy, and India, where he had delivered speeches and attempted, without success, to negotiate a resolution of the Dabhol fiasco.

Skilling walked in for a scheduled appointment. Lay greeted him, and they went to the conference table. Skilling brought out a pad of paper with a checklist on it and began running down several issues. It was pretty forgettable stuff. After ten minutes, Skilling set down his pad and looked at Lay firmly.

"There's another item," he said. "I've come to a decision that I need to share with you."

His voice was flat. "I've decided I want to resign."

Lay stared at him. "What?" he asked.

"I want to resign."

Lay knew Skilling had been struggling with his new job. He had anticipated that he might come asking for a sabbatical. But quitting? Maybe this was like that escapade a few years back, when Skilling was talking about working part-time. That passed; this might, too.

Lay placed his arm on the table. "Tell me more," he said. "I've got to understand what you're saying."

There wasn't a lot to it, Skilling said. "I've been thinking about this for a while. I'm concerned that the job is damaging my health. I'm facing enormous stress."

Then there was his family, Skilling said. He still had young kids at home. His daughter was about to leave for college, his older son would be leaving a few years later. And he wanted to spend time with his younger son.

"So I've decided for health reasons and for family reasons that it's best for me to resign."

Lay barely knew what to say. He was supposed to start at KKR by year's end, just months away. Did he have to walk away from that opportunity? Just to pick up after Skilling?

"Jeff, you know this is going to be a real shock to the board," Lay said. "And obviously, from a personal standpoint, this isn't something I wanted or expected to happen. I've kind of made plans for later in the year."

Skilling didn't respond.

"But more importantly," Lay continued, "I'm concerned this could do some harm to the company, damage investor confidence. Is there any way I can talk you out of this?"

"No," Skilling said. "I've thought about this really hard, and I believe this is the right thing for me."

Me. The word grated on Lay. Not what was good for the company. What was good for Skilling. "Jeff, obviously I just got back from a grueling trip, and I need to reflect on this," Lay said. "But I hope this weekend, you'll get some rest and reflect on this and see if there is maybe some alternative we can come up with."

"Okay, that's fine," Skilling replied. "But I'm pretty firm on my decision."

"If he won't change his mind, we need to think about what to do," Lay said. "We need to think about timing."

It was the next day. Lay was on the telephone with John Duncan from the board of directors, who was stunned by the Skilling bombshell—and perplexed. They should make every effort to change Skilling's mind, Lay said, but if they couldn't, they should move fast to contain the damage.

"If he's going to leave, then probably the sooner the change occurs, the better," Lay said.

Still, there was the matter of succession.

"Obviously, you can pick anyone to be chief executive that you want," Lay said. "I've made plans for later this year, but given that my life has been committed to Enron, if you feel it's best for the company for me to stay awhile, I would certainly give that serious consideration."

Duncan bubbled happily in response. Of course if Skilling left, they would need Lay to step into the breach. That went without saying.

Lay hung up. His wife, Linda, was nearby, disappointment written on her face. She had been looking forward to her husband cutting back on his travel. Now the hectic pace would resume. Maybe even get worse.

"Jeff really let you down," she said. "He let the board down, and he let the company down."

She couldn't understand how he could do this, she said.

"I just think it reflects great immaturity on Jeff's part that he thinks he can just flip a switch like this," she said. "He wants the job in February, and then in July he wants to give it back? What kind of behavior is that?"

Lay certainly couldn't disagree.

Early Monday morning, Lay wandered down the hallway to Skilling's office. His door was closed. Lay glanced over at Sherri Sera, Skilling's secretary.

"Is he in a meeting or on the phone?" he asked.

"No," Sera replied. "He's fine. Just go on in."

Lay clicked open the door, tapping on it as he entered. Skilling was at his desk, looking rested and at ease.

"Jeff," Lay said as he walked in, taking a seat at the conference table, "get some sleep over the weekend?"

Skilling smiled. "Yeah, slept like a baby."

The moment was uncomfortable. "Good," Lay said. "So maybe you've decided to change your mind?"

Skilling shook his head. "Nope. Haven't changed."

Lay felt himself sink a little into his chair.

"Are you sure?" he asked.

The two bantered for several minutes. It quickly became obvious that yes, he was sure. He was leaving. It was, he repeated, the right thing for him and his family.

"And probably," he added, "this is the best thing for the company, too."

That set Lay back. "Why?"

Skilling shrugged. "Given all the problems and everything going on, I think people might be reassured by you coming back in," he said.

Lay didn't understand. "What makes you think that?"

"Well," Skilling said, "certainly the stock price hasn't performed well. Maybe by you stepping back in, it will restore confidence that obviously we've lost."

Was *that* what this was about? Was Skilling taking the falling stock price personally, like some stock-market rejection of his leadership? Was he *that* thin-skinned?

"Jeff, that's tough to say," Lay replied. "I think there's a very large risk here that it will further shake confidence. You haven't been CEO very long, and for you to step down like this may not be perceived well."

Lay paused. "The directors have a question, Jeff."

"What's that?"

Well, Duncan and Winokur both had the same concern, Lay said. "Do you know something we don't know?"

The question surprised Skilling. "I don't think so," he said. Retail was fine, Skilling said, wholesale was ripping up the place. Broadband was troubled, but it had been folded into trading and might even eke out a small profit in a year. India—well, he said, he didn't know much about India, because Lay was handling that.

"But listen," he said. "I'll talk to Causey, just to make sure he's okay with everything. Make sure there's nothing out there I don't know."

All right, Lay said. He'd appreciate that.

Fifteen minutes later, Skilling headed down the hall into Causey's office and dropped into a chair.

"Rick," he said, "I need to ask you. Is everything okay? Anything on the horizon that worries you?"

Causey thought for a moment. "No," he said.

He stopped. "Well . . ." He paused. "The Raptors," he finally said. "We've got some that are in the money, some that are out of the money."

Skilling nodded. Some Raptors could meet their obligations; some were struggling. Okay, he understood that.

"That's just a wash, though," Causey continued. "No, I think things are about as good as they have ever been."

Skilling stood. "Okay, thanks."

He had the information he needed. Everything was fine.

Sherron Watkins watched carefully as two executives from retail drew a series of boxes on a whiteboard. It was the afternoon of July 30, and Jimmie

Williams and Javier Li were giving her a lesson about the Raptors. The more Watkins heard, the more horrified she became.

The Raptors were complicated to diagram, but all the lines and arrows did little to disguise their underlying problem: they did *nothing*. There was no real economic hedge here. Enron was simply using assets in one hand to protect the value of assets in the other. This whole construct was destined to collapse. Fastow, with LJM2, wasn't assuming much risk; he owned just three percent of the total, as best as she could tell. The rest of the risk was being borne by Enron itself.

After the lecture, Watkins decided to find out more. She reviewed Enron's filings for 2000 and saw a footnote suggesting that it avoided $500 million in losses through its use of the Raptors. This was unsustainable, and terrifying. Early in her career, Watkins had lived through the collapse of another employer that played fast and loose with the rules. She didn't want to go through it again. She wanted out.

That week, Watkins started looking for another job.

CHAPTER 18

MARK PALMER WATCHED ABSENTMINDEDLY as the numbers above the door of the crowded elevator blinked steadily toward the forty-seventh floor. It was August 10, a Friday, and Palmer, Enron's public-relations chief, was feeling relaxed. He had been out of the office for weeks, first on a fishing trip with his oldest daughter, then in California to extend an olive branch to local reporters. The West Coast electricity debacle had absorbed Palmer's time for months, and he felt relief as the glare of bad publicity receded.

The doors opened, and Palmer made his way down the hall. Turning a corner, he noticed Steve Kean, his boss, at his desk looking distracted. Kean glanced up.

"Come with me," Kean said. "I need to talk to you."

He headed down the hallway toward a conference room. Palmer followed, his mind racing. Was he in trouble?

In the conference room, Kean plopped down at the table, perching himself on the edge of a black Aeron chair. He brought both hands up, rubbing the bridge of his nose. Then he laid his arms down on the table and looked at Palmer.

"Skilling is leaving," he said.

The air blew out of Palmer's lungs. He eased himself down onto the edge of the small round table, which immediately tilted and sent him tumbling into a chair.

He spent a moment gaining his bearings. "Why?"

"Personal reasons."

"What, is he sick? What kind of personal reasons?"

Kean's face showed no emotion. "Personal reasons."

"Jesus, we've got to do better than that."

A moment's thought. "When?" Palmer asked.

"We're going to announce it Tuesday."

What? Doing this rapidly was public-relations suicide. Why the hurry?

"Who's going to take his place?"

"We don't know," Kean replied.

Palmer glanced at the floor. The only obvious candidate was Lay. But in recent years, he had become so out of touch, leaving things to Skilling. From Palmer's experience listening to him speak with reporters, Lay's information about Enron was usually years out-of-date. He was the world traveler, the glad-hander. He wasn't up to *running* things. Not anymore. Certainly not without Skilling.

They needed to prepare the announcement, Kean said—and not at the office. Advance word could not leak out. This weekend, he said, they needed to get together at his house and write up a press release. Palmer agreed and promised to tell no one, not even his wife. He stood and wandered out of the room, heading to his desk. He was numb. He had been hoping for smooth waters. Now this.

This would certainly be one of his toughest weeks ever, Palmer thought. Soon, he was going to need everybody on deck—his secretary, the full support staff—ready to work hard.

Palmer passed a large conference room, where a tense meeting was being held. Elizabeth Linnell, an executive from Kean's department, saw him and ran to the hallway. "I've got to talk to you," she said urgently.

She dragged him into the meeting. Faces around the table gazed at him somberly. She sat Palmer down and looked him squarely in the eye. "Your secretary is stealing from the company," Linnell said.

Palmer stared back at her. "*What?*" he asked sharply.

They couldn't mention Skilling's kids. Under any circumstances. Lay's instructions, relayed from Skilling himself, were clear. He didn't want his kids to think they were the reason he was leaving, even if they were.

Kean and Palmer were in an office on the second floor of Kean's house, cobbling together the materials for the big announcement. "Personal reasons" wasn't cutting it, so they were trying to guess what might fly with Skilling. In the draft press release, they had written "spend more time with his children" and "concentrate on his family," but those were knocked down. "Personal reasons" or nothing.

It was getting ridiculous. Kean phoned Skilling and spoke with him for a few minutes. Finally, Skilling suggested that he come over and help on the release. Kean agreed.

The knock on the front door came ten minutes later. Kean headed partway down the stairs, calling to Skilling to come in. The door opened. "Is Mark here?" Skilling asked.

"Yeah, he's upstairs, too," Kean said.

Skilling hustled up and strode into the office, in obvious high spirits. He was wearing green hiking shorts and boots, with a few days' beard growth shadowing his face.

"Hey!" he said, looking at Palmer. "How you doing?"

Palmer furrowed his brow. "I am *pissed*."

Skilling froze. "You're pissed?" he repeated. "Well, I guess I can see how you might be pissed."

How could Skilling be surprised? This was going to be hard enough, particularly with Palmer's secretary now on leave. If Skilling went into this with some rose-colored view of how things would play, it would make it worse.

"Jeff, you need to be prepared for a lot of people being angry," Palmer said. "You're our leader, and a lot of people are going to feel like you're abandoning us."

Skilling raised his eyebrows. "You really think so?"

"*God!*" Palmer exclaimed.

"Guys," Skilling said, "I had to do this. I had to."

Case closed. There was no discussing this.

The next morning, the senior executives on Enron's management committee had just finished discussing the last item on the agenda. Skilling looked around the room as his fellow executives gathered up their things.

"I have one more announcement," he said.

Everyone settled back down.

"I proposed to Rebecca," Skilling said, smiling at Carter, who was sitting in a chair near the conference table. "And believe it or not, she said yes."

Around the room, executives stood and rushed over to Skilling to offer their congratulations. But they pretty much ignored Carter. She considered the reaction bizarre.

"Now we'll turn to the chief financial officer's report," Pug Winokur said. "Andy?"

It was minutes before six that evening. Fastow clicked up his first slide. Nothing about Skilling had been announced yet; that would come after the committees concluded their work. For this meeting no one expected fireworks. But this time the directors were going to hear the unvarnished truth about Enron's condition. Until now, Fastow was just the CFO, always presenting the most comforting portrait of Enron's finances. Never before had he clearly explained the financial condition of the company, created by his years of incompetence and venality.

This day he was speaking not only in his role as CFO but also as head of corporate development, in charge of selling large assets. The board wanted the full picture. Now it was time to tell them in no uncertain terms the financial virtues of an aggressive campaign to rid Enron of its mistakes.

"Enron's total outstanding financings and debt, on and off balance sheet," he said, "totals $36.3 billion."

In truth, Fastow was wrong; he was overstating the numbers. The totals had been assembled sloppily, double counting some $2 billion in debt. But even the correct amount of $34 billion was staggering, almost three times the $12.8 billion that appeared on Enron's balance sheet.

And the situation was climbing out of control. Fastow clicked up another slide, showing that in just twelve months, debt had ballooned by over $14 billion, an increase of more than 62 percent. To pay the interest on debt, a company needed real, hard cash. Enron *had* been reporting cash on deposit from its trading partners as cash flow from operations. But now that the energy markets in California had turned, money was flying out the door—to the tune of some $2.3 billion in just six months, or half the previous year's total cash flow.

Huge, growing debt. Rapidly falling cash flow. This was corporate nitroglycerin, an explosive mix capable of blowing any business apart. The directors had every detail they needed. Fastow finished his presentation.

"All right," Winokur said. "Thank you, Andy."

They went on to the next topic.

At 8:10 that evening in the Austin Room at the Four Seasons, Lay tapped a glass with a spoon. The full board had been meeting for forty minutes, listening to the usual reports. Now it was time for the most important part.

"At this point I'm calling an executive session of the board," Lay said. "So if everyone would excuse us."

Several executives stood to leave. Rebecca Carter, the corporate secretary and Skilling's fiancée, was shaking as she moved toward the door. In the hallway she saw Sherri Sera, Skilling's secretary, seated on a couch. Carter sat down beside her and began to cry.

Back inside, Lay looked at the assembled group.

"As I've told most of you," he began, "Jeff has notified me that he wants to resign and leave the company."

Skilling glanced around. Some mouths were dropping.

"I've tried to talk him out of it, and I believe some of you have, too," Lay continued. "So far we've failed in that effort. But I do think it's appropriate now for Jeff to have some time to explain his reasons for leaving."

Lay turned the floor over to Skilling, who seemed shaky and uncertain. "This is a decision that has been very painful for me," he said. "But I think it is appropriate, a necessary one for me and my family."

He rattled off the reasons he had given Lay: the prospect of his children heading to college, his desire to be around them more. He paused with tears in his eyes.

"If I've disappointed some of you, I'm very sorry."

After repeatedly losing his composure, Skilling stopped speaking. Then questions—mostly from John Duncan and Norm Blake. Were there other reasons for this?

"I'm feeling a lot of pressure," Skilling said. "I'm having trouble sleeping. I think it's harming my health. But, primarily, I need to spend more time with my kids."

Blake bore in. Were there problems at Enron they needed to know about, anything that might be prompting this?

"Not causing this," he said. "But I've made no secret about my feelings about the international assets. We've wasted billions of dollars, and that still upsets me. And I'm not interested in being the one to fix that problem."

Of course, there was California, where they were still owed north of $600 million. And then Broadband.

"But is there anything *else*?" Duncan asked.

Skilling shook his head. "No," he said softly. "Just all the things I've told you about."

They came at him time and again, posing the question different ways. But the answer never changed.

"All right, Jeff," Lay said finally. "Now, if you'll excuse us, I need to have a few words with the board, and I'll see you in the morning."

Skilling nodded, wiping his eyes on the back of his hand. Then tears again. "I just want to thank everybody," he said as he stood. "I'm sorry I've disappointed you. But I think it's the right thing to do, and I hope it doesn't have serious consequences on the company."

He lingered for a moment. Then he turned to leave.

Outside the room, he saw Carter and Sera on the couch. He sat beside Carter. "How'd it go?" Carter asked.

Skilling sniffed. "I got a little too emotional," he said. "But it's done. It's over."

"Anything further that any of you think we ought to talk about tonight?" Lay asked.

The directors were ready to move past astonishment. Before the meeting, a few of those who knew what was coming had spoken to Lay and received assurances that he would return as chief executive for as long as he was needed.

"I'm sorry this happened," Blake said. "But, Ken, I'm delighted that you're here to pick up the pieces."

Lay had their support, the directors said. They would get through this. It was best, they decided, not to announce the resignation until the market's close the next day. They would formally accept it just before telling the world.

The meeting ended twenty minutes later, but no one quite wanted to leave. Directors gathered in small groups, gossiping. Lay glanced over at Mickey LeMaistre, a doctor and president emeritus at Houston's M. D. Anderson Cancer Center. The two approached each other. "Mickey," Lay said softly, "I'm very concerned about Jeff."

"I am, too," LeMaistre said. "I made notes while we were listening to him, and I didn't like how he sounded. I'll try to call him tomorrow and talk to him."

They paused. They didn't want to say the words. "I'm worried about his mental health," Lay admitted.

"Me, too," LeMaistre said.

The next day, a group of executives gathered in the small conference room off Ken Lay's office. They were reviewing all the final documents for the press announcement, making sure everything was in order.

The air in the room was heavy with unanswered questions. Mark Palmer glanced at Skilling. This wasn't the breezy, cheerful Skilling he saw Sunday; he looked terrible. His eyes were puffy, exhaustion drained his face; he seemed incapable of a smile. Palmer felt terrible for him.

It's going to be so ugly, he thought.

Suddenly, Skilling leaped up. "Wait a minute," he said, heading to the door. "I forgot something."

In a flash he was back with a piece of Enron stationery in his hand. On it he had written his sentence-long resignation from Enron. He held it out to Lay.

"Here," Skilling said. "I think you need this."

Lay took the piece of paper and glanced at it. An expression flashed across his face. Disgust? Disapproval? Annoyance? No one could quite tell.

For a moment, Skilling stood in the room, seeming out of place. Finally he turned to leave. The meeting quickly broke up, with Lay and Palmer lingering behind. Palmer decided to use this moment to push for the truth.

"Ken, do you know why Jeff is leaving?" Palmer asked. "Can you tell me, is he sick? I just want to know if he's sick because, frankly, he looks sick."

Lay's face hardened. "It depends how you define sick," he said, his voice icy.

Lay grabbed the letter, holding it by the edge like a used air-sickness bag. Then he left without another word.

Rumors flew through the building. Whalley and some others had been given the heads-up by Lay, and word spread quickly: Skilling was leaving. And no one was sure why.

Then a call went out to the top executives from Lay's office. An urgent management meeting had been scheduled for 3:30 in the Enron boardroom. Everyone should be there.

That same day, Sherron Watkins went out for lunch with two friends. At one side of the table sat Kathy Lynn, a Fastow favorite who worked with LJM2. They, too, tossed around gossip over the meal; even at their level, there were rumors that a big departure was coming.

Watkins mentioned that she had heard Kopper was buying out Fastow's interest in LJM2. "Michael must not have paid him very much with all those Raptor losses," Watkins said.

Lynn shot Watkins a cocky look. Whatever happened to the Raptors didn't matter to LJM2, Lynn said. "Andy put it together so that LJM2 got its money out first."

An amount equal to Fastow's full investment, plus profit, had been distributed to LJM2 before the Raptors hedged anything. Technically, Lynn said, LJM2 still had equity in the deal, but that was just more potential profit. If the Raptors blew up, LJM2 wouldn't lose anything.

Watkins was horrified. If LJM2 had nothing at risk, then Enron was hedging with itself. Enron would pay Enron to make up for its merchant-investment losses. No one could *ever* think the accounting rules allowed for that.

She had to step up her job search. Then, before she left, Watkins decided she would sit down with Skilling and tell him everything she had learned.

When 3:30 rolled around, not a seat was empty in the boardroom on the fiftieth floor. Skilling and Lay arrived and sat on the far side, their backs facing the windows.

"By now, all of you probably know that Jeff has decided to resign," Lay said. "He's doing it for personal reasons. We tried to talk him out of it, with no success. I'm not going to tell you I'm happy about this, but the board has asked me to step in as CEO, and I've agreed."

He turned to Skilling. "Jeff, do you have anything you would like to say?"

Skilling swallowed. "It's been really hard," he said. "And even though I've got to go, I'm still with you guys."

Distress washed over the room. Janet Dietrich, a top executive in Enron Energy Services, wasn't satisfied. "Jeff, what's going on?" she asked. "Are you sick?"

"No, I am not personally ill," he said. "I'm okay. I don't have a disease. It's just personal reasons."

The questions kept coming, but again and again, Skilling insisted there was nothing wrong with the company, that his departure was purely personal, and that no, he wasn't going to give details. His voice cracked.

"I want to thank you guys," he said. "It's been a tough decision, but it's the right thing to do." With that, Skilling bid everyone good-bye and walked out, leaving Lay behind to deal with his confused and angry executives.

"Ken, what is going on?" Dietrich said almost as soon as Skilling departed. "Why is Jeff leaving?"

Lay held up his hands. "He's explained his reasons to me. I respect his decision, the board respects his decision, and we're just going to have to move ahead without him."

For now, Lay repeated, he was going to be back in the driver's seat. "I know I'll have to change how I handle the job day to day," he said, "but I'm prepared for that."

Fifteen minutes later, the meeting was over. Small groups of executives huddled around the room and out in the hallways. There was a lot of bitter gallows humor.

Well, the forty-five-year-old quarterback couldn't handle the job anymore, one executive joshed, so Lay was coming off the bench. It was like calling Johnny Unitas, a star quarterback from the 1960s, in to play at the 2001 Super Bowl. The game had passed him by a long time ago. Few expressed confidence that Lay was up to the task.

Just down the hallway, Jeff McMahon and Ray Bowen were walking toward the elevator. The meeting had been oddly unsatisfying. They both smelled a rat.

"Unless Skilling is sick, or his kids are sick, this makes no sense," Bowen said. "He's bailing on us."

He took a deep breath. "The guy's a pussy," he said.

———

That afternoon, after Enron made the announcement, Lay and Skilling conducted a conference call with analysts and reporters. Their message was uni-
fied: Skilling's decision was purely personal, and the company was fine.

"I can honestly say that I have never felt better about the company," Lay
said.

Skilling agreed. He declined to explain his personal reasons, making vague
references to family issues.

"I feel a little bad that anything I do is somehow construed as something
related to the company," he said. "The company is in great shape."

Back to Lay. "There are no accounting issues, no trading issues, no reserve
issues, no previously unknown problem issues," he said.

Jordan Mintz didn't know what to think. Skilling was leaving? Maybe something big was going on. Well, Fastow always held himself out as Skilling's
buddy. He was sure to know the truth behind all the happy talk.

Mintz dialed Fastow's extension. "Andy, what do you know about this
thing with Skilling?" Mintz asked.

Fastow sounded annoyed. He had only just found out himself a short
while ago, he told Mintz.

"Well, what's going on?" Mintz asked.

Fastow snorted derisively. "I don't know," he said. "Maybe Jeff and
Rebecca just want to go out on the beach so he can buttfuck her all day."

Mintz hurried off the phone. He was flabbergasted. Skilling's supposed pal
doesn't know anything—then he deals with it by tossing out a nasty, sophomoric comment?

What, he wondered, was a guy this—*sleazy, immature, what was the word?*—
doing as chief financial officer?

Ken Lay's meeting with Rebecca Carter came that same day. Before he said
a word, she knew what was about to happen. The king was dead; most countries didn't keep the queen around for that much longer—even the prospec-
tive queen.

"Rebecca," Lay intoned, "the board has been discussing the situation, and
they are just not comfortable with you remaining in your current position."

Lay rambled on, saying things about finding her another job in the company, other than corporate secretary. But Carter didn't want to hear it. She
was devastated.

The next day, Watkins was at her computer, typing. She had been stunned by
the Skilling announcement. Enron had been his life. But now he was walk-

ing out, right as its last set of big ideas—broadband, retail, water—had flopped, with no new brainstorms in the wings. The Raptors were a disaster—no, a *scandal*—and had to be unwound.

Well, so be it. Enron had to take its lumps, admit its losses. She had decided to write to Lay to let him know everything she had discovered.

"Dear Mr. Lay," she typed. "Has Enron become a risky place to work? For those of us who didn't get rich in the last few years, can we afford to stay?"

Skilling's resignation would raise questions, she wrote, and investors would pull apart Enron's finances.

"I am incredibly nervous," she wrote, "that we will implode in a wave of accounting scandals."

Watkins finished her letter in less than an hour. She decided she wasn't ready to reveal her name to Lay. So she put the anonymous letter in an unmarked envelope and asked her secretary to deliver it to the box for employee questions. Then she placed another copy in an envelope and addressed it to her friend Jeff McMahon, so that she could hear his opinion. She signed her name on the envelope.

Later that afternoon, McMahon was digging through his in-box when he noticed a typed letter. His secretary, apparently, had removed it from the envelope. He picked the pages up and started to read.

Why am I getting a copy of this? It was addressed to Lay. He scanned to the bottom of the page. No signature. He read through it a couple of times. McMahon didn't know much about the Raptors or another deal it mentioned, Condor, but he was taken aback by the ferocity of the attack on their accounting. Andersen was all over them! McMahon would have thought that they would be bulletproof. But what amused him most was how the letter went after Fastow's premier deals. His old nemesis was sure to blow a gasket when he heard.

Where did it come from? McMahon called Bill Brown, described the letter, then read it to him.

"Wow," Brown said. "This is all Fastow. Is it true?"

"I don't know anything about these things," McMahon replied. "Raptor was the biggest secret around. *Nobody* got to know how it was structured."

"Where did you get it?"

"It's in my in-box. Is there a copy in your in-box?"

Brown checked. Nothing. The call ended, and McMahon walked down the hall to Ray Bowen's office. "Ray," he said, thrusting the letter out, "read this."

It wouldn't take long for word of this mystery letter to seep through the company.

Later, McMahon's phone rang. It was Sherron Watkins.

"Did you get my memo?" she asked starkly.

"What memo?"

"The one I wrote to Lay."

McMahon's mouth dropped. "That was *your* memo?"

Watkins's letter arrived that day in human resources and was sorted onto a stack of other notes from employees. But this one seemed serious and, since it was addressed to Lay, was delivered to his office that afternoon.

Lay puzzled over it. The language struck him as inflammatory—*wave of accounting scandals?*—and there were these suggestions Enron would have huge losses from the Raptors. It seemed wrongheaded. Enron was better than ever. Skilling said so. Fastow said so. Everybody said so.

Still, he couldn't ignore the allegations. This was exactly the kind of thing he should give to Jim Derrick, Enron's general counsel. He would know what to do.

Derrick didn't know what to make of the letter, either. The allegations were serious, but he wasn't in a position to decide whether they were right. He snapped up a pen and wrote "FYI" at the top of the first page of the letter. Then he scribbled the names of a few in-house lawyers, plus Fastow's and Causey's. They would know how to deal with this. Probably even had the answer at their fingertips.

The letter annoyed Causey. Some *nobody* wanted to look smarter about the Raptors than the lawyers and accountants who had reviewed and approved them? That was pretty nervy.

Still, he had to address the question, along with another about Andersen that had been forwarded to him. Both were submitted for the all-employee meeting the next day, but he didn't think the Raptor concerns should be discussed there. He began typing a response. He addressed the Andersen question first. Then he got to the anonymous letter.

"NOTE: I would not read this question," he typed.

If management did wish to allude to it, Causey wrote, the answer should be vague, saying simply that a question had arisen about Enron's structured transactions and the use of its own stock in those deals. Then they should dismiss it with a few words about how this stock was reflected in the calculations of earnings per share.

Watkins's letter asked nothing about earnings per share. Rather, it spelled out how Enron had recognized half a billion dollars in profits that weren't there.

Causey was sidestepping the question.

The employee meeting the next morning, August 16, had the frenzied atmosphere of a high-school pep rally. It was held in the Imperial Ballroom at the Hyatt Regency just down the block from Enron. Lay bounded in, dressed in shirtsleeves, waving at the applauding crowd.

"Well," he enthused, "I'm delighted to be back."

Lay described his excitement about the future, brushing aside whatever problems Enron was facing—in India, in California—as bumps in the road. There were some issues he knew about, he said. Since the announcement of Skilling's resignation, he had heard rumblings that Enron had strayed off the narrow path.

"Our values have slipped," Lay said. "But we're going to work on that. We're going to restore them."

Another chorus of applause.

Then the kicker. Things had been tough, Lay said, but now Enron was ready to turn a corner. In anticipation, he said, the company was giving all employees a onetime options grant, equal to five percent of their base salary.

"We want you," he said, "to enjoy the ride back up!"

Sitting close to the stage, Watkins listened to Lay's rousing speech with growing discomfort. Lay didn't even suggest that an accounting problem might be brewing. The anonymous letter had apparently missed its target.

As he wrapped up, Lay mentioned that his door was open to anyone with concerns. Just make an appointment, he said, through Cindy Olson from the human-resources group.

Soon the meeting was over and Watkins crossed the street with the crowds of employees heading back to Enron's office building. Climbing on the elevator, she pushed the button for sixteen, Cindy Olson's floor.

It took more than an hour, but Olson finally appeared. The two sat down at a small conference table, and Watkins brought out a copy of her letter, saying that she had sent this to Lay anonymously. Olson slowly read it.

She glanced up, looking ill at ease. "I'll tell you," she said, "Ken gravitates toward good news. It's one of his greatest strengths and greatest weaknesses."

The only way to really get action would be to sit down with Lay face-to-face. Would Watkins, she asked, be willing to do that?

"Absolutely," Watkins replied.

In the Los Angeles offices of *The Wall Street Journal*, John Emshwiller was on a couch, chewing sugarless gum. He hadn't been around the day of the Skilling resignation, but now his boss, Jonathan Friedland, wanted him to jump in.

"We need a second-day story on the Skilling departure," Friedland said.

Emshwiller wasn't happy with the assignment. Corporate resignations are choreographed affairs. Enron had selected its dance step and wasn't likely to change it now. Plus, Emshwiller didn't know many people there. This wasn't a company that he covered day to day.

"I might not be able to get much today," he warned.

Friedland's phone rang. "Do what you can," he said before grabbing the receiver.

It couldn't be put off any longer. Lay was back at Enron—for how long, no one knew. The job offer with KKR wouldn't, and shouldn't, wait for him. He had to decline. From his office, Lay telephoned George Roberts.

"George," he began, "I'm sure you've seen the news."

Skilling was home, putting together a list on a pad of quadrille paper. He had blown out of the office immediately after the announcement, leaving the packing to his secretary, Sherri Sera. Now, he was plotting his new life.

Finances. Office. Estate Planning. Those needed to be organized. His brother Mark would help him out there.

Reputation. Make sure his departure hadn't damaged his image with the business world.

Family. Spend more time with his kids, arrange some trips with them.

Health. Obvious. *Community.* Reach out into Houston, play a bigger role in the city.

There were plenty of details needed, but that was basically it. A business plan, just without a business.

It was section eight, called "Related Party Transactions," that got John Emshwiller's juices flowing.

After being assigned to follow the Skilling resignation, Emshwiller had put in a request for an interview, then scrounged up a copy of Enron's most recent SEC filing in search of any nuggets.

What he found startled him. Words about some partnerships run by an unidentified "senior officer." Arcane stuff, maybe, but the numbers were huge. Enron reported more than $240 million in revenues in the first six months of the year from its dealings with them.

One fact struck Emshwiller in particular. This anonymous senior officer, the filing said, had just sold his financial interest in the partnerships. Now, it said, the partnerships were no longer related to Enron.

The senior officer had just sold his interest, Skilling had just resigned. The connection seemed obvious.

Could Enron have actually allowed Jeff Skilling to run partnerships that were doing massive business with the company? Now *that*, Emshwiller thought, would be a great story.

Emshwiller was back on the phone with Mark Palmer. With no better explanation for Skilling's resignation, he said, the *Journal* was going to dig through everything it could find. Right now he was focusing on these partnerships. Were those run by Skilling?

"No, that's not Skilling," Palmer replied, almost nonchalantly. "That's Andy Fastow."

A pause. "Who's Andy Fastow?" Emshwiller asked.

The message was slipped to Skilling later that day. A *Journal* reporter was pushing for an explanation of his departure and now was rooting around, looking for anything he could find. Probably best just to give the paper a call.

Emshwiller was at his desk when the phone rang.

"Hi," a soft voice said. "It's Jeff Skilling."

It was a startling moment. Emshwiller had been on the hunt, and suddenly the quarry just walked in and lay down on the floor, waiting for him to fire. So he did: why was Skilling quitting his job?

"It's all pretty mundane," Skilling replied. He'd worked hard and accomplished a lot but now had the freedom to move on. His voice was distant, almost depressed.

He had been ruminating about it for a while, Skilling went on, but had wanted to stay on at the company until the California situation eased up. Then, he took the conversation in a new direction.

"The stock price has been very disappointing to me," Skilling said. "The stock is less than half of what it was six months ago. I put a lot of pressure on myself. I felt I must not be communicating well enough."

Skilling rambled as Emshwiller took it down. India. California. Expense cuts. The good shape of Enron.

"Had the stock price not done what it did . . ." He paused. "I don't think I would have felt the pressure to leave if the stock price had stayed up."

What? Had Emshwiller heard that right? Was all this stuff about "personal reasons" out the window? Had Skilling thrown in the towel because of *the stock price*?

"What was that, Mr. Skilling?" Emshwiller asked.

The employees at Enron owned lots of shares, Skilling said. They were worried, always asking him about the direction of the price. He found it very frustrating.

"Are you saying that you don't think you would have quit if the stock price had stayed up?"

Skilling was silent for several seconds.

"I guess so," he finally mumbled.

Minutes later, Emshwiller burst into his boss's office. "You're not going to believe what Skilling just told me!"

That son of a bitch.

Mark Koenig, Enron's director of investor relations, heard that same night about *The Wall Street Journal*'s interview with Skilling. The news infuriated him.

They had discussed this resignation for days, pressing Skilling for an explanation. *What's the reason, Jeff? What's the reason?* And every time, the same answer. *Just personal, nothing to do with Enron. Kids, exhaustion.*

Then, one day later, when everyone had already walked the gangplank of Skilling's story, the son of a bitch *changed* it! The stock price was *all about* Enron. If that was his problem, why didn't he just say so in the first place? Why wait until everybody at the company had made jackasses out of themselves by parroting his line?

Koenig glanced at Lay. The two were on an Enron jet along with a handful of other executives, including Fastow and Whalley. They had just spent a day with analysts in New York and were on their way to Boston to meet with investors there. The idea was to calm the market, to let the Street know that no surprises were coming. Then Skilling turns around and dumps one big, fat surprise in everybody's lap.

"Ken, Jeff's comments are really going to undercut everything we said yesterday," Koenig fumed.

Lay shared Koenig's unhappiness, but there wasn't much to say. Koenig set his jaw. "What is the *matter* with him?" he seethed.

The marketplace chatter about Enron was terrible. Steve Kean, Lay's chief of staff and top government relations executive, had heard a lot of it, and thought the criticism was too close to the truth. Lay needed to reposition Enron, explain that he recognized its problems and was planning to fix them.

With Lay on the road meeting with institutional investors, Kean composed an e-mail designed to explain the challenges that he thought Enron faced in the marketplace.

He began by reiterating his faith in the company. "I believe everything we have been saying," he typed. "We are making great money, we are growing, we are addressing our issues and we have all our capabilities intact."

Still, Kean typed, Enron was having difficulties because of its soured reputation in the marketplace.

"We're faced with too many bad, but true (or at least plausible) allegations that we have to deal with every time we try to tell our story," he typed.

They ran the gamut. Too much aggressive accounting, impenetrable financial reporting, hyping of unproven businesses. On top of that, Enron was believed to have a mercenary culture that drove away talented people. Worse, Kean wrote, it had gained a reputation for hiding problems until they became very big. The company needed to stop spinning, to make business decisions based on the economics of a deal rather than a desire to hit earnings or avoid a write-down. None of this meant there was a problem in investor relations or the accounting group, he wrote; they were the finest in the industry. But to improve its reputation, Kean wrote, Enron needed to reassess itself.

He sent the e-mail. If the top brass addressed these issues head-on, he thought, Enron could set itself right.

The Fastow partnerships were in play, that Palmer knew. Once Emshwiller started asking questions about them, it was only a matter of time until he came back looking for more. Not that there were any secrets to uncover, Palmer reflected. After all, Fastow had sold his interest, and his dealings were disclosed. Probably the way to handle the reporter's suspicions, Palmer figured, was to be up front about everything.

He called Fastow, asking him to speak with a *Journal* reporter about the LJM funds. Fastow audibly stiffened.

"I *don't* want to talk about LJM," he said. "It's a slippery slope, Mark. We'll answer this question, then they'll just have another one. It's a slippery slope."

Fastow was overreacting, Palmer thought. Yeah, like the whole world was suddenly going to be so interested in a bunch of Enron off-books partnerships.

The *Journal* wasn't going away. With Skilling having muddied up the water in his interview, the paper was going full bore to find out what was really going on inside of Enron.

Emshwiller was teamed up with Rebecca Smith, an energy reporter in Los Angeles. The strongest thread that the two of them had was this stuff about the Fastow partnerships. What were those? Did anyone on Wall Street even understand them?

They set out on their reporting. Maybe, they figured, they could pull together enough string on the partnerships to put out a basic story. Then they could just stand back and see what else came in.

Sherron Watkins was at her desk, hammering out a new memo for Lay. If she was going to sit down with him, she wanted to organize her thoughts first.

There was a Vinson & Elkins lawyer who might be able to help, but Watkins couldn't remember his name. Well, her friend Kristina Mordaunt, who now worked with Fastow in corporate development, was tight with that firm. Watkins called Mordaunt, asking for the name of the lawyer.

Mordaunt hesitated. "Why do you want to know?"

"I'm going to be meeting with Ken Lay on some issues and might want to recommend him for a project."

"What issues?"

Watkins invited Mordaunt to drop by her office so she could explain them in person. When her colleague arrived, Watkins handed her the original letter. Mordaunt read it and looked up, scowling. "Why are you doing this?" she said sharply. "Are you trying to bring down the company?"

Nobody seemed to be taking Watkins seriously. Mordaunt greeted her revelations with annoyance and skepticism, urging her to speak with the legal department before seeing Lay. Watkins took the advice and met with Rex Rogers, a top attorney in the general counsel's office.

Rogers's reaction was polite but patronizing. Would Watkins really want to take this to Lay? After all, every top expert—Arthur Andersen, Vinson & Elkins, Causey, Fastow—had signed off on these deals. The unspoken message was clear: the big boys knew what they were doing. Who was Watkins—who was anyone—to question their decisions? These were top people. They didn't make mistakes.

What e-mail was Ryan Siurek talking about?

Siurek, an architect on the Raptors, had been speaking with Andersen accountants about some technical detail involving $1.2 billion booked as "notes receivable" from the Raptors, or commitments to pay Enron, which related to the company's agreement to contribute stock to the entities. That had resulted in Enron's increasing its reported equity by the same amount. Siurek said he had raised the issue during the March restructuring in an e-mail to Patricia Grutzmacher, a member of the Andersen team.

But Grutzmacher had never heard about this, never saw the e-mail, and now was being asked about it. She dug through her old Lotus Notes files. Sure enough, there, in March, was an unopened e-mail from Siurek to her, with copies sent to other accountants on the Andersen team. None of them had ever discussed it with her. She opened it and found the notes-receivable question. She dialed Siurek.

"Ryan, I found that e-mail you were talking about from last March," she said. "But I never opened it. I never got back to you. This is the first time I've ever seen it."

A second's hesitation. "Well, when you didn't get back to me," Siurek said, "I just assumed you were approving the entry. I figured it was all okay."

It wasn't. Enron and Andersen, until recently the financial darlings of Wall Street, were on the verge of discovering a mistake. A $1.2 billion overstatement of Enron's total equity. One that might have been stopped if an e-mail had been opened.

Ray Bowen had been out of the office for days, returning finally on August 20, eager to learn more details about Skilling's resignation. The only person who might know, he decided, was Andy Fastow. He made an appointment to see him.

When the time came around for the meeting, Bowen walked in and dropped into the chair in front of Fastow's desk, skipping all the pleasantries.

"One question, Andy," Bowen said. "Why did he quit?"

Fastow raised his arms. "Ray, I don't know. I'm angry with him for quitting on me, but I'm as surprised as you are." He shook his head. "You know, I love the guy. I wouldn't be where I am today without him. But I don't know if he's got a kid problem or a drug problem. It just doesn't make any sense to me."

"What do you think's going to happen, Andy?" Bowen asked.

"I think Ken will name somebody as president soon."

"Are you on that list?"

Fastow grimaced. "I don't *think* so," he said.

Rick Buy. Of course. Watkins should call him. He was chief risk officer. *He* would want to know about what she had found. She had worked with Buy in the past. He wouldn't stand for cutting corners on the accounting.

She dialed Buy's office, only to find he was on vacation. She left a message, asking him to call as soon as he could. He got back to her later that day.

"Rick, there's something very serious I need to talk to you about," Watkins said. She launched into a detailed description of the problems she had dredged up.

"I've got everything written up. I've gone back and done some longer memos on this," she said. "Would you like to see all of my materials?"

She heard a deep sigh. "No," Buy said, sounding deflated. "I'd rather not."

Watkins pressed ahead. Everywhere she turned, she heard the same tune: the entities were fine, because Andersen had signed off on them. Maybe so, but the real question was, did Andersen understand the mess it had approved? Watkins, a former Andersen accountant herself, decided to seek out Jim Hecker, an Andersen partner and an old friend from her days at the firm's Houston office.

"Jim, it's Sherron! How are you?"

Hecker settled in his chair. The call had come out of the blue, and as Watkins made small talk about the job market and Skilling's resignation, Hecker waited for her to come to the point.

The conversation hit a momentary lull.

"Jim," Watkins said, "do you know much about Enron's recent structured transactions?"

Hecker had never done any work for Enron, but Watkins's questions, and the details she had uncovered, worried him. Andersen had survived its walk through fire with the Waste Management case. The last thing it needed now was another scandal. Senior partners needed to know about this. And the Andersen team on the Enron account, too.

For a week Jim Derrick, Enron's general counsel, hadn't done much about the anonymous letter's allegations. He'd kicked it back to the executives who had created the Raptors to ask if *they* had any second thoughts; they didn't.

But by identifying herself as the memo's author, Watkins had inadvertently created a real legal issue. An employee had raised allegations against her *boss*. If they made a mistake, Enron could be sued.

Derrick spoke with a deputy general counsel, Sharon Butcher, and asked her to contact Vinson & Elkins to get some advice on the legal ramifications of the situation. Butcher telephoned Carl Jordan, an employment lawyer at the firm, and briefed him. Then she got to the question.

"Sherron Watkins works with corporate and ultimately reports to Fastow," she said. "What do we do with her?"

And suppose Enron decided to fire Watkins or demote her to a do-nothing job? What, Butcher wanted to know, were the dangers to the company?

Well, Skilling figured, it had been a week. Maybe now was a good time to drop back in at Enron. His brother Mark was in town to talk about helping manage Jeff's finances. It would be nice to give him the Enron grand tour.

They drove downtown, with Skilling eager for the visit. Probably, he figured, there would be lots of backslapping, with people congratulating him for striking out on a new life. In no time, the brothers were walking the halls at Enron, but the reaction was far from what Skilling had anticipated. People grew quiet as he approached, didn't say hello until he did. He had expected almost a hero's welcome, but instead he was getting the cold shoulder. Apparently, all anybody cared about was learning the reason he had left.

How many times did he have to explain this? What the hell was the matter with everybody?

Jeff McMahon was driving home. He had heard from Cindy Olson that day that Watkins had come forward, and learned that she was now scheduled to speak directly with Lay about her concerns. McMahon was pleased and figured he might help her out.

He punched the main number for Enron into his car speakerphone and asked for Lay's office. McMahon listened to the recorded voice of Lay's assistant, Rosalee Fleming, instructing callers to leave a message.

That's bogus. He hated it when executives didn't record their own voice-mail message. It was just too *regal.*

The line beeped. "Ken, it's Jeff McMahon," he said, giving his job title. He figured there was a good chance Lay might not know who he was.

He explained that he had heard about the Watkins letter and knew she was scheduled to meet with him soon.

"As a matter of background, I've known Sherron for twenty years and find her to be pretty credible," he said. He gave a quick rundown of his relationship with her.

"So, probably you're wondering why I'm leaving this message," McMahon continued. "I just wanted you to know that she's not some lunatic-fringe employee. She's knowledgeable enough to be concerned about these issues. So I'd just ask that you take her seriously."

He thanked Lay and hung up.

Just outside Lay's office door, Watkins was waiting. It was before one o'clock on August 22, the time of her appointment. She was terrified and anxious; she hadn't slept well in days. She had written a series of new memos explaining the problems, then rewritten them again and again to make them easier to understand.

At that moment, Lay was wrapping up a lunch with Greg Whalley, whom he had unofficially selected as Enron's new president. Heading into the waiting area, he saw Watkins and broke into a smile.

"Hi, I'm Ken Lay."

Watkins stood, shaking Lay's hand. "Sherron Watkins."

"Well, glad you could stop by. Come on in."

Lay headed into his office, escorting Watkins to the small conference table. They both sat down.

"All right, then," he began. "I understand you have some concerns about some transaction issues. I'd very much like to hear what those concerns are."

Watkins ran through her materials, laying out the problems she had found. The Raptors, she said, were set up in a way that would not withstand public scrutiny. LJM, which provided the necessary three percent equity, had gotten its money back out of other payments from Enron. It had no skin in the game. It all looked like one big bet on Enron stock, put together in hopes that a rising share price would bail the company out of its investment losses.

But everything had gone against Enron. Its stock had fallen; its merchant investments had soured. There was a cavalcade of other issues, including rumors of a handshake deal between Fastow and Skilling guaranteeing that the LJM funds would never lose money. Lay's eyes wandered, but he did seem to be paying attention. He interrupted.

"Andy's a good CFO, right?" he asked. "He's doing a good job, right?"

Watkins fumbled with her answer. "Well, uh, sure."

She went on. Soon Lay interrupted again.

"Are you saying that from the standpoint of the accounting, these are done inappropriately?" he asked. "Do you think something illegal's been done here?"

Watkins shook her head. "No, I'm not saying that. Technically, maybe the argument can be made that the accounting is correct. But in the end, this will not stand up to public scrutiny. It doesn't look right."

Although he wasn't sure of Watkins's facts, Lay was convinced that she was someone to take seriously. Obviously, a lot of thought had gone into this. Her material was too extensive to have been thrown together overnight. But there was still one matter that concerned him.

"Have you shared this with anyone outside the company?" he asked.

Watkins shook her head. "No," she said.

As the meeting approached its conclusion, Watkins offered her suggestions of how to clean up the mess.

If he was planning to promote Fastow or Causey in the wake of Skilling's departure, she said, Lay should postpone his decision. The company should hire an independent law firm to investigate—but *not* Vinson & Elkins, since that firm had worked on the deals. A large accounting firm—but *not* Andersen—should review everything. Then, once everybody understood the real impact of the transactions, Enron should develop a plan to fix everything—hopefully one that could be done quietly. But if not, then one with a complete public- and investor-relations campaign.

There were a few people that the lawyers should interview to find out if Watkins was wrong. She listed McMahon, Rick Buy, Mark Koenig, and Greg Whalley. Cliff Baxter was also mentioned by Watkins as someone with concerns. Lay asked if he could keep the memos that Watkins had brought in, and she agreed.

Lay suddenly became animated. "Now, what can I do for *you?*" he asked.

Watkins had thought about that. "I don't think I can keep working for Andy," she said. "It might be best if I moved to Cindy Olson's group until another job turns up."

Watkins seemed to have planned for everything.

"This doesn't have to be done today," Watkins said. "I'm taking a short vacation to Mexico starting tomorrow. Nothing would have to be set up until I'm back."

"All right," Lay said. "I'll speak to Cindy and see if we can get an answer before you return."

Lay thanked Watkins for coming. Whether she was right or wrong, he thought, he admired her for her courage.

After Watkins left, Lay carried her memos down to Jim Derrick and described his discussion with her. He held up Watkins's papers. "These are my only copy," he said, "but I'm going to leave them with you."

Watkins had raised serious issues, Lay said, and he wanted them investigated quickly. As for who should conduct the inquiry, though, Lay wasn't ready to accept Watkins's counsel. A new law firm would take weeks getting to know the players and the issues. If there really was a big problem, it should be evident to Enron's closest advisers.

So why not bring in Vinson & Elkins? The two men talked it through and agreed that consulting Enron's old law firm was the best course. Derrick raised a point about the complexity of revisiting all of the accounting again.

"We don't want to reinvent the wheel here," Lay said.

After Lay left, Derrick picked up the phone to call Joe Dilg, a senior partner at Vinson & Elkins. He talked about the anonymous letter and the new material from Watkins. Dilg promised to get started right away.

Derrick sent over the Watkins material. Other than the original, unspecific letter, he had never read any of it.

About that time, Vince Kaminski was downstairs at his desk, reviewing his e-mail. He noticed a message that had been forwarded to him earlier that day and clicked it open.

It was from one of his analysts, Rudi Zipter, raising a question about the Raptors. With the stock market getting hammered lately, it said, both Enron stock and the value of some of its largest hedged assets had been falling.

"OOPS!" Zipter wrote.

Zipter mentioned something about the finance group having put a collar on the Enron stock to prevent it from falling too steeply. Kaminski knew *that* wasn't right. Enron had required that the stock not be hedged and, as a result, sold it to the Raptors at a discounted price. A collar would mean there was a hedge. In other words, Enron would have sold its stock at a discount based on a lie. It couldn't be true.

Kaminski started typing a response. "Makes sense," he wrote, saying he would set up a meeting.

He thought for a second. "Another question," he wrote. "Do you know if the collar was hedged by the equity desk?"

Joe Dilg quickly assembled his investigative team. After reading the Watkins material, he realized that one of his partners, Ron Astin, had worked on several of the transactions. He discussed it with Astin, and the two decided that since Vinson & Elkins had played no role in *conceiving* of the deals, it wouldn't be conflicted in investigating them.

Next, Dilg recruited one of his litigation partners, Max Hendrick III, to help out. After being briefed, Hendrick got on the phone with Astin and ran through the issues. Astin mentioned that he had long been bothered by one aspect of the Raptors: the deal that had been struck to hand LJM2 an amount of money equal to the cash it kicked in, plus a 30 percent return, before the entities engaged in any hedging.

"This is the troubling part," Astin said. "As a practical matter, LJM has its investment back."

Still, that wasn't something Enron wanted Vinson & Elkins to worry about. The firm was told not to bother retaining another accounting firm. There was no need to second-guess everybody on this. Just a fact-finding mission.

The day after his meeting with Sherron Watkins, Ken Lay was hit with another margin call from his lenders. Enron's stock price had fallen again with the announcement of Skilling's departure, and the banks wanted more money. Beau Herrold took care of it. He borrowed from Enron for the cash, and then repaid it with company stock, just as they had arranged. Every penny went to pay down debt.

Fastow was in a rage. Word had finally gotten around to him that, in response to this letter to Lay challenging the Raptors, the company was bringing in lawyers to dig into his work. He gathered a few trusted lieutenants in his office and told them what was happening, furiously pacing the floor as he spoke.

"There's going to be a *fucking* investigation of this," he screamed. "Who the *fuck* wrote this thing?"

He pounded a fist on his desk. "It's fucking McMahon," he growled. "McMahon is behind this thing!"

The diatribe lasted several minutes. McMahon was angling for his job, Fastow said. That's what this was all about. When the meeting broke up, news of his outburst spread quickly through the division. It didn't take long for one of McMahon's friends to hear about it and call to fill him in.

Hanging up before hearing the whole story, McMahon dashed out of his office. He barked at his secretary as he passed. "Call Andy. Tell him I'm on my way up to see him!"

McMahon stormed down the hallway, not slowing as he approached Fastow's secretary, Bridget Maronge.

"Is he ready for me?" McMahon asked sharply.

"Well . . ." Maronge began to answer.

McMahon blew past without waiting for a response, shoving open

Fastow's door. From behind his desk, Fastow looked up, surprised. McMahon closed the door behind him.

He pointed a finger at Fastow. "I've gotta talk to you," he said. Fastow got up. The two executives stood on either side of the desk, glaring at each other.

"I hear you're telling people I wrote this memo about this Condor and Raptor stuff," McMahon snarled.

"I don't know what else to conclude!"

McMahon's face was hard. "First off, I didn't write it. But that's not even relevant, Andy. If you continue to slander me around here, you've got a problem with me. If you think I've done something, come see me. Don't start leaking stuff out. I didn't write it, so cut it out."

Fastow's eyes narrowed. "Well, I don't know who else would try to damage my—"

"Why are you so paranoid about me wanting your friggin' job?" McMahon snapped. "I don't want it! I never wanted it! I don't know what your issue is."

"I just figure there are people out to get me in the company," Fastow replied, "and *you're* one of them."

Man, McMahon thought, *something's wrong with this guy*.

"I could care less about what you do or how you do it, Andy," McMahon shot back. "And I want you to tell me right now that you're going to stop talking about this memo and me, *because I didn't write it!*"

The two stared at each other in silence. The air in the room was electric.

"Okay," Fastow finally said, backing down. "I'll take your word for it."

"Fine!" McMahon barked. He marched out of the room, passing Fastow's stunned secretary. Though his face was red with anger, he felt ecstatic. After all these years, the confrontation had felt great; he had finally let Fastow have it. And the delicious encounter was made all the sweeter by the fact that *he* knew the identity of the letter writer Fastow so desperately wanted to track down.

On the morning of August 28, a new article about Enron appeared in *The Wall Street Journal*. It wasn't a big scoop, just a "Heard on the Street" column, the feature that typically ruminates about a company's prospects—and, by extension, about the potential direction of its stock price.

The article was written by Rebecca Smith and John Emshwiller, the first from their reporting partnership. It described how Lay was promising to divulge more information to investors and to abandon the in-your-face management style that had apparently alienated so many of them.

Deep in the article, three paragraphs appeared—the first mention of the LJM funds in a national newspaper. The article didn't disclose the funds' name and reported that Fastow had sold his interest in them. Still, it described some of their workings and quoted Lay as saying that they had become a "lightning rod" for criticism of the company.

All told, the article was informative but not that damaging. Some Enron executives felt relieved at what they saw as kid-glove treatment. They had no idea that this was only round one.

He was a former Enron executive, one who believed the company had lost its way many years before. And there was no starker example than Fastow's LJM2 fund. It was just dishonest.

That morning, the former executive was reading the *Journal* article. The reporters, he thought, were sniffing in the right area but hadn't located their prey. Should he help them? He had access to an LJM2 offering memorandum. He knew details of the battles that had occurred over the funds. He could point the reporters in the right direction.

Still, Enron—and certainly Fastow—would lash back at him if they ever found out that he was spilling the beans to the press. But he knew the way the journalism game was played. He could extract promises of confidentiality from the reporters. His anonymity guaranteed, he could tell them everything he knew, give them documents, pile up the evidence he possessed against Fastow and the LJM funds.

He reached for the phone.

What is this?

Robert Hannan was at his desk at the Fort Worth regional office of the SEC, reading that morning's *Wall Street Journal*. Hannan, a lawyer with the enforcement division, had been reviewing the Enron article and quickly zeroed in on the paragraphs about the Fastow partnerships.

Enron has placed billons of dollars of assets and millions of shares of its stock into complex transactions with these partnerships . . . Enron executives say the transactions were perfectly proper . . . The company asked Mr. Fastow to take part in the deals, which were done to reduce the risk of fluctuating market prices.

Hannan wasn't quite sure what this meant, but it sure didn't sound good. Well, the Fort Worth regional office covered Houston. Maybe he ought to look into the matter. He fetched one of the office's data-entry forms, to establish what was known as a matter under inquiry, or MUI. He filled in all the necessary codes and status requirements. At the bottom, in a space reserved for comments, he scrawled: "Investigation into possible accounting and related party irregularities."

Lay made it official. He selected Greg Whalley as the company's president, giving him the post that Skilling had filled for so many years. Lay didn't necessarily consider Whalley to be the *best* person for the job, but at the moment, as someone who commanded the respect of the energy-trading desk, he was the right choice.

On the day of his selection, Whalley received a call from Lay, who said he had something that he wanted to ask about.

"Do you know Sherron Watkins?" he asked.

Never heard of her. "No," Whalley said.

Lay described the letter and the allegations it contained. He had met with Watkins to talk it all through.

"Now, Sherron says that she talked about this with Jeff McMahon," Lay said. "And Andy thinks that McMahon is behind all this, in some sort of power play for his job."

Fastow had lied to McMahon. After promising to drop his conspiracy theory, he had instead told it to Lay in an effort to debunk Watkins's statements.

It all sounded a little too Machiavellian for Whalley's taste. "I'll talk to Jeff about it," he said.

The next day, after hearing from Whalley, McMahon was fuming at Watkins. Why was she dragging him into this, saying he would back her up? *He didn't know anything about it!* What the hell was she talking to Lay about *him* for? It was just going to confirm Fastow's conspiracy theory. He called her repeatedly, leaving increasingly livid voice mails. Finally, Watkins called back, and he tore into her.

Why was she telling Lay that he supported her? He hadn't been treasurer for eighteen months; he didn't know anything about the Raptors. Watkins apologized, saying that Lay must have misunderstood her. McMahon would have none of it.

"This is *your* thing," he snapped. "Leave me out of it."

John Emshwiller was examining a document from LJM2. The call from the former Enron executive had been a godsend; here was someone who not only knew the inner workings of Enron but had records to boot: an offering memorandum for LJM2, something used to persuade private investors to sink their money into the fund.

Emshwiller read a page that listed the biographies of executives involved in LJM2, and stopped at Michael Kopper. He had heard a lot about Kopper;

he was portrayed as Fastow's alter ego. And here was a load of information about the man's background. This was a great document.

Emshwiller's eyes lit on a single phrase in the biography. It said that Kopper "manages the general partner of Chewco, an investment fund with approximately $400 million in capital commitments."

Chewco? No one had ever mentioned Chewco to Emshwiller before. As described in the offering document, Chewco was set up to purchase company assets from Enron. The document, in the finance department's typical sloppiness, was wrong. Chewco purchased nothing from Enron; it had bought its interest in JEDI from the California state pension fund, Calpers. But Emshwiller had no way of knowing that. He called his colleague Rebecca Smith and described what he had found.

"Sounds like Chewco is similar to LJM," she said.

The message on August 30 came from Fastow's secretary and was delivered to Watkins's secretary. The Enron CFO wanted both of them—Watkins *and* her secretary—out of the building within eight hours.

He had finally learned that Watkins was the anonymous letter writer, and was now bent on destroying her career. He phoned Cindy Olson in human resources, demanding that Watkins be fired and her computer seized. Olson left a message for Watkins to come by. Watkins arrived shortly and sat down, full of dread.

"Andy is not behaving appropriately," Olson said.

Watkins still had a job, but they needed to get her out of Fastow's group. Soon she had the new boss she wanted: Olson herself.

Mark Palmer could feel it coming. In the days since that "Heard on the Street" column, Emshwiller and Smith had called, pressing with questions about LJM. It was almost as if they had suddenly gained access to new information about the funds. Something big was in the works at the *Journal*.

And still Fastow didn't want to talk about it.

Dilg and Hendrick, the Vinson & Elkins lawyers investigating the Raptors, had been interviewing everybody. They had even had a session with Fastow, where he suggested that Watkins was just acting on behalf of somebody out for his job. Now, on August 30, they were meeting with Jeff McMahon, who had been rumored to be a big LJM critic.

"LJM presented an inherent conflict," McMahon said. "I was very vocal with Fastow and Skilling about that."

He mentioned the time Fastow called him at home to complain about his people negotiating too hard, as well as the concerns bankers had expressed about whether their continued relationship with Enron depended on doing business with LJM.

"But listen," he said, "I have no problem with Andy's motive or intent with LJM. My problem is on appearances."

In fact, McMahon said, LJM had been pretty good.

"There were a lot of LJM deals that were very beneficial to Enron," he told the lawyers. "Without it, a lot of them wouldn't have gotten done."

The sky over Santa Fe was perfectly clear as the Enron corporate plane lifted off on its way back to Houston. On board was Greg Whalley, the newly named president, along with Vince Kaminski. Whalley had been wrapping up some final business before starting his new duties and now was relaxing on board as he contemplated his plans.

"You know what," he told Kaminski. "This quarter is still on Skilling, but next quarter is on me. So I'm going to recognize all the losses we can this quarter."

Kaminski didn't like the idea. It was a typical trader's mind-set—dump the problems on the last guy, move on clean. But it might not work well.

"That's a risky move," Kaminski said. "You don't know how the markets would react to that. It could go badly."

Whalley shook his head. "I talked to Glisan. He told me not to worry about it, because it's a noncash event."

Kaminski worried that the markets might not distinguish between a cash and a noncash loss. This could be the kind of shock that Kevin Kindall had been warning about. But before he could say anything, Whalley glanced out the window.

"Wow, this is great weather!" he exclaimed. "The best weather for sky-diving!"

The Woodlands is an enclave north of Houston that is home to executives with paychecks that don't qualify them for River Oaks. In its suburban setting, the sounds of the city can be forgotten and the tensions of the workday swept away. It was, Lay decided, a lovely spot to hold a retreat for his managers, to give them a place to cast off the gloom occasioned by Skilling's resignation.

They gathered for two days in the first week of September at the Woodlands Resort and Conference Center. The meetings started early in the morning, with the executives gathered around a U-shaped table. In preparation, Enron had polled its employees—in what was dubbed the "Lay It on the Line" survey—about their concerns. What came back was anxiety—about aggressiveness, about accounting, about everything that in the past had defined Enron.

Steve Kean and Mark Palmer made the first formal presentation. They saw it as the best chance to shake the managers out of their lethargy. Bad news was raining down on the company—California, India, and now LJM. And yet the executive leadership of Enron was sitting on its hands. That had to change. Kean stood and faced the group.

"We've got enemies," he said. "They're looking for dirt. We've got dirt. They've found it. And that's a problem." He recited Enron's many woes.

"Now we've got something here we can't even get to the bottom of," he said. The word wasn't mentioned, but Kean was referring to LJM. Fastow sat in his seat silently.

Palmer took over. "Which means that this is a company entering into a crisis," he said. For any kind of crisis management, Palmer said, there were three *A*s—acknowledge, apologize, and act. The company had to acknowledge there was a problem, apologize for whatever it had done to cause it, and then present its plan of action to fix it.

At that, the room exploded. "We're not apologizing for anything!" John Lavorato, a top trader, roared.

"Absolutely not!" chimed in another senior executive, Dave Delainey. "There's nothing wrong with Enron. We don't owe anyone an apology for anything!"

Palmer shot them a look. "Well," he said, "will you acknowledge that we've got a crisis?"

Delainey folded his arms. "What do we have to acknowledge?"

Palmer threw up his hands. "Dave! The stock is dropping like a rock. No one trusts what we say, with things now at the point that people who don't like us are leaking information they think will be damaging to us. *The Wall Street Journal* wants to write a story about us. *And we're not cooperating with them!*"

The room erupted, with everyone speaking at once. At one point, someone mentioned the concerns expressed in the employee survey about Enron's accounting. Suddenly, a hand slammed down on the table. Everyone turned to see Causey, red-faced, bringing his arm up to slap the table again.

"I take that personally!" he snapped as he stood to speak. "Reasonable minds may come to different conclusions, but our accounting works!"

He looked at everyone around the table. "Our accounting is not aggressive!" he said. "Our accounting is complex. We do complicated transactions, and that makes it hard for people to understand. But I take it personally when you guys criticize it."

Causey was working himself into a lather. He almost seemed on the verge of tears. "I will stake my entire career on the fact that our accounting works," he blared.

The room went silent. No one wanted to challenge Causey. The man seemed so sincere. But in no time another point came up. Lots of employees seemed concerned about the quality of Enron's balance sheet, that the company might be overextended. Companies needed strong balance sheets to grow, to prosper. Too much debt could put a company in a financial bind, even push it into bankruptcy.

Fastow broke in. "The balance sheet of Enron," he said, "has never been stronger."

There was nothing to worry about, Fastow said. Nothing to hide. Everything at Enron was exactly as it appeared.

It was late in the evening days later when the BMW slowly rolled toward a garbage Dumpster hidden far out of view. Kopper, in the driver's seat, pulled to a stop. He stepped out of the car into the nighttime air.

Things were coming apart. The Vinson & Elkins investigation. The *Journal* article. All the questions about LJM2. Fastow and Kopper were both becoming unnerved.

The two had made a decision. For years, Kopper had tracked their side deals, keeping score in files on his laptop computer. With that data, the two could know who had made how many millions, which of them was ahead. It had been a wonderful way to ensure they both got their fair share.

All that information was right there, on the laptop, waiting for someone to find it. At Fastow's instruction, Kopper had already deleted information on the computers at work; he had destroyed a home computer that held other damaging details. Now they were down to this. The laptop, the scorecard. The ultimate proof that they had been working in concert, planning their crimes for years, doing everything they could to enrich themselves.

It had to go. They both agreed.

Kopper reached into his car, removed the laptop, and walked toward the Dumpster. He stood alone in silence, then brought back his arm as he readied the throw. The laptop landed inside, disappearing forever amid piles of garbage.

BOOK FOUR
SHATTERED

CHAPTER 19

GREG WHALLEY ARRIVED AT the office on the morning of September 10 for his first full day at headquarters as Enron's president. Since his selection by Lay, he had been on the road—in London, California, Santa Fe—wrapping up business, but now he was eager to plunge into his new job.

Getting a fix on accounting and finance was a priority. Whalley had heard rumblings that an accounting error in the Raptors had resulted in a huge overstatement in shareholder equity. Then there were rumors of other problems with some of the financial deals Enron had done in recent years.

Whalley arranged to meet with Causey and Glisan. Causey quickly homed in on one particular problem.

"We have a couple of issues because of the decline in New Power Company's stock price," he said.

New Power was Enron's residential-energy company with an Internet sales program. It had gone public the previous October, just as the air was starting to seep out of the dot-com bubble. Enron executives thought that they had locked in the value of the company's stake by hedging it with the third Raptor, which itself was nonsensically capitalized with New Power stock. But with New Power's stock price knocked to the curb, the Raptor hedge wasn't holding. It simply didn't have enough assets to be reasonably described as a true hedge. Enron might have to take a write-off if something wasn't done.

"There are ways we can recapitalize it," Causey said. "We have a number of options . . ."

Whalley raised a hand. "Whoa," he said. "Wait a minute. Is the value lost or isn't it?"

There was a pause. The value was pretty much gone, Glisan said, but there were alternatives to taking a loss.

Whalley made a face. "Guys, if it's gone, it's gone," he said. "Write it off."

It was a simple, economically rational decision. But in making it, Whalley had inadvertently pulled out a main support beam in what would prove to be a financial house of cards.

Early the next morning in Chicago, John Stewart was listening to the voices on his speakerphone. Stewart, Andersen's top accounting expert, had been brought in to speak with the Enron team, once again about the Raptors.

On the line were the two partners who knew Enron best—David Duncan, calling from Houston, and his predecessor on the account, Stephen Goddard, who was visiting New York.

"Enron is interested in unwinding at least one of the Raptors," Duncan said. "They're looking to us to give them an opinion on it."

Stewart could offer little advice. "This isn't an accounting issue," he said. "This is a business decision. I would be fine with it, but it's really their decision."

Still, Duncan knew there was a problem. In the efforts to keep the vehicles afloat, the Raptors had been inextricably linked, with some responsible for the obligations of the others. It was now the financial equivalent of a three-legged chair: all of the Raptors had to stay in place, or else the whole structure would come crashing down.

Duncan was asking Stewart if he could review some materials when someone interrupted with horrifying news. An airliner had just struck the World Trade Center.

It was the morning of September 11.

The terrified voices from New York echoed through the Enron trading floor. One Enron trader had been on the line with Cantor Fitzgerald, based on the upper floors of One World Trade Center, when the first plane hit. The firm operated a computerized trading-reporting system used by trading desks, including at Enron, and now their screens had gone blank.

"The building's burning," one trader on the line said. "We're supposed to get out. But I don't think we can."

Eventually the voices disappeared, and the Enron traders watched in horror as the two towers collapsed—first Tower Two, then, not long after, Tower One, where the people they had just been speaking with had been trapped.

Few at Enron wanted to stay in the office. An emergency meeting was convened, led by Whalley. Business, they decided, was shutting down for the day.

The partners from Vinson & Elkins investigating the Watkins allegations were in the final stages of their work, back to interviewing one of their own colleagues.

Since launching the inquiry, the partners, Dilg and Hendrick, had spoken to executives involved in the Raptors, including Fastow, Causey, and Duncan. Repeatedly, they heard all was well, the accounting was proper.

Now, on September 13, the lawyers were days from giving their unofficial blessing to the structures. But before they did, they sat down again with Ron Astin, their partner who had worked on a number of Fastow deals.

There were issues that had always bothered him, Astin said. He had never believed the LJM1/Rhythms transaction had been given adequate consideration by the company.

"LJM just seemed like a gift to Fastow," he said.

As Astin described it, there was plenty to make him uncomfortable with the setup. "I heard rumors that it was unlikely Fastow would lose money on the LJM transactions with the company. There was talk of a handshake deal, and that made me uneasy."

If true, this alone would have been enough for Enron's dealings with LJM to be improper, maybe even illegal. But everyone at Enron denied it. Whatever the rumors, Vinson & Elkins hadn't been able to prove them.

The next morning, Shannon Adlong, David Duncan's secretary, finished collecting copies of his file memos about the Raptors. She attached them to an e-mail, then shipped them to the Andersen accountants who had been involved in the transactions. For the first time they would see everything that Duncan and his team had done.

That morning in Chicago, John Stewart reviewed the Raptor memos with growing horror. Repeatedly, Duncan's memos said that Stewart and Carl Bass had agreed with his decisions *when the exact opposite was true*! Ideas that they rejected—such as the effect of allowing the Raptors to provide guarantees for each other's obligations—were presented as *approved*. There were plenty other shenanigans, such as the way Enron sold the Raptors stock at a discount, then turned around and allowed the entities to place price collars on them. That was just plain unallowable.

Andersen's official representation in these memos of the firm's opinion was *false*. This had to be fixed.

The September 11 attacks sent Glisan into a panic—about Enron. In the weeks since Skilling's resignation, he had been muttering to colleagues that a financial storm might be brewing. Now, as smoke rose over the ruins of the World Trade Center, the first thunderclaps sounded.

Most markets around the globe had closed in the wake of the terrorist attacks, but a critical one remained open—for commercial paper, the

short-term loans that every company depended on to finance daily operations. On Wednesday, Glisan learned the horrible news that Enron's paper had
no buyers. As it paid back short-term loans, new ones weren't replacing them.
Cash was running out of the company. It was a crisis that could blow up into
a calamity.

Glisan summoned his staff to his office. His happy-go-lucky demeanor
was gone; instead, he scowled. His eyes roamed the room, latching on to the
faces of the stunned lawyers and financiers, barking orders at them.

"Do we need to pull down the revolvers, or do we just wait?" Glisan
snapped. The revolving credit lines, set up with the banks, would provide
Enron with a flood of cash.

The answers were equivocal. Jordan Mintz began offering a few thoughts,
but Glisan broke him off.

"I don't need bullshit, Jordan!" he screamed. "I need some goddamn answers from you!"

Glisan finally calmed down. This was no time to panic. He consulted Fastow,
and the two weighed the situation. Pulling down the revolvers might signal
Enron was in trouble, they decided. Better to hold off.

Enron was skating on the edge of the financial cliff, but the gambit
worked. Within a day, its commercial paper found buyers. It required some
fancy footwork—acting disorganized, postponing payments—but the company weathered the threat with investors none the wiser.

They weren't the only ones in the dark. Ken Lay was told nothing of the
crisis. And neither was Enron's board.

During the commercial-paper crisis, certain payments went out, no matter
what.

As part of the Chewco buyout, Kopper had demanded an additional $2.6
million to cover the taxes owed. That, he insisted, was part of the original
deal, since Enron had given a tax-indemnification agreement. The argument
infuriated Mintz; there was no way, he knew, that Kopper was that dim. The
agreement covered cash shortfalls, in the event of a mismatch at Chewco between the amount of taxes owed and its cash on hand. Ultimately, the agreement made clear, the taxes were Chewco's to pay. Mintz raged about the
demand, telling Fastow it should not be paid.

But Fastow disregarded his lawyer, with good reason; that tax money was
already earmarked as part of Kopper's payment to Fastow for the purchase of
LJM2.

The very week Enron was juggling its obligations, it cut a check for

Michael Kopper's taxes. The amount was $2.6 million; Fastow authorized the payment personally.

Whalley wanted to know more. The business consumed a lot of cash, and with all the market jitters, he needed to understand how much money Enron had readily available.

He set up a meeting with Fastow and Glisan. When they got together, the two finance executives turned over reports they had just delivered to the finance committee. Whalley skimmed through until one entry stopped him short.

Thirty-six billion in debt? That couldn't be right.

He pointed at the number. "What is this?" he said.

"In essence," Fastow said, "that's all of the money that we owe, on and off balance sheet."

Whalley stared at him. "All of this is debt?" he said, disbelief in his voice. Well, Fastow replied, some of it was nonrecourse debt, meaning that the obligations would be owed from projects rather than from Enron itself.

"So," Whalley said, "if everything goes well, we owe thirty-six billion dollars." Fastow nodded.

Why was he just hearing this? How could the directors have seen these numbers and thought nothing of them?

"This is a lot of debt," Whalley said. "We need more equity."

Enron's share price had been in the rafters for months, and it hadn't occurred to anyone to issue stock and use the proceeds to pay down debt? What a lost opportunity.

Fastow seemed eager to agree. "Yeah," he said, "I think we need more equity."

That same week, Causey and Glisan came back to Whalley with their verdict on unwinding a single Raptor: it couldn't be done, not without a huge cost. If the Raptor providing the hedge for New Power was taken down, all of the structures would collapse.

"To close this whole thing out, it's going to cost us about $800 million," Causey said. "Those are the total amounts we're going to have to write off."

Instead of taking the losses, Enron should try something else, Causey began. The retail unit had a business that could be shifted into the Raptors. Then those entities could sign a note agreeing to pay Enron for the business later, and that could recapitalize—

"Wait," Whalley interrupted. "Guys, have we lost the money or not? Are the values there or are they gone?"

Causey bristled. "Well, the values are gone, but—"

"Then close it up!" Whalley barked. "What is the issue here? Write the thing off, and get on with it."

That day, Whalley went to see Lay to fill him in on what he had discovered. "Ken," Whalley said as he walked into Lay's office, "I've been taking a look at the Raptors, and I think we've got a serious problem."

Lay stared at his new president. "Raptors?"

Whalley explained them, and the hedges they provided. Lay remembered. These were some of the vehicles that Sherron Watkins had spoken to him about a month before.

There were serious capitalization problems, Whalley said. Worse, he simply didn't think the Raptors were effective. How could something intended to hedge Enron's risk instead keep requiring so much fresh capital from the company?

"This is probably something we're going to need to address," Whalley said. "We might need to make a decision before the end of the third quarter."

All right, Lay said. Just let him know.

Causey dropped by to see Lay soon afterward, complaining about what Whalley wanted to do.

For years, Causey's task had been to find creative ways that Enron—using superior accounting knowledge—could report superior results. Now Whalley scotches that and issues orders to take a loss? What kind of approach was that? Where was the creativity?

"There *is* a problem with the Raptors," Causey said, "but it's all about capitalization."

Until now, Enron had been shifting stock from one pocket to the other to keep the hedges going, he said. That wouldn't work now with the stock in the doldrums. Instead, if Enron parked good assets in the Raptors—like that retail business—then the hedges could still work. Plus, the business didn't trade on the open market. There wouldn't be any more sudden collapses in value.

The dispute was obvious. Clearly, Lay thought, his management team was moving at cross-purposes. He would have to call a meeting and get everybody on the same track.

At nine on the morning of September 19, more than half a dozen Enron executives gathered in Lay's office, itching for a fight over the future of the Raptors. With Fastow's muted support, Causey pushed again for saving the entities by shifting a business into them. But Whalley was unbending. Enron shouldn't throw good money after bad, he said. Losses were losses; nothing would make them come back.

Dave Delainey, the head of the retail group, agreed. "Why commit a business to this?" he asked. "Why take something that could have big value in the future and waste it trying to hedge something that's already lost value?"

Causey was not persuaded. "If you can avoid taking write-offs, you ought to avoid taking them," he said.

Lay sat back. "Well, apparently, that was the argument we used when we recapitalized last time," he said. "And here we are, facing the same problem. And who knows whether we'll have the same problem six months from now."

The time had come for Enron to cut its losses, Lay decided. "I want us to be on a good, solid foundation and be able to tell the Street that we are not going to have these recurring problems," Lay said.

The Raptors, all of them, would be shut down. And ultimately help topple Enron.

The two Vinson & Elkins partners handling the Watkins investigation scheduled an appointment with Lay for late on September 21. At the appointed time, the lawyers—Joe Dilg and Max Hendrick—arrived at Lay's office accompanied by Jim Derrick, Enron's general counsel.

Dilg kicked off the discussion. These were preliminary findings, he said, and Enron needed to tell the lawyers if they wanted to proceed further. Then Hendrick began explaining that everyone identified by Watkins had been interviewed. "None supported her. None thought there was a problem with the accounting or with these transactions."

They had also gone back to Andersen—in particular, to Duncan and his team. "They looked at everything again," Hendricks said, "and concluded there was no problem."

Even Watkins, they said, was concerned primarily about public reaction to the transactions rather than about accounting-rules violations. For about forty-five minutes, Lay tossed questions at the lawyers. He liked what he heard.

"All right," Lay said. "Begin writing up your report. But I'd like you to go back to Sherron Watkins and tell her your findings, and see if she's got anything else to add."

The lawyers headed out to finish their work, and that was that. If everyone was still comfortable after a second look, Lay figured there wasn't anything to worry about.

At about the same time, Andersen convened an emergency conference call to review the problems the firm had discovered with the Raptors—and the Raptor memos. The revelations were dynamite that, if not defused, could rip another hole in Andersen's reputation. A core group of accountants from Houston and Chicago was brought in on the calls. This, they knew, would take weeks to repair.

Palmer was on the phone with Fastow. Since September 11, the *Journal's* interest in Enron had seemed to dwindle—no surprise, since the paper's main offices in Manhattan had been rendered uninhabitable in the attack. But now Emshwiller and Smith were back, asking again about LJM. Palmer couldn't hold them off any longer; he needed Fastow's help.

"Andy," he said, "the *Journal* wants to talk about these LJM structures, about what their purpose was."

"And what do you think we ought to do?" Fastow asked.

The answer was clear. "We ought to talk about them."

Fastow's voice almost exploded through the phone.

"Are you crazy!" he bellowed. "That is the *dumbest* thing I've ever heard. I told you, it's a slippery slope!"

Palmer held the phone away from his ear as Fastow screamed. "Well, Andy," he said, "we've disclosed them, you're not in them anymore. We should explain them."

Fastow's rage built up. "It's complicated, they won't understand, they'll write terrible stories, and I don't want to go into detail about LJM."

"Why not?" Palmer shot back. *What is Fastow's problem?*

"Slippery slope, Mark!" Fastow shouted, whistling on each *s*. "We're not going there!" Fastow shouted a few more words, then fell silent.

But only for a second.

"I cannot believe," Fastow finally yelled, "that Enron has a PR guy who would come up with a strategy that is *this stupid*! I will *not* speak to *The Wall Street Journal*!"

Before Palmer could respond, Fastow hung up.

Palmer turned to fill in his boss, Steve Kean, who sat just a few feet away. Before he could say a word, Kean's phone rang. Palmer saw on the caller ID that it was Fastow.

"Oh," Palmer said, "Fastow's going to yell at you about this LJM thing."

Kean answered. Fastow instantly lit into him.

Later that same day, Palmer was back on the line with the *Journal*, trying to broker some sort of compromise.

"Guys, you need to help me," Palmer said. "They'd like a better sense of what you want to talk about."

It would help, he suggested, if they sent prepared questions, so that Enron could understand what the reporters wanted. The reporters didn't like the idea, but agreed.

Lay had a chance to slow his sales of Enron stock. He had just received ten million dollars from Enron, a bonus for returning as CEO. With the stock price still falling, Lay kept being hit with demands for cash from his banks, which he met by drawing down on his credit line at Enron. Now, with his new load of money, he had something to forestall future sales. So on September 21, two days after receiving another demand from Bank of America, Lay turned over the entire ten million dollars to the bank.

It was a onetime opportunity. All he could do from there was hold on to his Enron stock and wait for a rebound.

On the morning of September 22, a Saturday, Stephen Cutler was pushing his infant son in a baby carriage down a dirt path. Cutler, a forty-year-old lawyer, was acting director of the SEC's enforcement division and had been with the agency for two years, starting under Levitt. But these days, he was getting accustomed to the new boss, Harvey Pitt.

Pitt had been confirmed in August and had swept into the agency like a whirlwind. He had taken charge of its response to the September 11 attacks, working to get the markets reopened quickly. Days before, he had given the green light to an enforcement initiative known as a 21(a) report, providing guidelines to companies on the cooperation expected by the SEC if executives discover wrongdoing. But today that was far from Cutler's mind as he walked in the September breeze with his new son.

A buzz sounded. It was Cutler's BlackBerry, his portable communications system. He pushed the stroller to the side of the path and pulled out the device. It was an e-mail from Harvey Pitt, labeled "Draft 21a."

"Here, I've taken a crack at drafting this," the message read. Below that, a first version of an extended report, listing all the steps of cooperation required from companies. Cutler read the document in astonishment. It was good, very good. But this was *the chairman* knocking out a preliminary report. That was what staff was for. If Cutler had done it, *his* staff would have thought he was crazy.

Decidedly, Cutler thought, Pitt was cut from a different cloth than Levitt.

Accountants crowded the fourth-floor office of Michael Odom, an Andersen practice director in Houston. The mood in the room was tense as the accountants on the Enron engagement team spoke by speakerphone with PSG members in Chicago, debating the accounting used for the Raptors.

There was a knock at the door. It was Carl Bass, the accountant booted months before from dealings with Enron.

"What can I do for you guys?" Bass asked.

Bass had been summoned to the meeting on John Stewart's insistence. Not only was Bass one of Andersen's smartest accountants; he had also been intimately involved in many of Enron's transactions—often protesting them. His views were among those misrepresented in Duncan's memos.

Bass took a seat as someone explained the situation. A schedule of assets and liabilities was passed to him. He reviewed it quickly, and his eyes fixed at a number on the first page. *A loss of $993 million.*

His mouth gaped. *A billion dollars?* Enron had a billion dollars' worth of unrecognized losses? Wait a minute! Another number. An equity charge of $1.2 billion. They had overstated shareholders' equity. How did that happen?

He looked at Duncan, whose face was crinkled with stress. "What is this equity charge about?" Bass asked.

Duncan waved a hand. "Don't worry about that. It's not material. It was just a mistake."

Not material. That was the argument being pushed by Enron and now embraced by Duncan.

Listening intently to the accountants' recital of events, it didn't take long for Bass to realize that Duncan and his crew had ignored his advice months before. And now their cockiness had come back to bite them.

Bass spoke up. "Look, you guys, just so we're clear here," he said. "What you did is exactly what I told you not to do back in December when you called me on this."

The room was silent for a moment. "Yeah," Duncan said softly. "I know you had some views on this."

Days later, on September 25, Bass fought disgust as he reviewed the Raptor memos. Repeatedly, Duncan had misrepresented his advice, saying Bass had concurred with ideas that he had opposed tooth and nail.

Bass started typing an e-mail. He was going to expose every error he had found.

That day, Mark Palmer received the list of questions from *The Wall Street Journal.* Each was more aggressive than the last, shots across the bow signaling the reporters' unwillingness to keep wasting time playing footsie with the company's executives.

Did Enron know the general partner of LJM2 had a profit participation in the partnership that would earn him millions of dollars? . . . Were LJM2 investors promised they would receive special access to Enron investment opportunities, including the purchase of company assets?

Palmer winced. The company couldn't just ignore this. He needed to get past Fastow and push Lay to make a decision about how to deal with this.

At about 9:15 the next morning, Ken Lay ambled into a communications room on the forty-seventh floor of the Enron building. He was there for a session of "E-Speak," an opportunity for employees to ask him questions over the Internet.

A typist who would record his responses was there, and a number of questions had already come in. Lay settled into a chair, waiting for 9:30, when the first answers were scheduled to be posted. Minutes later, it was time to begin.

"Good morning," Lay said. The typist wrote his words and the questions poured in. Anxiety jumped off the screen. So many people had sunk their savings in Enron stock that a near rebellion was taking place as the price tumbled. In response to their fear, Lay went into his full booster mode.

"My personal belief is that Enron stock is an incredible bargain at current prices," he said. "And we will look back a couple of years from now and see the great opportunity that we have."

Employees should spread the good word, he said. The company was sound, its balance sheet strong, its liquidity never better. When asked why more senior executives weren't buying stock, Lay assured the questioner that plenty were, including himself. He mentioned nothing of his tens of millions of dollars in stock sales to the company to help meet his margin calls.

Lay's soothing words were exactly what the troops needed to hear. Everything would be fine.

September 28, 2001, the day that would forever change Nancy Temple's life, began normally enough for her.

Temple was a young lawyer in Arthur Andersen's Chicago office, having joined the previous year from the law firm Sidley & Austin. This morning her supervisor, Donald Dreyfus, came by to talk about a new assignment.

"There's going to be a conference call at one o'clock today to deal with some accounting issues for Enron's third quarter," Dreyfus said. "I'd like you to sit in on it."

Apparently, the team handling the Enron account was in deep disagreement with the Professional Standards Group. There had been some accounting issues that could result in either a restatement of Enron's performance from the first quarter or big charges in the third. Either way, the news would be bad, and Andersen might have problems. It made sense for the legal team to start becoming part of the discussions.

"Sure," Temple said. "I'll be there."

She thought nothing of it. Until that moment she hadn't even known Enron was an Andersen client.

The words were music to Ken Lay's ears: Enron stock was terribly undervalued. He was on the phone with Robert Hurst, vice chairman of Goldman Sachs, who was delivering the news that his top investment bankers had been studying Enron and were alarmed at the stock's market price.

"We are very concerned," Hurst said, "that Enron is in danger of being targeted for a hostile-takeover attempt by someone trying to buy it on the cheap."

Lay agreed to meet with the Goldman bankers and listen to their proposals for takeover defenses. Maybe, he figured, they might even have ideas for how to get the price back up.

Vince Kaminski was at his desk when two of his top analysts, Vasant Shanbhogue and Rakesh Bharati, appeared in the doorway. Both men seemed upset as they walked in.

"We have something very important to tell you," Shanbhogue said.

The two had been working for days on the Raptors. Once Enron decided to shut them down, Kaminski had been asked to calculate some values, and had assigned Shanbhogue and Bharati to the task. The job also gave Kaminski's group its first opportunity to see the full picture of the Raptors, and something terrible had emerged.

"What's the problem?" Kaminski asked.

Shanbhogue nodded to his colleague. "Rakesh has discovered that the restrictions against hedging and the hedges of Enron stock reside in the same vehicles."

The room went silent. Kaminski's face flushed as he asked to hear more of the details.

This couldn't be. Enron had sold stock at a discount to the Raptors because they were restricted from hedging. *But then the company turned around and agreed to hedge the shares for the Raptors?* The Raptors would pay Enron for losses in its merchant investments only after Enron paid the Raptors for losses in its Enron stock.

In essence, LJM was getting a huge ownership stake in Enron through the Raptors, then pushing any losses it incurred back onto the company. It was as if a man bought insurance on his house from his wife, with her backing up the obligation through the money in their joint bank account. It did nothing. It was meaningless.

Kaminski stayed silent for a full minute. His world, his career, just fell away. *This company . . . is criminal.* They were lying to investors. They were playing a shell game, hiding losses to make themselves look successful.

I have to fight this to the bitter end, Kaminski thought. *This is the end of my employment with Enron.*

"We have to deal with this," Kaminski said. "We have to talk to these people right away."

"All right, then," Lay said. "What are the choices?"

Sitting across from him were Mark Palmer and Andy Fastow. Palmer had requested the meeting to come up with a response to the *Journal*. Fastow's strategy—*stop returning their calls! ignore them!*—was definitely out of the PR Suicide Playbook. From the questions, this piece was going to be devastating. The paper couldn't be ignored.

Palmer spelled out the situation. "Ken, Andy says these things are too complicated. He says by the nature of their questions, the reporters don't want to know what the purpose was, they just want to beat up on us."

Palmer spoke for several minutes, with Fastow silent throughout most of the discussion. Finally, Fastow leaned forward. "Ken," he said, "if you want me to talk about LJM, I'll do that, if that's what you think is best."

Palmer glanced at Fastow, wanting to wring his neck. All the screaming, and now—*oh, whatever you want, Ken.* It was like something out of a movie, with Fastow in the role of the obsequious yes-man. Lay considered the situation.

"It goes against every bone in my body," he said. "But if the best thing is not to go into detail because they don't want to hear the truth, then we'll give them a written statement."

That was the decision. Enron would not offer up Fastow—or anybody else—to answer the *Journal*'s questions.

Kaminski stared at the speakerphone in the center of the table, struggling with his anger. At his insistence, he had been brought in on a discussion with accountants from Andersen and Enron who were involved in the Raptors. And he was letting them know that he believed, in the early days, they had deceived his analysts by withholding information.

Kimberly Scardino, an Andersen accountant, asked for the analysts' opinions about a valuation issue. Kaminski wasn't about to get drawn into this again.

"We cannot answer your question," he said. "We don't know the facts. We haven't seen the legal documents."

The line had been drawn. Kaminski was telling the accountants that he would no longer trust them, that he had to review everything—*everything*—to be sure his team's answers were not going to be used for illicit purposes.

Ryan Siurek, an Enron accountant, glanced across the table at Kaminski, looking annoyed. "Kimberly," he said, "give us a few minutes. We'll get back to you."

Siurek pushed a button on the speakerphone and disconnected the call.

There was no holding back anymore. Kaminski stood and walked to the whiteboard. Scribbling pictures and numbers as he spoke, he explained how the deals within the Raptors were filled with contradictions, shifting risk back and forth to no end, giving discounts for no purpose.

He turned to look at the group. "Something," he said, "is drastically wrong here."

Later that day, John Stewart was speaking to Nancy Temple from the Andersen legal department.

"What documents should we keep on all this?" Stewart asked. "Historically, we keep everything."

Temple asked how many records existed. Plenty, Stewart said.

"We've got three or four buckets of e-mails," he said. In addition, there were flowcharts, memos put together to justify certain decisions, and then lots of records of the back-and-forth debate over the last couple of weeks.

Andersen had a policy on document retention, Temple said. He should keep the original Duncan memos and final drafts. But everything else should be destroyed, including the e-mails. That's what the policy required.

"I *need* the earlier draft versions of memos," Stewart protested. "I need it for my own files, because it captures the work that the PSG did on this."

It couldn't be done, Temple said. "Andersen has a policy," she said. "You should follow it."

The next morning, Kaminski declared war. He had spent the night tossing in bed before deciding to make a clear break. He prepared an e-mail for Scardino at Andersen.

Questions could not be answered, he typed, until his team was given access to all of the underlying documents. He spelled out his concerns about the stock-price discounts and the vanishing hedge restrictions. It was basic, he wrote. No one could have their cake and eat it, too.

The following day, Kaminski burst into Rick Buy's office. If his career at Enron was going to go down in flames, he planned to make a lot of noise on the way.

"Listen, Rick," he said as he stormed in. "We have discovered a very serious problem with the Raptors."

Buy looked up from his desk, a pained expression on his face. He was tired of hearing all of the complaints about the Raptors.

Kaminski plunged ahead. "I am not going to sign off on anything related to the Raptors," he said. "And I don't care if I'm fired for it."

Buy raised a hand. "Whoa, wait a minute, I don't think you'll be fired," he replied quickly. "Now that Skilling's gone, we have a different mantra at Enron."

He looked Kaminski in the eye. "We're expected to be honest," he said.

The break between Kaminski's group and Enron Global Finance worsened with each passing hour. By October 3, he had instructed every analyst to refuse any assignments from the division unless they were provided in writing.

At the same time, Kaminski began to suspect a cover-up had begun. Analysts noticed that messages were disappearing from their Microsoft Outlook mailboxes. They had no idea how it was being done, but Kaminski wouldn't stand for it.

He went to speak to his team. "Everyone!" he said. "I want you to start forwarding your personal messages to private e-mail accounts!" If anyone was trying to hide the truth, he would do his best to stop it.

That morning at eleven, Kaminski and two of his analysts, Shanbhogue and Bharati, responded to a written request from the finance group for help. They met in a conference room on the nineteenth floor. When Kaminski and his staffers arrived, five finance executives were waiting.

Kaminski started speaking as soon as he stepped in. "I am very uncomfortable with what is going on," he said.

Ryan Siurek answered. "Vince, you aren't the only one. That's why we're unwinding the Raptors."

But before they went further, Siurek said, they needed to talk about Kaminski's e-mail to Andersen. The message really made waves around Enron. No one but Causey was supposed to communicate directly with the accounting firm.

"Okay, fine," Kaminski said. "If this is the procedure, I won't send any more messages to Andersen."

He pointed a finger across the table. "But I want you to know that what is going on is unacceptable. You guys made me look stupid and dishonest at the same time."

An executive with corporate finance spoke up. "We understand, Vince," he said. "But we need your help now. We have made a commercial decision to unwind the Raptors and pay Kopper and LJM a certain amount of money. And we want your help to calculate the numbers, so we can back into that amount." The total amount, thirty-five million dollars, wasn't mentioned.

Were these people insane? "How on earth can you justify paying *anything* to Kopper?" Kaminski said. "The Raptors are underwater!"

Well, the executive said, Raptor II had some positive value.

"And how is that? Not the last time *I* looked."

There had been a deal between Causey and Fastow, the finance executives explained. Back in May, the two had agreed to remove certain poorly performing assets from the hedges. So now Raptor II was worth more. The result was that Kopper, as the new general partner of LJM2, was owed money.

Kaminski threw up his hands. *It's a hedge until it loses money! Then Enron takes it back!* "This looks better and better!" he shouted. "Two insiders make a verbal agreement to benefit another insider!"

Kaminski could not contain his disgust; he stormed out. Siurek ran behind, begging him to return. Kaminski walked back in and stared at the finance executives.

"Listen, I want to make this very clear," he said. "We're not doing any work for you unless we see all the legal documents." He glared at the men.

"But I guarantee you," he growled, "I see something in those documents I don't like, I scream loud and clear."

Kaminski left the room, followed by Shanbhogue and Bharati. They were shaken. Shanbhogue sidled up to Kaminski.

"There's only one phrase to describe what they are doing," he said. "They're siphoning off company funds."

The Morial Convention Center in New Orleans, just walking distance from the French Quarter, was buzzing with activity on the morning of October 5. Andersen partners from all over had arrived in town for their first meeting under their new chief executive, Joseph Berardino.

Since taking over earlier in the year, Berardino had signaled his plans to reshape the firm and, for this meeting, wanted to rekindle its spirit. His speech would feature a dramatic stunt; in answer to a rhetorical question about who would lead Andersen into the future, the back wall of the stage would turn, becoming a line of mirrors that showed the reflection of the audience.

That would follow a video celebrating the best of Andersen's best, the partners who represented everything good about the firm. People like David Duncan, whose Enron work would be featured. Berardino had just notified Duncan that he had been selected for the CEO's advisory council, designed to help plot strategy; there was no better signal that Duncan was the type of partner others at the firm should emulate.

Berardino was hanging around the convention center, sipping coffee and talking shop with his partners. An Andersen official approached him, saying he had news.

"There's an issue down at Enron," the official said. "We've got people on the ground with the team, but it's going to be real hard, and we have some real hard decisions to make in the third quarter. We may need your help."

Fine. "Let me know what I can do," Berardino said. But he wasn't worried. Their team at Enron was top-notch.

Enron had finally calmed down. In early October, when the board arrived in Houston for the quarterly meeting, the company seemed poised to turn a corner.

In meeting after meeting, the news was upbeat. At the audit committee, Causey presented a list of charges the company would take against its third-quarter earnings—all nonrecurring events, he told the directors. David Duncan chimed in, assuring the assembled directors that the accounting associated with the Raptor losses was appropriate.

The audit committee heard about Sherron Watkins as well. Dilg and Hendrick presented the results of their investigation succinctly: While there was discomfort about the perceived pressure on employees created by the Fastow related-party transactions, the lawyers reported, everything about the deals appeared to be on the up-and-up.

"Our firm does not feel that any further investigation is necessary," Dilg said.

The directors asked a number of questions, then instructed the company managers to thank Watkins for coming forward.

Everything seemed under control.

The news out of the finance committee was equally upbeat. Fastow announced that Enron's liquidity—the cash available or accessible for operations—was significantly above the minimum levels required by the board.

"We have tested our liquidity for the possibility of very negative market events," Fastow said. "And even in such instances, it remains adequate."

Enron had already been through a big test in the aftermath of September 11, after all. Now, listening to Fastow's assurances, the directors felt confident this company could withstand whatever the world threw at it.

The meeting of the full board was a celebration of Enron and its potential. Bankers from Goldman made their presentation about the threats from the low stock price. The directors agreed to consider takeover defenses, to ensure Enron would not be at risk from a lowball hostile bid.

Then came the business presentations. Dave Delainey, head of Enron Energy Services, told the board that the retail division was putting in a great performance. The elements were in place, he said, for increased growth and profitability. The same held true for the wholesale division. Its head, John Lavorato, reported steadily increasing earnings, with volumes growing significantly.

Good news all around, the directors muttered happily. They had survived the Skilling resignation; they had survived September 11. Enron's future looked pretty bright.

That same week in Chicago, risk-management executives at Andersen ran Enron's financial figures through FIDO, a fraud-detection software. A staffer checked the results.

A red alert. Enron's financial statements filed the previous June set off a fraud warning. One of the executives running the test, Mark Zajac, wrote up an e-mail on October 9 to Duncan and two of his superiors, alerting them. It was always possible that this was a fluke, generated by legitimate business activity. But still, Zajac cautioned, the accountants needed to heed the warning.

"It is imperative that you evaluate the results carefully and objectively before reaching any conclusion," Zajac wrote, "because of the significant adverse impact of failing to detect a material financial statement fraud."

Kaminski had been out of the office for a few days, recruiting potential analysts from Berkeley. With him out of the way, the finance division struck. Executives descended, asking analysts to sign off on the numbers for the unwinding of the Raptors, including the thirty-five million dollars to LJM2. When mid-level analysts refused, the executives went down the chain to the associates.

But each time, the analysts sent the request to Shanbhogue, Kaminski's second in command. He killed every attempt. No approvals, he repeated, until Kaminski saw all the legal documents.

He never would.

Members of Andersen's Houston office were listening to Michael Odom, a practice director. It was the morning of October 10, and Odom was letting everyone know that they needed to be careful with their paperwork.

Andersen had a policy, he said, requiring the destruction of records that weren't needed for the finished audit files. It worked well, he said, and auditors in Houston needed to be sure they were in compliance.

"We've had several cases where we've produced documents in litigation recently where we found a lot of stuff that we shouldn't have retained," he said.

Of course, once the firm was sued, Odom said, nobody could destroy documents anymore. "But if it's destroyed in the course of the normal policy and litigation is filed the next day, that's great," Odom said. "We've followed our policy, and whatever there was that might have been of interest to somebody, uh, is gone."

The next day, John Stewart saw Nancy Temple walking down a hall at headquarters. He stopped her.

"Nancy," he said, "I have to tell you, I am still very uncomfortable with deleting the e-mails and destroying the draft documents in the Enron situation. It is the type of material that I very well could need in the future."

"Tell you what, John," Temple replied. "Why don't you get a set of the documents you want to keep, and I'll hold them for you. But otherwise, comply with the policy and dispose of the other material."

Stewart wasn't happy about the idea. But he agreed.

Temple was at the office early the next morning, October 12. With all of this discussion about documents, it was apparent that few in the firm understood Andersen's retention policy. Whatever they could dispose of had to go. The team working on the Enron account in particular had to understand that.

She typed an e-mail to Odom. "Mike," she wrote. "It might be useful to consider reminding the engagement team of our documentation and retention policy. It will be helpful to make sure that we have complied with the policy."

Temple included a link to the policy, contained on Andersen's internal Web site. Then, at 8:53, she hit "send."

That same day at Enron, top management was completing its draft earnings release for the third quarter.

There was some debate about what else to include. Of course, there was the matter of the $1.2 billion reduction in shareholder equity, caused by the accounting error. Causey argued it had no place in the press release; the announcement was about earnings, and the equity reduction was a balance-sheet issue. It should, he said, be released with Enron's quarterly SEC filing in a few weeks.

There was some debate, and a compromise was struck. They wouldn't disclose the equity reduction in the press release, but would mention it on the analysts' call. Besides, there was going to be plenty to absorb in the earnings release itself. Enron would be announcing a huge loss, largely as a result of shutting down the Raptors.

As they finished up the release, Lay reflected that the entities that had caused so much controversy in recent months were now going to vanish. "Well," he told the group, "this ought to please Sherron Watkins."

That evening, David Duncan was in his office, reading through the draft press release. His eyes fixed on the third paragraph:

Non-recurring charges totaling $1.01 billion after-tax, or $(1.11) per diluted share, were recognized for the third quarter.

There they were—the Raptor losses, blended in with a couple of other problems Enron was cleaning up. Still, a word in the release made him uncomfortable.

Non-recurring. That is what Causey always called the losses. But that might be misleading. Enron had reported the gains locked in by the Raptors as recurring; in other words, they could be expected to happen again. Now that there were losses, it wanted to shift to "non-recurring."

This wasn't something to ignore. Duncan had been through the fire the past few weeks over the Raptors. He wasn't about to sit on a decision like *this* without kicking it up the line. He went to consult with members of the risk-management group and legal. They would know what to do.

Two days later, on Sunday, Duncan finally spoke with Rick Causey.

"Rick, we recognize that press releases are solely the company's responsibility," he said. "But we have very strong concerns that labeling these charges as nonrecurring could be very confusing to investors."

There were instances, Duncan said, where the SEC filed actions against companies using such terms in a misleading way. Andersen's advice, Duncan said, was to consider removing the word, or at least have the lawyers review it to make sure it was not inappropriate.

Causey was calm. "I hear what you're saying," he said.

Shannon Adlong stepped off the elevator onto the thirty-seventh floor of Three Allen Center, Andersen's offices for its Enron team. Adlong, Duncan's secretary, had brought her teenage daughter to work with her that morning, but immediately began to worry this wasn't a day for family visitors.

The place bustled, the trash cans overflowed. And around the office she periodically heard the whirring sound from the firm's shredders. Obviously, people were getting rid of paperwork. She wandered by the break room and saw two large bags of shredded papers. Walking toward her office, Adlong noticed Kimberly Scardino, one of the auditors on the Enron account. She asked what was going on.

"Dave got an e-mail on Friday from the legal department in Chicago," Scardino said. "They want us to be in compliance with the document-retention policy."

Adlong nodded and headed back to her desk.

That same night, Duncan tracked down Causey to ask about the press release scheduled to go out the next day. What procedures had been conducted to make sure the use of the term "non-recurring" wasn't misleading? Duncan asked.

"Normal legal review," Causey replied. But no changes had been made. "Non-recurring" had been kept in the release.

The next morning, Rebecca Smith from the *Journal* stared at the laptop computer perched on the edge of her bed. She was checking the newswires, seeing if anything was happening that day that might need her attention.

Smith and Emshwiller were still hot on the LJM2 story. Enron had played hardball, refusing to provide any comment other than a terse written statement that said nothing. Probably, the reporters figured, the story would be ready to go soon.

The Enron release came across the wires. In the headline, Smith saw something about $1.01 billion in nonrecurring charges. The release attributed a chunk of that—some $544 million—to the termination of a structured-finance deal involving "a previously disclosed entity."

What the heck is that? Could it possibly be LJM?

Smith looked around for other details, but there was nothing to answer her question. There was a story hidden somewhere behind the obfuscation. She felt it in her gut.

She sent a message to her boss, Jonathan Friedland. Something was up.

"This is Ken Lay, chairman and CEO of Enron."

It was the next morning at nine. Lay was sitting at a table, looking down at a speakerphone, as he opened up Enron's third-quarter analysts' conference call.

"I will provide a brief overview of our quarterly results, and then open the call for questions."

At that time in Fredericksburg, Texas, Jeff Skilling was standing by a four-poster bed in a tiny bed-and-breakfast. He had traveled there with Rebecca Carter, along with his brother Mark and his wife. But before he joined the fun that morning, he wanted to find out about Enron's quarterly results.

Skilling held a phone to his ear. He had just dialed into the Enron conference call, hoping to hear about its performance. Lay's disembodied voice echoed over the line.

"For the third quarter 2001," Lay said, "Enron reported strong recurring operating performance, which included a 35 percent increase in recurring net income."

Whoa! Skilling thought. *That's strong as hell.*

He listened as Lay ran through a couple of other numbers; everything sounded wonderful. He hung up; that was all he needed to know. Heading out of the room, he saw his brother and slapped him a high five.

"Company's doing great!" he exclaimed.

Back in Houston, the call continued.

"As these numbers show, Enron's core energy-business fundamentals are excellent," Lay said. "We are recording nonrecurring charges of slightly over one billion dollars this quarter." Even so, Lay said, the company was on track to hit its fourth-quarter targets—and for 2002 to boot.

Later, he returned to write-offs. He spelled out the reasons for the charges: $287 million because of troubled Azurix assets, $180 million of costs associated with shrinking Broadband, and the termination of some structured-finance arrangements. He didn't call them the Raptors.

"In connection with the early termination, shareholders' equity will be reduced approximately $1.2 billion," he said, "with a corresponding significant reduction in the number of diluted shares outstanding."

He mentioned nothing about the accounting error responsible for the huge revision.

Emshwiller was on the phone with Mark Palmer, quizzing him about the write-downs disclosed in the earnings release.

"Is LJM that 'previously disclosed entity'?" he asked. "And if so, how much of the write-off was due to LJM?"

"You wouldn't be wrong if you said less than half but more than a quarter," Palmer replied.

Emshwiller tried to contain his excitement. "So maybe a little over $200 million?"

"Maybe a little under," Palmer replied.

After getting off the phone, Palmer figured he better double-check his information. He dialed Causey. "Rick," he said, "how much of the $544 million in the release is the cost of undoing the LJM deals?"

Causey didn't hesitate. "Thirty-five million."

"What!" Palmer exclaimed. *Oh, I hope I didn't hear that right.*

"Mark," Causey said, "if we hadn't hedged these deals, we would have lost this much money. The only charge attributable to undoing the deals with LJM is the thirty-five million we paid them to let us blow this up."

Palmer asked a couple of other questions, then hung up. He immediately dialed Emshwiller.

Palmer sounded out of breath.

"I was wrong; I made a mistake," he said. The $200 million wasn't from LJM.

"So how much was related to LJM?" Emshwiller asked.

"Thirty-five million," Palmer said.

"Thirty-five million," Emshwiller repeated, his tone sagging.

"That's right."

Emshwiller was disappointed. Still, the story wasn't dead. Enron lost thirty-five million dollars to the investment fund formerly owned by its CFO. That was still something.

Rebecca Smith had been tied up on another interview, so she had missed Enron's morning conference call. Still, she could review it. She called up a recorded version on her computer and hit "play." With time running short, she fast-forwarded through Lay's opening comments.

She went right over his statement about the $1.2 billion reduction in shareholder equity.

At his home sometime after five the next morning, Palmer padded into the downstairs office across the hall from his darkened bedroom. He was wearing shorts and a T-shirt and holding a glass of orange juice that he had just fetched from the kitchen. He sat at the desk. The computer was on.

He called up the Web site for the *Journal*. He saw the Enron article prominently displayed and clicked it open.

"Enron Posts Surprise 3d-Quarter Loss After Investment, Asset Write-Downs," the headline read.

Palmer gulped the juice as he read. Not the usual earnings article. After the first paragraph, it jumped straight into a piece about LJM. It hinted at the controversy, suggesting that Fastow may have made a lot of money. There were quotes from documents sprinkled around.

Palmer relaxed. The article seemed fair; the reporters had done a good job. But it certainly wasn't an atom-bomb kind of story. This one probably wouldn't cause much trouble.

In the Washington offices of the SEC that morning, Linda Thomsen, a senior lawyer in the enforcement division, was in a meeting. Two young lawyers, Doug Paul and Beth Lehman, appeared in the doorway, looking excited. They signaled for Thomsen, who came out to see them in the hall.

"It looks like Enron has a huge financial issue," Paul said. "I think we should open a case."

Thomsen listened as the lawyers described what they knew. A big write-off, tied to some related-party transactions involving the CFO. Sounded good.

"Okay," she said. "Go see if you can grab it."

About that same time, the phone rang on Palmer's desk. He glanced at the caller ID, and his heart sank.

"Fastow, Andrew," the screen read.

He reached for the phone. "Mark Palmer."

"Mark, it's Andy," Fastow said.

Palmer braced for the storm.

"The story was *fantastic*," Fastow enthused. "If that's the best they can do, we're in great shape. Everything they said had been out in the market already. I think that was a brilliant strategy you employed."

What? "Andy, it wasn't my strategy," Palmer replied.

"Well, I think it was a brilliant strategy," Fastow continued. "And I am going to remember this at the PRC."

Palmer hesitated. "Well, okay," he said. "I'm glad you're happy with the story, Andy."

He hung up the phone, seething. He had felt the thinly veiled slap—*see, Mark? I was right, you were wrong*—and it stung. But also, crediting Palmer with the way the story came out, and saying that he would get a boost at the Performance Review Committee, could work against him, too. When news articles were bad, would Fastow punish him?

Palmer turned around. Steve Kean was at his desk.

"Steve, you may get a call from Andy telling you that he's brilliant and that he loved the story."

Kean shrugged. "Well, the story's not bad."

Palmer looked him in the eye. "Steve," he said firmly, "this might not be the end of it."

John Emshwiller was at his desk, taking calls from readers about his LJM story that morning. One came in from a short seller he knew. "You missed something that could be really big," the short seller said.

"What exactly did we miss?"

The $1.2 billion equity reduction, the short seller said. Lay had mentioned it on the conference call, but nobody picked up on it. Emshwiller thanked the trader and called Smith. He asked if she remembered anything about an equity reduction during the conference call.

"Nothing," she said. "But I'll go back and check."

"We didn't bury it!" Palmer protested. "We talked about it!" He was on the phone with Smith, who was accusing Enron of having camouflaged the equity reduction.

"Well, how's it tied to LJM?" she asked.

Palmer already knew what was coming. No doubt, this was the *Journal's* story for tomorrow.

The word back wasn't good for the SEC lawyers in Washington. They had checked the division's internal computer system and found that someone in the Fort Worth office had already opened an Enron case months before.

Thomsen got on the phone. She reached Spencer Barasch, the associate district administrator in Fort Worth.

"Spence, you've got an Enron case," she said. "But we can't tell if it's related to what we're looking at."

Barasch was amused. With the announcement of the write-downs, everybody in Washington was dashing to investigate Enron. That morning, he had received the same call from Tom Newkirk, the chief lawyer on Waste Management. But the Fort Worth office read the *Journal*, too, and their case had been open since late August.

"It's ours," Barasch said. Already, he said, his lawyers were putting together a request for information from Enron, seeking documents about Fastow and his deals. It was going to Enron's general counsel that very day.

Jim Derrick had just received the fax from the SEC in Fort Worth. They wanted everything—the offering materials for the LJM funds, records on all the transactions, and an accounting of Enron's profit or loss on each deal.

Well, Derrick thought, at least this wasn't a formal investigation, just a preliminary inquiry. Perhaps it wouldn't amount to much. He picked up the phone and dialed Lay's voice mail. Lay himself was in New York for investor meetings. Derrick silently listened until he heard the beep.

"Ken, I hope the trip is going well," he said. "I've got some information I need to share with you."

He discussed the contact from the SEC.

"I wouldn't be overly concerned," Derrick said. "This is not necessarily a disclosable event, but it is something we probably ought to visit about in the next day or so."

With that, Derrick said his good-byes and hung up.

That evening in New York, Lay was in a car headed to the airport. The day had been going well; even with that *Journal* story this morning, the analysts had seemed upbeat. Now they would fly to Boston and get ready to do their presentations all over again for investors there.

As he rode along, Lay dialed into the Enron voice-mail system. He wanted to check his messages before boarding the plane. He listened to the one from Derrick, unconcerned.

Okay, he thought. *I'll get back to him tomorrow and see if there's anything we need to do.*

The next morning, a sedan moved through traffic in Boston, ferrying Enron executives to their meeting. In the backseat, Causey unfolded the third section of the *Journal* and scanned the lead headline.

Enron Says Its Links to a Partnership Led to $1.2 Billion Equity Reduction.

He read a couple of paragraphs, seeing words that seemed to criticize the company for not revealing the reduction in its earnings release. He slapped the paper on his lap and turned to Lay, who was riding beside him.

"This is just wrong!" Causey fumed. "We disclosed this in the conference call!"

Lay nodded, angry. The analysts had heard all about this. To him, it looked as though a couple of *Journal* reporters had a vendetta against Enron.

Another short seller was on the phone to the *Journal*, this time with Rebecca Smith. He had possession of a recent quarterly report for LJM2 investors, he said.

"Would you like to see a copy?" he asked.

An emergency meeting was convened an hour later in Derrick's office. Palmer had just heard from Smith, and she was furious. The *Journal* had obtained LJM2 documents, she had said, showing massive returns to the fund from investments in vehicles called the Raptors. Millions appeared to be going to Fastow, even to Kopper, she said. Then Smith had raised issues from a source that McMahon had heard bankers complain about being pushed to invest with Fastow to get business with Enron.

This was a disaster. If any of this was true, it would blow up into a full-scale government investigation. Derrick summoned Dilg and Hendrick from Vinson & Elkins and told them that they should reopen their interviews. They had questioned McMahon, and he never told them this. They needed to speak with him again right now.

McMahon was reached by telephone. Hendrick asked point-blank if he knew of bankers being threatened by Fastow. McMahon recounted his experiences: the call from a banker inquiring about a deal that he claimed had been promised in exchange for investing, along with the rumors that swirled about links between investing and getting business.

"I have no firsthand knowledge," he said. "I wasn't present when anyone pressured the banks to do anything."

Led by Lay, a group of Enron executives trooped up a flight of stairs inside Logan Airport. Word from Houston was that Enron was headed into crisis mode. The entire senior management needed to make some decisions.

Everyone walked into a conference room and congregated around the telephone. They dialed Derrick's office. The phone was answered on the first ring, and Derrick named all the people with him. The room in Houston was packed.

Lay opened the conversation. "Well, we've had good investor meetings the last two days, but our stock is now down four dollars in two days," he said. "We've got this notice from the SEC; we've got these articles in the *Journal*. So I want to hear what's happening there."

Derrick nodded to Rex Rogers, one of his lawyers who had been dealing with the SEC.

"Ken, it's Rex," he began. "Now, I don't want to overly concern people, but if we keep seeing articles appearing in papers like *The Wall Street Journal*, and we keep seeing our stock price drop, the SEC is going to want to come in and really take a look around."

"Well, what does that mean?"

"The investigation might go from informal to formal," Rogers replied. "Formal investigations are much less frequent, so that's something we may have to announce. We may even decide that we want to announce this either way, given all the activity in the stock."

Lay took a deep breath.

"Okay," he said. "How are we on the PR front?"

Palmer answered. "We have problems," he said. "We have been getting a lot of questions from the *Journal* about Andy and his role in the related transactions and what kind of compensation he may have gotten."

Lay was about to ask a question when a voice boomed out. "We went through all the necessary approvals with the board, Ken. You know that."

It was Fastow.

Fastow was whistling as he spoke, his face twitching with anxiety. "It's been reviewed by the outside auditors, the lawyers," he said. "We just looked at it with Vinson & Elkins! This has been checked every which way!"

This was just the *Journal* getting back at Enron because the company refused to cooperate, some executives grumbled. Something had to be done to stop them.

Lay glanced over at Koenig from investor relations. They were scheduled to travel to Philadelphia the next day for investor meetings there. But Enron was in trouble.

Koenig nodded. "If you need to go back to Houston, I'll understand. I don't think that'll be a problem."

Philadelphia was off. The team was returning home.

At 7:30 the next morning, the Enron building was unnaturally quiet, its executives knocked off balance by the tumult of the last few days. Lay was in his office, reading that day's *Journal*. This article was the worst yet. "Enron CFO's Partnership Had Millions in Profit," the headline read.

Well, okay. Investors ponied up hundreds of millions of dollars; it was hardly a surprise they earned millions in returns. But it was the third paragraph that held the most uncomfortable claim: that Fastow and possibly others had received seven million dollars in management fees during 2000.

This wasn't helping Lay's digestive tract. Definitely, he thought, these writers were on a crusade. But then again, how much money did Fastow actually make on these deals? Did anybody really know? Had anyone ever asked?

And then, down deep in the story was this mention of Michael Kopper, a former Enron executive who was described as now helping operate LJM2. Lay stared at the name.

Who in the world was Michael Kopper?

That morning at eleven, Enron's directors convened by conference call for a special meeting. Lay took charge.

"As you can imagine with these recent articles, there's renewed concern about the related transactions and Andy's role in them," he said. "There could come a point, whether there's anything wrong or not, that Andy's effectiveness as our CFO could come into question."

The directors discussed the issue of Fastow's LJM compensation. John Duncan worried that the seven million dollars reported in the paper sounded high. Pug Winokur dismissed that, saying it was all a matter of how much money Fastow had invested and how well the funds had done.

"Listen, on the *Journal*, I think we need to become more proactive," Winokur said. "We should directly respond to them. We need to explain the fact that this was all approved by outside auditors and outside lawyers."

The other directors grumbled in agreement. This was all being blown out of proportion.

Lay turned to Whalley. "Greg," he said, "give us an update on the effect this is having on the business."

Whalley's tone was stern. "We can't let this interrupt our management of the daily operations. And we have got to ensure we maintain our counterparties' confidence."

Counterparties. The other energy traders who participated in the gas and electricity markets, the ones who did business with Enron on faith that it would be able to pay for the energy it agreed to purchase.

"If we lose their confidence," Whalley said, "the consequences could be severe."

Ray Bowen was sick of waiting for the next shoe to drop. He dialed Whalley and reached his voice mail.

"Greg, it's Ray," he said. "I don't want to micromanage your life, but I've got a point of view on this." There was no reason to hold back now.

"Andy's a bad guy," Bowen said. "You need to get rid of him, and go out and hire an accounting firm that isn't Arthur Andersen to come in and look at these deals. That's the only way we're going to restore credibility. And I just think Andy's a bad guy and there's no way he survives this. So we just need to bite the bullet."

With that, Bowen hung up.

Whalley's secretary called back, saying her boss wanted to see Bowen right away. But their schedules didn't mesh. They put off their meeting until October 23. By then, everything would be further out of control.

The Fort Worth office of the SEC had to drop the Enron investigation. The case was getting too big and would take a lot of manpower. And like most everywhere in Texas, the Fort Worth office had too many people with connections to Enron. Spencer Barasch kicked the case up to Washington.

At the SEC's headquarters, Linda Thomsen walked into the office of her colleague Tom Newkirk. They both were eager to get going on the Enron case, which they knew would likely be the enforcement division's high-profile investigation that year.

"You know I really want it," Thomsen said.

"Well, I want it, too," Newkirk replied.

They were silent for a second. "Let's flip for it," Newkirk said, digging in his pocket.

He stood and tossed the coin. Thomsen called it, and it dropped to the floor. They both leaned over to look.

Newkirk shrugged. "It's yours," he said.

Greg Whalley wanted to know the numbers. Fastow and Glisan kept chirping that Enron was more than able to weather this bad storm. But Whalley didn't know these guys. He wanted them to spell out what money was where. He summoned them to a conference room.

"Okay, liquidity," Whalley said. "What have we got?"

"We're in a very good position," Fastow said. "We've got $3.8 billion in available lines of credit."

Glisan raised a hand. "Well, wait, Andy," he said. "We've already drawn down $500 million."

Fastow nodded, closing his eyes. "*That's* right," he said. "There's $3.3 billion available on the lines."

Whalley stared at him, stunned. He just asked his CFO for the most important financial number of them all and got an answer that was off by half a billion dollars.

He decided to dig a little deeper. "How much of the line is a backup to the commercial paper?" he asked.

Good companies maintain extra lines of credit with banks that are available to tap in the event of trouble in the short-term commercial-paper market. But those lines are considered a replacement for credit that might disappear and should never be counted as additional available cash. For every dollar drawn from those lines, the company would have lost the same amount in commercial paper.

Fastow fumbled with the number. "Umm, it's $1.8 billion backing the commercial paper."

Glisan nodded. "Right, that's right. So we've got $1.5 billion in available liquidity."

What the hell? Whalley stood up, disbelief etched on his face.

"You guys are out of your minds!" he said, turning to head out. "I walked in with $3.8 billion in liquidity, and I'm leaving with $1.5."

He shook his head. "I don't want to ask you another question. I don't think we can afford it!"

Fastow started to speak, but Whalley just pushed through the door, disgusted. Realization hit him like a splash of cold water. Enron's CFO *was incompetent*! The man didn't understand the basics of his job. The prospect unnerved Whalley. *My God*. How much damage had he done over the years?

As he stormed down the hallway, Whalley made up his mind. *This guy*, he thought, *has got to go.*

CHAPTER 20

ENRON'S MANAGING DIRECTORS SHUFFLED into the Dogwood room on the third floor of the Hyatt Regency. It was just before 8:30 on the morning of October 22, and the executives were feeling surly. The barrage of bad news—about LJM, the write-downs, the fumbling in the senior ranks—had left them furious at the company's leaders.

In the back of the room, juice and bagels had been laid out, and the executives crowded around the table, gossiping about Fastow and his self-serving deals. But their CFO was nowhere to be seen; Lay had asked him not to attend. Lay marched in, walking to the front as the executives found seats. The room quieted down.

"We're ready to start," he began. "This is going to be an open discussion of the issues we're facing."

With that, Lay launched into his presentation, explaining the previous week's earnings release and the problems it had raised. Enron was facing challenges to its credibility, he said, and was assembling a strategy to deal with that. But Lay's tone did nothing to calm the panic in the room. Enron was spinning out of control—*right then!*—and there wasn't time to pursue some long-term plan.

The first question came from a member of the merchant-investing group, asking about the *Journal*'s LJM articles. Lay delivered the familiar spiel: the funds had been created to give Enron a broader market for assets, there had been plenty of controls, everything was supervised. Both he and the board, he said, were firmly behind Fastow.

That set off a barrage of more questions. *What are you going to do about the mess? Why did you guys let Fastow take this on?* Finally, Ray Bowen raised a hand and was recognized by Lay.

"The only thing we can do is tell the truth," he preached. "If we believe this stuff is proper, we ought to invite people in, tell them the story."

He looked straight at Lay. "If we don't have anything to hide, let's apologize for not disclosing it better, but show them there was nothing wrong with it."

On one side of the room, Dave Delainey, head of Enron Energy Services, had had enough. "Oh, please!" he barked. "We don't need to apologize for anything!"

From his seat, Vince Kaminski had been listening to the proceedings with a growing sense of unease. He spoke up.

"I would like to give you my view of these transactions," he announced to Lay.

Lay nodded. "Why don't you come up to the podium?"

Kaminski rose and strode purposely down the aisle. Lay and Whalley stood to his left as he gripped the podium.

"I am in the terrible position of having to disagree with you," Kaminski said as he looked at Lay.

"Anyone can disagree with me," Lay replied.

Kaminski turned to face his colleagues. His anger at the side deals, the excuses, *the impropriety*, boiled over.

"What Andy Fastow did was not only improper; it was terminally stupid," Kaminski began. "What he did is cause a crisis of confidence that could bring the company down. And the only choice that we have is to come clean."

Kaminski's face hardened. He thought of Stinson Gibner, who left Enron because of the Raptors. "One of our best employees resigned over this, because he couldn't take pride in Enron," he said. "This was my view from the beginning. I told Buy that this idea was so stupid only Andy Fastow could have come up with it."

The room broke up in laughter. One executive involved in LJM1 interrupted. "Those were hedges!" he yelled.

Kaminski ignored him. He was on a roll. His face reddened, his voice cracked with emotion. *The company had been hedging its investments against its own stock! It was stupid! Enron has been dishonest!* Finally, Whalley placed a hand on Kaminski's shoulder.

"That's enough," he said. With a gentle shove from Whalley, Kaminski started back to his seat. He passed Bowen, who was sitting on the aisle. Bowen looked him in the eye.

"God bless you," Bowen said.

Later that day, Harvey Pitt stepped up to a podium at the Americana Ballroom in the Loews Miami Beach Hotel, where members of the American Institute of Certified Public Accountants had gathered for their fall meeting.

The previous afternoon, the SEC released the 21(a) report that Pitt had drafted just weeks before, announcing how the agency expected corporations to cooperate if they discovered wrongdoing. Now he was ready to announce the next stage of his plan: an effort to improve the relationship between the SEC and the accounting industry.

Pitt shuffled his papers, then pulled up the microphone.

"In recent years, the unremarkable notion of an SEC chairman meeting with this group has taken on considerable mental, if not physical, risk. The agency I am privileged to lead has not, of late, always been a kinder and gentler place for accountants, and the audit profession, in turn, has not always had nice things to say about us."

He pulled himself up straight. "Somewhere along the way, accountants became afraid to talk to the SEC, and the SEC appeared to be unwilling to listen to the profession."

He looked up. "Those days," Pitt said, "are ended."

The crowd of accountants cheered.

The essence of the new effort was cooperation, Pitt said, in hopes that the accountants could approach the agency with questions, and without fears of recrimination.

"Practices that reflect venality and disservice to public investors, however, will not be tolerated," he said.

But together, he said, the agency and the accounting profession could create an environment where information provided to investors could better reflect reality.

"We may need to reconsider whether our accounting principles provide a realistic picture," he said. "When rules get in the way of providing clear, reliable information to investors, then it is time to change them."

The crisis at Enron was not going unnoticed at the upper reaches of Andersen. In Los Angeles, Rich Corgel, a senior partner, contacted a trusted colleague, John Riley, urging him to get involved. There were more conference calls coming, Corgel said, and Riley should be on the line. More important, Houston seemed shaky. The firm wanted Riley there to get a handle on the situation. Riley agreed.

Just after three that afternoon, the directors of Enron gathered in the boardroom, some by conference call, for another emergency meeting. Glisan made a short presentation, saying that demand for the company's bonds was soft but that Enron still had more liquidity than it needed.

Lay recognized Causey. In the middle of all these troubles, the company had to deal with another issue: the rules had changed for the accounting of certain intangible assets. The arcane revision meant Enron would have to report a noncash reduction in earnings of $200 million in the first quarter of 2002. But it wasn't as bad as it could have been, Causey said. The intangible assets acquired in the purchase of Wessex Water by Azurix so many years before did not have to be written down. Causey left the meeting, and Lay turned to the most serious issue.

"I would like to open up a discussion, to see if any members of the board have a recollection of obtaining any information about the financial returns earned by Andy Fastow through the LJM structures," he said.

It was a roundabout question. In its simplest terms, Lay was asking: anyone ever find out how much cash Fastow was pulling out of these things? No one had.

The time had come for the answer, the directors agreed. Two directors, John Duncan and Mickey LeMaistre, were appointed to call Fastow and simply ask him.

The cream of Houston society gathered that night at the annual fund-raiser for the Holocaust Museum. A number of public figures mingled in the crowd, but in particular the dinner was honoring Salomon Smith Barney, which, when pressed by Fastow, had made a six-figure contribution. Fastow even kicked in some money of his own.

As dinner proceeded, Ken Lay was asked to say a few words. He stood before the crowd. "Obviously, we're delighted that Smith Barney stepped up and made the contribution they made," he said.

He turned and saw Fastow watching him. "But the person who really made this happen is Andy Fastow," he said. "So I think we ought to recognize Andy's contribution and see if he'd like to make a few comments."

The crowd applauded, and Fastow stood. He thanked Lay and joined in on congratulating Smith Barney. "We hope they'll keep making these kinds of contributions," he said. "Certainly, we'll keep encouraging them to do it."

There was some polite laughter. Fastow glanced toward Lay. "I would be remiss if I didn't acknowledge Ken and Linda Lay. Ken and Linda have become role models for Lea and me. Certainly, they are role models for the community. But they're also our personal role models."

The Lays had given so much to the community, Fastow said, creating so many reasons to admire them. "Lea's and my hope is that we can do just a small percentage of what they have done for our community. It's through their inspiration that we've set up our own family foundation."

The Fastow Family Foundation. The entity stuffed with all the stolen money from the Southampton scam.

"We're trying to get that foundation more fully funded," Fastow said. "We want to be very active in the community, give something back, just as the Lays have. We want to follow in the footsteps of our role models."

He gestured toward Lay. "So, Ken and Linda, thank you for the example you have set for us, and for Houston."

The crowd applauded. Lay felt slightly uncomfortable; he had never been quite so publicly slobbered on.

The e-mail that went out to Enron's thousands of employees that night at ten seemed like standard fare, a brief explanation about a change in company benefits.

"October 26 is fast approaching!" the e-mail began.

As everyone had already been told, the corporate savings plan was about to switch administrators, the e-mail said. So employees had just four days left to make changes in their retirement plans. The lockdown would stay in place, it said, until November 20. Whatever everyone held as of Friday would be what they owned for the month—including employees who invested almost exclusively in Enron stock.

The e-mail ended on a chipper note. "Enron benefits," it read. "*Keeping pace with your lifestyle.*"

As he drove to the office the next morning before eight, David Duncan called his secretary, Shannon Adlong, from his cell phone. Enron was about to announce the SEC's informal inquiry and had scheduled an analysts' call. Duncan asked Adlong to pull up the Enron Webcast on his computer so it would be ready when he arrived.

Minutes later, he was in the office. He summoned other accountants on the team—Deb Cash, Tom Bauer, Kimberly Scardino, among others—to join him and closed the door.

Shouts were echoing down the fiftieth-floor hallways of the Enron building. Fastow was yelling at Ron Astin, the Vinson & Elkins partner who had worked with him for years.

"I never wanted to do LJM!" Fastow screamed. "The board directed me to! It was Enron's idea, not mine!"

"Andy!" Astin shouted back. "We can't say that!"

Fastow argued, but Astin stood firm. "Andy, I don't represent you!" the lawyer shouted. "I represent Enron!"

For a second, Fastow glared at Astin. Then he turned on his heel and stormed away, toward a conference room off Lay's office where the analysts' call was about to occur.

At home in Houston, Jeff Skilling was dialing into the Enron conference call. He had been witnessing the unfolding chaos from afar and feared Lay might not be up to the challenge. He could only hope that he was wrong.

"This is Ken Lay. Thanks for joining us today."

The small conference room where Lay was sitting was packed. To one side sat Fastow, his jaw locked in anger. Causey and Glisan hovered nearby. Across the room, Astin was in a chair, staring at a briefcase on his lap. Palmer leaned on a wall near a tiny refrigerator, drinking a soda.

Like almost everyone in the room, Whalley looked uncomfortable. He didn't want to be here. They couldn't say what the SEC was doing, which was the main thing that the world wanted to know. This could only go badly. But Lay had insisted he attend. After all, he *was* president. Lay introduced the participants, then began his presentation.

That's my cue, Whalley thought. Lay could hardly stop the call to inform the analysts that his number two was walking out. Whalley stood and, without a word, left the room.

Enron was disappointed in its stock price, Lay said, particularly with its business going so well. But he and his messengers were prepared to speak with investors as often as they needed.

"There has been a lot of recent attention to the transactions Enron previously entered into with LJM. Let me reiterate a couple of things. We clearly heard investor concerns earlier this year, and Andy Fastow, Enron's chief financial officer, ceased all affiliations with LJM."

Lay went through all the issues: the SEC investigation; an explanation for the failure to disclose the $1.2 billion equity reduction in the press release; the reasons for the reduction—ones that said nothing about the accounting error. Then he turned the call over to Fastow, who put the company's liquidity position at $1.5 billion.

Lay took the floor again. "And with those brief comments," he said, "we would welcome your questions."

David Duncan rested his chin in his hand as he listened. Everyone in his office was silent. So far, things seemed to be going pretty well. No major problems.

Their tone was aggressive. But for the first few minutes at least, the questioners threw mostly softballs. Then Curt Launer, an analyst from Credit Suisse

First Boston, was recognized. What, he asked, would the 2000 earnings have been without the partnership transactions?

Lay glanced at Fastow, who didn't move a muscle. *Nothing*. Lay motioned to Causey. "Rick Causey, chief accounting officer," he said.

Causey told Launer that he should just review the footnotes from the past to figure out the earnings—the same ones that no one had ever been able to decipher. As Causey spoke, Lay shot a cold look at Fastow.

Minutes later, the operator announced a new questioner.

"We'll next hear from Richard Grubman with Highfield Capital," she said. A collective pall fell over the room.

Grubman. The short seller. The one Skilling had called an asshole months before. This was going to be tough.

Grubman sketched out some numbers he had calculated about the financing of Azurix. By his reckoning, he said, Enron may have to provide one billion dollars to support the structure. Had it taken reserves against that liability?

Causey fielded the question, arguing that Azurix had more than sufficient assets to handle its obligations. Grubman fired back, declaring that the value wasn't there.

"Richard, let me intercede here for a minute," Lay interrupted. Wessex was the remaining asset of Azurix, he said. Outside auditors had reviewed the company and concluded there was no need for a write-down of its value.

"I know you want to drive the stock price down," Lay said, "and you've done a good job of doing that, but I think that's that. Let's move on to the next question."

Skilling allowed himself a moment of quiet satisfaction. This was the guy who had provoked his blowup. And Lay wasn't doing much better with him.

Good, he thought. *You're losing your temper, too.*

"That's pointless!" Grubman shot back.

Lay scowled. "Let's go to the next question, Richard. You're monopolizing the conference. We've got a lot of people out there with real, serious questions."

Standing by the refrigerator, Palmer winced. *That just sounds defensive.* This was the wrong approach.

"I would appreciate an answer," Grubman said.

"I think," Lay replied, "in fact, we've answered the question, but you won't accept our answer. Let's move on."

———

Duncan's anxiety grew. Things were falling apart. He could see on his computer screen that Enron's stock price, which had been climbing in the first few minutes of the call, was starting to reverse course.

The pummeling kept coming. There were questions on the partnerships and LJM. Rather than tackle them head-on, Lay stayed defensive, talking about the controls. Finally, David Fleischer from Goldman Sachs came on the line.

"The company's credibility is being severely questioned, and there is really a need for much more disclosure," he said. "There is an appearance that you're hiding something or that you just don't want to . . ."

He hesitated. "That maybe there's something beneath the surface going on that is less than—that may be questionable."

Enron could no longer give vague answers, like directing analysts back to the footnotes. There needed to be more information, Fleischer said.

"David, I appreciate that," Lay responded. "Certainly, as I also said earlier, there are limitations with what we can or should talk about with LJM in particular or related-party transactions in general because of both lawsuits, potential lawsuits as well as the SEC inquiry."

No! God, no!

Skilling wanted to reach through the phone and shake Lay. He sets up an analysts' call, and then says he can't talk about the most pressing issue!

Skilling couldn't listen anymore. He walked away from the call, pacing the floor of his kitchen. This couldn't continue. Somebody had to take charge. Lay wasn't up to it.

He had to go back. Enron needed him.

Skilling dropped onto a white couch in the breakfast area near his kitchen and reached for the phone, dialing Lay's office. He told Lay's secretary to have him call as soon as he could.

"We're trying to provide information," Lay continued. "We're not trying to conceal anything. We're not hiding anything."

Duncan shifted in his seat. This was bad. This plan to settle the market with a conference call had turned into a disaster.

And there was nothing he could do to stop it.

The call continued for another few minutes. As Lay wrapped it up, he promised that the company would keep in contact, and set up another conference call for sometime in the near future.

"So again, thanks for participating in this call," he said. "And thanks for the questions."

Mark Koenig pushed the button on the speakerphone, disconnecting the line. Most of the people in the room stood up. Lay, still in his seat, looked at them.

"How did that go?" he asked.

There was silence. They all knew the truth. "Well," Causey said finally, "I don't think we hurt ourselves."

Not another word was said. Everyone left the room.

A disaster. A total, complete disaster.

Duncan shut down the Webcast. His colleagues agreed. Enron had fumbled the ball spectacularly. Duncan huddled with his partners. Eleven days before, he had seen an e-mail from Nancy Temple telling the team to get in compliance with the document policy and shred what was no longer needed. This seemed like a good time to reiterate her instructions.

"We should all work now on getting in compliance with the policy," Duncan told his colleagues. "And I would like each of you to go out and communicate the need to get in compliance with the engagement personnel you work with."

Perhaps, one partner suggested, Duncan should gather the troops and let them know. He agreed, and told his secretary to arrange a full meeting at 1:30 in conference room 37C1. That would get the files in order fast.

The phone rang in Skilling's house. It was Lay, just off the analysts' call. The two wasted no time on small talk.

"Ken, you've got to bring me back!" Skilling implored.

"*What?*" Lay couldn't believe what he was hearing.

"You've got to bring me back," Skilling repeated. "For the outside world, I think I have some credibility, and they're not going to believe someone would jump into the frying pan if they thought there was anything wrong."

It would send a good signal to the marketplace, Skilling continued, and from there, they could go to New York, make the rounds with the banks, and calm everybody down.

"Ken, it's a chance," Skilling said.

Lay pondered that. "Hmm, that's interesting," he replied. "Let me think about it."

Later that morning, Lay and his management team crossed Smith Street, headed back to the Hyatt hotel ballroom, site of his celebratory return nine weeks before. This time there were no ovations, no cheering. Just a collection of angry, confused, and bitter employees.

Lay greeted everyone. A chorus of good mornings came back to him. "There it is," he replied. "We've got a packed house again, and we appreciate that."

In an even tone, Lay commented that in any other circumstance, he would probably have a few words to say about September 11 and the heroes from that terrible day.

"But of course, today we're going to talk about Enron," he said, "because just like America is under attack by terrorism, I think we're under attack."

He turned the floor over to Greg Whalley, who gave a lengthy description of the performance of the company's business units. All the numbers sounded great.

Back to Lay. "As you can see, the underlying fundamentals of our business are very strong, indeed the strongest they have ever been," he said. "But, regrettably, that is not what Wall Street is focusing on."

The challenges they faced, Lay said, needed to be seen in context. It wasn't as though Enron was a stranger to tough times. There was the oil-trading scandal in the 1980s that almost brought the company down, he said. There was the J-Block contract, which could have cost billions. "In each and every case, the company has come back," he said. "And it has come back stronger than it was before."

He knew, Lay said, that the stock-price drop was causing pain for employees, raising concerns about paying for children's educations and meeting mortgage payments.

"For that I am incredibly sorry," Lay said. "But we're going to get it back."

Of course, Lay acknowledged, everyone wanted to know about LJM. While the board recognized that Fastow's role placed him in a conflict, the company had instituted more than enough controls to ensure that shareholders were protected.

"I have reconfirmed over the past few days," Lay said, "that these controls and procedures have been adhered to."

And despite everything the employees may have read, Lay said, there was no reason for anyone to have concern about Fastow's involvement in the LJM funds. "I and the board are also sure that Andy has operated in the most ethical and appropriate manner possible," Lay said.

Now, Lay said, all Enron employees were facing a test.

"Will we measure up to the challenge, or will we not?" he asked. "True character is born in times of crisis. We need to show our character as an organization."

He looked straight at the audience. "I will say this also," he said. "I am here until the board throws me out, or until we restore Enron to its greatness."

The crowd applauded.

The employees had been invited to ask questions anonymously on note cards. Most of the queries had to do with Enron's business prospects. Different members of the management team stepped forward to reply to the questions that fell within their area of expertise.

Lay glanced at a card and read it to himself. Then he took his turn at the microphone. "A lot of these I think I'm going to have to handle," he said. "Like this one."

He held the card up in front of his face.

"I would like to know if you are on crack," he read.

The crowd laughed. Lay looked up. "I'll come back to the answer," he said. More laughs.

"If so," he continued, "that would explain a lot. If not, you may want to start because it's going to be a long time before we trust you again."

The crowd laughed again.

"I think that's not a very happy employee," Lay said. "I'm sure a lot of you have some hatred."

He paused. "No, I'm not on crack," he announced.

Harvey Pitt was angry.

That morning, *The Washington Post* had reported on his Miami speech. But it played up his regrets about the SEC's reputation for not being a kinder, gentler place for accountants. The article made it seem as though he were kowtowing to the accounting industry.

But those remarks had been about *process*, not regulatory zeal, Pitt fumed. He had specifically said the agency was going to be aggressive in combating malfeasance! Pitt was speaking about another matter with Steve Cutler, his director of enforcement, and mentioned the *Post* article.

"How," Pitt complained, "could someone write about what I said at the beginning of the speech without taking note of everything I said afterward!"

Cutler listened, annoyed. The people in enforcement hadn't known the speech was coming; if they had, they could have warned Pitt that he was about to leap into political hot water.

"Harvey, even if you believe what you said, you can't say it," Cutler replied.

"But it was taken out of context!" Pitt complained. "The rest of the speech explained what I meant."

Cutler looked at him patiently. "Harvey, in Washington you don't get to utter the second sentence," he said. "So you can't say the first when you're chairman of the SEC."

Once Duncan's instructions had gone out to the full team, the slow trickle of document destruction that had begun a week before suddenly became a flood.

And Duncan didn't limit his orders to Houston. That day he called Andersen accountants in London and Portland who worked on Enron matters, letting them know to start complying with the firm's document policy.

In London, partners shredded volumes of documents related to Enron. But not in Portland. Given all the turmoil at Enron, the accountants there thought the idea of shredding records was crazy. They held on to everything.

The fax from Bank of America arrived that same day. Lay's decision in September to use his ten-million-dollar bonus to pay down debt had held off margin calls for a while. Now, with Enron's share price collapsing, the banks were nipping at his heels again, demanding cash.

In the fax, the bank said he had two days to meet the demands or it would take action. Lay and his advisers decided to pay back the Enron loan he had been carrying with company stock, then borrow from the line again, and use the cash to meet the margin call.

Ray Bowen headed up to Whalley's office to discuss the warning about Fastow he had given his boss in a voice mail the previous week. Whalley got right to the point.

"Do you have specific facts that Andy did something wrong?" he asked.

No, Bowen said. "I just know he's a bad guy."

Whalley pressed in. He wanted Bowen to think. There must be something Bowen knew that he could use.

"I just think he's gaming the system," Bowen replied.

Whalley tossed up his hands. "Let me tell you, Ray, I've been speaking with the board, and they're not going to do anything about Andy unless we've got specific facts."

He brought a hand up to his head. "They love him," Whalley said. "They just absolutely love him."

The two sat in silence for a moment. Whalley stood.

"Okay, get out," he said.

At a management committee meeting that afternoon, Lay brought up the proposal for Skilling's return. To his amazement, Skilling's acolytes, the people whose businesses he nourished, vehemently opposed the idea.

It was Skilling's idea to leave, they argued. And why? *Because he was tired?* Too damn bad.

"He made his decision and caused us a lot of heartache and pain," Dave Delainey said. "It's just a bad idea. We've got a team. We'll work through this."

Whalley agreed. "I think it's going to confuse the market about who's really running the company," he said.

Lay just didn't understand it. How could these people be so disloyal to the man who made their careers?

The conference call late that afternoon with Fastow was meticulously planned. Two directors, John Duncan and Mickey LeMaistre, had been selected to represent the board. Jim Derrick, the general counsel, had composed a script to make sure they asked the right questions. That way, the directors could finally learn how much money they had awarded Fastow by allowing him to form the LJM funds.

LeMaistre was in Colorado, Duncan in Houston; Derrick ran the call, connecting them to Fastow. LeMaistre glanced down at a copy of Derrick's script and began to read.

"Andy," he recited, "because of the current controversy surrounding LJM1 and LJM2, we believe it would be helpful for the board to have a general understanding of the amount of your investment and your return on investment in the LJM entities."

He posed the question: how much had Fastow made on each fund, including everything—salary, fees, profits from the investment? There was no wiggle room.

Fastow's tone was matter-of-fact. He'd made twenty-three million dollars on LJM1, he said. And another twenty-two million on LJM2. All told, forty-five million. LeMaistre felt his heart drop.

"Incredible," he scribbled on his script.

And untrue. Fastow's real take would later be found to be at least fifteen million dollars higher, making the total in excess of sixty million. All for two years of work on a job he had promised would take no more than three hours a week.

It couldn't be seen. It couldn't be heard. But on that day, October 23, the financial underpinnings of Enron were snapping apart. The first person to catch wind of the problem was an executive named Tim Despain. Enron's short-term loans in the commercial-paper market weren't rolling over. Institutions were taking the cash from maturing loans and not buying new paper. This was what had happened weeks before, after September 11. But that had been a market problem. This was more serious; it was an Enron problem.

Later, more bad news. Glisan had been working with some of Enron's bankers, trying to secure a loan. There were no takers. So long as Fastow was CFO, they told him, the banks would have no faith that Enron was a worthy credit risk. The news devastated Glisan. He hurried to tell Fastow.

Pug Winokur, head of the finance committee, was screaming at Greg Whalley. They had been speaking about the crisis at the company, and Whalley had suggested that perhaps it was time for Fastow to go.

"Andy Fastow is going to continue as CFO of Enron until the board says otherwise!" Winokur yelled.

Whalley's response was calm. "Don't misunderstand this, Pug," he said. "This isn't about me. Sure, get the board in to talk about this."

But there wasn't much of a choice. "The banks," Whalley said, "are already screaming 'Anybody but Andy.' "

For hours, Fastow and Glisan worked with the finance team, struggling to find a way out of the latest problem. But the markets, the bankers, everyone was steadfast. No one trusted Enron—or Fastow—with the money anymore.

They spoke to Whalley, and he suggested someone who might be able to help. Fastow, accompanied by Glisan and Causey, stood beside his desk. Then he turned on the speakerphone and started dialing.

That evening, Jeff McMahon was wandering through his kitchen, exhausted. He had just gotten back from a business trip and was looking forward to hitting the sack.

The telephone rang. McMahon glanced at the caller ID. *Enron Corp.* He picked up the receiver and said hello.

"Jeff," a detached voice said, "it's Andy, with Rick Causey and Ben Glisan. Have you got a minute?"

McMahon was momentarily taken aback. This was an odd group of people to be calling him—and at home? Something bad was up. This wasn't a conversation for the kitchen.

"Hold on," McMahon said. "Let me pick you up on a different phone." He pushed the hold button, then walked to his home study. He sat on a couch and reached for the line.

Fastow spoke. "Look, we've got an issue here, and we're trying to get all the smart financial minds in the company to address it, to see if we can get any ideas."

Okay, something is really wrong, McMahon thought. Fastow giving him a compliment? Calling him a smart financial mind? No way. McMahon chuckled. "Well, you guys must be really desperate if you're calling me *that*."

No one laughed on the other side.

"Okay," McMahon said. "What's up?"

Glisan leaned in to the speakerphone. "We were unable to roll the commercial paper today," he said.

McMahon snorted derisively. Glisan, Mr. Wonderboy, the company treasurer, didn't even understand the words he was using. Unable to roll the commercial paper? Couldn't happen.

"Ben, obviously you didn't mean you couldn't roll it," McMahon said. "You mean you weren't able to issue as much as you wanted. That's not a surprise in this market."

McMahon's statement was greeted with silence.

In Fastow's office, no one knew quite what to say. Finally, Fastow spoke into the speakerphone.

"No, Jeff," he said. "Ben's right. We were unable to find any buyers for our paper."

McMahon couldn't speak. He couldn't breathe. *No* buyers? How could that be? What the hell happened?

No one said a word for several seconds. McMahon rubbed his eyes. "Well, that is a major problem, isn't it?" he said matter-of-factly.

"Yeah," Fastow replied. "That's why we're calling to see if you have any ideas about this thing."

This was stupid. If the commercial paper didn't roll, there was only one option, McMahon thought. They needed to draw down the bank lines that backed the commercial paper. That was what they were there for. He told Fastow.

"I don't like that," Fastow replied. "I think that would show the market that we're desperate."

McMahon laughed. "Andy? Hello? We *are* desperate!"

After getting off the phone, McMahon ran the situation through his head. Fastow had asked him to come to a meeting the next morning. But he had to face the facts here. They weren't going to *meet* their way out of this problem. They had to pull the bank lines.

Enron was on the precipice; it could go under. Fastow didn't seem to understand the gravity of what was happening.

Greg Whalley. Had Fastow told him what was happening? Or was he keeping it quiet in hopes he could weasel his way out of it? McMahon knew Whalley well, considered him a friend. He decided to call him at home, just in case.

"Listen, Greg," McMahon said, "I just hung up the phone from Andy, Ben, and Rick—"

"Oh, they called you?" Whalley interrupted. "Good. I suggested they do that."

Okay. That explains it. "Are they right? We couldn't roll the commercial paper?"

Yeah, Whalley replied. That's what they had told him.

"Well, you understand, Greg," McMahon said, "this is a major liquidity crisis."

Whalley sighed. "Yeah, I get that, Jeff. I get that."

There weren't a lot of choices, McMahon said, but they needed some brainpower behind this. He told Whalley that he was going to call Ray Bowen and bring him along in the morning. Bowen was a former banker and would be invaluable.

Fine, Whalley said. Bring Bowen.

The next morning, October 24, Whalley was in his office early when Fastow dropped by. Fastow had already let Lay know about the problems with the banks. Now he and Whalley needed to talk things through.

Whalley closed the door, and Fastow took a seat. Enron's CFO looked dejected, almost at a loss for words. Everything had moved too fast for him. Fastow spoke first.

"I'm not sure I'm valuable to you as CFO anymore," he volunteered. "The banks are very uncomfortable with me."

Whalley's face showed no reaction. "I agree," he said. "I don't think this is going to work."

They were going to have to change things, Whalley said. Fastow said he could talk to members of his team, discuss it with McMahon, and they could figure out their next step.

Whalley nodded. He already knew what he was doing. He didn't need Fastow's input. The two stood, and Fastow headed to the door, with Whalley following. Fastow stepped out and saw McMahon, Bowen, and a few others waiting. He flashed a nervous smile. Whalley pushed past him.

"Okay, everybody," he said. "We're meeting upstairs. Go on up, and I'll be there in a few minutes."

Everyone headed to the elevator. Whalley walked briskly toward Ken Lay's office. They needed to talk.

Whalley found Lay at his desk, showing no obvious signs of distress. Whalley offered no pleasantries.

"We're getting rid of Fastow and replacing him with McMahon," Whalley said simply.

"Wait a minute, Greg," he said. "If you're serious, we need to take it up with the board."

Whalley had no patience for these formalities. The house was on fire, and Lay wanted to make sure everyone put on a topcoat and hat before running out into the street.

"We need to go to the board," Lay repeated.

"*You* need to go to the board," Whalley snapped.

Lay was beginning to regret ever having chosen Whalley as president and chief operating officer. "And what," he said sharply, "am I supposed to tell them?"

Whalley gave Lay a grin. "Tell them they're getting something new today. Either a new CFO or a new COO."

Whalley arrived on the mezzanine, and events moved quickly. Without waiting for board approval, he tossed Fastow out as CFO and appointed McMahon, stunning both of them. From there, the conversation turned to drawing down Enron's revolvers. Fastow objected, but no one listened.

In his first move as CFO, McMahon drafted Bowen as a deputy. Then the two executives assembled a financial SWAT team to sort out the company's books. McMahon announced that he wanted the team over in the new building, on the fourth floor, in thirty minutes. That would soon be the site of the financial war room, where the new group would struggle to save Enron from collapse.

Bridget Maronge, Andy Fastow's secretary, reached for the ringing phone.

"Bridget, it's Jeff Skilling. Is Andy there?"

Skilling knew nothing about Fastow's termination. He just thought the guy was getting a raw deal with all the publicity and wanted to buck him up.

Maronge put Skilling on hold and called for Fastow. He snapped up the telephone.

"Hello?"

"Andy, I'm so sorry."

"Fuck, *you're* sorry!" Fastow snapped back, his tone shocked. "This is just unbelievable!"

"What the hell happened?"

"I don't have a fucking clue," Fastow responded.

Well, Skilling asked, what was going on at the company? How were they trying to get on top of things?

"They don't tell me what's going on," Fastow said. "Lawyers are running around all over the place. I'm just sitting here in the dark about everything."

There was a pause. Skilling was shocked by Fastow's desolate state. "Andy, is there a problem?" he asked.

"There shouldn't be a problem," Fastow replied. "I just don't get it. I don't understand."

Skilling could offer no advice. "Andy," he said softly, "I just wanted to give you a call."

In the war room, the dirty secrets of the finance group's years of incompetence and mismanagement were just starting to spill out.

First, McMahon asked for a briefing on the commercial-paper market. How was Enron shut out so quickly? Tim Despain, an executive in finance, took charge of answering.

"We've been seeing the changes over the past number of days," he said. "Last week we couldn't issue thirty-day paper. We could only find buyers for two-week paper."

It just kept falling from there, Despain said. By early in the week, the market was shunning everything but Enron's overnight paper, meaning that investors only had faith that the company could repay its loans over twenty-four hours.

"Then," Despain said, "last night, we couldn't sell the overnight paper."

McMahon gaped at the people in the room. "So you mean to say that over the past week, we've been seeing this train wreck coming, *and nobody did anything about it?*"

Ten minutes later came another slap in the face.

"We don't have any method for tracking our *cash*?" McMahon sputtered. "That's *impossible*! We're a Fortune 50 company! We *have* to be tracking our cash!"

Bowen looked shaken. "Come on, guys. I mean, how can we manage our finances if we don't track our cash?"

Despain looked at his new bosses with a stricken expression. "Ray, I've never . . . nobody's ever asked us before to focus on it," he stuttered. "Nobody ever said this was something they wanted us to do."

McMahon sat back in his seat, lifting his eyes to the ceiling. *Oh. My. God.* This was Finance 101. Companies needed to track their cash to know when they were experiencing shortfalls, to know when they could pay their bills. It was the same reason that people *balanced their checkbooks*! If Enron didn't know how much cash it had, it couldn't know how much to draw down on the revolvers!

Apparently Fastow had always thought that Enron would have more than enough cash to spare. Nobody had any idea how much daily cash was collateral posted by trading partners and how much was being generated from business. Sure, the historical numbers could be pulled together over a few days. But Enron didn't have that kind of time.

Okay, if Enron didn't have a handle on its cash, then this SWAT team needed to look at when the bills were coming due. There was a lot of outstanding debt. All of it was going to mature at some point, and Enron would have to repay it. Right now, the company didn't have a lot of sources of new cash to grab to meet any of its obligations.

Bowen pointed at Glisan. "Ben," he said, "go get me the current maturities schedule." That would let him know, day by day, when Enron was expected to repay debt.

Glisan leaned back in his chair and grabbed his chin. "I think I can get somebody to pull that together."

The room went silent. Bowen's mouth dropped. This topped everything he had heard so far. Glisan *thinks* he can get one? He doesn't *have* one? They're not tracking their cash, and they're not tracking their debt maturities?

"Excuse me, Ben," Bowen said. "Am I wrong, or aren't you the corporate treasurer?"

Glisan bristled. "Yes."

"What do you mean, you *think* you can get one?" Bowen shot back. "This is the current maturities schedule of the company! The current *fucking* maturities schedule! Go get it! You *have* to have a maturities schedule!"

But they didn't. With all the focus on deals and earnings—with the finance group's transformation into a profit center rather than a division to support the business—the workaday, boring details had been sloughed off.

No one had realized it, but as Fastow and his team churned out entity after entity—Raptor, LJM, Braveheart, and the rest—winning plaudits and bonuses, they had simply ignored the basics of corporate finance. Enron had been flying blind financially for years.

Glisan got on the phone for half an hour with executives in the treasury division, asking them to manually figure out when the money had to be paid. When they reported back to him, he called out numbers to McMahon, who scribbled them on a whiteboard. Then he added them up.

Okay. More than thirty billion dollars in debt. The amount of that Enron had to repay in the next twelve months was . . .

He totaled the numbers up in his head. *Ten billion dollars.*

And, as best as McMahon could tell, Enron had no means to pay it. It would either have to renegotiate with the banks, find more cash, or go bankrupt. He couldn't imagine it could be much worse than this.

In fact, it was. In their rapid effort to cobble together a maturities schedule, Glisan and his team had overlooked debt that Enron owed. As daunting as the $10 billion appeared, it fell short of reality. By $2.6 billion.

McMahon turned to the group. "What else have we got out there?"

Well, someone replied, there's the equity forwards, which Fastow had used to finance entities like the Raptors. Those still made up a real number on Enron's books.

McMahon wasn't worried. How bad could this be? "Okay," he said, looking at Glisan. "Explain that."

Glisan approached the whiteboard and began drawing circles and boxes. As he spoke, the construct grew bigger and bigger. McMahon couldn't take it all in; he began trembling. Glisan was filling up the board.

"Ben, look, this is all very interesting, but what's the bottom line?" he said. "Tell me the total obliga—"

"I can't," Glisan responded. "I can't tell you until you tell me where our stock goes."

What? McMahon didn't understand.

Glisan started scribbling different answers, showing how the amount Enron owed would climb as its stock price fell. The truth was beginning to dawn on McMahon.

"You're telling me," he said forcefully, "that there's several billion dollars in this, *and that it's not done*? It can *grow* if things get worse?"

Glisan turned. "Yeah."

McMahon looked over at Bowen. This was not the time for recriminations. They had to plunge forward.

"Okay," McMahon said, "so what number do we put on the board? I don't know the number to put."

The room was silent. "Well," Bowen said, "I guess we put the only number we know. The amount we owe now."

Glisan wrote it down. McMahon shook his head. He couldn't have made this up. Enron was in a death spiral.

"Wait," Glisan said. "There's something else."

McMahon looked back at him. *No . . . no more.* But Glisan had now transformed. His attitude was like that of a government informant, casually ratting out his old colleagues.

Glisan started to explain. Enron had owned a company for years called Enron Oil & Gas, or EOG. It had spun the entity out as its own company some time before, holding on to a slug of its shares. That EOG stock, Glisan explained, had been used as capital in one of Fastow's securitization deals. As part of that transaction, Fastow had committed Enron to make up for any losses in the value of EOG shares. Since then, EOG's stock price had fallen. So now, Glisan said, Enron was obligated to make up the difference.

This confused McMahon again. Enron owned EOG shares back when *he* was treasurer. It had been unable to sell the stock because of restrictions when EOG went public. So the company had devised a bond deal. In it, investors purchased bonds that were exchangeable—one for one—with shares of EOG stock in the future. That allowed Enron to get the cash value of the shares without selling them. But of course, all those shares still had to be available for the investors who purchased the bonds.

So how could there be EOG shares in another Fastow partnership? They were already committed to the bond investors. Did Enron own other EOG shares that he didn't know about? McMahon asked.

"No, it's the same stock," Glisan replied.

McMahon just stared at him. Did Enron buy back the bonds, then? Give the investors cash? No, Glisan replied.

"Well," McMahon said, "where's the stock from?"

"We just took those shares out and put them in this structure," Glisan replied.

This wasn't getting through. "Well, what are we going to pay the bondholders with?" McMahon asked.

"Oh," Glisan said, "we'll have to go to the market and buy EOG shares."

It was a shattering moment. Fastow not only used every asset that wasn't nailed down to put together his deals; he had used one twice, leaving Enron on the hook to repurchase a gargantuan number of shares in its former division. McMahon did his best not to show any anger.

"Okay," he said. "So how much does that mean we would owe at current prices?"

They wrote the number down on the board.

The chaos of Enron's finances had at long last been laid out for everyone to see. A series of emergency groups were set up—one to come up with a way to track cash, another to reexamine the debt and figure out maturities. At 10:30, as McMahon struggled with what he recognized was a train wreck, the phone rang. His secretary let him know that Andy Fastow was on the line. McMahon picked up.

"Look," Fastow said, "I just want you to know, if there's anything I can do to help, you know I'm behind you. You know I've always been a big supporter of yours, Jeff."

McMahon felt a wave of disgust.

Fastow kept talking. "I'm sure you're going to be able to solve this crisis, and I'm here if you need anything."

This was a moment for diplomacy. "Thanks, Andy," McMahon replied. "I appreciate that."

Seconds later, he hung up. He stared at the phone, shaking his head. "Thanks for nothing, Andy," he muttered. "We're in this crisis because of you."

Forty minutes later, Ken Lay was meeting with the Enron directors. A few hours before, he had heard from Fastow about the problems with the bankers and now was making the case that Enron needed a new CFO. He had no idea that Fastow had already been thrown out of the job by Whalley.

"There are some serious questions about Andy's current effectiveness," he said. "We have bankers refusing to do business with us so long as Andy remains CFO."

It would be best, Lay said, for Fastow to be replaced by McMahon. The directors began discussing that suggestion.

John Duncan jumped in. "I think I need to mention something," he said. "Yesterday, Mickey and I spoke with Andy about Andy's earnings from the LJM vehicles."

The number was far higher than anything they had been led to believe, Duncan said. Fastow admitted receiving forty-five million dollars from LJM1 and LJM2. The words were numbing. Lay felt disoriented. There wasn't much that anyone could say.

Norm Blake exploded. "That's outrageous!" he shouted. "We've got to find out what that money was paid for!"

The stunned directors began discussing the issue. Blake broke back in. "We've got to terminate him," he said.

The room went silent. Then Lay spoke. There was no doubt in his mind. Fastow had deceived him all these years.

"I agree with Norm," Lay said. "My recommendation is that he has to be terminated."

But it wasn't so easy. Fastow's contract had just been renewed. Enron needed specific cause to fire him. So Blake made a motion. It carried unanimously. Fastow was officially out as Enron's CFO, placed on a leave of absence. McMahon was his replacement, effective immediately.

Things couldn't keep going like this, Mark Palmer knew. The barrage of bad news was killing the company. Every day the management team waited for the *Journal*'s call, to hear what was really happening in their own company.

Palmer consulted with Larry Rand, a public-relations expert with the firm Kekst and Company. Rand's advice was strong: Enron should launch its own investigation, hiring top-flight lawyers to find out what Fastow had been up to all these years. Rand even suggested a name: Bill McLucas, former head of SEC enforcement, who was now a partner at the firm Wilmer, Cutler & Pickering.

The idea appealed to Palmer, and he brought it up with executives around the company. Nobody was interested. Things were bad enough already; they didn't need another investigation on top of everything else.

Skilling.

He had called the day before, offering to come back to Enron. The management team had opposed it, but maybe Skilling's return could calm the market's waters, Lay thought. He persuaded Whalley to go speak with him, to take measure of the situation. The meeting was set up for that day at Skilling's house. It would create too much of a flurry if he came to Enron at this point.

Whalley drove up in his Jeep to the wrought-iron gates outside Skilling's new, multimillion-dollar mansion. He pressed a button on an intercom. Skilling's voice came through, and the gate slid open. Whalley drove in, pulling to a stop on the circular driveway.

Skilling walked out of the house before Whalley emerged from the Jeep. "Greg," Skilling said, "what the fuck is going on?"

"Jeff, this is bad. This is really, really bad."

"What happened?"

Whalley shook his head. "Liquidity. It's drying up."

"What's needed? Three?"

"Well, we think three-point-two."

Big numbers. Enron needed $3.2 billion, or its trading business would die. This demanded fast action.

"We've got to be on the next plane to New York," Skilling said. They had to sit down with the bankers—Chase, Citi, Credit Suisse, all of them.

"We've got to look these people in the eye and tell them that there's not a problem, tell them we'll pay them back, but that for now we need some money," Skilling said.

"Yeah, we probably really need to do that."

This whole situation had to get stabilized, Skilling said. "What's this shit with Andy, anyway?"

Whalley pulled a face. "We're firing him."

Skilling was bowled over. "You've gotta be kidding," he said. "That's the dumbest thing. I mean, your CFO, you need to raise money, and you're *firing* him?"

"Hey, I don't know if he did anything wrong," Whalley said. "But that's beside the point."

Why? Skilling wanted to know.

"Jeff," Whalley said, "Andy was a *really* shitty CFO."

Whalley returned to Enron as a convert. Skilling should come back. He told Lay, and the two decided to hold another management meeting to discuss it.

Skilling waited by the phone for an answer, but no one called. *There isn't time for this. We need to head up to New York tonight.* Didn't they know how urgent this was?

His impatience growing, Skilling called Whalley to find out what the holdup was. "Well, we need to discuss this among the members of the management committee," Whalley said.

"What are you going to do? Put it to a vote?" Skilling asked sharply.

"Ken wants to have a management committee meeting."

"Greg!" Skilling shot back. "We don't have time! We have to get up to New York!"

Nothing could be done, Whalley said. Lay wanted a meeting.

In a hospital just outside St. Louis, Chuck Watson was looking for a pay phone. Watson, the chairman and CEO of Dynegy, Enron's largest competitor, was in town tending to his mother, who was undergoing heart surgery. That morning, his people in Houston had sent word of market rumors that Dynegy, fearing an Enron collapse, was refusing to trade with the company. The stories weren't true, but Watson knew that even the *suspicion* of such a development could cripple Enron. Sure, he wanted to beat Enron, but not by exploiting a panic.

He found a phone and pulled out his AT&T calling card. In a few minutes, he was on the line with Lay.

"Look, Ken, there's some rumors out there about us not doing business with you," Watson said. "You've got enough to worry about without having to spend your time on rumors. This one's not true, and I would be happy to put out a statement saying so, if you'd like."

"Thank you, Chuck," Lay said. "We'll probably make some sort of public comment on that."

Lay's tone was calm. Watson couldn't help but think that the man would be a great poker player. "Well, okay, Ken," Watson said. "If you want our help, let us know."

It was an offer that would go much further than Watson could ever have intended.

The management committee stood firm. Skilling could not return. Once again his natural allies led the opposition. He had made his bed; let him lie in it.

"Okay," Whalley said. "Then I guess we don't do it."

The Wall Street firms hardly knew what to do. Enron was flaming out; it looked like a company in its death throes. Investors in the stock should probably get out.

Then again, what if Enron pulled it out? What if it survived this war, then surveyed the battlefield to see who had backed the company when things looked dire? Who would get Enron's investment-banking business then?

So some firms decided to split the difference. Publicly, they pronounced their faith in Enron, encouraging investors to buy or hold on. But privately, they notified their firms' investment arms to steer clear of Enron shares.

The hypocrisy outraged some on the Street. Wade Suki, an associate analyst at J. P. Morgan Chase, sent an e-mail to members of the research division, pointing out that they were now advocating contrary positions.

"How has your rating helped clients?" Suki asked. "You're telling me one thing, but clients a different story? Sounds a little shady to me."

The analysts needed to take one position, Suki wrote.

"Strap it on, man!!!" Suki wrote. "Afraid to lose the banking business??? Are you an investment banker or an equity research analyst???"

John Riley, the senior Andersen partner appointed to oversee the unfolding problems with Enron, arrived in Houston that afternoon and telephoned David Duncan.

"Listen, John," Duncan said, "it's late. There's no reason for you to come to the office now. Why don't you just relax at the hotel and come by tomorrow morning?"

Fine. Riley agreed to come by early the next day.

Duncan and his team could continue their feverish shredding without worrying about watchful eyes.

Now, Sherron Watkins thought, she had a chance. With Fastow out and her buddy McMahon taking over, she could get a leg up on her career.

Almost as soon as she received the company-wide e-mail announcing the appointment, Watkins started typing a message to McMahon. In the subject heading of the e-mail she typed, "Your new CFO spot and the job I want."

She offered her congratulations and immediately suggested that he get rid of Glisan, perhaps replacing him with Bill Brown. But she had another reason for writing.

"My issue, and I feel very strongly about this, is that I want to be on the crisis management team to determine how we save our trading franchise. I have clearly proven myself to be the only person at Enron that had the character, at great risk to my own career, much less personal risk, to go to Ken Lay and let him know what was going on here."

By that point, others, of course, had begun criticizing the Raptors. But that just infuriated Watkins.

"I resent all these late comers joining the band wagon. It's damn easy to make a statement now, when Ken has made the hard decision to unwind these deals and write them off."

Mainly, Watkins typed, she resented being kept on ice, without the responsibilities she deserved.

"I hope to meet with Ken Lay soon," she typed. "But I'd like to talk to you about my role in the 'inner circle,' because I firmly believe that I deserve it."

Then she hit "send."

From the war room, McMahon telephoned Lay's office. Lay still seemed to believe Enron was just having a problem with bad press. He needed to let the boss know the truth.

"Okay, Ken," he said, "here's our position."

Enron had more than thirty billion dollars in debt, McMahon said. Best they could tell, about ten billion of it was current.

"Frankly, we're completely illiquid right now," McMahon said. "We are at our lenders' mercy."

The only thing to do, McMahon said, was get lenders together and renegotiate the debt. They would have to get commitments from everyone not to make any rash moves; that would cripple Enron and hurt everybody. But just in case, he said, Enron needed to get advice from bankruptcy and restructuring specialists.

"So we're going to need to start negotiating," McMahon said. "We have to sit down with the banks."

The line was silent for a moment. "Is it really that dire?" Lay said softly.

More than thirty billion dollars in debt and almost no cash flow?

"Yeah, Ken," McMahon said. "It's really that dire."

McMahon called Whalley right afterward. "The only solution I see is that we sit down with the banks," he said, "and get a workout."

"Or a merger," Whalley shot back.

A merger? "Yeah," McMahon said, thinking about it. "Merge with someone with a much stronger balance sheet."

"Yeah," Whalley replied. "I'm working on that."

Scores of e-mails were piling up in McMahon's account. He noticed one from Sherron Watkins and clicked it open. He read it and went back to work. He was trying to save the company. He didn't have time to worry about her career.

Late that night, the crowds were thin at Kenneally's, an Irish pub on South Shepherd, ten minutes from the Enron building. Dark and dank, the bar hadn't changed in two decades. A small collection of regulars were there, tossing back beers and devouring the bar's fabulous pizza.

After midnight, McMahon walked in, followed by Bowen. It was late, and Whalley had called McMahon some time before, inviting him to stop by the pub to unwind.

Minutes later, Whalley arrived, accompanied by Mark Muller, one of Enron's deal makers. They glanced around, then made their way over to McMahon's table. The bartender brought over some beers and joked about how terrible everyone looked. For thirty seconds the men just sat, staring at their beers, saying nothing.

"Well," Whalley finally said, "this is a tough situation we're in, guys."

McMahon picked up his beer and chuckled. "Yeah, that's kind of an understatement." He looked at Whalley.

"By the way," McMahon said, "thanks for the promotion."

Whalley smiled. "Yeah, I suppose you're not really thanking me."

McMahon took a sip of his beer. "Not yet," he said.

As the beer flowed, the executives wrestled with possibilities. What about Whalley's idea of a merger?

"Would a merger solve all of this?" Whalley asked.

"Yeah," McMahon laughed. "With Exxon."

"Well, who could do a merger?" Bowen asked. "Who'd be willing?" The executives kicked around the idea for a while. Then Mark Muller jumped in with a brainstorm.

"You know who we could do it with, and who would do it fast enough, is Dynegy," he said. "They've always been the Burger King of the energy business."

Whalley chuckled. McMahon stared at Muller. *Burger King?*

"I don't get it," McMahon said.

"Well, you know, McDonald's does market research to figure out where to site one of their franchises, and then Burger King builds one across the street," Muller said. "That's the Dynegy view. They just wait to see what Enron does, and then they do it in a smaller way."

They all laughed and went back to their beers.

The idea was planted. *Dynegy.* That was the answer.

The lunch scheduled for October 25 was nothing special. Every few weeks Steve Bergstrom, Dynegy's president, had a meal with Stan Horton, a friend who headed Enron's pipeline group.

But Thursday morning Horton left a message asking if Whalley and Mark Frevert, Enron's new vice chairman, could join them that day. Bergstrom was intrigued. He had been pushing Enron to combine their European trading operations with Dynegy's. Maybe, he thought, with the company's financial crisis, that idea had gained a new appeal.

He phoned back Horton. "Listen, it'll be fine if Whalley and Frevert come along," he said. "Maybe I should arrange for us to meet in a private room?"

Horton was way ahead of him. "I've already got one booked," he said, "at the Plaza Club."

Already booked? Now Bergstrom was certain. Enron wanted to combine European operations. This was great.

———

What in the world is that noise?

John Riley, the Andersen partner helping manage the Enron crisis, was in a room across from Duncan's office. He had arrived that morning, been set up by Duncan, and given a number of files to review. But as he worked, Riley couldn't block out the sound of a dull, high-pitched whine. It continued for hours, almost without interruption. He couldn't imagine what it was. At one point, Duncan dropped in for a moment, and Riley decided to ask about it.

"Hey, David," Riley said, "what is that whining noise I've been hearing all morning?"

"Oh, that's the shredder."

Riley fixed Duncan with an even look. "You know, David, this wouldn't be the best time for you to be shredding client documents."

Duncan nodded. "It's just routine shredding of some client information," he said.

He gave Riley a smile. "I can imagine for what you do that it would be the worst-case scenario for you to come into an office where documents are being shredded."

They both had a good laugh.

Andersen's destruction of Enron records was proceeding swiftly. The shredders in Three Allen Center were going full blast, from early morning until late at night. But even that wasn't enough. They needed to pick up the pace.

There was a way. Andersen used an outside company named Shred-It for big jobs; its trucks were called in to help. And Andersen's main office in Houston had more, and better, shredding machines. Requests for trunks were submitted. That way the paperwork could be packed up and carted over to that office, where it could be destroyed.

A bouquet of fresh-cut flowers had been placed in a crystal vase at the entryway of the Plaza Club. From there, on the forty-ninth floor of the One Shell Plaza building, members could see a breathtaking view of Enron Field, the baseball stadium that had helped transform the company into Houston's most beloved corporate citizen.

Whalley, accompanied by Frevert and Horton, stepped briskly past the floral display without giving it a glance. The three men were escorted back to their private room for their meeting with Bergstrom. The executives chatted about their European trading operations, just as Bergstrom had anticipated. Then the conversation took an abrupt turn.

"Truthfully, Steve, we're not here today to talk to you about Europe," Whalley said.

"All right," Bergstrom replied.

"We want to talk to you about a combination with the entire company," Whalley said simply.

Bergstrom stared at Whalley in shock.

In just an hour of talks, the two sides covered a lot of ground. Then Bergstrom interrupted the discussions.

They had to hear from Lay, he said. Chuck Watson would not even consider a merger unless Lay told him this was what Enron wanted. If so, maybe they could get it done.

Not a problem, Whalley replied. Lay would make the call.

That day, Enron announced its plans to draw down its bank credit lines—some three billion dollars. Of that, more than half would go to repurchase all of its commercial paper, eliminating that financial problem from Enron's growing list of woes.

In the *Journal's* Los Angeles bureau, John Emshwiller and Rebecca Smith began cobbling together an article about the drawdown. Perhaps, they decided, this was the time to mention Chewco. They had learned the name weeks ago, in Kopper's biography in the LJM2 offering memoranda.

At this point, the reporters didn't know much else new about Chewco. But now the Enron story was hot. They wanted to get the name out there before someone else did. While writing that part of the story, Emshwiller telephoned Palmer to ask if Enron had any comment on Chewco.

"Never heard of it," Palmer replied.

Emshwiller explained that the documents he had read showed—incorrectly, it later proved—that Chewco had purchased $400 million in assets from Enron and that it had been run by an Enron executive named Michael Kopper.

Palmer promised to get back to Emshwiller with answers.

In minutes, Palmer tracked down Whalley in his office. "Hey, Greg," he said, "have you heard of Chewco?"

Whalley's work came to an abrupt stop. His chief public-relations guy was asking about Chewco. That meant somebody—somebody in the press—was asking Palmer.

"Oh," Whalley said, "that's not good."

Chuck Watson from Dynegy was just back from Missouri and was driving home in his silver Mercedes 500 when the car phone rang. He tapped the button on the speakerphone.

"Chuck, it's Ken Lay."

Watson greeted Lay. Apparently, what he had been hearing from Bergstrom about a possible Enron merger might be true. The two spoke almost in a form of code. There were problems, Lay said, and Enron had options it was pursuing. But talking with Watson was an important one. They needed to meet, Lay said, just to see what they might put together.

They compared schedules. Friday was booked and didn't work. Lay suggested they get together Saturday morning at his home in the Huntingdon. Watson promised to be there.

The news on Chewco was horrible. The biggest problem, Palmer realized, was that people at Enron either didn't know it existed or simply didn't want to talk about it.

As the details trickled out—Kopper ran the thing, his gay lover was the chief investor, Enron had repurchased it for a price that gave Kopper ten million dollars, McMahon had fought to block the deal—Palmer recognized Chewco for what it was. It could be the final nail in Enron's coffin, proof that the company had been out of control for years.

The calls from Emshwiller kept coming, and the information *he* knew seemed better than what Palmer could learn in the company. Palmer spoke to his boss, Steve Kean.

"The *Journal* knows more about what's going on here than *we* do!" he barked. "Get Ken down here, get Whalley down here, get McMahon! We've got to go through this!"

Minutes later, Palmer was on the phone when someone let him know the senior management was waiting for him in a conference room, ready to discuss Chewco.

He hung up and headed down the hall.

Waiting inside the doorway of the conference room, Whalley saw Palmer dashing toward him. How bad was it this time? What was the *Journal* going to say? He darted over to his public-relations chief.

"What do they know?" he asked hurriedly.

Palmer looked at Whalley and said nothing. Whalley noticed Palmer's eyes were watering.

––––––

Palmer's mouth filled with saliva. A wave of nausea washed over him. He was about to vomit, right in front of Whalley. He could feel it coming.

He turned, dashing into the men's room. He ran to the farthest sink and stood over it, prepared to throw up. His stomach heaved, and he spit out the saliva flooding his mouth. The wave of nausea passed, and he splashed some water on his face. He grabbed a fistful of paper towels and was wiping his face when Whalley pushed into the bathroom. He walked over and put an arm around Palmer's shoulder.

"Hey, come on," Whalley said, escorting him out of the bathroom. "Come on. Come sit down."

He took Palmer into a small, empty room and sat him down at a table. Palmer wiped his face.

"Fuck it, Greg!" he barked. "I want out!"

Whalley looked at Palmer with surprise. "You want out why? We're going to be okay. We'll get through this."

Palmer shook his head. "No, we won't, Greg! The *Journal* knows a lot more about what's going on around here than *I* know, a lot more than Ken and the rest of you. I don't know how I can do my job! No one is giving me answers!"

Well, there was a problem, Whalley said. Most of Enron's executives had lawyered up; they were now all worrying about their personal liability. There weren't going to be a lot of straight answers coming out of anyone.

He pointed at Palmer. "But we're not giving anybody any outs here," he said. "You go, you're gone. Nobody's getting a severance package. Nobody."

Palmer closed his eyes. He couldn't afford to walk away without a severance package. He didn't have another job lined up. He stood. "All right," he said. "Let's go back to the conference room."

Palmer wandered in to the conference room, escorted by Whalley. All the seats in the room were filled. He walked to a back wall and sat down on the floor, covering his face with his hands.

Ken Lay came in and stood at the head of the table. Soon, he was listening to a briefing on Chewco delivered in almost militaristic tones by Steve Kean.

Everyone tossed in the bits and pieces that they knew. McMahon mentioned to Lay the story of the Chewco buyout, explaining how he had fought it, stopped it. But then, once he lost the treasurer's job, it had gone through anyway. Kean picked it up again from there.

"Now, one issue here is that the equity holder in Chewco is Michael Kopper's partner," he said.

Lay looked at Kean, confused. "His partner? What, we have *another* partnership in this?" he asked.

"Uh, no, Ken . . ."

"So what is he, a business partner?"

Several executives shifted uncomfortably. McMahon broke in. "No, Ken. It's his lover. Michael's gay lover."

The room was silent for a moment. Lay glanced at the faces around the table and blinked.

"He's got a fucking *gay lover*?" Lay shouted.

He waved his arms in the air. "*What the fuck is going on here?*" he screamed.

From the back of the room, there was a sharp pounding. Everyone turned to look. Palmer was slapping his hand on the floor, hard enough to hurt himself. He looked up at Lay.

"I'll tell you what's going on, Ken!" he shouted. "*The Wall Street Journal* knows more about what's going on at your company than *you* do!"

He slapped the floor again, punctuating each word.

"This . . . has . . . to . . . stop!" he shouted. "We have got to hire someone, someone who can do an investigation and tell us what the *fuck* has been going on around here!"

The explosion of anger silenced the room.

Lay looked down at the table, then back at Palmer.

"We're going to find out what's been going on," he said simply. The meeting broke up.

Twenty minutes later, Palmer was back at his desk when the phone rang. He saw from caller ID that it was Jim Derrick, Enron's general counsel.

"Mark, do you have a number for Bill . . ."

He stumbled on the last name.

"Bill McLucas?" Palmer asked. The former head of SEC enforcement. The lawyer recommended by Larry Rand at Kekst.

"Yes. Bill McLucas. Who is he with?"

"Wilmer, Cutler," Palmer said. "I'll get a number."

He hung up the line and called Larry Rand.

"Larry?" he said. "Do you have the number for Bill McLucas? We need him down here."

CHAPTER 21

THE TRADING ROOM IN the new Enron building was a swarm of activity. McMahon was on the phone with Enron's bankers, discussing plans to draw down the lines of credit. Nearby, Glisan was helping plan where to put the cash. Whalley was supervising the chaos, knowing any misstep could leave Enron without the money it needed to stay alive.

Steve Kean appeared, his usual composure strained, and approached Whalley. "Greg, I need to talk to you," he said.

Whalley waved him away. "Steve, I don't have time right now," he snapped.

"No, Greg," Kean said. "I need to talk to you *now*."

The urgency of Kean's tone grabbed Whalley's attention. "Is this about a press release?" he asked.

"No, it's not."

Whalley studied Kean. "Okay," he said. He followed Kean into a private office, then shut the door.

They both sat down. "Okay," Kean said. "You need to go get on the phone with the Special Agent in Charge of the FBI's Houston office, because we've been contacted by both the FBI and the Houston police."

Whalley laughed. "Steve, tell them I'll turn myself in at five o'clock. I just don't have the time right now."

"No, you don't understand," Kean protested. "It seems last night a woman turned herself in to the FBI."

The woman, Kean said, was a drug addict. She claimed that she had found a duffel bag in a parking lot and took it to a crack house. She told the FBI that inside the bag, she found foreign passports, plane tickets to Nairobi, weapons, and ammunition. And a piece of paper referring to the Enron building and October 26.

What? September 11 was just weeks earlier. Now there was a terrorist threat—*against Enron?* For tomorrow? They had three billion dollars coming in, the company was teetering toward collapse, and now they might get *attacked*?

"You've got to be kidding me!" Whalley said.

At that moment, McMahon wandered in, looking lost. "Hey, Jeff," Whalley called. "You've got to listen to this. I'm hearing the building's blowing up tomorrow."

McMahon didn't flinch. "You don't understand," he said flatly. "The building's blowing up today."

Then he walked away.

That same day in midtown Manhattan, Tom Roberts was at his desk in the offices of Weil, Gotshal & Manges. Roberts, a longtime Texas deal maker, was now the partner in charge of the corporate department, helping push the firm—best known for its work on huge corporate bankruptcies—into other, equally lucrative legal fields.

Roberts was getting ready for a trip to Dallas the next day to visit Southern Methodist University, which his daughter was hoping to attend. As he was wrapping things up, some of his partners dropped by. The Dallas office had just been contacted by Enron.

"Okay," Roberts said. "What's it about?"

No one was quite sure. Enron just wanted *something*. The call had come from some junior person in the legal department of the company's wholesale-trading business.

That's strange. This wasn't a call from the general counsel but from some lower-level guy. There was grumbling around the room. This sounded like a loser assignment. A few lawyers protested that they had commitments on Saturday.

Roberts held up a hand. "Look, I'm going to be down in Texas this weekend anyway," he said. "I'll visit with them and take some of our folks from Dallas."

Everyone agreed that was a fine idea. Fly in, have a quick meeting, fly out. No big deal.

"So what's the situation?" Whalley asked. "Are we open for business tomorrow or not?"

He was on the phone with the FBI. Agents had just completed a search of the crack house and found the duffel bag. There were some plane tickets inside, some bullets, but no weapons. And no reference to the Enron building.

Whalley sighed. "So we're coming to work tomorrow?"

The New York bankers were doing everything they could to dissuade Enron from drawing down three billion dollars. They argued with McMahon, who refused to back down. Send the money, he told them.

The bankers were apoplectic. Sure, they had provided Enron with three-billion dollars in credit lines, but none of them had ever figured the company would suck down all the cash in one go. In his office, Lay received a telephone call from Michael Carpenter, CEO of Salomon Smith Barney, a division of Citigroup. As McMahon listened in, Carpenter argued that pulling down the full lines was a bad idea.

"It will send a very negative signal, Ken," Carpenter said. "If you just take some of it and leave the rest in the bank, it will be much less of a negative signal."

"Mike, we've got to pull it all down," Lay replied. "I understand what you're saying, and it's a valid argument. But we think this is the most prudent thing for us to do."

Carpenter could sense the conversation was over.

"I have to respect your judgment, Ken," he said. "And if that's what you want to do, of course we'll cooperate."

Lay hung up and decided to make one more call. One of Enron's other banks, J. P. Morgan Chase, had as a vice chairman an old-line Texas banker named Marc Shapiro, a longtime friend. Shapiro should know what was happening, Lay decided. Maybe he would have some ideas on how to help.

Later that day, Jimmy Lee, a Morgan vice chairman, was in his glass-walled office just off the bank's trading floor. As Lee scanned his Bloomberg monitor, the intercom on his desk crackled to life.

"Mr. Shapiro's on the line," Lee's secretary said.

Lee snapped up the phone. "Hey, Marc!" he enthused.

"Hey, Jimmy. I know someone, he's on a couple of big boards, and he really needs your help."

"Who is it?" Lee said quickly.

"Ken Lay with Enron. He has a problem, and I think he could really use your help."

"Okay, what's his number?"

He didn't recognize Lay's name, but he knew Enron. Lee thought nothing of it. Just another company running out of cash or struggling with a bad balance sheet. He'd seen plenty of them and was eager to toss another corporate giant up onto the operating table. He hadn't lost a patient yet. No reason Enron should be any different.

The next morning, the streets around Enron were blocked, and security tightened. Regardless of what was found in the crack house, law enforcement had decided to take precautions. Whalley was making his way to the building when an employee saw him and called out.

"Hey, Greg! What's with all the stepped-up security?"

Whalley smiled. He wasn't about to announce that Enron was working through a possible terrorist threat.

"Well, we pulled a three-billion-dollar revolver, and we put it in small bills on the fourth floor," he replied. "So we're just making sure to guard it."

The thankless job had been handed to Glisan. Find out about Chewco, dig through the documents, brief the board. He met with executives to discuss the deal, including Rodney Faldyn, head of accounting transactional support. Faldyn never knew much about Chewco, but now, the more he heard, the more uncomfortable he felt. It didn't sound like the accounting should work. He went to see Causey.

"Rick, I think we've got a serious problem with Chewco," he said.

Soon after, Tom Bauer, an Andersen partner on the Enron team, received a call from Faldyn and Ryan Siurek.

"I need to ask," Faldyn said, "about the requirements for the three percent equity standard, what it takes for a special-purpose entity to be considered valid."

Again? Bauer had explained this concept to Enron repeatedly, and *it just wasn't that hard*! For an off-books partnership to be valid, three percent of its capital had to come from an investor independent of the company. Simple. But year after year, Enron just tortured this rule. *What about this? What about that?* It was tiresome.

"What's the issue?" Bauer asked.

"Does the three percent have to be exclusive or any related-party equity?" Faldyn asked.

A no-brainer. It wouldn't be independent equity if it was from a related party. Bauer recited his answer. His words were greeted with silence.

"This is what I've said for years," Bauer said. "It's what I told you on Chewco and on the LJM transactions."

The silence continued. "Well," Faldyn said, "based on some new information, Chewco might not meet the standard."

It couldn't be true, Bauer thought.

Chewco had been used to buy out Calpers's interest in the pool of energy assets known as JEDI. Those produced lots of cash flow. There was no shortage of investors who would have wanted three percent of *that*.

And the consequences of a mistake on Chewco could be devasting. If the three percent wasn't there, then the partnership wasn't independent. Instead,

Chewco *was* Enron. That would knock over the next domino. If Chewco was Enron, it couldn't be half-owner in JEDI. So *JEDI* was Enron, too. None of them was off-books. All of JEDI's revenue and income would have been Enron's. All of the company's numbers, all of them, would have been wrong, dating to the day Chewco was formed. Back four years. To 1997.

It couldn't be true.

Skilling was going out of his mind.

For days he waited to hear from Enron, knowing precious minutes were being lost. Finally, on Friday, he couldn't delay anymore. He was scheduled to fly to Florida that day with Rebecca Carter to attend a boat show with Cliff Baxter. Skilling had to know if he could leave.

He called Whalley. "Okay, Greg, what's been decided?"

Whalley reacted as if he hadn't thought about Skilling for months. "Oh, yeah. We decided not to do it."

Skilling dropped into a chair. "*What!*"

"We had a management committee meeting, and the sense of the group was that it wasn't a good idea."

Skilling could almost feel Enron slipping away.

"*Why?*" he asked plaintively.

"No one knew how this would play out in the press," Whalley said. It would just confuse people.

Skilling listened. "Okay," he said. Then he hung up.

He sat on his couch, his eyes closed. The reasons were weak; he knew what this was about. Fastow looked dirty. He had taken a lot of money. Fastow had been his guy. Skilling had no doubt. His buddies must suspect he was in on it.

Rebecca Carter wandered in. Skilling was sitting on the couch, looking wrecked. He looked up at her.

"They don't want me back," he said softly.

"What?"

"They don't want me back," he repeated.

He looked down at his lap. "This may be the end."

Jordan Mintz seethed. What the hell was the matter with everybody? How could he possibly be scheduled to have a meeting that morning to justify forcing LJM people out of the building? *What did it take?*

Mintz had been fighting this battle for months, picking up where McMahon left off. But nothing happened. So finally, with the world crashing down, Mintz found some receptive ears, willing to consider booting LJM out. Then, Kopper protested. He needed more time, he said.

Mintz couldn't believe Kopper's chutzpah. All his dirty little deals had pushed Enron to the edge of collapse, and now he wanted more time to get out? The man wasn't even an *Enron employee* anymore! He was working full-time for LJM! The meeting was scheduled for 10:30. Glancing through the glass walls of the conference room, Mintz saw Kopper making his way down the hall, right on time. *Unbelievable.* The guy was actually willing to argue his case, right in the middle of all this chaos.

Kopper arrived, and Mintz shot him a look of contempt. Raising his hand, Kopper pointed a finger at him.

"Don't *start* with me!" he snapped.

The discussion began, and for once Kopper had no supporters in the room. It looked as though finally Enron was going to do the right thing. As the meeting came to an end, Kopper brought out an envelope and tossed it to Mintz.

"You guys need to take care of that," he said.

Mintz pulled open the envelope, and his stomach sank.

It was a bill for several hundred thousand dollars. Kopper was charging Enron for the expenses that LJM2 incurred on the wind deal. The one Enron never wanted the fund to do.

The Enron board met that afternoon at 12:10, joined by a stern-looking, mustached man. If not for his expensive suit, the man might have been mistaken for an Irish cop.

Lay opened the meeting and gestured toward their guest.

"Joining us today is Mr. Bill McLucas from Wilmer, Cutler & Pickering," he said. McLucas was in Houston at Enron's request, Lay said, to help on the current crisis.

McLucas stood. He summarized the events of the past few weeks, describing the challenges Enron faced. "It is critical that Enron both establish credibility with the SEC and create confidence in the marketplace," he said.

The way to accomplish that, McLucas said, was to form a special committee of independent directors. That group, he said, should engage lawyers—who in turn would hire forensic accountants—to review the related-party deals.

Lay picked up the theme. "If a special committee will help instill confidence, I would urge we proceed down that path," he said.

The directors warmed to the idea, then took things a step further, discussing whether to add a new director to the board, someone uninvolved in the decisions of the past who could lead the special committee in its investigation.

Jim Derrick thought he knew the perfect person. But first he needed to run the idea by Vinson & Elkins.

Rick Causey just stared at Ben Glisan.

"You have got to be *kidding* me!" he said.

All day, Causey had been going back and forth with Glisan, Faldyn, and a few others about Chewco. At each step, with each new disclosure, the story got worse.

The Chewco paperwork was a shambles. No one seemed to have a complete set; documents were filed haphazardly all over the place. The secrecy imposed around Chewco had allowed everyone to be slipshod in handling the records. Now Enron was paying the price.

Even so, the fragments that had been assembled painted a gruesome picture. It appeared Kopper may have invested in Chewco, but it wasn't clear yet how much. And Dodson, Kopper's lover . . . How did the accounting rules view homosexuality? If Dodson was Kopper's *wife*, they both would have been considered related parties to Enron. That would obliterate the three percent outside equity.

Worse, Kopper had presented the cash put into Chewco by Barclays as independent equity. But there were problems. When Enron repurchased Chewco for thirty-five million dollars, Kopper took a ten-million-dollar cut. Barclays, which put up all the real cash, got its money back, plus a bit. The money from Barclays sure *looked* like a loan.

Then there were Kopper's instructions on where to send some Chewco distributions. Not to Barclays. Not to the general partner created. Instead, to the attention of Lea Fastow. At her home address. Causey shuddered.

Was it possible there was *no* outside equity in Chewco?

It was early evening in Houston, and Ken Lay was sitting at his desk, building up to his next move. He had no choice. He called to his secretary. "Rosie, I need to talk to Alan Greenspan."

Within minutes, Lay was connected to the Fed chairman.

"Alan, I was calling to update you on our situation," Lay said. "We've had a pretty rough ten days or so."

"Yes, Ken, I've been reading in the papers," Greenspan replied. "Sorry you're going through all this."

"Thank you," Lay replied. "Well, things are still very rough. We're beginning to see troubles with our trading partners."

He gave a rundown of the events of the last few days and of Enron's desperate attempts to shore up its liquidity.

"I think it would be a good idea for the Fed and the Treasury to begin monitoring what's going on," Lay said, "just to see what might happen if we don't pull this out."

Of course, Lay said, he fully expected Enron would survive. "But," he said, "I think it's best to have an effort to monitor things, just to prepare for the worst."

By early that evening, Lay had tried to alert every top finance official in the government of Enron's precarious state. In addition to Greenspan, he had phoned his friends Don Evans, the Commerce Secretary, and Paul O'Neill, the Treasury Secretary. Neither had been in, but an O'Neill assistant had suggested that Lay phone the Secretary on Sunday at his Washington apartment in the Watergate complex.

Lay didn't have big plans for the calls. He wouldn't explicitly ask for government assistance, but he would let his old friends know how dire Enron's situation was. If one of them offered to extend a lifeline, all the better.

At seven o'clock, Lay walked down the hallway to Jim Derrick's office. His general counsel had just called him to say that they needed to meet. Causey was there, looking distraught.

"You need to hear this, Ken," Derrick said.

Causey explained that they had been reviewing Chewco. They hadn't yet drawn definitive conclusions; they still needed more documents. Lay felt the anxiety creeping over him. This was too much throat clearing.

"Okay," he said. "So what do we suspect?"

Causey glanced at the floor, then looked at Lay.

"We may have a serious problem," he said.

The lockout began that same night. After weeks of warnings to employees, both in home letters and in e-mails, Enron's retirement plan was officially changing administrators. Now, scheduled for weeks to come, employees could make no changes in their retirement accounts until all of the paperwork was transferred. That day, Enron's share price had closed just below fourteen dollars.

After passing the security gate at the Huntingdon condominiums, Chuck Watson drove toward the parking area. It was the morning of October 27, a

Saturday. The meeting that day with Lay probably wouldn't amount to much, Watson figured; a merger between Dynegy and Enron seemed far-fetched.

On the elevator, Watson pushed the button for the thirty-third floor. A minute or so later, the doors opened; the entire floor was Lay's. Watson stepped off, and Lay appeared. The two men greeted each other and headed to a kitchen area.

"Would you like some coffee?" Lay asked. "I made it myself."

Soon they were in the living room, loaded up with coffee and sweet rolls. Watson brought out a handwritten list of issues he wanted to discuss. Lay had a typed version of the same thing. Watson quickly took charge.

"If this happens, Ken, it's going to have to be as a merger of equals, with no premium," he said.

Lay was taken aback. Watson was talking about buying Enron at its current market price, with no added cash for shareholders. That, he thought, just wasn't right.

"This is a company that not long ago was trading at ninety dollars a share," Lay protested. "The only reason our share price has fallen so far, the only reason we've had recent problems, is because of short sellers and the media."

Watson studied Lay. His voice was strong and emphatic. Lay either believed everything he was saying, Watson thought, or was the most accomplished liar he had ever met.

"Ken," Watson said, "if you want me to step in front of the train, this is the only way it's going to happen."

They reached several understandings. A deal had to happen quickly; Enron was fading fast. Watson also wanted Lay to formally stand behind the company's numbers, including its projections for 2002. Lay agreed.

Dynegy wasn't going to take everything. The international projects looked like dogs; in fact, Watson wanted nothing outside of North America, except London trading.

"I have to ask you, Ken," he said. "Is there another shoe to drop?"

Lay shook his head. "The banks, the lawyers are all over the company. They haven't found anything."

What about the name of the new company? "I believe it should be called Enron-Dynegy," Lay said.

No way, Watson retorted. "Ken, the Enron name has to go," he said. "It just has become too sullied."

Lay protested. If not Enron-Dynegy, what about Dynegy-Enron? Again, no. After a few more times at the plate, Lay gave in, for now. He tentatively agreed to plain "Dynegy." Watson said he would run the merged company; Lay could stay on the board, perhaps as chairman emeritus. As for management, Watson said he would keep Whalley. But that was it.

After hours of fighting for scraps, Lay had had enough for one day. Now they were both getting hungry. Lay glanced at the kitchen.

"Nobody left any food," he said.

Later that day, a contingent of Andersen accountants trooped into Causey's office for a Chewco update. The group, including Duncan, Bauer, and Deb Cash, was shown a whiteboard where a sketch of the Chewco structure had been drawn. Bauer took out a piece of paper and copied it down.

Causey laid out the details, beginning with Kopper's possible control and the role of his lover, Bill Dodson. Bauer was astonished; he had worked on Chewco, and this was the first time he had heard about Dodson's connection.

From there, Causey described the issues that had emerged relating to Barclays, the failure of the bank to receive a significant return from the Chewco purchase, and the decision to send distributions to Andy Fastow's wife.

Causey looked stricken. "I didn't know about any of this until I spoke with Ben," he said. "I promise."

The room was heavy with tension. "This is deeply troubling, Rick," Duncan said.

Bauer agreed. "Based on this information, it looks like Enron may have actually sponsored Chewco," he said.

But they still didn't have enough evidence to prove it.

The first team of lawyers from Weil, Gotshal arrived in Houston that afternoon. Tom Roberts and Mary Korby, a partner from the Dallas office, were led through Enron, meeting executives in the trading division.

From the beginning, some things seemed oddly out of whack. For one, the lawyers still hadn't met with Derrick, the general counsel—and effectively, they never would. The trading division was in revolt, struggling to salvage itself, regardless of what happened to the rest of the company. That made Mark Haedicke, the top lawyer in that division, Weil, Gotshal's primary contact.

Then the executives themselves seemed almost psychologically damaged by the past few weeks. One top trader kept pulling his shirt over his head in the middle of conversations. Other corporate chieftains spoke in too rapid a clip, racing after solutions that weren't there.

Finally, Roberts and Korby were taken to a conference room, where they met with Whalley, McMahon, and the trading team. The executives spent hours describing Enron's structure, communicating a strong message: the traders cared only about saving their operation, the rest of Enron be damned.

One suggested finding an equity fund, like the Blackstone Group, to inject a few hundred million into trading. Another brought up the idea of borrowing money against company assets. But there wasn't a lot to choose from. All of the international projects were underwater, worth less than the amount already borrowed against them.

Then someone raised an idea that had been knocking around for days. The pipelines! The assets at Enron's foundation that threw off hundreds of millions in cash every year, that had been treated with such derision by Skilling's acolytes. They could borrow against the pipelines.

The meeting dragged on, and Roberts and Korby missed the last flight back to Dallas. This was going to be a lot harder than either had imagined. The two of them headed out to a local Target Superstore. They hadn't planned to stay in Houston. They needed to buy some toiletries and clothes to get through the weekend.

That night at the Delano Hotel in Miami Beach, Rebecca Carter rushed out of her hotel room, crying. Earlier in the evening, their first in Florida, Skilling had fallen apart at a jazz club and had just thrown Carter out, telling her to get away from him. This debacle at Enron was wrecking him. He was drunk, unsteady. Carter couldn't leave. She had to wait, to see how he was after he sobered up.

She headed to the lobby and approached the front desk. "Do you have another room available this evening?" she asked shakily.

The next morning, the hotel room telephone was ringing. Bleary-eyed, Skilling struggled to pull himself across the bed and reached for the receiver.

"Jeff? It's Rebecca."

He sighed. Why was she calling him from Houston? "I don't want to talk to you," he grumbled. "Stay away."

Then he hung up.

For the top players at Enron, there was no escape from the unending grind of work. There were no weekends, no evenings. Just hour upon hour of crisis management.

The only visible hopes, as far as McMahon was concerned, were the pipeline solution, a Dynegy merger, or both. Potential lenders and Dynegy had to be briefed on the state of the company. It was a process known on

Wall Street as performing due diligence, a fancy term that meant little more than examining a company real hard. McMahon couldn't handle the task; he had other roles to play. Plus, he was assembling a presentation for Enron's banks, hoping to persuade them to give Enron some breathing room.

Glisan, he decided, had to take over the job of helping everyone with their due diligence for the merger. But McMahon had concerns. Had Glisan allowed himself to get embroiled in Fastow's schemes? If so, he couldn't be trusted to take on the responsibility.

There was only one way to deal with this. He called Glisan into his office and told him to take a seat.

"Ben," he said, "I need to know where you were on all this partnership stuff."

McMahon's face was stern. "I want to know if you're involved in LJM or any of these other partnerships," he said. "I cannot afford to have you working on deals to save the company if you've been compromised. So I need you to assure me. Do you have any involvement in any of this?"

Southampton. Glisan had received a million dollars from Fastow and Kopper just weeks after making a fifty-eight-hundred-dollar investment. He had been compromised.

"I'm not involved in anything," he said. "I have no interest in LJM or any of these other things."

McMahon studied Glisan as he answered. "You understand, Andy's out because he had conflicts. We need to be the new guys coming in who aren't involved in any of that."

"I'm fine with that," Glisan said, holding up his hands. "I'm not involved in any of it."

A few hours later, Paul O'Neill, the Secretary of the Treasury, was enjoying a Sunday afternoon in his apartment at the Watergate. The telephone rang, and he walked over to answer. "Please hold for Ken Lay," a woman's voice said.

The line clicked. "Paul," Lay said, "I appreciate you letting me call you at home today."

"It's fine, Ken. Good to hear from you."

"I'm just calling to update you on what's been going on at Enron," Lay said, "and to recommend that you have somebody at Treasury monitor what's going on here."

Given the size of Enron in the energy and financial markets, Lay said, it would make sense for the government to have contingency plans in place.

"Things have moved very fast in the past ten days or so," Lay said. "We're hoping all the bad stuff's out, and if it is, maybe we'll start stabilizing."

O'Neill reflected for a moment. "I think the perfect person to monitor this will be Peter Fischer," he said. Fischer was one of his top people at Treasury and had helped manage the government's response to the collapse a few years back of Long-Term Capital Management, a giant hedge fund.

Probably the best contact for dealing with Fischer was Greg Whalley, Lay said. He knew all about trading.

It was afternoon, and Skilling had finally sobered up when the phone rang. Rebecca again. He made a comment about her return to Houston.

"I'm still in Miami," she said. "I'm in the hotel."

"You're kidding," Skilling replied.

"No, I'm not."

Skilling needed Carter with him. "Okay," he said, choking back tears. "Come on up."

That same night, at his home in the historic Kalorama section of Washington, D.C., Harvey Pitt gripped a copy of that day's *New York Times* in fury.

He was reading a lengthy article about Enron in the Sunday Business section. The article provided a comprehensive review of everything that had happened at the company in recent weeks, and the investigation set off by the events. But there was a paragraph that set Pitt on edge. It was a comment from Mark Palmer, Enron's spokesman.

Mr. Palmer of Enron disputed any suggestion that Mr. Lay did not have a grasp of the investments at issue, saying Mr. Lay was handicapped in talking about them because of the S.E.C. investigation. "There is not a whole lot we can say, or should say, about them," Mr. Palmer said.

Enron was refusing to answer the most basic questions investors could ask—and blaming the SEC! *Despicable!* What did these people think they were doing?

Pitt hefted himself out of his chair, heading to his study. He wanted to reread this article, mark it up with a highlighter, and then call a staff meeting right away.

It was past nine on Sunday night. No matter. If Enron was going to blame the SEC for its decision to keep investors in the dark, Pitt decided, then it was up to the SEC to smoke the company out.

Pitt was sitting at the desk in his study, speaking into the telephone. "Their statement here just drove me through the wall," he said. "We can't have people claiming that they would tell the world what was going on but for the fact they're under investigation."

On the line were several SEC staffers, including Steve Cutler, head of enforcement, and Linda Thomsen, who was running the Enron inquiry. For several minutes the group thrashed through the issues.

Then the idea struck Pitt. *Section 21(a).* The rules on cooperation they had just been revising, the ones Pitt himself had drafted. The rules could be used to compel Enron to talk. It had never been done; a company had never been forced to explain what was going on right in the middle of an investigation. But why not?

"I want to send them a demand under 21(a) that they file something explaining what's happened," Pitt said. Enron certainly couldn't refuse. And it might jump-start the investigation. The SEC staffers agreed that the agency needed to put as many people on it as possible and convert it to a formal inquiry.

"Let's get it done quickly," Pitt said.

The next morning, October 29, Don Evans, the Commerce Secretary, returned from a trip to St. Louis and found Lay's message to call. He phoned right back.

"Don, thanks for calling," Lay said. He launched into his familiar monologue about Enron's problems and his suggestion that it called for government monitoring.

But this time he pressed for a favor.

"Our biggest concern is with the credit-rating agencies in New York," he said. "If we lost our investment-grade rating, it would probably destroy us. If there's anything appropriate that Commerce could do to be helpful on that, we'd love to have that kind of help."

Evans's response was noncommittal. "I'll look into it," he said.

Around lunchtime, Evans was in the Treasury building for the weekly meeting of the Administration's economic team. The policy makers were making their way into the small conference room used by Paul O'Neill.

Evans pulled O'Neill aside. "I wanted to tell you, I received a call from Ken Lay," he began.

He recounted their conversation. "We've decided that we're not going to intervene in this situation," he said.

"Ken called me, too," O'Neill replied, keeping his eyes on Evans as he moved toward the conference room. "We've made the same decision."

Greg Whalley was sitting at his desk, a smirk on his face, when McMahon walked in to speak with him.

"Oh, man, Jeff, you gotta see this," Whalley said.

More bad news? "What? What's up?"

They just received a fax from Dynegy, Whalley said, seeking records so that it could judge whether to do a merger.

"And guess what was the number-one document they asked for?" Whalley said, smiling broadly.

Schedule of liabilities? Profit projections? "What?" McMahon asked.

"The Enron Field naming-rights agreement!" Whalley roared. "First thing they want to know! They want to rename the ballpark after Dynegy!"

The two executives broke out laughing. Whalley pointed at McMahon. "Chuck's horny for this deal," he said. "This deal's gonna get done, 'cause Chuck's horny for it!"

It was an Indian summer's day in Manhattan, with pedestrians swarming along Columbus Avenue. Among them was a tourist, William Powers, the dean of the University of Texas Law School, in town for an alumni event.

As Powers walked south, the Nokia cell phone in his pocket began to ring. It was Harry Reasoner, a friend and the managing partner with Vinson & Elkins.

"So, Bill," Reasoner said, "have you been following what's been going on at Enron?"

"Not really," Powers replied. "I've seen a little in the paper, but I haven't really followed the details."

There was an issue at the company involving some transactions done with related parties, Reasoner said. "Now Enron wants somebody to join the board and investigate these transactions. They'd like it to be you."

Powers was still walking down the street. "Well, I'll think about it," he said. "When do they need to know?"

That same afternoon, Bill McLucas and his partners from Wilmer, Cutler received a call from the SEC. It was Linda Thomsen, alerting them to the agency's concerns about both the partnership transactions and Enron's failure to provide more detailed information to the public about them.

"You guys need to explain a lot, in pretty short order," Thomsen said.

Enron had until November 5, Thomsen said, to disclose what it knew about LJM and any similar arrangements. It needed to file a document, known as an 8-K, laying out every detail. In exactly seven days.

One thing was already becoming apparent to Jimmy Lee from J. P. Morgan Chase. Enron was a lot sicker than most of his corporate patients. While Enron had billions of dollars in assets, they were almost all junk. All they had were the pipelines. It was as if Enron had spent the past decade just throwing cash out its doors.

But all was not lost. The pipelines could definitely be used to secure loans for a billion dollars. Then this Dynegy deal was brewing. Maybe, he figured, if Dynegy wanted Enron, it would inject some money into it first, to help keep the company afloat. Big money.

Scores of trunks lined the hallways in Andersen's main offices. They had been loaded with documents and carted over from Three Allen Center, where the Enron team worked, so the paper could be destroyed quickly. But even with the higher-speed equipment in the main office, the shredders couldn't keep up with the demand.

Mike Luna, a facilities manager, wandered down the hallway, perplexed. Why were trunks everywhere? He noticed Sharon Thibault, the supervisor of records, digging through a box, reviewing each document before it was shredded.

Some time later, Luna saw Thibault again and walked over to speak with her. The main topic of conversation was the implosion of Enron and the chaos that had set off for Andersen.

"Well," Thibault said, "maybe that's why they sent over some shredding. Maybe they are cleaning the office."

Mark Palmer was in a conference room on the thirty-third floor when one of his colleagues came by with a message: Ken Lay wanted to speak with him right away. Palmer picked up a nearby phone and called Lay's office.

"Look, Mark," Lay began, "the reason we can't right the ship is we're not doing a good job in dealing with the press."

The real issues surrounded the *Journal*, Lay said. "They've got a hate-on for us."

Palmer closed his eyes. "Ken, we cannot say that. If you want the media to really go crazy, blame them for our problems. You can't do that."

"Well, I wouldn't," Lay responded, his voice edged with anger. "But that's our real problem here."

"Ken, you can't even think that. We've got forty billion dollars in obligations and no cash flow. *That's* the problem."

How can Lay not understand this? "The one thing you've got to accept, Ken," Palmer said, "the facts keep turning out to be *worse* than the reporting!"

In the late afternoon of October 29, Steve Bergstrom, Dynegy's president, strode into the Hyatt Regency hotel through a door off the garage. Directly ahead, he spotted Greg Whalley, waiting at a table in the sunken bar.

The negotiations for a possible Enron-Dynegy merger were only a couple of days old but had already hit choppy waters. Enron was acting haughty, dragging its feet. Bergstrom wanted to get things back on course.

Over drinks, the two men discussed possible stumbling blocks and painted their visions for what the combined business would look like. Bergstrom asked about what had happened at Enron. Whalley took a swig of his beer.

"Corporate guys screwed up," he said. "Made a mess with these partnerships. But it can be cleaned up."

The explanation was a little too glib for Bergstrom's taste. Whalley was brushing off a disaster as a distraction. But he chose not to challenge him for now.

Bill Powers was back in his Austin office the next morning, on the phone with Jim Derrick, whom he considered a friend. And that was the problem. Before he could take this Enron job, he needed to know what Derrick's role had been in the meltdown.

"I need to ask, Jim," Powers said. "Are you being investigated?"

"Not to my knowledge," Derrick replied.

Powers asked about the inquiry, and Derrick described the conflicts of interest in the Fastow deals.

"You know, I'm not a corporate lawyer," Powers said. "I'm not an accountant."

"That's not going to be necessary," Derrick replied. "You'll have experts at your disposal. You'll be overseeing things. We want somebody who is neutral in all of this."

He needed an answer soon, Derrick said, and Powers promised to call back. It took him a few hours to decide, but he agreed to oversee the first major investigation of Enron.

Later that day, Derrick glanced up from his desk. One of his best lawyers, Kristina Mordaunt, now the general counsel in corporate development, was standing at his doorway. Anxiety was written all over her face.

"Kristina?" Derrick said. "What can I do for you?"

Mordaunt walked in. She seemed at a loss for words. "There's something I want you to be aware of," she finally said. "I don't want you and Ken to be surprised." She paused. "And I don't want you to hear it from someone else and be disappointed in me."

Mordaunt glanced at the floor, then plunged ahead. "I invested with an entity affiliated with LJM," she said.

She didn't say the word "Southampton." She didn't mention the million-dollar return shoveled her way after a few weeks. Derrick's reaction was almost grandfatherly.

"Kristina," he said, "we've all done things we regret." But this had to be examined more closely, he said.

"Go down and find the folks from Wilmer, Cutler," he said. "I want you to share this with them."

Mordaunt nodded slowly. "Where are they right now?"

Within the hour, Mordaunt was in a room with Joe Brenner and Reed Brodsky, two Wilmer, Cutler lawyers handling the investigation.

"I have a duty as an Enron employee to answer your questions, and I'll fully cooperate," she said. "But I don't want to be part of any political witch hunt."

She told the tale without embellishment. She had been approached more than a year before by Kopper, who she thought was acting on Fastow's behalf. He presented this investment opportunity, and she took it.

"Why do you think Kopper came to you?" Brenner asked.

"I don't know."

"Was anybody else approached?"

Mordaunt shook her head. "I don't know."

A pause. "I can't get into Andy's head," she said.

Mordaunt promised to provide all of her records from the investment, and the meeting ended. No one asked her how much money she made on her investment or how fast.

It was that deer-in-the-headlights look.

David Stulb, head of Andersen's forensic investigation unit, had seen it before in the faces of partners threatened with litigation. Now it was David Duncan's turn. Stulb almost felt sorry for him. Every Enron decision he had ever made was being dissected in search of errors.

On October 31, Halloween, Stulb was standing on Andersen's floor in Allen Center with Duncan, who was reviewing a hard copy of an e-mail, along with attachments. It had been written months before by the Andersen accountant who was contacted by Sherron Watkins about her concerns. The e-mail jokingly suggested that everyone review the attached memo about that call, in search of "smoking guns that you can't extinguish." Duncan almost winced.

He grabbed hold of the top page. "Another smoking gun," he muttered. "We don't need this."

Stulb watched in shock as Duncan prepared to tear off the top sheets of the document. "Dave!" Stulb interjected. "I'm not sure if you've had any discussions, but you really need to keep all this information."

Duncan looked back at him impassively.

"There's a strong likelihood that we'll be the subject of litigation," Stulb said. "And the SEC, the Justice Department, and everybody else might be interested in this type of information."

Duncan shrugged and put the document down. It was saved. But Andersen's destruction of thousands of other Enron records continued unabated for another nine days.

The first package of information provided for Dynegy's due diligence arrived from Enron that same day. Hugh Tarpley, Dynegy's head of mergers and acquisitions, pored through the numbers, trying to calculate the potential financial performance of this would-be merger partner.

Tarpley found the answer deep in the package. Enron projected earnings per share of $1.80 for 2001. But the real delight was 2002—$2.25 a share. *Impressive.* But *how?* There was nothing explaining what Enron was planning to do to achieve such stellar results.

During a negotiating session later that day, Tarpley decided to ask. He looked across the table at Dave Delainey.

"Dave," Tarpley said, "I'd really like to get a copy of Enron's business plan for 2002."

Couldn't happen, Delainey said. "We don't have a business plan available," he said.

How then, Tarpley asked, did Enron get its 2002 projections if it didn't know what it was planning to do?

Delainey shrugged. "We just increased the prior year's results by 25 percent," he said simply.

Since returning from Florida, Skilling had desperately been trying to devise a plan to save Enron. He had phoned business associates in Germany, seeking someone, anyone, to invest in the company. Cash would solve the problem.

But on November 1, Kevin Scott, an old friend from California, called Skilling to propose he shift his energies to a different project: saving his own skin.

"This could get bad, really bad," Scott said. "You need to put your team together."

"What are you *talking* about?" Skilling asked.

"You need the best lawyer you can get your hands on. You need an accountant. And you need a psychiatrist."

Scott said he had a friend for Skilling to call, a lawyer at O'Melveny & Myers. Skilling took down the name.

"Are you sure?" Chuck Watson said.

Standing in front of him, Andrea Lang, the head of human resources at Dynegy, nodded as she stared at the piece of paper in her hand. "I don't think Enron lied to us," Lang said. "So I'm sure the numbers are right."

Watson was almost breathless. Lang had been meeting with her counterpart at Enron, discussing personnel issues. In the process, she had learned what Enron was paying its employees. The numbers were unlike anything Watson could have imagined. Enron paid at least 25 percent more—sometimes as much as *double*—what Dynegy people received for the same jobs. Even Enron's human-resources chief commanded a sharply higher salary.

Enron's profligacy was starting to unnerve Watson. He was beginning to suspect what had really gone wrong at the company. Enron's people had been contaminated by too much money.

Lang could see the humor in it. "Well, I'll tell you, Chuck," she said. "All I'd like is to get the same salary as my Enron counterpart. Nothing more."

Watson chuckled. "Sorry, Andrea, but no," he said. "That's why they're in trouble."

Vince Kaminski was wandering the twenty-eighth floor when he noticed a rush of activity in one of the conference rooms. He stuck his head in and saw a group of executives—Mordaunt, Glisan, Faldyn, and others—enmeshed in some obviously troubling discussion. Something about Chewco.

He spoke a few words of greeting, but no one seemed eager to talk. So Kaminski headed down the hallway toward Rick Buy's office. He was about to walk in when he noticed Buy in a small conference room.

Buy was alone, seeming agitated, pacing as he muttered to himself. Kaminski could hear the words clearly.

"I couldn't have stopped the Raptors," Buy said as he paced. "Yes, I could, I could have."

He turned. "No, I couldn't. I couldn't have stopped them. Skilling wouldn't have let me. I couldn't."

Kaminski lingered for a few more moments, watching the small human drama play out. Then he turned and walked away, leaving behind a man in obvious torment.

"I've got to explain something to you," Causey said.

McMahon had just walked into Causey's office and immediately saw the panic on his face. Causey went to the whiteboard and drew the increasingly familiar Chewco structure. He spoke for several minutes, communicating a single theme: he didn't think the accounting worked.

"Rick, what I'm hearing you saying is that you don't think it works because you presume Kopper has a direct interest in it," McMahon said.

"That's right," Causey replied. "But we haven't actually found the link."

"So until you find the link, wouldn't you presume it *does* work, since so many lawyers and accountants spent so much time on it on the front end?"

Causey shook his head. "I don't believe it. We're going to find the money trail back to Michael. I know it."

That presented big problems, Causey said. "I don't think we can file the financial statements," he said.

McMahon looked back at him, stunned. "What do you mean we can't file the financial statements?"

The quarterly records were due to be filed soon. Failing to do so would announce to the market that Enron's finances were in shambles.

Causey pointed at the diagram on the whiteboard. "Well, this is wrong," he said.

"Show me where the accounting for Chewco is wrong!" McMahon barked. "Show me that."

"I don't have it yet."

McMahon threw up his hands. "So you're willing to not issue financial statements because . . . of *what*, Rick? You don't have a basis for this!"

"You're right," Causey replied. "But I don't want to file and find out we're wrong and have to restate."

McMahon spit out his words in disgust. "Oh, this is just great. So now, on top of everything else, *we can't issue financial statements*?"

McMahon tracked down Ken Lay. Causey was making a decision that could be the deathblow to Enron, he said.

"I think Rick's chasing ghosts," he said. "We're talking about a deal that's *freaking four years old*! He can't say why the financial statements are wrong. But he's not going to issue them!"

Lay considered that. "Well, we can just issue the financial statements anyway," he said.

McMahon stared at him. *Does he not understand how the company works?* "We can't issue them without the chief accounting officer signing off on them, Ken," he said.

Then what to do? Wait a minute, Lay said. Wilmer, Cutler was in the building; *they* were the experts here. McMahon agreed to track them down and get their advice.

———

Within minutes, McMahon found Joe Brenner, a partner from Wilmer, Cutler, and briefed him on the latest crisis.

"Right now," McMahon said, "it's just totally going down the path of 'I don't know what Andy did. I don't know what Michael did. I don't know what anyone did. So I'm never going to issue financial statements again.' He didn't say that, but that's the road we're heading down."

Brenner promised to speak with Causey. But without final proof, this was going to be a hard call.

The proof arrived that same week, on November 2, a Friday. It came in one of several cardboard boxes, forwarded by Wilmer, Cutler to David Duncan. McLucas and his partners had been rooting around for records and dug up a bunch related to Chewco. Now they were sending copies to everyone they could think of, just to get their views.

Duncan handed the records over to be examined by two of his partners, Tom Bauer and Deb Cash. After more than an hour of work, Bauer reached into box number seven and pulled out a file. Inside was a two-page letter agreement, dated December 30, 1997. It was signed on behalf of the company by Jeremy Blachman, an Enron vice president. Kopper had signed for Chewco.

The document perplexed Bauer. It provided that a six-million-dollar distribution from JEDI would fund some sort of reserve account. He read it through again.

What reserve account? What in the world was this?

Over the next twenty-four hours, the Andersen accountants struggled to piece together the mystery of the two-page letter. It soon became apparent that this information, never disclosed to Andersen, changed everything about the accounting for Chewco.

This was the proof of a secret side agreement used to get the Chewco deal closed. The six million dollars had been placed in a reserve account to secure a portion of the money provided by Barclays Bank. Enron could argue all it wanted that Barclays's cash was really equity and not a loan. It didn't matter anymore. Chewco had been constructed with *exactly* three percent independent equity. With six million dollars secured, Barclays did not have that cash at risk. Even assuming Barclays's money was equity, Chewco was short the three percent by at least six million dollars.

There could no longer be any question. The accounting failed. Chewco was not a valid special-purpose entity. It was Enron.

———

The Dynegy negotiations crept on through the afternoon of November 3, a Saturday, this time with a detailed discussion about LJM2. Dynegy needed to understand all of Enron's deals with the fund and their implications.

Enron sent Glisan to handle the presentation. He distributed a small report, which included a one-paragraph description of each deal. Keith Fullenweider, Dynegy's deputy general counsel, still had concerns.

"I need to ask, Ben," Fullenweider said. "Does anyone else at Enron who's involved in these negotiations have any interest in these partnerships?"

Glisan was silent. Then he changed the subject.

"Chewco is not a failed SPE," Causey said confidently. "It's valid."

It was that same evening. Causey's team had been working furiously as time inched toward the SEC's deadline two days away for Enron to disclose more information about the partnerships. Ten people had been roped in for this meeting—seven from Enron, one from Vinson & Elkins, and two from Andersen—to make the final assessment on Chewco. After Duncan and Bauer arrived, Causey announced they had formally concluded Chewco was fine.

"What's your view on Dodson as an equity holder?" Bauer asked.

"I'm not sure he can be counted as a related party," Causey replied.

Kristina Mordaunt picked up the point. "Texas state law doesn't legally recognize homosexual relationships."

Unreal. Enron was hanging a huge accounting decision—impacting income statements and balance sheets going back years—on state antisodomy laws.

"I believe for accounting purposes, the assessment of whether Dodson is a related party has to rest on a lot more than just the legal status of their relationship," Bauer said.

But there was a more important issue, he said. "How were you able to conclude that Chewco is valid, given the impact of the side letter?"

Causey stayed silent for a moment.

"What side letter?" he asked.

Bauer's bombshell set off a frantic search in the conference room as everyone dug through the original files, looking for the letter. They found it among a pile of records on a side table. Causey read it, blanching.

"I've never seen this before," he mumbled.

The lawyers had left earlier, and Causey called them back. None recognized it. He summoned Glisan to the meeting and thrust the letter toward him. As Glisan read the document, a look of terror gradually shadowed his face.

"I've never seen this before," Glisan said. "Why would they do this? I've never seen this!"

Bauer watched him, disbelieving. Glisan placed the document down on the table and closed his eyes.

"We're toast!" he exclaimed.

At Skilling's house that Sunday afternoon, the phone was ringing. He walked into the kitchen and answered.

"Hello," a voice said. "This is Bruce Hiler from O'Melveny & Myers."

The O'Melveny partner Skilling had called days before had referred him to Hiler, a securities-law specialist. Skilling had called the lawyer on Friday and left a message for him. Now Skilling felt a little awkward.

"Hi," he said. "My name is Jeff Skilling. I'm the former chief executive of Enron."

"Yeah," Hiler said. "I've been watching this."

"So what do you think?" he asked.

Hiler pulled no punches. "I think this is going to be a real problem," he said. He began to spell out the issues. Skilling was impressed; Hiler had clearly done his homework.

"Well," Skilling said, "I think I need a lawyer. Would you be willing to take me on?"

Hiler didn't hesitate. "Yes," he said.

That same day, McLucas broke the news to Enron's board.

"Chewco failed," he said. "And unfortunately, that means that everything that touched Chewco has failed."

There would have to be a restatement, he said, dating back to Chewco's creation. JEDI was now solely owned by Enron. Its results had to be joined with the company's.

The room was raw with frustration. "How do we manage the public communications on this?" Lay asked. "We need to be able to talk about this in a way that manages people's fears and lets them know we can recover."

That was not advisable, McLucas said. "It's a bad idea to make any definitive statements about these structures until the special committee has finished its work."

As the bruised directors shuffled out of the room, Mark Palmer, who had arrived minutes before, approached McLucas and his colleague Charles Davidow to introduce himself. McLucas began dishing out instructions.

"All right, Mark, you need to understand, you need to speak to me before you answer any questions from the media. And if you can't reach me, you talk to Chuck."

For *any* call? That made no sense to Palmer.

"I'm sorry, I don't know how well that's going to work," Palmer said. "The situation is really fluid, and we're on a twenty-four-hour news cycle."

McLucas's face was stern. He cupped a hand and held it up in the air, aiming it at Palmer.

"All right, Mark, I want you to imagine the spotlight," McLucas said. "You're in a small room with an SEC examiner across from you, and the light is shining down on you. And he says, 'Mr. Palmer, when you made this statement, did you know it was true? How did you know it was true?' What are you going to say then, Mark?"

Palmer's eyes went wide.

"Mark," McLucas said, "*you* could be liable if you misled investors. Not Enron. *You*, Mark Palmer."

Oh, my God. It all came crashing down. Palmer didn't know the truth. He didn't know who was lying. Everybody was running for lawyers, as Whalley said. Yet they expected *him* to stick his neck out by peddling their stories. Maybe he needed to worry about his *own* exposure.

He took a deep breath. "Thank you," he said.

About that time, emotions were running high in an Enron conference room, where the accounting and financial teams were finishing their final analysis of the Chewco disaster.

McMahon still didn't fully understand what had happened, and asked Glisan to explain it. For several minutes, Glisan filled him in on the side deal, the reserve accounts, and the effects these had on the accounting.

He spoke with mounting anger. "I was responsible for the accounting! But nobody told me this document existed! If I had known, I never would have signed off on it."

The room greeted the outburst of righteous indignation with silence. Causey crossed his arms; McMahon screwed up his face in disgust.

Both men thought Glisan was lying.

Monday, November 5. The deadline for filing the information demanded by the SEC. But too much had happened. The Chewco failure had thrown everything into disarray. Enron pleaded for time. The SEC gave three days. No more.

An entirely new accounting team, this time from Deloitte & Touche, swarmed over Enron's financial records. This time the accountants weren't working for the company; instead, they had been retained by Wilmer, Cutler on behalf of the special committee.

By that morning, the Deloitte accountants were digging into multiple issues, including this odd Southampton transaction, which they learned about from Kristina Mordaunt. Since her interview, Mordaunt had provided a road map for the investigators to follow and handed over all of her records. Other details turned up in Enron's own files.

An accountant was reviewing a document when something jumped off the page. He consulted his colleagues, then the Wilmer, Cutler lawyers. They all were agreed. The special committee needed to be notified immediately.

"A million-dollar return on a five-thousand-dollar investment?" Bill Powers asked.

Yes, the Deloitte accountant said.

"Well," Powers replied, "that's not normal."

Deloitte & Touche had figured out everything. The huge return on Southampton. The millions of dollars that flowed to Fastow and Kopper. The millions more that went to Glisan and Mordaunt, two executives still with the company who were supposedly helping guide it through this crisis.

Andersen had discovered other discrepancies. Swap Sub, the LJM1 entity that was used to hedge Rhythms and was purchased by Southampton, never had enough capital. It couldn't be treated as independent of the company. Enron had been hedging Rhythms with itself, and it had paid Southampton to purchase what it already owned.

"We need to arrange a full board meeting," Powers said. "The directors have to be told about this."

Glisan was at his desk later that day when David Oxley, an executive from human resources, approached.

"Ben, I'm sorry, but you need to go home," Oxley said.

Glisan had heard about the committee's discovery. Still, he looked bewildered. "Am I fired?" he asked.

Oxley nodded. "Probably."

McMahon had just heard about Southampton and Ben Glisan. *That son of a bitch lied to me.* He was *part of it!*

"Sue!" McMahon called to his secretary. "Get me Ben Glisan on the phone! He's at home!"

It would take hours to track Glisan down.

That evening, McMahon finally reached Glisan.

"Ben," he said, "I specifically sat you down before I gave you this important job. I asked you if you had any involvement in these things, and you told me no."

But wait, Glisan argued. Southampton wasn't LJM. It was a one-off deal, a closed-end entity that completed a single transaction involving LJM more than a year earlier.

McMahon steamed. "Ben, I have no idea what the hell you're talking about. The one word I heard in that was LJM. And that's enough. You told me no problem. And now you're coming back to me and telling me LJM."

"Yeah, but through a closed-end entity . . ."

"It doesn't matter, Ben!" McMahon shouted. "Do you realize the jeopardy you have put this entire merger into? You lied! Did you intend to do that?"

"That was never my intent," Glisan replied.

McMahon paused. "Well, I think you need to consider yourself terminated from this company," he said.

Mordaunt was thrown out with equal speed. It didn't matter that she had come forward, she was told. She never should have invested in the deal. Her Enron career was over.

Dynegy had to be informed. Its managers were days from presenting a merger deal to their board. Now Enron knew that Glisan, who had provided Dynegy with much of the the information it needed for its multibillion-dollar deal, was a liar. Maybe even a crook.

Derrick, along with Pug Winokur and an outside lawyer, phoned Dynegy's deputy general counsel, Keith Fullenweider.

"We have some new information," Derrick began.

McMahon handled the job of breaking the news to Dynegy's financial team. He went over to the offices of the law firm Baker Botts, which was advising Dynegy. Rob Doty, Dynegy's CFO, was there crunching some more numbers.

"I've got to tell you guys something," McMahon said. "We found some other employees who received payments related to LJM. And one of them was Ben Glisan."

Doty brought a hand to his head and sighed. "Every time I talk to one of you guys, you tell me another new revelation. What else are we going to find out?"

"Look," McMahon said, "as near as we can tell, everything he's told you so far has been right, but you needed to know this. It's probably going to be disclosed shortly, and he's not with the company anymore."

Enron had a new treasurer, McMahon said. Ray Bowen would take over Glisan's job. Doty shook his head silently.

"I don't know how you guys put up with this," he said.

That same day, a handful of Dynegy directors met with a few of their counterparts from Enron. The time had come to convey an uncomfortable message: Ken Lay had to go.

Otis Winters, a Dynegy director, tried to be polite, saying that Dynegy appreciated everything Lay had accomplished but that the company needed new leadership.

"It's our position that the Enron board should ask Ken to step down," Winters said.

John Duncan, one of five directors at the meeting, was almost indignant. That wouldn't work, he said. Lay had to be a director and the interim chief executive. His expertise in public relations and government issues would be crucial to the success of the merger.

"You *need* Ken," Duncan said. "He built this company. You don't understand his importance."

The Dynegy directors were thunderstruck. They had made it clear that Ken Lay could pull this deal apart, and the Enron directors wouldn't budge. Winters tried again.

"Of course," Winters replied, "it's Enron's call, but Dynegy feels very strongly about this."

What the hell is all this?

Chuck Watson was studying a draft of Enron's 8-K filing that the SEC had demanded. No one had given him a warning; Enron had just shipped over a copy, revealing the details it had learned of the partnership debacle.

Watson could only shake his head. A restatement of five years of earnings. The Southampton scandal. The revelation that the $1.2 billion equity adjustment was the result of an accounting error, not the closing of the Raptors, as Enron had said. And *another* error on Swap Sub.

Watson contacted Lay. "Ken, you told me when we first met there was nothing else. You gave me your personal assurances! So why are there all these new revelations?"

Lay's voice was calm. "Chuck," he said, "I'm as surprised as you are."

The merger was still going forward, with the final negotiations about price. This was an all-stock deal, Dynegy shares for Enron shares. The issue, of course, was the ratio. Lay and Watson hammered out an agreement based on the relative prices of Enron and Dynegy shares. Bergstrom and Whalley took it from there. It was pretty basic arithmetic.

Then some investors apparently got wind of the deal. Enron's share price shot up, rising from about seven dollars to the nine-dollar range. Enron was suddenly more valuable than just hours before.

That evening, in separate meetings, the boards of Enron and Dynegy were scheduled to conduct their final reviews of the agreement. It had plenty of moving parts, calling for Dynegy to inject $1.5 billion in new cash into Enron immediately and another billion at closing.

An hour before the Dynegy board meeting, a new document arrived from Enron. It was Ken Lay's employment agreement. Andrea Lang, the head of human resources at Dynegy, gave it a quick review.

She almost gasped.

Sixty-one million dollars. If the merger went through, Lay would be entitled to a sixty-one-million-dollar severance. Lang took the information to Watson, who presented it to the board. The Dynegy directors debated Lay's employment agreement for some time. But it was a legal document. There was pretty much no way around it. They voted to approve the deal.

Past 8:30 that evening, Lay glanced around the Enron boardroom. The demoralized directors had been meeting for more than an hour. It was time. There was no choice.

"All right, then," Lay said. "I'm calling for a motion to approve the proposed merger transaction."

John Duncan made the motion. It was approved unanimously. The deal was all but sealed. Or so it appeared.

That night, Ray Bowen signed the documents, writing his name hundreds of times. He was at Baker Botts, surrounded by lawyers and financiers for both companies.

Past midnight, almost there. Clusters of tired executives and lawyers stood around, ironing out minor details. Everyone was giddy from exhaustion; there were laughs and jokes. They had done it. They had saved Enron.

Jeff Donahue, an Enron managing director in corporate development, spied Dynegy's draft release about the deal on a table. He leaned over to read it, chuckling. He picked up the release and waved it in the air, thrusting his chin toward Keith Fullenweider, Dynegy's deputy general counsel.

"Hey, Keith!" Donahue called out. "You've got a typo in your press release."

Fullenweider stood, showing little concern. "Let me see," he said, irritation in his voice.

He walked over and took the release. He read it over.

What's he talking about? "Jeff, there's no typo."

Donahue smiled. "You missed it!" he said, pointing at a section of the release. "It's right there. Look at the price it says your board approved."

Fullenweider read the words: *Enron shareholders will receive 0.2685 Dynegy shares per share of Enron common stock.* He shrugged. "So?" he said. "That's no typo. That's the price our board approved."

Donahue's face fell. "Well," he said, "that's not the price *our* board approved."

An uproar engulfed the conference room.

The Dynegy and Enron boards had voted on different merger agreements and didn't know it. Dynegy had approved an exchange rate of 0.2685 shares for Enron stock, while Enron had approved a higher ratio of 0.2885, based on the sudden pop that afternoon in the stock price. That translated into a difference of about $400 million.

Fullenweider grabbed the release and tore through Baker Botts, looking for McMahon and Mark Muller, Enron's chief deal maker. He found them in another conference room.

"Your chairman fucked up!" Fullenweider snapped. "You guys can't even get the goddamn merger price right! What the hell is the matter with you?"

Muller was stunned. "What are you talking about?"

"The exchange ratio! It's .2685!"

"No, it's not," Muller said. "It's .2885."

"No, it's not, you idiot!" Fullenweider shouted.

"I've got the board minutes right here!" Muller shouted. "That's what they approved!"

Fullenweider threw up his hands. "Yeah! I know! That's the problem!"

He shook his head in disgust. "They approved the wrong goddamn deal!" he shouted.

The two sides, battling fatigue, retreated to separate rooms to ponder the latest disaster. Muller was on the phone, tracking down Whalley. Bowen meandered in, watching lawyers and executives scurry about. A second later, William Joor, a Vinson & Elkins partner, began tapping his head against the wall while simultaneously kicking it.

"Oh, my God," Joor muttered. "I can't believe this."

Joor turned around, rubbing his head. "How are we going to explain this in the proxy?" he asked the group. "We look like the biggest bunch of idiots on the planet!"

Bowen sat beside Rob Walls, a senior lawyer with Enron. "You know," he said to Walls, "this is really shitty."

He chuckled. "But, you've got to admit, it's just too funny to be true."

Past three in the morning. The Dynegy team had walked out in disgust, leaving the Enron executives to clean up the mess.

Muller motioned toward McMahon. "You're the CFO," he said. "You need to call Ken."

"Oh no," McMahon shot back. "This isn't my deal. *You're* supposed to get the darn numbers right, Muller. *You* call Lay at three in the morning and wake his ass up."

Muller thought about it. "Yeah, all right."

The Lays were asleep when the phone rang. Linda rolled over in bed and picked up the receiver.

"Hello?" she mumbled.

The Enron team listened in.

"This is Mark Muller from Enron. I need to speak to Ken Lay. I'm sorry I woke you up."

A pause. "Can I tell him what it's about?"

"Yeah," Muller said. "You can tell him our merger's all screwed up because of him."

Linda turned over and passed the phone to her husband.

"Ken, this is Mark," Muller said. "We've got a major problem here with the numbers."

Muller spelled out what he knew.

"Okay," Lay said. "Well, you know, the number Dynegy has is not the one Chuck and I discussed. He got it wrong. Let me call Chuck, and I'll take care of it."

Minutes later, Watson was on the line from his home.

"Ken," he said, "that ain't the deal."

Somehow, there had been some horrible miscommunication, Watson said. Enron was using the closing price, Dynegy the price from when the deal was struck. But the deal had already been sent for final approval to the board of Chevron, Dynegy's largest investor. It couldn't be revised now.

Lay was silent for a moment. "Well, then I've got to call my board," he said.

"Okay," Watson replied. "Then call your board."

Lay called back his team. "Chuck isn't going to budge," he said simply. "He's not going to negotiate."

The room was silent.

"I'll call a board meeting," Lay said, sounding defeated. "We have to get this fixed."

CHAPTER 22

UPSTAIRS IN HER HOUSE, Rebecca Carter stepped into a game room, passing her teenage son's collection of sports trophies that filled a built-in cabinet. She pulled out a chair and sat down at his computer. Within moments, she was on the Internet, typing in the Web address for the SEC.

It was early on the morning of November 8, and Carter was hoping to learn the latest on Enron. She pulled up the list of filings, and noticed something new had been added that morning, an 8-K. She moved the computer mouse and clicked it open.

Carter's eyes widened. A restatement—going back five years? Chewco? Accounting errors?

I can't believe what I'm reading here. The nineteenth page was the biggest shock of all. There, Carter read about Southampton and the investments made by Enron executives.

Kristina Mordaunt? Kristina was a friend of hers! She'd invested in some Fastow entity—and now was getting fired? And Ben Glisan! He was a Boy Scout. *What is going on?*

Carter jumped up and ran downstairs. That morning, she knew, Skilling was in Washington, meeting with Bruce Hiler, his new lawyer. Somebody had to tell them about all of this. She searched frantically for Skilling's itinerary. After locating it, she grabbed the phone and dialed Hiler's office. A secretary answered.

"I need to speak with Jeff Skilling," Carter said.

"I'm sorry, he's in a meeting with Mr. Hiler."

Carter didn't hesitate. "Interrupt them," she said.

Skilling was deep in conversation with Hiler when he heard Carter was on the line. Annoyed, he wandered over to a phone and picked up.

"Why are you calling me out of a meeting?" he asked.

"Enron's restating the financials! And there's more . . ."

"*Restating the financials?*" Skilling interrupted.

The words caught Hiler's attention. "Put this on speaker," he said.

Minutes later, Carter's voice filled the office as she read portions of the 8-K. She mentioned that the financial restatements went back five years.

Hiler was bothered but not surprised. "This is going to be a problem," he said.

Skilling shrugged. *Okay, new accountants have a different opinion from other accountants. So what?*

"But then this is the worst part," Carter said.

She read the statement about a deal that had involved numerous Enron executives as investors, including Fastow and Kopper. Then she read the names of the investors. "Ben Glisan, Managing Director and Treasurer of Enron Corp.; Kristina Mordaunt, Managing Director and General Counsel of an Enron division . . ."

Skilling staggered into a chair. "You've got to be *kidding*!" he exclaimed. "You've got to be kidding!"

His mouth was open. He didn't know what to think.

"Kristina? *Ben?*" Skilling asked.

"Yeah, that's what it says."

For a moment, he couldn't speak. For days, he had been reading the papers, thinking that he had known everything that had happened at Enron. But not this. Not this.

Oh, shit.

Early that same morning, Ray Bowen was getting ready to head back to work, but was already feeling exhausted. With the high-wire act the night before, he had only been able to grab a few hours of sleep.

But today, the final hurdles waited. The proposed merger had been presented to the credit-rating agencies to make sure that they would let Enron keep its investment-grade rating; without it, Enron's trading business would dry up. Then Dynegy's largest shareholder, Chevron, had to give its blessing for the deal. After that, smooth sailing.

Bowen glanced at the clock. By now, McMahon must have heard *something* from the credit-rating agencies. The suspense was too much to bear. Bowen picked up the phone and dialed McMahon's number. It rang and rang. Not a good sign.

Finally, a click. "Yeah?" It was McMahon.

"Hey, Jeff, it's Ray. Is everything okay? Did we get the right answer from the credit-rating agencies?"

McMahon's tone was desperate.

"No, Ray," he said. "They're fucking us."

An hour later, McMahon and Bowen were in Whalley's office, struggling to come up with some strategy to please the credit agencies. The big problem was Moody's Investors Service, which believed the deal offered Dynegy too many outs from the merger before it closed. In particular, Moody's was concerned about the material adverse change, or MAC, clause, which allowed Dynegy to bolt if there was any dramatic deterioration in Enron's prospects.

The three executives got on conference calls with Moody's, then with Jimmy Lee at Chase. They debated the possibilities; Dynegy was soon brought in. Without changes, this deal was dead. Backed into a corner, Watson agreed to toughen up the provisions allowing Dynegy to scotch the deal, and to make a few other revisions to satisfy Moody's.

The executives at Enron couldn't have been more pleased. Now it would take some sort of financial tsunami for Dynegy to get out of this merger.

Enron had to pay its bills that day. But if Moody's didn't give the nod, the merger, its last chance for survival, would slip away. It would go bankrupt, and then deeply regret having wired out all of its cash.

Bowen came in to see McMahon and Whalley, pressing them to make the call: pay the bills or not?

"Okay, here's the problem," Bowen said. "I've got like $400 million in cash on hand. If Moody's shoots us down and we're on the path to bankruptcy, that's money that I would rather have here. But we've got a lot of bills due today that would eat up most of that cash."

Whalley ran a hand through his hair, exhaling. "What happens if we don't pay our bills?"

There could be problems, Bowen said. A lot of the bills were related to settlements of energy trades. That money normally would already have been shipped out. Trading partners were probably wondering where it was, getting itchy about extending Enron any more credit. If Enron stiffed them, it could easily be shut out of the markets.

The three men thought in silence for a moment.

Whalley decided. "Ah, the hell with it, let's wait," he said. "Don't pay them."

Bowen called Mary Perkins, Enron's executive in charge of cash transfers. "We're not going to pay our bills today," he said simply.

Perkins paused. "Oh," she said. "Okay."

Got to admire her composure, Bowen thought. He had no doubts that his instructions had thrown her off stride.

In the morning, Bowen said, they were going to hear from Moody's. If the credit agency gave the green light to the merger, then everybody would have to be paid immediately. That meant all the wires needed to be set up, ready to go.

"Well," Perkins said, "I can get the payments loaded into the Fed system early in the morning. Then the payment will flow when the Fed opens."

Fine, Bowen said. In that event, Enron would pay what it owed, plus overnight interest. Everybody would likely just assume Enron was a little more disorganized than usual.

The answer from Moody's came back early the next morning. It agreed to grant Enron a BBB-minus rating, the lowest ranking within the critical investment-grade level. It wasn't great, downgrading Enron by one notch, but it would keep the company alive. Bowen immediately called Perkins.

"It's a go!" he said. "We're making the payments."

"Thank God!" She hit the button.

The next morning, a voice mail and an e-mail were waiting for David Duncan when he arrived in the office. They were from Nancy Temple, the Andersen lawyer working on the Enron debacle. Andersen, she told him, had finally been served by the SEC with a subpoena in the investigation. He should suspend the use of the firm's document policy, she said.

Duncan punched a few buttons on his phone, forwarding Temple's message to his secretary, Shannon Adlong.

"This is from Nancy Temple," he said. "Make sure everyone is notified to suspend the policy."

Just past noon, Adlong listened to the message. She opened up an e-mail, addressing it to most of the assistants in the office. She placed the cursor in the subject heading.

No more shredding, she typed.

But it was too late; the crime had been committed. Hundreds of e-mails had been deleted, and thousands of pieces of paper documenting details of Andersen's dealings with Enron were now little more than confetti.

Late that afternoon, what seemed to be the final obstacle to the merger was cleared away. The Chevron board approved the deal. Chuck Watson called Lay to let him know.

"It's all set," he said. "They signed the merger papers." Dynegy would now invest $1.5 billion in Enron to keep it afloat and was authorized to invest $1 billion more at closing. Lay felt both relieved and deflated. His company was saved; he was losing his company.

"Congratulations, Chuck," he said softly, muttering a few words about how far they had come so quickly.

Watson was eager to proclaim his victory. "We want to announce it tonight," he said, "as soon as possible."

Lay sighed. "We'll be right over."

The press conference that Friday night embittered Enron's senior managers. Any hopes they had of clinging to shreds of power, or even respect, were shattered.

Watson placed strict limits on the number of them who could attend, and Lay was given all the prominence of the janitorial staff. He was allowed to say virtually nothing and made little effort to hide his dissatisfaction. Dynegy was the victor. Enron was on its knees, vanquished by its smaller rival; the white flag had been unfurled.

That night, the younger Enron managers went to Kenneally's, the dimly lit Irish pub. Gloom hung in the air. These were executives who for years had delighted in deriding Dynegy as a cheap imitation of Enron. Now the upstart was running the show—and rubbing their noses in it.

Someone tried to liven up the mood. Dave Delainey, the head of retail, hoisted a glass. "Guys, this is a reverse merger," he thundered. "They may think they're buying us, but give it two months, and we'll be running the place!"

Nearby, Ray Bowen laughed and swigged his Foster's lager.

"Maybe," he said softly. "Whether this merger happens or not, time will tell."

Three days later, Monday, November 12, one of Andy Fastow's last remaining financial land mines exploded.

The shambles of the finance division's records made it almost impossible for the new team to find every detail—in particular, the triggers embedded in structured deals. To get better pricing for the deals, Fastow had agreed to terms allowing banks and investors to demand money or stock from Enron if its share price fell to certain levels or its credit rating dropped—usually below investment grade.

But not always. There was one deal where the critical trigger had been placed at BBB-minus, one notch above junk. The rating just bestowed on Enron by Moody's.

The first person at the company to learn about it was Bowen, in a call from Bill Fox, a banker from Citibank.

"Hey, Ray," Fox said, "now that you guys are BBB-minus, I seem to remember that Rawhide had a trigger event at that level."

Rawhide. Bowen knew it was one of the finance group's off-books entities, used to raise more than half a billion dollars a few years back. He didn't know anything about the terms, but he couldn't imagine this was true. What idiot would put an *investment-grade* trigger in a finance deal?

"Why don't you guys go check it and see if we've got an issue here?" Fox asked.

Bowen got off the phone and called someone in finance. "Hey, can one of you guys go look at the Rawhide documents, 'cause Bill Fox is telling me we've hit a ratings trigger."

The answer came back soon. Fox was right. And the trigger was a doozy. Enron owed all the money it had borrowed through Rawhide. Some $690 million, due fifteen days after the trigger was hit. And until Fox called, no one at Enron knew the repayment clock was already ticking.

"That *can't* be right," McMahon protested, throwing up his hands. "That's just insane!"

Bowen was standing in front of McMahon, having just broken the news of the Rawhide trigger.

"It's right," he said simply.

"Ray, we've *never* done deals where we allow for debt acceleration in the investment-grade category!" he shot back. "Why would someone *do* that?"

Bowen shrugged. "I have no idea. But we've checked it. That's what they did."

McMahon put a hand over his face. This was too much.

In Washington, a mealtime crowd filled Il Radicchio, an Italian restaurant near Capitol Hill. A waitress made her way through the mass of people, placing an iced tea in front of David Cavicke, a staff member on the House Energy and Commerce Subcommittee on Oversight and Investigations. At the other side of the two-person table sat Mark Paoletta, chief counsel and a top investigator for the subcommittee.

For days, Cavicke had been lobbying Paoletta to go all-out on Enron. The subcommittee investigated issues relating to business and energy, with a bent toward potential wrongdoing. By that standard, Enron seemed to hit the trifecta. Cavicke, who spent years working on Wall Street, had been telling Paoletta that the Enron affair seemed huge. So today Paoletta had taken Cavicke out to lunch, giving him the time to make his case.

"What happened at Enron is amazing," Cavicke said, his voice animated. "It is just the most massive fraud!"

Cavicke had been reviewing the documents, particularly the recently filed

8-K. He spelled out everything he had learned from the records. More important, he said, this pointed up fundamental issues relating to the reliability of company financial reports. It was *exactly* the kind of thing the subcommittee should be jumping on.

For about an hour, Cavicke walked through the details of what happened at Enron. By the time Paoletta's chicken sandwich arrived, he had pretty much made up his mind. This was something he needed to raise with Jim Greenwood, the congressman who chaired the subcommittee.

Enron employees had been blocked from making changes in their retirement plans for ten workdays. But too much was happening; it was, executives decided, a terrible time to prevent the workers of Enron from being able to make decisions about their investments, particularly since the vast majority of them held huge stakes in the company's stock.

So on November 12, the lockout was ended. Employees could go in and buy and sell whatever shares they felt necessary. In the ten days of trading they had missed, the stock had dropped to $9.98 a share, a decline of $3.83. In some ways, that worked to their advantage: the stock price now was *higher* than it had been on five of those days. Anyone who wanted to sell could make more money than was possible during half of the lockup period.

But the end of the restrictions did not bring on a flood of selling. Instead, Enron employees, apparently believing this was a great opportunity to snap up cheap shares, became net buyers of the stock.

Chuck Watson was on the road, busy selling investors on the Dynegy-Enron merger. No one had told him about the Rawhide debacle unfolding back in Houston. But then again, no one at Dynegy would know about it for days.

Instead, Enron and Dynegy spent the days haggling over less weighty issues: the number of Enron executives allowed to accompany Watson on the road show; whether Dynegy executives could use Enron planes; whether an Enron executive could be flown to a session on a Dynegy plane.

The bickering was already souring the relationship. Watson had wanted to come by Enron, to visit his new employees. Lay and Whalley refused; such a visit, they argued, would be demoralizing and should be delayed until they could hold their own meeting. Instead, Watson shot a video, welcoming Enron to the Dynegy family.

No one at Enron watched it.

Somehow, word got out, all over the Internet and the radio. Ken Lay stood to make sixty-one million dollars in severance if the Dynegy deal went through. Among Enron's traders, the response was outrage. Why, they argued, should Lay walk away from this debacle with so much cash?

Two executives, John Lavorato and Louise Kitchen, stormed up to Lay's office after hearing the news. Lay was sitting at his desk when they arrived.

"Ken, you can't take sixty million dollars out of the company," Lavorato said. "The place will go nuts."

Lay was taken aback. "I've got that contractual right, but it's not built into the merger agreement," he said.

He'd already discussed reducing the payout with Chuck Watson, he said, but certainly he was owed something.

"That won't do it, Ken," Kitchen said.

"If you take anything at all, there's going to be a riot on the trading floor," Lavorato interjected.

Lay considered that. "Okay, okay, I hear you," he said. "Do you mind if I speak to my wife first?"

After calling to make sure Linda was there, Lay drove home to speak with her. He described the reaction among the traders. The prospect of forgoing the money her husband was due did not please her.

"We've already lost so much money," she said. "We're struggling to find what we can to pay off debt and pay taxes and keep us out of bankruptcy."

Hundreds of millions of dollars of their wealth had vanished in the stock-price collapse, but Lay thought he had little choice. "I know I have a legal right to this money. But I think I need to walk away from it."

Tears welled up in Linda's eyes. But she agreed.

In Enron's trading room, the market was evaporating. Despite the announced Dynegy merger, competitors still worried Enron might disappear without having paid its obligations under new trades. Every transaction with Enron was an act of faith they were no longer willing to take.

John Lavorato was furious. Even Dynegy, the only company selling physical gas with Enron, was refusing to make trades extending beyond one year. Lavorato got on the phone with Matt Schatzman, the head of Dynegy's trading operation.

"You're not helping us," Lavorato grumbled.

"Our credit exposure to Enron is high, and if the merger falls apart, we're on the hook," Schatzman said. "We owe a duty to our shareholders. I've told our brokers not to treat you guys with any favoritism."

Lavorato exploded. "What about the merger agreement?"

Schatzman's tone could not have been calmer. "I don't care," he said. "This is business."

There was a solution, the Enron traders decided.

If other companies were afraid Enron couldn't pay, why not pay up front? *That* would keep the business going. All the traders had to do was post cash collateral, essentially turning hard currency over to their trading partners as a partial—or in some cases total—guarantee of payment.

After years of disregard, Enron still lacked meaningful controls over division spending or the means to track cash. Now money had arrived from Dynegy, piles of it, ready to help Enron traders prove that they were still in business. They grabbed it by the fistful, thrusting it into the outstretched hands of their trading partners.

Hundreds of millions of dollars were disappearing on a daily basis. And, as the cash drain picked up speed, none of the top executives at either company had a clue that it was happening.

"You need to call Dynegy," Bowen told McMahon. "We've got this Rawhide default to deal with."

It was later that same week, and Dynegy had still not been notified of the Rawhide trigger. Bowen figured the problem could be averted; if the bank called in the cash, Enron could implode. Surely a solution could be negotiated.

But McMahon was swamped and simply hadn't gotten around to giving Dynegy the heads-up. Still, he promised Bowen that he would make the call to Enron's new merger partner. Very soon.

In Chicago, the mood in the board meeting at Andersen was grim. The firm's lawyers had briefed the directors about the deepening crisis at Enron, then talk had turned to the threat from an onslaught of litigation. Joe Berardino did his best to assure everyone that Andersen was on top of everything. There was no reason for fear.

"We've got our top legal counsel on it, our top risk managers all over it," he told the board. "We've got all the processes in place now to manage this risk."

Still, there was no doubting the consequences, he said.

"We're going to lose business over this," he said. "It is just too big. But we can't panic."

He looked at the worried faces around him. "We just have to live our values. Then we can get through this."

On Friday, November 16, Lay relaxed in his Galveston home, reading a draft of Enron's upcoming quarterly report, known as a 10-Q. Despite Causey's earlier misgivings, Enron had managed to pull everything together in time to meet an extended deadline. It was all set to be filed on Monday.

There were plenty of new details in the document, some pretty horrifying. There was information about Enron's rating setting off a trigger, putting it on the hook for almost $700 million. And details of how the cash position was worsening. This was sure to bother the folks at Dynegy. Well, by now, Lay assumed, *somebody* at Enron had forwarded it to Watson or one of his top executives. Dynegy, he thought, would have plenty of time to absorb the news.

He was wrong.

The next day, Saturday, a full contingent from the finance staff was in the office. There was much work to be done, with the quarterly financial filing due and a meeting scheduled between Enron and its banks.

Mark Muller mentioned Rawhide to McMahon, saying that Rob Doty, Dynegy's CFO, needed to be told about the default.

"You need to call," Muller said. "It's going to be a headline issue in the 10-Q."

McMahon nodded. "Yeah, you're right. I've got to do that, I guess. I'll go give him a call right now."

He wandered into an office and picked up the phone. Doty wasn't in on Saturday; the voice-mail system picked up.

"Hey, Rob, Jeff McMahon," he began. "Listen, Enron made a mistake." The Rawhide financing, he said, had a trigger at BBB-minus, not at a junk rating like the rest of Enron's deals. The company was now technically in default on Rawhide, and debt repayment had been accelerated.

"It will all be disclosed in the 10-Q we're filing Monday," McMahon said in the recording.

Rob Doty was beside himself. He had arrived at the office early Monday and heard McMahon's bombshell. Now he was trying desperately to get Enron's quarterly report. It was about to be filed with the public, and Dynegy, which had just sunk a billion and a half dollars into Enron, still hadn't seen the damn thing.

Doty got on the line with the finance group. "Look, I don't *care* if you don't have a final version," he snapped. "At least send me the draft copy!"

It arrived by e-mail at 10:53 that morning. The teams at Dynegy set to work reviewing the pages. Then, in the afternoon, Enron filed its final version with the SEC. Dynegy received its copy at about the same time every investor in the country had access to it.

Doty was flipping through the latest document, when he stopped short. "Wait a minute," he told his colleagues. "There are pages here that weren't in the earlier draft."

More than $1.5 billion! Gone!

Doty and his team hit the roof. The filing was *loaded* with information that Dynegy knew nothing about. The money it had recently injected into Enron had disappeared, just like that. But where had it gone? Doty had no way of knowing that Enron's traders had gotten hold of it and were tossing it out the door to stay in the market.

The business was falling apart, too. Trading activity was dropping, and fourth-quarter results were expected to be a train wreck. The European trading profits were all but wiped out. Then there was the debt-maturity schedule. Doty had believed Enron would have at most $800 million of debt to repay by year-end, but that had grown by *two billion dollars.* What was going on? How had Enron not known this earlier? Had this company not had a debt-maturity schedule prepared long ago?

On top of it all, Enron had just announced that, technically, it was *insolvent.* It had $2.8 billion in almost immediate obligations, and only $1.2 billion in cash. Why would anyone have faith in a company in *that* position?

Doty rushed out of the room. He needed to find Chuck Watson. It was very possible that, even with the tight restrictions that kept Dynegy from walking away from the merger, Enron may well have just met all of the requirements.

"Why did you put this out without telling us? What in the world are you doing?"

Watson was on the phone, chewing out Ken Lay. Nothing Lay said would calm his fury. He had taken a personal risk, injected his own company's cash to salvage Enron. And for what? To get refused access to the employees? To stand by idly while Enron burned through every penny he had given them? To be kept in the dark about ominous developments until the rest of the world already knew about them?

"Well, didn't you review this, Chuck?" Lay asked.

"We didn't get a copy until today!"

"I can't understand that," Lay said. "I got mine on Friday. I read the whole thing myself over the weekend."

Watson seethed. "Why didn't I get a copy, Ken?"

"I just assumed you did. I didn't know you didn't. Didn't even think to ask."

They needed to meet the following day, Watson said, at the Coronado Club in downtown Houston. "I've got a host of problems to discuss with you, Ken," he said. "Plan to be there about two or three hours."

What, Lay asked, were the primary issues?

"Ken, I am a billion dollars short!" Watson snapped. "And your guys can't tell me where it is!"

"We're going to need to take a look at the Raptor transactions," the Deloitte accountant said. "They involved a very aggressive accounting position."

The Raptor transactions? Bill Powers, head of the Enron board's special committee, wasn't sure what the accountant was talking about. It was that same afternoon, and Powers was receiving a primer on special-purpose entities. They had already discussed Chewco when the Raptors came up.

"Okay," Powers said. "So explain the Raptors."

The accountant launched into a monologue, describing how Enron shifted stock into the Raptor entities, took a small investment from LJM2, and then used the vehicles to avoid losses on its merchant investments. The concept confused Powers. *Enron* contributed the capital? Then how would it get losses compensated by the Raptors?

I guess I don't quite get it, he thought.

It would be weeks before Powers would realize the horrible truth. He did get it. The Raptors made no sense.

In the Rayburn House Office Building in Washington, Jim Greenwood, a Republican congressman from Pennsylvania, was standing up from his desk when he saw someone in the doorway.

"Hey, Mark, come on in," Greenwood said.

Mark Paoletta, chief counsel for the Energy and Commerce Subcommittee on Oversight and Investigations, crossed the room and took a seat, placing a pad of paper on the table. Greenwood joined him. Paoletta flipped open a folder, glancing at a list of issues he wanted to discuss.

After several minutes, Paoletta looked down at the next item. *Enron,* it read. He pulled out a few news articles he had brought along.

"Enron," he said, handing the articles across the table. "It's unbelievable what's going on there."

Greenwood skimmed through them. A look of recognition flashed in his eyes. "Oh yeah," he said. "I've seen this. It looks really interesting."

Paoletta spent a few minutes filling him in on what he had been told by his colleague David Cavicke days before over the Italian lunch. Greenwood was intrigued. "This sounds like an interesting one," the congressman said. "Can we do a hearing on this?"

Paoletta nodded. "We'll take a look at it and see if we can pull something together."

On November 20 at eleven o'clock, Chuck Watson strode off the fifth-floor elevator in the old Southwest Bank building and headed toward the entrance of the Coronado Club. Both Watson and Lay were familiar fixtures in the stately eatery, a prime magnet for Houston's power-lunch crowd. Watson was greeted effusively by the maître d' and whisked to a table.

Lay and Watson said their hellos and took their seats. Their discussion was civil but tense. The Coronado was not a place where patrons glided from table to table, chatting with acquaintances. Even so, both Lay and Watson could ordinarily count on being interrupted a few times. But no one came near them today as they huddled over their meals.

Watson brought out a typed list of issues that had arisen since the deal was signed and read them to Lay. The communications breakdowns. A too-rich severance plan.

"But the most important issue here is the missing cash, the $1.5 billion," Watson said. "We need an accounting of that, of where it went, by tomorrow."

There was another matter that had to be dealt with, Watson said. He looked across the table into Lay's eyes.

"A management change at the top of Enron is needed right away," he said. "It has to happen if we're going to stop the train and restore confidence and credibility."

Lay didn't change his expression. "I'll talk to the board," he replied.

Enron was cracking open. The quarterly filing had unnerved both the market and the credit-rating agencies. Its debt was put under review again, and its shares were the most actively traded on the New York Stock Exchange. That day, November 20, Enron stock fell almost 23 percent, closing at just about seven dollars a share.

Looking exhausted, Steve Kean walked across the fourth floor of the new building, holding a piece of paper in his hand. He spotted Ray Bowen and headed over to him.

"I've got a press release that Ken wants us to put out," Kean said, his voice weary. "Could you look at it?"

Bowen read it. It was silly; just a statement about Enron's trading volumes.

He made a face. "We can't put this out," Bowen said. "What do we accomplish by doing this?"

"Ray, I understand that," Kean replied.

He sighed. "But *you* have to understand, I'm working for a delusional chairman who thinks all the company has is a PR problem that can be solved with a press release."

On Wednesday, November 21, Dynegy's president, Steve Bergstrom, was sitting in Whalley's office, trying to get his head around Enron's cash situation. The levels had kept dropping and now, Whalley said, were down to $500 million.

"The traders have been pretty anxious to prove they're still in business," Whalley said. "They've been putting up cash collateral for big trades."

But they had hit a snag, Whalley said. The cash collateral didn't *keep* anyone doing business with Enron. Instead, once the company posted cash, other traders closed out the position from the individual trade, pocketed the money, and walked away. Enron's payments weren't fooling anyone.

"Greg, you've got to conserve cash over anything else," Bergstrom said. "That's the most important thing."

Whalley shrugged. Enron made markets. Conserving cash would kill the culture. It wasn't going to happen.

"Look," Whalley said, "we really stepped in it. But now we've got to get the merger back on track."

It was Friday, November 23, the day after Thanksgiving. A squad of managers from Enron surrounded him. Across the conference table, three Dynegy executives—including Keith Fullenweider, the deputy general counsel, and Rob Doty, the CFO—peered back at them skeptically.

The Enron managers had come with several messages. First, things were getting worse. The revelations in the quarterly filing had sent the trading business back into a tailspin. Enron's huge debt, on and off the books, had placed a stranglehold on the company. Doty argued that Enron had to meet with its banks and extend the repayment schedule.

"You're right," McMahon said. "We renegotiate with the banks or else we have to file bankruptcy."

Whalley held his index finger to his head. "Hey, I'll tell the banks I've got the gun to my head," he said.

But concessions from the banks alone couldn't solve all the problems with the deal. Enron was now dramatically different from what anyone had thought just two weeks before. New capital had to come from *somewhere*. Otherwise Enron wouldn't be able to survive long enough for the merger to close.

Bold action was needed. Negotiations had to be reopened, the two sides agreed. They would meet with the bankers and try to strike a new deal.

Enron's new GT Gulfstream corporate jet took off early the next morning. The cabin space was packed with executives, among them Lay, Whalley, McMahon, and Bowen. The plane was headed to the Westchester County Airport in New York. From there, the executives would travel by car to meetings at the Doral Arrowwood, an executive conference center and hotel, for the final negotiations with Dynegy and the banks.

Almost everyone on board was emotionally drained. The weeks of leaping from crisis to crisis, the endless negotiations, the grueling travel, the lost sleep had pushed them to their limits. Whalley alone seemed to have caught his second wind and was preaching about skydiving, a hobby he had relished since his days in the military.

"I'll tell you, you guys ought to try it," Whalley said. "Best adrenaline rush you'll ever get."

Lay was tired of the lecture, tired of Whalley. He turned to face him. "Greg, I've got enough of an adrenaline rush right now. I don't need to add to my list."

That morning, Jimmy Lee and a few colleagues from J. P. Morgan Chase squeezed in a round of golf before making their way to Arrowwood for the Enron meetings. It was a beautiful day, and the contingent arrived still dressed for the links.

"Okay," Lee said as he took a seat, "here's where we stand." Best estimate, Lee said, Enron needed three billion dollars, but that could be overcome. Citi would kick in a billion, Chase would step up for a billion. Then another billion from Dynegy, plus a public recommitment to the merger.

"That would take care of everything," Lee said.

Rob Doty from Dynegy answered. "We're committed to this transaction, and we will step up for our third," he said. "But we have concerns that have to be addressed."

Price was issue one, Doty said. Enron had gone down the tubes; the original merger price was out of whack.

Lay listened to the harangue, achingly aware that his counterpart, Chuck Watson, wasn't in the room. In fact, Watson hadn't bothered to come up to the meeting at all and was instead down in Mexico, vacationing. He was leaving success or failure in the hands of his lieutenants.

This, Lay knew, was a bad sign.

———

That night, Ken Lay and most of his management team got drunk. Nothing much had been accomplished that day, though the discussions were scheduled to pick up again the next morning. So, desperate for a reprieve, the Enron executives had ordered steak dinners at the hotel restaurant, and then downed bottles of wine.

"Here," Lay said late in the evening to McMahon. "Let me pour you some more."

Whalley was silent at the table. Repeatedly that day, he had warned the banks and Dynegy that three billion dollars might not be enough to save Enron; if it had to keep prepaying for physical gas, he told them, the company would burn through the new cash before the end of December.

As the night wore on, Bowen grew increasingly uncomfortable. Across from him sat Lay, looking broken. This was Ken Lay—*Ken Lay!* Mr. Houston!—tranquilizing himself. It struck Bowen as all so terribly sad.

"The banks are just stupid," Lay complained. But it would all work out, he promised. Enron would be saved.

An hour later, Lay headed up to his room. Soon after, McMahon needed to leave; he was so drunk he was unable to speak. His lips locked together, and he staggered off leaving his briefcase behind.

Bowen and Whalley sat alone at the table for a moment.

"I have no idea if this is going to work out or not," Whalley suddenly said. "But I'm going to fire every weapon I've got. Everything I can do to save this company. I'm not going to die with any bullets in my chamber."

He puffed a cigarette. "But if this Dynegy deal doesn't close and we end up bankrupt, I guess I'm going to spend the next couple of years giving depositions."

It would be months before Bowen would realize how accurate that prediction was.

The next morning at ten, everybody was back to work.

"Look," Jimmy Lee said. "There has got to be a restructuring of this deal, with three billion dollars of new cash."

He looked at the other faces in the room. "That has to be ready to be announced tomorrow," he said. "Or the right thing for Enron to do is just file bankruptcy."

After four hours of discussions, Dynegy was ready to issue their list of demands. Keith Fullenweider did the honors. "We've got an eight-point plan," he said.

The terms were harsh. Dynegy traders would move onto Enron's floors now. Banks would convert three billion dollars in debt into an ownership stake in the merged company and come up with three billion dollars in new credit. The acquisition price would be cut by more than half. And on and on.

Fullenweider looked across the table at Lay and McMahon, who were leading the discussions for Enron.

"We need a change in management," Fullenweider said brusquely. "Ken needs to step down. And we need a new CFO."

McMahon wrote that down. *Wow. They're firing me.*

"Okay," he said once the presentation was done. "Let us go over this, and we'll be back." The Enron executives left the room to talk through Dynegy's demands.

They returned in two hours. McMahon sat at the conference table and was the first to speak.

"Let me start this off, so everyone's sensitivities are okay," he said. "Ken is fine with leaving."

McMahon smiled. "Now, as appealing to me as replacing the CFO sounds—I mean, I would love to let someone else take the job right now—we're concerned. You haven't told us a name. So we would withhold approval until we know who you want, because this is a pretty critical role now."

Other than that, McMahon said, there were no issues.

What else did you think we were going to say? "No" isn't exactly an option for us anymore.

That afternoon, Steve Bergstrom, Dynegy's president, was in Houston. He called his negotiating team for an update on the Enron talks, then consulted a few of his financial experts. What, he asked, would the ratio of debt to capital be in this new merged company?

The answer came back quickly: 65 percent.

Bergstrom was thunderstruck. He had never imagined such a lopsided number. Enron's debt was impossible to overcome. It was like a virus, and as soon as Dynegy absorbed the body of Enron, it, too, would become infected. He contacted Watson.

"This deal will not work," he said. "Our trading business will not survive."

Watson was silent for a moment. "Let's try to finish it," he said.

The next day, Tuesday, November 27, Skilling was in a conference room at O'Melveny & Myers, scarcely able to contain his excitement. Three of his lawyers, including Bruce Hiler, were in the room. Then three more arrived—Bill McLucas and two of his colleagues from Wilmer, Cutler.

Skilling wanted to talk, to tell everyone his view of what had happened at Enron, how the company had been financially crippled by excessive spending on the international side and other silly mistakes. The lawyers took their seats.

Steven Rosen, a young Wilmer, Cutler lawyer, asked the first question. "Have you ever heard of a partnership called Southampton?"

Skilling didn't hesitate. "Nope," he said.

The whole interview struck Skilling as unpleasant. This wasn't the collaborative effort, the chance to expound on his views that he had been hoping for. These lawyers clearly thought he was *responsible*. He couldn't believe it.

"Would it surprise you to find out Fastow made about thirty-five million dollars from LJM in the last two years?" McLucas asked.

Skilling shrugged. "Depends on what he had at risk," he said. "You guys should do a value-at-risk analysis."

They haggled over the LJM approval sheets. Fastow had told the board that Skilling was approving each deal, McLucas said. That wasn't the process, Skilling retorted. Only Causey and Buy were formally meant to approve each deal. McLucas brought out an approval sheet for a deal named Margaux, the sole LJM transaction signed by Skilling.

"You signed this one," McLucas said. "There is a list of questions with answers, and you signed it."

"Now, wait a minute," Skilling shot back. "My signature doesn't mean I've reviewed these questions independently and satisfied myself the answers are right."

McLucas crossed his arms. "What does it mean, then?"

Skilling pointed at the signature page. "Right here, I saw Causey and Buy already signed," he said. "The fact that they signed it was good enough for *me* to sign without reviewing the same facts again."

That afternoon, the Dynegy deal was done—yet again. The Enron team had even hung around in Manhattan an extra day, waiting in the offices of Weil, Gotshal to receive a faxed copy of the revised deal-term sheet. It came over at about five o'clock, with Watson's signature at the bottom.

With work wrapped up, a limo drove everyone to Teterboro Airport, where the Enron plane was waiting. Lay took his seat, looking morose but satisfied. The plane was just getting ready to pull out toward the runway when a radio message came across to the pilot. The engines slowed. The pilot stood and walked back into the passenger cabin.

"Mr. Lay?" he said. "There's a Mr. Watson who needs to speak to you right away."

The four executives dragged themselves off the plane.

"My God!" McMahon exclaimed. "Will his ego never cease?"

They walked into the terminal and were directed to a room with a speakerphone. On the line was Watson, who was soon joined by Jimmy Lee from Chase, and Michael Carpenter from Salomon Smith Barney.

Watson's tone was ponderous. Something was up.

"I've been talking to my guys over the last number of days, and there are still some problems," he said. "We're very concerned about the debt-to-capital ratio of the merged company. Plus, there have been so many surprises."

Watson started ticking off the familiar list. The Rawhide debacle. The problems with the quarterly filing. The Glisan scandal. McMahon slumped into a chair and slapped his hand to his head. *Okay, I know!* That was why Enron had agreed to everything Dynegy had demanded.

Lay was impatient. "Chuck, we've been all through this," he said, his voice hoarse from a brewing cold.

"Well, but we have concerns," Watson began again.

Everyone in the room knew where this was going. Watson wanted to knock down the price again, and there was nothing they could do. They just had to take it. They waited for him to lower the boom.

"And that's why we've decided," Watson said, "that we're not going to pursue this merger."

The room went silent.

Lay argued. The deal was dead? Over the same problems everyone already knew about? *That* was why everyone had come to New York, he said, to help work through Dynegy's concerns. Jimmy Lee joined in, scolding Watson; the term sheet had just been signed, he said. Watson didn't back down, but he agreed to speak again with his team and consult his board. He promised to get back to them by morning.

The Enron team trudged back to the airplane. It was over. Their company, their careers. All of it was over.

As the plane took off, Lay heard a crack in his ear. The changing cabin pressure, combined with his cold, had caused some damage. He had just lost not only his company but his full hearing as well.

The next morning, November 28, Dynegy's traders stopped doing business with Enron. At 8:30, a desperate call came to Dynegy from Susan Pereira, an Enron trader.

"You're cutting us off!" she shouted. "Everyone has cut us off! I don't even know why I'm here."

The comments circulated through the trading room and quickly spilled out into the market. The world was waking up to the fact that Enron was on its last legs.

Less than two hours later, Lay and his senior management were waiting in the Enron boardroom for final word from Chuck Watson, hanging on to what they knew was a false hope for a miracle. No one was speaking.

At Dynegy, Watson had convened a board meeting by conference call and informed the directors that there had been some dramatic changes in the Enron deal.

"We don't believe we can proceed," Watson told the directors. Liquidity at Enron was drying up, its disclosure of information was repeatedly proving to be inadequate, and its top management was not exiting gracefully.

Steve Bergstrom took it from there. "It's not clear what we'll be getting if we buy them now. Their trading business has evaporated. Europe is just gone. We will be taking a significant risk, for very little benefit."

The discussion was brief. And the vote unanimous.

The phone rang in the boardroom. Lay hit the button on the speakerphone. Watson was on the line.

"I've tried really hard, and I've talked to my board," he said. "But I'm just not comfortable . . ."

That's it. Without waiting to hear another word, Ray Bowen hustled over to another phone in a corner. There was no need to hear any more; Enron, he knew, was bankrupt.

He had to move fast. Some $400 million was sitting in accounts at Citibank, which would now be owed far more than that in the bankruptcy. The bank might seize the money as its own. Bowen needed to move it. Enron owed basically nothing to Goldman Sachs. That's where it would go. He dialed the number for Mary Perkins, the assistant treasurer.

"Pull every penny we've got out of Citibank and wire it over to Goldman Sachs," he said. "Do it now."

McMahon immediately called the ratings agencies to let them know. Standard & Poor's was the first to downgrade the company. Its debt was now rated at junk levels. Trading in Enron shares was suspended. When it resumed, the price plummeted 75 percent, to just above one dollar.

Computer-support technicians at Enron watched as the commands went through. Millions and millions of dollars were moving out of Enron's bank accounts. They had no doubt what was going on. Someone was stealing all of Enron's cash.

One executive made a decision. He had to stop it. He telephoned the first reporter he could think of.

Goldman Sachs didn't want Enron's money. The case was too high-profile. The executives at the firm worried they were going to be dragged into something they weren't part of: the biggest bankruptcy in American history.

At first, Goldman refused to credit Enron's account. Instead, it parked the money while its executives anguished over what to do. Enron rattled its saber, threatening to sue if Goldman didn't deposit the cash.

The next morning, November 29, Ted Leh, an executive with the firm who handled the Enron account, telephoned Enron to announce that Goldman was getting out.

"We want your cash out of here by the end of the day," he said. "You guys are too hot. We don't want your money here. Take it somewhere else."

The rumblings in Houston were just beginning to shake the nation's capital. The Enron fiasco was already shaping up as a classic business scandal, one that raised fundamental questions about securities and accounting rules—and involved a close friend of the President's to boot. Suddenly, political reporters who rarely followed business news were questioning the nation's leaders about Enron.

The opening salvo came that Thursday during a regular press briefing held by Tom Daschle, the Senate Majority Leader. One reporter mentioned that Enron was teetering on bankruptcy. Would the Senate investigate? And should that change the public's view of electricity deregulation?

"Well, we're certainly going to try to find answers to the questions involving the collapse of Enron," Daschle replied. "I don't think that anybody knows yet just how this happened, and how it happened so quickly. I think we need to find as much information as possible."

Some $400 million was burning a hole in Ray Bowen's pocket, and he couldn't find a financial institution anywhere that was willing to take it.

Some people at Enron had a relationship with senior executives at Frost Bank, a sizable regional company, and arranged for an account to be opened there. But once everything was lined up, the bank's board of directors got skittish. Late that night, they nixed the arrangement.

Finally, Bowen found a tiny bank in Houston, a subsidiary of the International Bank of Commerce, that would take the money. Enron wired it over immediately.

People at Enron needed to be paid a lot more, just to make sure they didn't jump ship when the company filed for bankruptcy. If they did bolt, there was no way it would be able to come close to repaying its creditors.

The payment of so-called retention bonuses to senior managers at collapsing companies is a common practice, serving to lock them in place; if they accept, they are forbidden to leave for a period of time. Enron's board approved the immediate distribution of fifty-five million dollars to key executives, hoping to stem a tide of departures.

Now all the payments would have to come out of the tiny branch of the International Bank of Commerce. But Enron didn't even have checks for the account, and didn't want to risk having them bounce. It would have to pay the bonuses with cashier's checks.

That same night, Bowen got a call from Charles Delacey, the Enron executive working with the bank to assemble the fifty-five million dollars in cashier's checks. The bankers were on edge, he said, worried that something fishy was going on.

Now, Delacey said, there was a new problem. The new head of Enron's wholesale division, John Lavorato, was insisting on coming out to the bank to supervise the check writing. Lavorato was a typical trader—rambunctious, loud, and demanding—exactly the sort of personality that should be kept away from a bunch of edgy, starched-shirt bankers.

"I'm worried he's going to make them more nervous, Ray," Delacey said. "It could be a problem."

Bowen promised to call the man off. He hung up, then tracked down Lavorato's number.

"Hey," Bowen said, "I hear you're planning to show up at IBC tomorrow. I think that's a bad idea."

Lavorato stiffened. "I just want to make sure things are going okay," he said.

"John, don't go. These guys are already nervous."

"I just want to make sure it goes well."

Bowen sighed. "John, one bank has already thrown us out. If you go there and start throwing a temper tantrum and make these guys even more nervous, everybody's going to get screwed here. We're not going to have a bank to house our money. We're not going to be able to pay our people."

Lavorato paused. "Well, can I sit in the parking lot?" he asked.

"John, you can do whatever you want. But if they know you're there, I'll kill you."

Lavorato's voice broke. "I'm sorry, Ray, I'm sorry," he said. "I just want my money. I've never had a big payday. I just want my money."

Bowen almost gagged. Lavorato was a division leader. He had hundreds of people depending on him. And all he was talking about was his own cash.

"John, I don't give a shit," Bowen said. "I don't care about you." He hung up.

The next morning, the lobby at the International Bank of Commerce was jammed with Enron executives. The paperwork seemed to last forever, but eventually the bankers produced a small box, filled with cashier's checks.

A portion of the bonuses was going to be paid another way. But these checks for the remainder had to be purchased; they couldn't be used to draw down a specific client account. The bank president came toward Bowen, carrying another blank check, the kind that any of the local customers would receive when opening a new account.

"You need to fill out this check for the cashier's checks," the president said.

Bowen looked down at the check. Blank, nothing. No name, no logo. Just an account number. He started writing.

$38 million. Thirty-eight million and 00/100.

It was the largest check he had ever seen, much less written. He handed it to the bank president. The box of cashier's checks was turned over to David Oxley, an executive from Enron's human-resources division.

Oxley looked at Bowen. "See ya," he said.

He and a colleague, Robert Jones, ran out to their car, so they could deliver the checks to Enron's top employees.

Jones and Oxley parked their car and were hustling toward the Enron building. Before they could even get in, they stumbled across Lavorato and another division president, Louise Kitchen, who were waiting for them. They both demanded their checks right away. Oxley fished them out of the box and handed them over.

Kitchen and Lavorato hurried away. They wanted to get to their banks and deposit the checks while there was still a chance they would clear before Enron went under.

During the afternoon briefing that day, Ari Fleischer, the White House Press Secretary, pointed to a reporter midway back in the rows of seats filling the room.

"Senator Daschle is calling for an investigation into the collapse of Enron," the reporter said. "Does the President support that?"

Congress has an oversight role, Fleischer responded. "That includes anything that, in a case like this, the Senate sees fit, in terms of an investigation into the collapse of a company," he said. "That's the purview of the Congress."

Next question.

"All right," Lay announced. "I'm calling this meeting of the Enron board to order."

It was 8:12 the next night, December 1, a Saturday. Most directors were taking part in the meeting by phone. None had much stomach for what they had to do.

"All right, Greg," Lay said, looking at Whalley. "Please update us on the efforts being made to maximize the value of our wholesale-trading division."

Whalley nodded. Enron was in negotiations to strip wholesale trading out of the company and hand it off to UBS Securities. Enron would get basically nothing for the division, other than a piece of future profits. There were a few questions. Then Whalley stood and walked out. There was no better signal that he no longer considered himself responsible for anything other than the trading operations.

McMahon gave the final presentation on the company's cash position. It ended the week with $424 million in cash—practically nothing in the corporate world.

"All right," Lay said. "We now have to consider our option here for Enron to file for bankruptcy. Does anyone have any thoughts?"

The room was silent for a moment. "Who would've thought this?" Pug Winokur said. "I just can't believe this is happening."

There was little other discussion. "All right, do I hear a motion for that recommendation?" Lay asked.

John Duncan raised a hand. "So moved," he said.

"All in favor?" Lay asked.

Unanimous. "The motion carries," Lay said.

Tom Roberts, the Weil, Gotshal partner who had worked at Enron for just over a month, caught up with Bowen outside the boardroom. He and his partner, Glenn West, looked solemn.

"I guess you're the lucky guy," Roberts said.

Bowen shot him a look. "What do you mean?"

Roberts held up a document. "You need to sign the bankruptcy filing," he said.

Hours later, on the morning of December 2, the miracle of broadband finally transformed Enron, but not in the way the company's executives had once dreamed.

The lawyers worked for hours perfecting the paperwork before handing it off to their staff to convert into a digital format. In the Houston office of Weil, Gotshal, the records were provided to Steven Vacek, a paralegal.

Vacek signed on to his computer, using his high-speed connection to call up the Internet site for the United States Bankruptcy Court in New York. The Weil, Gotshal lawyers had urged Enron to file there; New York had the most sophisticated bankruptcy judges, they argued, and this was going to be one of the most complicated cases of all time.

Moving the mouse for his computer, Vacek clicked on the words "Document Filing System," then entered a password. At 4:28 in the morning, Vacek clicked the "submit" button, sending the papers to New York. Enron was officially bankrupt.

CHAPTER 23

IT WAS MONDAY MORNING, December 3, and Enron's offices were like a tomb. Armed guards roamed every floor, keeping watchful eyes on employees whose remaining time at the company could be counted in hours. Word was out that mass layoffs would be announced that very day. Already some division chiefs, nervous about confronting angry employees in the office, had simply fired them at home by phone.

Ray Bowen was responsible for eliminating jobs in two divisions: the treasury operations, which he now ran, and Enron Industrial Markets, where he had worked weeks before. In that second group, he had to let hundreds of people go, and he summoned them all together to deliver the bad news. Some wept. Others cursed. A woman in front raised a hand.

"How will I be able to file for unemployment and food stamps?" she asked plaintively.

Employees poured out of Enron into the streets of Houston. About four thousand people had been laid off, more than half its Houston workforce. Senior managers had fought to provide generous severance payments, but the lawyers had forbidden it. Creditors would just sue to get the money back, they said. They capped the payments at around five thousand dollars.

Reporters swarmed the plaza outside the Enron building as employees lugged boxes of belongings to the sidewalk. Many ignored the media's questions, but some were willing to share their thoughts and anger.

"These people who made $50 million a year, they destroyed the company because of their greed," Charles Weiss, once with the broadband division, told a reporter. "They're putting families at risk."

Someone was sitting outside Bowen's office, waiting for him to arrive.

It was Jim Bouillion, the executive in charge of purchasing Enron's insurance. The executive who, years before, had been unsuccessfully championed by McMahon at the PRC for bonuses and promotions. The executive whose contribution had been waved aside by top officers as insignificant, not in the same league as the work done by the whiz kids who put together deals like the Raptors.

As part of the reorganization of finance, Bowen now oversaw insurance, making him Bouillion's new boss. As he approached his office, Bowen greeted Bouillion and invited him in. Bouillion took a seat in front of the desk, and the two discussed the new arrangement for several minutes.

Bouillion swallowed. "Ray, I just want to thank you."

"For what, Jim?"

Bouillion's eyes filled with tears. "For not firing me," he said. "I've lost everything."

His kids were all out of college, Bouillion said, and he had thought that he was heading into the home stretch of his career. "But now, if I didn't have this job," he said, "I would literally be broke."

The words hit Bowen hard. Here was a man who had done his time, was happy to have survived, felt guilty that others hadn't. He saw the fear in Bouillion's eyes.

"Jim," Bowen said, "we're going to figure out how to make this as good as we can, no matter how shitty it was."

Bouillion thanked him and left the room.

In the weeks and months that followed, the new management became very familiar with the insurance that Bouillion had purchased for Enron. It was as complicated as McMahon had said years before when he had lobbied for him at the PRC, hardly a job, as other executives laughingly described it, that a monkey could handle. Bouillion's work had been spectacular; the insurance was ironclad. Enron and its executives were protected for every contingency, including the one they now found themselves in.

The financial structures and machinations so celebrated by the PRC were all gone; only Jim Bouillion's insurance remained. And now the executives who had once dismissed him as a nobody clung to his top-notch work like a life raft, hoping it would protect them from the hundreds of lawsuits they now faced.

"Is your name Jeffrey Skilling?"

Paul Minor, a former chief polygraph examiner with the FBI, watched as chart paper scrolled past, marking a spot where he had asked his question. Across from him sat Skilling; his shirt was off, with tubes wrapped around his chest and head, and wires attached to his fingers.

It was the next day. Skilling was in an interior conference room at O'Melveny & Myers, submitting to a lie-detector test. He wasn't quite sure why his lawyers wanted him to take it; they had said something about the benefit of having the results available. But he suspected that, in truth, they wanted to make sure he wasn't deceiving them.

He was terrified. What if he failed? Would his lawyers drop him as a client?

"Are you concerned that you might fail this test?"

"Yes," Skilling replied.

After a minute, Minor asked the first relevant question. "While president of Enron, were you aware of any improper financial arrangements that were concealed from the board of directors?"

"No," Skilling replied.

Over two separate tests, Skilling was asked questions about his own and Enron's finances. Repeatedly, he replied that he had done everything properly, taking only money that had been approved by the board and always believing the accounting for the partnerships was correct.

Minor made a few more marks on the paper, then stopped the machine. "Thank you very much," he said.

Skilling hesitated. "How did I do?" he asked.

Minor began removing the wires and tubes. "I'll communicate with your lawyers tomorrow with my written conclusions," Minor said.

Oh, God. He failed. He knew it.

Skilling put on his shirt as Minor left. In minutes, he headed to another room where his lawyers were waiting. He pushed open the door. Members of his team, Hiler and Elizabeth Baird, were waiting for him. Baird grinned.

"What?" Skilling asked. "What are you smiling at?"

"He told us you were telling the truth, with no attempt to deceive," she said. "Congratulations."

Skilling sighed and lowered his head onto the table.

"Oh, thank you, God," he said.

With the polygraph completed, three of Skilling's lawyers accompanied him the next morning to the SEC's Washington offices, where he would testify. Nine SEC lawyers, accountants, and other staffers were there. Skilling sat in the middle, watching Christopher Cutler, the SEC attorney who asked most of the questions.

"Mr. Skilling," Cutler asked, "when did you join the Enron Corporation?"

Skilling sniffed. "August 1, 1990," he answered.

The interview went on for two days. On the second morning, at 9:40, Cutler went back on the record. He picked up a document—the presentation made by Fastow to his LJM2 investors in the fall of 2000—and handed it to Skilling. As he flipped through it, a number jumped out at him on page 20.

It was the internal rate of return, or IRR, that LJM2 had obtained from the Raptors. And it was huge.

Skilling held up the document. "I would like to start out by saying that this is an interesting document."

He pointed out the column he had been studying. "The numbers, the current IRR and the projected IRR number, for a number of these transactions would strike me as being totally not understandable," he said.

If he had seen this document, Skilling said, he would have demanded that Fastow provide proof that LJM2 took sufficient risk to justify the huge returns. And he would have given him twenty-four hours to come up with it.

It was the closest Skilling had ever come to suggesting that Fastow might have cheated the company.

At about that same moment in Houston, three staffers from the House Energy and Commerce Committee, including Mark Paoletta and David Cavicke, were being escorted into a conference room on the forty-ninth floor of the Enron building.

The congressional competition was on. Numerous committees were scrambling to put together hearings on Enron. In a perfect world, the Energy and Commerce hearings would have been held in December, but they had already given up on that idea as unrealistic. There were too many documents to review, too many people to question.

Today, the staff was beginning that process. For days, Paoletta had been on the phone with Enron, trying to arrange for interviews. Finally, Enron had agreed to make McMahon, the new CFO, available for a few hours in Houston.

The men found their seats. Minutes later, McMahon, accompanied by Enron lawyers, swooped in. He made no effort to hide his impatience. His company had filed for bankruptcy four days ago, and now he was being forced to waste precious time. The congressional staffers, for their part, bridled at what they saw as McMahon's haughtiness.

"All right," Cavicke said. "I want to start off asking you about Enron's book of derivatives."

McMahon was clenching his teeth. Two hours into the interrogation, Cavicke was pressing him about the Rhythms hedge and the defects that led to the Swap Sub restatement.

"Look, I know what's in the 8-K," McMahon said sharply. "This transaction was done years ago. I didn't play any role in this. I really don't know the details."

Cavicke bristled. "You are the CFO of this company," he said sharply, "and you don't know the answer?"

"I've been the CFO for six weeks!" McMahon snapped back. "And I've been kind of busy."

"Well, what was the due diligence that Enron did in respect to this transaction?"

"I don't know."

The discussion veered into a recounting of the board meetings where LJM1 had been approved. What had McMahon thought about it at the time?

"I was bothered by the conflict and surprised that the board approved it," he replied.

For another hour the staffers hit him with more questions. *What about the financial incentives to managers? Explain Chewco. Tell us about Michael Kopper.*

One question came close to the mark. "Was there a whistle-blower letter relating to Swap Sub?"

To Swap Sub? There was the Watson letter relating to the Raptors and Condor. But they didn't ask about that.

"Not that I'm aware of," McMahon replied.

At the end of the interview, the House staffers weren't quite sure what they had. McMahon, they thought, hadn't been very helpful; his information had been scant.

They didn't realize how close they had come to the mother lode. McMahon had volunteered nothing that wasn't specifically requested, and they hadn't asked the right questions. So he didn't mention the bankers complaining of pressures to invest in Fastow's deals, or his efforts to get Skilling to rein things in, or the Watkins letter.

It would take weeks for those details to emerge.

The next day, Ken Lay sat waiting in the office of a Vinson & Elkins partner, ready for his secret meeting. Weeks before, after the first of a wave of shareholder lawsuits were filed, he had hired civil lawyers to represent him. But now things had entered a new dimension.

Prosecutors in several U.S. attorneys' offices had started investigating the company's collapse—in Houston, San Francisco, and New York, just to name a few. Lay was the executive at the top of the heap. He needed to be prepared.

A lawyer told him that the expected guest had arrived. Lay walked into an adjoining conference room. There, a white-haired man with a cherubic face was waiting. It was Mike Ramsey, one of Houston's best-known criminal lawyers.

Lay thrust out his hand. "Hi, Mike. How are you?"

The criminal defense of Ken Lay had begun.

David Duncan was sitting behind his desk at the Andersen offices, lost in thought as he looked through his office window, watching the downpour outside.

A partner in the Houston office, Emily Madison, dropped in. She was helping Andersen comply with subpoenas and had come to ask Duncan a few questions. He answered in a flat voice. He turned to look back out the window.

"You know," he said softly, "I guess I just didn't realize what my job was out here."

On the morning of December 12, Congressman Richard Baker pounded a gavel. It was the first congressional hearing into Enron's collapse ten days earlier. But what the hearing—sponsored by two subcommittees of the House Financial Services Committee—accomplished in speed, it sacrificed in detail; no Enron executive would testify, and few of the principals had even been interviewed at length.

After taking a moment to criticize Lay for choosing to attend a proceeding in bankruptcy court rather than appear at the hearing, Baker turned the floor over to the ranking Democrat, Paul Kanjorski of Pennsylvania.

"Thank you, Mr. Chairman," Kanjorski said. "Today's hearing will help us understand at least some of the factors that contributed to the downfall of Enron."

While he had not reached any conclusions about the events, Kanjorski said, there were certain issues of great concern that he had already identified.

"I would like to learn more about the serious financial harm done to thousands of Enron employees," he said. There had been press reports, he said, that employees had been blocked from selling shares in their retirement plans as the company careened into bankruptcy.

"Those hard-working Americans had to watch helplessly as their savings shrank without any recourse, while Enron's executives could apparently sell their stock options and avoid the financial pain," he said. "That is wrong."

The first myth about the Enron fiasco was taking root. For years to come, the story would be repeated endlessly, in tones of righteous indignation. The greedy bigwigs at Enron had blocked the rank and file from selling their Enron shares, perhaps in a bid to slow the stock collapse.

But the story was false. In reality, over just five days, circumstance had prevented Enron employees, including senior officers, from slightly decreasing a loss of $3.83 a share in their retirement accounts. And when the chance came to sell, many bought. But in the public consciousness, heart-stirring mythology won out over lackluster fact.

The hearing lasted most of the day. Just before the afternoon, a tall, gangly man with a slick of black hair joined others at the witness table. It was Joe Berardino, Andersen's chief executive, who had volunteered to testify.

Baker nodded slightly toward Berardino. "Before I recognize you for your comments, Mr. Berardino, I just want to, by way of personal acknowledgment, express my appreciation to you and the manner in which you have responded to the committee," he said. "I wish all officials who had similar participation in the issues before the committee had exercised your judgment."

Relief swept over Berardino. A good beginning. "That's very kind of you, Mr. Chairman," he said.

He glanced down at his prepared text. "I'm here today because faith in our firm and the integrity of the capital markets has been shaken," he began.

It was imperative, he said, for the causes of Enron's downfall to be understood, so that actions could be taken and policies adopted to restore public confidence.

Defects with two special-purpose entities had forced Enron to restate its financial results, he said. He didn't divulge the names, but he was referring to Chewco, which was undone by the reserve account, and Swap Sub, which didn't have the capital to be treated as independent.

"Of the larger of these, which was responsible for 80 percent of the SPE-related restatement, it appears important information was not revealed to our team," he said, referring to the Chewco side deal.

He looked up at the faces of the congressmen on the panel. "We have notified the audit committee of possible illegal acts within the company," he said.

The next morning, Causey stormed down a hallway on the fiftieth floor, carrying a copy of the morning newspaper. Near his doorway, he veered left, heading into McMahon's office.

"Can you *believe* what Berardino said?" he fumed. "They told the board about illegal acts? *I* never heard that. Ever."

McMahon squinted at Causey, puzzled. "Well, do the minutes reflect anything like that?"

"No!" Causey shot back. "And Lay said they were *never* told by the auditors about illegal acts."

McMahon paused for a second. "So what are you telling me? That he lied to Congress?"

Causey shook his head. "I don't know," he said. "He certainly didn't tell the facts."

Berardino hadn't lied, but he had been mistaken. The team that had drafted his comments had, in fact, not been aware of many of the details of the Chewco transaction and the events that followed the discovery of the side deal.

So while several accountants had concluded that the hidden reserve accounts might constitute a crime, David Duncan never formally conveyed those suspicions to the audit committee, a group he appeared before on November 18, fifteen days after the discovery of the secret deal.

Andy Fastow had fled the country. Maybe to Israel, possibly to Brazil. The rumor rocketed rapidly around Houston and Washington and in no time turned up in news reports.

There were good reasons to believe it. On November 14, Fastow had been subpoenaed to give testimony to the SEC. But on the agreed-upon day, Fastow didn't show. The SEC had gone to court, asking a judge to compel his appearance. Ken Johnson, a spokesman for Energy and Commerce, added fuel to the fire by stating that House investigators couldn't find him.

Simply denying the rumor would do little to convince a skeptical public, Fastow's lawyers realized. So on the afternoon of December 12, David Boies, a topflight litigator who at that point was leading the defense, called a press conference at his Manhattan offices. Once the reporters were settled, Boies strode into the room, followed by Fastow. The two men took seats behind a table cluttered with reporters' microphones.

Fastow, wearing a gray suit and a red tie, smiled wanly. Boies addressed the crowd. "There have been increasingly over the past twenty-four hours a variety of reports that Mr. Fastow was not available," he said. "He has not fled the country. He is going to respond to inquiries. He will provide documents."

Fastow sat still, looking ill at ease. Reporters began pressing questions, and Boies fielded them all, refusing to let Fastow speak. The mood in the room grew testy; couldn't Fastow say *anything*? Boies turned to his client and prompted him.

"Hello," Fastow said. "I wish you a happy holiday season, and thank you for coming."

And that was it.

At nine on the morning of December 14, Lay's secretary notified him that Joseph Berardino was on the line. Lay leaned over his desk and picked up the phone.

"This is Ken Lay," he said.

"Hi. Joe Berardino."

Lay's lawyers had instructed him days before on what to say when the time came for this conversation.

"I appreciate the call," he said. "But I've been advised it's not wise for us to discuss this matter. I regret that, but that's where it is."

Berardino poked around a little bit, trying to see if he could get some sort of dialogue going.

"Joe, I'm sorry," Lay said. "I can't do this."

A minute later, the two corporate chieftains, each trying to smother the flame of scandal licking at his feet, bid one another a polite good-bye.

Fastow walked through the doorway of Michael Kopper's house. The two had been speaking on and off during the unfolding debacle at Enron. But now, on this day in December, they knew the magnitude of what was unfolding. There were investigations, both criminal and civil. They needed to be sure their story was straight.

There was one thing particularly worrying Fastow, a single transaction that he feared posed the greatest threat to him. He looked at Kopper.

"Now you know," Fastow said, "I never received any money from RADR."

RADR. Their first successful crime together. The one that had resulted in Kopper funneling huge sums of cash from front investors to his boss. Fastow's statement now was a lie. Kopper knew it. He understood.

"Yes," he said.

He was the first major player in the door, the first Enron executive promising to tell criminal investigators everything he knew. He agreed to testify for immunity.

A secret meeting was arranged between the FBI and the executive. It was an event known in law enforcement as "queen for a day," when a potential defendant could come in and spill his guts to the government, in hopes of striking a deal. If prosecutors didn't like what they heard, the statements couldn't be used as direct evidence.

For hours that December day, the FBI agents threw questions at the executive. The answers were always pretty much the same: sure, there were suspicious things he had seen, but he had never committed a crime, never done anything that wasn't on the up-and-up.

The interview ended, and it didn't take long for the government to reach its conclusion. As far as prosecutors and agents were concerned, Ben Glisan was lying.

"How come we're not defending the company!" John Duncan shouted. "How come we're not defending the board!"

Duncan, the head of the board's executive committee, was on the phone with Kean and Palmer, the executives running Enron's communications strategy. The news stories were just terrible, he said. They never gave Enron's side. How come Enron wasn't putting up more of a fight?

Kean responded. "John, there's not a lot we can say, because we don't know the facts. We've got Bill Powers's investigation that's going on to reveal the facts."

"Bill Powers!" Duncan shot back, furious. "Bill Powers does not represent the company. I don't know what he's going to say. It could be terrible! I just want to know who is going to defend the company!"

Finally, after several minutes, Duncan calmed down. "Listen, I know this is impossible for you guys. I just needed to get that off my chest. It's so frustrating."

The wheels were coming off the Enron criminal investigation. With so many prosecutors' offices involved, different and often conflicting demands for evidence were being delivered to the company from all over the country. Nobody was in charge of an overall strategy.

Then, a key player in the probe dropped out. The U.S. attorney's office in Houston withdrew, ruling that too many of its top prosecutors were conflicted in a case involving what had once been the city's premier corporate citizen.

By that time Robert Bennett—the Washington super-lawyer with Skadden, Arps, Slate, Meagher & Flom who had represented former President Clinton—had begun working on Enron's behalf. And his first task was simple: get the prosecutors to decide who was running the show.

Bennett telephoned David Margolis, the associate deputy attorney general.

"Enron wants to cooperate," he said. "We just don't know who to cooperate with."

Word of Bennett's complaint soon reached Michael Chertoff, the wiry and aggressive chief of the Justice Department's criminal division. For months, Chertoff had been spearheading the division's antiterrorism efforts and had been only vaguely aware of the goings-on in Houston.

Now, after hearing about Bennett's concerns, Chertoff made himself familiar with the Enron inquiry. With Houston out of the picture, a unique opportunity had been created, he thought. He contacted Margolis.

"We should step in and set up a task force," Chertoff said. "Recruit top assistant U.S. attorneys to put this case together, really give it the prominence and attention that it seems to deserve."

Margolis agreed. The Enron case would have its own team of prosecutors to dig down every rat hole until they figured out what crimes had been committed and by whom.

Scouting around for someone to lead the task force, Chertoff sounded out Robert Mueller, the former U.S. attorney in San Francisco who had been appointed director of the FBI just months before.

"You might want to look at Leslie Caldwell," Mueller said. "She was really terrific when I was out at the U.S. attorney's office in San Francisco."

Chertoff knew Caldwell by her reputation as a no-nonsense, aggressive prosecutor who had taken on tough criminals in Brooklyn before moving to San Francisco, where she ran the office's securities-fraud unit. She had handled complex accounting-fraud cases. She was perfect.

But before he could call her, a sudden development emerged that rapidly transformed the criminal case.

In Andersen's Houston offices, a lawyer flicked on a laptop computer. Within minutes the lawyer—from Davis Polk & Wardwell, now representing Andersen on Enron—clicked open an e-mail program and began scrolling through messages, looking for information to help prepare partners for interviews with the Energy and Commerce Committee.

There wasn't a lot there. Everything after November 9 looked normal, but before that it was thin. In no time, the lawyer and his colleagues were examining other laptops. Time and again, they found the same thing—a lot that seemed to be missing before November 9. It was almost as if someone had purposely deleted the information.

The lawyers decided to contact Andersen's general counsel, Andrew Pincus.

Early the next morning, January 3, a Thursday, Joe Berardino was in his Chicago office at Andersen when he received a telephone call from Pincus.

"Joe, we may have a new issue down in Houston."

"What's happening?"

"Our lawyers have been getting people ready for their testimony and looking through their e-mail records," Pincus said. "But the files are just too clean. We don't know what that means yet, but I'm worried."

Thoughts rushed through Berardino's mind. He and his team had been working so hard to pull Andersen through this Enron mess. His congressional testimony had all been part of that, and he had come away satisfied he had accomplished a lot. But if somebody was out there destroying records . . .

He didn't want to think about it. Not until he knew more. "Follow up on this fast," Berardino said.

"We are. We're interviewing people now. And we're scheduled to keep interviewing right through the weekend."

"Fine," Berardino said. "Give me a call early tomorrow morning, and update me on what you learn."

The call to Berardino came the next morning at eight, and the information was devastating. Pincus, calling with a Davis Polk lawyer on the line, pulled no punches.

"We've got a big problem," he said. "We've talked to a lot of people, and it seems that a lot of them have been deleting e-mails in recent weeks."

Berardino sucked in a deep breath. "What kind of quantity are we talking about?"

Staggering, Pincus replied.

The three men discussed alternatives, then Berardino issued his instructions. First, Andersen should notify the government right away. Then he wanted people in Houston interviewed night and day until the firm knew what happened. Finally, he wanted technicians brought in to try to recover the e-mails from the Houston and Chicago servers.

None of them knew that the situation was far worse than they imagined. Regardless of how many e-mails Andersen recovered, tens of thousands of documents had already been destroyed. And nothing could bring them back.

The news from Andersen knocked the wind out of official Washington. How could it have happened? How could a modern company have had such terrible procedures that employees could destroy evidence without being detected?

After being briefed on the matter, Michael Chertoff decided to alert Larry Thompson, who, as deputy attorney general, was second in command of the department. Chertoff popped into Thompson's expansive office that afternoon.

"Larry, you got to hear this one," Chertoff began.

Thompson sank back in his thick leather chair and listened in astonishment. He shook his head. *Wow*, he thought, *somebody really screwed up here.*

"How could the lawyers let that happen?" he asked. "They didn't know to send out a memo telling everybody not to destroy everything?"

This, the two men agreed, was a new avenue of investigation. And Justice still hadn't started putting together its team for this new task force. That was something Chertoff decided to fix that very afternoon.

In San Francisco, the day was winding down for Leslie Caldwell, the city's top white-collar prosecutor. After work, she was planning to go with friends for drinks at Stars, a local hangout. But just when the workweek seemed almost finished, Chertoff called from Washington. This, she knew, could only mean something important was brewing.

Chertoff got right to the point. "We're forming a task force to handle the Enron investigation," he said. "Bob Mueller thought you would be the perfect person to be the head of it, and I wanted to see if you were interested."

Caldwell knew a fair amount about Enron; her team had already opened its own investigation into the company's collapse. Still, she wasn't ready to jump without giving the idea more thought. Not on a Friday afternoon.

"Let me think about it over the weekend," she said. "I'll give you an answer on Monday."

That was fine, Chertoff said. But when he hung up, he was confident that he had bagged his prey.

The weekend was hell for Joe Berardino. He stayed huddled at his Connecticut home, receiving periodic updates from Houston, and by Sunday, the ugly truth had emerged. This wasn't just about e-mails; there had been a wholesale destruction of Enron-related documents, all taking place when the firm knew an SEC investigation was under way.

Berardino began planning his counterattack. First thing Monday, he decided, he would notify the firm's five-member Global Executive Committee. Then the public had to be told. But how? A misstep here could spell ruin; if public companies feared Andersen had committed a crime, the firm could lose its client base. He was in anguish.

What do we do?

Holding her ticket in one hand, Leslie Caldwell stood with a line of passengers, waiting to board a plane to Washington. It was January 9, a Wednesday, and she was on her way to her new job as head of the Enron Task Force.

It had been an easy decision. Over the weekend, she had consulted friends and colleagues, and their verdict was unanimous: how could she ever consider *not* taking the job? So, that Monday, she had phoned Chertoff to let him know she was coming aboard. Chertoff told her to get to Washington quickly; Andersen's problems were apparently much worse than anyone had anticipated. With that, Justice announced the creation of the task force.

Caldwell walked onto the plane and found her seat. For the next few hours, she fretted. This was going to be the biggest stage she had ever performed on, yet she had no idea whether a crime had even been committed at Enron. That was scary. If there was nothing to find, would the whole world see her as having blown the investigation?

What if there's no case? What if it doesn't exist?

The next morning at 9:10, a crowd of government officials entered the Oval Office. The atmosphere was calm and relaxed. In the wake of the September 11 attacks, Bush had won soaring public support for his quick responses, including a war in Afghanistan to root out terrorists. Now, his Administration was turning to domestic matters.

On the front burner this morning were the Administration's plans to protect pensions and improve internal oversight at corporations. The Enron debacle had been front-page news, with heartrending stories abounding of employees and investors who were wiped out. It was an issue that demanded the attention of the nation's leaders.

As they stepped in, the officials—members of Bush's economic team and a few political and communications staffers—jostled for seats. Paul O'Neill, the Treasury Secretary, found one in the center of the room; Don Evans, the Commerce Secretary, sat nearby.

Bush sailed in and took charge, conveying an air of excitement. "What are we going to do about this pension problem?" he asked, sounding jovial.

The mood in the Oval Office was dismayed, almost regretful. Enron's sudden, precipitous collapse and the suspicions of wrongdoing were shocking, the officials agreed. So many people had been harmed; perhaps the Administration could have minimized the damage, someone said.

"It's too bad that none of us spoke with the folks in Houston," Bush mused.

O'Neill interrupted. "Wait a minute, Mr. President," he said. "I *did* talk to Ken Lay not long before Enron filed for bankruptcy. And I know that Don did, too."

All eyes turned to O'Neill and Evans. Suddenly, the wished-for contact between the Administration and Enron didn't seem like such a good idea after all.

Bush held up a hand. "Tell me all about it."

O'Neill unveiled the whole story. Lay, he said, had clearly been angling for a federal bailout while never explicitly asking. In the call to Evans, O'Neill said, Lay had pressed for the government to lean on the credit agencies. But no one took any action, he said. Evans spoke up, agreeing with O'Neill's version of the events.

Bush considered that. "We should tell the media that this happened immediately. Get it on the record."

The decision was made. Ari Fleischer, the White House Press Secretary, would let the media know. But not until after Bush himself met with reporters to announce the plans for the Administration's pension initiative.

Minutes later, at 9:42, reporters arrived in the Oval Office, where Bush sat surrounded by his economic team.

"Thank you all very much for coming," Bush began. "One of the things that we're deeply concerned about is that there have been a wave of bankruptcies that have caused many workers to lose their pensions."

So now, Bush said, the Treasury, the SEC, and other federal agencies were working together to come up with recommendations for reforming the system.

"This is an important part of, obviously, other investigations that are ongoing," Bush said. "The Justice Department announced and informed us late yesterday that they're in the process of investigating aspects of the Enron bankruptcy. The Administration is deeply concerned about its effects on the economy."

Bush opened the floor for questions.

"When was the last time you talked to either Mr. Lay or any other Enron official about the—about anything?" one reporter asked. "And did the discussions involve the financial problems at the company?"

"I have never discussed with Mr. Lay the financial problems of the company," Bush began. "I have not met with him personally."

There was a question about whether the Administration had concerns about the political fallout of the debacle.

Bush was almost nonchalant. "He was a supporter of Ann Richards in my run in 1994," Bush said. "She had named him the head of the Governor's Business Council. And I decided to leave him in place, just for the sake of continuity. And that's when I first got to know Ken, and worked with Ken, and he supported my candidacy."

The words left no doubts among the reporters in the room. Bush was distancing himself from a man who for years had been one of his biggest political boosters.

About that time, investigators from a range of federal agencies gathered in the SEC's Washington offices. The enforcement staff, including Thomsen and Steve Cutler, were there, joined by Leslie Caldwell. The FBI sent over Special Agent Joe Ford, who had spent months tracking terrorists' cash before being attached to the Enron team. Surrounding that core group were lawyers, investigators, and others now part of the sprawling inquiry.

The SEC had been digging into the case far longer than anyone else in the room but had only scratched the surface. Some of the key witnesses, like Fastow and Kopper, had so far refused to testify before the agency, so many pieces of the puzzle were still missing.

"It's just our initial view," one SEC official warned. "But there may well not be a criminal case here, outside possibly obstruction of justice at Andersen."

Linda Thomsen agreed. "Admittedly, what we are seeing is limited," she said. "But we don't see the criminal angle yet. We see it more as a disclosure case."

Joe Ford spoke up. "I think it's highly unlikely there's no criminal case," he said, "particularly given the speed and the severity of Enron's meltdown."

"I agree," Caldwell interjected. "The magnitude strongly suggests a likely crime in this case."

In the middle of the conversation, Caldwell's cell phone rang. She pulled it out and clicked a button. It was a police officer from Sausalito, California, where Caldwell lived.

Oh, this can't be good.

"I was calling to let you know that your apartment's been burglarized," the policeman said. A lot of material had been thrown all over the place, he explained.

The officer said that he had tracked Caldwell down to her San Francisco office, only to find that she had gone to Washington to take over the Enron investigation.

"So I was wondering," he said, "if you think this might have anything to do with the Enron case?"

Not likely. "I don't think so," Caldwell replied. "I don't think they even know I'm doing the case yet."

Reporters were practically swarming Ari Fleischer, the White House Press Secretary. That morning, in the last moments of an informal briefing, Fleischer had mentioned the contacts between Lay and members of the Cabinet. Now, as the formal briefing got under way at 12:20, reporters were demanding more information.

Was Lay asking for a bailout? Did O'Neill know about Enron's losses before investors did? Did Evans and O'Neill tell the President about the calls? Why wouldn't they have told the President? Shouldn't they have told the President? Is the President disappointed they didn't tell him? Did anybody tell the Vice *President?*

Fleischer showed no signs of his frustration. "I just want to remind everybody," he cautioned, "the difference between communication and contact and wrongdoing."

But it was too late; what had been a flagging, dying news story about a company that had gone bankrupt a month before was suddenly transformed. Now, however tangentially, the case seemed to have touched the White House. Still, the chronicle of events remained dense, creating an immense thicket of information too convoluted to capture the public imagination. All that was needed was a spark, a development so simple to grasp that this simmering scandal could explode across the front pages.

Hours later, the spark.

In Chicago, Joe Berardino signed off on the Andersen press release announcing the discovery of document destruction in Houston. The release attributed the actions to "individuals in the firm." The announcement was distributed to reporters around the country.

The firm was barraged with questions, and within hours Andersen put out another release, straightening out a few matters of confusion. Among them— yes, those "individuals in the firm" were indeed Andersen personnel.

That same afternoon, John Ashcroft, now the United States Attorney General, met with his staff. His relationship with Lay was certain to be an issue. Lay had raised money for his Senate bid and, at the secret behest of the Bush campaign, done the same for his aborted presidential effort. If a Justice Department task force was handling this case, Ashcroft decided, his obvious conflicts barred him from playing a role.

Ashcroft informed his staff that he was recusing himself from the Enron investigation and handing responsibility for it to his deputy attorney general,

Larry Thompson. At that moment, Thompson was in Tucson, mingling with federal judges at a committee meeting for the Judicial Conference. He was called on his cell phone, and told he was needed back in Washington, to take over supervision of the Enron criminal investigation.

"He was a supporter of Ann Richards in my run in 1994."

Ken Lay sat in front of his home television that night, listening to George Bush's comments from earlier that day. He watched as Bush portrayed him as simply a holdover from the administration of Governor Ann Richards, seeming to suggest that they had never really been all that friendly.

True, he had always been closer with the President's father, but even so, it seemed silly to imply their relationship had somehow been a distant one.

Linda shook her head. "It's really surprising to me that he's doing that," she said.

Her husband shrugged. It was just politics, though likely *bad* politics, he figured.

"Probably it'll do him more harm than good," he said. "Probably just better to acknowledge the obvious, acknowledge the relationship."

Lay's point was proven weeks later when Ann Richards—the sitting governor he had helped defeat by supporting Bush—went on *Larry King Live*. In plainspoken terms, Richards proclaimed her admiration for Lay and her surprise at Enron's collapse. Then, she chastised Bush for glossing over his relationship with a man who helped elect him.

"Wasn't that silly of George Bush?" she said, laughing. "What a stupid thing."

Skilling was sitting in his office, on the telephone with his lawyers, when he glanced through the windows into his kitchen. He saw Cliff Baxter, his long-time friend and once one of Enron's best deal makers, just standing there. Baxter caught his eye and gave a quick wave.

Rebecca Carter appeared in the office. "Cliff's come by," she said. "What do you want me to do?"

"Just a second," Skilling said to Hiler, putting the call on mute. "Look, I'm going to be stuck on this thing for at least a couple of hours. Tell Cliff I'll call him."

"Okay," Carter said. She headed back to the kitchen.

Baxter didn't leave. Instead, he hung around the house, at one point helping Carter unpack the dishes. Hours later, Skilling emerged from the office.

"Hey, Cliff, I'm really sorry," he said.

Baxter raised his hands and smiled. "No problem," he said. "Let's go shoot the shit."

They headed out back, taking seats in the screened-in porch. Baxter started talking. He was furious—*furious*—at the plaintiffs' attorneys suing Enron. Because of them, he said, Enron's executives were being trashed.

"I'm not giving them a penny," Baxter said. "I'd rather pay my lawyers and fight this to the death."

The worst, Baxter said, was his boat. He had ordered a new one before the scandal broke, but his lawyers told him to cancel the contract because it would look bad. His boat! These lawyers were wrecking his life!

Suddenly, the tone of the conversation changed. "You know, I understand why my father was the way he was," Baxter said. "He was just a good guy trying to get by."

Wow. This is different. As long as Skilling had known Baxter, he had listened to his friend rage against his father for his drinking and other personal flaws. Now that was all put aside.

"I understand what it's like to battle the world now," Baxter said. "I didn't realize how bad the world could be. I bet my father knew that."

The moment slipped by. Together, the two men railed against the legal system, which had led to all of these investigations. "We're good people!" Baxter shouted.

"I know, Cliff. I'm there, man."

"Can you believe this is allowed to happen?"

They talked for hours. Finally, as the sun was setting, Skilling began to ease his friend toward the door. Baxter turned and looked at him.

"You know what this is like?" he said. "It's a beautiful day, the sun is shining, and you walk out of your house. And the temperature is perfect, and all the kids in the neighborhood are riding bikes and throwing baseballs, and all the adults are chatting over fences. It's just one of those great, great days. And you're talking with the kids and throwing the ball and waving to your neighbors."

Baxter shook his head. "And then, all of a sudden, your next-door neighbor comes up to you and says, 'You're a goddamned child molester.' Then turns around and walks back into his house and closes his door."

Then, he said, the neighborhood goes silent. "All the neighbors heard it, all the kids heard it. You're going, wait a minute, one minute ago it was as good as it can get, and then all of a sudden you're a child molester."

He looked Skilling in the eye. "And from then on, it doesn't matter what you say. It'll never wash off."

Skilling wasn't quite sure what to say. It wasn't that bad. Baxter, he thought, was getting a little overheated.

The men muttered a few parting words, then Baxter went on his way, leaving Skilling behind to forever wonder about the clues he had missed the last time he saw his friend alive.

By Friday afternoon, January 11, the somber mood in Andersen's Houston office had decayed into despair. One at a time, employees and partners were escorted into private offices where lawyers grilled them about the shredding. By then, everyone had already told about the e-mail from Nancy Temple urging the Enron team to get in compliance with the document policy. It was an uncomfortable set of facts.

Shannon Adlong, David Duncan's secretary, was asked to meet with the lawyers. She felt torn; she didn't think Duncan had done anything wrong. He had followed orders, and now the firm was hanging him out to dry. After her meeting, she tracked down her boss to let him know what had happened.

"Well, you know," Duncan said, "all I can tell you is to tell the truth and to be honest."

He glanced away. "I don't know what's going to become of all this. I wish I had never received that e-mail."

Boxes of documents were piled high around the offices of the Energy and Commerce investigations subcommittee. The records had been shipped over by Enron in response to a document request, and now staffers were digging through the paper, searching for anything that might be useful at a hearing.

A committee staffer, Peter Spencer, was thumbing through a stack of papers. One looked different; it had no letterhead, no signature. It was apparently a personal letter addressed to Ken Lay. Spencer started reading.

Dear Mr. Lay, Has Enron become a risky place to work? For those of us who didn't get rich in the last few years, can we afford to stay?

Spencer's astonishment grew. This letter had been written to Lay, accusing Enron of engaging in an accounting fraud! He hurried over to find his boss.

The letter that Sherron Watkins had toiled over months before had found a newly receptive audience.

Oh, my God! It's a smoking gun!

Mark Paoletta, the chief counsel for the subcommittee, read the anonymous letter that had been left on his desk. It was his job to put together the

Enron hearing, and now he wanted to know everything he could about this warning that had been sent to Lay.

He quickly learned that Watkins had been the author. It was all too delicious. This was a document that could drive an entire hearing. He wanted to think about it, to decide how best to handle this stunning revelation.

All he had to do was outlast Lay. It couldn't be much longer. Mark Palmer was sure of it. Maybe a few more days.

Palmer had been quietly battling Lay's worst impulses for weeks. Over and over, Lay seemed to argue that Enron's troubles were just caused by bad publicity, not by a flawed business model, not by a mismanaged balance sheet.

Signs of Lay's resistance to the truth were everywhere. An old favorite, Beth Tilney, who specialized in happy-face posters and who had been arguing about the need to defend Lay, was suddenly at his side again. There was no better sign that Lay didn't understand what was happening. Tilney, whose husband, Schuyler, was a Merrill banker in charge of the Enron relationship, was an investor in LJM2.

So it was no surprise to Palmer when Lay summoned him up to his office to let him know that he had a new boss.

"Mark, I'm going to have Beth Tilney in charge of public relations," he said. "What do you think of that?"

Palmer was past the point of corporate diplomacy.

"Well, Ken, it stings," he said simply. "And I don't think the two of you are seeing the big picture here."

Lay sat back in his seat. "What do you mean by that?"

"Ken, if all we're going to focus on is salvaging your reputation, it's going to look like that's all we're doing," Palmer responded. "The best way to do that is to pay everybody back. That should be the message."

Palmer gave Lay a stern look. "We can't change the past, we can't define the past, and I'm sure as hell not going to defend the past," he said. "Now we have to focus on moving forward, focus on the future."

Lay was silent for a second. "Beth's going to be your boss," he said simply.

Fine, Palmer said. He turned to head out the door.

I just need to outlast this guy.

On the morning of January 12, a Saturday, *The Washington Post* splashed the latest damaging article about Enron across its front page. "Hidden Numbers Crushed Enron," the headline read. " 'Partnerships' Shielded $600 Million Debt."

At his home, Mark Paoletta from Energy and Commerce read the article in a fury. It revealed the role played in Chewco by Barclays Bank. This was information that Paoletta's staff had already figured out, and he had been considering exploring the issue at the upcoming hearing. But now this article—leaked by whom? the bank? the subcommittee's Democratic staff?—had preempted him. A lot of work for nothing. But there wasn't much he could do about it now. He was supposed to take his seven-year-old daughter to her basketball game that morning, and they needed to get going.

About an hour later, Paoletta was sitting in the gym, stewing as he watched his daughter play, when suddenly it hit him. *Sherron Watkins*.

If the Barclays information wasn't fresh, why not use the Watkins letter for a hearing? Or better yet: put out a letter now from the committee and subcommittee chairmen, demanding to know what Enron did about the allegations. With untold numbers of congressional committees grabbing pieces of the Enron inquiry, that letter would put Energy and Commerce at the lead of the pack.

At halftime, Paoletta walked out to the hallway. He needed to call his staff director and get this idea in motion.

Two days later, David Duncan was walking down Fifth Street in northwest Washington, accompanied by three lawyers from the firm of Sullivan & Cromwell. He was feeling anxious and uncomfortable. No surprise, since he was about to meet with representatives of the FBI, the Justice Department, the SEC, and the Internal Revenue Service to answer their questions about Enron and the document destruction.

Duncan and his lawyers walked into 450 Fifth Avenue, the modest headquarters for the SEC, and were escorted upstairs to a conference room. It was packed with people.

"Mr. Duncan, I'm Leslie Caldwell, and I'm a prosecutor with the U.S. attorney's office in San Francisco."

The Enron Task Force's new director—a title she had not yet adopted as her own—looked hard at the Andersen partner who had overseen the disaster at Enron.

"I'm relatively new to the Department of Justice's case," she said. "Because of that, I'm not prepared to say whether you're a target of this investigation. If you were, I would tell you. But right now, I just don't know."

Duncan nodded silently. The gravity of the moment was setting in on him.

First, the logistics. Both the SEC and Justice had agreed to hold these discussions with Duncan under terms that his statements would not be used against him in the future, except to challenge later testimony or unless he lied. But Charles Clark, a top SEC official in the room, noted that Duncan's agreement with the prosecutors was separate and apart from his deal with the agency.

"Now," Caldwell said, "the focus of our discussion today will be the destruction of documents relating to the auditing and other services Andersen performed for Enron."

She eyed Duncan. He was pale and jittery. "Why don't you offer your understanding of those events?" she asked.

Duncan nodded. He'd done nothing wrong. He just followed the lawyers' intructions. He needed to make that clear.

"It all began on October 12, when Mike Odom forwarded an e-mail to me from Nancy Temple in our legal department."

At the office of Energy and Commerce, the final touches were going on a letter to Lay. It was all about the Watkins memo, quoting extensively from it and demanding related records. The letter, signed by Congressmen Billy Tauzin and Jim Greenwood, mentioned nothing about Watkins as the memo's author. The committee decided to leave her name out of it for now.

It was as if the world had exploded. Within minutes of the letter's release, Watkins's name was being reported as the Enron whistle-blower. The story now had a full cast of characters, including a heroine who appeared to have tipped off Lay to problems months before Enron's collapse.

Scores of telephone calls poured into the offices of the Energy and Commerce subcommittee, where Ken Johnson, a spokesman, was ready with a statement.

"Obviously," Johnson told callers, "this is an explosive new development in our investigation."

After being grilled all day long, a frazzled David Duncan went out to dinner with his lawyers. He had answered every question—about the document destruction, the Raptors, Chewco, everything. Throughout, he insisted that he had done nothing illegal.

As dinner wore on, one of his lawyers' cell phones rang. It was a reporter. Andersen had just announced that Duncan was being fired, the reporter said, asking for comment. In a minute, the lawyer got off the phone and informed Duncan of what he had been told.

Duncan was stunned. Before announcing his ouster to the world, no one at the firm had bothered to inform him.

Bill Powers opened his eyes and glanced at the clock. About four in the morning. Again. He turned over in bed, in what he knew would be a difficult effort to get back to sleep.

His mind raced. By this point, the special committee had discovered enough to know that something had gone terribly wrong in Enron's last years. The company had used and abused the accounting rules to *create* results rather than to determine the financial consequences of decisions.

But now, it had also become an emotional touchstone for the nation, a symbol of—something. Greed? The go-go '90s? Everyone in it, everyone touched by it, could be stained. Even, Powers realized, himself.

He was already hearing rumblings from reporters and public-interest groups. Didn't Enron give money to the law school where he served as dean? Didn't he have a relationship with Enron's general counsel? Wasn't he hopelessly mired in conflicts? Shouldn't he resign?

Powers considered the allegations hurtful and wrongheaded but knew that at some point they would find their way into print. It was just that kind of story.

All I can do is tell the truth. Some people will be happy; some people won't. That's all I can do.

He rolled over in bed and tried to get back to sleep.

Andy Fastow was sitting at a conference table in the Houston law offices of Smyser Kaplan & Veselka.

"Is this interview privileged, even though I'm a former employee?" he asked.

Chuck Davidow from Wilmer, Cutler answered. "The company's position is that the interview is privileged."

Fastow nodded. "I understand."

After weeks of effort, the special committee had finally arranged to sit down with Fastow. Already he was seen as the key to many of the company's decisions in recent years. He attended with three lawyers—David Gerger, Jennifer Ahlen, and Richard Drubel.

The conversation began with Chewco. "I'm not really that familiar with the details of that," Eastow said.

There was a quick round of questioning. One of Fastow's lawyers, David Gerger, broke in. "Andy's not going to answer any questions about who came up with the idea of making an Enron officer the manager of Chewco," he said.

That set the tempo for the meeting. Fastow would utter a few words, then Gerger would announce that his client would not discuss the issue in detail.

He wouldn't talk about whether he asked Kopper to run Chewco; he wouldn't discuss whether he knew how much Kopper had invested.

They turned to the repurchase of Chewco, the one that McMahon had stopped when he was treasurer, the one that gave Kopper the ten million dollars in profits that he used in his purchase of LJM2.

"I knew Enron repurchased Chewco in 2001," Fastow said. "But I intentionally didn't become involved in those discussions with Michael."

"And why was that?" Davidow asked.

"Michael was already a partner with me in LJM," he said. "I just thought communicating with him about the Chewco repurchase would be inappropriate."

Fastow was lying, and Davidow knew it. He pulled out a three-page handwritten document addressed to "Andy." It was all about the Chewco repurchase and had been prepared by Kopper when he was fighting McMahon's objections.

"Do you recognize this document?" Davidow asked.

Gerger took the pages and read them. "I need a moment to confer with my client," he said.

They were gone for fifteen minutes.

When Fastow and his lawyers returned, it quickly became evident the interview was over. Fastow would not answer any questions about the handwritten note. Nothing about the governance of LJM. Nothing about Southampton.

Gerger then launched into a statement on Fastow's behalf, portraying him as the pliant participant in Enron's desire to create off-books entities. Fastow would never have done anything, Gerger said, without approvals. Richard Drubel, another Fastow lawyer, took it from there.

"Andy did not prepare the accounting documents regarding the transactions," he said. "Andy was not responsible for Enron's accounting."

The next day, Bill Powers walked into a conference room at the Enron building, accompanied by his team of lawyers and accountants. He had never before attended the Wilmer, Cutler interviews, but this was an exception. He wanted to hear for himself what Ken Lay had to say.

Everyone found a spot at the table. Powers and Lay launched into a short discussion before the interview began. By then, Powers had come to recognize that the Raptors had been a sham designed to allow Enron to hide huge losses—by his team's estimate, a billion dollars' worth. He had to know what Lay understood.

"Ken, I do have one thing I want to ask," he said. "Did you think the Raptors were real economic hedges?"

Lay gave him a puzzled look. "I'm sorry?"

"The Raptors. Did you believe they were real economic hedges that protected Enron against loss?"

Lay seemed like a man trying to comprehend an irrational question. "Well, of course," he said.

The history of Enron was one of almost miraculous reinvention and discovery, Lay explained to the group.

At first it had all been pipelines. But then wholesale energy took off, and Enron branched out. Electricity. Retail. International power plants. Dabhol. Brazil. By 1998, he said, about 60 percent of its earnings came from businesses it hadn't been in ten years before. And that was before broadband came along.

"And of course, in 1998, we tried to get into the water business," he said. "We had the right concept, but the implementation of it was wrong."

Naturally, such fast-paced growth put enormous demands on Enron's financing abilities. Put simply, Lay said, the balance sheet wasn't large enough to handle the expansion.

"So we had a choice," he said. "We could either significantly decrease the growth rate or continue to grow rapidly through utilizing off-balance-sheet transactions."

He glanced around the room. "We opted to continue focusing on rapid growth," he said.

The consequences of that decision were now on the examining table. They began with Chewco; Lay said he had joined the board meeting where Chewco was discussed after the presentation had ended. He didn't know Michael Kopper, he said; in fact, he first learned of Kopper's name that fall, when he read it in *The Wall Street Journal*.

Then LJM1. He had never asked Fastow about his compensation, Lay explained. The worries his CFO had aired about the possibility of his partnership work damaging his Enron career left Lay with no doubt that the compensation from the fund was minimal. Same with LJM2. Why, again and again, Fastow had expressed reservations about his participation, stressing that he was taking part only to benefit Enron.

They ran through a series of transactions and discussed the deals where LJM2 purchased an Enron asset, only to sell it back months later at a profit.

"I was unaware that was happening," Lay said. "What were the reasons for buying them back?"

The discussion about the Raptors was the ugliest. The structure of the deals was laid out for Lay in excruciating detail. He had never known that the sole capital available to one Raptor was shares in the New Power Company, which were being used to hedge Enron's investment in New Power.

Lay shook his head. "I don't understand the logic of that structure," he said.

They discussed a presentation that Causey had made to the board about the Raptors in early 2001. Lay didn't remember hearing anything about there being any problems.

Chuck Davidow spoke up. "At the time of that presentation," he said, "two of the Raptor structures owed Enron $175 million and didn't have the capacity to pay."

Lay was silent for a moment. "That was a significant omission," he said. "I trusted Causey to bring something like that to the board."

In a recent annual filing known as a 10-K, Davidow said, Enron stated that it recognized $500 million of revenue from dealing with related parties.

"That disclosure refers to the Raptors," he said.

Lay shook his head. "I don't remember hearing anything about the revenues we were recognizing from the Raptors."

Davidow looked at him evenly. "But did anyone question how Enron could recognize $500 million from Raptor when the value of the investment was going *down*?"

A pause. "The disclosures in our filings were signed off on by Arthur Andersen and Vinson & Elkins," Lay said. "So I was confident in the 10-K."

The interview lasted several more hours. By the end, Lay had started to show fatigue, both physical and emotional. Bill Powers had one more question.

"Ken," he said, "do you still think the Raptors were real economic hedges?"

This time Lay understood exactly what Powers meant. "No," he replied in a firm voice. "Of course not."

It was Vince Kaminski who first heard the new allegation. Enron executives on the nineteenth floor had been shredding documents. A former employee named Maureen Castaneda said so. She had turned the information over to an investigator for Bill Lerach, a class-action lawyer suing Enron on behalf of its shareholders. Lerach was headed to court with a box of shredded paper from Castaneda and would be holding a press conference—but not until the ABC evening news ran its exclusive story about the allegations.

Kaminski alerted others to the development and took charge of the floor. The company had informed everyone, repeatedly, not to shred anything. And Kaminski wasn't going to let anyone get near the shredders. If this had been happening, it was stopping. Now.

Rob Walls, the deputy general counsel, began alerting executives about the allegation. He tracked down Ken Lay, who was meeting with legal advisers in another Houston building at the time. Lay, in turn, called Kaminski, who assured him that no one would get near the shredder again.

A conference call with the lawyers was arranged. Bob Bennett, Enron's top Washington lawyer, took charge. There was no doubt, once this got out, the FBI would descend on Enron with a warrant. There was only one choice to make.

"We've got to invite the FBI in," Bennett said on the call, "so they can come down and secure the location."

"Fine," Lay said. "Tell them they've got free, open access to anyplace in the Enron building."

Dozens of agents arrived the next morning and began checking computer systems, searching for paper records, and examining the shredders. Two agents wandered through Fastow's office; they were surprised when, while they were checking the walls, a panel popped open to reveal a hidden closet. But it was only used for coats and umbrellas.

Several agents set up shop in Lay's office, working at his conference table as they reviewed documents. Boxes of paperwork were sealed and taken away. Even some of his communications with his lawyers got swept up in the search.

But for all the digging, the allegation that had set everything in motion proved to be a dry hole. On the *ABC News* report, horizontal strips had been held up as evidence of the shredding that was taking place, but the shredders on the floor where the effort was supposed to have taken place pulverized the paperwork into confetti, not strips. After several days the FBI concluded that nothing of value had been destroyed and that—unlike with Andersen—there had been no concerted, illegal effort to shred documents at Enron.

The unenviable task of notifying Lay that his career was over fell to Tom Roberts, one of Enron's lawyers with Weil, Gotshal. On the evening of January 22, the day the FBI descended on the company's offices, Weil, Gotshal had met with Enron's lead creditors in the bankruptcy. They had issued the demand for Lay to leave. He was no longer an asset to the company, they argued, and was simply too enmeshed in the events of the last few years. He had to go.

Now it was about 9:30 New York time on the following morning. Sitting at his desk in the Manhattan offices of Weil, Gotshal, Roberts got on the telephone and dialed Lay in Houston. He came on the phone right away. Roberts explained about the meeting and the creditors' demands.

"You can stay on the board, and they'd like you to do that," he said. "But you have to step down as chairman and chief executive."

There was a long, gut-wrenching pause.

"All right," Lay said softly, trying hard to maintain his professional dignity. "I guess we need to hold a board meeting, don't we?"

Roberts was sitting back in his chair. "Yes, that needs to be scheduled," he said.

Lay was silent again. "Tom," he said suddenly, "pray with me. Pray for the company, and for all of us."

Roberts sat up in his seat. He didn't know what to do. He had never prayed by phone before. "All right," he said.

The line went silent. Roberts closed his eyes, unsure of what to think or say. Then the moment passed. Lay was the first to speak.

"Thank you, Tom," he said. "Thank you."

The next night, the weather in Sugar Land, Texas, was cool and overcast. Just past 2:15 in the morning, Deputy Constable Scott Head from Fort Bend County was driving east down Palm Royale Boulevard. On the other side of the street, he saw a black Mercedes four-door, driven by a man he recognized. It was Cliff Baxter.

Head considered the situation and decided to find out where the car was going. He pulled left and made a U-turn. He was less than three minutes away from Baxter's car.

Baxter pulled his car between two medians, stopping almost in the middle of the eastbound and westbound lanes.

He was still dressed for bed, wearing pajamas and moccasins. He hadn't wanted to make too much noise before leaving and had shut off the security system at his home so it didn't chirp when he headed out to the garage. There, he had left an envelope on the dashboard of his wife's car, with a note inside explaining why he had made this decision.

The engine was still running. The car's headlights illuminated the median. Baxter brought out a .357 Magnum revolver and held it to his right temple.

Constable Head didn't hear the gunshot. But he arrived within a minute, at 2:23, and saw the car sitting in its awkward position between the medians.

He came to a stop, first calling in to report what appeared to be a disabled car. He approached the Mercedes and looked inside. All of the car doors were locked. In the driver's seat sat Baxter, dead with a gunshot wound to the head.

Hours later, at about 7:30, Skilling struggled to wake up. The phone was ringing, and he was confused. He glanced around; he was in the den at Rebecca Carter's house. She had come home from surgery days before and wasn't able to climb stairs yet, so the two had spent the night downstairs on a pull-out bed. Carter reached for the phone.

"Is Jeff there?" It was Ken Rice, his voice shaky.

"Yeah," she said. "Hold on."

She rolled over toward Skilling. "It's Ken Rice," she said. "Something's wrong."

Skilling quickly sat up in bed, grabbing the phone.

"Jeff? It's Ken."

Carter was right. Rice sounded distraught. "What's going on?" Skilling asked.

"Are you sitting down?"

"Yeah, I'm sitting down."

Rice paused and took a deep breath. "Cliff shot himself," he said, his voice breaking.

"Shot himself? Is he okay?"

Rice choked back a sob. "No, Jeff. He's dead."

A long pause. "Suicide?" Skilling finally asked. His voice broke; he couldn't speak anymore.

He passed the phone over to Carter, then collapsed back into the bed, sobbing uncontrollably.

"Oh, God!" he screamed. "Oh, God!"

The suicide of Cliff Baxter hit Enron like a final body blow, something that made the surreal events of the last few months all too concrete. Nothing compared with it—not the bankruptcy, not the end of Lay's career. Suddenly all that seemed distant, unimportant. A friend had died alone. Because of what happened at this company.

There was anger, mostly at the news media, something that only intensified as camera crews showed up that morning at Baxter's home in hopes of catching a moment with his widow. Making it all the worse were the instant rumors, fueled largely by the Internet, that Baxter had been killed because he knew something. The public wouldn't know for years that there was no mystery in his death, and that Baxter had been seen alive and alone minutes before by the police constable who discovered his body.

For Lay, it was all gone now. The spot he had reached in the world, the company he had built, the excitement and dynamism he had always believed it generated. Now, it was all infused with the stench of death and failure.

That same afternoon, Lay slowly headed into the office of Ray Bowen. It was strange to think of it as Bowen's office. It had been Fastow's for so long.

Things were changing in the new management team; Whalley would soon be gone, following the trading division over to UBS. McMahon, the instant chief financial officer, would soon be the instant president. And assuming Fastow's old job would be Bowen himself.

In their last few months together, Bowen had always struck Lay as level-headed, calm. Lay wanted to talk to him. He took a seat in front of Bowen's desk and chatted about the coming changes, about the bankruptcy-workout specialist who had already started up at the company, taking Lay's job.

After discussing the personnel issues, Lay shifted topics. "What do you think the Powers report's going to say?" he asked.

"I don't think it's going to be very nice to Rick Causey or Rick Buy," Bowen replied.

"Yeah," Lay said, his voice almost a whisper. "I've heard that."

He took a deep breath. The conversation seemed almost painful to him. "What do you think of Sherron Watkins?" Lay asked. "What was she trying to accomplish?"

Bowen shrugged. "I think Sherron, in her clumsy fashion, was trying to be helpful," he said. "I think her motivation was trying to help the company survive."

Lay gazed down at the floor, considering the words. "Yeah, I agree," he said. "That's exactly how I feel."

Another pause, the longest yet. Lay glanced up, staring Bowen in the eye. "What about me?" he asked. "What do you think happens to me in all this?"

Bowen looked back at Lay, a man he had admired for years, a man who had traveled in a different stratosphere, a man who now sat before him, dispirited and broken.

"Well," he said, "there are two possible outcomes here. One is you look incredibly stupid and look like you did a bad job."

He held his gaze steady. "And the other is they try to put you in jail."

The words, known but unspoken for so long, hung in the air. Lay brought up a hand and touched his chin.

"I know," he said softly. "I know."

For a moment Lay just sat there, saying nothing. Then he looked up. "Well," he said, "have a nice weekend."

With that, Ken Lay stood, not saying another word as he wandered out of the office into the empty, silent hallway.

EPILOGUE

LIVE ROCK-AND-ROLL music echoed through the newly built, rambling estate where hundreds of members of Houston's elite had gathered for a holiday party. It was mid–December 2002, the night of the big social event at the Bayou Breeze, the home of Abbott Sprague, who had made his fortune in fund management and now was one of Houston's richest men.

Taking part in the festivities were a number of executives, bankers, and lawyers who had been swept up in the Enron catastrophe. This year, there was no pressing business, no burning of the midnight oil at the end of the quarter to keep them away. And there would be no Christmas bash at Enron either. This event was as close to a corporate holiday reunion that any of them would see.

More than a year had passed since Enron had filed for bankruptcy, and for almost everyone touched by the scandal, the world had transformed into a radically different place.

Whatever doubts might have persisted about the magnitude of the deep problems within the company had been obliterated in February, ten months before, by Bill Powers's final report to the Enron board. It spelled out in painful detail how the now-infamous off-books entities—Raptor, LJM, Chewco, Southampton—had been used by Fastow and his accomplices both to enrich themselves and to deceive investors about Enron's finances. The revelations swept away the final vestiges of Enron's former management. Rick Causey and Rick Buy, who had been responsible for managing the conflicts with LJM, had been ushered out the door, never to return. Even Ken Lay had been forced to relinquish his last, frayed connection to the company, stepping down as a director just weeks after resigning from management.

The Powers Report set the stage for what became a national spectacle—the congressional hearings on Enron. The House Energy and Commerce subcommittee took the lead, issuing subpoenas to all of the primary players in the Enron saga. Almost everyone—Fastow, Kopper, David Duncan, Causey, Buy—declined to testify, citing their Fifth Amendment rights. With the release of the Powers Report, even Lay heeded his lawyers' advice and declined to appear before the committee. When a Senate committee subpoenaed him weeks later, he, too, took the Fifth.

Skilling chose a different path, testifying under oath and assuring members of Congress that he had done nothing wrong. He was not, Skilling insisted, an accountant, and had relied on Andersen and Causey to provide him with the proper judgments.

Sherron Watkins also appeared, playing the role of Enron heroine. Watkins, who by then had agreed to co-author a book on Enron, was an eager witness who ventured beyond her actual knowledge in her testimony. She accused Skilling of working with Fastow to dupe the board and portrayed Lay as a scapegoat of underlings' manipulations without citing evidence to justify her allegations. No one on the committee pressed her for details.

Other executives who had attempted to unmask Fastow and his collaborators and expose their partnerships' dealings did not fare as well. Jordan Mintz was praised, but also challenged by some committee members who seemed not to understand the role he had played. Jeff McMahon was at first lauded for standing up to Fastow, but soon after condemned for his role in the Nigerian barge transaction. Vince Kaminski and Carl Bass, the executive and the accountant who had campaigned the loudest and longest against the partnership dealings, were never called to testify. And the name of Kevin Kindall, the Enron executive who discovered the threat to Enron's survival and tried to stop it, was never mentioned in any public hearing.

By May, another bombshell emerged. The memo about the California trading strategies—crafted largely by Stephen Hall of Stoel Rives in Portland, under the direction of Christian Yoder at Enron—was turned over by the company to federal energy regulators, who promptly made it public. The document once intended to notify senior Enron management of bad doings by traders instead became smoking-gun evidence of the illegal trading.

Some politicians jumped on the trading strategies as proof that the California energy crisis was solely caused by manipulation—a position largely dismissed by reputable economists, who considered trading abuses a contributing factor to a problem fueled mostly by supply and demand mismatches. Hall and Yoder entered the Enron media firestorm, were hauled before Congress, and ultimately celebrated for their integrity.

As time passed, executives and professionals with ties to Enron worked to move on with their lives. A number of them—including Rebecca Mark, Amanda Martin, and Jeff McMahon—found quiet spots in business, handling family-related ventures, doing consulting work, or managing their own investments. Greg Whalley, the short-lived president of Enron, moved to

Connecticut to join his traders then at UBS; as the investigations of Enron heated up, he would eventually leave and return to Houston.

Professional survival often seemed to depend on how far Enron executives and others had managed to move from the epicenter of the scandal—either through the objections they raised at the time or their wisdom in getting out when the getting was good.

After her celebration in Congress, Watkins went on to form her own career as a speaker and corporate ethics consultant; she would ultimately be named as one of *Time* magazine's people of the year. Mintz leaped from his job at Enron to a position on the legal staff of a major American homebuilding company. Kaminski found work as a risk analyst with another financial firm, but changed jobs as the tumult in the energy markets left by Enron's collapse roiled the industry.

But no one walked away from Enron with less damage than the man whose departure cleared the way for the elevation of Jeff Skilling. Rich Kinder, the onetime Enron president whom board members feared would be unable to move the company forward, became the richest and most successful of the bunch. Now a billionaire, Kinder transformed the small energy company he cofounded, Kinder Morgan, Inc., into a steadier, more reliable, and more profitable enterprise than Enron ever was. From 2000 to the end of 2002, Kinder Morgan shareholders saw a 113 percent return; Enron's investors, of course, lost everything.

The efforts by Arthur Andersen to limit the fallout from the document destruction proved fruitless. After urging the Enron Task Force to quickly resolve the matter, Berardino and his legal team were shocked when the prosecutors came back with a decision to file criminal charges. With the firm already under a court injunction as part of the Waste Management settlement, prosecutors felt that, given the role of Andersen's legal department in the document destruction, they had little choice but to push this case into the criminal realm.

Andersen sought to settle but fumbled. The government demanded an admission of criminal liability, and at one point the two sides seemed close to a deal. But in the end Andersen balked, and the government walked away from the negotiating table.

By that time a top prosecutor on the Enron Task Force, Andrew Weissmann, had secured a secret weapon: David Duncan. After mulling the matter for months, Duncan acknowledged that he must have destroyed documents with the knowledge that he would be keeping them away from the SEC. He agreed to plead guilty to one count of obstruction, and to serve as the chief witness against his former employer.

The Andersen indictment for obstruction of justice ended the company's last hope of survival. Clients fled in droves, unwilling to allow a firm charged with a crime to serve as their financial watchdog. Around the globe, Andersen partners jumped to competing firms. By the time of Andersen's conviction in June, only a small shell of the once great firm remained, and it announced that it would cease auditing public companies.

The fates of Andersen's partners varied. Berardino resigned from the top post in a futile attempt to forestall its indictment; after Andersen's collapse, he opened his own consulting firm. Duncan would still be awaiting sentencing for his crime some three years after his guilty plea. John Stewart, Andersen's expert on accounting rules, remained with the firm for many months, finally leaving to also set up a consulting shop. And Carl Bass, who made so much trouble for Enron that he was forced to end his dealings with the company, was snapped up by a competing accounting firm, where he works when not being consulted as one of the government's favorite witnesses.

The death of Andersen triggered public criticism that the prosecutors had gone too far in charging the firm. But within days of its conviction, it became apparent that, had this fatal blow not fallen, another would have: WorldCom, the telecommunications giant, announced the discovery of its own massive accounting fraud, involving billions in unreported expenses. The accounting firm that missed the scam was none other than Arthur Andersen.

Until that moment, the Bush Administration had been resisting calls from Congress for sweeping corporate reform. But the one-two punch of Enron and WorldCom changed all that. Within weeks, new rules for corporate America would be adopted by Congress and signed by the President. Called Sarbanes-Oxley, after its chief sponsors, the act represented the most dramatic overhaul of securities laws since the aftermath of the Depression.

The exposure of so much corporate skulduggery also proved the undoing of Harvey Pitt. His ill-timed "kinder and gentler" speech served as red meat to Administration opponents, and, despite his aggressive moves against Enron and WorldCom, he made repeated political missteps that undercut his role in the Administration. The night of the midterm elections, with the Republicans winning a decisive victory, Pitt resigned under pressure from the White House.

By that time, it had become clear that the criminal investigation into Enron was going to penetrate deeply into the company's executive ranks. The government started in what seemed an unusual place—at Greenwich NatWest. Grand jury subpoenas had uncovered the e-mail traffic among the three bankers who had first proposed to Fastow and Kopper what eventually became Southampton. But for the most part, it was Kopper's name, not Fastow's, all over the documents.

Leslie Caldwell and her team decided to send a strong message to Kopper. In late June, they filed a criminal complaint against the bankers, loaded with damning evidence of their misbehavior—and of Michael Kopper's as well.

Kopper took the hint. Within weeks he came in, eager to cut a deal. He told the prosecutors everything—about the front investors in RADR, the kickbacks from Chewco, the rigged LJM deals, even the Global Galactic agreement. Topping it off, he told of the laptop he had used to track his deals with Fastow, the one that, at his boss's behest, now rested in a garbage dump somewhere in Texas.

A deal was reached, and in late August, Kopper pleaded guilty in a Houston federal courtroom to two felonies related to Chewco, RADR, and Southampton. As part of the deal, he surrendered twelve million dollars to the government; more than two years later, he had yet to be sentenced.

Five weeks afterward, on October 2, it was Fastow's turn. Early that morning, he arrived at the FBI's Houston office and surrendered to agents there. He was handcuffed and led to the courthouse, where he was charged in a criminal complaint with securities and wire fraud, money laundering, and conspiracy. Fastow pleaded not guilty.

The rush of prosecutions and revelations weighed heavily on a number of the partygoers attending the Sprague celebration. Just a few days earlier, a mid-level nobody, Larry Lawyer, had pleaded guilty to a tax crime for failing to report money he made on a Fastow partnership. Now prosecutors were hitting hard on Broadband executives, accusing them of lying to investors about the business's prospects. Ken Rice, Joe Hirko, and a number of others had already been informed that they stood to be indicted soon.

Amid the laughter and tinkling of glasses, Ray Bowen, now Enron's CFO, was standing near the mansion's vast multistory entryway, just feet from a large staircase. He felt a tap on his shoulder. He turned to see Rebecca Carter behind him. His face registered a moment of shock.

"I just wanted to say hi," she said. "How are you doing?"

"We're okay."

"Still at Enron?"

Bowen nodded. "Yeah."

Carter shrugged. "Well, we can't talk about that."

Bowen understood. The criminal case. Longtime friends hadn't spoken to each other for months. Certainly acquaintances couldn't discuss Enron, not without the conversation likely being recounted to a grand jury.

"Well, I'm glad to see you're doing well," she said.

Bowen thanked her, his anxiety growing. Carter was at the party. *Is Skilling here, too?* The thought made him uncomfortable. He hadn't seen Skilling since he resigned. He had heard the man was telling everyone that he had done nothing wrong, and Bowen didn't want to listen to his protests. Like a lot of Enron executives, he was angry at Skilling.

Then he saw him. Bowen had just walked down a hallway to pick up a beer and, with drink in hand, was on his way back when Skilling emerged from the dining room.

"Ray," Skilling boomed, "how are you doing?"

Bowen stopped. Skilling looked awful. He had aged and gained weight. Bowen muttered a greeting.

"Why don't you want to see me?" Skilling asked.

What? It was true, but Bowen hadn't told anyone that night. Maybe Carter had read it in his face.

"I don't think I ever said that," he responded.

"Do you not want to see me because you think I did something wrong? Is that it?"

How can that be answered? "Jeff, I don't know."

Skilling pressed in. "Do you think I did something wrong?" he repeated.

Bowen backed into a corner. "Jeff, I don't know," he repeated. "I have no idea."

"I didn't do anything wrong!" Skilling shouted. "I didn't know about any of this stuff!"

Skilling's tone was emotional. Unbeknownst to anyone, he had just received a letter from the federal prosecutors, notifying him that he was likely to be indicted.

"Jeff," Bowen said, "I don't think we should be talking about this."

"I didn't know about Andy and all that stuff," Skilling said. "I didn't know about the kickbacks from Kopper. You worked for him! Did you know about this?"

This was becoming a scene. "Absolutely not!" Bowen responded. "I didn't work for Andy for two years."

Skilling wouldn't let it go. "I need to know, do you think I did something wrong?"

Bowen stood up straight, feeling angry. "I'll tell you what I do know, Jeff," he said. "I know that the financial position of this company wasn't anywhere close to what the world was led to believe. And that happened on your watch. Was that right or wrong? I don't know."

"You're not answering the question, Ray. Do you think I did anything wrong?"

Bowen stiffened. "I don't know, Jeff. And that's what I'm telling everybody that asks me. But again, I don't think we should be talking about this."

"Okay," Skilling said. "Okay."

There was a pause. Bowen stared at him for a moment.

"How are you doing, Jeff?" he asked.

Skilling cleared his throat. "Well, Ray, if you want to know the truth, it's god-awful. It just sucks."

"I can't imagine," Bowen said. "This is a big tragedy. Lots of people are getting fucked in this thing."

Skilling looked him in the eye. "I know, I feel bad about that. But, Ray, I didn't do anything wrong."

Bowen didn't want to hear it. Whether Skilling had committed a crime or not, Bowen still held him accountable. He had created a get-rich-quick culture and failed to control it, he thought. Then, at the end, he abandoned them all. He blamed Skilling.

"I gotta go," Bowen said, taking a step forward. "I wish you the best."

The party wound down, and the crowds moved to the front of the house, milling about as valets brought their cars around on the long driveway. Bowen and his wife, Jennifer, found themselves behind Skilling and Rebecca Carter. Like four old friends, they chatted until a black Mercedes coupe arrived. Skilling and Carter climbed in and drove off.

Jim Timmins, the Enron executive who left in protest over LJM, happened to be behind Bowen. As the Mercedes pulled away, his own anger at Skilling boiled over.

"Can you believe that asshole had the fucking gall to show up at this party?" Timmins sneered.

His eyes followed the departing car. "Hope you have a good time in jail!" he called out.

The others in line laughed.

In the year that followed, the walls closed in on Andy Fastow. By early 2004 any hopes he harbored for an acquittal had been shoved aside.

By then, he had been formally indicted by a grand jury on ninety-eight counts, including one for obstruction of justice stemming in part from his role in the destruction of Kopper's laptop. All of his closest allies had taken plea deals. Ben Glisan had pleaded guilty the previous September to conspiring to commit fraud, admitting that the Raptors were structured in ways that violated accounting rules so that Enron could exaggerate its financial performance. He was sentenced to five years in prison.

But the real trap was of Fastow's own creation. In constructing the RADR scheme, he had secured the help of his wife, Lea. The money siphoned by Kopper from the bogus investors had been delivered in the names of Fastow's wife and children. And then the Fastows failed to declare it as income, leaving Lea open to a criminal tax charge.

Prosecutors informed Fastow that they would shelve plans to charge Lea if he would plead guilty. Fastow refused and Lea was indicted. Suddenly, the Fastows faced the prospect that their two young sons would have to be raised by others while they served lengthy prison terms. The time had come for Fastow to admit the truth.

"All rise."

At 2:05 on the afternoon of January 14, 2004, U. S. District Judge Kenneth Hoyt walked past a marble slab on the wall as he made his way to the bench of courtroom 2025 in Houston's Federal District Courthouse. Scores of spectators attended, seated in rows of benches. In front of the bar, Leslie Caldwell, the head of the Enron Task Force, sat quietly watching the proceedings as members of her team readied themselves at the prosecutors' table.

Judge Hoyt looked out into the room. To his right sat an array of defense lawyers surrounding their client, Andy Fastow, who was there to change his plea. Fastow, whose hair had grown markedly grayer in the past year and a half, sat in silence as he waited for the proceedings to begin.

Minutes later, under the high, regal ceiling of the courtroom, Fastow stepped before the bench, standing alongside his lawyers.

"I understand that you will be entering a plea of guilty this afternoon," Judge Hoyt asked.

"Yes, your honor," Fastow replied.

He began answering questions from the judge, giving his age as forty-two and saying that he had a graduate degree in business. When he said the last word, he whistled slightly on the *s*, as he often did when his nerves were frayed. He was taking medication for anxiety, Fastow said; it left him better equipped to deal with the proceedings.

Matt Friedrich, the prosecutor handling the hearing, spelled out the deal. There were two conspiracy counts, involving wire fraud and securities fraud. Under the deal, he said, Fastow had agreed to cooperate, serve ten years in prison, and surrender $23.8 million worth of assets. Lea would be allowed to enter a plea and would eventually be sentenced to a year in prison on a misdemeanor tax charge.

Fastow stayed silent as another prosecutor, John Hemann, described the crimes he was confessing. In a statement to prosecutors, Fastow acknowledged his roles in the Southampton and Raptor frauds and provided details of the secret Global Galactic agreement that illegally protected his LJM funds against losses in their biggest dealings with Enron.

Hemann finished the summary, and Hoyt looked at Fastow. "Are those facts true?"

"Yes, your honor," Fastow said, his voice even.

"Did you in fact engage in the conspiratorious conduct as alleged?"

"Yes, your honor."

Fastow was asked for his plea. Twice he said guilty.

"Based on your pleas," Hoyt said, "the court finds you guilty."

The hearing soon ended. Fastow returned to his seat at the defense table. He reached for a paper cup of water and took a sip. Sitting in silence, he stared off at nothing, suddenly looking very frail.

His hands cuffed behind him, Jeff Skilling was led by FBI agents into the backdoor of Houston's federal courthouse. It was early in the morning of February 19, the day the Enron Task Force unsealed its forty-two-count criminal indictment against him.

In the weeks since the Fastow plea, the corporate dominoes at the top of Enron's former management team had begun to fall as the former corporate CFO provided prosecutors with evidence against his onetime colleagues. Already Rick Causey had been charged with fraud for his role in a number of Fastow dealings, including Global Galactic. Now Skilling was being added to the Causey indictment, charged with a broad array of crimes.

Escorted by the FBI, Skilling was brought to the elevator banks in the courthouse. The doors opened, and inside stood a man dressed in a prison-issued jumpsuit, wearing handcuffs. Skilling recognized him instantly. It was Ben Glisan, being brought from prison for an appearance before the Enron grand jury.

"Hey, Ben!" Skilling said jovially as he climbed onto the elevator. "How you been doing?"

"Hey, Jeff," Glisan said uncomfortably. "Guess I've been better."

Skilling was escorted to a holding cell, where he was left alone for almost half an hour. He stewed; all of this, he was convinced, was just some mind game the government was playing with him—the appearance of Glisan, the time alone. He made a decision. He wasn't going to show any weakness. He wouldn't let them win.

At 9:20, Skilling was brought to room 704, where he sat at a table with his lawyers, including Bruce Hiler and a new member of the team, Daniel Petrocelli. Sam Buell, a lead prosecutor in the case, stood before Magistrate

Judge Frances Stacy and was soon joined by Skilling and his lawyers. Magistrate Stacy began to recite Skilling's rights and mentioned that he had a right to an attorney.

"It looks like you have an embarrassment of riches in that regard," she said.

The magistrate then turned to Buell, who recited the charges that Skilling faced. It was a grab bag of allegations, the most serious involving Fastow and his dealings. It charged that, along with Causey, he knew that the LJM funds were being used to manipulate Enron's earnings through deals like the Raptors and Cuiabá sale. He was also charged with fraud for what the government said was his involvement with Causey and Fastow in Project Grayhawk, the transaction designed to allow Enron to profit from the increase in its own stock price following the 2000 analysts' conference.

But most of the allegations had nothing to do with Fastow and instead were spread across a wide range of Enron's businesses. In the wholesale division, Skilling and Causey were charged with manipulating earnings in 2000 and 2001 through the establishment of the reserves to hold the profits from California trading. In retail, they were charged with disguising losses by shifting the division's trading book into the wholesale division in early 2001. And in Broadband, Skilling was charged with lying to investors about its prospects and technology.

As Buell spoke, Skilling turned to face the prosecutor, clasping his hands in front of him. He didn't flinch when Buell said that the charges could bring a maximum of 325 years in prison.

Magistrate Stacy asked Skilling for his plea.

He stood up straight. "I plead not guilty to all counts," he said.

Five months later, on July 8, the final domino fell.

Early that morning, a silver Crown Victoria pulled into space 35 in the parking area behind the Houston courthouse. Special Agent Paula Schanzle pushed open the front passenger-side door and emerged from the car. She opened the back door, reaching inside and grasping a man beneath the arm. He turned and stepped out of the car.

It was Ken Lay. After three years of investigation, he had been indicted. He was dressed in a blue sports coat and red tie, and seemed relaxed despite the handcuffs binding his arms behind him. As Schanzle escorted him toward the courthouse, reporters called out from behind a fence, asking if Lay had anything to say.

"A little later today I will," he said, sounding almost nonchalant.

He was the thirtieth defendant. By then, executives from Broadband had been indicted, including Ken Rice, who would soon plead guilty to misleading analysts about the state of the company's technology at the 2001 conference. Six executives from Merrill and Enron who participated in the Nigerian barge deal had been indicted—and five of them would eventually be convicted. Only a lowly Enron accountant named Sheila Kahanek would be cleared.

With criminal cases pushed forward following the discovery of the Stoel Rives memos, federal prosecutors stepped up their efforts in investigating possible illegal trading in the California energy markets. Ultimately, the three Portland electricity traders most involved in the California manipulations—including Belden and Forney—would plead guilty.

But all of those cases would be little more than a sideshow to this day: the opening salvo in the criminal prosecution of Ken Lay.

Lay was taken inside the courthouse. He was placed in a holding cell with two men in leg irons, both charged in the smuggling-ring deaths of nineteen undocumented workers.

One of his cell mates looked at Lay curiously. "I think I saw you on TV last night," he said.

For three hours, Lay waited in the cell, where he emerged as the jailhouse celebrity. One prisoner hit him up for some investment advice.

"Well, I've not really thought much about that recently," Lay responded.

Later, at 11:40, he was brought into courtroom 701. Standing alone, he glanced around the gallery, looking for a moment at his wife, Linda. He walked to the defense table, sat down, and slowly rocked in his chair.

Everyone stood when Magistrate Judge Mary Milloy strode into the room. Lay walked before the bench with his lawyers. He stood nervously, swaying on his heels. Again the procedure was the same, including the discussion of the criminal charges.

Lay had been added as the third defendant to the indictment of Causey and Skilling, but the case against him was markedly different. He was not charged with involvement in or knowledge of the Fastow manipulations; indeed, the case focused on what he said and did in the final weeks before Enron's bankruptcy. His statements of confidence in the company and its prospects, the indictment said, had been a lie. He was charged with misleading Arthur Andersen that fall about Enron's plans for its Wessex Water plant, in an effort, the government said, to minimize the impact of an accounting change. And he was accused of lying to the banks that lent him money, by improperly using some of the cash to purchase stocks on margin.

Lay was asked for his plea. "Not guilty, your honor."

But the day didn't end there. Ken Lay and his lawyers decided to take his case public right away. They arranged for a press conference at the

DoubleTree Hotel, down the street from what had once been Enron headquarters.

Reporters, family members, supporters, and former employees packed the room. Lay, accompanied by his wife, stepped onto a makeshift stage, with Linda taking a seat in the back. Lay strode up to a podium lined with microphones.

"Ladies and gentlemen, number one, we're pleased that you came over to spend a few minutes with us," he began. "It has been a tragic day for me and my family. But we also know that an indictment came down that should not have."

He accepted responsibility for what happened at Enron, he said, but added that did not mean he committed any crime. "I firmly reject any notion that I engaged in any wrongful or criminal activity," he said.

He had believed in the company, he said. He had never lied. Now he wanted a speedy trial. "We are anxious," he said, "to prove my innocence."

He invited questions and answered everything thrown at him, insisting repeatedly that he had done nothing improper. After thirty minutes he signaled that he was done.

He and his legal team were ready to keep answering questions in the days and weeks to come, Lay said.

"We are entering into this new period," he said. "You will be hearing quite a bit from us."

He thanked everyone and walked over to Linda. As the couple headed off the stage, a group of supporters on one side of the room stood and applauded, cheering on Lay as he entered into his last and most desperate battle.

ACKNOWLEDGMENTS

THIS BOOK HAS PLENTY OF UNSUNG heroes. It's time to sing about them.

At *The New York Times*, Brent Bowers played the essential role of primary reader, adviser, editor, and sprinkler of magic. His keen insights and suggestions found their way onto every page. From the first day that I made the long jump from tracing terrorist financing to covering Enron's demise, Glenn Kramon, then the business editor, was an enthusiastic supporter. Jim Schachter, then deputy business editor, was with me every step of the way, fielding innumerable late-night and weekend phone calls from me as we wound our way through the Enron morass.

Rich Oppel was the first to introduce me to players in the Enron tale, and his wise counsel has been an important asset for me ever since. David Barboza, a top-notch reporter, ripped up Houston as he delved into aspects of the story; during this project, Dave was always available with thoughts, advice, and assistance. And, as always, Floyd Norris was there, serving as a guide to Enron's complex financial machinations. He is, quite simply, the smartest financial reporter in the business today.

As the years passed, new players took over at the paper, and I owe them my thanks. In particular, Larry Ingrassia, who arrived as business editor during my work on this book, has been endlessly patient and encouraging. As deadlines passed with no end in sight, his support was critical in allowing the manuscript to finally see the light of day. Others at the *Times* to whom I owe thanks include Diana Henriques, Donna Anderson, and Maureen Balleza.

I also had the support of numerous researchers and document managers. In Texas, David Wethe, now at the *Fort Worth Star-Telegram*, was an eager and top-notch investigator, with both the skills to conduct a penetrating interview and the work ethic to dig through thousands of pages of documents rapidly. In California, Nick Grudin, now a graduate student at the Kennedy School, dove into projects with an endless enthusiasm, digging up sources and records at a blinding pace. More than a few times, I was delighted to see a giant box of new documents arrive at my home, courtesy of Nick's dogged efforts.

When I hired him, Jordan Wolf was a seventeen-year-old with a willingness to handle the unenviable task of placing tens of thousands of documents in chronological order. After he demonstrated an industriousness and maturity far beyond his years, his responsibilities soon branched out to more complex research tasks. Now in his first year at Yale University, I have no doubt that all of us will be hearing great things of Jordan in the future. When Elizabeth Keeler, a dynamo and a friend, stepped in to take over for Jordan, I was astonished at her alacrity, good cheer, and efficiency. Elizabeth, you made so much possible. Thank you.

Finally, I had two assistants who provided endless support. Diane Obara, with me on a book for the third time, was always available during the hard slogging, ready to take on any task I threw at her. And this go-round, she was joined by Debra Piedra, who amazed me with her ability to jump in on any last-minute assignment, providing not only what I needed but also tossing in special extras from name indexes to additional research. She is an absolute delight.

Friends played key roles. Tim Perkins was my resident computer genius, directing me to software I needed and teaching me to download thousands of Enron documents stored on compact discs. Others read the manuscript and offered suggestions, including Denton Watumull, Deborah and David Michel, Robert Keeler, and Margie Tippen.

I also want to thank (and apologize) to Elva Eichenwald, Tim and Samantha Durst, Laurence and Alma Alden, Margie and Terry Tippen, Greg and Cynthia DeMars, Marcia Jones and Jeannie Caldwell, Linda and Joe Altick, Katherine and David Stewart, Magdelana Malczyk, and Errington Thompson. The guys of *2010 Blues*—David, Denton, Greg, Robert, and Terry—were amazingly patient with my troubled schedule and frequent exhaustion. And Freya Manston was once again there for me, offering her keen insights as this book moved from idea to manuscript.

My agent, Andrew Wylie, was an enthusiastic supporter of this project from its inception and, along with Jeff Posternak, was always available with solutions to problems I encountered. Andrew and Jeff were an absolute delight.

At Doubleday Broadway, my editor Stacy Creamer suffered through experiences that are sure to be cited in some future nomination for sainthood. Her fabulous assistant, Tracy Zupancis, was always there to gently nudge me along to meet my next obligation. And Ingrid Sterner put in what was simply the most amazing performance I have ever witnessed by a copyeditor.

She saved me in more ways than I could express. Meanwhile, Sean Mills, the production editor, served as my air traffic controller inside the publishing house, bringing us all in for a safe landing. There are far more people in the Doubleday Broadway family to whom I owe my gratitude; put simply, they are total pros who made this experience enjoyable. I thank you all.

I'm at a loss how to express my debt to my family. My wife, Theresa Eichenwald, never wavered in her support—bucking me up, assuming extra workloads, keeping me sane. I love her dearly, and cannot thank her enough. Theresa, you are the greatest gift in my life—with the possible exception of our three boys, Adam, Ryan, and Sam. Their endless patience and support made all of this possible. Guys, I love all of you and cannot thank you enough. Now, let's start having game night, just like I promised.

NOTES AND SOURCES

THIS BOOK GREW OUT of my three years of covering the Enron scandal for *The New York Times*. It is based on more than one thousand hours of interviews with more than one hundred participants in these events, as well as thousands of documents. Every person who plays a significant role in this story was contacted—either directly or through a representative—and given the opportunity to be interviewed.

The primary documents for this book filled more than two hundred thick three-ring notebooks. Secondary documents took up twenty file-cabinet drawers. The records included notes of interviews prepared by various government bodies, including the Federal Bureau of Investigation and the Securities and Exchange Commission, as well as secret testimony before a federal grand jury investigating the Enron and Andersen debacles, the SEC, the Federal Energy Regulatory Commission, the Commodity Futures Trading Commission, and the bankruptcy examiner in the case. In addition, notes of interviews conducted by various other groups and bodies, including congressional investigators and lawyers, were obtained.

Other documents included e-mails and memos, internal government records, personal diaries and notes, schedule books, expense and travel records, telephone logs, SEC filings, board minutes, bank documents, video and audio tapes of described events, contemporaneous transcripts, reports, and presentations, an array of other investigative records, books, and newsclippings.

All of the interviews—with both principals and others whose names are not generally known but who witnessed specific events—took place during the time of ongoing criminal and regulatory investigations as well as untold numbers of civil suits. As a result, those who agreed to speak with me, almost without exception, did so on the condition that their identities not be revealed.

At times, recollections and documents conflicted. To resolve these problems, I established standards of credibility: Tapes and transcripts of events trumped all other recollections and documents. Second were contemporaneous documents: expense records, e-mails, travel documents, diaries, notes, memos, schedule books, phone logs, and so on. Following that were sworn testimony or statements provided to government investigators. Last were interviews. In essence, the story was built on a foundation of documents, then fleshed out with information from interviews that was corroborated by those records. No one got a free ride; the renditions in this book are the events in which the interviews and the documents are in agreement or are consistent.

Some dialogue comes from direct transcripts of conversations. However, most of them were reconstructed with the help of participants or witnesses to conversations, or documents that describe the discussion. In a few instances, secondary sources were informed of events or conversations by a participant. If the secondary sources agreed on what they were told, and it was corroborated by documents, the dialogue was used. The dialogue and events reconstructed with secondary sources were never incriminating.

Because of the many sources used in reconstructing dialogue, readers should not assume that any individual participant in a conversation is the source of the statements or even among the sources. When a person is described as having thought or felt something, it comes either directly from that individual, from a document written by that individual, from notes or other records of that individual's comments to a third party, or from others to whom the individuals in question directly described their experiences.

Of course, I am not claiming that the dialogue in these pages is a perfect transcript of events dating back some twenty years. It does, however, represent the best recollection of these events and conversations by participants, and more accurately reflects reality than mere paraphrase would. Invariably, subjects of interviews would find that my pressing them for ever more detailed descriptions and dialogue—at times aided by documents I placed before them—led to greater recall of the events.

In some instances I was unable to determine the exact date that an event occurred. In those cases I have presented the relevant scene at the point in the narrative that is most consistent with the information contained in related documents and interviews. In such scenes I give no indication of the event's date. For ease of reading, if a scene was moved a few days out of order to allow for a theme in one chapter to be completed, the next chapter moved back in time to an unrelated event, launching a new story line. Such instances are described in these notes.

Descriptions of individual settings come from interviews, documents, or personal observation. Most details of weather conditions come from records on file with the National Climatic Data Center.

PROLOGUE

1 Details of Ken Lay's car from records on file with the Texas Department of Transportation, Vehicle Titles and Registration Division, for a 1993 Mercedes-Benz 600 SL Roadster, vehicle identification number WDBFA76EXPF079413.

1 Information about River Oaks from personal observation, and from Claudia Feldman, "Casas Grandes," *Houston Chronicle*, Oct. 27, 2002, Lifestyle section, 1.

6 Details of Fastow's Oct. 24, 2001, e-mail to his wife from the original document.

7–9 Details of Jazid from observation of the location and interviews. Also see Ben Crandell, "Rubies and Jade in a Perfect Setting: A Cool Night at Jazid," *South Florida Sun-Sentinel*, Nov. 23, 2001, 58.

CHAPTER 1

15 Date of the meeting between Lay and the internal auditors from documents prepared for the presentation, and details from Woytek's schedule book.

15 Weather conditions of that morning from the National Climatic Data Center of the National Oceanic and Atmospheric Administration. The data were collected on the morning of Feb. 2, 1987, at the William P. Hobby station in Houston, which climatologists said was most reflective of the conditions in the downtown area.

15–16 Details of the Mastroeni and Borget account at Eastern Savings Bank from an internal memo at the bank's successor, Apple Bank for Savings, Jan. 29, 1987. The memo relates to account no. 0704101069 in the name of InterNorth International Oil. It lists transactions in the account, showing $4.8 million wired in and some $2.25 million disbursed in Mastroeni's name. Also, some details from an investigative memo prepared Feb. 1, 1987, detailing questions that the Enron internal-audit department wanted to have answered.

16 The traffic and related conditions of Houston as of Feb. 1987 in the wake of the oil bust from David Maraniss, "Houston Learns There's More Than Growth to Growing Up," *Washington Post*, Feb. 4, 1987, A3.

16–17 Details of the contents of the packet of documents provided by Borget from the original records, headed "CONFIDENTIAL/Memo for the File: Enron Oil Corp. Banking Program," Feb. 2, 1987. This includes purported Teletypes to Isla Petroleum, Southwest Oil, and the other bogus entities.

17 Copies of both the original and the forged bank statements for account 0704101069 at Eastern Savings Bank, a.k.a. Apple Bank for Savings, were obtained by the author.

17–18 The Borget explanation, in part, from the Feb. 2, 1987, memo headed "CONFIDENTIAL/Memo for the File: Enron Oil Corp. Banking Program."

18–19 The transactions involving the oil trader from the original banking records, with supporting details from the trader's personnel records and a Feb. 6, 1987, memo written by Mark van den Dries, an executive in the oil-trading division, to David Woytek and John Beard. Additional information from certain tax records of the trader, as well as a June 1, 1984, memo written by Thomas Mastroeni about the conditions of the trader's employment. Details are also from a preliminary report, "Reporting of $250,000 Payment to Former Employee," Feb. 9, 1987, which was prepared by the internal-audit group.

20 Certain details of the 1948 truck accident from current residents of Raymondville, Missouri. The truck accident was first written about publicly by Bryan Gruley and Rebecca Smith, "Anatomy of a Fall: Keys to Success Left Kenneth Lay Open to Disaster," *Wall Street Journal*, April 26, 2002, A1.

20–24 Some details of the Lays' early life first came to the author's attention from Gruley and Smith, "Anatomy of a Fall." Other articles providing information included Kyle Pope, "Big Business May Not Be Big Enough for Enron Chairman," *Houston Chronicle*, Oct. 13, 1991. Also see Loren Fox, *Enron: The Rise and Fall* (Wiley, 2003), 7–11; Mimi Swartz with Sherron Watkins, *Power Failure* (Doubleday, 2003), 21–30; and Bethany McLean and Peter Elkind, *The Smartest Guys in the Room* (Portfolio, 2003), 4–14.

22 Some details regarding the end of Lay's first marriage from civil action no. c1-61-4126, captioned *In re the Marriage of Kenneth L. Lay and Judith A. Lay*, filed in Orange County State Circuit Court.

24 Some information relating to Lay's trip to Zurich from the original itinerary.

23–24 Some details of Lay's move to HNG from "Houston Natural Gas Chairman Resigns Under Pressure," Dow Jones News Service, June 6, 1984.

26–28 Some details of Skilling's background from a transcript of his secret deposition before the SEC on Dec. 5–6, 2001. Other details from his deposition of Sept. 19, 1997, in the case of *Bernard H. Glatzer v. Bear Stearns & Co.*, 95 civ. 1154, filed in U.S. District Court for the Southern District of New York, 10–14. Other details from Peter Tufano and Sanjay Bhatnagar's case study for Harvard Business School, "Enron Gas Services," number N9-294-076, March 4, 1994. Also see an untitled Jan. 6, 2001, draft of an article by Professor Christopher A. Bartlett for the *Harvard Business Review*. In addition, see McLean and Elkind, *Smartest Guys in the Room*; Fox, *Enron*; and Swartz with Watkins, *Power Failure*.

29–30 Some details of the contentious board meeting of Nov. 12, 1985, from the official minutes. The documents, which are not public, were obtained by the author. Details of the movie production from Steve Millburg, "Movie Crew Ends Omaha Stay," *Omaha World Herald,* November 26, 1985.

31–32 Some details of the audit committee meeting of Jan. 20, 1986, from the official minutes.

33–34 Details of the Enteron debacle from Matt Moffett, "HNG/InterNorth Goes to Pros in Bid to Get New Name." *Wall Street Journal*, Feb. 20, 1986, sec. 1, 12. Also see "Enteron, Is It?" *Inside FERC*, Feb. 24, 1986, 6; and "HNG-InterNorth Scraps Proposed Name Because of Publicity over Meaning," Associated Press, March 7, 1986.

34–35 Details of the original Valhalla investigation come from several confidential records, created preceding, during, and after the review. They include a document Woytek wrote dated Jan. 30, 1987, "Summary of Conversations in Regards to InterNorth International Oil, Inc.," and the preliminary report submitted by the internal-audit department to Kinder on Feb. 9, 1987, "Investigation of 'Off-Balance-Sheet' Cash Transaction of Enron International Oil, Inc." Unsigned notes of discussions that took place surrounding the investigation, dated Feb. 9, 1987, are included in the official corporate file relating to this investigation and describe some of the events that occurred. In addition, the author relied on details from the Feb. 9, 1987, report, "Enron International: Special Project."

35–36 Details of the Andersen investigation from the confidential report of April 22, 1987, written by the firm to Mick Seidl, president and chief operating officer of Enron. Also see a March 12, 1987, letter to corporate auditing from Steve Sulentic.

35–36 A copy of the confidential private investigations report, conducted by Intertect Inc. of Houston and dated Dec. 13, 1987, was obtained by the author.

36–37 Some details of the April 29, 1987, audit committee meeting from the official minutes.

37 Some details of the meeting between Seidl and Borget from McLean and Elkind, *Smartest Guys in the Room*, 22.

38–39 Some details of the oil-trading scandal from Enron's official release on the matter, "Enron Discontinues Subsidiary," Oct. 22, 1987.

CHAPTER 2

41–45 Some details of the development and functioning of the Gas Bank from Skilling's SEC deposition of Dec. 5–6, 2001, as well as his Sept. 19, 1997, deposition in *Glatzer v. Bear Stearns*, 27–29. Other details from Tufano and Bhatnagar, "Enron Gas Services," and the untitled Jan. 6, 2001, draft of the Bartlett article for the *Harvard Business Review*.

46–48 Details of the events surrounding the economic summit from a variety of sources, including a transcript of the June 21, 1990, White House briefing conducted by Marlin Fitzwater, the Press Secretary; a transcript of the July 11, 1990, broadcast of *ABC World News Tonight*; Sean McCormally, "Sherpas and Snappers, Nocturnal and Otherwise," United Press International, July 12, 1990.

46–47 Much of the information on Lay's relationship with the first President Bush from an array of White House documents, including personal papers of the President. These include a May 18, 1989, memo written by a White House official named Patricia Mack Bryan to C. Boyden Gray, the White House counsel, relating to Lay's approaches on locating the Bush library in Houston; a March 21, 1989, letter to Bush from Lay; and a personal letter dated Oct. 11, 1989, from Bush to Lay. Bush directly communicated with Lay regarding the summit in a handwritten note, Jan. 23, 1990; a typed note, June 5,

1990; and a typed letter, Sept. 7, 1990. Some information also came from a follow-up letter from John Sununu, the White House Chief of Staff, to Lay, July 24, 1990.

46 Bush chastised his staff for failing to forward him a Lay letter in a May 30, 1991, memo he typed to Phil Brady, a White House staffer. This resulted in a series of written communications that day between Bush, Brady, and Shirley Green, a special assistant to the President, culminating in a personal letter from Bush to Lay, May 31, 1991.

47 Bush described his feelings about the event in Houston in his remarks at the "Thank You Houston Celebration," which were transcribed in *Public Papers of the President*, vol. 26, doc. 1085, July 11, 1990. All of Bush's public dialogue comes from that transcript, and certain events that had just occurred, including his thoughts, were described in his speech.

49–50 The timing of the conversations between Spencer Stuart and Fastow was established by the dates automatically printed on faxes that day that went to both Fastow and Enron.

50 Portions of Fastow's background from his 1997 deposition in *Glatzer v. Bear Stearns*. Also see David Barboza and John Schwartz, "The Financial Wizard Tied to Enron's Fall," *New York Times*, Feb. 6, 2002, A1. Other information from a copy of Fastow's 1990 résumé.

50 Fastow's encounter with the cabdriver was chronicled by Ann Marie Lipinski and Hanke Gratteau, "What Some Cab Riders Suffer Is a Crime," *Chicago Tribune*, May 27, 1986.

50–51 A copy of the document faxed from Spencer Stuart to Skilling was obtained by the author. It contains an automatically printed fax "telltale," which reveals the time and date it was sent.

52 Details of Fastow's employment from a Dec. 3, 1990, Personnel Action Form, maintained by Enron's human-resources department and specifying the terms of his deal. Other information from a Nov. 27, 1990, memo for Enron's human-resources department, written by Sheila Knudsen and addressed to Glenda Czaplewski, spelling out additional terms of Fastow's arrangement.

53–54 Some details of the early days in the finance group from Tufano and Bhatnagar, "Enron Gas Services," and the untitled Jan. 6, 2001, draft of the Bartlett article for the *Harvard Business Review*.

54 Some details of the mechanisms used in structured finance from Vinson & Elkins, "Structured Finance Overview," April 1999.

54–55 The perceptions within Enron Gas Services of mark-to-market accounting are drawn from a number of documentary sources. They include a June 1990 document, "Summary of Example of Mark-to-Market Accounting," and a preliminary internal report from the same month, "Criteria for Adoption of Mark-to-Market Accounting." Also see the report "Enron Gas Services Mark to Market Accounting Memorandum to the Securities and Exchange Commission," June 11, 1990, as well as a June 28, 1991, letter signed by Jack Tompkins and George Posey and submitted to John Albert, the SEC's associate chief accountant. Details of mark-to-market accounting from an Arthur Andersen document dated Oct. 11, 1999, commissioned for Enron, entitled "Application of Mark-to-Market and Fair Value Accounting."

55–59 A copy of the application to the SEC by Enron Gas Services pushing for a change in the division's accounting was obtained by the author. Dated June 11, 1991, it was signed by Tompkins and Posey and sent to George Diacont, then the SEC'S acting chief accountant.

57–58 The conversation between Posey, Tompkins, and Albert comes from contemporaneous notes of the discussion, which Posey and Tompkins transcribed that same day into a single, agreed-upon rendition of everything that had been said.

59–60 A number of records documented Skilling's presentation to the SEC. They include a copy of the presentation itself, "Presentation by Jeff Skilling, CEO, Enron Gas Services," Sept. 17, 1991, as well as an outline of additional comments made at the meeting, and unsigned notes that were taken during the discussion, which were obtained by the author. Also see an Oct. 4, 1991, letter from Posey of Enron to Mike Foley in the office of the chief accountant at the SEC.

60 The questions to Enron from the SEC are documented in a number of letters from Posey. These include one to Diacont, Nov. 5, 1991; another to John Albert, Dec. 5, 1991; and a final one to Albert, Dec. 16, 1991. Enron officials met a second time with the SEC, on Dec. 19, 1991, and the author obtained the written presentation for that meeting.

60–61 A copy of the Jan. 30, 1992, letter from the SEC to Enron was obtained by the author. Signed by Walter Schuetze, the chief accountant, it was addressed to Tompkins.

61 Enron's decision to utilize mark-to-market accounting effective Jan. 1, 1991, is revealed in a Feb. 11, 1992, letter from Tompkins to Schuetze. The motivation for that move was discussed with the author by Enron officers involved in the decision.

61–62 Some details on the history of Mark's division and the India power project from Minority Staff, U.S. House of Representatives, Committee on Government Reform, "Background on Enron's Dabhol Power Project," Feb. 22, 2002. Also see the 2002 case presentation number A07-02-0008 at Thunderbird, the American Graduate School of International Management, by Professor Andrew Inkpen, "Enron and the Dabhol Power Company," and Inkpen's case presentation number A07-97-0004, "Enron Development Corporation," 1997. Specific details from original documents, including the minutes of the 118th meeting of the Central Electricity Authority, Dec. 11, 1993; and the confidential minutes of the Foreign Investment Promotion Board, Oct. 11, 1993. Some background of Mark from Toni Mack, "High Finance with a Touch of Theater," *Forbes*, May 18, 1998, 140.

61–62 Some details of the arrangement between Enron and its international power-project developers from a copy of their contract.

61–62 Some details of the meeting between the Indian delegation and Rebecca Mark from "U.S. Tour by Indian Delegation Ups Proposal Tally to over 7,300 MW," *Independent Power Report*, June 19, 1992.

CHAPTER 3

63 The financial performance of Enron Gas Services from the company's 10-K, filed with the SEC, for 1992.

63 Some details of Amanda Martin's background and role at Enron from a copy of her executive employment agreement, renewed as of Jan. 1, 1998.

65 Details of the agreement between Baker, Mosbacher, and Enron from the company's Feb. 22, 1993, press release, "Enron Corp. Signs Arrangement with Former Secretary of State James Baker and Former Secretary of Commerce Robert Mosbacher." Also see "Baker and Mosbacher Are Hired by Enron," *New York Times*, Feb. 23, 1993, D5.

65 Some details of the Dabhol plant from Abhay Mehta's fascinating book, *Power Play: A Study of the Enron Project*, published in India in 2000. Also see Claudia Kolker and Tom Fowler, "Dead Enron Power Plant Affecting Environment, Economy, and Livelihoods in India," *Houston Chronicle*, Aug. 4, 2002, Business section, 1. See also the May 20, 1998, memo for the file from Carl Bass and Michael Jones, "Report for Dabhol Power Company."

65–66 Some details of Bower's hunt for investment opportunities and the subsequent effort in developing JEDI from Christopher Palmeri and Ronald Grover, "Too Close for Comfort?" *Business Week*, March 18, 2002, 78–80, and from internal documents, including "Monitoring Plan for California Public Employee Retirement System's Investment in Energy Asset Development Limited Partnership," June 9, 1993, and "Formation of Joint Energy Development Investment Limited Partnership," June 29, 1993.

66 Some details of the executive committee meeting on May 17, 1993, from the official minutes.

67 Details about the cover and contents of Enron's 1992 annual report from the original document.

67 Mack's article "Hidden Risks" was printed in *Forbes*, May 24, 1993, 54.

68–69 Some details about Enron's clean-fuels division from the company's 1993 annual report.

69–70 Some details of Lay's golf game with Clinton, Ford, and Nicklaus from "Clinton Plays Bipartisan Golf, Then Switches to the Sax," Associated Press, Aug. 15, 1993, and Thomas Ferraro, "Clinton, Ford Engage in Bipartisan Golf," United Press International, Aug. 14, 1993.

73–74 A copy of the consultant's report on the Richmond plant was reviewed by the author.

75 Information about the Guatemalan financial transactions from "Report of Staff Investigation of Enron Corp. and Related Entities Regarding the Guatemalan Power Project," CP-108-15, issued by the Senate Finance Committee, March 2003.

75 Some details of the Dominican Republic deal and the subsequent battle with Bayside Inn from *Hotelera del Atlantico v. Smith-Enron et al.*, filed with the arbitrage court of the Santo Domingo Chamber of Commerce.

76 Kopper's background from a copy of his résumé, his written performance review at Enron for 1995 and the first six months of 1996, and a July 11, 1996, e-mail from Kopper to Causey and Fastow headed "Year to Date Performance." Also see "Exhibit A to Executive Employment Agreement Between Enron Capital Management and Michael Kopper," for July 1, 1998, through June 30, 2000. See also Kopper's testimony of Sept. 27, 2004, in the case of *United States of America v. Daniel Bayly et. al.*, H-CR-03-363, in Federal District Court in Houston. Among the trips taken by the Fastows with Kopper and Dodson was a weekend jaunt to California wine country to the $550-a-night Auberge du Soleil, which is documented on an itinerary for May 26–29, 2000, with the heading "NAPA TRIP."

77 Details of the Shiv Sena rally from Madhu Nainan, "Foreign Investors Jittery as Hindu Militants Take Charge in Bombay," Agence France Presse, March 19, 1995. Also see Emily MacFarquhar, "A Volatile Democracy," *U.S. News & World Report*, March 27, 1995, 36.

77 Background of Thackeray from John F. Burns, "A Violent Goal: Hindustan for Hindus," *New York Times*, Nov. 3, 1995, A6; Burns, "Another Rushdie Novel, Another Bitter Epilogue," *New York Times*, Dec. 2, 1995, sec. 1, 1; Julia Eckert, "The Charisma of Autocracy," *Manushi*, issue 130 (2002); and Praveen Swami, "Let Off, for Now," *Frontline: India's National Magazine*, Aug. 5–18, 2000. Details of Thackeray's relationships with violent mobs from "Demagogue of Hate," *Asia Week*, Dec. 29, 1995; Ajay Singh, "The Emperor's Troubles," *Asia Week*, Sept. 13, 1996; and "Little Hitler Calls the Shots," *South China Morning Post*, Nov. 13, 1995, 19.

77 Details of the World Bank findings from its April 30, 1993, report, which was forwarded to the Indian Secretary of Finance.

77 Enron's decision to respond to the World Bank report by hiring a public-relations firm from a June 28, 1993, letter written by Joseph Sutton from the international division to Ajit Nimbalkar, chairman of the Maharashtra State Electricity Board.

77 Total amount spent on education in India by Enron from the testimony of Linda F. Powers, vice president of global finance with Enron Development Corporation, before the Foreign Operations Subcommittee of the House Committee on Appropriations, Jan. 31, 1995.

79–80 Some details of Jim Alexander's efforts, and his conversation with Kinder, from John Schwartz, "An Enron Unit Chief Warned, and Was Rebuffed," *New York Times*, Feb. 20, 2002, C1. Also see Julian E. Barnes, "How a Titan Came Undone," *U.S. News & World Report*, March 18, 2002, 26.

81 Details of Burns's new job from "Union Pacific Railroad Brings in an Outsider," Associated Press, July 28, 1995.

82–83 Details of the Lay and Mark trip to India and Matoshri from a copy of Lay's personal itinerary from Oct. 20 through Nov. 3, 1995.

82–83 Details about India, its culture, and its political circumstances come from an assortment of sources, including interviews. Basic information came from David Collins's book, *Mumbai (Bombay)* (Lonely Planet, 1999). A more complete picture of the country and its economic forces came from Gurcharan Das, *India Unbound* (Knopf, 2001), and John Keay, *India: A History* (Grove Press, 2001). Additional information from Burns, "A Violent Goal."

83–84 Some descriptive details of Matoshri from a series of external and internal photographs of the residence obtained by the author, including one taken during the meeting between Lay, Mark, and Thackeray.

84 The death of Meena Thackeray was described by Naresh Fernandes, "Wife of Maharashtra State's De Facto Leader Dies," Associated Press Worldstream, Sept. 6, 1995.

85 The article read by Clinton was by Allen R. Myerson, "Tentative Pact Allows Enron to Continue Project in India," *New York Times*, Nov. 22, 1995, C1. Clinton's reaction to the article was first reported by Michael Weisskopf, "That Invisible Mack Sure Can Leave His Mark," *Time*, Sept. 1, 1997, 21. Weather conditions were obtained from records on file with the National Climatic Data Center.

85 Some details of the plant renegotiations from Mehta, *Power Play*; Minority Staff, U.S. House of Representatives, Committee on Government Reform, "Background on Enron's Dabhol Power Project," Feb. 22, 2002; and Inkpen, "Enron and the Dabhol Power Company," and "Enron Development Corporation," 1996.

CHAPTER 4

89–90 Some details of the atmosphere and style at Armando's from Eric Lawlor, "Armando's Gets a New Chef—and a New Attitude," *Houston Press*, Jan. 8, 1988.

90–91 Some details of Fastow's work and role within the retail unit from a May 1, 1996, e-mail he wrote, which included a draft memo for distribution discussing his role.

92 Some descriptive details of Portland's World Trade Center and surrounding areas from Bill Greer, "At Peace in Portland," *The Tennessean*, Sept. 12, 1999, Travel 1. Some details of their discussion from a Schedule 14A proxy statement filed with the SEC by Portland General on May 21, 1997, 24–25.

93 Some details of Kaminski's background from the notes of his interview with lawyers from Wilmer, Cutler & Pickering, Dec. 19, 2001.

95 Some details of Watkins's background and experiences at Enron from the book she wrote with Mimi Swartz, *Power Failure*, 72–75.

95–96 Watkins acknowledged her salty tongue in *Power Failure*, 12.

97–98 A copy of Beerel's undated analysis was obtained by the author.

99 A copy of Fastow's untitled report to Skilling was obtained by the author.

107–8 Some details of the management committee meeting from a set of unsigned notes contained in Enron's official files and obtained by the author.

110–11 Some details of the Phoenician meetings between Enron and Portland General from the May 21, 1997, Schedule 14A proxy statement, 27–28. Anita Marks, "Enron Deal: A Marriage Made in Phoenix," *Business Journal—Portland*, July 26, 1996, 1. Additional information about the merger from an internal Calpers analysis, prepared for the pension fund's investment committee by the Pacific Corporate Group, Aug. 19, 1996.

111 Some details of Lay's meeting with Portland General employees from Bill MacKenzie, "Big Guy in Town Makes Big Power Play," *Oregonian*, July 27, 1996, E1. Also see MacKenzie, "PG Employees Optimistic," *Oregonian*, July 24, 1996, C1.

CHAPTER 5

112–13 Details of Lay's trip to Morristown from the flight plan filed by the pilots. Information about the plane from the official records for the aircraft maintained by Enron.

115 Some details of Wilson's signing of the electricity deregulation bill from "California Set for Massive Electric Deregulation," Reuters, Sept. 24, 1996. Also see "SD Electric Law," City News Service, Sept. 23, 1996. Information about the legislation itself was found at www.energyquest.ca.gov/time_machine/1990ce-2000ce.html.

115–16 Information regarding the structure of the California electricity system from Will McNamara, *The California Energy Crisis: Lessons for a Deregulating Industry* (PennWell, 2002); and James L. Sweeney, *The California Electricity Crisis* (Hoover Institution Press, 2002). Also see the March 2003 report prepared by the staff of the Federal Energy Regulatory Commission, "Final Report on Price Manipulation in Western Markets," docket no. PA02-2-000.

120 Details of the basement inspection, and the technician's failure to properly use the equipment, from records produced in the National Transportation Safety Board's investigation of the San Jaun explosion, as well as the final NTSB report, "Pipeline Accident Report: San Juan Gas Company Inc. Enron Corp. Propane Gas Explosion in San Juan, Puerto Rico, on November 21, 1996," PB97-916501 NTSB PAR-97/01. The company's history of safety violations, and the total fines it paid, from the NTSB report.

124 Details of the San Juan explosion, and the events surrounding it, from redacted copy of testimony before the NTSB, as well as the final report, "Pipeline Accident Report." Also see Hilario de Leon, "Explosion Turns Day into Night on Busy Street," Associated Press, Nov. 21, 1996.

125–26 Some details of the board's decision on Lay and Kinder from Lay's employment contract, Dec. 18, 1996.

125–26 Some details of Kinder's decision to leave Enron from Michael Davis, "Lay Staying, So Kinder Will Leave," *Houston Chronicle*, Nov. 27, 1996, Business, 1.

127–28 Details of the party at the Museum of Natural Science from planning and billing records obtained by the author. Some descriptive information from the Web site for the Houston Museum of Natural Science, www.hmns.org.

131 Some details of Skilling's elevation from the company's official announcement, Dec. 10, 1996.

CHAPTER 6

137–38 Some details of the unveiling of the new corporate logo from Enron's official announcement of Jan. 14, 1997. Other details from Skilling's schedule book for that day.

138 Some details about the selection of Duncan as the lead member of Andersen's Enron engagement team from a Form 302—the FBI notes of an interview—for D. Stephen Goddard Jr., reflecting his statements to Special Agents Greg Ruppert, Paul Holdeman, and Paula Schanzle, Feb. 28, 2002. The notes are part of case file nos. 196C-HO-59147 (the Enron investigation) and 196C-HO-59147-AA (the Andersen inquiry).

139 Details of Duncan's background, including his purchases for the co-op and use of illegal drugs both during and after college, from a series of his FBI 302s in cases 196C-HO-59147 and 196C-HO-59147-AA. These include notes from interviews conducted by Special Agents John S. Hummel and David Michael Hays on Jan. 14 and 16, 2002. They also include notes from interviews conducted by Special Agents James E. Jewell and Paul Holdeman on March 21 and April 5 and 6, 2002.

140 Some details of Bass's background from his FBI 302 from his interview of Feb. 1, 2002, with Special Agent Omer Meisel.

142 Some details of the Enron and Calpine deal from the Calpine press release of March 31, 1997, "Calpine to Acquire Interest in 827 MW of Gas-Fired Power Plants." No similar release was issued by Enron.

142–43 Some details of Fastow's effort to bring friends into deals, and the creation of Alpine Investors, from a government affidavit of Special Agent Omer Meisel, filed as part of a criminal complaint against Fastow on Oct. 1, 2002, at Houston's Federal District Courthouse, case no. HO-2-889-M. Also see the internal Andersen 1997 document "Joint Ventures, SPE's, Partnerships."

143 Melcher's role as an investor with Fastow was revealed by a number of sources, including the notes of the Jan. 12, 2002, interview with Kristina Mordaunt by Wilmer, Cutler. Also see the Wilmer, Cutler notes from the Dec. 6, 2001, interview with Carol St. Clair, an assistant general counsel with Enron.

143 Some background of Mintz and details of his job from a copy of his executive employment agreement with Enron Capital & Trade Resources Corp., Dec. 1, 1997.

144 Some details about the collapse of Alpine Investors, and its replacement by the RADR structure, from the Oct. 1, 2002, Meisel affidavit.

144–46 Some details of the May 14, 1997, presentation to Calpers from the report used by Fastow, "Discussion with Calpers." Also see a confidential May 27, 1997, memo prepared by Sheryl Pressler for Barry Gonder of Calpers, "Comparison of the Proposal Made by Enron to Staff Concerning a New Relationship Versus What PCG Has Communicated to Staff," which summarizes the events of May 14, as well as a draft, unsigned memo to Pressler from Enron Capital Management, May 29, 1997. Also see details from the June 10, 1997, meeting within Enron about the Calpers presentation, as shown in unsigned, handwritten notes taken in a meeting that included Fastow and Jeremy Blachman, an executive in the finance division.

147 Bill Brown described his early role in the special-projects group during his Dec. 5, 2001, interview with lawyers on the Wilmer, Cutler team. Copies of the official notes from that interview were obtained by the author.

147 Some details of Glisan's background from his employment application with Enron, dated Aug. 1996, as well as his résumé. Also see Glisan's Commercial Support Performance Review, Sept. 3, 1996.

147–48 Some details of Astin's review of the investment proposal from the notes of his interview with Wilmer, Cutler, Dec. 11, 2001. Other details from Wilmer, Cutler's notes from the Jan. 11, 2002, interview with Mordaunt, and also from the firm's notes of the Dec. 6, 2001, interview with St. Clair. There were what appeared to be some factual conflicts between Astin's and Mordaunt's accounts—unless Mordaunt was describing subsequent meetings, many of which took place that summer. However, the author reviewed contemporaneous handwritten notes taken during the summer of 1997 that confirmed Astin's account of the events portrayed here.

148–49 The problems with the Portland General contract were revealed in the minutes of Enron's audit committee meeting on Oct. 12, 1998. Ultimately, those numbers were disclosed by Enron in its Nov. 8, 2001, announcement of its intent to restate its financials, dating back to 1997.

150–51 Some details of Enron's initial forays into broadband from the company's April 22, 1998, release, "First Point Communications Inc. and Optec Inc. Join Forces to Become Enron Communications."

152 Some details of the wire transfer from the criminal information filed Aug. 21, 2002, in *United States of America v. Michael J. Kopper*, no. H-02-0560, in the Federal District Court in Houston, as well as the criminal complaint filed in *United States of America v. Andrew S. Fastow*, no. H-02-889-M, filed in the Federal District Court in Houston, Oct. 1, 2002. Also see the superseding indictment in the case of *United States of America v. Andrew S. Fastow et al.*, no. H-02-0665, filed on April 30, 2003. Also, the author reviewed copies of wire-transfer documents used in the transaction.

152–53 Some details of Astin's response to his review of Sept. 4 from the notes of his Dec. 11, 2001, interview with Wilmer, Cutler. Also see *Final Report of Neal Batson, Court Appointed Examiner*, vol. 4, app. C, 111, filed in the case of *In re Enron Corp. et al.* filed in U.S. Bankruptcy Court for the Southern District of New York, case no. 01-16034 (the Batson Report).

153–54 Some details of the Sept. 8, 1997, meeting from handwritten notes prepared by Bob Baird, as well as a sworn statement given by Astin to the bankruptcy examiner on July 18, 2003, 57–62. Also see the notes of the Dec. 11, 2001, interview with Astin by Wilmer, Cutler, as well as the Batson Report, vol. 4, app. C, 111–112. Also see notes of the Wilmer, Cutler interviews with Mordaunt on Jan. 11, 2002.

154–55 The decision to substitute Kopper for Fastow is described in the Wilmer, Cutler interviews with Mordaunt on Jan. 11, 2002, as well as the firm's interview with St. Clair on Dec. 6, 2001. See also the facsimile, including a structure of the proposed Chewco deal, sent by St. Clair to Vinson & Elkins on Oct. 31, 1997.

155–56 Some details of Fastow's meeting with Skilling from a transcript of Skilling's nonpublic testimony before the SEC, Dec. 5, 2001.

156 The effort to arrange the Barclays "consulting agreement" from minutes of the Oct. 20, 1997, Barclays operations committee meeting, as well as a Sept. 10, 1997, memo from John Meyer of Barclays to Helen Calvelli, Richard Williams, and John Sullivan—all from the bank—relating to the structure of the deal. Also see the Batson Report, vol. 3, app. F, 43–44.

156–57 Some details of the Chewco tax-indemnification agreement from "Report of Investigation by the Special Investigative Committee of the Board of Directors of Enron Corp." (the Powers Report), Feb. 1, 2002, 64–66. Also see the Wilmer, Cutler notes from the Jan. 9, 2002, interview with John E. Lynch, a partner with the Vinson & Elkins tax group, and the notes from the law firm's Nov. 15, 2001, interview with Mintz.

157 Some details of Brown's potential role in Chewco, and his discussions about the negotiations with Fastow, from the notes of his Wilmer, Cutler interviews of Dec. 5, 2001, and Jan. 5, 2002. Also see Brown's undated memo to Fastow and Kopper "1997 Accomplishments," which describes his work on the negotiations for Project Chewbacca, and Kopper's Jan. 7, 1998, memo to Rocky Jones of Enron's human-resources department, "Bill Brown."

158–60 Some details of the Enron management committee meeting from a distribution office memo from Vanessa Groscrand of Enron, "1997 Enron Management Conference, November 5–7, 1997," issued in late Oct. 1997.

158–59 Some details of the changes relating to the company's European business from a memo issued by Lay and Skilling, "European Responsibilities," Nov. 19, 1997.

161–62 Ephross's role in drafting the side letter from his Dec. 16, 1997, memo to Kopper, Mike Edsall, George McKean, and Sarah Ward. A copy of the Chewco side deal, signed by Kopper and Blachman, was obtained by the author.

162–63 Terms of the deals completed that night from the closing documents. Also see the original subscription agreement, "Subscription Agreement Among Joint Energy Development Investments Limited Partnership, Enron Capital Management Limited Partnership, and Chewco Investments, LLC," Nov. 6, 1997. Also see the Aug. 11, 1997, letter from Barry Gonder of Calpers to Enron Capital Management.

Moreover, additional details are provided by the Aug. 20, 1997, confidential presentation from Enron to Calpers, "JEDI II: Investment Opportunities," and an investment term sheet sent by Ron Astin of Vinson & Elkins to Dulcie Brand of Jones, Day, Reavis & Pogue on Oct. 31, 1997. Some details of the EES investments from Fastow's Aug. 19, 1997, letter to Gonder; the Sept. 15, 1997, document "Bylaws of Enron Energy Services"; the Aug. 21, 1997, presentation from Enron to Calpers, "Enron Energy Services"; and a package of documents, sent by Blachman on Sept. 30, 1997, to Calpers, the Pacific Corporate Group, and J. P. Morgan with an attached memo headed "EES Due Diligence Questions." Details for both transactions were found in a Sept. 22, 1997, letter prepared by Calpers's lawyers with Jones, Day for Gonder's signature, and addressed to Enron Capital Management. Additional details were found in a Sept. 15, 1997, presentation by Calpers's staff to the system's investment committee and in a term sheet sent to the Pacific Corporate Group by Jim Timmins of Enron on Oct. 3, 1997.

163–64 The structure of Chewco was clearly explained both in the Powers Report, 60–65, and in the Batson Report, vol. 4, app. C, 108–14. Additional information from the handwritten notes of St. Clair, Dec. 11, 1997, and undated notes apparently from that same month. Also see the July 18, 1997, memo from St. Clair to the Chewbacca Working Group, "Registration Rights and Procedures." Also, some details from the FBI 302 from the agency's Feb. 15, 2002, interview with Patricia Grutzmacher.

164 The decision to create the file on the laptop computer was first disclosed by Kopper in his discussions with the government in anticipation of his plea deal. The existence of the laptop, with few details about it, was revealed in the government's April 30, 2003, superseding indictment of Fastow.

164 A copy of the "Top 10 Reasons" parody was obtained by the author.

164 Details of the second-quarter write-off caused by J-Block and MTBE from the Enron press release "Enron Corp. Reports 1997 Second Quarter Earnings Per Share from Operations of $0.40, Announces Reduced Earnings Expectations, and Plans a 10 Million Share Repurchase by Year End," July 15, 1997. Also see the June 3, 1997, analyst report by Curt Launer, then of Donaldson, Lufkin & Jenrette, "Enron Corp. Settles 'J-Block Contract,' Second Quarter 1997 Earnings Per Share Indication Below Consensus."

164 The fifty-one million dollars in profits from the Bonneville power contract were later restated in Enron's 8-K of Nov. 8, 2001.

164–65 The overstatement of income to EES from the Batson Report, vol. 2, app. O, 13–16. Also see the Feb. 7, 1998, e-mail from John Stewart, of the Arthur Andersen Professional Standards Group, to Grutzmacher on the Enron engagement team.

CHAPTER 7

167–68 Some details of Levitt's personal background and of the early days of the accounting wars from his book *Take on the Street* (Pantheon Books, 2002), 3–7, 105–24.

168–69 Details of Stewart's e-mail from the original document.

170–71 Details of Skilling's visit to Washington from entries in his daily schedule.

171–72 Some details of the finance meeting with Fastow from unsigned, handwritten notes taken during the discussion. Additional information, and details of the Moody's presentation, in the document "Enron Rating Agency Presentation to Moody's Investors Service," Feb. 17, 1998. Also see the Dec. 17, 1998, document from Toronto Dominion, "Toronto Dominion Speedy Review," which states that Enron has informed the bank it is entering into prepay transactions with it to satisfy its commitments to the ratings agencies to decrease its debt; such deals lowered on-books debt while raising total debt.

173–74 Some details of Skilling's meetings over these days from entries in his schedule book.

174–75 Details of the Rhythms purchase and Skilling's approval from the document "Enron Capital Management Deal Approval Sheet" with "Deal Name: Rhythms," March 3, 1998, which was signed by Skilling two days later.

176 A copy of the announcement e-mail was obtained by the author. Also see a copy of the personal letter to Fastow from James F. Burgoyne, managing director for GE Capital Services, March 24, 1998.

176 Some details of Buy's background from notes his confidential Jan. 17, 2002, interview with staff members of the House Energy and Commerce Committee's Subcommittee on Oversight and Investigations. The notes are incorrectly dated as having been taken on Jan. 17, 2001.

178–79 Details of the use of the "management fee" accounting gimmick from the Powers Report, 57–58.

179 Some details of McMahon's assumption of the treasurer's position, and his meeting with Fastow about it, from the notes from his Jan. 21, 2002, interview with Wilmer, Cutler.

179–80 Some details of the Ashcroft fund-raiser from documents on file relating to his presidential bid and "Spirit of Victory" political action committee.

181 The weather details from records on file with the National Climatic Data Center, from William P. Hobby station in Houston, April 17, 1998.

181 Some details of the April 17 finance committee meeting from the official minutes.

181–83 Some details of the discussion between Tilney and Fastow are described in an April 18, 1998, memo from Tilney and Rick Gordon of Merrill to Herb Allison in the firm's New York headquarters.

183 The telephone call from Allison was recorded on a call log that morning.

184 Copies of the Tilney faxes—from April 28, April 30, and May 4—were obtained by the author.

185–86 Some details of the Kopper and Fastow trip to England to visit with the executives of Greenwich NatWest from a copy of Kopper's travel itinerary for May 17–20, 1998, and a May 15, 1998, memo issued by Kelly Boots to Fastow, "Greenwich NatWest Meeting." Also see Fastow's itinerary issued for the week of May 18, 1998.

186 Terms of Olson's firing from an internal Merrill document, "Termination Authorization Form," with a proposed firing date of June 1998. Also see a May 25, 1998, e-mail from Susan Preli of Merrill global research to Margot Leffler of the firm's human-resources division regarding Olson's termination. Finally, other details came from Olson's May 22, 1998, e-mail, "Last Wednesday's Events," to Andrew Melnick of the research department. In his testimony before the House Energy and Commerce Committee's Subcommittee on Oversight and Investigations on Feb. 7, 2002, Olson alluded to, although he did not discuss explicitly, Enron's efforts in his case and its attempts to reward analysts who spoke favorably of the company and punish those who did not.

187 Some details of the presentation to Lay were identical with those later presented on June 22, 1998, to the board of directors in the report "Project Trident: Creating a Global Water Company."

187 The time and place of the Martin meeting with Skilling from an entry in Skilling's schedule book.

188–89 A copy of the proposal presented to Skilling regarding the Elektro deal, "Project Hubcap Update," was obtained by the author.

189–90 Some details of the July 14, 1998, executive committee meeting from the official minutes.

190 Some details of the auction for Elektro from "Elektro Auction Should Be Model for Integral Subsidiary," Gazeta Mercantil Invest News, July 16, 1998; Geoff Dyer, "Elektro Stake Bids to Start at $744 Million," *Financial Times*, 40; "Enron-Led Consortium Wins Elektro Auction," *Business News Americas*, July 16, 1998; and Karen Santos, "Enron Buys into Utility in Brazil," *Houston Chronicle*, July 17, 1998, Business section, 1.

190–93 Some details of the special meeting of the Enron board of directors held on July 21, 1998, from the official minutes. Also see the July 24, 1998, "Letter to All Employees," written by Lay and Skilling. The Marlin financing is described in a March 18, 1999, memo written by Roger Willard of Andersen for the Azurix Corp. and Atlantic Water Trust files, "Pushdown Requirements for Azurix and the Atlantic Water Trust." Also see a series of e-mails between Bass and Stewart of Arthur Andersen, Aug. 7–8, 1998, e-mails between the two men of Aug. 13–14, 1998, as well as the Sept. 22, 1998, Andersen e-mail, with attachments, from Michael Patrick to Richard Petersen and John Stewart.

193–94 The efforts to work through the financing of Elektro are reflected in a 1998 memo from Bowen, copied to Fastow and McMahon, "Elektro—Debt Refinancing and Equity Syndication Action Plan."

194 Timing of Olson's dismissal from his official notice of termination.

194–95 McMahon testified about his efforts to bring in an outside person to manage an Enron equity fund in his appearance at hearings before the House Energy and Commerce Committee's Subcommittee on Oversight and Investigations on Feb. 7, 2002. He discussed certain specifics of his efforts to recruit Jakubik in his Jan. 21, 2002, interview with Wilmer, Cutler, which are reflected in the notes of that session.

195–96 Details of Levitt's "numbers game" speech from a transcript and video of the event. He also described this speech in *Take on the Street*, 118–19.

196 Data about the performance of the Dow Jones Industrial Average from www.djindexes.com.

CHAPTER 8

197–99 These events occurred on September 11, 1998, seventeen days before the Levitt speech that closed Chapter Seven. However, for the sake of clarity and because the two closely set events are completely unrelated, I reversed the order of their presentation. This allowed for the chapter about Levitt to come full circle, and for the main arc of the Jakubik story to start in this chapter.

197 Details of the effects of Tropical Storm Frances from Eric Berger, "Frances Catches Area by Surprise," *Houston Chronicle*, Sept. 12, 1998, A1.

197–98 Some details of the timing of these events from entries in Skilling's schedule book for Sept. 11, 1998.

199–200 Some details of the audit committee meeting of Oct. 12 from the official minutes, the unofficial handwritten notes taken during the discussions by the corporate secretary, and a copy of the formal presentation made by Duncan and Causey.

200–1 Some details of the subsequent board meeting from the official minutes, the unofficial handwritten notes taken during the discussions by the corporate secretary, and a copy of the formal presentation made by Skilling.

201 Details of the guarantee authority granted to Fastow from a copy of the resolutions presented to the board on the morning of Oct. 13.

201–2 Timing of the meeting with the Chase bankers from entries in Skilling's official schedule as well as an Oct. 21, 1998, memo to Fastow and Skilling from Kelly Boots regarding the meeting. Also see the Oct. 23, 1998, memo from Rick Walker of Chase to Jimmy Lee regarding the upcoming meeting with Fastow and Skilling.

202 Details of Fastow's travels from a series of Sept. 29 memos from Kelly Boots, laying out his meetings with Banco Bilbao Vizcaya in Madrid; Société Générale and Crédit Lyonnais in Paris; Greenwich NatWest and Barclays in London; Banco Nazionale del Lavoro in Rome; and several others.

202–3 Serice described portions of the meeting and the subsequent encounter with Lyness in an e-mail the following day, dated Nov. 4, 1998, and addressed to Rick Walker of Chase, among others.

203–4 Much of this argument came to be voiced at a board meeting on Aug. 7, 2000, as Enron was attempting to decide what to do with billions of dollars the company, incorrectly, expected to be arriving soon. The argument was presented in the paperwork handed out for the meeting of the audit and compliance committee.

204 Some details of the discussions between Hannon and Rice from a transcript of Hannon's testimony before the Securities and Exchange Commission on Jan. 4, 2002.

204–5 Some details of Enron's move into broadband, its purchase of Modulus, and the challenges it faced from the FBI 302 from the interview of Rex Shelby, dated Aug. 15, 2002. Also see the Modulus document "Creating a Unique Advantage in Distributed Computing," April 1998; the Jan. 1999 internal Enron document "Q&A: Enron Communications"; and the sworn testimony of Kevin Hannon before the SEC on Jan. 4, 2002.

205 Timing of this meeting was established through entries in Skilling's schedule book.

206–8 Some details of McMahon's discussion with Brown and his subsequent meeting with Fastow from the Wilmer, Cutler notes of his Jan. 21, 2002, interview.

208 Details of the wire-transfer authorization from the original document. Details of Kopper's checks to Fastow from the superseding indictment in *U.S. v. Fastow et al.*

210–11 Some details of the effort to obtain Fastow the *CFO* magazine recognition from unsigned notes about the idea, which appear to have been put together by members of the public-relations office.

214 Details of Franco's efforts and statements from Mac Margolis and Michael Hirsh, "The Samba Effect," *Newsweek*, Jan. 25, 1999, 34.

214–15 Details of the 1999 analyst conference from the summary report, "Analyst Conference, Houston, Texas, January 20–21, 1999," including the attached agendas.

215–16 Some details of the board's trip to India from Lay's itinerary of that week, as well as packets of materials prepared for the board members.

219 Some details of the Azurix strategy from an undated document, "Azurix Private Placement Offering."

220 Some details of this conversation from a March 16, 1999, e-mail from Holloman to James Reilly of Citigroup.

221–22 A copy of the draft Enron Merchant Partners offering document was obtained by the author. The discussions between Merrill and Fastow are documented in a Dec. 3, 1998, internal Merrill memo from Schuyler Tilney to Dan Bayly, with the subject heading "Andy Fastow."

CHAPTER 9

223 Details of the performance of Rhythms from a stock-price listing from that day. Data about the performance of the Dow Jones Industrial Average from www.djindexes.com. See also "Rhythms Netconnections Announced Sale of $250 Million," *Bloomberg Business News*, Feb. 29, 2000.

223 The effort to develop hedges through the merchant-investment committee is disclosed in an April 8, 1999, e-mail from the Enron Capital & Trade Office of the Chairman to all ECT personnel, "Merchant Finance Organization Memo."

223 Some details of Skilling's meeting from entries in his schedule book for that day.

224 Details of the announcement about Enron Field from Mark Babineck, "New Astros Ballpark to Be Called Enron Field," Associated Press, April 7, 1999. Also see the internal e-mail of that same day from Skilling and Lay to all Enron employees in Houston, "Enron and Astros Name New Ballpark 'Enron Field.' "

226 Dialogue of Skilling's discussions with analysts on April 13, 1999, from a transcript of the telephone call.

227 Details of Lay's campaign contributions to Bush and Richards from Don Van Atta Jr., "Enron Spread Campaign Contributions on Both Sides of the Political Aisle," *New York Times*, Jan. 21, 2002, 13.

227 A copy of the April 14, 1999 handwritten note from Bush to Lay was obtained by the author.

227–28 Some details of Fastow's conversation with Skilling regarding the fund that would become LJM from the notes of Skilling's Nov. 27, 2001, interview with Wilmer, Cutler and his confidential testimony before the SEC on Dec. 5, 2001. Timing of the events from entries in Skilling's schedule book.

228–29 See the confidential testimony of Kevin Hannon, later of Enron Broadband Services, before the SEC on Jan. 4, 2002, and the FBI 302 of Shelby. The timing of this event from entries in Skilling's schedule book.

229–30 Details of the AGOSBA bid and the initial analysis from "Enron Risk Assessment and Control Summary Approval Sheet" with "Deal Name: AGOSBA," April 25, 1999. Also see the June 14, 1999, presentation to Azurix by Merrill Lynch, "Regarding North American Strategic Alternatives."

230–31 Some details of Azurix's successful bid for AGOSBA from the company's 8-K filing with the SEC, July 7, 1999. Also see the Azurix 10-Q filing with the agency of Nov. 15, 1999.

231–32 Timing and location of the Skilling/Martin meeting from Skilling's schedule book.

232 The direction of the communication—from Fastow to Howard, from Howard to his Greenwich colleagues—from the Batson Report, vol. 4, app. E, 37.

232–33 Fastow's insistence on total secrecy and the name of the project, Martin, in part from contemporaneous documents presented to Greenwich and a May 26, 1999, e-mail from Bermingham to Howard, both of Greenwich. Also see David Duncan's June 18, 1999, e-mail to John Stewart, along with attachments. Some details of the effort also from the Feb. 15, 2002, FBI 302 with Grutzmacher.

232–33 A copy of Bermingham's May 28 e-mail was obtained by the author. Details of his suspicions from that e-mail, and one that preceded it on May 26.

233–34 Details of the e-mail communications between Neuhausen and Duncan from the original documents, May 28 and June 1, 1999.

234–35 Details of the efforts to set up a merchant-investing review group from a July 14, 1999, memo to members of Enron North America, a division of the wholesale group, from Cliff Baxter and Kevin Hannon.

235 A copy of the Lay letter to *CFO* magazine was obtained by the author.

235–36 The timing of the meeting between Fastow and Skilling from entries in Skilling's schedule book. Some details of the meeting from Skilling's Dec. 4, 2001, testimony before the SEC.

236–37 Timing and location of the Skilling/Rice meeting from Skilling's schedule book.

237–38 Some details of Shelby's thoughts and opinions about Enron's broadband effort from the 302 of his FBI interview on Aug. 15, 2002. Also see the undated presentation "Enron Communications," which was subsequently distributed throughout the company on July 27, 1999.

238 Some details of Jeffe's conversation with Fastow from the Batson Report, vol. 4, app. F, 39–40.

238–39 Details of the events surrounding the Nordstrom offering from "Nordstrom Gets a Leg Up with a Move to Big Board," *Seattle Post-Intelligencer*, June 10, 1999, F4. The offering price of Azurix from the company's press release; its daily performance and closing price from Adam Jones, "Azurix Makes a Modest Debut," *Times (London)*, June 11, 1999.

240–41 The timing of these events involving Kaminski has been incorrectly cited in numerous official reports. Repeatedly, the reports declare that they began on June 2; however, in each instance, the reports cite the Wilmer, Cutler notes from a Dec. 19, 2001, interview with Kaminski as its source. The eight-day discrepancy is significant: the timeline laid out by Kaminski in his Wilmer, Cutler interview would suggest that Buy's later protestations that the deal was too far along to stop were false. However, a review of Kaminski's actual schedule, as well as the schedule of outside meetings he attended that played a role in the way these events unfolded, demonstrates conclusively that these discussions began on June 10, and that Buy's subsequent statements were correct. The author has independently confirmed this conclusion that was based on a review of the documents.

241–45 Some details of Kaminski's efforts to understand LJM and price the options from his Dec. 19, 2001, Wilmer, Cutler interview. Also see the Batson Report, vol. 4, app. D, 62–63; Skilling's testimony before the SEC on Dec. 4, 2001; and the Wilmer, Cutler notes from the Dec. 28, 2001, interview with Vasant Shanbhogue.

244 Timing of the meeting from an entry in Lay's personal schedule.

244–45 Some details of the meeting with Lay from a copy of the PowerPoint presentation; Skilling's testimony before the SEC on Dec. 4, 2001; and the Wilmer, Cutler notes from the Jan. 11, 2002, interview with Mordaunt, who was also in the room at the time. Also see the Wilmer, Cutler notes from the Jan. 16, 2002, interview with Lay and the Batson Report, vol. 4, app. D, 63.

246 Some details of Kaminski's discussions with Buy from his Dec. 19, 2001, Wilmer, Cutler interview. Also see the Batson Report, vol. 4, app. D, 62–63.

246–47 A copy of the Ellison e-mail was obtained by the author.

247 Details of the controversy within CSFB from the Batson Report, vol. 4, app. F, 40–41, 45–46.

247–48 Details of the LJM papers in the Cayman Islands from the original documents on file in the office of the Registrar of Limited Partnerships.

248 Some details of Castleman's discussion with Glisan from the notes of his Dec. 6, 2001, interview with Wilmer, Cutler.

248 Some details of Kaminski's discussions with Buy from his Dec. 19, 2001, Wilmer, Cutler interview. Also see the Batson Report, vol. 4, app. D, 62–63.

248–49 Details of Gramm's experience from her sworn statement of Aug. 20, 2003, to a lawyer from Alston & Bird, Neal Batson's law firm.

249 Some details of the June 28, 1999, board meeting from the official minutes, the unofficial hand-written notes taken by the corporate secretary, and the PowerPoint presentation "Project LJM Board Presentation."

250 Some details of the Kaminski discussion from his sworn statement of May 9, 2003, to a lawyer from Alston & Bird. See also notes of his Dec. 19, 2001, Wilmer, Cutler interview.

CHAPTER 10

251–52 Baxter expressed his frustration with Skilling's approach to Fastow in his interview with Wilmer, Cutler on Jan. 10, 2002.

254 Details of the management committee meeting from agenda documents prepared for it. A copy of the Fastow/McMahon presentation was obtained by the author. Also see the Batson Report, vol. 3, 15–16.

254 The mismatch in the performance of the hedge is described in a memo to the file by Beth Lehman from the SEC, dated Jan. 17, 2002. The memo describes statements by David Duncan taken from his interview three days earlier in case number H0–9350, *In the Matter of Enron Corp.* Some details of the LJM structure from the June 30, 1999, letter, with attachments, from Enron Corp. to LJM Cayman LP and LJM Swap Sub LP. The attachments include the amended and restated limited-recourse promissory note of fourteen million dollars, dated June 30. Also see the confirmation pages for the equity-option transaction, sent by fax to LJM Swap Sub from Enron and on that same day, and notes of Kaminski's Dec. 16, 2001, interview with Wilmer, Cutler.

255 Some details of the lunch between the Enron engagement accountants and Goolsby from the 302 of the FBI's Feb. 8, 2002, interview of Cash, as well as the 302 of the bureau's interview with Goolsby on Feb. 28, 2002.

256 Some details of Kopper's presentation on Lipshutz and Glisan from their employment reviews from that period.

257 Some details of the British water announcement from Michael Harrison, "Byatt Faces Water Challenge," *Independent*, July 28, 1999, Business, 17.

259–60 Some details of the Aug. 5 meeting from the CSFB document "Materials Prepared for Discussion: LJM Caymans L.P., August 5, 1999." Other details from an Aug. 6 e-mail from Bermingham to Howard describing the previous day's meeting. Also see the Batson Report, vol. 4, app. E, 48–51, and app. F, 50–52.

260–61 Some details of the Banham interviews from notes taken during the phone calls. Also see Russ Banham, "Andrew S. Fastow—Enron Corp.," *CFO* magazine, Oct. 1, 1999.

261 Fastow's demand for the semiannual management fee from a letter he wrote, Aug. 12, 1999. Also see the wire-transfer request of Aug. 11, 1999.

262–64 Some details of the Cuiabá discussions from Wilmer, Cutler's notes from the Dec. 6, 2001, interview with Castleman; the Dec. 5 and 7, 2001, interviews with Lipshutz; and the notes of the Dec. 21, 2001, interview with Causey. Also see Castleman's memo for the file, "Sale of EPE Equity Interest to LJM," Sept. 30, 1999.

264–65 Details of Fastow's return from his Sept. 16 presentation to Merrill Lynch.

265–66 A transcript of Fastow's presentations, and copies of his PowerPoint presentations, were obtained or reviewed by the author.

266 A copy of Jimmy Lee's handwritten notes, scribbled on the cover sheet of the LJM2 presentation, was obtained by the author.

266–67 Details of the efforts by Chase to review the LJM2 investment from a series of internal e-mails, memos, and notes compiled at the time that the deal was considered. These include unsigned, handwritten notes from a Sept. 27, 1999, discussion with Arnie Chavkin; handwritten notes labeled "Follow-up on Arnie Chavkin's questions" that were taken by the same individual from a conversation with Fastow on the same day; handwritten notes from a Sept. 16, 1999, presentation to Chase by Fastow about LJM2; and an Oct. 25, 1999, memo written by Todd Maclin and Rick Walker to Bill Harrison, Jimmy Lee, and seven other bank executives which was headed "Andy Fastow/Enron Corp.—$10 MM Request for Equity Investment."

267 A copy of the questions sent to Fastow from Merrill Lynch was obtained by the author.

267 Quotes from Banham, "Andrew S. Fastow—Enron Corp."

268 Some details of the Tilney, Furst, and Skilling conversation from an Oct. 12, 1999, memo written by Furst for the LJM due-diligence file, which summarized the conversation.

268–69 A copy of the agenda and the briefing materials for the Oct. 12, 1999, board meeting was obtained by the author.

269 Some details of the Oct. 12 finance committee meeting from the official minutes. Others from handwritten notes taken by the corporate secretary. Also see "Chief Financial Officer's Report," the presentation made by Fastow at the meeting. Also see the 1999 private-placement memorandum for "LJM Co-investment L.P."; the Dec. 15, 1999, document "LJM2 Co-investment LP Supplement Number One to Private Placement Memorandum"; the draft internal LJM talking points, e-mailed by Fastow to Scott Sefton on Nov. 10, 1999; and "LJM2 Co-investment L.P. Amended and Restated Limited Partnership Agreement," Dec. 20, 1999. Also see the Dec. 31, 1999, memo to the files written by David Duncan and other members of the Andersen team, "LJMII Partnership Structure"; and the Oct. 4, 1999, memo from Bob Baird to Scott Sefton and others, headed "LJM2."

269 Some details of the board meeting from the official minutes.

270–71 McMahon testified about his discovery of potential conflicts among the banks at hearings before the House Energy and Commerce Committee's Subcommittee on Oversight and Investigations on Feb. 7, 2002. He also discussed certain specifics from the same encounters in his Jan. 21, 2002, interview with Wilmer, Cutler, which are reflected in the notes of that session.

271 Weather conditions in Scottsdale from records on file with the National Climatic Data Center, from the Scottsdale Municipal Airport station.

271 Some details of the discussions regarding Enron Communications from a presentation package from the meeting, "Enron Communications," as well as information provided to the Enron board on Nov. 18, 1999.

272 Some details from the final press release, "Azurix Corp. Reports Third Quarter 1999 Net Income of $18.8 Million and $.16 per Share and Discusses Financial Outlook," Nov. 4, 1999.

274–75 Dialogue from the Nov. 4 broadcast on CNN from a transcript. The performance for Azurix shares from the company's officially reported stock prices.

275 Some details of the Astros' "fashion show" from "Astros Will Wear New Look in New Stadium Next Year," *Fort Worth Star-Telegram*, Nov. 5, 1999, Sports, 3.

275–76 A copy of the international presentation was reviewed by the author.

278 Merrill's emphasis on EBITDA is reflected in its June 14, 1999, presentation to Azurix, "Regarding North American Strategic Alternatives."

279–80 Details of the Nov. 18 board meeting from the official minutes, unofficial handwritten notes taken by the corporate secretary, and a copy of Skilling's presentation.

CHAPTER 11

281 Some details of the 1999 management conference from the official agenda for the meeting. Details on Milken's background from James B. Stewart, *Den of Thieves* (Simon & Schuster, 1991).

282 Fastow's travels in Europe are revealed in his official itinerary for the week of Nov. 7, 1999.

283 Details of the Bermingham e-mail from the original document, Dec. 1, 1999.

283 Information about the Mandanas report from the original Dec. 8, 1999, document, sent from Mandanas to Chuck Ward, the co-head of investment banking, and other senior CSFB bankers. Mandanas's estimates were in fact understating the magnitude of Fastow's returns, according to his tax records. Two Schedule K-1s for Fastow, for 1999 and 2000, show that he earned $14.4 million and $17.7 million directly from LJM1. This did not include payments under the Southampton scheme or other payments he received from the fund.

283–84 Some details of McMahon's run-in with bankers from Feb. 7, 2002, testimony before the House Energy and Commerce Committee's Subcommittee on Oversight and Investigations, as well as notes by subcommittee staffers from their Jan. 17, 2002, interview with Rick Buy. Also see the notes from McMahon's Jan. 21, 2002, interview with Wilmer, Cutler.

284–85 Dialogue from a transcript of the session. Additional details from McLean and Elkind, *Smartest Guys in the Room*, 241–42.

286 The array of pockets at Enron is laid out in a May 2000 Enron document entitled "Global Finance: Funding Vehicles." Background on the Condor deal from the Batson Report, vol. 2, app. J, annex 5. Details on Whitewing from the May 15, 2000, document "Whitewing Liquidity." Also see the Batson Report, vol. 2, app. G.

286–87 Details of the Ephross e-mail from the original document.

287 Walker's statements from an official transcript from the event. A copy of the Dec. 9 Andersen e-mail was obtained by the author.

288 Some details of the Dec. 13 finance committee meeting from the official minutes, as well as handwritten notes taken by the corporate secretary and McMahon's presentation, "Enron Corp. Treasurer Report, December 13, 1999." Also see "Enron Corp. Projects and Amendments, December 13, 1999," "Supplement for December 13, 1999, Finance Committee Meeting," and "Enron Corp. Chief Financial Officer's Report, December 13, 1999." At least one director, Robert Belfer, described his discomfort with what he was hearing in testimony to the bankruptcy examiner, as revealed in the Batson Report, vol. 4, app. D, 126. Also see the Batson Report, vol. 4, app. D, 139.

288–89 Some details of the board dinner from the official agenda for Dec. 13, 1999, and from an unsigned document, "Board Dinner, Monday, December 13, 1999."

289 Bass described his discussion with Duncan in an e-mail to John Stewart, Dec. 18, 1999.

289–90 Details of the early days of the Raptor hedge from Skilling's Dec. 4, 2001, testimony before the SEC; the notes from Wilmer, Cutler's Jan. 9, 2002, interview with Wes Colwell; and Causey's Wilmer, Cutler interview on Dec. 21, 2001.

290 Some details of Lay's visit with Murdoch from entries in his personal schedule.

290–91 A copy of the Collins e-mail was obtained by the author. Also see Kurt Eichenwald and John Markoff, "Deception, or Just Disarray, at Enron," *New York Times*, June 8, 2003, sec. 3, 1.

291–92 Some details of the Brown and McMahon episode and McMahon's subsequent tussle with Fastow from McMahon's Feb. 7, 2002, congressional testimony and notes from his Jan. 21, 2002, interview with Wilmer, Cutler. Also see the Wilmer, Cutler notes from the interviews with Brown on Dec. 5, 2001, and Jan. 5, 2002.

292–93 The aggregate effects of the final weeks of 1999 are described in the Batson Report, vol. 3, 13. Also see "LJM2 Year-End 1999 Transactions," Jan. 5, 2000. Some details on the Polish power-plant deal from the Dec. 17, 1999, document "LJM Approval Sheet," with "Deal Name: Nowa Sarzyna." Also see the Powers Report, 140, and the Batson Report, vol. 2, appendix L, annex 4, 20–21.

293 Kopper described the details of his meeting with Fastow about the possibility of LJM2 investing in the Nigerian barges, and his subsequent determination of the related problems, in his testimony of Sept. 27, 2004 in *U.S. v. Bayly et al.*

293–94 Some details of McMahon's call on the Nigerian barges from the Dec. 22, 1999, memo by James Brown of Merrill to the firm's debt markets commitment committee. Also see the Dec. 21, 1999, fax, including the handwritten comments on the cover sheet, from Robert Furst of Merrill to Brown, which included an offering memo, "Preferred Stock Representing a Set Duration 90% Economic Interest in Enron Nigeria Barge Ltd," and an internal report of Nov. 30, 1999, "Nigeria Barge Project, Capital Pricing Analysis." Also see Dan Bayly's testimony before the SEC of July 10, 2002; the Dec. 17, 1999, document, "Nigeria Barge Project Sell Down Transaction and Shareholder Structure"; and "Apachi Transaction Approval Sheet: Nigerian Selldown Executive Summary," Dec. 29, 1999; and the testimony of Ben Glisan Jr. on Oct. 6 and Oct. 7, 2004, in the case *U.S. v. Bayly et al.* Finally, also see "Enron Risk Assessment and Control Deal Approval Sheet" for the deal entitled "Nigeria Barges," from Oct. 21, 1999.

294–95 That Merrill understood the purpose of the electricity trade is clear from a May 30, 2000, e-mail from Schuyler Tilney of the firm to Dan Gordon and Robert Furst from the firm. Some details from "Confidentiality Agreement Between Enron North America Corp. and Merrill Lynch Capital Markets," Dec. 8, 1999. Also see Gordon's Dec. 28, 1999, e-mail to Christine Gonzalez and other Merrill employees and executives, which discussed the transaction. Other details from the Batson Report, vol. 3, app. I, 37–44. Some details about Enron's electricity-trading effort from Ted Jackson, "End Run," *Financial World*, Dec. 16, 1996.

295 Some details of this portion of the Yosemite transaction from the Wilmer, Cutler notes from the Jan. 16, 2002, Astin interview, and the Jan. 25, 2002, Brown interview. Also see the Powers Report, 142. Also see the LJM Approval Sheet for the Yosemite deal, dated Feb. 8, 2000.

296 Some details of Brown's reaction and the meetings at Merrill from his Sept. 25, 2002, testimony before the United States Grand Jury in the Southern District of Texas, Houston division. Bayly described portions of this meeting in his July 10, 2002, testimony before the SEC. See also the Dec. 21, 1999, e-mail from Marianne Bonici to Vincent DiMassimo and Paul Wood, all from Merrill; the Dec. 29, 1999, loan agreement between Enron Nigeria Power Holding Ltd. and Ebarge, LLC; and the Batson Report, vol. 3, app. I, 26–29.

297–98 Some details of the Sun visit from entries in Skilling's and Lay's schedules. Also see "Itinerary: Cupertino, CA, December 22, 1999," which was assembled for Lay. Some details about the presentation derived from the 1999 document "Enron Communications," which provides a detailed description of the BOS. One participant in these discussions said that this document was used in this presentation, but that could not be confirmed.

298 Fastow's thoughts during the call from undated excerpts of the 302 from the FBI's interview of him following his decision to plead guilty and cooperate. Also see the Batson Report, vol. 3, app. I, 28.

298–300 Some details from notes from McMahon's Jan. 21, 2002, interview with Wilmer, Cutler. Also see the Wilmer, Cutler notes from interviews with Brown on Dec. 5, 2001, and Jan. 5, 2002. Details about the Yosemite transaction from the Powers Report, 142. Also see the undated memo from Brown to McMahon "Re: 1999 Accomplishments"; see the LJM Approval Sheet for the Yosemite deal, dated Feb. 8, 2000; the Feb. 27, 2000, memorandum from Vinson & Elkins to three financial institutions, entitled "Yosemite Securities Company Ltd"; and the Feb. 23, 2000, interoffice memo from Dave Gorte to Rick Buy headed "LJM2 Investment in Certificates of Beneficial Interest in Yosemite Securities Trust." After this, according to notes of Gorte's Jan. 4, 2002, interview with Wilmer, Cutler, Buy told him to no longer write such memos and just initial the LJM approval sheet.

300 Details of the MEGS deal from the Powers Report, 141. Also see "Enron Risk Assessment and Control Summary Approval Sheet" with "Deal Name: Project Pluto, Dec. 29, 1999. Also see the Batson Report, vol. 2, app. L, annex 4, 30.

300–1 Details of Project Nahanni from the Dec. 17, 1999, document "Marengo L.P. Amended and Restated Limited Partnership Agreement Among Marengo, Yellowknife Investors, Enron Corp., and Nahanni Investors L.L.C."; the Dec. 14, 1999, "Execution Approval Memorandum to GCS Commitment Committee" at Citibank; the internal Enron document prepared in Oct. 2001 "Nahanni Financing Presentation"; and Enron's annual report (10-K) for the year ended Dec. 31, 1999, which disclosed that the company had redefined "merchant investments" to include government securities. Also see the Batson Report, vol. 4, app. C, 66–72; vol. 4, app. B, 142; and vol. 2, app. I, annex 3. Also see the undated memo from Brown to McMahon "Re: 1999 Accomplishments."

301 Some details of the Yosemite transaction from the Powers Report, 142. Also see the LJM Approval Sheet for the Yosemite deal, dated Feb. 8, 2000; the Feb. 27, 2000, memorandum from Vinson & Elkins to three financial institutions, entitled "Yosemite Securities Company Ltd."; and the Feb. 23, 2000, interoffice memo from Dave Gorte to Rick Buy headed "LJM2 Investment In Certificates of Beneficial Interest in Yosemite Securities Trust"; and the Batson Report, vol. 2, app. L, annex 4, 32.

301–2 Some details from a Dec. 29, 1999, e-mail and attachment from Dan Gordon to Jeff Kronthal and Christine Gonzalez, all of Merrill. The attachment was titled "Handout for STRC Meeting." Some additional information from the Batson Report, vol. 3, app. I, 39–41.

302 A copy of Causey's letter, addressed to Merrill Lynch Capital Services, was obtained by the author.

302 Enron announced its fourth-quarter and annual profits on Jan. 18, 2000, in a release entitled "Enron Continued Strong Earnings Growth." Also see Michael Davis, "Enron's Earnings Skyrocket 29 Percent in Fourth Quarter," *Houston Chronicle*, Jan. 19, 2000, Business, 1.

302–3 Details of Glisan's conversations with McMahon from Glisan's testimony on Oct. 6 and 7, 2004, in *U.S. v. Bayly et al.*

303 Some details of the Scottsdale meeting from the official agenda and packets of materials distributed to executives, including a copy of Rice's "Enron Communications" presentation.

304–5 Some background on Grayhawk Golf Club from John Davis, "Scottsdale Revels in Status as Elite Golf Paradise," *Arizona Republic*, April 7, 2003, 1C. The role of the golf game was first revealed by Kurt Eichenwald, "U.S. Inquiry Tracks Insiders at Enron," *New York Times*, April 15, 2002, A1. Some details of the Grayhawk scheme from *United States of America v. Jeffrey K. Skilling and Richard A. Causey*, case no. CR-H-04-25, filed in Houston's Federal District Court on Feb. 18, 2004.

305–6 Some details of the analysts' conference from a copy of the packet materials distributed to the analysts, including the document entitled "Enron 2000 Analyst Conference, January 19–20, Houston, Texas." The dialogue from the meeting, and visual descriptions, come from a transcript of the event and a video taken on Jan. 20, 2000. Also see the press release from Sun Microsystems and Enron on that day entitled "Enron and Sun Microsystems Inc. Team to Accelerate Adoption of Broadband Internet Services."

306–7 Enron's stock performance from "Thursday's Most Active Stocks," Associated Press, Jan. 20, 2000.
307 The Grayhawk profits from *U.S. v. Skilling et al.*

CHAPTER 12

309–10 Once again, for chapter clarity, the presentation of unrelated events has been shifted a little. The last chapter ended shortly after the analyst's conference of Jan. 20; the Kaminski meeting in fact took place two days earlier, on Jan. 18. However, this allowed for the full circle of one story—the Sun Microsystems and Project Grayhawk tale—to be told before launching the next story of the spreading recognition of Enron's risk. Some details of Kaminski's presentation from the document he prepared that weekend, "Discussion Notes for RAC Research," Jan. 16, 2000.

311–12 Details of the efforts to develop the Raptor program and its ultimate structure from the Wilmer, Cutler notes from interviews with Kevin Jordan on Jan. 11 and 15, 2002; Ryan Siurek on Dec. 11, 2001, and Jan. 31, 2002; and Wes Colwell on Jan. 9, 2002; as well as the original March 28, 2000, memo to file written by Duncan and other members of the Enron engagement team, "Raptor Transaction." Also see the Powers Report, 97–128; the Feb. 2, 2000, performance review for Glisan written by Kopper; the March 31, 2000, Enron document "Project Raptor; Fairness Analysis"; the April 2000 memo to the files by Siurek and Jordan "Project Raptor"; the Aug. 3, 2000, document "Raptor I Derivative Proposal Sheet"; and the 302 of the FBI's interview with Debra Cash of Andersen on Feb. 21 and 22, 2002.

313 Astin's discomfort with the Raptor payment to LJM2 is confirmed in the Batson Report, vol. 4, app. C, 141–42, and the handwritten Vinson & Elkins notes of the Aug. 23, 2001, interview with Astin during the Watkins investigation. Also see the March 2000 memo from Causey to Mary Perkins, "Project Raptor," which seeks payment of the forty-one million dollars.

313–14 Some details of the efforts to unwind Chewco from the Wilmer, Cutler notes of the Dec. 5, 2001, interview with Brown, as well as the Jan. 21, 2002, interview with McMahon. Also see the undated handwritten notes by Kopper to Fastow, providing his analysis of the value of Chewco.

314–15 Some details of Bermingham's efforts from his e-mail to Darby on Jan. 29, 2000. Also see the affidavit of C. Jeanne Simpson, an FBI special agent, filed on June 27, 2002, in support of the criminal complaint against Mulgrew, Darby, and Bermingham.

315–16 Some details of the Andersen meeting from Bass's Feb. 4, 2000, e-mail to Stewart, and Stewart's response of the same day.

316–17 Some details of the Azurix board meeting from the original minutes. Details of the water2water strategy from Rebecca Smith, "Azurix Is Launching Online Exchange for Buying and Selling Water in West," *Wall Street Journal*, Feb. 9, 2000, A4; "Azurix Launching Website for Liquid Assets Trading," *Houston Chronicle*, Feb. 10, 2000, Business, 2; and an Azurix release of Feb. 28, 2000, "Azurix Corp. Expands Water2Water.com to Become First Internet-Based Vertical Marketplace in the Water and Wastewater Industry."

317–318 Some details of the audit committee meeting from the official minutes, as well as copies of the presentations prepared for the meeting. The fact that Causey failed to mention certain transactions comes from a reconciliation of the deals that were done versus what he is recorded in the minutes—and in his official presentation—as having said. Also see the Batson Report, vol. 4, 109, and vol. 4, app. D, 110.

320 A copy of the Bermingham e-mail was obtained by the author.

320–21 Details of the Houston meeting from a copy of the bankers' presentation. Also see the Simpson affidavit of June 27, 2002.

321 Details of Project California, and the role played by Morgan Stanley, from a Feb. 2000 presentation put together for the effort, "Project California Discussion Materials."

322 Some details of the Enron and Blockbuster negotiations from a May 1, 2000, copy of the document "Non-binding Term Sheet."

322–23 Some details of the trip to the Caymans from the Simpson affidavit of June 27, 2002.

323 Some details of the presentation to Skilling from an undated document by the wholesale division laying out the situation in California. The document is titled "The Supply/Demand Imbalance Has Been Masked by Several Years of Above-Normal Hydro."

323–24 Some details of the efforts to bring Glisan and Mordaunt into what eventually became the Southampton transaction from the Wilmer, Cutler notes of an Oct. 30, 2001, interview with Mordaunt. Also see the March 20, 2000, document "Southampton Place L.P. Amended and Restated Agreement of Limited Partnerhsip," as well as the cooperation agreement signed by Kopper as part of *U.S. v. Kopper*.

324 A copy of the MEGS DASH, as signed by McMahon, was obtained by the author. Some details of his response to the signing and his subsequent discussions with Baxter from the notes of his Wilmer, Cutler interview of Jan. 21, 2002.

324–25 Details of the concert from Michael D. Clark, "Crosby, Stills, Nash & Young Can Still Rock," *Houston Chronicle*, March 8, 2000, 1.

327 Some details of the *Fortune* photo shoot from entries in Skilling's and Lay's schedule books. Also see Brian O'Reilly, "The Power Merchants," *Fortune*, April 17, 2000, 148.

327 A copy of McMahon's handwritten notes was obtained by the author.

327–28 Timing of the McMahon meeting from the schedules of McMahon and Skilling. Some details of their discussions and thoughts from the McMahon notes, and the testimony of both men before the House Energy and Commerce Committee's Subcommittee on Oversight and Investigations, as well as the notes of McMahon's Jan. 21, 2002, interview with Wilmer, Cutler.

329 Some details of Sutton's involvement in the McMahon complaint from "Affidavit of Joseph W. Sutton," signed on March 6, 2002. The document appears never to have been formally submitted to any public case file involving the Enron litigation. In his affidavit, Sutton states that he believes his meeting with Skilling occurred on March 20, 2000. However, other information reviewed by the author suggests that this recollection must be inaccurate. Skilling and Sutton do have a scheduled meeting the days preceding that, and on March 18, according to schedules and travel records, Skilling left the country for Brazil and did not return for several days. Other reporting suggests that, indeed, the meeting with Sutton took place the week prior to March 20. McMahon's recollections of his contacts, as laid out in his Jan. 21, 2002, interview with Wilmer, Cutler, also contradict Sutton's beliefs on the timing and coincide with the sequence presented in this book.

329 Some details of the trip to the Caymans from the Simpson affidavit of June 27, 2002.

330–31 Some details of Sutton's involvement from his March 6, 2002, affidavit. Also see the notes of the Jan. 21, 2002, Wilmer, Cutler interview with McMahon.

332 Some details of the final days before the creation of Southampton from the Simpson affidavit of June 27, 2002. Also see the Wilmer, Cutler notes of the Oct. 30, 2001, interview with Mordaunt; the March 20, 2000, document "Southampton Place L.P. Amended and Restated Agreement of Limited Partnerhsip"; the Kopper cooperation agreement that is part of *U.S. v. Kopper*; and the March 6, 2000, letter from Kopper on behalf of LJM2 to Darby of Greenwich NatWest. Also see the Batson Report, vol. 4, app. C, 121.

332–33 Some details of Skilling's return and discussions with Sutton from the Sutton affidavit, as well as entries in Skilling's schedule book.

333 The Polish plant repurchase was first described in the Powers Report, 140.

334 Some details of McMahon's trip to Barton Creek, and his return, from entries in his computerized schedule. Other details from his Jan. 21, 2002, interview with Wilmer, Cutler.

334 Timing of the Whalley meeting from an entry in Skilling's schedule.

334–35 Some details of the meeting between McMahon and Fastow from the notes of McMahon's Jan. 21, 2002, interview with Wilmer, Cutler.

335–36 Timing of the Raptor meeting from Skilling's schedule book. Some other details from Skilling's Dec. 4, 2001, testimony before the SEC.

336 Some details of the Skilling, McMahon, and Whalley meeting from notes of McMahon's statements in the Wilmer, Cutler interview of Jan. 21, 2002.

336–37 McMahon's change of jobs was announced internally on April 7, 2000, in an e-mail from Fastow.

CHAPTER 13

339–40 Certain details, including the minute that the Golden Knights landed and Lay's outfit and seating, from photographs taken by a number of fans during the opening-night festivities. Additional information from Carlton Thompson, "Phillies Spoil Opener for Astros," *Houston Chronicle*, April 8, 2000, Sports, 1; and David Barron and Eric Berger, "All Aboard for the New Ballpark," *Houston Chronicle*, March 30, 2000, A1. Also see the internal Enron document "April 7, 2000: Enron Field Opening Day."

340 Some details of Wanda Curry's experiences from McLean and Elkind, *Smartest Guys in the Room*, 299–301. Other details from audits of EES from the draft document "Enron Energy Services Business

Audit Review" for the years 1998, 1999, and 2000. Also see the Jan. 24, 2000, "tentative and preliminary" memo to the file from the EES accounting department, "EES Contract Accounting"; and the April 20, 2000, document "Enron Energy Services Risk Management: A Presentation to RAC."

340–41 Details of the time and place of the Badr El-Din meeting from entries in Skilling's schedule book. Some details of Badr El-Din's background from "Offsets in Defense Trade Fifth Annual Report to Congress," *DISAM Journal*, Sept. 22, 2001; and M. Satyanarayan, "Ghantoot Wins Opening Tie in Polo," *Gulf News*, Jan. 13, 2000. Some details of his ties of Enron from "UAE's Dolphin Project to Maximize Gas Value Chain, Industrial Zone," *Offshore*, April 2000, 54; David Barboza, "Enron Sought to Raise Cash Two Years Ago," *New York Times*, March 9, 2002, C1; and the 1999 presentation "Project Dolphin."

341–42 Some background of Belden and the Portland trading effort from testimony before the Commodity Futures Trading Commission and the Federal Energy Regulatory Commission. These testimonies include those of Richard Sanders on July 9 and 10, 2002; Christian Yoder on June 2, 2002; John Arnold on Aug. 9 and 10, 2002; and an undated transcript of the testimony before the same bodies by Stephen Hall. Also see the Aug. 17, 2000, e-mail from James Steffes of EES to Belden and other members of the trading team, "FERC Investigation in CA—What Should They Be Looking For?" and the documents titled "Daily Position Report" for Jan. 17, 2000, through the end of that year, which lay out the trades of every division within Enron, including the western markets for power trading.

342–43 Dialogue on the Forney transactions from a transcript of the recorded April 15 call obtained by the FERC.

343 Details of the trading strategies from the testimonies before the CFTC and the FERC by Sanders on July 9 and 10, 2002; Yoder on June 2, 2002; and Hall's undated transcript. Also see a copy of the Dec. 6, 2000, memo from Yoder and Hall to Sanders, "Traders' Strategies in the California Wholesale Power Markets/ISO Sanctions."

344 Details of the wire transfers from the original documents. Also see *U.S. v. Fastow* and the Simpson affidavit of June 27, 2002.

345–46 Details of the May 1 finance committee meeting from the original minutes, as well as handwritten notes taken by the corporate treasurer and the presentation prepared by Glisan. Also see the Batson Report, vol. 3, app. C, 25, and the Wilmer, Cutler notes from the Jan. 29, 2002, interview with Norm Blake.

346 Details of the Southampton wire transfer from the superseding indictment in *U.S. v. Fastow*.

346 Some details of the May 22, 2000, stage-two emergency from Nancy Rivera Brooks and Zanto Peabody, "Heat Triggers Moderate Power Emergency," *Los Angeles Times*, May 23, 2000, B2.

347 A copy of the Quaintance e-mail was obtained by the author. See also the Batson Report, vol. 4, app. B, 64.

350–52 Some details of the meeting between the accountants and the SEC from Levitt, *Take on the Street*, 127–28.

352 Andersen's work on the Raptors from the original March 28, 2000, memo to file "Raptor Transaction" written by Duncan and other members of the Enron engagement team; also see the Feb. 1, 2000, e-mail from Bass to Stewart and others headed "Enron Transaction," as well as the response on the same day from Debra Cash and another response, "Clarification: Enron Transaction," from James F. Green. Fastow's and Glisan's efforts to obtain authorization for Raptor II from the minutes of the meeting of the executive committee of the board on June 22, 2000, as well as the presentation from that meeting, "Project Raptor II." Also see the LJM2 approval sheet of June 26, 2000, for the deal titled "Raptor II"; the July 21, 2000, memo to the files by Duncan and the Enron engagement team, "Raptor II Transaction"; the Powers Report, 97–128; and the Batson Report, vol. 4, app. D, 73, and vol. 2, app. L, annex 5.

353 Details of Larry Lawyer's tax fraud relating to RADR from the criminal information that was part of his guilty plea to the charges in *United States of America v. Lawrence W. Lawyer*, filed on Nov. 26, 2002, in Federal District Court in Houston. Other details of the transaction from the deal-approval sheet for "Bulk Fiber Sale," June 28, 2000, and the same sheet for "Project Backbone," June 30, 2000. This is the sheet signed by Lay. Mordaunt's role in EBS from the document "Status Change Form," Feb. 1, 2000, and the Wilmer, Cutler notes from her Jan. 12, 2002, interview. Also see the June 2000 presentation by Enron Broadband Services "Project Backbone," and the "Operation, Maintenance, and Repair Agreement" between EBS and LJM2 (listed on the cover page as "purchaser"), June 28, 2000. Also see the Batson Report, vol. 2, app. L, annex 4, 34–35.

353–54 Details of the efforts to sell off the Nigerian barges from the Batson Report, vol. 2, app. L, annex 4, 36–37; the Wilmer, Cutler notes from the Jan. 29, 2002, interview with Quaintance and from the Jan. 11, 2002, interview with Kevin Jordan. Also see the June 13, 2000, e-mail from Kira Toone of Merrill Lynch to Alan Hoffman of Whitman Breed Abbott & Morgan; and the Merrill Lynch "Credit Flash Report" for the week ending Dec. 23, 1999. Dialogue from Kopper's testimony in *U.S. v. Bayly et. al.;* additional details of the buyback proposal from Glisan's testimony in the same case.

354 Details of the Cochise transaction from the Batson Report, vol. 3, app. G, 51–52.

354 The excessive number of faxes arriving at Buy's home in New Hampshire was described by Kaminski in his interview with Wilmer, Cutler on Dec. 19, 2001.

354 Details of the stage-two alert from "Heat, Humidity in Southern California Force Regulators to Declare Emergency," Associated Press, June 26, 2000.

355 Some details of Skilling's African trip from entries in his schedule book and travel records.

355–56 Details of Fastow's declared distribution from "LJM Cayman L.P. Analysis of Accounts," Nov. 16, 2000; a July 14, 2000, wire-transfer request from LJM Cayman to LJM2 Capital Management. Also see the Batson Report, vol. 4, app. F, 60. Background on the Fastow Family Foundation from the certificate of incorporation filed for the group on March 14, 2000, with the office of the secretary of state for Delaware.

356–57 Details of the timing of Lay's meeting from his schedule book and his personal itinerary, headed "New York/London/Nice, July 18–23, 2000, KLL Itinerary." Also see the Aug. 16, 2000, document "Blockbuster Transaction Summary."

357–58 Details of the effort to bump up Enron's earnings to thirty-four cents from the superseding indictment in *U.S. v. Skilling et al.* Also see the Enron release from July 24, 2000, "Enron Reports Second Quarter Earnings of $0.34 per Diluted Share."

358 The dialogue in the second-quarter conference call from an official transcript, July 24, 2000.

358–59 Details of the summer problems in California from Betsy Streisand, "Power to the People," *U.S. News & World Report*, Aug. 21, 2000, 50; David Lazarus, "PUC Calls for Probe of Deregulation," *San Francisco Chronicle*, Aug. 2, 2000, A1; Lazarus, "Davis Acts to Bridge Energy Gap," *San Francisco Chronicle*, Aug. 3, 2000; and Sweeney, *California Electricity Crisis*, 128–44.

359–60 Some details of Lay's movements during the Republican National Convention from a copy of his itinerary for that week, headed "Republican National Convention, August 1–4, 2000, Philadelphia, Pennsylvania, Itinerary for KLL and LPL." Background on the convention and the Regents from Mike Allen, "For 'Regents,' a Special Class of Party Favors," *Washington Post*, Aug. 3, 2000, A15; and Jim Drinkard, "Party Never Forgets Royal Treatment for Big Donors," *USA Today*, Aug. 4, 2000, 5A.

360 The words of Bush's acceptance speech from a transcript of the speech. Also see Frank Bruni, "Bush, Accepting G.O.P. Nomination, Pledges to 'Use These Good Times for Great Goals,' " *New York Times*, Aug. 4, 2000, p A1.

360 Details of the Project Summer transaction from the confidential Aug. 1, 2000, presentation to the Enron board titled "Project Summer"; the minutes from that special meeting; the document "Project Summer" presented to the full board on Aug. 8, 2000; and the draft document from Aug. 9, 2000, "Project Summer Q&A." Also see the July 25, 2000, document "Project Summer Update" and the Aug. 3, 2000, memo to the file by Rodney Faldyn, "Project Summer Dabhol Total Return Swap."

360–62 The events in this meeting were recounted by multiple attendees. However, while I believe I have copies of all Enron board and committee minutes back to 1985, no one could precisely place when these events occurred, although all agreed they took place sometime in Aug. 2000. Minutes in several meetings, which are written in a very diplomatic style, have different events that could be these discussions. Also, many of the presentations were faxed to board members before or after the actual meeting, so it is difficult to ascertain which precise meeting these events occurred in. The possibilities are the finance committee meeting of Aug. 7, the full board meeting of Aug. 7–8, or the full board meeting of Aug. 1. Rather than guess, I have relied on the reconstruction provided by participants, coupled with the reports that were faxed to the directors around that time. Those include Skilling's "return analysis" for the international division from 1994 to 2000.

362 The signing of the Project Summer agreement from the term contract, Aug. 11, 2000.

362–64 Some details about the collapse of Mark's career from Rebecca Smith and Aaron Lucchetti, "Water Venture Sinks an Enron Career," *Asian Wall Street Journal*, Aug. 29, 2000. Timing of the meeting from entries in the schedules of Skilling and Lay. Also see the Azurix press release of Aug. 25, 2000, "Rebecca P. Mark Resigns Azurix Chairman and CEO Post."

364 The timing of Skilling's meeting with the international group from an entry in his schedule.

CHAPTER 14

367 Some details of Sheikh Zayed's surgery from "UAE President Undergoes Successful Kidney Transplant," Xinhua General News Service, Aug. 28, 2000; Olivera Perkins, "Sheik Undergoes Kidney Transplant," *Plain Dealer*, Aug. 29, 2000, A1; Sarah Crump, "Blossom Bonanza with Sheik in Town," *Plain Dealer*, Sept. 1, 2000, B7; Regina McEnery, "Sheik's Age Makes Transplant at Clinic Unusual," *Plain Dealer*, Sept. 18, 2000, E1; Bob Dyer, "A Big Wallet Can Bring Big Adventures," *Beacon Magazine*, Oct. 22, 2000, 4; and "Sheik Touched by Get-Well Letters Donates $30,000 to School," Associated Press, Nov. 22, 2000.

367–68 Copies of the Zisman memo, one dated Aug. 31, 2000, and another dated Sept. 1, 2000, were obtained by the author. Also see the internal Enron memo by Mike Galvan, "Troubled Assets—Raptor," Sept. 6, 2000; notes of the Wilmer, Cutler interview with Zisman on Dec. 12, 2001; and the Batson Report, vol. 4, app. C, 143–44.

368 Details of Raptor III from the Sept. 2000 memo to the file of Kevin Jordan, Clint Walden, and Alan Quaintance, "Project Raptor 3"; and the Sept. 20, 2000, memo from the same executives, "Project Raptor." Also see the Powers Report, 114–18, and the Batson Report, vol. 4, app. C, 135–44; Wilmer, Cutler notes from the Jan. 11 and 15, 2002, interviews with Jordan, and the Dec. 11, 2001, and Jan. 31, 2002, Siurek interviews; the LJM approval sheet for Raptor IV, Sept. 11, 2000; the Oct. 20, 2000, memo from Enron Corp. to Talon I LLC, "Equity Swap Transaction"; the Nov. 9, 2000, memo to the file by Duncan and other members of the Enron engagement team, "Raptor 3 Transaction"; and the Dec. 27, 2000, memo to the files by the engagement team, "Raptor IV Transaction." Additional information from the FBI 302 of Deb Cash from her Feb. 21, 2002, interview.

370 Details of Lay's situation from downloaded data in a financial navigator program, showing all of the family's transactions from 1998 through 2001, as well as personal balance sheets for 1999, 2000, and 2001. Details of the individual drawdown on the credit lines from individual drawdown requests submitted on Lay's behalf.

370–71 Timing of the meeting, and some details of the discussion, from entries in Mintz's personal schedule. Also see the Wilmer, Cutler notes from the Oct. 20, 2001, interview with Mintz, and his May 16, 2003, deposition taken as part of the Batson investigation.

371 Timing of the meeting from entries in the executives' schedules. A copy of the purported "Global Galactic Agreement" was obtained by the author. The agreement, along with the fact that it had been written down, was also described in *U.S. v. Skilling*. Fastow has represented to the government that this agreement was approved by both him and Causey. While Causey's initials are also present on this document, Causey had pleaded not guilty in this case, and I cannot state with absolute certainty that he himself is the person who placed his initials on the document.

372 Some details of these discussions from Sanders's July 9, 2002, testimony before the CFTC and the FERC, 33–36.

372 Some details of the conversations between Haedicke and Yoder from Yoder's deposition before the CFTC and the FERC on June 7, 2002, 35–40.

372 Details of Zisman's conversations with Haedicke from notes of his Dec. 12, 2001, interview with Wilmer, Cutler. Also see Zisman's sworn statement of April 21, 2003, to lawyers with Alston & Bird;

the Batson Report, vol. 4, app. C, 143–44; and notes of Haedicke's Jan. 21, 2002, interview with Wilmer, Cutler.

373 Timing of Baxter's visit from an entry in Skilling's appointment book.

373–74 Some details of the SEC's struggles with Capitol Hill over the accounting proposal from Levitt, *Take on the Street*, 132–34.

374 The collapse of Project Summer is reflected in the flurry of activity involving the board of directors. On Sept. 15, Rebecca Carter, the corporate secretary, sent out notification by fax to the directors calling for a special board meeting on Sunday, Sept. 17, according to the original documents. Included in that invitation was an updated packet of material on the economics of Project Summer. However, with the deal still struggling, the meeting was postponed on that Sunday, followed by the collapse of Project Summer the next morning.

375 Some details of Weil's reporting effort from Scott Sherman, "Enron: Uncovering the Uncovered Story," *Columbia Journalism Review*, May/June 2003. Also see Jonathan Weil, "Energy Traders Cite Gains, but Some Math Is Missing," *Wall Street Journal (Texas Journal)*, Sept. 20, 2000.

375–76 A copy of the Duncan letter written for Lay was obtained by the author. Some details of the letter from Duncan's testimony of May 15, 2002, in *United States of America v. Arthur Andersen LLP*, criminal action no. H-02-121 in Federal District Court in Houston. Also see Duncan's Sept. 11, 2000, e-mail to Jeffrey Peck of Andersen, headed "Enron SEC Letter."

376 Some details of Chanos's efforts from his testimony of Feb. 6, 2002, before the House Energy and Commerce Committee's Subcommittee on Oversight and Investigations. Also see Jonathan R. Laing, "The Bear That Roared," *Barron's*, Jan. 28, 2002, and McLean and Elkind, *Smartest Guys in the Room*, 319–21.

378 Levitt described his efforts to reach out to Berardino in *Take on the Street*, 134–36.

378–79 Timing and some details of the Davis and Skilling call from handwritten notes taken during the conversation and from an entry in Skilling's schedule.

379–80 Some details of the Portland meeting from the FERC and CFTC testimony of Sanders on July 9 and 10, 2002; Yoder on June 7, 2002; and an undated transcript of the Hall testimony. Also see unsigned, handwritten notes of the meetings of Oct. 3 and 4, 2000, and the billing records of Stoel Rives for Oct. 1–31, 2000, as reflected in the invoice issued by the firm to Enron North America, Nov. 27, 2000.

380 Yoder described his encounter with Forney in his June 7, 2002, testimony before the FERC and the CFTC.

380–81 Some details of the accident in Palm Beach from "Palm Beach," *Palm Beach Post*, Oct. 7, 2000, 2B.

381 Details of the Oct. 7 meeting of the Compensation and Management Development Committee from the official agenda and minutes, as well as handwritten notes taken by the corporate secretary.

381–82 Some details of the Oct. meeting of the finance committee from the official agenda and minutes, as well as handwritten notes taken by the corporate secretary. Also see the presentations at that meeting titled "Chief Financial Officer Report" and "LJM3." Also see the Wilmer, Cutler notes from the Nov. 30, 2001, interview with Causey; the Jan. 29, 2002, interview with Blake; and the Nov. 27, 2001, interview with Skilling; as well as the Batson Report, vol. 4, app. D, 145.

383 Some details of the Oct. 7 board meeting from the official agenda and minutes, as well as handwritten notes taken by the corporate secretary.

383–84 Some details of the meeting with Fastow from entries in Mintz's personal schedule book, which he used to take notes. Copies of the LJM approval sheets were obtained by the author. Some details of Mintz's early days in global finance from the Wilmer, Cutler notes from the Oct. 20 and Nov. 21, 2001, interview with Mintz; his May 16, 2003, deposition taken as part of the Batson investigation; and his Feb. 7, 2002, testimony before the House Energy and Commerce Committee's Subcommittee on Oversight and Investigations.

384–85 Details of the Raptor problems and the use of the costless collars from the Powers Report, 110–11, and the Batson Report, vol. 4, app. C, 135–44; Wilmer, Cutler notes from the Jan. 11 and 15, 2002, interviews with Jordan, and the Dec. 11, 2001, and Jan. 31, 2002, Siurek interviews; a Nov. 14, 2000, memo to the files by Ron Baker of Enron, "Raptor Vehicle Issues"; and the documents headed

"Daily Position Report and Summary" for each Raptor vehicle in the months of Oct. and Nov. Also see the Wilmer, Cutler notes of the Dec. 20, 2001, interview with Rakesh Bharati.

385–86 The timing of the Oct. 23 meeting from the two men's calendars. Some details of the discussion from contemporaneous notes taken by Mintz during the meeting. Also see the Wilmer, Cutler notes from the Oct. 20 and Nov. 21, 2001, interview with Mintz, and his May 16, 2003, Batson deposition.

386 Mintz's discussion with Buy from the Wilmer, Cutler notes from the Nov. 21, 2001, interview with Mintz, and his May 16, 2003, deposition taken as part of the Batson investigation. Also see the notes from Buy's Jan. 17, 2002, interview with Congressional staffers.

386–87 Some details of the Mintz meeting with McMahon from notes in Mintz's schedule book.

387–88 Some details of Skilling's experience at the LJM conference from his testimony of Dec. 4 and 5, 2001, before the SEC, as well as entries in his schedule book for Oct. 26 and a copy of his itinerary. A copy of the presentation made by Fastow, "LJM Investments, Annual Partnership Meeting, October 26, 2000," was obtained by the author. Other specific details from an invitation labeled "LJM2 Co-investment LP Conference," and welcoming material distributed to the attendees. Also see the document "LJM2 Co-investment LP Conference, October 26–27, 2000, Agenda and Attendee List."

388–89 Some details from notes and entries in Mintz's schedule book. Also see the Wilmer, Cutler notes from the Oct. 20 and Nov. 21, 2001, interviews with Mintz, and his May 16, 2003, Batson deposition. Also see notes from Buy's Jan. 17, 2002, interview with Congressional staffer.

389 Some details of the follow-up meeting in Portland from Sanders's July 9, 2002, deposition before the FERC and the CFTC.

390 Some details of the negotiation breakdown and Berardino's follow-up from Levitt, *Take on the Street*, 136–38.

391 Some details of Chanos's efforts from his Feb. 6, 2002, testimony. Also see Laing, "The Bear That Roared."

391 Some details of Yoder's decision to try to capture management's attention with a memo from Hall from his June 2, 2002, testimony before the CFTC and the FERC.

391 Some details of Curry's examination of EES from McLean and Elkind, *Smartest Guys in the Room*, 299–301.

392 Some details of the Derrick meeting from the Sanders testimony of July 9 and 10, 2002.

392–93 Some details of Mintz's conversation with Fastow from notes written in his schedule book for that day. Also see the private-placement memorandum for LJM2, Dec. 15, 1999, and the draft memorandum for LJM3, Dec. 2000. Also see the Dec. 2000 investment-recommendation memo from the Pacific Corporate Group to Calpers, "LJM3 Co-investment LP," and Mintz's Dec. 7, 2000, memo "Private Placement Memorandum for 'LJM3.' "

393 Details of the tree lighting from Nancy Vogel, "Crisis Darkens State Christmas Tree," *Los Angeles Times*, Dec. 6, 2000, A1. Also see Colleen Valles, "Facing Power Shortage, Plea to Turn on Holiday Lights Late," Associated Press, Dec. 5, 2000.

393–94 Some details of Hall's effort from the undated transcript of his testimony before the CFTC and the FERC; a copy of the Dec. 6, 2000, memo from Yoder and Hall to Sanders, "Traders' Strategies in the California Wholesale Power Markets/ISO Sanctions"; and Yoder's June 7, 2002, testimony before the two bodies. Also see the billing records of Stoel Rives to Enron North America for Dec. 1–7, 2000, as reflected in an invoice issued on Jan. 30, 2001; and the Jan. 11, 2001, memo to Sanders from Gary Fergus of the Brobeck firm, "Status Report on Further Investigation and Analysis of EPMI Trading Strategies."

394 Sanders described his reaction to the Yoder memo in his July 9, 2002, deposition before the FERC and the CFTC.

394 Yoder described Haedicke's reaction to the memo in his June 7, 2002, testimony.

395 Some details of the draft of Mintz's memo from the original document, "Private Placement Memorandum for 'LJM3,' " Dec. 7, 2000. Also see the Wilmer, Cutler notes from the Oct. 20, 2001, interview with Mintz, and his May 16, 2003, deposition taken as part of the Batson investigation, and the revised memo, a copy of which was obtained by the author. Also see the Batson Report, vol. 4, app. C, 167.

395–96 Some details of the Dec. 12 board meeting from the official minutes.

CHAPTER 15

397–98 A copy of the deal-approval sheet for Fishtail was obtained by the author. Details of the transaction from an Oct. 1, 2000, memo to the file by Enron Transaction Support, "Accounting Enron's Investment in Fishtail LLC." Some details from the subsequent Mintz e-mail of that day, Jan. 4, 2001, to Nicole Alvino, Barry Schnapper, and Ryan Siurek, "LJM Approval Sheets for Avici, Catalytica." Also see the notes from Wilmer, Cutler's Dec. 12, 2001, interview with Schnapper and the Nov. 21, 2001, interview with Mintz; and the Batson Report, vol. 3, app. C, 90.

398 Some details of Bass's work on Fishtail from his March 4, 2001, e-mail to Stewart, headed "Enron"; also see the FBI 302 from the Feb. 8, 2002, interview with Stewart.

398–99 Some details of Project Braveheart from the Dec. 2000 internal presentation "EBS Blockbuster Monetization and More: 'Project Braveheart' "; a Dec. 29, 2000, memo to the file by Roger Willard and Clint S. Carlin of Arthur Andersen, "Content Services LLC Formation and Securitization Issues"; a Dec. 29, 2000, memo to the file by Kimberly Scardino of Andersen, "Project Braveheart—Sale of EBS Content Systems Membership Interests"; and a Jan. 2001 Enron document, "EBS Blockbuster Monetization, 'Braveheart—the Sequel.' " Some details of the accounting debate over the effort from the 302 prepared by the FBI from an interview with Bass on Feb. 1, 2002; and from a Bass e-mail to Stewart, "Blockbuster Update," Dec. 20, 2000. The near collapse of the deal is revealed in the March 8, 2001, letter from John Antioco, chairman and chief executive of Blockbuster, to Rice from Enron Broadband Services; also see the fourth superseding indictment in *United States of America v. Kenneth Rice et al.*, filed in Houston Federal District Court on July 22, 2004.

399 According to the 302 of his Feb. 1, 2002, interview, Bass described the CIBC controversy to the FBI.

399–400 The problems regarding the flipped fee, known as negative UDC charges, are disclosed in an undated Enron document created in late Jan. or early Feb. 2001 and headed "EES—Confidential," which lays out the financial impact of those charges. Some details of the California reserves, taken through a document known as Schedule C, are described in the FBI 302 from the Feb. 8, 2002, interview of Thomas Bauer from Andersen. Also see *U.S. v. Skilling et al.*, as well as some of the individual calculation documents used in assembling Schedule C and Skilling's Dec. 5, 2001, testimony before the SEC.

400–1 Some details of the efforts to find answers to the Raptor problems from the FBI 302s from the Feb. 1, 2002, interview with Bass and the Feb. 21, 2002, interview with Cash; and a Nov. 29, 2000, memo to the file by Ron Baker of Enron, "Raptor III–IV Cross-Guarantee Loss Contingency." Also see the memo to the files by Duncan and other members of the team, "Raptor Structures Update," Dec. 28, 2000; the undated, unsigned document "Raptor Vehicles Credit Capacity Issue Solutions"; and another undated, unsigned document, "Raptor Realignment Steps." Also see the Powers Report, 119–20; the Batson Report, vol. 4, app. C, 138; the Wilmer, Cutler notes from interviews with Kevin Jordan on Jan. 11 and 15, 2002; Ryan Siurek on Dec. 11, 2001, and Jan. 31, 2002; Wes Colwell on Jan. 9, 2002; and Ron Astin on Jan. 16, 2002.

402 Details of the Duncan memo from the original document. Also see the Batson Report, vol. 4, app. B, annex 1, 4.

402–3 Some details of the Davis, Greenspan, and Summers meeting from Noam Neusner, "Greenspan, Davis Meet to Discuss Electricity Crisis," *San Francisco Chronicle*, Dec. 27, 2000, B1; and "California Briefing for Fed Governor," *Houston Chronicle*, Dec. 27, 2000, Business, 4.

403–4 Some details of the meeting between Lay and Davis from Lay's itinerary for the week and handwritten notes taken during the discussion.

404–5 Details of the Azurix buyback from the 8-K filed by Azurix with the SEC on Dec. 15, 2000. Also see "Enron Throws Azurix a Lifeline," *Global Water Intelligence*, Nov. 2000.

405 The issues surrounding the use of collateral as cash from operations from Enron's 2000 10-K, filed with the SEC on April 2, 2001; and the May 6, 2001, analysis of Enron issued by the Off Wall Street Consulting Group.

406 Some details of Davis's State of the State address from an official transcript of the speech. Also see Dan Morain, "Davis Urges Electric Overhaul to End 'Energy Nightmare,' " *Los Angeles Times*, Jan. 9, 2001, A1.

406 Some details of Causey's demand to remove Bass emerge in the 302s from the FBI interviews with David Duncan on April 5, 2002; Bass on Feb. 8, 2002; Bauer on Feb. 8, 2002; as well as Bass's testimony of May 9, 2002, in *U.S. v. Arthur Andersen.* Berardino's trip is described in a Jan. 24, 2001, e-mail from Shannon Adlong of Andersen to David Duncan, and a Feb. 16, 2001, e-mail from Adlong to the Enron engagement team, "Joe Berardino Visit to Enron—Feb. 21st."

407 Kaminski described his frustration with the Raptors, and his conclusions about them, in his Dec. 16, 2001, interview with Wilmer, Cutler.

408 Some details of the meeting from Lay's itinerary for Jan. 13–15, 2001, headed "Los Angeles CA Itinerary; KLL/SJK/RS."

408–12 The events in the video conference call were reconstructed by multiple participants in the meeting who were in attendance in either Los Angeles or Washington.

412–13 Details of Mintz's meeting with Fastow from notes in his schedule book, his May 16, 2003, deposition taken as part of the Batson investigation, and his Feb. 7, 2002, testimony before the House Energy and Commerce Committee's Subcommittee on Oversight and Investigations. He also recounted this conversation in his e-mail to Astin and Rogers of that day. Also see a hard-copy printout, complete with handwritten notes by Mintz, of his Jan. 31, 2001, e-mail to Astin and Rogers, "LJM Proxy Disclosure—RhythmsNet"; the Batson Report, vol. 3, app. C, 34, and Mintz's handwritten transcription of Fastow's May 1, 2001, voice mail pertaining to how he would like to handle potential disclosure of his LJM income.

413 A copy of Mintz's Jan. 16, 2001, e-mail was obtained by the author, as was the subsequent forwarded e-mail from Walls to Derrick of that same day. Also see the Batson Report, vol. 4, app. C, 129–30. Walls recounted his discussion with Astin in his sworn statement to the bankruptcy examiner of Sept. 25, 2002.

414–17 Some details of the Lays' trip to Washington from their official itinerary for Jan. 18–21, 2001. The document is headed "2001 Presidential Inauguration; Kenneth and Linda Lay; Washington, D.C.; January 18–21, 2001; Itinerary." Also see Kurt Eichenwald with Diana Henriques, "Enron Buffed Image to a Shine Even as It Rotted from Within," *New York Times,* Feb. 10, 2002, A1.

417 Dialogue from the conference call from the official transcript.

418 A copy of the Lay family balance sheet for the year ended 2000 was obtained by the author.

418 Some details of Chanos's efforts from his Feb. 6, 2002, testimony before Congress, and from McLean and Elkind, *Smartest Guys in the Room,* 320–21.

419 Some details of the meeting between Mintz and Causey from notes in Mintz's schedule and from a Feb. 1, 2001, e-mail from Mintz to Causey headed "Re: Related Party Transactions." Also see Mintz's May 16, 2003, deposition taken as part of the Batson investigation; his Feb. 7, 2002, congressional testimony; notes from his Oct. 20, 2001, interview with Wilmer, Cutler; and the Batson Report, vol. 4, app. C, 130.

419–20 Skilling described his meeting with Fastow in his Dec. 4 and 5, 2001, testimony before the SEC; a copy of what appeared to be the Fastow estimate was reviewed by the author.

420 Details of Fastow's actual financial performance from *U.S. v. Fastow, et al.,* and from the April 30, 2003, criminal indictment in *United States of America v. Lea W. Fastow,* filed in Federal District Court in Houston.

420 A number of details of this meeting, including the dialogue, from McLean and Elkind, *Smartest Guys in the Room,* 299.

420–21 Some details of the EES book shift from the FBI 302 taken during the proffer of Debra Cash on Feb. 21 and 22, 2002; from *U.S. v. Skilling et al.,* and the indictment filed Oct. 29, 2003, in *United States of America v. David Delainey,* in Federal District Court in Houston. Delainey pleaded guilty to the crimes charged. Also see the 10-Q filed by Enron with the SEC on May 15, 2001, which disclosed the shifting of the risk-management book. Also see the Feb. 7, 2001, e-mail from Lay and Skilling to all of Enron, "Organizational Changes."

421 Some details of the Feb. 12, 2001, audit committee meeting from the official minutes, handwritten notes taken during the meeting by the corporate secretary, and a copy of Causey's formal presentation, "Review of LJM Procedures and Transactions Completed in 2000." Also see Mintz's May 16, 2003, deposition taken as part of the Batson investigation; his Feb. 7, 2002, congressional testimony; the Wilmer, Cutler notes from the interview with Winokur on Jan. 8, 2002, and with Causey on Nov. 30, 2002; and the Batson Report, vol. 4, app. C, 128–31, and vol. 3, 130.

422–23 Some details of McLean's work and her call to Enron from McLean and Elkind, *Smartest Guys in the Room*, 321–22, as well as from entries in Skilling's schedule book. Also see Bethany McLean, "Is Enron Overpriced?" *Fortune*, March 5, 2001, 122, and handwritten notes taken by one participant during the McLean and Skilling call.

424–25 Some details of the *Fortune* interview from McLean and Elkind, *Smartest Guys in the Room*, 322–23.

CHAPTER 16

426–29 Some details of Bass's removal from the 302s from the FBI interviews with Duncan on April 5, 2002; Bass on Feb. 8, 2002; Bauer on Feb. 8, 2002; and Stewart on Feb. 8, 2002. Also see the March 4, 2001, Bass e-mail to Stewart, as well as Bass's May 9, 2002, testimony in *U.S. v. Arthur Andersen*, Stewart's testimony at the same trial on May 30 and 31, 2002, and the handwritten, unsigned notes taken from a March 12, 2001, Andersen meeting.

428 Some details of Mintz's briefing to the legal team from a March 7, 2001, memo, "LJM Legal Review," as well as entries from his personal schedule, his May 16, 2003, deposition taken as part of the Batson investigation, and his Feb. 7, 2002, testimony before Congress. Also see the Batson Report, vol. 4, app. C, 155. The testimonies and schedule book also provide details on the effort to forward information to Fastow. A copy of the forwarded memo, "LJM Approval Process—Transaction Substantiation," dated March 8, 2001, was obtained by the author. Also see the Wilmer, Cutler notes of the Nov. 30, 2001, interview with Causey.

429–32 Timing of the reviews and discussions from notes in Glisan's schedule. Some details of the meeting between Kaminski, Glisan, and Kindall from the Kindall report, written with Li Sun and dated March 9, 2001. While there was no daily cash reporting, Andersen analyzed Enron's cash flow on a quarterly basis, as evidenced by the June 30 and July 30, 2000, memo to the file of Michael Croom from Andersen, "ECM Cash Flow Review."

432 Details of Glisan's family trip to Colorado from the "Travel Itinerary/Agenda" for "Ben Glisan and family," for the week of March 10–17, 2001.

432–33 Some problems with the Blockbuster deal are revealed in the March 8, 2001, letter from John Antioco, chairman and chief executive of Blockbuster, to Ken Rice. Also see the fourth superseding indictment in *U.S. v. Rice et al.* and Anne Marie Squeo and Bruce Orwall, "Enron and Blockbuster Terminate Partnership for Video-on-Demand," *Wall Street Journal*, March 12, 2001, B9.

433–34 The Reuters article was dated March 9, 2001. A copy of the e-mail correspondence between Bass and Stewart on March 10 was obtained by the author. The failure to take a loss from *U.S. v. Rice et al.* Also see Bass's March 13, 2001, e-mail to Stewart, "EBS Blockbuster Memo."

434–35 Timing of the Mintz, Causey, and Buy meeting from notes in Mintz's personal schedule. Also see his May 16, 2003, Batson deposition; and his Feb. 7, 2002, congressional testimony.

435–36 Skilling described his frustration in watching the stock price fall in John Emshwiller, "Enron's Skilling Cites Stock Price Plunge as Main Reason for Leaving CEO Post," *Wall Street Journal*, Aug. 16, 2001, A2.

436–37 The Raptor restructuring is described in clear detail in the Powers Report, 121–25. Also see notes of the Wilmer, Cutler interviews with Kaminski on Dec. 19, 2001; Jordan on Jan. 11 and 15, 2002; Siurek on Dec. 11, 2001, and Jan. 31, 2002. Also see the March 30, 2001, memo to the files by Duncan and the Enron engagement team, "Enron-Raptor Entity Note Impairment"; and Siurek's April 12, 2001, memo to the files, "Raptor Restructuring."

437 Siurek described his contact with Skilling in his Wilmer, Cutler interviews.

437 Some details of Pitt's background from Andrew Hill and John Labate, "A Reluctant Street Fighter," *Financial Times*, May 11, 2002, 9; and Stephen Labaton, "Praise to Scorn: Mercurial Ride of S.E.C. Chief," *New York Times*, Nov. 10, 2002, sec. 1, 1.

438 Timing of the Skilling and Martin meeting from entries in Skilling's schedule.

439 Timing of the Skilling and Fastow meeting from entries in Skilling's schedule. Also see Skilling's testimony before the SEC on Dec. 4 and 5, 2001.

439–40 Mintz described how the wind deal proved to be a breaking point for him in his congressional testimony of Feb. 7, 2002, and in his May 16, 2003, Batson deposition. Also see his memo of April 12, 2002, to Baxter, Metts, and Causey, "Proposed Sale of Enron Wind to LJM—Disclosure Issues." Also see the notes of Wilmer, Cutler's Jan. 17, 2002, interview with Derrick; the Jan. 18, 2002, interview with Rex Rogers; and the April 18, 2001, letter from Ron Astin to Mintz and Lance Schuler, "Proposed Transaction."

440–41 A version of Fastow's e-mail to Skilling was obtained by the author from an electronic duplicate of Skilling's e-mail account. Timing of the arrival in Fastow's office from Mintz's schedule book.

441–44, 445 Some details of Lay's trip to Washington from his itinerary headed "Eli Lilly—Indianapolis, Indiana; Vice President Cheney—Washington, D.C.; April 16–17, 2001," as well as the April 13, 2001, letter from Carolyn A. Cooney from Enron's Washington office to Debbie Heiden on Cheney's personal staff and an April 13, 2001, briefing memo from Linda Robertson and Tom Briggs of Enron's Washington office to Lay and Kean. The precise details of what was discussed in the meeting were heavily documented. Lay's talking points, headed "Discussion Points for Lay/Cheney Meeting," were obtained by the author, as were the multiple position papers left with Cheney. The papers, some of which were prepared for other lobbying efforts, are headed "National Energy Policy: Priorities," "Examples of Problems Due to Lack of Open Access," "Emergency Measures for Western Power Markets," "Action Plan for Implementing Findings & Principles for Joint Action on Western States Power Markets," "ESPA Letter on Open Access," "Summary of Democratic Alternative Bill," "Federal Demand Buy-Down ('Negawatt') Proposal," "LNG," and "Carbon Dioxide." Finally, the author also reviewed copies of notes taken during the meeting by a participant.

442–45 Dialogue of Skilling's conference call from an official transcript of the discussion.

445–46 Several news outlets reported the Skilling gaffe. For example, see "Skilling, Analyst Verbally Butt Heads," Reuters, April 18, 2001; and "Skilling Speaks His Mind," *Gas Daily*, April 18, 2001.

446 Skilling's proposal to increase the VAR was documented in the April 30, 2001, presentation to the finance committee written by Skilling and Buy, "Recommended Changes to the Risk Management Policy."

447–48 A copy of Skilling's initial resignation letter was obtained by the author.

449 Some details from the May 6, 2001, analysis of Enron issued by the Off Wall Street Consulting Group. Also see Trebor Banstetter, "Some Saw Through Enron's Ploys," *Fort Worth Star-Telegram*, Feb. 10, 2002, Business, 1.

449 Baxter's departure was formally announced on May 2, 2001, in a company-wide e-mail sent out by Lay and Skilling headed "Cliff Baxter."

450 Lay's location from an entry in his schedule. A copy of the Bank of America margin call was obtained by the author.

450–51 Timing of Mintz's meeting from entries in his schedule. Other details from the Wilmer, Cutler notes from the Oct. 20 and Nov. 21, 2001, interview with Mintz; his May 16, 2003, Batson deposition; and his Feb. 7, 2002, congressional testimony. Also see the Batson Report, vol. 4, app. D, 143–45.

451 The article read by Mintz was by Stephen Labaton, "White House Picks Chairman of S.E.C.," *New York Times*, May 8, 2001, A1. Other details from Mintz's Feb. 7, 2002, congressional testimony. Also see Mintz's May 10, 2001, letter to Richard Steinwurtzel of Fried, Frank.

452 The article read by Lay was by Peter Eavis, "Why One Firm Thinks Enron Is Running Out of Gas," TheStreet.com, May 9, 2001.

CHAPTER 17

453–54 Details of the bank meeting in Miami from papers laying out the attendees and events titled "Bank Attendees," May 17, 2001.

453 Bush's announcement from David Sanger with Joseph Kahn, "Bush, Pushing Energy Plan, Offers

Scores of Proposals to Find New Power," *New York Times*, May 18, 2001, A1. Details of the stock performance of the industry and of Enron from a transcript of *Nightly Business Report*, May 17, 2001.

454–55 Some details of Lay's trip to California from his itinerary for that week, headed "Itinerary for KLL; California."

455 The author reviewed the report of the National Energy Policy Development Group, "Reliable, Affordable, and Environmentally Sound Energy for America's Future," May 2001, and compared it head-to-head with the issues papers and talking points presented to Cheney and his staff during the meeting with Lay. While there has been much public speculation that the Cheney task force may have bowed to Enron's demands, in fact the Lay analysis is accurate: Enron's central request for the establishment of regional transmission organizations was not adopted by the Administration. Certain specific Enron requests for what the Administration should *not* do were adopted as policy recommendations. All in all, the comparison of the Lay presentation and the Cheney recommendations shows that both voiced a commitment to power deregulation. That, however, has been a central tenet of Republican Party policy for more than a decade; it flies in the face of history and reason to argue that the Administration advocated deregulation because of Lay's commitment to such a position.

455 The Emshwiller article, "California Blame Game Yields No Score," appeared in *The Wall Street Journal* on May 22, 2001, A2. Details of Emshwiller's interview with Lockyer from Rebecca Smith and John R. Emshwiller, *24 Days* (Harper Business, 2003), 14–15.

455–56 Details of Skilling's meeting from entries in his schedule book. Other details about this meeting from Skilling's sworn testimony before the SEC on Dec. 4 and 5, 2001. There are numerous reasons to believe that this scene, as portrayed, is accurate. As of this writing, the government now has Fastow as a witness, has already charged Skilling with crimes, but has not suggested Skilling perjured himself in his SEC testimony in regard to this matter. The surrounding evidence, both documentary and through interviews, makes it undoubtedly clear that the motivation for the Fastow withdrawal from LJM came from Skilling; in the days leading up to this meeting, Fastow was working hard to capture every advantage for LJM. He walked away from this meeting trying to find ways to maintain a position in the fund without creating a disclosure obligation. Fastow also contemporaneously told some witnesses about Skilling's demand, and his recounting at that time mirrors in every particular the comments made by Skilling in his sworn SEC testimony.

456–57 Some details of Lay's visit to KKR from his travel itinerary, May 21–23, 2001.

457 Some details of Belden's decision to hire a lawyer from Sanders's testimony before the CFTC and the FERC, July 9, 2002, 113–14.

457–58 Details of Mintz's efforts to get Skilling to sign the LJM approval sheets from the Wilmer, Cutler notes from the Oct. 20 and Nov. 21, 2001, interview with Mintz; Mintz's May 16, 2003, Batson deposition; and his Feb. 7, 2002, testimony before Congress. In his testimony before the same congressional body that day, Skilling said he never saw the memo sent by Mintz; Skilling's schedule shows that he would have been heading out of the office about the same time the package was sent, and that he did not return to the office for a week. Also see a copy of Mintz's memo to Skilling, "Company Approvals for Transactions with LJM," May 22, 2001; and the notes from Skilling's Nov. 27, 2001, interview with Wilmer, Cutler.

458 Fastow's efforts to get a smaller portion of ownership in LJM, and the subsequent rejection of that idea, from a May 21, 2001, letter from Jordan Mintz to Richard A. Steinwurtzel and James H. Schropp of the Fried, Frank law firm; Mintz's typewritten notes headed "LJM Legal Review," dated May 22, 2001; Mintz's June 4, 2001, memo to Fastow headed "LJM Proxy Disclosures (2002)"; a June 4, 2001, memo from James P. Baetzhold of Fried, Frank to Steinwurtzel, Schropp and Lanae Holbrook, headed "Enron Proxy Disclosure."

458 The timing of Mintz's meeting with Fastow from Mintz's schedule book. Other details from Mintz's testimony before Congress on Feb. 7, 2002.

459 Details of the Skilling and Fastow meeting from Skilling's sworn testimony before the SEC.

459–60 Details of the dealings on Cuiabá, and the decision to shove the closing date forward, from documents. including the March 28, 2001, share repurchase agreement between LJM BrazilCo and Enron de Brazil Holdings Ltd.; the Aug. 15, 2001, document headed "EPE Holdings Ltd. Transfer of Share from LJM BrazilCo. To EPE Holdings Ltd."; the Wilmer, Cutler notes from the Dec. 6, 2001, interview with Castleman and from the interviews of Dec. 5 and 7, 2001, with Lipshutz. Also see the Batson Report, vol. 2, app. L, annex 3, 7–8; and Jordan Mintz's typewritten notes headed "LJM Update" and dated May 7, 2001.

460–61 Some details of Watkins's personal situation, and her run-in with Fastow, from Swartz with Watkins, *Power Failure*, 262–64.

461 Some details of Lay's meeting from his travel itinerary, headed "European Trip; E7 Summit; May 29–June 10, 2001; Lays/Seidls/Reasoners/Duncans."

461–62 Details of the negotiations for LJM, and the final purchase price, from a number of documents, including the July 24, 2001, purchase agreement between Fastow and Kopper; the term note and pledge agreement of July 31, 2001, by Kopper in favor of Citicorp, which financed the loan for the LJM2 purchase; an Aug. 29, 2001, letter from Kopper to Citicorp. Also see the criminal complaint filed in *US v. Fastow et al.* and the Batson Report, vol. 2, app. L, annex 4, 41–43.

462–63 The changes to the PRC process are described in a Skilling e-mail to all employees, "Changes to PRC Process," May 9, 2001.

463–64 Details of Skilling's presentation from a video of "Strategic Directions 2001," a technology conference sponsored by Tibco.

464 Details of the Andersen Waste Management settlement, and Goolsby's role in that resolution, from the paperwork filed by the SEC in the case of *Securities and Exchange Commission v. Arthur Andersen LLP et al.* filed in Federal District Court in Washington, D.C. These documents were filed at the time the settlement of June 19, 2001, and include "Order Instituting Public Administrative Proceedings, Making Findings and Imposing Remedial Sanctions Pursuant to Rule 102(e) of the Commission's Rules of Practice," Administrative proceeding file no. 10513; "Final Judgment as to Defendant Arthur Andersen LLP"; "Consent of Defendant Arthur Andersen LLP"; and the formal civil complaint.

464–65 The FERC decision and its effect on Enron stock from Christian Berthelsen, "Texas Power Firm's Shares Falling," *San Francisco Chronicle*, June 22, 2001, B1.

465–66 Some details of Skilling's meeting with the lawyers from entries in his schedule book, along with the Sanders testimony of July 9, 2002, 162–65.

466–67 Details of Herrold's efforts and the answers he received to his questions from a series of handwritten notes he took beginning on June 20, 2001, in his conversations with Rex Rogers.

467 Skilling testified about the events in San Francisco before the SEC on Dec. 5, 2001. The author obtained an audiotape of the events that transpired in the meeting room. Also see Karen Gaudette, "Enron CEO Gets a Pie in the Face," *Associated Press Online*, June 21, 2001.

468–69 Details of the Fastows' trip to Florida from a series of documents, including Fastow's "Company Airplane Transportation Request" of May 30, 2001, which was approved by Skilling; an itinerary headed "Fastow Foundation Travel; Cheeca Lodge, Florida; June 21–24, 2001," which includes multiple copies with handwritten notes about events participated in; the flight schedule and plan submitted by the pilots of the Hawker for June 21, 2001; an undated printout of an e-mail from Bridget Maronge to a travel agent at Travel Park and three others from her to Fastow's siblings; bills from the Cheeca Lodge from June 21 through 24, 2001, for Andy Fastow; copies of reimbursement requests submitted to the foundation through Maronge; and the attachment "SIFL Detailed Summary Report," which was provided to Fastow in a July 6, 2001, memo from Kristi Monson headed "Personal Use of Corporate Aircraft."

468–69 Details of the foundation meeting from the document "Fastow Family Foundation Annual Meeting, June 22, 2001." Also see the foundation's 990-PF form (Return of Private Foundation) filed with the Internal Revenue Service for the tax year ending Dec. 31, 2000.

469–70 Some details of Skilling's trip from entries in his travel book. The type of transaction being pursued by Nacchio, known as a capacity swap, was part of the regular form of business at Qwest for years. According to Qwest's filings with the SEC, the accounting used by Qwest for such swaps was approved by Arthur Andersen; however, in 2002, after Qwest brought in new accountants from KPMG, the telephone company began to restate its financial performance for those transactions. For example, on Sept. 22, 2002, Qwest filed documents with the SEC announcing that it was reversing $1.48 billion in revenue, with more than $1 billion of that amount reported in 2001. However, while the accounting proved to be incorrect, there is nothing about Nacchio's proposal that is on its face illegal or clearly improper; it made little business sense for Enron, however. That Qwest discussed such swaps with Enron is confirmed in the congressional hearings "Capacity Swaps by Global Crossing and Qwest: Sham Transactions Designed to Boost Revenues?" before the House Energy and Commerce Committee's Subcomittee on Oversight and Investigations, Sept. 24, 2002. In that hearing Nacchio testified, "During my tenure as CEO, to my knowledge, every purchase of capacity by Qwest was with the intent of furthering the company's business plan," and not for the purpose of booking revenues on a quarterly basis. That several parties in June 2001 were negotiating with Enron to do a broadband swap deal is documented in a June 11, 2001, e-mail from Nancy Davidson on behalf of Gary Winnick, CEO of Global Crossing, to Tom Casey, another Global Crossing executive, in which Winnick describes recent discussions with Skilling about broadband deals.

470 Details of Watkins's discovery from Swartz with Watkins, *Power Failure*, 268–70.

471 Some details on the troubles in broadband from an internal "news" article distributed over the Enron corporate Web site on July 12, 2001, "Enron Reports Strong Q2 Earnings Despite Broadband Loss."

471 Mordaunt discussed her approach by Fastow to join him in her Jan. 12, 2002, interview with Wilmer, Cutler.

471 Some details of the transfer of $750,000 to Mordaunt from the RADR conspiracy were disclosed in the indictment in *U.S. v. Fastow et al.*

472–73 Timing of the Skilling meeting with Buy and other details from entries in Skilling's schedule book.

473–74 Some details of the meeting between Lay and Skilling from the two men's schedule books.

476–77 Some details of Watkins's meeting with Williams and Li from a printout of an entry in her electronic schedule book. Also see Swartz with Watkins, *Power Failure*, 269.

CHAPTER 18

479–80 Copies of some of the draft press releases were obtained by the author.

480–81 Details of the finance committee meeting from the official minutes, handwritten notes of the corporate secretary, and a copy of Fastow's presentation. Also see the Batson Report, vol. 4, 105; vol. 4, app. D, 135; and vol. 2, app. E, 6.

481–83 Some details of the board meeting from the official minutes.

484 Some details of Watkins's reaction from Swartz with Watkins, *Power Failure*, 270–71.

486 Details of the Skilling and Lay conversation with analysts and reporters from an official transcript. The announcement of Skilling's resignation was sent out in an e-mail from Lay and Skilling on the morning of Aug. 14, 2001, to employees worldwide. Also see Jonathan Friedland, "Enron's CEO, Skilling, Quits Two Top Posts," *Wall Street Journal*, Aug. 15, 2001, A3.

486–87 Some details of the letter from a copy of the undated, unsigned document. Timing of the delivery of the document from an entry in a mail-tracking registry, headed "Log of Incidents," maintained by the company's legal department. Some details from Swartz with Watkins, *Power Failure*, 275–76.

487–88 Some details of the initial response to the Watkins letter from Swartz with Watkins, *Power Failure*, 276.

488 Some details of Derrick's response to the Watkins letter from his September 26, 2003, sworn statement to the bankruptcy examiner. Also see the Batson Report, vol. 4, app. C, 159–61.

489 Causey's response to the Watkins letter is contained, in part, in an e-mail he sent on Aug. 15, 2001, to Mary Clark of Enron, with copies to Steve Kean and Derrick.

489–90 Dialogue and other details of the employee meeting from a transcript of the event.

489–90 Some details of Watkins's reaction to the Lay meeting, and her subsequent visit to Olson, from Swartz with Watkins, *Power Failure*, 278–79.

490 Details of Emshwiller's meeting with Friedland from Smith and Emshwiller, *24 Days*, 12–13.

490–91 A copy of Skilling's plan for his future was obtained by the author.

491 Details of Enron's disclosures from its 10-Q filed August 14, 2001. Other details from Smith and Emshwiller, *24 Days*, 18–19, 21.

491–92 Some details of Skilling's conversation with Emshwiller from Smith and Emshwiller, *24 Days*, 22–24. Also see the Batson Report, vol. 4, app. D, 14.

492–93 Some details of the trip from Lay's itinerary headed "Analyst Meetings—New York/Boston; August 16–17, 2001." The article read by Koenig was Emshwiller, "Enron's Skilling Cites Stock Price Plunge as Main Reason for Leaving CEO Post."

493 A copy of the Kean e-mail was obtained by the author.

494 Details of the *Journal*'s decision to put together a partnership story from Smith and Emshwiller, *24 Days*, 25–26.

494–95 Some details of Watkins's efforts to reach out to Mordaunt and Rogers from Swartz with Watkins, *Power Failure*, 281–83.

495 Some details of the unopened Siurek e-mail from the FBI 302 of agents' interview with Grutzmacher on Feb. 15, 2001.

495–96 Some details of the Fastow and Bowen meeting from Bowen's appointment book.

496 Some details of the Watkins and Buy meeting from her Feb. 14, 2002, testimony in hearings before the House Energy and Commerce Committee's Subcommittee on Oversight and Investigations. Also see Watkins's June 6, 2003, deposition before the Enron bankruptcy trustee and Swartz with Watkins, *Power Failure*, 284–85.

496 Some details of Watkins's call to Hecker from an Aug. 21, 2001, memo of the call written by Hecker to the file, with copies to Duncan and the Enron engagement; Hecker's Aug. 23, 2001, e-mail to Duncan, "Documentation of Client Call," which included a copy of the Aug. 21 memo; Hecker's May 8, 2001, testimony in *U.S. v. Arthur Andersen*; Duncan's memo to the files of Oct. 16, 2001, "Enron Employee Assertions Regarding Certain Transactions"; the FBI 302s of agents' interviews with Shannon Adlong on Feb. 5, 2002; David Duncan on Jan. 14, March 21, and April 5, 2002; Nancy Temple on Feb. 13, 2002; and the SEC notes of the interview with Duncan from Jan. 14, 2002. Also see Swartz with Watkins, *Power Failure*, 285; and the Batson Report, vol. 4, app. C, 174.

497 Derrick's limited action during the first week after reviewing the Watkins letter is documented in the Batson Report, vol. 4, app. C, 159. Some details of the concern about legal liability involving Watkins from an Aug. 24, 2001, e-mail written by Carl Jordan of Vinson & Elkins to Sharon Butcher of Enron. Also see the Batson Report, vol. 4, app. C, 159.

498–99 Details of the timing of Lay's meeting with Watkins from his schedule book. Copies of the documents prepared by Watkins for the meeting were obtained by the author. Also see Swartz with Watkins, *Power Failure*, 287–89.

500 Details of Derrick's call to Dilg, and his failure to review the Watkins material before sending it to Vinson & Elkins, from his sworn statement to the bankruptcy examiner on Sept. 26, 2003. Also see unsigned, handwritten notes from Vinson & Elkins regarding the assignment.

500 A copy of the Aug. 22, 2001, e-mail—originally from Zipter to Ding Yuan of Enron, and then forwarded by Zipter to Kaminski—along with Kaminski's response, was obtained by the author.

500–1 Details of Dilg's efforts to assemble an investigative team from certain handwritten notes compiled by the lawyers. Also see the Batson Report, vol. 4, app. C, 161–62. Other details from Dilg's sworn statement of Aug. 14, 2003, and Astin's sworn statement of Sept. 10, 2003, to the bankruptcy examiner. Also see Hendrick's handwritten notes from the Aug. 23, 2001, discussion with Astin, and the Batson Report, vol. 4, app. C, 162–63.

501 A copy of the overnight letter announcing the margin call from Bank of America was obtained by the author.

502–3 The Smith and Emshwiller article, "Heard on the Street: Enron Prepares to Become Easier to Read," was published in *The Wall Street Journal* on Aug. 28, 2001, C1.

503 By analyzing certain details, the author was able to determine the identity of the *Journal*'s source, and then confirmed that finding directly with the source. However, that confirmation was provided on a not-for-attribution basis.

503–4 A copy of the MUI form filed by Hannan on Aug. 28 was obtained by the author.

504 Some details of McMahon's call to Watkins from Swartz with Watkins, *Power Failure*, 290–91.

504–5 Details of the reporting by Emshwiller and Smith from Smith and Emshwiller, *24 Days*, 47–50, 73–75.

505 Some details of Watkins's learning of Fastow's anger, and Olson's response, from her congressional testimony of Feb. 14, 2002; her June 6, 2003, deposition before the Enron bankruptcy trustee; the Vinson & Elkins memo to the file regarding their interview with Fastow as part of the Watkins investigation, which documented his anger; and Swartz with Watkins, *Power Failure*, 291. Also see the Batson Report, vol. 4, app. C, 159.

505–6 Some details of the Aug. 30, 2001, Vinson & Elkins interview with McMahon from the lawyers' Aug. 30, 2001, memo to the file on the discussion. Also see the Batson Report, vol. 4, app. C, 169.

506–8 Some details of the Woodlands meeting from handwritten notes taken by one of the participants. Also see the Aug. 31, 2001, e-mail to the management committee from Joannie Williamson of Enron, along with the attached agenda; Whalley's Sept. 3 e-mail to Lay and Kean about the agenda; and notes of Lay's Jan. 16, 2002, interview with Wilmer, Cutler.

508 Kopper later admitted his destruction of the laptop, which was never recovered, in interviews with the FBI given as part of his effort to secure a plea deal in July and Aug. 2002. These acts resulted in obstruction-of-justice charges being filed against Fastow in *U.S. v. Fastow*. He also discussed it in his testimony of Sept. 27, 2004, in *U.S. v. Bayly et al.*

CHAPTER 19

511 The structure and problems that emerged with the third Raptor vehicle are described in the Powers Report, 114–18. Some details of the decision from the Wilmer, Cutler notes from the Jan. 9, 2002, interview with Rodney Faldyn.

512 Some details of the Sept. 11, 2001, discussion between Stewart, Duncan, and Goddard from an FBI 302 of Stewart's interview with agents on Feb. 8, 2002. Also see the 302s of the FBI's Feb. 28, 2002, interviews with Goddard and with Goolsby. Also see the Batson Report, vol. 4, app. B, 52.

512–13 Details of the Dilg, Hendrick, and Astin meeting from Astin's sworn statement to the bankruptcy examiner of Sept. 10, 2003, and from Hendrick's contemporaneous notes from the meeting. Also see the Batson Report, vol. 4, app. C, 170–71.

513 A copy of Adlong's Sept. 14 e-mail, "Raptor Documentation," and the ten attached Raptor memos, were obtained by the author. Also see the Batson Report, vol. 4, app. B, 52.

513 Details of Stewart's reaction to the Raptor memos from the 302 of his Feb. 8, 2002, interview with the FBI and from his Sept. 25, 2001, e-mail to Cash, Duncan, and other members of the Enron team, "Enron Raptor Memos." Also see the Batson Report, vol. 4, app. B, 104.

513–14 Some details of the Glisan meeting from undated, handwritten notes taken by one of the participants. Also see the Wilmer, Cutler notes from the Jan. 18, 2002, interview with Tim Despain.

514–15 Some details of the $2.6 million tax payment from the Wilmer, Cutler notes of its Nov. 19, 2001, interview with Mintz. Also see the Powers Report, 64–65.

515 A copy of Fastow's report to the finance committee from Aug. 13, 2001, was obtained by the author.

516–17 Timing of the meeting at Lay's office from his official schedule.

517 Some details of the oral presentation by Vinson & Elkins from unsigned notes, "Outline Points to Discuss with Ken Lay and Jim Derrick," Sept. 21, 2001, that were prepared for the meeting. Also see Eichenwald with Henriques, "Enron Buffed Image"; and an Oct. 10, 2001, and an Oct. 15, 2001, copy of the report from Vinson & Elkins, sent to Derrick, both headed "Preliminary Investigation of Allegations of an Anonymous Employee."

518 The Andersen meeting is disclosed in an e-mail that morning from Bonnie Lamberth of Andersen to Duncan, Stewart, and other Andersen employees. Duncan's appearance in the video is revealed in the 302 of his March 21, 2002, interview with the FBI. See also the Batson Report, vol. 4, app. B, 53.

519 A copy of the Bank of America margin call from Sept. 19 was obtained by the author. Also see Kurt Eichenwald, "A Company Man to the End After All," *New York Times*, Feb. 9, 2003, Sunday Business, 1.

519–20 A copy of the draft 21(a) report e-mailed by Pitt was obtained by the author.

520 Some details of the meeting from the 302 of the FBI's interview with Bass on Feb. 1, 2002. Also see Bass's Sept. 25, 2001, e-mail to Cash, Duncan, and other members of the Enron team, "Raptor Memos."

520–21 A copy of the e-mailed questions from *The Wall Street Journal* was obtained by the author. Also see the Batson Report, vol. 3, app. C, 92.

521 Quotes of the E-Speak conference on Sept. 26, 2001, from a transcript of the event.

521–22 Some details of Temple's first day of involvement on Enron from the 302 of her interview with the FBI on Feb. 13, 2002. Also see "Government's *In Limine* Motion of Law," filed April 29, 2002, in *U.S. v. Andersen.*

522–23 Some details from notes of the Wilmer, Cutler interviews with Kaminski on Dec. 19, 2001; Shanbhogue on Dec. 20, 2001; and Bharati on Dec. 28, 2001. Also see the Sept. 2001 memo by Siurek and Ron Baker "Project Raptor—Addendum," and the unsigned document from Sept. 2001 "Project Raptor, Proposed Alternatives."

523 The decision to only provide a written statement is demonstrated with the Sept. 27, 2001, e-mail "LJM Statement," from Derrick to Dilg, with the attached statement that was intended to be provided to the *Journal*, and the reply of the same day, headed "68055 1.doc" from Dilg to Palmer, containing a revised statement.

524 Some details of the discussion between Temple and Stewart from Stewart's 302s from his Feb. 8, 2002, interview with the FBI, and Temple from her Feb. 13, 2002, interview. Also see Stewart's May 30, 2002, testimony in *U.S. v. Andersen* and Temple's handwritten notes from the conversation. Andersen's document-destruction policy, dated Feb. 1, 2000, is titled "Client Engagement Information: Organization, Retention, and Destruction."

524–25 A copy of the Kaminski e-mail to Scardino was obtained by the author. Other details from notes of the Wilmer, Cutler interviews with Kaminski on Dec. 19, 2001; with Causey on Dec. 21, 2001; with Gordon McKillop on Dec. 20, 2001; as well as the 302 of Scardino's interview with the FBI on Feb. 13, 2002.

525 Some details of Kaminski's run-in with Buy from notes of his Wilmer, Cutler interview on Dec. 19, 2001.

525–26 Some details of the meeting from notes of the Wilmer, Cutler interviews with Kaminski on Dec. 19, 2001; Shanbhogue on Dec. 20, 2001; and Bharati on Dec. 28, 2001.

526–27 Some details of the Andersen meeting in New Orleans from a package of materials provided to partners on their arrival at the Oct. 5 gathering.

527 Some details of the audit committee's Oct. 8, 2001, meeting from the official minutes and the agenda, as well as from Causey's two presentations, "Third Quarter Earnings Update" and "Review and Update for Accounting for Goodwill."

527–28 Some details of the finance committee meeting of that same day from the official minutes.

528 Some details of the full board meeting from Oct. 8 and 9, 2001, from the official minutes, as well as copies of the full presentations made by Enron Energy Services and Enron North America.

528 A copy of Zajac's Oct. 9, 2001, e-mail regarding the results of the FIDO test was obtained by the author.

528–29 Details of the struggle with finance during Kaminski's absence from notes of the Wilmer, Cutler interviews with Kaminski on Dec. 19, 2001, and Shanbhogue on Dec. 20, 2001.

529 Details of the Oct. 10 "current topics" meeting from a videotape of the discussion. Also see the agenda, dated Oct. 10 and headed "Current Topics Agenda," and the attendance sign-in sheet for the event.

529 Some details of the discussion between Temple and Stewart from Stewart's 302s from his Feb. 8, 2002, FBI interview, and Temple from her Feb. 13, 2002, interview. Also see Stewart's May 30, 2002, testimony in *U.S. v. Andersen.*

529 A copy of Temple's Oct. 12 e-mail to Odom, "Document Rentention Policy," was obtained by the author. Also see the 302 and the SEC's notes from the Jan. 14, 2001, interview with Duncan.

530–31 Duncan described the failed attempts to persuade Causey to drop the term "non-recurring" from the press release in an Oct. 15, 2001, memo to the file. Also see the notes of the Wilmer, Cutler interview with Bob Butts, the Enron controller, on Jan. 15, 2002, and Duncan's Oct. 13, 2001, e-mail to assorted Andersen officials, "Press Release Verbage."

531 Details of Adlong's morning on Oct. 15 from the 302 of her Feb. 5, 2002, interview with the FBI.

531 Details of the final discussion between Causey and Duncan from the Oct. 15, 2001, memo to the file written by Duncan, "Enron Press Release Discussions." Also see the Oct. 16, 2001, e-mail from Temple to Duncan, "Re: Press Release Draft."

531–32 Details of Smith's morning and her reaction to the Enron release from Smith and Emshwiller, *24 Days*, 105–9. Enron's Oct. 16 release was headed "Enron Reports Recurring Third Quarter Earnings of $0.43 per Diluted Share."

532–33 Dialogue from the conference call from an official transcript.

533 Some details of Emshwiller's discussion with Palmer from Smith and Emshwiller, *24 Days*, 109.

533–34 Smith's decision to fast-forward through the recorded version of the analyst call from Smith and Emshwiller, *24 Days*, 114–15.

534 The story by Emshwiller and Smith, "Enron Posts Surprise 3d-Quarter Loss After Investment, Asset Write-Downs," appeared in *The Wall Street Journal* on Oct. 17, 2001, C1.

535 The call from the short seller to Emshwiller, and the way he reacted to it, are described in Smith and Emshwiller, *24 Days*, 122.

536 A copy of the Oct. 17, 2001, fax from the SEC to Rogers and Fastow at Enron was obtained by the author. Also see the 302 from the FBI's Jan. 14, 2002, interview with Duncan.

536–37 Some details of the locations of Lay and Causey from Lay's itinerary, headed "3rd Quarter Analyst Reviews; October 16–19, 2001; Itinerary for Ken Lay."

537 The short seller call to Smith from Smith and Emshwiller, *24 Days*, 129.

537 Details of Enron's reaction upon hearing Smith's statements about McMahon from the Vinson & Elkins notes from the Oct. 18, 2001, interview with McMahon. Also see the Batson Report, vol. 4, app. C, 169.

539 The Emshwiller and Smith article, "Enron CFO's Partnership Had Millions in Profit," appeared in *The Wall Street Journal* on Oct. 19, 2001, C1.

539–40 Some details of the Oct. 19 special board meeting from the official minutes.

CHAPTER 20

542–43 Some details of the managers' meeting from the Wilmer, Cutler notes from Kaminski's Dec. 19, 2001, interview.

543–44 Details of Pitt's speech before the AICPA from a videotape of the event.

544 Corgel's efforts to bring Riley into the Enron mess at Andersen's Houston office from the 302 of the FBI's interview with Riley on Feb. 14, 2002.

544–45 Details of the special board meeting of Oct. 22 from the official minutes. Also see the Batson Report, vol. 4, app. D, 114, and the Senate hearings titled "The Role of the Board of Directors in Enron's Collapse," held before the Governmental Affairs Committee's Permanent Subcommittee on Investigations on May 7, 2002.

546 A copy of the company-wide e-mail was obtained by the author.

546 Details of the preparation at Andersen for the Oct. 23 conference call from the 302 of the FBI's Feb. 5, 2002, interview with Adlong. Also see the Cash 302 from the Feb. 5, 2002, interview and the SEC notes of the interview with Duncan on Jan. 14, 2002.

549–50 Dialogue from the conference call from the official transcript.

549 Enron's stock performance from a price chart from Bloomberg, Oct. 23, 2001.

549–50 Duncan testified about his disappointment in the Oct. 23 conference call during *U.S. v. Andersen*. Also see the 302s of the FBI interview with Duncan on March 21 and April 5, 2002; Adlong on Feb. 5, 2002; Roger Willard on Feb. 6, 2002; Grutzmacher on Feb. 15, 2002; Kate Agnew on April 4, 2002; and Bauer on Feb. 2, 2002. Also see the undated, unsigned report prepared in 2002 by lawyers for Andersen, entitled "Summary of Document Destruction Facts."

551–52 Dialogue at the employee meeting from a transcript of the event. Also see an undated memo from Lay to Enron employees, "All Employee Meeting."

552–53 The story read by Pitt was David S. Hilzenrath, "SEC Chief: 'Gentler' Agency," *Washington Post*, Oct. 23, 2001, E1.

553 Duncan testified about his effort to push compliance with the Andersen document policy during his testimony in *U.S. v. Andersen*. Also see the 302s of the FBI interviews with Duncan on March 21 and April 5, 2002; Adlong on Feb. 5, 2002; Willard on Feb. 6, 2002; Grutzmacher on Feb. 15, 2002; Agnew on April 4, 2002; and Bauer on Feb. 2, 2002; and the "Government's *In Limine* Motion of Law," filed April 29, 2003, in *U.S. v. Andersen*. Also see the testimony of Timothy McCann on April 11, 2002, before grand jury no. 02-2 in the case *Re: Investigation of Enron*.

553 A copy of the Oct. 23 margin call from Bank of America was obtained by the author.

553 Some details of the Whalley and Bowen meeting from both men's schedules.

554 Some details of the management committee meeting from entries in Lay's schedule book.

554 Details of the Duncan and LeMaistre call with Fastow from both men's testimonies of May 7, 2002, before the Senate Governmental Affairs Committee's Permanent Subcommittee on Investigations. A copy of their script, along with LeMaistre's handwritten notes, was obtained by the author.

559–63 The chaos that emerged as the reality of Enron's finances was discovered was reconstructed from confidential interviews with a number of participants in these events.

563–64 Details of the Oct. 24 board meeting from the official minutes. Also see the Lay e-mail of that day addressed to Enron worldwide, "Jeff McMahon Named CFO," and the press release of the same day, "Enron Names Jeff McMahon Chief Financial Officer."

565–66 Some details of Watson's phone call with Lay from undated, unsigned notes of interviews compiled by Dynegy's lawyers from an interview with Watson.

566–67 A copy of Suki's Oct. 24, 2001, e-mail was obtained by the author. Also see the Batson Report, vol. 4, app. F, 34.

567 Some details of Riley's arrival from the 302 of his FBI interview on Feb. 14, 2002, and from the 302 of Duncan's interview on Jan. 14, 2002.

567 A copy of Watkins's Oct. 24, 2001, e-mail to McMahon, "Your new CFO spot and the job I want," was obtained by the author.

569 Some details of the preparations for the Bergstrom-Horton lunch meeting from undated, unsigned notes compiled by Dynegy's lawyers from an interview with Bergstrom.

570 Some details of Riley's encounter with Duncan while hearing the shredding from a 302 of Riley's FBI interview on Feb. 14, 2002. Also see his June 3, 2002, testimony in *U.S. v. Andersen*.

570 The retention of Shred-It from copies of invoices issued for the Houston office's shredding assignment. Also see the Agnew 302 of the interview on April 4, 2002.

570–71 Some details of the Plaza Club lunch from undated, unsigned notes compiled by Dynegy's lawyers from an interview with Bergstrom.

571 Enron's announcement came in the release "Enron Continues as Market-Maker of Choice, Says CEO Lay; Transaction Volume Shows Strength of Core Businesses; Company Draws Down Credit Facility to Address Investor Concerns." Some details of Emshwiller's efforts on the Chewco story from Smith and Emshwiller, *24 Days*, 168–69.

572 Some details of the discussions between Watson and Lay from undated, unsigned notes compiled by Dynegy's lawyers from an interview with Watson.

CHAPTER 21

578–79 Some details of the Bauer discussions with Faldyn and Siurek from Bauer's Nov. 2, 2001, memo to the file, "Chewco Investigation." Also see the 302 of Bauer's Feb. 2, 2002, interview with the FBI.

579–80 Mintz's continuing efforts to move LJM2 out of the Enron offices are documented in an e-mail he wrote a few weeks before, dated Oct. 11, 2001, addressed to Derrick, and headed "LJM—Status Report." A copy of Kopper's separation agreement and release from Enron, dated July 23, 2001, was obtained by the author.

580–81 Some details of the board's Oct. 26 meeting from the official minutes.

581 Some details of Causey's discoveries about Chewco from Bauer's Nov. 2, 2001, memo to the file and the 302 of Bauer's Feb. 2, 2002, interview with the FBI. Also see the confidential notes from Causey's Jan. 18, 2002, interview with staffers from the House Energy and Commerce Committee's Subcommittee on Oversight and Investigations.

582 Timing of the lockout from the Oct. 23 all-employee e-mail. See also Enron's official press release, "Enron Explains Basic Facts About Its 401k Savings Plan," Dec. 14, 2001.

582–84 Some details of the discussions between Watson and Lay from undated, unsigned notes compiled by Dynegy's lawyers from an interview with Watson.

584 Some details of the Chewco meeting from Bauer's Nov. 2, 2001, memo to the file and the 302 of Bauer's Feb. 2, 2002, interview with the FBI.

586 Some details of McMahon's conversations with Glisan from his Feb. 7, 2002, testimony before the House Energy and Commerce Committee's Subcommittee on Oversight and Investigations.

587–88 The article that infuriated Pitt was by Alex Berenson and Richard A. Oppel Jr., "One Mighty Enron Strains Under Scrutiny," *New York Times*, Oct. 28, 2001, Sunday Business, 1.

588 Details of Evans's discussion with O'Neill from Eichenwald with Henriques, "Enron Buffed Image."

588–89 A copy of the Dynegy fax was obtained by the author.

589 Some details of William Powers's day from entries on his official schedule.

590 Luna testified to his experiences with Thibault during his 2002 deposition in *Newby v. Enron et al.*, H-01-3624, filed in Federal District Court in Houston.

590–91 Some details of the discussions between Bergstrom and Whalley from undated, unsigned notes compiled by Dynegy's lawyers from an interview with Bergstrom.

591–92 Details of Mordaunt's admission to Derrick, and her subsequent interview on Oct. 30, 2001, with Wilmer, Cutler, from notes the lawyers took.

592–93 Some details of Stulb's encounter with Duncan from Stulb's testimony of May 22 and 23, 2002, in *U.S. v. Andersen.*

593 Some details of the discussion between Tarpley and Delainey from undated, unsigned notes compiled by Dynegy's lawyers from an interview with Tarpley.

596–98 Details of the Andersen discovery of the Chewco side letter, and its ramifications, from Bauer's Nov. 2, 2001, memo to file; the 302 of Bauer's Feb. 2, 2002, interview with the FBI; the 302 of Cash's Feb. 8, 2002, interview; and the 302 of Duncan's Jan. 14, 2002, interview. A copy of the side letter was obtained by the author, as was a listing that showed which box the document had been placed in. Also see the notes from Causey's Jan. 18, 2002, interview with Congressional staffers.

598–99 Some details of the board meeting from the official minutes.

601–3 Some details of the merger discussions, including the disclosure of the Glisan scandal, from undated, unsigned notes complied by Dynegy's lawyers from interviews with Fullenweider, Doty, Winters, and Watson.

603 Some details of the Enron board meeting from the official minutes.

604–6 Copies of the two conflicting press releases were obtained by the author. Also see the undated, unsigned notes compiled by Dynegy's lawyers summarizing the findings of their interviews with the company's executives, bankers, and lawyers.

CHAPTER 22

607–8 Some details of what Carter saw from the SEC Web site, www.sec.gov, and from the 8-K filed by Enron on Nov. 8. Also see the Nov. 8, 2001, e-mail from Lay to Enron employees, "SEC Information/Earnings Restatement."

610 A copy of the Andersen subpoena, issued Nov. 8, 2001, in the case *In the Matter of Enron Corp.*, HO-9350, was obtained by the author, as was a letter of that day from John Loesch, SEC senior counsel, to Andrew Pincus, general counsel of Andersen, which delivered the subpoena. Also see the Nov. 9, 2001, e-mail from Nancy Temple to Caroline Cheng and others at Andersen, "Enron Subpoena"; Adlong's response that same day to a copy she received of the Temple e-mail; Adlong's e-mail that same day to the engagement team, "No More Shredding"; Temple's handwritten notes from meetings that day; and the FBI 302s of interviews with Adlong on Feb. 5, 2002; Temple on Feb. 13, 2002; Cash on Feb. 8, 2002; and the SEC notes from the interview with Duncan on Jan. 14, 2002.

610–11 Some details about the Dynegy merger from an internal Enron document, "Talking Points—

11-9-01"; the joint press release issued Nov. 9, "Dynegy and Enron Announce Merger Agreement"; and the document of that same day "Merger FAQ's (Internal)."

611–12 Some details of the Rawhide debacle from Enron's Nov. 19, 2001, 10-Q; annex 7 to the Nov. 14, 2003, report by Harrison Goldin, a court-appointed examiner in the Enron bankruptcy, filed in the United States Bankruptcy Court in Manhattan; and the Batson Report, vol. 3, 52.

613 Some details from a tracking of the Enron daily stock price, as recorded on Bloomberg, for the period from Oct. 26 through Nov. 12, 2001. See also Enron's Dec. 14, 2001, release, "Enron Explains Basic Facts About Its 401k Savings Plan."

613 Some details of the aftermath of the merger from the undated, unsigned notes compiled by Dynegy's lawyers summarizing the findings of their interviews with the company's executives, bankers, and lawyers.

613–14 Some details of the demands that Lay surrender his severance from Richard A. Oppel Jr. and Floyd Norris, "Enron Chief Will Give Up Severance," *New York Times*, Nov. 14, 2001, C5.

614–15 Some details of the problems between the Enron and the Dynegy trading rooms from unsigned, undated notes compiled by Dynegy's lawyers summarizing the findings from an interview with Schatzman.

615 The change in position by Enron traders from the Dynegy lawyers' interview notes with other traders; internal cash documents maintained with the Enron wholesale-trading division; and the 10-Q filed by Enron on Nov. 19, 2001.

616–17 A copy of the draft 10-Q, as it existed on Nov. 16, 2001, was obtained by the author.

616–17 Some details of the McMahon call, the response from Doty, and the wider response to the final copy of the 10-Q from the unsigned, undated notes compiled by Dynegy's lawyers summarizing the findings of their interviews with the company's executives, bankers, and lawyers. Specific financial information from comparisons between the final 10-Q, as filed on Nov. 19, 2001, and the draft that existed on Nov. 16, 2001.

619 Some details of the luncheon meeting at the Coronado from unsigned, undated notes compiled by Dynegy's lawyers summarizing the findings of their interviews with Watson.

619 Enron's stock price from historical price information maintained by Bloomberg.

620–23 Some details of the discussions between Enron and Dynegy, including the talk between Whalley and Bergstrom, from the unsigned, undated notes compiled by Dynegy's lawyers summarizing the findings of interviews with the company's executives, bankers, and lawyers.

623–24 Some details of Skilling's Nov. 27, 2001, interview with Wilmer, Cutler from the lawyers' notes of the meeting.

625–27 Some details of the collapse of the Enron-Dynegy merger from the unsigned, undated notes compiled by Dynegy's lawyers reflecting interviews with the company's executives, bankers, and lawyers.

629 Daschle's statements from a transcript of his Nov. 29, 2001, press briefing.

629–30 Dialogue at the Nov. 30, 2001, White House press briefing from the official transcript of the event.

630 Some details of the Dec. 1, 2001, board meeting from the official minutes.

631 Details of the Enron bankruptcy filing from Eichenwald with Henriques, "Enron Buffed Image."

CHAPTER 23

632 Some details of the termination of Enron employees, and the aftermath, from David Kaplan and L. M. Sixel, "Enron Lays Off 4,000," *Houston Chronicle*, Dec. 4, 2001, A1.

633–34 Some details of Skilling's polygraph from a Dec. 4, 2001, report prepared by American International Security Corporation on subject "Jeffrey K. Skilling."

634–35 A transcript of Skilling's testimony before the SEC was obtained by the author.

635–36 Some details of the Dec. 4, 2001, McMahon interview with the House staffers from notes taken by Wilmer, Cutler lawyers who attended the discussion.

637–38 Details of the discussions before Congress from the official transcript of the Dec. 12, 2001, hearings titled "The Enron Collapse: Impact on Investors and Financial Markets," before two subcommittees of the House Financial Services Committee: the Subcommittee on Capital Markets, Insurance, and Government Sponsored Enterprises and the Subcommittee on Oversight and Investigations.

639 The unfamiliarity of the team that helped craft Berardino's statements to the congressional panel was revealed in Berardino's letter of Jan. 21, 2002, to Representative Michael Oxley, chairman of the Financial Services Committee, in which he explained that he had made certain technical errors in his presentation about Chewco. Those errors occurred, he said, because the officials helping with his statements did not have the familiarity with Chewco that members of the Andersen team on the Enron account did. Finally, a review of all of Duncan's appearances before the Enron audit committee shows no instance in which he alerted the directors to possible illegal acts, and no documents filed with the committee by Andersen maintaining such a claim. However, the statement did accurately reflect Andersen's opinion at the time, and it is possible that the opinion could have been shared informally with a member of the audit committee; that, however, would not rise to the level of official notification.

639–40 Details of the Boies press conference from Laura Goldberg and Ralph Bivens, "Enron's Former CFO Surfaces," *Houston Chronicle*, Dec. 13, 2001, Business, 1; David S. Hilzenrath, "Auditor Hints of 'Illegal Acts' at Enron," *Washington Post*, Dec. 13, 2001, E1; Jessica Sommar, "Enron Ex-CFO Hires Top Defense Lawyer," *New York Post*, Dec. 13, 2001, 42. Other details from photographs taken at the briefing.

640 Timing of the Berardino call from an entry in Lay's schedule.

640 Some details of the Fastow/Kopper meeting from Kopper's Sept. 27, 2004 testimony in *U.S. v. Bayly et al.*

640–41 Some details of Glisan's efforts to secure a cooperation deal, from Kurt Eichenwald, "Enron Executive Said to Be Aiding in Federal Inquiry," *New York Times*, Feb. 26, 2002, A1. Also see Glisan's testimony of Oct. 6, 2004, in *U.S. v Bayly et al.*

642–44 Some details of Andersen's discovery of the e-mail destruction, and Berardino's subsequent involvement, from Kurt Eichenwald, "Miscues, Missteps, and the Fall of Andersen," *New York Times*, May 8, 2002, C1.

645–46 Some details of the Oval Office meeting from Ron Suskind, *The Price of Loyalty* (Simon & Schuster, 2004), 203–7.

646–47 Details of Bush's meeting in the Oval Office with reporters from a White House transcript, "Remarks by the President in Meeting with His Economic Team," Jan. 10, 2002.

648 Details of the Jan. 10, 2002, press briefing from the official transcript.

648 Andersen's Jan. 10, 2002, press release was headed "Andersen Notifies SEC, Justice Department, Congress That a Significant but Undetermined Number of Enron-Related Documents Were Disposed Of." The follow-up press release that day was headed "Additional Andersen Statement on Enron-Related Documents."

649 Ann Richards's statements from a transcript of the Jan. 30, 2002, broadcast of *Larry King Live* on CNN.

651 Details of Adlong's conversation with Duncan from a transcript of her testimony in March 2002 given as part of an inquiry by class-action lawyers suing Enron to determine the scope of Andersen's document destruction. See also Kurt Eichenwald, "Andersen Misread the Depths of the Government's Anger," *New York Times*, March 18, 2002, A1.

652–53 The *Washington Post* article, by Peter Behr, ran on p. A1 on Jan. 12, 2002.

653–54 Details of Duncan's first meeting with the government on Jan. 14, 2002, from the 302 prepared by the FBI agents in attendance, and by the SEC notes of the interview prepared as a memo for the file by Beth Lehman from the agency. Copies of Duncan's agreements with both the SEC and the Justice Department, which allowed for his cooperation on this day, were obtained by the author.

654 Details of the Jan. 14, 2002, letter from Tauzin and Greenwood to Lay from the original document.

654 Some details of the response to the Tauzin and Greenwood letter, and the comment from Johnson, from several news articles, including Don Van Atta Jr. with Alex Berenson, "Enron's Chairman Received Warning About Accounting," *New York Times*, Jan. 15, 2002, A1; and James Kuhnhenn, "Enron's Chairman Was Warned of Impending Crash, Memo Shows," *Knight Ridder*, Jan. 15, 2002.

654 Some details of the events surrounding the Duncan dinner where he learned of his termination by Andersen from a 302 of his March 21, 2002, interview with the FBI.

656–57 Some details of Fastow's Jan. 15, 2002, meeting from the Wilmer, Cutler notes of the interview.

657–59 Some details of Lay's Jan. 16, 2002, meeting from the Wilmer, Cutler notes of the interview.

659–60 Some details of the Castaneda allegations from a transcript of the ABC news report that ran on the program *World News Now*, Jan. 22, 2002. See also Peter Behr, "Manager Says Enron Documents Shredded," *Washington Post*, Jan. 22, 2002, A1; and Paul Duggan and Susan Schmidt, "Firm Calls Agency After Allegations of Data Shredding," *Washington Post*, Jan. 23, 2002, A1.

661–62 The news reporting on the Baxter suicide at times appeared to suggest that he might have been a victim of foul play in an effort to silence him. Such innuendo was picked up on numerous Internet sites, and became part of the mythology of Enron that has been widely accepted as fact. But the episode serves solely to underscore how easily falsehoods enter into the public consciousness. Every detail related in this book was available in the voluminous records, made public shortly after the investigation concluded but apparently only skimmed by most who obtained them. The fact that Head saw Baxter alone, driving his car, minutes before his death is revealed in the file for case 02-000599 with the Sugar Land Police Department. That case file contains scores of individual documents running close to a thousand pages—from witness reports to descriptions of police actions to crime-scene photographs and autopsies—that leave no doubt that Baxter was a suicide. The pain inflicted on the Baxter family from the swirling cloud of rumor following his death marks one of the despicable consequences of a society all too willing to believe conspiracy theories over documentation, and a media that fails to review complex yet solid records to inform the public of the truth.

EPILOGUE

664–65 The Powers Report was formally released on Feb. 2, 2002; despite the criticisms leveled at Powers in the run-up to the document's public disclosure, it stands as one of the most masterful, hard-hitting reports to ever be issued from an internal corporate investigation. As a testament to its success, the voluminous other reports that have been issued—from bankruptcy examiners, congressional committees, and the like—have never achieved the clarity and ultimate simplicity of the Powers report, and have not added significant new details that brought a different understanding to the reasons behind the Enron bankruptcy.

664–65 Details of the appearances and statements before the House Energy and Commerce Committee's Subcommittee on Oversight and Investigations from the transcripts to the hearing titled "The Findings of Enron's Special Investigative Committee with Respect to Certain Transactions Between Enron and Certain of Its Current and Former Officers and Employees," Feb. 5, 2002; "Financial Collapse of Enron," Feb. 7, 2002; and "Financial Collapse of Enron Corp.," Feb. 14, 2002.

666–67 A detailed rendition of the events surrounding Andersen's efforts to forestall indictment—and the government's decision to charge the firm—from Eichenwald, "Andersen Misread the Depths of the Government's Anger." Also see Eichenwald, "Miscues, Missteps, and the Fall of Andersen"; and Duncan's 302 from his FBI interview, conducted by Weissmann, on April 5–6, 2002.

667 The fall of Harvey Pitt was chronicled by Labaton, "Praise to Scorn."

667–68 The criminal complaint against the bankers—Bermingham, Darby, and Mulgrew—was filed on June 27, 2002, in Federal District Court in Houston. The affidavit in support of the complaint by Special Agent Simpson laid out the details signaling to Kopper that he faced a high probability of indictment. The three bankers were subsequently indicted in Houston on Sept. 12, 2002, and as of this writing are facing extradition from England to stand trial.

668 Kopper's guilty plea was witnessed by the author. Some of his statements to prosecutors are detailed in the criminal charges against him along with his cooperation agreement, filed on Aug. 20, 2002, in Federal District Court in Houston. Other details of his statements from the affidavit of Special Agent Omer Meisel, filed on Oct. 2, 2002, in support of the criminal complaint against Fastow.

668 The author witnessed Fastow's surrender and guilty plea. The criminal information against Larry Lawyer was filed in Federal District Court in Houston on Nov. 26, 2002. The first wide-scale broadband indictment—brought against Enron executives Ken Rice, Joe Hirko, Kevin Hannon, Kevin Howard, Scott Yeager, Rex Shelby, and Michael Krautz—was filed in the Houston court on April 29, 2003.

670 The superseding indictment in *U.S. v. Fastow* was filed in the Houston court on April 30, 2003.

Glisan's plea agreement and admission of guilt to count five of his original indictment were filed in the court on Sept. 10, 2003. The indictment of Lea Fastow was filed on April 30, 2003, and she ultimately entered into a plea agreement with the government, which was filed on Jan. 14, 2004.

671–72 The author witnessed Andy Fastow's change of plea, and details of the hearing come from personal observation. Dialogue comes from a transcript of the proceeding on Jan. 14, 2004.

672–73 The superseding indictment, naming Skilling and Causey as defendants, was filed under seal in the Houston court on Feb. 18, 2004. Some details of Skilling's encounter with Glisan from Mary Flood, "Skilling Colleague Passed by on Chain Gang," *Houston Chronicle*, Feb. 21, 2004, Business, 1. The author witnessed Skilling's arraignment, and details come from personal observation. Dialogue comes from a transcript of the proceeding on Feb. 19, 2004

673–74 Details of Lay's being escorted by the FBI agents into court, including the dialogue, from a videotape of the event shot by KPRC, Channel 2 news in Houston. Some details of Lay's time in jail from Mary Flood, "Lay Describes Time in Cell, Reveals Hope for Future," *Houston Chronicle*, July 10, 2004, 1.

674–75 Lay's arraignment and his subsequent press conference were witnessed by the author, and the details come from personal observation. Dialogue from a transcript of the hearing of July 8, 2004. The press conference dialogue is from a videotape by KPRC in Houston and transcript of the event.

Q&A With Kurt Eichenwald
Author of Conspiracy of Fools

Q: Kurt, what attracted you to the Enron story?

A: Enron, I was probably the last person persuaded that it was a good book. I was very hesitant about it for a while until I finally realized that there was a spectacular narrative arc to the story—that you were talking about people at the pinnacle of power who very arrogantly went along doing very foolish things, at times very criminal things, and seeing their mistakes celebrated by the market, by the government, by investors, by everybody. And it all comes crashing down. It is almost Greek mythology in the way the narrative arc unfolds. And the more I learned about it, the more I realized this thing was a Grisham book, this thing was a story of greed and power unbridled and it went through this fabulous tale where you got to see these people rise up and fall down and so the challenge there was to figure out how to tell the story in a way that would give people that roller coaster excitement, give them that feel of being in the story, give them that sense of excitement that would leave them wanting to flip the page and not quite turn out the light yet, and in the end I hope that's what I did.

Q: Do you feel the behavior of Arthur Andersen was more the exception or the rule when considering the few remaining accounting giants?

A: The answer to that is sort of twofold. I think Andersen was in a unique position in that the firm had had a lot of internal battles in previous years and had, in fact, recently just lost its rather lucrative consulting practice and was setting up a new one. That created a mindset, I believe, of trying to keep big business. Enron was the biggest business they had. Ultimately, today I think most accounting firms recognize that they do this kind of stuff at their peril. The death of Arthur Andersen—Arthur Andersen got the death penalty. I think when you go through the book and see what happened, Arthur Andersen deserved the death penalty. They were not public accountants. They were not acting on behalf of public interest. And I think that failure—they paid a very heavy price for it, but I think it's a price that was ultimately deserved. It was a company that had experienced these kind of violations in the past, and didn't do enough to make sure that it didn't happen again.

Whether the other firms were better or worse during the 1990s . . . I would just say, I was writing a lot about corporate fraud, and it wasn't always Andersen that came up. I saw a lot of the other firms who did a lot of squirrelly things as well. I just think they are all much more frightened now about the prospect of becoming an Arthur Andersen.

Q: Based on the evidence you have collected, can you comment on whether you believe Lay and/or Skilling deserve to be convicted of crimes and should go to jail?

A: One of the things I think is sort of a sign of the arrogance of the press is we tend to believe that the information we gather is the kind of stuff that allows us to reach those kind of conclusions. Ultimately, all I can do is say "this person has an involvement in these events," "this person does not have an involvement in those events," "this person may or may not have an involvement in the third events." The nature of corporate fraud is that you can have the exact same actions committed by an individual and unless you are able to determine what his *intent* was, what he was meaning to do, you can have those same actions in one instance be completely legal and in another be a crime. I am not going to venture out and say "I know, in my opinion this person committed a crime, in my opinion this person did not." That's really up to a jury.

What is clear is that the case against Lay is much narrower than anybody would believe given the run-up of reporting about it, and the accusations in Congress, and the pounding of the table about his knowledge of the special purpose entities that were manipulating the company's income state balance sheet. Because, ultimately, Lay isn't being charged with any of that. The Enron task force investigated him very extensively and they charged him only with crimes relating to certain statements he made in the last twelve weeks of the company's life. And most of that time, and actually during *all* of that time not a single one of these transactions was done. So that case is narrower than people think it is. The Skilling and Causey side of the case is sort of the broad piece, the one that gets into those transactions.

What they did, how they did it, the book lays out those facts, it tells where everyone was. I kind of look at it as an impressionistic painting. Everyone can look at it and make their own judgments about what they think the intents were. I don't think that's my job.

INDEX

© Fred R. Conrad

KURT EICHENWALD has written for the *New York Times* for more than seventeen years. A two-time winner of the George Polk Award for excellence in journalism and a finalist for the 2000 Pulitzer Prize, he has been selected repeatedly for the *TJFR Business News Reporter* as one of the nation's most influential financial journalists. His last book, *The Informant,* is currently in development as a major motion picture. He lives in Dallas with his wife and three children.